Greetings dea

thank you for choosing this

Allow me to introduce our story.
The author of this book is father to 2 children;
a son and daughter aged 2 and 5.
Every day he tells his children stories
he has created for them
and the one they love the most
is written in this book.

This is the story of a little Snowflake
who wanted to know all about Christmas.
You will be taken on an epic adventure
that finally helps her understand
that togetherness, family and love
is the true meaning of Christmas.

Want more?

Please visit us at

WWW.SNOWFLAKE-AND-CHRISTMAS.COM

to download our free coloring pages.

Welcome to the fairy tale

Once upon a time in the sky,

Among the clouds and way up high,

Lived a white Snowflake so very small,

She looked down on Earth and heard it all.

The people spoke of Christmas and fun,
She asked the wind, not the moon or sun,
"Wind, above the Earth you always fly,
Christmas is so special why oh why?"

The Wind answered on a gentle breeze,
"It's a holiday with presents and trees,
Houses are decorated with holly,
The people are so happy and jolly."

★ How many lights can you find on the tree?

The Snowflake said,
"Wind, Wind can you help me?
By taking me to Earth so I can see?
What Christmas is
and what people do,
This would be
the best present from you."

Can you find a golden snowflake?

"Of course, little Snowflake hold on tight,
Christmas is such a wonderful sight."
While they were flying up through the air,
They saw people rushing everywhere.

★ Can you see the green light twinkling in the Christmas garland?

BAKERY

"Why do the people hurry around?"
The Snowflake asked watching the ground,
They flew some more and the Wind replied,
"To be with their families at Yuletide."

Santa is here! Can you find him?

On their way, the Snowflake did see,
A family decorating their tree,
They were all helping and having fun,
It was such a good time for everyone.

Where is the square toy on the Christmas tree?

This made the Snowflake happy and glad,
They were all helping including Dad!
In the next house, they both could see,
A family having dinner with glee.

The little Snowflake was filled with delight,
Seeing families together was a highlight,
The Wind took the Snowflake to a Christmas tree,
Decorated so beautifully for all to see.

Christmas carols were being sung so loud,
This made the Snowflake happy and proud,
For the Snowflake now knew what Christmas meant,
Being with family and time together spent.

Focused activity

Help little readers get involved

Page №8 - How many lights can you find on the tree?

Page №10 - Can you find a golden snowflake?

Page №12 - Can you see the green light

twinkling in the Christmas garland?

Page №14 - Santa is here! Can you find him?

Page №16 - Where is the square toy on the Christmas tree

Want more?

Please visit us at

WWW.SNOWFLAKE-AND-CHRISTMAS.COM

to download our free coloring pages.

For notes

_____

_____

_____

_____

_____

_____

_____

_____

_____

CPSIA information can be obtained at www.ICGtesting.com
Printed in the USA
LVIW01n0059201217
560343LV00016B/608

35332695R00287

Made in the USA
San Bernardino, CA
09 May 2019

Fyodor Dostoevsky, *Crime and Punishment,*
Read and Understood by Robots
Double Distilled Machine Translation, 2015
Vision and Idea of Eugene Efuni and Dmitry Glukhovsky
© **Cover illustration by** Sergey Kritsky, 2015
© **Cover design by** Ilya Yatskevich, 2015

WARNING: TOTAL ABSURD!

EPILOGUE   **448**

CHAPTER I   448
CHAPTER II   455

PART 5   303

CHAPTER I   303
CHAPTER II   317
CHAPTER III   328
CHAPTER IV   340
CHAPTER V   355

⟨⟨≪≫⟩⟩

PART 6   367

CHAPTER I   367
CHAPTER II   376
CHAPTER III   388
CHAPTER IV   397
CHAPTER V   406
CHAPTER VI   419
CHAPTER VII   431
CHAPTER VIII   439

⟨⟨≪≫⟩⟩

PART 3   163

CHAPTER I   163
CHAPTER II   175
CHAPTER III   185
CHAPTER IV   197
CHAPTER V   208
CHAPTER VI   225

←«»→

PART 4   235

CHAPTER I   235
CHAPTER II   246
CHAPTER III   257
CHAPTER IV   264
CHAPTER V   279
CHAPTER VI   296

←«»→

CRIME
AND PUNISHMENT

BY FYODOR DOSTOYEVSKY

MCH\E & TR\SLTD

PART 1

<« CHAPTER I »>

In early July, exceptionally hot evening, a young man came out of his closet, which is hired from tenants in C - m lane on the street and slowly, as if in thought, to K. - also a bridge.

He successfully avoided meeting the hostess on the stairs. His attic under the roof of the five-story high and was more like a closet than a room. His hostess that he attic with lunch and a visit, lived under the stairs, in a separate apartment, and every time you go out, he was obliged to pass her kitchen, almost always wide open otvorennoy the stairs. And every time a young man passed by, I felt sick, frightened feeling that shame and that frowned. He was hopelessly mistress and feared to meet her.

Not that he was a coward and scored, quite the contrary; but for some time it has been in irritable state on the brink of hypochondria. He was so self-absorbed, and retired from all that he was afraid of meeting, not only meeting with the mistress. He was crushed by poverty; but even stopped discomfort lately weigh ego.Nazhatie his works, he stopped completely and do not want to deal with. No hostess, in fact, he was not afraid that it is not in a conspiracy against him. But to dwell on the stairs, listening to all sorts of nonsense about all this shit every day, to which he does not care, all these payment harassment, threats, complaints, and at the same time to dodge, to apologize, to lie - No, really, it is not better glide like a cat on the stairs and sneak away to unnoticed.

However, this time the fear of meeting with his kreditorsha even hit him in the face the street.

"On what business want to try, and at the same time, which is a bit scary

ROBOTS READ

- he thought, with a strange smile. - Um ... yeah ... all in the hands of man, and yet he is past the nose, only one cowardice ... it is an axiom ... I wonder what people are most afraid of? new step, a new own words, they are more afraid of everything ... And yet, I talk too much. That's why I do. Nothing that chatter may however, and so do :. because chatter that I do not do anything that I have learned in the last month talking, lying for days on end in the corner ... and think about the days of yore, why. ??. I have to go Am I able to do this seriously is not serious So, for the sake of fantasy to entertain yourself !; toys Yes, I think that the toys! "

On the street the heat was terrible, besides closeness, crush, everywhere lime, wood, brick, dust, and that special summer stench, so familiar to all St. Petersburg man, who can not afford to hire a cottage - all at once unpleasantly shocked already frustrated nerves boys. Unbearable stench from the taverns that in this part of town a special set, and drunken, constantly faced, despite the time, weekday, completed disgusting and sad coloring of the picture. A deep sense of revulsion flashed for a moment from the point of view of a beautiful young man. By the way, it was nice looking, with beautiful dark eyes, dark Russia, higher than the national average, a slim and slender. But he soon fell, as if deep in thought, even, or rather, as if in some forgotten and gone, no longer noticing the others, and not wanting him to notice. Only occasionally he muttered something under his breath, the habit of monologues in which he admitted to himself now. At the same time he was aware that his thoughts sometimes go to jail, and that he is very weak: the second day, as it's actually almost nothing at all to eat.

He was so badly dressed, sometimes even familiar people, ashamed to go to the day of rags on the street. However, a quarter of the dress will be difficult to surprise someone. The proximity of the Haymarket, the number of establishments in the first place, seminars and working class people crowded in the middle of the street of St. Petersburg, and alleys, sometimes dazzled general panorama of such entities, that it would be strange and wonder at a meeting with inoyu figure. But so much has accumulated bitterness and contempt in the soul of a young man, that despite the sometimes very young, weakness, it is less likely minded his rags on the street. Another thing, when they met with friends and former teammates with whom he did not like at all to meet ... And yet, when drunk, which for some unknown reason, and taken somewhere at this time on the street in a big cart, drawn huge draft horse, suddenly shouted, passing, "Hey, you, German hatter" - And cried

with laughter, pointing at him - a young man suddenly stopped and frantically grabbed his hat. This hat was a tall, round, tsimmermanovskaya, but completely worn out, very red, full of holes and stains, no fields and most unseemly angle to the side of the crease. But it's not a shame, but quite another feeling akin to fear seized him.

"I knew it! - He muttered in confusion - I thought it was just a free-electron laser is a kind of any stupidity, every detail has gone, the whole idea can spoil Yes, too conspicuous hat .. funny and so conspicuous !.. .. In my rags, of course, you need a hat, at least the old pancake some, but not this freak. Not one of them is not far from the notification, remember ... The main thing, remember, and shows. Here you have to be invisible ... Trifles, trifles thing! .. Here are some little things and always ruin it ... "

He had to go a little; he even knew how many steps from the gate of his house: exactly seven hundred thirty. After he counted them when he had dreamed. As long as he does not believe that these dreams and was only tantalizing himself their hideous but daring recklessness. Now, a month later, he began to look differently and, despite all that he mocked monologues about his own impotence and indecision, "ugly" dream somehow do not necessarily come to think of now, but still do not believe it myself. He even went to do now fetch your company, and with every step his excitement grew stronger and stronger.

With a sinking heart and a nervous tremor, he went to the big house, on one side looked at the ditch, and others - th Street. This house stood in a tiny apartment houses and was inhabited by all kinds - tailors, mechanics, cooks, Germans kind of girls living as best they could, petty clerks, and so on. Inbound and outbound and through two gates and two vessels house. There had three or four janitor. The young man was very glad to solve any of them, and slipped unnoticed through the door on the right to lestnitse. Lestnitsa was dark and narrow, "black", but he already knew, and knew he liked all these surroundings: in such darkness even the most inquisitive eyes were not dangerous. "If the time shu I'm so afraid what would happen if I really like, and what happened before it came? .." - thought he unwittingly passing on the fourth floor. Were blocking his path retired soldiers porters, transfer from one apartment furniture. He already knew before that lived in the apartment with the help of a German officer: "So, it moved from the German, and, consequently, on the fourth floor, the stairs and on this site, is, for some time, only one Starukhin employment. This is good ... just

ROBOTS READ

in case ... "- he thought again and called the apartment of an old woman. Until blurted out weakly, as if it were made of tin, not copper. In these small apartments in these homes, almost all such calls. He forgot bell, and now it's a special signal, as if he suddenly remembered something and clearly presented ... He shuddered, too already weakened nerves this time. A little later, the door opened a tiny crack: the old woman looked at her visitor with a clear gap of mistrust, and nothing could be seen shining in the dark eyes. But when he saw many people on the court, she grew bolder, and opened the door. The young man entered the dark corridor, was cordoned off from the tiny kitchen. The old woman silently in front of him and looked at him questioningly. It was a tiny, lean old woman of sixty, with sharp malignant eyes and a sharp nose and bareheaded. Colorless, a few gray hairs thickly smeared with oil. Her thin long neck, like chicken legs was tied to some flannel cloth, and on his shoulders, despite the heat, all hung tattered, yellow fur short jacket. The old woman coughed and groaned constantly. It must be the young man looked at her with a special look, because in her eyes suddenly flashed again mistrust.

- Raskolnikov, a student, was you back in a month - hastened to mutter a young man with a half bow, remembering that you have to be polite.

- I remember, sir, I'm very good at what you have, remember - clearly said the old woman, still not taking his inquisitive eyes from his face.

- So, with ... and again, on the same order ... - Raskolnikov went on, a little confused and surprised distrust year-old woman.

"It may, however, it is always the case, but at the time I did not see," - he thought with an unpleasant feeling.

The old woman was silent, as if in thought, stepped to the side and pointing to the door of the room, she said, allowing visitors the lead:

- Go on, sir.

Small room, which was a young man with yellow wallpaper, geraniums and muslin curtains on the windows, was at that moment brightly lit by the setting sun. "And then, therefore, so the sun will shine! .." - As if by accident, flashed through the mind of Raskolnikov, and a quick glance he scanned everything in the room as possible to learn and remember the location. But the room was nothing special. Furniture, all very old and of yellow wood, consisted of a sofa with a huge bent wooden back, an oval table in front of sofa, bathroom with a mirror in the pier, chairs along the walls so that two or three pennies photos in yellow frame with a picture of German women

4

with birds in their hands - that's all. In the corner, before the torch burning. Everything was very clean and the furniture and the floors were brightly polished; all shone. "Lizavetina work" - thought the young man. No dust can be found throughout the apartment.

"This is from the evil one and the elderly widow is so clean," - went on to himself and Raskolnikov looked curiously at the cotton curtain in front of the door to the second, tiny room, where there was an old woman bed and chest of drawers, and where it has never looked before. The entire apartment consisted of these two rooms.

- Anything? - Strictly said the old woman, entering the room and still in front of him to look him straight in the face.

- Mortgage brought, here, sir! - And he took out a silver watch old apartment. On the back was engraved globe. Circuit steel.

- Why, and still the mortgage term. Even the third day of the month before last.

- I'm still interested in the past month, I will give; Bear with me.

- And that, my good will, sir, or tolerate their job now sell.

- And for many hours, Allen I.?

- Walk with nothing, sir, nothing dignity, not worth it. Call the last time you two rubles, and it and buy something new in it to the jeweler, and half a possible ruble.

- The ruble to give something four, I will save the father. I'll get the money.

- Fifty percent of a forward and if you want, sir.

- One and a half rubles! - Said the young man.

- Your will. - And the old woman handed him back the clock. The young man took it and was so angry that he was on vacation; but then changed his mind, remembering that there is nowhere else to go, and that he also came after another.

- Let Us! - He said hoarsely.

The old woman took the keys from his pocket and went into another room behind the scenes. The young man, left alone in the middle of the room, it is interesting to listen to and think about.Could be heard as she unlocked the trunk. "This should be top drawer - he thought. - Keys, therefore, in the right pocket ... all in one bundle, steel ring ... And there's one key, the more three times, with the transfer of the beard, of course, from the chest ... So, there is some framework Ali laying ... This is curious. In the packaging of

all such keys ... And yet, how ugly everything ... "

The old woman returned.

- That, sir, sir, if USD per month with the ruble, as half of the ruble prichtetsya you fifteen cents a month ahead, sir. Yes, two former ruble you still have, in accordance with the same bill forward twenty cents. In general, therefore, thirty-five. We must now do you get for your clock ruble and fifteen cents. Here's get-to.

- How! so now the ruble and fifteen cents!

- Besides, sir.

The young man did not argue and took the money. He looked at the old woman and was in no hurry to leave, as if he still had something to say or do, but as if he did not know that ...

- I told you, Alyona Ivanovna, maybe one of these days, one more thing ... bring money ... well ... papirosochnitsu one ... that's how I will depart from each other ... - He was embarrassed and silent .

- Well, then we'll talk, sir.

- Farewell to ... And you're still sitting at home alone, sister, do not you?
- He asked how to facilitate, leaving the front.

- What are you to him, sir, is not it?

- Oh, nothing special. I asked. Since you now ... Goodbye, Alain Ivanovna!

Raskolnikov went into the decisive confusion. Confusion more and more increasing. Going down the stairs, he even stopped a few times, as if something suddenly udaril.Nakonets, on the street, he exclaimed:

! "Oh my God, how disgusting it all And in fact, I do not ... No, that's nonsense, it's ridiculous! - He added firmly. - And can such horror could come to my mind, that kind of dirt that is capable of However?, my heart is important :! dirty, dirty, disgusting, disgusting .. And I, for a month ... "

But he could not express in words or exclamations of his excitement. A sense of infinite disgust begins to oppress and torture his heart while he was just going to the old woman, had by now reached such size and so clearly revealed that he did not know where escape from his wretchedness. He walked along the pavement like a drunken man, oblivious passers-by, and when confronted with them, and came to the next street. Looking around, he noticed that stands next to the tavern, which was the entrance from the sidewalk down the stairs to the basement. Of doors, just at that moment, two drunken men came out and supporting each other, and a curse, climbed up on the street. Without thinking, Raskolnikov went straight down. Never

before put it into the tavern, but now his head was spinning, and besides burning thirst tormented him. He wanted to drink a cold beer, the more that his sudden weakness, he refers to the fact that he is hungry. He sat in the dark and dirty corner of the sticky table, beer and asked eagerly drank the first glass. All at once relieved, and his thoughts proyasneli. "All this is nonsense - he said with hope! - And there was nothing to be ashamed of simple physical disorder some one glass of beer, a piece of dry bread - and that, in an instant, strengthens the mind, yasneet thought harden intentions! Ugh, that all this pettiness! .. "But in spite of this scornful spitting, he looked fun, as if suddenly released from some terrible burden, and looked through the eyes of a friendly audience. But even at that moment he was vaguely aware that it was the best sensitivity to pain, too.

In the tavern, while there were few people. In addition to these two drunks that were caught on the stairs, and then the same time still have the whole gang, one of the five, with a single servant and harmony. After them, it was quiet and spacious. Stayed one step, but a little sitting for a beer, apparently the merchant; his companion, fat, huge, in anthrax and with a gray beard, very drunk, asleep on a bench, and sometimes, suddenly, as if asleep, and began to snap your fingers, hands, spread, and failures in the upper body, not getting off the bench and sang some nonsense, trying to remember the verses as:

Whole year caressed his wife,
Goal-ly the same year, and Las cal ...

Or suddenly waking up again:

Podyacheskaya went on
His former found ...

But no one shared his happiness; silent companion looked at him all these explosions even hostile and distrustful. There was also another man who looked like as if the retired official. He sat apart before his posudinkoy, sometimes stretching and looking around. It is also, as if some excitement.

⇜«»⇝

⪡ CHAPTER II ⪢

Raskolnikov was not accustomed to the crowd and, as already mentioned, running any society, especially in recent times. But now he suddenly pulled something for people. Something to do with it, as it was new, and at the same time it became apparent some people crave. He was so tired from all this month focused his wretchedness and gloomy excitement that, although now it's like to breathe in another world, even if it does not matter that he could, and, in spite of all the dirt of the situation, he was happy to stay in tavern now.

The host organization was in another room, but often come mainly down to her from somewhere on the steps, and especially showed his stylish blackout boots with big red lapels. He was terribly greasy coat and black satin jacket, no tie, and his whole face was like a greased, only iron lock. For zastoykoy was a boy of fourteen, and there was another younger boy, who served with what was offered. Were chopping cucumbers, black crumbs and chopped pieces of fish; it's all very smelly. It was stuffy, so it was even unbearable to sit and everything was steeped in wine to smell, which seems to be one of the air can be five minutes to get drunk.

There are other meetings, it is even with strangers we, the people, we begin to be interested at first sight, somehow suddenly, suddenly, before you say a word. What is your impression of Raskolnikov's guest, who was sitting a little way off and looked like a retired officer. The young man several times, and then remembered the first impression and even attributed his anxiety. He always looked at the clerk, of course, but also because he looked at It is difficult, and it was clear that what really wanted to start a conversation.

Otherwise, the former tavern, not excluding the host, the official looked somehow familiar and even boredom, and at the same time with a touch of haughty disdain, as if people with lower status and development, with whom he has nothing to say, he was a man in his fifties, of medium height and solid build, with gray hair and a big bald head, swollen from constant drinking yellow, even greenish face and swollen eyelids , because of which shone tiny as slits, but alive reddish eyes. But there was something in it very strange, in his eyes shone as if even enthusiasm - was probably the meaning and reason - but at the same time broke madness. He was dressed in old, tattered black coat completely collapsed with buttons. One only kept it, and that he and buttoned, obviously not wanting to go decency. From under nankeen waistcoat stuck shirtfront, all wrinkled, dirty and flooded. His face shaved, bureaucratic, but a long time, so that the already densely began performing blue-gray beard. And in his manner was really something hard-bureaucratic. But he was in trouble, disheveled hair and propped up sometimes in anguish, his head both hands, elbows on the torn slippery and sticky table. Finally, he looked straight at Raskolnikov and loudly and firmly said:

- And, I, my dear sir, I beg you to speak decent? For though you have not significantly, but my experience is different in you educated man to drink unusual. Sam always respected education, coupled with heart feelings, and, in addition, belong to the titular counselor. Marmalade - the name, the titular counselor. I dare to learn how to serve you going next?

- No, I'm ... - replied the young man, somewhat surprised and ornate special tone of voice, and the fact that so directly in the face, turned to him. Despite the recent instant desire even any kind of community with people, he first really spoke to him the word suddenly felt his usual nasty and irritated feeling of disgust to every person touches a stranger or someone just wanted to touch his personality.

- The student, therefore, or former student! - Cried officer - so I thought! Experience, sir, repeated experience! - And a sign boasting he put his finger to his forehead. - There were a student or graduate of place! Let ... - He stood up unsteadily, grabbed posudinku, glass, and sat next to a young man, some of them askance. He was a hop, but he spoke freely and boldly, only occasionally puts stumbling a bit, and tighten it.With some even eagerly pounced it Raskolnikov, exactly one month too, no one spoke.

- Sir, - he said, almost with solemnity - poverty is not a vice, it is the truth. I know that alcoholism is not a virtue, and it is even more so. But poverty,

sir, poverty - the vice-C. In poverty you still retain their innate sense nobility in poverty never anyone. For poverty is not even stick a broom down and removed from the human to the offensive was, and just because I'm the first in poverty, that he was willing to offend you. And, therefore, the salon! Dear Sir, month ago that my husband beat Mr. Lebezyatnikov, and my wife is not what I am! You see, sir? Let me ask you, because, at least in the form of simple curiosity: you are happy to spend the night on the Neva River on barges hay ?

- No, it did not happen, - said Raskolnikov. - What is it?

- Well, I was there, and already the fifth night, with ...

He poured a glass, drank and thought. Indeed, in his clothes and even hair in some places can be seen sticking out of grass hay. It is very likely was that he did not undress for five days and does not wash. Especially hands were dirty, greasy, red, with black nails.

His conversation seemed to be cast in general, although lazy attention. The boys at the bar began to giggle.The owner seems to be deliberately left the top of the listening room "fun," and sat down at a distance, lazy, but it is important, yawning. Obviously, marmalade was here long been known. And pretentiousness acquired speech, probably because of the habit of frequent kabachnym conversations with various strangers. This habit is drawn from other drinkers in need, and mainly in those house stands firmly and pushed around. That's why, and drinking in the company, and they always try to ensure that as an excuse, and, if possible, even respect.

- Fun! - loudly said the host. - Do not work on the cha cha do not serve if officially?

- Why did not I serve, sir, - raised Marmeladov, referring exclusively to Raskolnikov, as if he had asked him a question - why did not I serve? Is my heart does not hurt that I cringe vain? When Mr. Lebezyatnikov that a month ago, My husband beat his own, and I was lying drunk, I do not suffer? Excuse me, young man happened to you ... um ... well, at least seek to borrow money hopeless?

- Sometimes ... it's so hopeless?

- That is completely hopeless, knowing what would come of it. So, you know, for example, in advance and carefully, that this person is well-intentioned and naipolezneyshy citizen who would not give you money, why, I ask, he will? He knows that I will not give up. Out of compassion? But Mr. Lebezyatnikov that watches new ideas, explained the other day that compassion in our time, even science is forbidden and what has been done in England,

where political economy. Why then, they ask, it will give? And now, knowing that it will not, you can still go on a trip and ...

- Why walk? - Added Raskolnikov.

- And if not for everyone, if nowhere else to go! We must give every person who at least somewhere could poyti.Potomu that there is a time when all means have at least somewhere to go so! When my only begotten daughter for the first time in the yellow ticket went and I went ... (for my daughter to live with a yellow card ...) - he added in parentheses, with some concern looking at the young man, - Nothing, sir Nothing! - He hurried at once, and apparently calm, say when snorted and boys behind the counter smiled and owner. - Not at all! Sim shaking chapters, do not hesitate because everyone already knows everything and all the secret becomes clear; and not with contempt, and with humility to this position. Let! and let! "Behold the Man!"Excuse me, young man, you can ... No, Explain stronger and well you do not you can, and you dare, at the moment, looking at me and said, yes, I'm not a pig?

The young man did not answer a word.

- Well, - he continued, solid and even with the government, this time should wait again followed by a giggle rooms. - Well, I let a pig, and she is a lady! I have a wild way, and Katerina Ivanovna, my wife - and daughter educated man born ofitsera.Pust head, let me wretch, it is also the heart of a highly refined senses and education are made. And yet ... and oh, if she felt sorry for me! Sir, sir, we have to give that every man, At least one such place, where would feel sorry for him! And Katerina Ivanovna lady though generous, but fair ... And although I understand that when she pulls my hair, then pulls them only as pity heart (because, I repeat, do not hesitate, she pulls me curls, young man - he confirmed, with particularly worth hearing again giggles), but my God, what if it is at the time ... But no! no! all these things for nothing, and have nothing to say! nothing to say! .. Because it happened more than once to be desired, and not once have felt sorry for me, but ... this is my hell, and I were born cattle!

- You bet! - Said, yawning, master.

Marmalade strongly banged his fist on the table.

- This is my hell! You know, you know, sir, that I even stockings propyl? No shoes, sir, for that at least some will not like the order of things, and stockings, stockings with her handkerchief from her propyl goat down too propyl, gift, old, her own, not my !; and we live in a cold coal, and this winter's cold

and cough have already passed blood. Children we have three, and Katerina Ivanovna in from morning till night, and scratches cleans and washes the children, for the purity in izmaletstva used to, but with the breast and weak consumer inclination, and I feel like it. Do not I feel? And the more I drink, the more and feel. Drink and disgusting that the seed of compassion and a sense of looking . Not fun, but the general malaise looking for ... Pugh, just because I want to suffer! - And he, as if in despair, bowed his head on the table.

- A young man - he continued, straightened again - in the face of your I read as if some grief. How come I read it, and therefore immediately and addressed to you. To tell you the story of my life, not to disgrace themselves want to put before these prazdnolyubtsami, who already know everything, and sensitive and educated man looking for. Know that my wife in the noble provincial nobility Institute educates and leaving the shawl dance with the governor and other persons to whom the gold medal and received a certificate of merit. Medal Medal ... well, to sell something ... so long ... um ... for services still is not in the trunk, and recently showed his mistress. And although the hostess in her naibespreryvneyshie struggle, but at least until someone wanted to be happy and proud to announce about past days. And I am not guilty, not guilty of them, because in the past from her and left her in his memoirs, and other things crumbled Yes, yes !; hot lady, proud and unbending. Sex itself washes and sits on black bread, and disrespect will not be allowed. That's why Mr. Lebezyatnikov rude, he did not want to go down and when nailed her Mr. Lebezyatnikov, it is not so much from the beatings, but from a sense of laying in bed. The widow took her three children, one less than.She married her first husband, an infantry officer, for love, and with him ran out of my parents' house. My husband loved too, but in game of cards blank, was on trial because he died. Biwa he did in the end; and though she did not take it as far as I know for documents and known, but still remembers him with tears and reproaches me with it, and I'm happy, I'm happy, because although their imagination sees himself only happy ... And she stayed with him after three young children in the county and far Cruel, where I was then, and remains so poor, hopeless, I though many different kinds of adventures and even can not describe. My relatives otkazalis. Da and proud was too proud ... And then something, sir, I am also a widower, and his first wife, with fourteen year old daughter, held out his hand because he could not look at such suffering. It is possible to judge because

the extent to which it has reached a disaster, it is formed and educated and well-known names for me to agree to go! But it was a lamentation and wailing and wringing hands - gone!Because there was nowhere to go. You see, you see, sir, this means that if you have nowhere to go? No! Then you still do not understand ... And a whole year I performed my duties pious and holy, and do not touch it (he pointed to polushtof), because I have a feeling. But Sim failed to please, and then lost his place, and through no fault, and change the state, and then touched! .. and a half years ago, will have, as we found ourselves finally, after much wandering and misery, this magnificent and decorated with numerous monuments of the capital. So I took ... a place to get lost again. You see, sir? There's already lost through their own fault, because my dash came ... now living at the same angle, the owner of Amalia Fyodorovna Lippevehzel, but how we live and what we pay I do not know. To live well there, and many besides us ... Sodom, with ugly ... um ... yeah ... And in the meantime increased, and my daughter from his first marriage, and that she only suffered my daughter, his stepmother age that I glossed over. For though Katerina Ivanovna and determined generous feelings, but the lady is hot and irritation, and tear off ... Yes, sir! Well, there's nothing to think about it! Education as You can imagine, Sonia has not received. I tried for about four years, the geography and history of the world to go, but as I am in the knowledge of this and was nekrepok, and a decent operating instructions were not available, which is available for the book. .. um .. Well, now they are not these books, so did all the training, on the Persian Cyrus stopped. Later, reaching adulthood, she read several books a romantic content, but in recent years, through Mr. Lebezyatnikov, one book - "Physiology" Lewis, if you please to know, sir? - with great interest and even read aloud to us fragments said, that's all her education.Now turn to you, my dear sir, from himself to the issue of privacy: how many you can think of a poor but honest woman to earn an honest living? .. Fifteen cents a day, sir, will not work, to be honest, and has a special talent, and that the hand is not hard at work! And then State Councillor Klopstock, Ivan - were happy to hear? - Not just money for half a dozen Dutch sewing shirts have not yet, but even with the crime took her, stamping his feet and called indecent, under the guise of alleged shirts gates are not sewn up and the jamb.And then the children are hungry ... And Katerina Ivanovna, wringing her hands, walks around the room, but they were red spots on her cheeks act - it is a disease, and it is always like this: "You live, they say, you darmoedka, we eat, drink is, and use the heat,

"but what they drink and eat, and when the kids something to three days peel can not see anything! I was lying then ... well, yes it too! Lying drunk-with, and hear, says my Sonia (unrequited she, and her voice was so gentle ... belokurenkaya, pale face always slender), said: "Well, Katerina Ivanovna, do the same thing to me this thing go?" And Daria Frantsevna, evil woman and the police often known, two or three times through the mistress broke. "And what - is responsible Katerina Ivanovna, in Hippolais -?!, Which protects Eco treasure" But do not blame, do not blame, sir, is not to blame! Not in his right mind would say that these things, and when anxious feelings, in sickness and at the cry of the children who did not eat, and it is said for the sake of more abuse than in the strict sense ... to Katerina Ivanovna is a lot of character, and rasplachutsya as children, even if hunger, immediately begins to beat them. And I see advertisements in the sixth hour, Sonia got up, put on a handkerchief, put burnusik and apartments went up, and at the ninth hour ago and returned. Come and chat to Katerina Ivanovna, and on the table in front of her thirty-one rubles silently laid. Not a word did not say, even if looked, and took only our great dradedamovy green scarf (general example we have a handkerchief, dradedamovy), covered them completely head and face and lay on the bed, facing the wall, just a hanger body, so that all tremble ... And I, as now, in the same form, with lay ... And then I saw a young man, I saw how Katerina Ivanovna, and, without saying a word, went to Sonya and all the little crib evening at her feet knelt, kissed her feet, did not want to get up, and then only two, and sleep together, arm in arm ... two ... two ... yes sir ... and I was lying ... pyanenkoy - p.

Marmalade pause, as if his voice broke. Then, suddenly, hastily poured and drank and grunted.

- Since then, sir, - he continued, after a pause, - on the one side and in the representation of evil persons - which was especially promoted Daria Frant-sevna because, although she, as appropriate, honoring skimp - my daughter Sophia Semyonovna, yellow ticket was forced to accept, and together with us on the occasion of these things could not stay. For the mistress, Amalia Fyodorovna, they do not want to admit (as herself in front of Daria Frant-sevna contribution), and Mr. Lebezyatnikov ... um ... Here's something for Sony and reached its history with Katerina Ivanovna. At first he tried to Sonya, and here and ambitions suddenly: "How, they say, I'm so enlightened man in an apartment with takovskie will live" And Katerina Ivanovna did not disappoint, got up ... and there ... and Sonia comes to us now more in the

twilight, and Katerina Ivanovna easier and possible means of delivering the same ... He lives in an apartment on the tailor Kapernaumovs, apartments and removes them Capernaum chrome and tongue-tied, and all his large family too vague. And his wife, too tongue-tied ... In one room are placed, and Sonia has its own special, with a partition ... Um, yeah ... people are poor and inarticulate ... yes ... just got up in the morning, I was with, clothed my rags, threw up his hands and went to his excellency Ivan Afanasievich. His Excellency Ivan Afanasevicha deigned to know? .. No? Well, God does not know the man! This - wax ... wax before the Lord; Thou wax melts! .. Even the tears, you will hear everything. "Well said, marmalade, once you have deceived my expectations ... I you once again for your personal responsibility - and said - remember, they say, to go," I kissed the dust of his feet, mentally, because it really does not have former dignitaries and people new government formed and thoughts; returned home, and as announced that the service again enlisted and get paid, my God, that was then! ..

Jam stopped again in great excitement. At this time came from the street a bunch of drunk, drunk already, and there were at the entrance to the sounds of the hurdy-gurdy and hired children, seven-year cracked voice, singing "Farm". Become noisy. Master and servant engaged novichka.Marmelad ignoring included, began to continue the story. He seemed to be very weak, but it becomes more fun, so get slovoohotnee. Memories of the recent success in the service as it will be revived and even reflected in his face some radiance.Raskolnikov listened attentively.

- That, sir, five weeks ago. Yeah ... just found out that they both, Katerina Ivanovna and Sonia, my God, I've just moved into the kingdom of God. Sometimes are like cattle, only swearing! And now: walking on tiptoe, children hard: "Semen Zaharych service tired, resting, TM"! Coffee before my service to water, boil the cream! This cream for starters, you hear! And where did they put together their obmundirovku decent eleven rubles fifty cents, I do not understand? Boots, calico shirt - great shape, all for eleven and a half cooked in great shape, sir. I came on the first day of the morning service, see: Katerina Ivanovna cook two dishes, soup and corned beef with horseradish, and what concepts are still not available. The dress does not present it does not ... I mean, not with, then just visit came dressed up, but not something so, out of nothing will not be able to do everything: pricheshutsya, the collar is there a clean cuffs, a completely different person goes, and younger and more beautiful. Sonia, my love, only money contributed the most, tell me

now, ahead of time, you often have inadequate, so that if, in the twilight, that no one has seen. Hear, hear? I went to sleep in the afternoon, so you think it did not suffer Katerina Ivanovna: A week with the landlady, Amalia Fyodorovna, the latter had a falling out, and a cup of coffee here is called. Two hours and all were whispers: "Tell me, now Simon Zakharych service and receives a salary, and His Excellency himself, and His Excellency came out, all told to wait and seeds Zakharych past all handmade office." Hear, hear? "I, of course, says Simon Zakharych memorization skills, and even if you were in this frivolous weakness, but since you are now promised, and that beyond that without you we went bad (Hear, hear!), And I hope that says Now on your word of honor ", that is all I can tell you, went and came, not what I was frivolous, to boast one! No, sir, she believes all things, his own imagination amuses itself , by Jove, sir, I do not blame them; No, I do not blame her! .. When, six days ago, I pay my first - twenty-three rubles forty cents - fully brought shrimp called me, "said Shrimp, you some! "And alone, with, you know? Well, so what, I think, for beauty, but what I wife? No, pinched his cheek:" Shrimp you some "- says.

Marmalade stopped, tried to smile, but suddenly his chin began to twitch. However, he refrained. This tavern, perverted views, five nights in the hay barges and Damascus, and at the same time, this painful love for his wife and family knocked him putat.Raskolnikov students listened attentively, but with a sense of painful. He was annoyed that he came here.

- Sir, sir! - Exclaimed Marmeladov restored - my dear sir, you can be all the laughter, as a friend, and I only bother you stupid all these meager details of my family life, well, I can not laugh! Because I can feel it all ... and all the heavenly day of my life and all night, I myself in my sleep volatile transferred, and this is how I would do it all, and children will wear, and she will give Spock and daughter My only-begotten a disgrace to the family will bring ... And much, much ... It is permissible, sir. Well, you're my father (Marmeladov suddenly as if startled, looked up and stared at the audience) Well, the next day, after all these dreams (ie, it will be exactly five days ago that) in the evening, I cunning deception, like a thief in the night, stole Katerina Ivanovna of his key trunk, took what was left of the wages earned, as I do not remember, and that, sir, look at me, everyone! The fifth day of the house, and there I was looking for, and the end of life, and his uniform in a tavern on the Egyptian bridge lies, in exchange for which these things and got clothes ... and the end of all things!

Marmalade banged his fist on the forehead, clenched his teeth, closed his eyes and leaned his elbow firmly on the table. But a moment later, his face suddenly changed, and some mock cunning and audacity wrought looked at Raskolnikov, laughed and said:

- Today, Sonia went to ask a hangover! Heh-heh-heh!

- Really gave? - Someone shouted from the arrivals, cried and laughed at full throat.

- Here are the most polushtof her money and bought - said Marmeladov, referring exclusively to Raskolnikov. - Thirty cents made with their own hands, the past, all that was, he saw ... He did not say anything, just looked at me in silence ... It's not on the ground, and there ... people are grieving, crying rather than reproach do not blame them! And it hurts with the patient's, when you do not blame them! .. Thirty cents, yes, sir. And yet, and now they need it, eh? What do you think, my dear sir? In the end, she now has to comply with chistotu.Podtyanutost costs money, something special, you know? You know? Well, there's too sweet to buy, because you can not, sir; starched skirts, shoes kind, pofiglyarnee set the pace when the pool will have to move.You see, you see, sir, that smartness means? Well, here I am, blood father of thirty-something, these cents and got to hang! And to drink, sir! And it propyl, sir! .. Well, who like me, excuse me?and? I'm sorry now, sir, or not? They say, sir, excuse me, or not? Heh-heh-heh-heh!

He wanted to pour, but there was nothing. Polushtof was empty.

- Yes, what you regret that? - Cried the host, appeared again with them.

Was laughter and even curses. Laughing and swearing and listen neslu-shayte, so looking only for one piece of a retired official.

- Pity! Why feel sorry for me! - Suddenly shouted Marmeladov standing with outstretched hand in the decisive inspiration, as if just waiting for those words. - Why am sorry, did you say? Yes I am! I regret that I did not at all! I should be crucified, crucified, and not regret! But crucify judge, crucify, and crucified, have pity on him! And then I'll go to your propyatie, because it's no fun thirst and sorrow and tears! .. How do you think the seller, it is your polushtof I will gladly go? Sadness, grief, I was looking at its bottom, sorrow and tears, and eat, and found; and deliver us from the one who took pity and everyone knew everyone and everything that he is one, he and the judge. It comes in one day and asked, "Where is the daughter of the evil stepmother and hectic, that children and young stranger betrayed? Where the daughter that the earth drunk avoid her father, not the terrible atrocities, excuse

me? "And said," Come! I've already forgiven you once ... just once ... you are forgiven, and now thy sins harbored many, for what loved much ... "And forgive my Sonia, sorry, I know that I just ... just now as it was in my heart felt! .. And will judge and forgive, and good and evil, and wisdom, and myrrh ... And when finishing first and foremost, and then vozglagolet us: "Well, tell me you leave drunk, weaken, soromniki go! "And we will leave all without shame, and let us. And they say:" Pigs Beast you picture and print it; but come and thank you! "And vozglagolyat wise, vozglagolyat reasonable," Lord, why have you priemlesh now? "and said," Because of its purpose, wisdom, because acceptable, reasonable, that none of them, he did not consider himself worthy of this ... "stretch us rutse yourself, and we fall down and cry ... ... and understand everything! Then everyone will understand! .. And everyone will understand ... and Katerina Ivanovna ... and she will understand ... Lord, Thy kingdom come!

And he sat down on a bench, exhausted and exhausted, anyone not looking as if he had forgotten the environment and in deep thought. His words made some impression; for a moment there was silence, but soon heard the old laughter and cursing:

- It will be the judge!
- Zavralsya!
- Official!

And so on. And so on.

- Come on, sir, - said Marmeladov suddenly raised his head and turning to Raskolnikov - bring me home ... a goat in the yard. It's time ... to Katerina Ivanovna ...

Raskolnikov had long wanted to leave; help him, as he thought. Marmalade was much weaker than in the legs than in the speeches, and leaned hard on the young man. Go was two or three hundred paces. Confusion and fear mastered more drunk as you approach the house.

- I do not Katerina Ivanovna now afraid - he murmured excitedly - and not the fact that he begins to tear his hair. What hair! .. Blah hair! I'm talking about! It's even better if she starts to vomit, and I am not afraid ... I am afraid of her ... eyes ... eyes ... yes ... red spots on her cheeks too afraid. .. And more - her breathing Vidal afraid ... Do you know how to breathe this disease ... unsettling feeling? The baby cries too afraid ... Because, if Sonja is not supplied, then ... I do not know! I do not know! And I'm not afraid to beat ... You know, sir, that I was beating so not only does not hurt, but there is joy ... For

without this, I myself can not do. It's better. Let the beat, soul ... it will take better ... But the house. Cosel house. Locksmiths, German, rich ... the lead!

They entered the yard and went to the fourth floor. Ladder farther, the darker. It was almost 11:00, and although at this time in St. Petersburg, there is no real night, but on the top of the stairs was very dark.

Little smoky door at the end of the stairs, at the top, was opened. Ignited lit room poorest ten paces in length; All of this can be seen from the passage. All were scattered in disarray, especially for children of different cloth. Through the back corner was full of holes stretched sheet. Behind her, probably posted bed. In the same room there were only two chairs and very ragged oilcloth sofa, in front of which stood an old pine kitchen table, unpainted and in no way covered. At the end of the table was a fat burning candle in an iron candlestick. It was found that marmalade was placed in a special room, not in a corner, but the room was contact. The door to the room or further cell into which Amalia Lippevehzel apartment was ajar. Was noisy and flashy. Laughed. It seems, played cards and drank tea. Sometimes words flew most netseremonnye.

Raskolnikov immediately recognized Katerina Ivanovna. It was terribly emaciated woman, thin, quite tall and slim, but with a beautiful dark brown hair, and with flushed cheeks to stain. She paced back and forth in his small room, his hands folded on his chest, with dry lips and uneven, jerky breathing. Her eyes glittered like a fever, but the look was sharp and motionless, and the painful impression of consumer and excited person in the past weakening light candles trembled on her face. Raskolnikov she appeared about thirty years old, and did not really have a couple ... Marmeladov Inbox she did not hear and did not notice; thought she was in some kind of trance, do not listen and did not see. The room was stuffy, but she did not open the windows; carried down the stairs stinks, but the door to the stairs was not the shutter; from the interior, through nepritvorennuyu door, a wave of smoke, she coughed, but the door does not apply. The little girl, six years old, sleeping on the floor, for example, sitting, squatting and bury his head in the couch. The boy, a year older than she, trembling in a corner and cry. Its probably just arrived. The older girl, nine years old, vysokenkaya and thin as matches, one thin and everywhere torn shirt and bare shoulders thrown over the old dradedamovom burnusike sewn to her, probably two years ago, because it does not reach to the knees, and now stood in corner next to the little brother around his neck, his long, withered arm, as matches. She seems

to have rebuked him, whispered something to him, he strangles, he somehow did not whined again, and at the same time with the fear of the mother watched her big, big dark eyes, which seemed to be more on her haggard and frightened face. Marmalade, not entering the room, stood in the doorway to his knees, and Raskolnikov pushed forward. Woman, seeing a stranger, absently stopped in front of him for a moment, as if waking up and wondering why he entered into it? But, really, she immediately imagined that he goes to the other room, as they had communicating.Realizing is not paying more attention to him than she went to the door of hay to pretend to them, and suddenly shouted, seeing on the threshold of her husband on his knees.

- Ah! - She screamed in a frenzy - is back! Convict! Monster .. And where is the money? What's in your pocket, show me! And the dress is not so! where your dress? where is the money? Tell me! ..

And she ran to look for him. Marmalade immediately obedient and submissive his hands on both sides to facilitate the search karmane.Dengi were not a penny.

- Where's the money? - She was crying. - Oh, God, he still propyl! After twelve rubles left breast! .. - And suddenly, in a rage, she grabbed him by the hair and dragged room.Marmalade in itself contributes to its efforts humbly crawling over her lap.

- And this is my joy! And I'm not in pain, and in us-premium denie, milo-o-ho-ho-Gift Su - he shouted, stunning hair and even just bumping his head on the floor. Sleeping on the floor of the child awoke and began to cry. The boy in the corner could not stand, trembled, cried and rushed to his sister in a terrible fright, almost in a fit. The older girl was shaking like a leaf from a dream.

- Propyl! everything, everything propyl! - I cried in despair poor woman - and not a dress! Hungry, hungry!(And, wringing her hands, she pointed to the children). Oh, damn life! And you, shame on you - suddenly attacked his Raskolnikov - the tavern! Have you seen him? You, too, drank with him! Get Out!

The young man hurried away without saying a word. In addition, the inner door opened wide, and from it came a few curious. Stretch arrogant laughing with head and cigarette tubes, in yarmulkes. Could see figures in robes and completely wide open in the summer obscene costumes, with other cards in their hands.Especially comical they laughed when Marmeladov, pull hair, shouted that it was his joy. They even began to enter the

room; came finally sinister screech: it is their way forward Amalia herself Lippevehzel produce daily in their own way, and for the umpteenth time to scare the poor woman forcibly order to remove the apartment tomorrow. Before leaving, Raskolnikov had to stick his hand in his pocket, Zagreb copper coins inherited from him in exchange tavern ruble, and inconspicuously placed on the window. Later, on the stairs, he changed his mind and wanted to return.

"Well, what is this nonsense, so I did - he thought - they have Sonia and I'll have to." But, judging that it is impossible to return, and that made it no longer took, he waved his hand and went to his apartment. "Sonia sweet, too, need, - he continued walking down the street, and smiled sarcastically - worth the money dexterity ... Hmm But Sonia something, maybe yourself today obankrutitsya, because the same risk, hunting red beast. .. gold mining! ... here they are, consequently, for tomorrow beans without my money somehow ... Oh, Sonya! What is good, however, managed to dig up! and enjoy! That is because there is! And used. cry, and are used to. To all scoundrel, a man accustomed to! "

He wondered.

- Well, if I lied - he exclaimed involuntarily - if not really a scoundrel man, all in general, the whole human race, that is, it means that everything else - prejudices, not afraid of anything, except themselves, and there are no obstacles, then it must be so! ..

←«»→

←« CHAPTER III »→

He woke up late the next day, after a restless sleep, but sleep did not support it. He woke up bilious, irritable, angry, and stared at his cubicle. It was a tiny closet, six paces in length, which had the most miserable with their little yellow, dusty and everywhere behind the wall wallpaper, and so low that a man becomes just above it terribly, and everything seemed about to stukneshsya head on the ceiling. Furniture corresponded to the room: there were three old chairs, it is not working properly, painted table in the corner, on which lay a few notebooks and books; Already, as they were dusty, it was not obvious that they no longer bother Hand draw; and finally, the big clumsy sofa, which occupied almost the entire wall and half the width of the entire room as soon as cotton is soft, but now in tatters and served as Raskolnikov's bed. He often slept on it as it was, without undressing, without sheets covered with his old, decrepit, student coats and shooting with a pillow on his head, under which puts all that was linen, clean and worn to make it higher headboard. Front of the sofa stood a small table.

It was hard to fall more and obneryashitsya; Raskolnikov, but it was nice even in his present state of mind. He strongly ahead of all, like a turtle in its shell, and even face maid obliged to serve him, and sometimes look in his room, woke him bile and seizures. This is what happens in other delusions, too something to focus on. Mistress of his two weeks as he stopped to dish, and he had not thought yet to talk to her, though, and sat without dinner. Nastasya, the cook and the maid only mistress, kind of glad that it is the tenant and the mood completely stopped it clean and place, so only once a week, by chance, was made sometimes on a broomstick. She woke him now.

CRIME AND PUNISHMENT

- Come on, that you sleep! - She was crying over it - the tenth hour. I brought you some tea; he loves tea, then? Go exhausted?

Tenant opened his eyes, startled and learned Nastasya.

- Tea something from the hostess, huh? - He asked, slowly and with a pained look, sitting on the couch.

- Kako from the mistress!

She set before him a cracked kettle with tea already asleep, and put two yellow lumps of sugar.

- Here, Nastasia, take, please, - he said, fumbling in his pocket (he slept dressed), and pulling out a handful of copper, - go out and buy me Saikou. And take a sausage sausages, although a bit cheaper.

- Saikou I bring sow minutes, loves, and whether it is instead of sausage-Ing it? Good soup, yesterday.Yesterday you put down, but you have come too late. Good soup.

When the soup was brought and he made them, Nastasya sat down beside him on the sofa and began to talk.That women of the village and very talkative woman.

- Praskovya Pavlovna in a police sting on what you want, - she said.

He frowned hard.

- The police? What does she want?

- Money is not paid and do not agree with Vater. It is known that it is necessary.

- Uh, this feature is still not enough - he muttered, skrypya teeth - no, I now ... Report ... Dura it - he added aloud. - Today I go to her and talk.

- Fool fool, the same as I do, and you know what a clever man, lying like a sack of anything you do not see?Firstly, you say you went to teach children, and now, why do not you do it?

- I do ... - reluctantly and sternly said Raskolnikov.

- What do u do?

- The Work ...

- Kaku work?

- I think - seriously he replied after a pause.

Nastasia and roared with laughter. She was cheerful, and when rassmeshat, laughed softly, rocking and shaking all over, yet not too violently ill.

- Money is a lot, and came up with? - She finally managed to say.

- No shoes can not teach children. Oh, and do not care.

- You do not spit into the well.

ROBOTS READ

- For children with copper wages. What penny? - He said reluctantly, as if responding to their thoughts.

- And you would be right all the capital?

He looked at her strangely.

- Yes, all the capital - he said firmly, after a pause.

- Well, you little by little, and then ispuzhalsya; scary actually sharpened. Saikou for something to go or not to go?

- As you wish.

- Yes, I forgot! Write a letter yesterday, because without you it.

- Letter! for me! from whom?

- From whom do not know. Penny postman gave her. You will give, or what?

- Conduct So, for God's sake, bring! - Shouted in excitement all Raskolnikov, - Lord!

A minute later, the letter was. That's right: mother-P - th province. He paled even take it. For a long time did not receive his letters; but now has something else suddenly squeezed his heart.

- Nastasya, go away, for God's sake; Here are your three pennies, but for God's sake, hurry to leave!

Letter trembled in his hand; he does not want to print with him: he wanted to be alone with that letter. When Nastasya came out, he quickly lifted it to his lips and kissed her; Then for a long time staring at the addresses handwriting, in a familiar and dear to him sheep and handwriting kosenky his mother, who taught him once to read and write. He hesitated; he even seemed to be afraid of something. Finally published: Letter was a big, dense, in two lots; two large leaves finely mail-namelko inscription.

"My dear Rodia - wrote to his mother -. Within two months of the weird, as I have not talked to you in writing, from which she suffered and even at night did not sleep, thinking, But maybe you do not accuse me of this involuntary My Silence. You know how I love you, you are one with us, for me and Dunya, you're everything to us all hope, our hope, that happened to me when I learned that you have a few months left for the University. than the lack of support for themselves, and that the lessons and other means to stop! How could I have my one hundred and twenty rubles a year boarding school for you? fifteen rubles I sent you four months ago, I took, as you know, because of the the same pension at the local merchant Athanasius Ivanovich our clothiers. He's a good man and still a friend of your father. But by giving him

the right to receive a pension for me, I had to wait for payment of debts, and it is only now it turned out that I did not could all the time to send you. But now, thank God, I think I can send you to others, and now we can even boast of fate, which I hasten to tell you. And above all, do not you think, dear Rodia, that your sister lives in six weeks with me, and we are no longer separated in the future. Thank God, it ended torture, but I'll tell you all right, so you know how it was, and we of you are still in hiding. When you wrote to me two months ago that he had heard from someone like Dunya tolerate much rudeness in the house of the Lord Svidrigailov, and asked me to accurate explanations - that I could write you back? If I wrote you the truth, then you probably would have dropped everything and even on foot, and come to us, because I feel like your character, and you know, and you would not give offense to his sister. I myself was in despair, but what could I do? I did the whole truth I do not know then. Importantly, the difficulty was that the Dunya, joining last year in his native governess took forward a hundred rubles, subject to a monthly deduction from wages and, consequently, it was impossible to leave the place, do not pay their debts. The same number (now I can explain to you all the invaluable Rodia) took it upon themselves to send you sixty rubles, which then, as appropriate, and that you and received by us in the past year. Then we were deceived, wrote that it was due to a buildup Dunya old money, but it was not so, and now tell you the truth, because now everything has changed overnight, according to the will of God, and for the better, and that you know how to love you Dounia and that her precious serdtsa.Deystvitelno Mr. Svidrigailov first treated her very rudely and made it another rudeness and ridicule at the table ... But I do not want to deal with all these heavy parts to do not bother you for nothing, when it's all over, short, despite the noble and treatment of Marfa Petrovna, Mr. Svidrigailov wife, and all the houses, Dounia was very hard, especially when Mr. Svidrigailov was an old habit of his regiment, under the influence of Bacchus. But what happened? Imagine that this madcap long Duns conceived a passion, but it is hidden under the mask of cruelty and contempt for her. Perhaps he was ashamed and terrified, seeing myself in years, and the father of the family, with such frivolous hopes and so angry with Dunya involuntarily. Or maybe the fact that he rudeness of his conversion and ridicule just wanted to cover the whole truth of the other. But in the end could not resist myself to make a clear and Duns proposal, promising a variety of awards and, in addition, to drop everything and go with her to another village or perhaps

abroad. Can you imagine all her suffering! Leave Now place it was impossible, not only because of the monetary debt, but also to spare Marfa Petrovna, who can suddenly understand the suspicion and, therefore, would have to live in the family discord. And for Dounia will be a great scandal; it really was not. There were many different reasons, so that six weeks before Dunia would not expect to get out of this terrible home. Of course, you know, Dunya, you know, she's smart and what a strong character. Dunya can withstand a lot, and even in the most extreme cases, to find a lot of generosity, not to lose its firmness. She did not write to me about everything, so as not to upset me, and we often passed on the news. Decoupling also come unexpectedly.Marfa Petrovna overheard her husband begged Dunya in the garden, and understand all wrong, in all of its own and accused think that this is the whole point. They occurred there in the garden horrible scene: Marfa Petrovna even struck Dunya would not listen, and she cried for an hour, and finally ordered to take immediate Dunya me into the city on a simple peasant cart that fell all his belongings, underwear , dresses, everything as it happened, and do not involve unfolded. And standing in the pouring rain, and Dunya, insulted and disgraced, had to go with a guy seventeen miles on the bus Cart. Think now that I could write you a letter in response to yours, I got two months ago, and what to write about? I myself was in despair; really do not dare to write to you, because you would be very unhappy, upset and indignant, and what you would do? Maybe even destroy themselves, and Dunia is prohibited; and fill out a letter and trivia about anything, but in my heart so sad that I could not. The whole month we walked around town gossip about this story, and before too realized that we were even in the church could not go any further with Dunya scornful glances and whispers, and even loud when we were talking. All something familiar alienated from us, everything stopped even onions, and I probably learned that employees and clerks will make us poor insult, smeared with tar gate of our house, some merchants so that the owners began to demand that we have moved from the apartment, it was the cause of Marfa Petrovna, who managed to accuse and contaminate Dunya in all homes. She is familiar with each and every minute of this month is coming to town, and since she was a little talkative and loves to talk about their family affairs and, in particular, complain about her husband, and all, which is very bad, then pitched the entire history for a short time, not only in the city but also in the area. I got sick, I Dounia also stronger, and if you've seen it all, and gave birth to

me, comforted and encouraged! She is an angel! But, by God's grace, Our meal was reduced: Mr. Svidrigailov repented and changed his mind, and perhaps regretting Dunya not presented Marfa Petrovna a complete and compelling evidence of innocence throughout Duns, namely a letter Dunya still until when Marfa Petrovna found them in the garden, was forced to write and tell him to give up the personal explanations and secret meetings at which he insisted, and who, because of Dounia, remained in the hands of Mr. Svidrigailov. In this letter she most ardent and full indignantly rebuked him for it neblagorodstvo hold its relatively Marfa Petrovna, delivered him to pretend that he is a father and a family man, and that, finally, how disgusting his side torment and misery of already poor and defenseless girl . In a word, my dear Rodia, the letter was so nobly and touchingly written that I cried while reading it, and still I can not read without tears. In addition, in order to justify the Dunya, were finally and certificates employees who saw and knew much more than I expected, and himself, Mr. Svidrigailov, as it will always be found. Marfa Petrovna was completely shocked and "Rekilled", as she admitted to us, but he is convinced of the innocence of Duns and the next day, Sunday, came straight to the cathedral, on his knees and tearfully begged the lady to give her strength to bear this new challenge and to do his duty. Then, right out of the cathedral, in order not to stop, came to us and told us all, bitter and full repentance embraced Dunya cried and begged her to forgive. That same morning, without delay, directly from us, did not go to all the houses in the city and elsewhere in the most flattering for Dounia point, shedding tears, regained her innocence and nobility of her feelings and behavior. In addition, all displayed and read aloud Dunya autograph letter to Mr. Svidrigailov and even allowed to make a copy (which I think is too much). Thus, it has been several days to go around the city, as well as others were offended that others favored and thus dilute all, so that in every house lay ahead, and everyone knew that in such and such that day Marfa Petrovna would be something to read this letter, and each reading is once again going even those that letter several times and listened to in their own homes, and other friends, one by one. My opinion is that many, many things, there was too much; but Marfa Petrovna has such character. At least, he completely restored the honor of Dounia, and all the enormity of this case is an indelible disgrace to her husband as the main culprit, so I even feel sorry for him; too strictly deal with this MADCAP. Dunya once was invited to give lessons in some homes, but she refused. In general, all of a sudden

he began to be treated with special respect. All this contributed to a large extent, and unexpected, with which I can now say that all our destinies.You know, dear RODIA that Dunya persuade the bride, and she has already given his consent, and I hasten to tell you how it's done, you can skoree.Hotya without your advice, but you probably will not be to me or to my sister in the claim as he will see out of business just wait and save to get your answer will be impossible for us. Yes, and you could not discuss all correspondence accurately. It's the same thing happened. He has a court counselor, Peter Luzhin, and a distant relative of Marfa Petrovna, who was very helpful with this. Began by saying that through it expressed a desire to meet with us as it was to be adopted, drinking coffee, and the next day sent a letter in which he explained very politely asked his proposal and the speedy and decisive response.Man he business and employment, and in a hurry now in St. Petersburg, so cherish every moment. Of course, we were very impressed at first, because it all happened so quickly and unexpectedly. Think, and we thought the whole day. Man, he is trustworthy and security in two places and already has his capital. Nevertheless, he was forty-five years, but it is very beautiful and still can like women, and the people he is very solid and decent, just a little surly and seemingly arrogant. But it is, perhaps, the only way it seems at first glance. And I warn you, dear Rodia, as can be seen with him in St. Petersburg, what will happen in a very short period of time, do not judge too quickly and passionately, as is typical for you, if first you do something does not seem, I say this is the case, though I am confident that he will make a good impression on you. And, in addition to any man was mistaken, you have to treat it slowly and carefully, so as not to fall into the error and prejudice, which are very difficult to fix and after to make amends. And Peter, at least, in many ways, a man highly esteemed. During his first visit, he told us that he is a positive, but has many, as he put it, "the latest generation of our beliefs," and the enemy of all prejudices. And much more, he said, because the kind of little vain and likes to be listened to, but it's hardly a crime. Of course, I understand a little, but Dounia explained to me that he is a man of education, although small, but smart and seems to be good. You know the nature of your sister, Rodia. This girl is a solid, sensible, patient and generous, albeit with a passionate heart that I learned that it was good. Of course, neither of his or her hand a special love here, but Dunya, except that a smart girl - at the same time and be noble, like an angel, and the debt will put yourself happy husband, who, in turn, will take care about her happiness, and

recently we have, for the time being, a big reason to doubt, although skorenko admitted to do business. In addition, he is a man very prudent and, of course, he sees that his family fortune will rather than his Duns be happier. And that there are irregularities in nature, some old habits and even some differences in ideas (which in itself a happy marriage can not be bypassed), on this account Dunya, she told me that she hopes; that there is nothing to worry about, and that it has a lot to move, provided that the future relationship will be honest and fair. For example, he first and seemed as if sharp; but it can happen just because a simple man, and, of course, wrong. For example, the second visit, has already received consent, in a conversation he had put that much before, not knowing Dunya, put the girl to take, to be honest, but without a dowry, and, of course, the one that has experienced heavy; because, as he explained that the husband does not have to be his wife, and a lot better if the wife believes her husband of his benefactor. Add that he put a little softer and kinder than I wrote, because I forgot to submit an expression, and remember only one idea, and, in addition, he said that was not intentional, but obviously said in the heat of the conversation, so that even then tried to restore and soften; but I still thought it was a bit like sharply, and then I told Dunya. But Dunya even angrily responded that "the word wrong," and this is certainly true.Before deciding Dounia did not sleep all night, thinking that I was asleep, got out of bed and all night walking up and down the room; Finally, knelt down and prayed fervently and before the image, and the next morning I was told that she decided.

I have already mentioned that Peter is now in St. Petersburg. He received great things, and he wants to open in St. Petersburg public law office. He has long been involved in walking on the various claims and litigation, and recently just won an important battle. In St. Petersburg the same, and therefore it is necessary that there was one major thing in the Senate. Thus, dear Rodia, he can be very useful, even in all things, and we have already put Dunya you, even at the present day the same, of course, would like to start my future career and considered his fate is already clearly defined, ah, if it's true! It would be such a benefit, it is necessary to consider it as nothing but direct to us by the grace of God. Dunya just dreaming about it. We ventured to say a few words on this topic Peter. He put it mildly, and said that, of course, since he can not do without a secretary, of course, it is better to pay wages relative than a stranger, if only he will be able to send (of course, you could not!) but immediately and expressed doubt that your university

studies will not leave you time to practice in his office. At this time, no matter ended, but Dunya about anything, moreover, is not thinking. She now has a few days, just a little heat and have a project that later you can be a partner or even companion Peter in his controversial research, the more that you are on the faculty. Rodia I quite agree with her and share all her plans and hopes, seeing in them the total probability; and, in spite of the present, due to the very evasiveness Pyotr Petrovich (because he does not know you), Dunya firmly believes that reaches all its beneficial impact on the future of her husband, and that she was sure. Of course, we said Peter ostereglis though about anything from these dreams of our future and, most importantly, that you will be his companion. He is a man positive and probably would have taken a very dry, as it all seemed to him alone dreams. In addition, neither I nor anyone syllable Dunya not talked to him about our strong hope that he will help us promote you money while you at the university; because it did not say that, firstly, he will be later and he probably without further ado, he will offer (of course he denied it something Dunya) is more likely that you yourself can become his right-hand man to the office and get this care is not as good deeds, but as you honor salary.So Dunya wants to set up, and I quite agree with her. But, secondly, because I did not say that I particularly wanted to put you with him at the upcoming meeting of our present, on a flat foot.When Dunya told him about you with delight, he replied that everyone should first examine themselves and closer so that he judged, and that he gives himself to meet with you to make you an opinion. You know that my invaluable Rodia, I think a number of reasons (though not related to Peter Petrovich, and, according to some of my whims, personal, even, perhaps, the old woman, women) - it seems to me that I might be better to do, if I live after their marriage, the more that are currently living, not with them. I'm sure it is, that it will be so noble and gentle, he invited me and offer me not to be separated from her daughter, and if you did not say, so far, of course, because without words, so it is assumed; but I refuse. I noticed that my time of life that Tiffany is not very husbands are in the center, and not only do I not want to be at least someone, even in the slightest load, but also the desire to be completely free, now I at least some of its part because children like you and Dunya.If you can, I'll stop next to both of you because Rodia is something good, I have accumulated at the end of the letter, know well, my dear friend, that perhaps very soon we will get together again all together and embracing all three after the separation of almost three years! Already

, probably decided that I leave Dunya in St. Petersburg, where he is, I do not know, but in any case, very, very soon, maybe even a week. It all depends on the order of Peter Petrovich, who, as soon as consideration in St. Petersburg, immediately and let us know. He immediately wanted to, according to some estimates, as much as possible to speed up the wedding ceremony, and even if it is possible, as a wedding gift in a meat-eater, and if you can not, in the short term, after gospozhinok. Oh, how happy I am, you press down on my heart! Dunya in all the excitement of joy goodbye to you, and said again, a joke that already from this will go to Peter Petrovicha.Angel it! Now she did not explain to you, but only told me to write that she was so much to talk to you so that now her hand is not raised, and take up the pen, because in a few lines do not write, but only the upset; order the same hard hug and send you a lot of kisses. But, despite the fact that we can be very soon going to do in the face, I did the other day you send as much money as I can. Now, as everyone will know that Dunya for Peter Petrovich, and my credit has increased suddenly, and I probably know that Afanasy Ivanovich, believe me now, due to retirement, even up to seventy-five rubles, so I can be twenty rubles -Five or even thirty send. Sent to more, but I fear for our travel expenses; and although Peter was kind enough to take on the part of the cost of our trip to the capital, namely voluntarily at their own expense, to take our luggage and a large chest (once he got through a friend), but the world is all we need to consider arrival in St. Petersburg, which can not be shown without a penny, at least for the first few days. We, however, are calculated from Dun accuracy, and it was that way will nemnogo.Dlya railway from us just ninety miles, and we, in any case, in agreement with one known to us, man-cabin; and there we Dunya preblagopoluchno ride in the third grade. So maybe I'm not twenty-five, and probably manage to send thirty rubles. But enough; two sheets upisatsya circle, and place a very long stay; All our history; Well, yes and accidents as accumulated! And now, my invaluable Rodia, keep you close to our goodbye and bless you with my motherly blessing. Love Dunya, his sister, Rodia; I love the way she loves you, and I know that it's you infinitely more love. She is an angel, and you, Rodia, you have everything - all our hopes and all hope. Could you just be happy, and we pray to God schastlivy.Vy, Rodia, and still believe in the goodness of whether our Creator and Redeemer? I fear in his heart, not been there, and you the latest fashion unbelief? If so, I pray for you.Remember, expensive, even in childhood, during his father's life, you murmured a prayer on his knees and as

we all were happy then! Good-bye, or better,goodbye ! Hug you tight and kiss countless times.

Your to death

Pulcheria Raskolnikov.

Almost all the time, like Raskolnikov read from the beginning of writing, his face was wet with tears; but when he was finished, he was pale, twisted spasm, and severe, bile, evil smile curled his lips. He lay his head on his thin and well worn pillow and thought long thought. Pounding his heart, and greatly concerned about their thoughts. Finally, it was stuffy and cramped in this little room yellow, like a closet or trunk. Eyes and thought, please space. He grabbed his hat and went out, this time, not being afraid to meet someone on the stairs; he forgot about it. The path that he took to Vasilevsky Island on B - First Avenue, as if hurrying there for business, but, according to his custom, went without noticing the road, whispering to himself and even speaking aloud to him, very surprised passers-by. Many mistook him for a drunk.

←«»→

←« CHAPTER IV »→

Letter exhausted his mother. But in relation to the main, capital item doubt that it was not even for a minute, even in something else, as he read the letter. The main crux of the matter was resolved in his mind and finally decided: "Do not go to this marriage, while I am alive, and to hell with Mr. Luzhin"

"Because it is the obvious thing - he muttered, grinning wickedly and triumphant success of the promotion of their decisions.! - No, Mom, no, Dunya, you can not fool .. And I'm sorry that my advice was not given, and Case decided without me! However, I think it's too much and you can not beat to see lzya or not! I'm sorry, that capital "because it supposedly business man Peter, a business man, and marry that otherwise could not, as in the post, almost on the railroad. "No, Dounia, all that I see and know what you're doing to me a lot of conversations going, and I know that you thought all night, pacing the room, and that he prayed to Our Lady of Kazan, who have mothers bedroom .. Calvary is difficult to grow Um ... So, then finally decided too: for business and rational person would be willing to go, Avdotya Romanovna, with its capital (already having their capital, is a solid, impressive) serving two places and share the belief of our newest generations (writes his mother), and "seems good, "she says Dunya. It seems to be just great! And the same for the same Dunya think married! .. Excellent ! Very Well! ..

... It is curious, but then, what about the mother "a new generation of something," I wrote? Just to characterize a person or with a further purpose: to cajole me in favor of Mr. Luzhin? On the sly! It is interesting to know one

more thing: the extent to which they were both frank with each other sisters, day and night, and in all subsequent time? Are all the words between them were clearly stated, or both realized that one and the other in the heart and mind, so it's not easy to say out loud something for nothing so to speak. Perhaps in part because it was; The letter is clear: Mom, he seemed stiff, a little bit, but naive mother and got to Dunya with his comments. And this, of course, angry and "meet with disappointment." Of Course! Who does not enrage when it is clear and without naive questions, and when he decided that there was nothing to talk about. And she writes to me: "Love Dunya, Rodia, and it will never be longer loves itself"; I do not remorse, if this is the secret torment for being the daughter of his son agreed to donate. "You are our hope, you are everything to us!" Oh, mother! .. "Seething with anger in him more and more, and if you met him now, Mr. Luzhin, he seems to have killed him!

"Hmm, it's true - he went on, following a whirlwind of thoughts swirling in my head - it is true that a person should" approach slowly and carefully to find out, "but Mr. Luzhin clearly important ,." business man, and it seems to be good! ":? Joke luggage took over, a large chest at his own expense delivers There is not good, and they somehow, the bride and her mother, a peasant contract many in the basket, mats covered (I started attending) Nothing Just because that ninety miles, "and there preblagopoluchno drive in the third grade," thousands of miles and wisely:!. on clothes a stretch in the legs, so what do you say, Mr. Luzhin, what? After all, it's your bride .. . And he could not know that his mother under his pension on the road holding? Of course, here you have a total commercial turnover, the company is mutual benefit and in equal proportions, means and costs twice, with bread and salt together and spend one from each other, as they say And then a little business man podnadul :. swag something cheaper rate with them, and maybe go for nothing. Well, they both do not see, and that al purposely did not notice? And it's pretty, pretty ! And I think that is just the beginning, but the real fruits to come! In the end, what is important here: there is no greed, not skaldyrnichestvo important, but the tone of it all.This is the future tone after marriage, a prophecy ... And that's what a good mother, however, carousing? What she Petersburg will be something? With three of the ruble al with two "ticket", says ... old ... ahem! Than to live in St. Petersburg, she hopes, then what? In the end, she was somehow able to guess what her with Dunya can not live together after marriage, even in the early days? Cute man probably once here

let slip made itself felt, although the mother and dismisses both hands on this: "Sam, they say, give up." That it is, in hopes that a hundred and twenty rubles pension, with net debt to Afanasy Ivanovich? Winter scarf she knits, embroiders cuffs yes, her eyes the old port. Why Shawl only twenty rubles a year added to one hundred and twenty-something rubles, I know that. So, still on the generosity of feelings Mr. Luzhin hope: "Sam, they say, offer, ask to be." Keep your pocket! And so that's always these beautiful souls Schiller: until the last moment ryadyat peacock feathers man until the last moment for good and not evil hope, and even anticipating turnover of medals, but would like to submit in advance of the word did not reprimand; warps from one of his thoughts; both arms fire from the truth, as most since painted their own nose to stick with it. It is interesting whether Mr. Luzhin Order; I bet the mortgage on that Anna in his buttonhole, and what he did for lunch contractors and vendors is. Maybe wear their wedding! And yet, to hell with it! ..

Yes ... Well, let's mother, so God bless her, she really was, but that Dunya? Dunja, my dear, because I know you! In the end, you have the twentieth year was then, as we have seen for the last time: the nature of something I already knew yours. Mother won writes that "Dounia much can carry." I know that, sir. This is me two and a half years ago, already knew, and since then two and a half years of thinking about it, that's exactly what "Dounia has much to carry." Oh, when Mr. Svidrigailov, with all the consequences can carry, it is true that a lot can carry. Now imagine, with his mother, and that Mr. Luzhin can carry, we present the theory of the superiority of his wife taken from poverty and make good husbands, and even presents little in common with the first date. Well put, this "slip", although a reasonable person (so maybe not slip, namely in mind that quickly explain), but something Dunya Dunya? After her man something clear, and even a place to live with a man. In the end, it is black bread still drink water, not to mention his soul will not sell, not to mention his moral freedom does not give comfort; for the whole of Schleswig-Holstein will not give, not what Mr. Luzhin. No, it was not Dunya, as I knew, and ... well, yes, of course, does not change now! .. What can I say! Heavy Svidrigailov! Hard two hundred rubles for life as a governess for provinces wander, but I still know that my sister and go to negros planter or Latvians Baltic Germans than opodlit his spirit and his moral sense in conjunction with a person who does not respect and with which it has nothing to do - ever, from its own profits! And whether even Mr. Luzhin all one of pure gold, or from one of the diamond, and then refused to become

law concubine Mr. Luzhin! Why now agree? What is the thing, then? What is the solution? The thing is clear: for themselves, for their comfort, even to save himself from death itself will not sell, and for foreign markets! For cute, adorable person to sell! That's what our whole thing, and it's something: his brother because his mother to sell!Everything will be sold! Oh, here we are, on occasion, and give our moral sense; freedom, peace, even conscience, all, all in a little market demolished.Intermittent life! If only these beloved creatures we were happy. In addition, his own casuistry coined the Jesuits and learn for a while, perhaps, to convince myself to convince myself that it is necessary, in fact, need for a good purpose. That is what we are, and everything is clear as day. Obviously, this is none other than Rodion Romanovich Raskolnikov course and is in the foreground. Well, somehow, his happiness can be organized at the university include Companion done in the office, his whole future secure; may subsequently rich, honored, respected, and perhaps even a good man ended his life! And the mother? Why, then, Rodia, an invaluable Rodia, the firstborn! Well, as for the first-born as a daughter and do not donate! About cute and unjust heart! But why: here we have a lot of Sonia may not give up! Sonya Sonya Sonya Marmeladova eternal, and the world! Sacrifice something, sacrifice something you both measured completely? Right? By virtue of this? In favor of this?Does it make sense? Did you know Dunya that Sonechkin not much Fel lot with Mr. Luzhin? "Love can not be here," - says my mother. And what if, in addition to love something, and respect can not be, but, on the contrary, already have an aversion, contempt, disgust, then what? And then go out and, again, therefore, the "purity observe '' have to. It's not that it? You see, you see that smartness means? Do you understand that the purity of Luzhin would like Sonia and purity, and perhaps even worse, nastier, meaner, because you, Dounia, still in a calculation of comfort, and is simply a question of hunger is! "Expensive, expensive, Dunya, smartness! "Well, if you can not afford it becomes, to repent? Tribulation something much grief, curses, tears, something to hide from everyone, how much, because you do not Marfa Petrovna? A mother with that then? In the end, it is also now a restless, tormented, and when all is clear you see? And I? .. But what you really me something to think about? I do not want your sacrifice, Dounia, I do not want my mother, do not come to while I'm alive, does not happen, does not happen, do not take it! "

He suddenly woke up and stopped.

"It would not be? And what did you do to make it not happen? Ban? And

what right have? What can they promise to turn to the right to be? All of their destiny, they devote all future when he finished and place get it? We have heard it, but it beeches, and now? After all, here we now have to do something, you know? And what do you do now? fleeced of their own. In the end, the money under their hundred-dollar pension and under masters Svidrigailov under the mortgage gets! Svidrigailov From then on something Athanasius I. tailors than them shalt thou be the next millionaire, Zeus, their fate is? more than ten years? Yes, in ten years time mother blinded by kerchiefs, and possible, and tears quickly ischahnet and sister Well, guess minutes, which can be with her sister Ali ten years in ten years, I know "??

So tormented and teased himself with these issues, even with a certain pleasure. However, all these questions are not new, unexpected, and the old, painful, long. Long since they began to torture him and tormented his heart. Once upon a time, as it appeared in the modern all the pain grows and accumulates recently matured and concentrated, taking the form of a terrible, wild and fantastic question that tortured his heart and mind, irresistibly demanding resolution. Now a letter to his mother suddenly hit him in the thunder. It is now clear that it was necessary not to miss, so as not to suffer passively, some arguments that the issues can not be resolved, and, of course, something to do, and right now, and as soon as possible. In what may be necessary to determine that at least some, or ...

"Or to give up life at all! - Suddenly screams in ecstasy - obediently accept fate as it is, once and for all, and to stifle a whole, renouncing any right to act, to live and love!"

"You see, you see, sir, this means that if you have nowhere to go? - Suddenly remembered against him yesterday Marmeladova question - because it is necessary that everyone, at least somewhere you can go ... "

Suddenly he started with one, too, yesterday, the thought flashed again in his head. But he did not flinch, because the thought flashed. He knew that he had a premonition that she would "sweep", and was waiting for her; Yes, and this idea is not yesterday. But the difference is that a month ago, and even yesterday, it was only a dream, and now ... now suddenly not a dream, but in some new, horrible and rather unusual form, and suddenly he knows it ... . He knocked on the head, and dark eyes.

He quickly looked around, he was looking for something. He wanted to sit down, and he was looking for a bench; Then he went on K - th Avenue. Bench can be seen in front of a hundred paces. He went quickly as he could;

but on the way happened to him one little adventure that is within minutes of his attention.

Looking bench, he saw before him, at twenty paces, a woman walking, but at first did not dwell on this attention, like all still flickering before him questions. He more than once happened to pass through, for example, at home, and I do not remember the road on which he walked, and he was so used to going. But the woman, walk was something strange and, at first glance, it appears that little by little attention to its beginning it involves - at first reluctantly, as if with vexation, and then more and more. He suddenly wanted to understand that this woman is so strange? Firstly, it must be very young girl was on such znoyu bareheaded, without an umbrella and without gloves, something ridiculous waving his arms. She was dressed in silk, lightweight material ("tissue") dress, but also as something very wonderful to wear, barely buttoned at the waist and back, at the beginning of the skirt, torn; beam back and hung dangling. Small shawl was draped over the naked neck, but got stuck somehow crookedly and sideways. To end, the girl went, staggering, stumbling and staggering in all directions. The meeting opened in the past, all the attention of Raskolnikov.He became friends with a girl, bench, but when he reached the bench, and she fell on her in a corner, threw his head back on the bench and closed her eyes, apparently from extreme fatigue. Looking at him, he knew right away that she was very drunk. Strange and wild look at this phenomenon. He even thought that he was not mistaken. Before him was a very young person, sixteen, even, perhaps, only fifteen - small, belokurenkoe, beautiful, but all flushed and as if swollen. The girl seems to be very few really understood, one foot is placed on top of the other, and put it far more than I should, and, apparently, very bad knowing that he is on the street.

Raskolnikov sat down and would not go away, and stood before her with a grain of salt. This boulevard and always deserted, but now, in the second hour, and in this heat, it was almost empty. Yet Well aside fifteen steps, on the edge of the boulevard, stopped a gentleman who, apparently, is also very much like to approach a girl with some goals. He also probably saw her from afar and catch up, but he was prevented from Raskolnikov. He gives him a dirty look, trying, however, that he did not notice them, and waited impatiently for their turn when accidents torn leaves. This was understandable. This gentleman was about thirty years old, fat, fat, blood and milk, with pink lips and mustache, and very elegant. Raskolnikov is very angry; He

suddenly wanted to somehow offend this fat dandy. For a moment, he left her and went to the master.

- Hey, you, Svidrigailov! What do you want here? - He shouted, clenching his fists and laughing their zapenivshimisya rage lips.

- What does this mean? - Strictly asked Mr. frowning down and surprised.

- Get out, that's what!

- How dare you, you scoundrel! ..

And he waved his whip. Raskolnikov rushed at him with his fists, not even hoping that the Lord could handle firmly with two like him. But the moment someone grabbed him from behind tightly between them became a cop.

- Well, gentlemen, if you do, please do not fight in public. What you want? Who's that? - Strictly he turned to Raskolnikov, making out his rags.

Raskolnikov looked at him. It was a gallant soldier face with a gray mustache and sideburns and a reasonable view.

- You are just what I need - he shouted, grabbing him by the arm. - I am a former student Raskolnikov ... That you can learn - he said to the lord - and you Come on, I'll show you something ...

And they took the hand of the police, he dragged him to the bench.

- Here, look, quite drunk, now on the Boulevard: Who knows what, and it does not seem to craft. Rather, as soon as somewhere watered and cheated ... the first time ... you know? yes and let the street. See how torn dress, to see how it should be: because it is dressed, and not she dressed, and wore a clumsy hands, man. This can be seen. Now look here: dandy, with whom I now wanted to fight, unfamiliar to me, the first time I've seen; but he said that he, too, is expensive, drunk something he did not remembering something, and now he really wants to come up and catch her - because she is the state - to deliver somewhere ... and it's probably because : Believe me, I'm I'm not mistaken. I saw the way he looked at her and looked, but I prevented him, and now he is waiting for all when I'm gone. There he now moved little worth if cigarette rolling ... How can we not give it? How should we send her home - think for a minute!

The policeman immediately understood and realized. The fat man was, of course, of course, were a girl.Soldier leaned over her to see closer and sincere compassion to portray his features.

- Oh, sorry, it's true! - He said, shaking his head - just as a child. Deceived, it's simple. Look, ma'am, - he began to call her - where are you going next live? - The girl opened her eyes tired and stupidly looked at posolovelye

investigators and waved.

- Look, - said Raskolnikov, - that (he fumbled in his pocket and pulled out a twenty cents, there was), here, take a taxi and tell him to deliver the address. Just for the solutions that we know!

- The young lady and the young lady? - Police began again, taking the money - I'll take a taxi, and you alone are sent. Where would you like? a? Where are you going next Lodge?

- Pshla! .. Stay! .. - She murmured again and waved.

- Oh, oh, how bad it is! Oh, the shame something like, girl, shame, what! - He shook his head again, shame, regret and indignation. - In the end, this is a problem! - He turned to Raskolnikov, and then, briefly, once again looked him up and down. Strange, is not it, and it seemed to him, in such tatters, and he gives the money!

- You are far l find them? - He asked him.

- I'll tell you in front of me was stunning, right on the boulevard. As for the bench came in and fell.

- Oh, what a shame now find themselves in the world, O Lord! Nemudrenyh kind, and, of course, drunk!Deceived, this is how it is! Vaughn and dress them broke ... Oh, how debauchery something Nona went .. And perhaps this is noble, poor public ... Nona many of these materialov.Po type something like from the tender, if in fact the young lady - and again he leaned over her.

Maybe he grew up the daughter of the same - "as if the young lady, and the tender", with the manners of a well-educated and all have absorption modnichanem ...

- Home - fussed Raskolnikov - this is a wretch like no! Well, it is still above the outrage! The heart can see what he wants; ish villain, not a waste!

Raskolnikov spoke loudly and pointed at him with his right hand. He heard and wanted to get angry again, but changed his mind and was limited to one scornful look. Then slowly walked ten steps and stopped again.

- Do not give them something that's possible, sir, - said the non-commissioned officer thought. - Now, if only they were told where they provide, and then ... The young lady and a young lady! - He leaned back.

It really opened my eyes suddenly looked as if realized something, got up from the bench and went back in the direction from which it came.

- Fu, shameless, stick! - She said, waving again. She went quickly, but still varies greatly. Dandy went for it, but for a different avenue, not taking his eyes off her.

- Do not worry, I will not, sir, - said categorically barbel and went after them.

- Oh, debauchery something like Nona went! - He repeated aloud, sighing.

At this moment, as if something had stung Raskolnikov; at the time, seemed overturned.

- Hey, hey! - He exclaimed after barbel.

- Leave it! What do you want? Drop! Let him great pleasure (he pointed to the dandy). You what?

The policeman did not understand and looked me in the eye. Raskolnikov laughed.

- Oh-oh! - A soldier said, waving his hand, and followed a dandy and a girl, probably taking Raskolnikov il hurt, or something even worse.

"Twenty cents blew my - angrily said Raskolnikov, left alone. - Well, even so, too, will be released and the girl with him, and the end ... And then I came here to help Oh, yes I can help! I have l I have the right to help Yes, let pere-glotayut each other alive? - some to me, and I dared to give these twenty cents Are they mine. "?

Despite these strange words, it has become very difficult. He sat on the left bench. His thoughts were distracted ... And in fact it was hard to think at this point any further. He would like to completely forget, forget everything, and then wake up and start all over again at all ...

"Poor girl! .. - He said, looking at the empty corner of the bench. - Wake up, cry, and then the mother finds out ... First, will beat, and then whip hurt and offended, perhaps the tides. .. And do not Squeegee, so to still get wind Daria Frantsevna and start throwing my baby, yes here and there ... Then, when the hospital (which is always with those who are mothers live very calm and fair play tricks on them), and there .. but then again the hospital ... ... wine taverns ... and the hospital ... in two or three -. cripple, total plaguing her nineteen al eighteen years, with all the ... Am I not seen this? And how do they do? Yes, well done ... Ugh! And let them! This, they say, and it should. This percentage, say, you must go every year ... somewhere ... hell, should be to relax and refresh them not to interfere percentage nice, however, they have these little words:.!, they comfort, he said :. scientific interest, then do not worry now if. another word, well then ... it was would probably be restless ... And, as Dun and percentage fall! .. Not one, so the other? ..

And where do I go? - He suddenly thought. - Strange. In the end, for some reason I went. How to read the letter and went ... on Vasilevsky Island,

ROBOTS READ

Razumikhin, I went there, I remember now .... But why, though? And the idea to go to Razumikhin flew me now in my head? That'S Great ". He wondered to himself. Razumikhin was one of his former colleagues at the university. It is remarkable that Raskolnikov, when he was studying at the university, there was almost no friends, all off anyone and do not go for the adoption difficult. However, he soon turned all. Neither the general meetings or in conversations or games, all that he somehow did not participate. He worked without sparing himself, and he was respected for it, but no one liked. He was very poor and somehow haughtily proud and unsociable; as if to hide something.Otherwise, his friends thought he was looking at them at all, as a child, down, as if he had them all beat up and development, and knowledge, and beliefs, and their beliefs and interests as he looks at something less .

With Razumihina he somehow became friends, this is not something that has converged, and was with him to communicate, to be honest. However, since it was impossible to be Razumikhin in other respects. It was an unusually cheerful and sociable guy, well ease. However, with the door hidden simplicity and depth and dignity. Most of his friends knew, everyone loved him. Was he really is not stupid, but sometimes really a simpleton. His appearance was expressive - tall, thin, always bad-shaven, dark-haired. Sometimes he brawled and had a reputation for strong. One night, in the company, he was put off in one fell swoop guardian growth twelve inches. He could drink forever, but he could not drink; Leprosy sometimes inappropriate, but could not, and leprosy. Razumikhin was still so great that it does not fail never troubled and poor conditions, could not seem to hold him. He could not even apply for the roof, to endure a hellish hunger and unusual cold. He was very poor and very strong, one of which contains itself, getting Coy what works for money. He knew that the gulf sources where I could see earnings rate. After he had spent the whole winter has not sunk into her room and claimed it was even better because in the cold better sleep. Currently, he also was forced to resign from the university, but not for long, and because of all the forces in a hurry to correct the circumstances, to be able to continue.

←«»→

⟵ CHAPTER V ⟶

"In fact, I recently Razumihina still wanted to work asks him to me or took lessons or anything ... - think of Raskolnikov - but that now he can help me let the lessons would get install even the last penny share if ? he has a penny, so you can even buy boots and fix the suit to go to class ... um ... Well, and then? on the coin, what can I do? I just want now? Right, it's funny that I went to Razumihina ... "

On the question of why he went now to Razumikhin troubled him even more than he thinks; anxiously looked at him a sinister meaning for himself in this seemingly most ordinary actions.

"Well, I really wanted it all to fix one Razumihina and all the results found in Razumikhin?" - He asked himself in surprise.

He thought and rubbed his forehead, and, oddly enough, somehow accidentally, suddenly and almost by itself, after a very long deliberation, came to him a very strange idea.

"Um ... to Razumikhin, - he said suddenly, quietly, as if in the sense of a final decision - I will go to Razumikhin, of course ... but it - not now ... I'm on it ... the other day, after how that I will go when it is finished and will be when everything is new will ... "

And then he came to his senses.

"After this - he exclaimed, jumping up from the bench - yes unless it ? will not really be? "

He threw the bench and went almost ran; he wanted to return to the house, but home he suddenly felt terribly disgusting: there is something in the corner, it's horrible wardrobe and matures allthis for a month, and he

went aimlessly.

Willies it turned into some sort of feverish; he felt even chills; in this heat he felt cold. As if with an effort he began, almost unconsciously, by some inner necessity, to peer into all the subjects faced, as if searching for hard fun, but it is poorly managed it, and he always fell into a reverie. When once again, shuddering, raised his head and looked around, then immediately forgot that currently thought, and even where he was. So he went all the Vasilevsky Island, went to Malaya Neva, crossed the bridge and turns into the island. Greenery and freshness liked his tired eyes in the first place, accustomed to urban dust, lime and huge, displacing and oppressive home. There was no stuffiness, no stench, no taverns. But soon these new, pleasant sensations passed into painful and razdrazhaet.Inogda he stopped in front of some of the cottage, decorated with green, looked at the fence, I saw in the distance, on balconies and terraces, discharged women and children running around in his interest sadu.Osobenno flowers; He watched them all for a long time. Met him too magnificent carriages, horsemen and horsewomen; He watched them curiously eyes and forget about them before they hid from the eyes. Once he stopped and counted his money: There were about thirty cents. "Twenty police, three Nastasya for the letter - so Marmeladovs gave yesterday and forty-seven cents Ali fifty" - he thought, somehow expected, but soon forgot even and why the money out of your pocket. He thought about it, passing one edible places like taverns, and felt that he would like to eat. Enter the tavern, he drank a glass of vodka and ate with a sort of pie filling. He finished his back on the road. He is a very long time to drink vodka, and it instantly worked, although there was only drunk one glass. Legs suddenly heavy and he began to feel a strong desire to sleep. He went home; but before reaching the island of Peter, stopped completely exhausted, left the road, went into the bushes, and fell on the grass and at the same time falling asleep.

In the state of the disease is characterized by frequent dreams Extraordinary convex, brightness and extraordinary resemblance to reality. Consists picture sometimes monstrous, but the atmosphere and the whole process all representations thus likely before and with such subtle and unexpected, but artistically relevant data completeness image that they did not actually invent the same dreamer, whether it is the same artist Pushkin or Turgenev. Such dreams, painful dreams, always remember for a long time and made a strong impression on the already excited and upset the human body.

Raskolnikov had a terrible dream. He dreamed of his childhood, even in the city. He is seven years old, and a walk on holiday, in the evening, along with his father in the country. Time gray, gasping day, the area in the same way as experienced in his memory even in his memory, much more worn than it is now in a dream. The city is open, at first glance, a circle or a willow; somewhere very far away, on the edge of the sky turns black forest. A few steps from the last town garden stands a tavern, a great pub, always makes a bad impression on him, and even fear, as he passed him, walking with her father. There has always been such a crowd, so shouting, laughing, cursing, ugly and hoarse singing and so often fought; Circle Tavern wandered always drunk and scary faces ... When meeting with them, he lies against the father and trembling. Tavern near the road, dirt road, always dusty, and dust on it is always so black. It meanders further steps and three hundred rounds right to the city cemetery. Among the cemetery stone church with a green dome, in which he once or twice a year went with his father and mother in the church, when he served as a memorial service for his grandmother, who died long ago, and that he had never seen. At the same time, they always took with him kutyu on a white plate, napkin, and was Kutya sugar rice and raisins dent in cross Fig. He loved the church and old on her way, mostly without pay, and the old priest trembling grave head.Beside my grandmother, who was a stove, and was a little grave of his younger brother, who died six months later, and he also did not know and did not could remember ,; but he was told that he had a little brother, and every time he is on a visit to the cemetery, religious and respectful cross over the graves and bowed to her and kissed her. And the dream to him, they go with his father on the way to the cemetery and walk past the tavern; he holds his father's hand and looking fearfully at the tavern. Special circumstance attracts his attention: this time, it seemed, holidays, crowd, dressed meschanok, women, their husbands and chern.Vse drunk all sing songs, and near the porch kabachnogo worth cart, but a strange cart. This is one of those big carts drawn by a large draft horse and transport them into products and wine barrels. He always liked to look at these huge dray horses dolgogrivyh, with thick legs, walk calmly at a measured pace, and pulling it some whole mountain, not nadsazhdayas, as they carts even easier than without carts. But now, oddly enough, in such a large wagon drawn was a small, skinny, Roan Peasant klyachonka one of those - he often saw it - fatigue sometimes with some high wood or hay, especially if WHO stuck in the mud or in the track, and at the same time so painful, so

painful to beat guys always spurs, sometimes even on the face and eyes, and he felt so sorry, so sorry to look at it that he almost crying, and my mother always took his out of the window. But then suddenly becomes very noisy: out of the tavern, shouting, singing, drunk with a balalaika-prepyanye such great people in red and blue T-shirts with a coat saddle. "Sit down, sit down all - Cries one, still young, with a thick neck and a fleshy, red as carrots, face - all'll take, take!" But immediately hear the laughter and cheers:

- What nag so lucky!
- Yes, you Mikolka in mind that if you: like a mare in Taku cart zapreg!
- But savraske about twenty years without fail so will my friends!
- Sit down, all'll take! - Again Mikolka shouts, jumps into the cart first, takes the reins and gets in front of his full height. - Doubling the bay with Matthew gone - he shouts from the cart - the mare and Etta, my friends, my heart just cried, so it will be, I think she was killed, a gift of bread to eat. I say sit down! Gallop comin!Gallop go! - And it raises the whip gladly whip savrasku.

- Yes, sit down, then! - Laughter in the crowd. - Hey, come at a gallop!
- It gallop something really ten years, I believe, do not jump.
- Returned!
- Do not be sorry, my friends, to take all the whips, zgotovlyay!
- And then! Seki it!

All climb in Mikolkinu cart laughter and jokes. Nalezlo six people, and another can be planted. Take with thee one woman, fat and rosy. She calico in Kichko with beads on his feet cats presses nuts and giggles.Circle in the crowd laugh, too, and really, they do not laugh: like Lyada mare yes Taku will bear the burden of a gallop! Two guys in a shopping cart at once to take a whip to help Mikolka. You hear: "Well!"Klyachonka pulls hard, but not limited to a gallop, and even a little step can only handle minced feet, moaning and squats on three lashes, rolling in it, like peas. Laughter in the cart and in the crowd but udvoivaetsya Mikolka angry and furious blows flogs accelerated mare just really believes that she will ride.

- Allow me, my friends! - Cries razlakomivshiysya one guy from the crowd.
- Sit Down! All sit down! - Cries Mikolka - all lucky. Race against the clock! - And gushing, gushing, and did not know that and hit the madness.
- Dad, Dad - he screams father - Dad, what do they do? Dad, Poor horse to beat!

- Come on, come on! - Says his father - a drunk, naughty, fools Well, do not look! - And he wants to take him, but he pulled out of his hands and, beside himself, runs to the horse. But too bad the poor horse. She gasps, stops, pulls back, almost falling.

- Seki to death! - Cries Mikolka - on this issue. Race against the clock!

- What are you on the cross, or something, no, damn! - The old man shouted from the crowd.

- View oh, what a nag Taku carrying the load - adds another.

- Zamora! - Cries third.

- Do not touch! Oh my God! What I want, I do. Sit! All sit down! I want to go into a gallop without fail! ..

Suddenly heard a volley of laughter and covers everything: the mare did the frequency of shock and helplessness start kicking. Even the old man broke down and chuckled. And indeed: Sort Lyada mare, and still kicking!

Two guys from the crowd to get more whip and flog run to cut her hand. Everything works in their favor.

- On the face of it, in the eyes of trenchant in his eyes! - Cries Mikolka.

- Song, brothers! - Someone shouts from the basket and everything to cart to pick up. Distributed violent song bryakaet tambourine whistle choirs. Wench presses nuts and giggles.

... He runs beside the horse, he runs forward, he sees how it is cut along the eyes, most eye! He cries. Heart it rises, tears flow. One of the intersecting hurt him in the face; he does not feel that he breaks his hand, shouting, rushing to an old man with a gray beard, who shakes his head and condemns it all. One woman takes him by the hand and wants to take; but he escapes and runs back to the horse. That even in the latter effort, but once again begins to kick.

- Meanwhile, the goblin! - Screaming furious Mikolka. He throws a whip, bends down and pulls out from the bottom of the cart shaft long and thick, takes her by the end with both hands and firmly swing over savraskoy.

- Broke! - Range of screams.

- Will Kill!

- Oh my God! - Cries Mikolka and with all his might down the shaft. Dealt a severe blow.

- Seki Seki it! What started! - The voices cry out from the crowd.

Mikolka namahivaetsya another time, and another blow with all his lies on his back miserable nags. It all comes back all but jumps and pulls, pulls

all the recent strength in different directions to take; but on all parties to take her six whips and the shaft again rises and falls for the third time, then a fourth, roughly speaking, in a big way. Mikolka furious that he could not kill a single blow.

- Tenacious! - Range of screams.

- Who will fall without fail, my friends, and it end! - The cries of the crowd one amateur.

- Axe it, then! Put an end to this once - shouts a third.

- Oh, they eat mosquitoes! Make way! - Passionately crying Mikolka throws shafts, rear bends and pulls a cart in a scrap. - Heads Up! - He shouts, and that there are forces Blindside waved a bad cut. The blow fell;mare staggered down, tried to pull, but declined again with all his lies on his back, and she falls to the ground, although it is again brought down all four legs.

- In order to achieve! - Shouting and jumping Mikolka, as I do not remember the cart. A couple of guys are too red and drunk, grab awful - whips, sticks, tree, and run to the dying mare. Mikolka becomes the side and begins to beat with a crowbar nothing on the back. Nag stretches person sighs and dies.

- To finish! - Creek in the crowd.

- Why not go galloping!

- Oh my God! - Cries Mikolka, with a crowbar in his hand and with bloodshot eyes. He stands as if regretting that much more confident to beat.

- Well, actually, to know that you do not have to cross! - Shout out from the crowd for many voices.

But the poor boy was beside himself. With a cry he breaks through the crowd to savraske, covers the dead, bloodied face and kisses her, kisses her eyes, lips ... Then suddenly jumps up and throws herself into a frenzy with his fist on Mikolka. At that moment, my father, for a long time to chase him, he taketh him, and finally emerges from the crowd.

- Let'S Go! let's go! - He says it is - let's go home!

- Dad! What they ... ... poor horse was killed! - He cried, but it captures the breath and shouts words, taken from his chest.

- Drunk, naughty, not our business, let's go! - Says his father. He wraps his arms around his father, but his chest squeezes close. He wants to take a breath to scream and wake up.

He woke up in a sweat, wet with sweat, hair, nose, and sat down in horror.

"Thank God, it's only a dream - he said, sitting under a tree and deep

breathing - but that's what I do not will the fever in me !. disgusting dream!"

His body was as disturbed; dim and the dark heart. He put his elbows on his knees and bowed his head with both hands.

"Oh my God! - He exclaimed, - yes really good, very good, I really take an ax, I hit on the head, smash her skull ... I will slip in the sticky, warm blood, break the lock, steal and tremble; hide all blood ... with an ax ... Lord, surely? "

He was shaking like a leaf, let it.

"Yes, that's me! - He went on, straightened again, as if in deep amazement - ?, Because I knew that I can not stand, so why am I still torturing yourself after yesterday, yesterday, when I went to do it ... the court, as I understand it very well yesterday, that can not tolerate ... What am I, then? What am I even still doubt it? After all, yesterday, down the stairs, I said to myself, it's disgusting, nasty, low, low ... because I have one thought in fact sick and horror thrown ...

No, I can not, I can not! Suppose that, even if there is no doubt that in all these calculations, whether it's all decided this month, it's clear as day, as a true arithmetic. O Lord! In the end, I still would not dare! I do not wear it, can not bear! .. What is that and still ... "

He got to his feet and looked around in surprise, as if wondering and what you came here and went to the T - bridge. He was pale, his eyes were burning, exhaustion was in all his limbs, but he suddenly felt as if it is easier to breathe. He felt that he had dropped off the terrible burden davivshee it for so long, and his heart was suddenly easy and peaceful. "The Lord - he pleaded - show me my way, and I renounce this accursed ... my dream!"

Walking across the bridge, he quietly and calmly looked at the Neva, on the bright sunset bright, red sun.Despite the weakness of his, he did not even feel tired. In addition, an abscess in his heart, ran for a month, suddenly broke. Freedom, freedom! Now he is free from these spells, sorcery, charm, from glamor!

Later, when he recalled this time and everything that happened to him in those days, minute by minute, item by item, feature by feature, he hit superstition always one thing, but actually is not very unusual, but it seemed to him forever then as if somehow the fate of his destiny.

What he could not understand and explain himself why he was tired, worn out, that would be most beneficial to return home and the shortest direct route back home in Haymarket Square, where it was completely unnecessary to go. Hook was small but obvious and totally unnecessary. Of

course, it happened dozens of times to go home, not remembering the streets through which he walked. But for some reason, he always wondered why such an important, such a strong for him, and at the same time, such a high chance meeting at the Haymarket (for which even he had no reason to go) came only now this hour, for a minute his life, this is the spirit of his spirit, and thus, it is the circumstances under which he could only this meeting to make the most resolute and decisive influence on the whole of his future? Similarly, there is waiting for him on purpose!

It was about nine o'clock when he came to the Haymarket. All merchants on the tables, on trays, in shops and stores locked institution or removed and cleaned up their goods, and went home, as well as their clients.About pubs in the lower floors, on the dirty and stinking courtyards of the houses Haymarket Square, and in most taverns crowded a lot of different and various industrialists and lohmotnikov. Raskolnikov mostly loved these places, as well as all the surrounding streets, when he left without a purpose outside. Here his rags do not draw attention to themselves, no one is arrogant, and you could go in any form, no skandaliziruya. Next to the K - on the corner of an alley, a trader and a woman, a wife, traded with two tables Goods: Threads, ribbons, scarves and so on calico. N. They also raised the home, but lingered, talking with the approach familiar. Know it was Lizaveta, or just like everyone called her, Lizaveta, the younger sister of a very old woman Alyona Ivanovna, collegiate reception and a lender who yesterday was Raskolnikov comes to pawn his watch and do your sample ... He had known all about this Lizaveta, and even then, I knew him a little bit.She was a tall, awkward, shy and modest girl, almost an idiot, thirty-five years, the former in full bondage his sister, who worked on it day and night, in awe of her and Hurler it even beatings. She was lost in thought with a knot in front of Baba and the man in the street and listen attentively to them. Those something special with her warmth interpretation. When Raskolnikov suddenly saw her, a strange feeling, as the deepest astonishment seized him, though at the meeting, which was not surprising.

- Could you, Lizaveta Ivanovna, and decided to do it myself - talking loudly trader. - Well-TCR hours tomorrow in SEM-ies. And they will come.

- Tomorrow? - Drawl, and thoughtfully said Lizaveta, as if embarrassed.

- Ek because you Alyona Ivanovna asked some fear! - Rattled the wife of a merchant lively girl. - Look at me to you just what you want robenok little. And sister, she will not be home, and details, but some will take it.

- Yes, you in this time Alyona Ivanovna, do not say anything, sir, - interrupted by her husband - that's my advice, sir, but we're not going to ask. This is beneficial deal-with. Then my sister themselves can understand.

- Al go?

- In the family hours tomorrow; and from those arriving relative; personally decided to do, sir.

- And put a samovar, - added his wife.

- Well, well, - said Lizaveta, still wondering, and slowly began to pull away.

Raskolnikov is already here and have not heard any more. He walked calmly, quietly, trying not to miss a single word. The initial amazement gradually replace the horror as if frost has passed on the back. He learned he suddenly, suddenly and unexpectedly learned that tomorrow, at seven o'clock in the evening, Lizaveta, the old woman and her sister only a concubine, not at home and that, therefore, the old woman, at 7:00 in the evening, stay alone at home at home.

Prior to his apartment only a few steps away. He came to himself, like a man condemned to death. All that he did not completely reasoned and could not speak; but his whole being suddenly felt that he had no more reason neither liberty nor will and that all of a sudden decided.

Of course, even if for many years he had to wait for the opportunity, and then, with the idea that it was impossible to count, probably more obvious step to the success of this plan, like the one that seemed to suddenly now. In any case, it would be difficult to know before and probably with greater accuracy and with the least risk, without any dangerous requests and track tomorrow, at a certain hour, the old woman, who is preparing to attack, but the home odinehonka,

←« CHAPTER VI »→

Subsequently, Raskolnikov was somehow know exactly why the trader and the woman invited him Lizaveta.It was very common and does not contain anything osobennogo.Zabednevshee visitors and families to sell things, dress and so on. All the women. Since the market is not profitable to sell, market and looking for a woman, and Lizaveta did it: I took the commission went on business, and had a lot of practice, because it was a very honest and always said the final price: say what price, so be it. Said you were very little, and, as already mentioned, was modest and shy ...

But Raskolnikov has recently become superstitious.Traces superstition remained in it for a long time in the future, almost indelibly. And in all this, he was always inclined then to see some strange, mysterious, as if the presence of some special effects and accidents. In winter, one other student, he won, leaving in Kharkov, told him in a conversation when the address of an old woman Alyona Ivanovna, if in case he had to lie down. For a long time he did not go to her, because the lessons and somehow made its way yes. A month and a half ago, he remembered the address; he had two things are going well for a mortgage: old father silver watch and a small gold ring with three red stones, a gift from my sister goodbye, as memory. He decided to take the ring; finding an old woman, at first glance, even without knowing anything about him a lot, he felt invincible repugnance, took her two "ticket" and went on the road to a lower traktirishko. He asked me for a cup of tea, sat down and thought. Strange idea in motion in his head like a chicken with egg, and very, very busy with it.

Almost beside him on another table sat a student, whom he did not know

and could not remember, and the young officer. They played pool and drank tea.

Suddenly he heard that the student says officer of pawnshop, Alena Ivanovna, collegiate secretary, and tells him her address. This one thought Raskolnikov in a strange way he is now, and there's just the same thing about her. Of course, an accident, but he can not get rid of that now one very extraordinary experience, and that's when it seemed someone fawning: student suddenly starts to inform someone about this Alyona Ivanovna different parts.

- It's nice that - he said - it is always the opportunity to have the money to get it. Rich as a Jew, can immediately give five thousand, and the ruble mortgage and brezgoval.Nasha many call it in.Only awful bitch ...

And he began to tell what is evil, capricious, it is worth only one day overdue mortgage and lost thing. Gives four times less than the cost of things, and interest on the five and even seven takes a month, and so on. D. student freely and said, moreover, that the old woman had a sister, Lizaveta, she was so small and bad beats per minute and keeps in perfect enslavement as a young child, while Lizaveta, at least eight inches of growth . ..

- There is also a phenomenon! - Exclaimed the student and laughed.

They started talking about Lizavety.Student talked about it with some special joy, and everyone laughed, and the officer listened with great interest and asked the student to send him this Lizaveta to mending. Raskolnikov did not utter a single word at a time and learn everything: Lizaveta was younger, resume (in different mothers), the sister of an old woman, and she was thirty-five years. She worked for her sister day and night, in a house instead of a cook and laundress, and sewed for sale, even wash floors to hire and all sister dala.Nikakoy order and no work had not dared to take the old woman without permission. The old woman had already made a will in which was known to most of Lizaveta, who by will not receive a penny, except movable property, chairs and other things; all the money designated in the monastery in N - th province, saying eternal dushu.Lizaveta as everyman, not official, a virgin, and terribly uncomfortable, increase remarkably high, with long, splayed like a beetle-crusher, always wore boots gantry and keep yourself clean. First of all, which surprised and laughing student, was that Lizaveta was constantly pregnant ...

- Why do you say that ugly? - The officer said.

- Yes, it's dark, the soldiers under the guise of, but you know, do not worry.

ROBOTS READ

She has such a kind face and eyes. Very even.Proof - many people like.Quiet so gentle, meek, agree, agree on everything. A smile from her, even very good.

- Why is it and do you like it? - Director laughed.

- Out of strangeness. No, this is what I tell you. I damn old woman killed and robbed, and I assure you that without a gap of conscience - with added fervor student.

The officer laughed again, and Raskolnikov shuddered. As it was weird!

- Let me ask you a serious question like - zagoryachilsya student. - I am now, of course, a joke, but look: on the one hand, stupid, senseless, useless, evil, sick old woman, no one needs and, on the contrary, all harmful, he did not know that he lives, and he that shall die tomorrow. Do you understand? Do you understand?

- Well, you know, - said the officer, looking intently into the hot companion.

- Listen. On the other hand, young, fresh forces without losing support, and it's in the thousands, and it's everywhere! Hundred, a thousand good deeds and undertakings, which can be arranged and improve on the old woman's money, doomed to the monastery! Hundreds, thousands, maybe people are focused on the road; dozens of families to escape from poverty, from decay, from death, from depravity, from the venereal hospitals - all of her money. Kill her and take her money, so that with their help, and then devote himself to all humanity and a common cause: what do you think, can not be cleared if one tiny prestuplenitse thousands of good deeds? In a single life - thousands of lives saved from decay and decomposition. One death and one hundred lives in exchange - why, then arithmetic! And what does this mean for the overall balance of this hectic life, stupid and wicked old woman? No more than the life of lice, cockroaches, and not worth it, because the old woman is harmful. It captures the life of someone else: it is a day Lizaveta finger bitten by malice; just cut off!

- Of course, it is not worthy to live, - said the officer - but because nature.

- Oh, brother, but it's the nature of fixed and direct, and without it would drown in prejudices. Without it, no one will be a great man was not. They say, "duty, conscience" - I do not want to speak against duty and conscience - but because, as we understand them? Wait, I'm still going to ask one question. Listen up!

- No, you stand; I ask the question. Listen up!

- Well!

- Here and now you say oratorstvuesh, and I tell you, to me, you're going to kill yourself an old woman or not?

- Of course not! I'm for justice ... I have no here, and then ...

- Not And in my opinion, so you decide to do not no justice! Come to another party!

Raskolnikov is full of excitement. Of course, all this was the most common and most frequent than once already heard it in other forms, and only to other topics, young conversations and thoughts. But why now he had to listen to this conversation, and it was such thoughts when his own head just born ... the exact same thoughts? And why now, as soon as he brought the germ of his thoughts from an old woman, and gets him to talk about the old woman? .. The country has always seemed to him a coincidence. This small tavern conversation extraordinary influence on him in the future development of the case, as if there really was some kind of predestination, designation ...

. . . .

Returning to the Haymarket, he threw himself on the sofa and sat down for an hour without moving.Meanwhile, it was dark; candles he was not, and it never occurred to me to light. He could not remember: whether he thought about anything at that time? Finally, he felt daveshny fever, chills, and happily realized that the sofa can be and go. Soon strong lead sleep fell on him, as if pressed.

He slept unusually long and dreamless. Nastasya, which became for him at 10:00 the next morning, violence dotolkalas it. She brought him tea and bread. Tea again and again slept in his Maker.

- Ek after sleep! - She cried indignantly, - and yet he sleeps!

He sat down with force. His head ached; He rose to his feet turned into a closet and fell onto the couch.

- Again sleep! - Exclaimed Nastasia - yes you are sick, or what?

He did not answer.

- I look at what he loves?

- After - he said firmly, closed his eyes again and turned to the wall. Nastasya stood over him.

- Indeed, it may be bad - she said, then turned and walked away.

She came back two hours later with soup. He lay as before. Tea stood untouched. Nastasya even hurt and anger began to push it.

- What dryhnesh! - She cried, looking with disgust at him. He sat down,

but did not say anything to her and looked at the ground.

  - Sick or not? - Asked Nastasia, and again received no reply.

  - You are on the street likes to go out - she said, after a pause, - he loves you wind blew. There will be something, eh?

  - Once - he says weakly, - go! - And waved.

She was a little more compassion looked at him and left.

After a few minutes he raised his head and looked at the tea and soup. Then he took bread, picked up a spoon and began to eat.

He ate little, no appetite, spoons three or four, as if an afterthought. His head ached less. After dinner, he again reached on the couch, but I could not sleep, and lay motionless, face down, his face buried in the pillow. He still dreams, and they were all strange dreams: often it seemed to him that he is somewhere in Africa, in Egypt, in some oasis. Caravan of camels resting quietly lie; Circle of palms grow in a circle; All lunch. He continues to drink water straight from the stream, which is right there in the side streams and noise.And so great and wonderful, wonderful, such blue water, cold, running on a multi-colored stones and pure gold sequined sand ... Suddenly he clearly heard the clock strikes. He shuddered, woke up, looked up, looked out the window, I realized the time and suddenly jumped up, his feelings completely, as if someone pulled him off the couch. He tiptoed to the door, he opened it and listened quietly down the stairs. His heart was beating terribly. But on the stairs was quiet as everyone was asleep ... Wild and wonderful it seemed to him that he could sleep in a trance from yesterday and nothing has been done, nothing has prepared ... And yet, perhaps, and six hours drums ... . and extremely restless and some fuss in confusion seized him suddenly, instead of sleeping and dullness.Preparations, however, was not enough. He spared no effort to understand everything, and do not forget; and his heart was beating all Stukalo, so it was hard to breathe. Firstly, it was necessary to make a loop and sew a coat - a matter of minutes. He put his hand under the pillow and found stuffed in her underwear under the complete collapse of the old, dirty shirt. From rags he tore braid inches wide and eight inches long. This braid folded it in half, took a broad, strong, out of some thick paper material summer coat (his only coat) and began to sew both ends of the ribbon under the left arm inside. When sewing hands were shaking, but he overcame, and so that the outside could not see anything when he put on his coat again. Needle and thread have with him for a long time and have been prepared in the table, in the paper sheet. As for the cycle, it was a very clever invention

of his, the loop is assigned an ax. It was impossible to carry out in the street with an ax in his hands. And if you hide under your coat, you still had to hold his hand, it would be noticeable. Now, with a loop, one has only to put in it the ax blade, and he will hang quietly under his arm inside, all the way. Running the same hand in the side pocket of his overcoat, and he may end clumsy pen to hold that it does not hang; and the coat was very wide, this bag, it might not be noticed by others, that he had something to pass pocket has. This cycle he did two weeks ago came up with.

This done, he put his fingers into a small gap between his "Turkish" sofa and floor, fumbled around the left corner and pulled out a long time already cooked and hidden there mortgage. This mortgage is not, however, mortgage and wooden smoothly planned range, size and thickness of not Moreover, as it could be silver papirosochnitsa. This tablet he accidentally found in one of his walks, on the same yard where the house located on a workshop. Then he added to the plaque smooth and thin strip of iron - probably from something fragment - which is also located on the street, at the same time. Adding the two plates, of which iron less wood, he bound them together firmly, cross-wise thread; then thoroughly and vigorously uvertel them in a clean white paper and tied with a thin tesemochkoy, too wise, and feature node so that pomudrenee undone.This is done in order to temporarily divert the attention of the old woman when she starts messing around with a bundle, and so Seize the moment. Iron same dish was to add weight to the old woman, even in the first moment I realized that the "thing" of the tree. All of this could not help him to time under divanom.Tolko that he received a loan, when somewhere in the courtyard someone was screaming:

- Sema hour long!

- For A Long Time! Oh my God!

He rushed to the door and listened, grabbed his hat and began to descend down his thirteen steps, carefully, quietly, as koshka.Esli be the most important thing - to steal from the kitchen ax. The fact that this should be done with the ax, it was decided long. He was still a folding knife garden; but on the knife, and especially on their own strength, he had no hope, and, therefore, focused on the ax finally. Pay attention to the way one feature over all final decisions already taken by them in this case. They had a strange property: Final they became more monstrous, ridiculous, and immediately became in his eyes. Despite the painful internal struggle on their own, he never for a moment he could not believe in the feasibility of plans, for all

this time.

And even if he happened since then that has everything to the last point would have to be dismantled and finally decided, and, of course, there would be no more than - where it would seem, he dropped everything, and from the point of absurdity, and inability to monsters. But the outstanding moments of doubt and still remains a chasm. How, where to get the ax, it is a trifle, he did not worry because there was nothing easier.The fact that Nastasya, and especially in the evenings, every minute was not at home: or flee to a neighbor, or in the store, and always leaves the door wide open.The hostess only because of this and fell out with her.Thus, it should be administered only slowly, when the time comes, in the kitchen and take an ax, and then an hour later (when it was over), enter and put back. But, it seems, and I doubt that he is suppose to come in an hour to put back, and Nastasya here gate. Of course, it is necessary to pass and wait until it is released again.But what if at the same time will be missed ax begins to look, raskrichitsya - is suspected, or at least suspected case.

But it still was the little things that he did not think of, and there was no time. He thought about the main thing, and trivia postponed until he is satisfied with everything. But the latter seemed decidedly inappropriate. Thus, at least, seemed emu.V any case, he could, for example, to imagine that someday he will think out, to stand up and - just go there ... Even the recent sample them (ie to visit order to finally see the place), he justtried to be done, but not how good, "Give me, they say, go and try this dream something" - Just could not resist, spat and fled himself frenzy. At the same time, it would seem, all the tests, in the sense of moral resolve the problem, it has already been put an end to them: casuistry cut with a razor, and to himself, he is no longer conscious objections. But in the latter case, he simply did not believe myself and thrust, slavishly, sought objections to the parties and groping as if someone pulls him and forced. On the last day, so unexpectedly arrived and decided to do everything at once, affected him almost mechanically, as if someone took her by the arm and pulled him along, irresistibly, blindly, with unnatural force, without objection. In addition, he received a piece of clothing in the wheel of a car, and its roots in her draw.

First of all - however, has long before that - he took one question: Why is it easy to find and subject to almost all crimes and so clearly illustrated by the following almost all criminals? He came gradually varied and interesting conclusions, and, in his opinion, the main reason is not so much the material

impossibility to hide the crime, both in the criminal ,: he was a criminal, and almost everything in the time of the offense is subject to a reduction of will and reason, are replaced, on the contrary , children's phenomenal levity, and it was at a time when most needed reason and caution. To convince him, it seemed that this eclipse of reason and decline will cover the person as the disease develops gradually and reaches its highest point just before the commission of the offense; continue in the same way in the time of the crime and some time after that, in accordance with human rights; Then tested in the same manner as any disease passes. Question: whether the disease generates most crime or crime itself as something special in its nature, is always accompanied by a special disease? - He did not feel able to solve.

Having reached these conclusions, he decided that he himself, in his case, there can be such a painful shock that the mind and stay with him, in fact, throughout the execution of their plans for the sole reason that conceived them - "No offense "... We cut the whole process by which he reached the final decision; we too ran forward ... only to add that the actual, purely financial difficulties of the case as a whole has played in my mind the most minor role. "We need to keep them all over the will and the whole mind, and they, in due time, all will be defeated when it is necessary to meet the slightest subtlety with all the details of the case ..." But it was not started. Final, he continued his solutions are less inclined to believe, and when the hour, it all went wrong, but somehow accidentally, even almost unexpectedly.

One minor circumstances to put it to a standstill, even before he came down the stairs. Drew level with her kitchen, as always otvorennoyu open, he looked into her eyes to look around, especially if there was, in the absence of Nastasya, most housewives, and if not properly closed the door to her room, so she too, as there -nibud not look as it enters the ax? But what was his surprise when he suddenly saw that Nastasya not only this time at home, in the kitchen, but also engaged in the business: pulls out of the basket and the laundry hanging on a clothesline! Seeing him, she stopped hanging, turned to him and always looked at him as he passed. He turned and walked as if noticing nothing. But it was not over: no ax! He was struck by terrible.

"And the fact that I took - he thought, going under the gate, where I took it all means at this point will not be home Why, why, why I probably decided that?" He was crushed, even somehow humiliated. He wanted to laugh at him with anger ... blunt, brutal rage boiled in it.

He paused in thought at the gate. Back on the street, so to mind a walk,

it was disgusting; back home - still disgusting. "And the fact that it is lost forever!" - He muttered, standing aimlessly under the gate, directly in front of a dark closet janitor, too otvorennoy. Suddenly he started. From the janitor closet that were with him a few steps from the shops just something flashed in his eyes ... He looked around - nobody. He tiptoed to the bed, went down two steps and a faint voice called janitor. "It's not at home! Somewhere close, however, in the yard, because the door was not locked wide open." He rushed headlong to the ax (it was an ax) and pulled it out from under the bench, where he lay between two lazy; immediately, leaving no, attach it to the loop, both hands stuffed in his pockets and walked out of the box; no one noticed! "I do not mind, because the devil!" - He thought that strange smile. This case encouraged him enormously.

He walked quietly expensive and gradually, slowly, so as not to present any suspicion. Not only he looked at passers-by, even tried not to look at the person and not be noticeable. Then he remembered his hat. "Oh, my God! And the money the third day, and he could not find a place in the hat!" Curse broke out of his soul.

Glancing casually, with one eye in the store, he saw that there, on the wall clock, 7:10. It was necessary to take the time and at the same time to make a detour: come to the house, passing the other hand ...

Earlier, when he happened to represent all this in mind, it is sometimes considered to be very afraid. But it is not very afraid now, not even afraid at all. Occupied it at this point even some extraneous thoughts, but for a long time. Turning the Yusupov garden, he was even too busy thinking about the high fountains and how they are very refreshing air in all areas. Little by little, he moved to the belief that if the Summer Garden to extend to all the Champ de Mars, and even connect to the Mikhailovsky palace garden, it would be great and a good thing for the city. And suddenly interested him: why, in all major cities, people are not what one needed, but somehow especially inclined to live and settle in these parts of the city, where there are no gardens, no fountains, where dirt and stench, and dirty . Then he remembered his walks through the Haymarket, and for a moment he woke up. "What nonsense - he thought. - No, nothing at all is better not to think!"

"It's true, those which led to his execution, digested thoughts on all subjects, they meet on the road" - flashed through his mind, but only flashed like lightning; he repaid as soon as possible ... But this idea was close and this home is a goal. Somewhere suddenly the clock struck one blow. "What

is it, in fact, half of the eighth? This can not be true, run! "

Fortunately for him at the gate again went well. Moreover, even, as if on purpose, at this very moment just before entered the gate huge hay completely overshadow all the time, as he passed along the path, and only slightly, who had to leave the gate to the yard, he quickly slid to the right. There, on the other side of the basket, he could hear the shouts and arguing a few votes, but no one noticed and no one got to meet. Many windows, leaving this huge area of the yard was not locked at the moment, but he did not look - there was no power. Stairway to the old woman was close, now out of the gate on the right. He was already on the stairs ...

Moving spirit and shook his hand, Bob heart, and immediately felt the ax again straightened, he was carefully and quietly climb the ladder, constantly listening. But the ladder at the time was empty; All the doors were locked; one never met. The second floor has one apartment was empty, however, the solution is open, and he worked as an artist, but they never looked. He was, I thought, and went on. "Of course, it would be better if they did not exist here, but ... over them two more floors."

But this is the fourth floor, and a door, and that the earth is flat opposite; blank. In the third floor, apparently apartment, which is located directly under the old woman, also empty: business card, nailed to the door gvoz- dochkami, shot - left! .. He gasped. For a moment the thought flashed through his mind the thought: "Do not leave it?" But he did not give himself the answer and began to listen to the old woman apartment: dead silence. Then he listened down the stairs, listening for a long time, then looked ... for the last time, crawled, recovered and again tried to ax loop. "Not pale ... I actu- ally -? He thought - not special excitement I suspect it ... Do not wait any longer ... until the heart stops ..?"

But the heart is not stopped. On the contrary, as luck would have pounded stronger, stronger, stronger ... He could not resist, slowly stretched out his hand to the bell and rang the bell. Half a minute later again rang loudly.

No answer. Call nothing nothing, but he did not do so below. The old woman, of course, was at home, but it suspiciously and one. He would know her habit ... and again firmly put his ear to the door. Whether his feelings were just as confused (which is usually hard to imagine), or really was very audible, but then he saw a cautious whisper hand into the keyhole and han- dles like the rustling of dresses of the door. Someone stood quietly next to the castle and in the same way as it is here, on the street, listening to, except

for inside and seems to be too put his ear to the door …

He deliberately turned and muttered something aloud, and therefore did not give any indication that hides;Then called a third time, but quiet, solid and without impatience. Referring to this post, bright, clear - this time minted in it forever - he could not understand where it has so many tricks, the more his mind, as if pomerkal moments, and his body, and he almost did not feel to me … A moment later, he heard that from constipation.

↤« CHAPTER VII »↦

Door, and then opened a small crack, and reopen two eyes and look incredulously stared at him from the darkness. Here Raskolnikov was lost and made an important mistake.

Fearing that the old woman was afraid that they were alone, and not hoping that his appearance to dissuade her, he took the door and pulled her to the old woman, do not try to lock up again.Seeing this, she jerked the door in the back, but did not release the lock and handle, so he almost pulled it together with the door to the stairs. Seeing as she stands in the doorway across and not give him a pass, he went straight at her. She jumped in fright, tried to say something, but did not seem to be able to look at him with wide eyes.

- Hello, Alena Ivanovna - he said as much ease, but his voice did not listen to him, broke off and shook - I brought you some ... thing ... but it's better than here ... let the light .. . - And he threw it, he directly, without an invitation, entered the room. The old woman ran after him; her tongue untied.

- The Lord! But why would you? .. Who are you? What do you want?

- Excuse me, Alena Ivanovna ... your friend ... Raskolnikov ... that brought the mortgage, which promised the other day ... - And he held out a mortgage.

The old woman looked at was the mortgage, but then he looked straight into the eyes of my eyes intruders. She looked closely, viciously and disbelief. It took about a minute, it seemed to him, even in her eyes something like a mockery, as if she knew everything. He felt that he had lost, he was almost scary, scary before, she seems to look so do not say a word, even for half a minute, he ran away from her.

- What do you see, just do not know? - Suddenly, he said, too angry. - Do you want to take it, but no - I go to the other, I have no time.

He did not think to say, as well, very unexpected reprimand.

The old woman came to her senses, and decisive tone of her guest, apparently encouraged.

- Yes, you, sir, so suddenly ... what? - She asked, looking at mortgage.

- Silver papirosochnitsa: as I said last time.

She held out her hand.

- Yes, quite often lose what you pale? This shake hands! Bathed, and, sir?

- Fever, - he answered dryly. - One is forced to become pale ... if there is nothing - he added, barely get the words out. Force again left him. But the answer seemed plausible; The old woman took a mortgage loan.

- What is it? - She asked, looking around again Raskolnikov intently and weighing the mortgage on his arm.

- Thing ... papirosochnitsa ... silver ... watch.

- Yes, quite often lose something, as if he had no silver ... Look navertel.

Trying to uncover snurok and turned to the window, to light (all the windows were locked in it, despite the stuffiness), she does it a few seconds before the end and started it back. He unbuttoned his coat and freed the ax out of the loop, but not yet pulled out completely, and just stick with his right hand under his clothes. His hands were terribly weak; he heard them, every minute, more and more numb and dereveneli. He was afraid that it will release and drop the ax ... Suddenly his head as if spun.

- Yes, he was here navertel! - Angrily exclaimed the old woman and stirred in his direction.

No instant can not lose more. He took an ax at all, swung with both hands, barely feeling, and almost without effort, almost mechanically, fell head-butt. His power here, as it was not. But he lowered his ax, was born here and is a force.

The old woman, as always, was bareheaded. White with gray, thinning hair in his usual bold oiled, braided pigtails in rats and agreed with the splinter horn combs, poking his head. Shot hit the top of the head, assisted by his small stature. She screamed, but very little, and suddenly everything has been decided on the floor, but still managed to raise both hands to his head. In one hand was still keep the "mortgage". Then it hit hard, and other times, all stock and all over the head. Blood gushed as from an overturned glass, and the body fell backwards. He stepped back and gave the fall and

immediately bent down to her face; she was already dead. His eyes, as if to jump, and forehead, and his face was wrinkled and distorted cramp.

He put the ax on the floor beside dead, and immediately reached into his pocket, trying not to get dirty blood flows - in the right pocket, from which he was the last time, remove klyuch.On was in full mind, eclipses and dizziness was not, but it hands still shaking. Then he remembered that there was even a very careful, cautious, careful not to get dirty ... all the keys he immediately pulled; all, as then, were in tandem, in a steel obruchke. Immediately, he ran into the bedroom with them. It was a very small room, with a huge kiot images. Another wall was a large bed, very clean, with a silky, layout patchwork quilt. The third wall was a chest of drawers. Strange to say, but as soon as he began to match the keys to the chest, just heard them ringing like a spasm passed over it. Suddenly he again wanted to give up and leave. But it was only a moment;It was too late to leave. He even laughed at himself, suddenly another disturbing thought occurred to him. He suddenly seemed to him that the old woman, perhaps, is still alive and can still wake up. Throw the key, and a chest of drawers, he ran back to the body, grabbed an ax and namahnulsya again to the old woman, but not lowered. There was no doubt that she was dead. Leaning back and looking at it closer, he saw clearly that the skull was crushed and even svorochen little storonu.On wanted to touch a finger, but jerked his hand; yes no longer be seen. Blood between natekla is the whole pool. Suddenly he saw on her neck snurok, pulled it out, but he was strong and snurok not broke; Furthermore, in the blood soaks through. He tried to pull out because of his shirt, but something prevented stuck. He impatiently again swung the ax was immediately rubnut on a shoestring, the body, from the top, but did not dare, and hard to get dirty hands and an ax, after a two-minute rush, cut snurok, without touching the body with an ax, and took off; He was not wrong - purse. On the rope were two crosses, cypress and copper, and, in addition, filigree blade; and then with them hung a small, suede, fat wallet with steel rim and rings. Purse was very tightly packed; Raskolnikov put it in his pocket without looking back, crosses the old woman fell on his chest, and took this time and an ax, rushed back to the bedroom.

He was in a hurry awful, grabbed the keys and again began to tinker with them.But once all failed: they were put in the lock. Not that his hands were shaking so, but it is not: and see, for example, that the key is not the same, is not suitable, and all this fuss is about. Suddenly he remembered and

realized that a big key, with rough beard, who immediately hangs out with other small, does not necessarily have to be from the chest (the last time he came to mind), but with some style, and in this package can be hidden from all. He threw his chest and immediately crawled under the bed, knowing that the laying usually old women put under the bed. That's right: there was a significant style, lots of yard in length, with a convex roof, upholstered in red Morocco, studded with steel nails on it. Key gear just came and unlocked. Above, under white sheets, lay cleft coat covered with red suite; that under her silk dress, a scarf, and there, inside, everything seemed to lay a cloth. First of all he took was going to destroy the red put their soiled with blood. "Red, well, red blood invisible" - it seemed good to him was, and then he came to himself, "Lord, mad or something, I mean?" - He thought he was in turmoil.

But as soon as he moved his rags, when suddenly out of wool, slipped a gold watch. He ran all perevertyvat. Indeed, between the rags were mixed gold items - probably all mortgages repayments and outstanding - bracelets, necklaces, earrings, pins, and so on. Some of them were in other cases simply wrapped in newspaper, but cautiously and carefully, in double sheets, and tied with ribbons circle. Without the slightest delay, he began to fill their pockets pants and coat, not looking and not disclosing the components and cases; but he did not score a lot of ...

Suddenly he heard in the room where there was an old woman, go. He stopped and fell silent, as if dead. But all was quiet, so imagined. Suddenly clearly heard a slight cry, or as if someone quietly and abruptly moaned and fell silent. Again, silence for a minute or two. He squatted in the chest and waited with bated breath, but suddenly jumped up, grabbed an ax and ran out of the bedroom.

Middle of the room stood Lizaveta with a big knot in his hands, and stared blankly at the dead sister, all white as a sheet, as if not to cry. Seeing his end, she was shaking like a leaf, trembling, and ran around her face cramps; raised her hand, opened his mouth, but still screamed and back slowly began to pull away in the corner, looking straight, looking at him, but he did not cry, though she did not have enough breath to scream. He lunged at her with an ax;Her lips trembled so pitifully, as very young children when they start something frightened, frightening look at your subject and are going to scream. And before this unfortunate Lizaveta was simple, crowded and scary once and for all, that even hands raised to protect his face, but it was

most necessary natural gesture at that moment, because the ax was raised directly over her face. He barely raised his free left hand, not to his face and slowly handed him forward as if pushing it. Shot went just over the skull of the island, and immediately break through the entire upper part of the forehead, almost to the top of the head. She collapsed. Raskolnikov was completely lost, grabbed her website, threw it again and ran into the hallway.

Fear covers it more and more, especially after this second, quite unexpected murder. He really wanted to get out of here. And if at this point he was able to see and correct to argue ,; If only he could understand all the difficulties of his position, all the despair, all the ugliness and all the absurdity of it, at the same time to understand how a lot of difficulties, and perhaps even more brutality to overcome it and commit to get out of here and return home, then it may very well be that he would have thrown everything at once went to declare themselves and not from fear, even for themselves, but only from one of horror and disgust at what he did. Disgust especially rose and it grew with each passing minute. In no event in the world he would not go now to the chest and even in the room.

But some confusion, as if even reverie, began to gradually acquire their minutes, he seemed to have forgotten, or simply forget about the main thing, and shall cleave unto detalyam.Odnako looking into the kitchen and saw on the bench bucket half full of water, he realized wash their hands and an ax. His hands were covered in blood and stuck. He dropped the ax blade into the water, grabbed lying on the window, on a silver platter split, a bar of soap and began to chat in a bucket to wash their hands. After washing them, he pulled the ax, washed the iron, and long, with three minutes, washed tree where zakrovyanilos tries blood even soap. Then all Otter linen, which immediately dried on a rope stretched across the kitchen, and then a long and carefully considered the ax at the window. Not a trace, only the shaft was still wet. He carefully put the ax in the noose under his coat. Then, as foreseen in the dim light of the kitchen, looked at the coat, pants, boots. Outside, at first glance, as if nothing had happened; Only the boots were stains. He damp cloth and otter boots. He knew, however, that it is not good to look at, maybe there is something striking that he does not notice. In meditation, he stood in the middle of the room. Painful, dark thought grew up in it - the idea that he is mad, and that at this moment can neither judge nor defend themselves, making, maybe we should not be doing what he's doing right now ... "My God I have to run, run! "- he muttered, and rushed to the front. But here expecting

such a horror, a course he had never experienced before.

He stood and looked and could not believe my eyes: the door, the outer door from the hallway to the stairs, which he called this morning and went, was not locked, even for a half-open palm or lock or locks on all the time for all this time! The old woman did not shut the might of caution. But ah! In the end, he then saw Lizaveta! And how could he, since he could not guess that, because it came from somewhere! Not through the wall of the same.

He rushed to the door and put the constipation.

"But no, again! We have to go, go …"

He took off his constipation, opened the door and listened to the stairs.

For a long time he listened. Somewhere far away, at the bottom, probably under the gate, loud and shrill screams someone two voices arguing and swearing. "What is it? .." He waited patiently. Finally all was quiet, how to cut; dispersed.He was about to leave, but suddenly the floor below the noise opened the door to the stairs, and someone has to go down, humming a tune."How are they all so noisy!" - Flashed through his mind. Again he closed the door and waited. Finally, all was quiet, not a soul. He already went a step on the stairs, when he again heard someone new steps.

These steps could be heard far away, at the beginning of the stairs, but he is very good and well to remember that from the very first sound, and then began to suspect the reason is that it is, of course, here in the fourth floor in the old woman. How Come? Sounds that were so special, meaningful? Steps were heavy, smooth, unhurried. It really he was on the ground floor, there was still; all that can be heard more audible! Had a severe shortness of inputs. This is really the third started … Here! And suddenly it seemed to him that he was just stunned that this is in sleep, when dreams that are catching up, close, want to kill, and he just rooted to the spot and can not move his arms.

Finally, when it began to grow in the fourth floor of the visitor, but then all of a sudden and more quickly and deftly slip back porch apartment and closed the dver.Togda grabbed constipation and quietly, calmly, put them in the course. Instinct helped. When he had finished all that he hid his breath at the door. Intruder was already at the door, too. Now they faced each other, and now he and the old woman when the door separating them, and he listened.

There are several times more otdyhnulsya. "Thick and large, it should be" - thought Raskolnikov, clutching an ax in his hand. In fact, just dreamed it all. Guest grabbed the bell and rang the bell.

As soon as the bell rang tinny sound as if he suddenly felt as if the room was moved. For a few seconds he even listened serezno.Chelovek called again, still waiting, and suddenly, impatient, struggling started to pull the door handle. Horrified, Raskolnikov looked at jumping in the loop hook constipation and a dull ache waiting that is about to pop out now and constipation. Indeed, it seemed possible: so much pulled. He was taken to the head to hold the lock arm, but he could not guess. His head, as if again starts to rotate. "Here you drop!" - Flashed in it, but the stranger spoke, and he immediately came to his senses.

- Yes, they eat, sleep and suffocate them who? Trrreklyatye! - How he roared out of the barrel. - Hey, Alyona Ivanovna, the old witch! Lizaveta, indescribable beauty! Opens! Y, the damned, they sleep, or what?

Again, ostervenyas him a dozen times at once, all the urine, pulled the bell. Yes, of course, it was a man overbearing and short in the house.

At this point, suddenly very small, hasty steps were heard on the stairs around. Approach someone else. Raskolnikov and did not hear the beginning.

- Do not have one? - Loudly and cheerfully shouted came directly addressing the first visitor, still continues to pull the bell. - Hi, Koch!

"Judging by his voice, must have been very young," - thought Raskolnikov.

- God knows, almost broke the lock, - said Koch. - And how do you know me are you going next?

- Here you go! The third day, "Gambrinus", three games in a row to take you in a pool!

- Ah ...

- So they do not have, then? Strange. Silly, but it's terrible. Where would an old woman now? I have a job.

- Yes, I do, sir, the case!

- Well, what do you do? So back. Eh! And I thought to get the money! - Said the young man.

- Of course, the back, so why register? I myself, the witch, the appointed hour. I actually hook. And where the hell she is stuck, do not understand? Year-round sitting witch kisnet, legs hurt, and suddenly a walk!

- Do not ask whether the janitor?

- What?

- Where and when he comes?

- Um ... hell ... Why ask ... Well, it does not go anywhere ... - and again he pulled the handle and lock. - Hell, do nothing, do not go!

- Stop! - Shouted suddenly a young man - see see how the door if yank?
- Well, what?
- So, it is not closed, and constipation, that is on the hook! Hear how bryakaet constipation?
- Well, what?
- Yes, how do you not understand? So, some of them home. If all goes as the key will be locked from the outside, not the inside of constipation. And then - hear bryakaet constipation? And to the castle gate from the inside, you have to be at home, you know? Thus, to stay at home, but not unlocked!
- Bah! Yes, indeed! - Yelled surprise Koch. - So what they're there! - And he desperately started to pull the door behind him.
- Stop! - Again exclaimed the young man - do not pull! There is something so wrong ... because you called, pulled - not unlocked; means, or both of them fainted, or ...
- What?
- Here's what: Let's janitor; Let wake them himself.
- Case! - And moved out.
- Stop! Stay in the moment you're here, and I'll run down to the janitor.
- Why stay?
- And you never know what? ..
- Maybe ...
- I'm getting ready to judicial investigators! There is obviously Pts-che-na-seen something like that! - Hot exclaimed a young man and went for a run down the stairs.

Koch, again rose quietly challenge, and he called one hit; then quietly, as if thinking, and saw, began to move the door handle, pulling and lowering it again to make sure it is one of the constipation. Then he leaned forward, panting, looked through the keyhole; but he was stuck inside the key and, therefore, could not see anything.

Raskolnikov stood clutching an ax. He was just delirious. He is even ready to deal with them when they go.When the knock and conspired, several times he suddenly occurred to me to finish it all at once and shout them out the door. Sometimes he wanted to start a fight with them, tease them, do not just release. "Hurry up a lot!" - Flashed through his mind.

- However, it is the devil ...

As time went on, minute, and the other - no one came. Koch began to stir.

- But, damn! .. - He suddenly shouted impatiently, throwing his guard,

too, went down slowly and the sound of boots on the stairs. Steps subsided.

- My God, what are you doing!

Raskolnikov did not take the lock, opened the door - do not hear anything, and suddenly, he was no longer thinking went out and closed the door tightly as he could for himself and let down.

He had come down three stairs, when suddenly there was a loud noise below - where to go! Everywhere it was impossible to hide. He ran back to the apartment was.

- Hey, the devil, the devil! Here You Go!

With a cry burst someone down some of the apartments, and not something that escaped, and just fell down the stairs, shouting in a loud voice:

- Mitya! Mitya! Mitya! Mitya! Mitya! Clown for those and and!

Cry cry composition; the last sounds heard already in the yard; all was quiet. But at the same time, several people talking loudly and often became noisy climb stairs. There were three or four. He heard the sonorous voice of the young. "They Are!"

In desperation, he went straight to meet them, come what may! Stop, all is not lost, do not miss, too, everything was gone: Remember. They have already agreed; among them there was one entrance - and suddenly the rescue! A few steps to the right, empty and wide open unlocked apartment, the same apartment on the second floor, where the painted work, and now, unfortunately, gone. They are, however, and now ran screaming. Just painted floors, rooms are among kadochka clay pot and paint Bogomazov. In an instant, he slipped through the open door and hid behind a wall, and it was time they stood on the site itself. Then appeared and passed the fourth floor, talking loudly. He was waiting for came on tiptoe and ran down the stairs.

No one on the stairs! Under the gate too. He walked quickly down the path and turned left down the street.

He knew very well that he knew very well that they are, at the moment, in the apartment, which is very surprised to see that it is unlocked, then as now was locked, they are already looking at the body and that it would take no more than than a minute, they suggest, and was well aware that he had just been a murderer and had somewhere to hide, sneak past them, run away; I think, perhaps, that he was sitting in an empty apartment, while they were up to. Meanwhile, under any circumstances, he did not dare to add a very step, but before the first turn of a hundred yards. "Do not roll down the road if some and wait somewhere on an unfamiliar stairway? No problem! And

do not throw Does where the ax? Should not take a taxi? Trouble! Trouble!"

Finally here is a lane; And he turned him half-dead; Then he was half saved and understood this: less suspicion, besides the people here strongly curved, and he rubbed it as grain sand.But all these tortures before he weakened that he could barely move. Sweat drops came out of it; neck was all the moisture. "Look was cut!" - Someone called out to him when he went into a ditch.

He is now remembered himself; further worse. He did, however, remember when he went into the ditch, he was afraid that a few people here, and it shows, and was about to turn back into the alley. Despite the fact that almost falling, it still did hook and return home on the other side at all.

Not fully conscious, and he passed through the gate of his house; at least he has already passed on the stairs, and then remembered topor.Mezhdu those faced with a very important task: to put it back, and as unobtrusively as possible. Of course, he was not able to understand that maybe it would be much better, he did not put the ax to its original location, and throw it, though later, somewhere in the courtyard of the opponent.

But everything went well. The door to the house was open, but not at the castle, so most likely it was that the caretaker of the house. But before he had lost the ability to figure out something that went straight up to the house and its solutions. If the janitor asked him: "What do you want?" - It can be so straight and give him the ax. But, again, was a janitor, and he had to lay the ax to its former place under the bench; even magazine covers anyway. No, the soul, then he met in his room; Mistress of the door was locked. Going to her, he threw himself on the sofa as it was. He did not sleep, but he was in a trance. If someone entered his room while he would have immediately jumped up and screamed. Notes and fragments of some thoughts and swarmed in his head; but it can not have any idea, no one could stop, despite the efforts of ...

←«»→

PART 2
<< CHAPTER I >>

He lay for a long time. It so happened that he seemed to wake up and, in these moments notice that long night, and wake up to it arose. Finally, he noted that even the light of day. He lay on his back on the couch, still stunned by the recent oblivion. Before him came sharply terrible, desperate cries from the street, which, however, he listened every night in his window at 3:00. They also woke him now. "Oh, it's too tavern drunk - he thought - the third hour - and then suddenly jumped up as if he ripped someone off the couch. - What's the third time already!" He sat on the couch - and we all remember! Suddenly, in a moment remembered everything!

For a moment he thought he was crazy. Terribly cold seized him; but it was cold and fever, which has long started with him in a dream. Now suddenly hit the cold that just jumped teeth and all that is in it and call. He opened the door and began to listen: everyone in the house completely subsided. With amazement, he looked around and everything in the room, and do not understand how he could have it yesterday, went into the house, and not to lock the door and throw the hook on the couch, not only deprived, but even in the hat she slipped and then lying on the floor near the pillow. "If someone came, what would he think? That I'm drunk, but ..." He rushed to the window. Light was enough, and he became a hurry to look around, everything from head to toe, all the clothes: there is no trace But since it was impossible: chills fever, he began to take off all round and check again. He perevertel every last thread and pieces, and, not trusting himself, repeated the examination three times. But there was nothing, it seems, no trace; the place where the bottom of the pants fell silent and hung on the edge of the strip is left thick

traces of dried blood. He grabbed a folding knife and cut off a large fringe. Moreover, it seems nothing. Suddenly he remembered that the purse and the fact that he pulled out of the trunk of an old woman, all are still pockets lie! He never thought that so far, to remove them and hide! I did not think about it even now, when considered dress! What is this? Instantly he rushed to remove them and throw on the table. The choice of everything, even reversing pocket to make sure that there is not even the fact that he survived all this heap in the corner. There, in the corner, at the bottom, in the same place were torn from the wall wallpaper stragglers, he immediately began to shove all in this hole under the paper: "! Included in all fields of view and wallet too" - Fortunately, he thought, standing and staring blankly into a corner, a hole in the provocation. Suddenly, it all started with horror: "Oh my God, - he whispered in despair - that to me is what is hidden if it is so hidden?"?

True, he did not count on things; he thought that the money alone, and therefore did not prepare in advance places - "But now, now I'm glad that? - he thought. - Is that so hidden really mind if I leave ?!" As he sat down exhausted on the couch and immediately unbearably cold shook it.Mechanically pulled beside him lying on a chair, a former student of his winter coat, warm, but almost in rags, covered himself with them, and sleep, and delirium again embraced him. He forgot himself.

No more than five minutes later, he did not get up again, and once, in a frenzy, rushed back to his clothes. "How could I go back to sleep, while nothing was done That's right, that's right hand hinges :! still has not taken off, I forgot about this fact forgotten This is the key!" He pulled out of the cycle and be in a hurry to break it into pieces, stuffing them under the pillow in his underwear. "Scraps of canvas in any case not to arouse suspicion, it seems, so it seems like it!" - He repeated, standing in the middle of the room, and with rapt attention to the pain again began to look round on the floor and everywhere, whether it is something else remember? Confidence that everything, even the memory, even simple argument to leave him, began to torment him unbearably. "What really really begins, it really is punishment comes? Look, over there, that's right!" Indeed, trimming bangs, which he cut his pants and lay down on the floor of the room to see the first! "But what is it with me!" - He shouted again, as lost.

There came to him a strange thought that perhaps all his clothes in the blood, which can be a lot of places, but he just does not see them, does not notice because his argument is weakened, fragmented mind is darkened ...

.. . Suddenly he remembered that there was blood on the purse. "Bah! So, so, in your pocket, too, must be in the blood, because I'm still wet purse then shoved it in his pocket!" Instantly he was reversing his pocket, and - indeed - have lined the pockets of marks, spots! "So, do not leave as yet very reason, therefore, have the same philosophy and memory when he caught himself and realized - he thought triumphantly, deeply and sighed happily with all the chest - just slabosilie fever, delirium for a moment "- and he tore the whole lining of the left pocket of his trousers. At that moment, a ray of sunshine lights up the left boot: on the nose, which looked out of the boot, it seemed signs.He threw the boots, "really marks the whole point of the sock soaked in blood!"; it should be in the pool, then accidentally left ... "But what do I do? What should I do with this sock stripes in your pocket?"

He scooped it all in his hands and stood in the middle of the room. "In the oven? But in the oven in the first place to start digging. Burn? Yes, and burn? Matches do not even have. No, it is better to go somewhere and throw it. Yes! It is better to quit! Away - he repeated, again sitting on sofa - - and now, at this moment, do not hesitate .. "But instead of a head lay back ;! again froze its unbearable chills; He again put on his coat. Over time, a few hours, it still represented gusts that "it would be now, without delay, to go some- where and throw everything so much out of sight, hurry, hurry!" He fought off the couch a few times, I had to get up but could not. Finally he woke up a loud knock at the door.

- Yes, open, alive or not? And all the while he slumbers - Nastasya cried, banging his fist on the door - a day after day, like a dog napping! Dog! Open, da.Odinnadtsaty hour.

- Mauger, not at home! - Said the man's voice.

"Bah! That voice janitor ... What does he want?"

He jumped up and sat on the couch. His heart was beating so that even hurt was.

- And who else was locked hook? - Answered Nastasia - ish, was impris- oned! Very, yes, will be? Open mind, wake up!

"What do they want? Why janitor? All we know. To counter or open? Dis- appears ..."

He stood up, leaned forward and picked up the phone.

His whole room was of a size that can remove the hook without getting out of bed.

That's right: it's the janitor and Nastasia.

Nastasya strange way he looked. He was defiant and desperate view looked at the janitor. He silently handed him a gray, folded in half sheet of paper, sealed with wax bottle.

- Agenda in the office - he said, handing the paper.
- What office? ..
- The police, then call the office. It is known that office.
- The police! .. How Come? ..
- And how do I know. Require and go. - He looked at him, looked around, and turned to leave.
- No, not really started to hurt? - Said Nastasia, watch him. Janitor also put his head for a moment. - Since yesterday in the heat - she added.

He did not answer, and held the paper without printing.

- Yeah, do not get up - continued Nastasia, soften, and seeing that he pulls off the couch legs.- sick and not go: will not burn. They are the ones in the hands of something?

He looked at his right hand was cut off part of the fringe, sock and rags torn pocket. And slept with them. Then, thinking about it, he recalled that in the heat and poluprosypayas, tightly clutching all of this and so went back to sleep.

- Look what rags and sleeping with them, even the treasure ... - And Nastasya rolled painful laugh nervously. Instantly put it under his coat and stared at her eyes.Though very little could he have at the moment is quite reasonable figure, but I felt that people did not use to be when they come to accept it. "But ... the police?"

- I look like a drink? He likes what? Bring; left ...
- No ... I'll go, I'll go, - he muttered, getting to his feet.
- Come, and you will not down the stairs?
- Go ...
- How he loves.

She left behind a janitor. He immediately rushed to the light to examine the sock and the fringe, "there are spots, but not really noticeable .. All dirty, stuck and had disappeared Who does not know in advance - not disassemble Nastasia, so anything from afar could not take it, thank God "Then he opened it with trembling agenda and began to read !; read it for a long time and finally realized. It was an ordinary summons from quarters to come today, at 9:30 am, in the office of the head of each quarter.

"Yes, it happened No, she is not for the police and why now -?!? He thought

bereavement -. O Lord, make haste to much!" He was brought to his knees to pray, but even he laughed - not a prayer over and over itself. He quickly began to dress. "Disappearing so fucking still wear Sock -! Suddenly it occurred - more clobber in the dust, and traces disappear." But as soon as he put on, and immediately pulled him with disgust and horror.Pulled, but, realizing that there is no other, and he took and put again - and again laughed: "Everything is relative, everything is relative, it all. one type - he thought briefly, only one corner of his mind, and tremors - because it's put on the back he finished as what to wear! "Laughter, however, immediately replace despair." No, can not afford. .. "- he thought. His legs were shaking." Fear "- he murmured to himself. Dizzy and sick from the heat." This trick is to me that they want to lure trick and suddenly bring down on everything - he said to himself, climbing stairs. - I wish I was delirious ... I can not lie to do something stupid ... "

On the stairs he remembered all the things that leaves wallpaper in the hole - "and here, perhaps, deliberately without looking" - and remembered ostanovilsya.No so desperate and so, if I may say cynicism death suddenly grabbed him, he waved his hand and walked away.

"Just to make haste! .."

On the street again, the heat was unbearable; even a drop of rain during all these days. Again, dust, brick and mortar, again the stench of shops and taverns, constantly drunk again, Finn-hawkers and dilapidated cabbies.Sun shone brightly in his eyes, so he began to look and very dizzy - normal feeling feverish, coming suddenly into the street on a bright sunny day.

When he reached the turn in yesterday's street, he was tormenting fear, looked into it to at home ... and immediately turned away.

"If they ask, I may be, and say," - he thought, going to the office.

The office was away for a quarter of a mile. She had just moved into a new apartment in a new building on the fourth floor. At the same apartment he once caught, but a very long time. Going under the gate, he saw a straight staircase that went a man with a book in his hands, "the janitor, it means that there is an office," and he began to walk at random. Ask anyone, or that did not.

"I'll go, I'll be on my knees and tell everyone ..." - he thought, entering the fourth floor.

The stairs were narrow and steep and covered with debris. All kitchens of all the apartments in all four floors were opened to the ladder and stood there almost all day. Because it was not terribly stuffy. Up and down up and

down wipers with books under his arm, and hozhalye different people of both sexes - visitors. The door to the room was too wide open.He came and stood in the hallway. It all stood and waited for some men.There was also an extreme closeness and, in addition to nausea tossed in a fresh nose, even nevystoyavsheyusya rotten drying oil paint on newly painted rooms. After waiting a little, he reasoned, move up another forward into the next room. All the tiny dwarf and had rooms. Terrible impatience drew him farther and farther away. No one noticed him. In the second room sits and writes several scribes not dressed if its a little better look at all strange to some people. He turned to one of them.

- What do you want?

He showed a summons from the office.

- Are you a student? - Asked one look at the agenda.

- Yes, a former student.

Scribe looked at him, but without any curiosity. It was a particularly disheveled man with an obsession in his eyes.

"The fact that I do not know, because he does not care" - thought Raskolnikov.

- Go back to the clerk, - said the scribe, and pointed forward, pointing to the last room.

He entered the room (fourth order), close and jam-packed with audience - people, some dressed cleaner than those komnatah.Mezhdu visitors were two ladies. One in mourning, badly dressed, sat at the table with the clerk and wrote something under his diktovku.Drugoe lady, very complete and purple-red, spotted, outstanding woman, and something so very richly dressed, with a brooch on his chest, the size of a tea saucer, stood on the sidelines and waiting for something. Raskolnikov clerk shoved agenda. He looked at her and said, "Wait," and continued to work with the mourning lady.

He breathed freely. "Probably not!" Little by little he began to encourage him to exhort all the forces in a good mood and recover.

"That stupid, any small indiscretion, and I can give all of himself Hmm ... sorry that there is no air - he added - stuffy head spinning and ... more ... mind, too ..."

He felt around him a terrible mess. He was not afraid sovladet with him. He tried to cling to something, and that is something to think about is not related, but it does not work out.The clerk strongly, however, interested him: he still wanted something to guess at his face to see through. It was a very

young man, twenty-two years old, with a dark complexion and mobility, it seemed his old age, dressed in the fashion and sulfate, parted on the back of his head, brush and raspomazhenny, with many rings and rings on white otchischennyh brush fingers and gold chains vest . On the one former foreigner here, he even said a few words in French, and very satisfactory.

- Louisa Ivanovna, you have - he said briefly, wearing a purple-red lady who stood there as if she did not dare to sit down, but the chair was near.

- Ich Danke, 1 - she said softly, with a silky noise, sank into a chair. Light blue with white lace dress her up like a balloon, spread around the chair and took almost half of the spirits room.Suffered. But the lady is obviously shy, which occupies half of the room, and it's because of her perfume, but cowardly and cheeky smile together, but with obvious concern.

Funeral lady finally finished and started to get up. Suddenly, with some noise, very smartly and somehow especially povertyvaya shoulders with each step, entered the officer threw his hat with badge on the table and sat down. Curvy lady and jumped from their seats, his envy and some special pleasure began to squat; but the officer did not pay any attention to it, but she did not dare to sit down with him anymore. It was a lieutenant, assistant warden quarterly, with horizontally protruding on both sides of a reddish mustache and a very small features, nothing special but for some audacity expressing exception. He narrowed his eyes and glared at partially Raskolnikov too was dressed in a suit of the area, and despite all the understatement is still in action is not carried; Raskolnikov, by chance, too straight and looked at him for a long time, so he was offended.

- What do you want? - He shouted, probably wondering what a ragamuffin, and do not think that will ever remain in his lightning glance.

- Demanded ... on the agenda ... - posted something like Raskolnikov.

- This is a matter for the restoration of money from them, with the student - hurried clerk looked up from his work. - Here, sir! - And he threw the book Raskolnikov, pointing to its location - Read!

"Money is what money? -? The thought Raskolnikov - but ... well, well, probably not that ! " And he began with joy. He suddenly felt terribly, indescribably easy. All flew down from his shoulders.

- And at what time you come to a written milostisdar? - Shouted the lieutenant, more and more unknown than offended - you're nine, and now the twelfth hour!

- I brought the whole quarter of an hour ago - loud and shoulder

Raskolnikov answered, also suddenly and unexpectedly wrath and even find some pleasure in it. - And what beautiful, I was sick with a fever came.

- Do not you scream!

- I did not cry, but it is to say, but you scream at me; and I am a student and yell at yourself will not.

Assistant to the burst in the first minute, and he could not say, and only a fine spray flew out of his mouth. He jumped to his feet.

- Please, ma-and-a-lchat! You are in the presence of. Not GR-R-rubiyanit, sir!

- Yes, and you are in the presence of, - said Raskolnikov, - and, moreover, that cry, cigarette smoke, so we all mankiruete. - Having said that, Raskolnikov felt an inexpressible pleasure.

Clerk with a smile looking at them. Hot lieutenant, obviously puzzled.

- It's none of your business, sir! - He shouted, finally, unnaturally loud - but all right-ka to present an overview that you nuzhno.Pokazhite him, Alexander Grigoryevich. Complaints about you! Money does not pay! Look how clear the falcon flew!

But Raskolnikov listened greedily grabbed the newspaper, looking for clues as quickly as possible. I read once, twice, and do not understand.

- What is it? - He asked the clerk.

- This is the money you borrowed to record demand recovery. You either have to pay all expenses and other foam or give written feedback, when you can pay, and at the same time the obligation not to leave the capital to pay and do not sell or hide their assets. The lender has the right to sell your property, and you will act in accordance with the laws.

- Yes, I ... no one should!

- It's not our business. And here came to us to recover overdue and legally protest letter loan of one hundred and fifteen rubles issued you a widow, collegiate asessorshe Zarnitsina back up to nine months, and was transferred from the widow Zarnitsina pay court counselor Chebarovu, so we invite you to read.

- Why is it my mistress?

- Well, then, that the mistress?

The clerk looked at him with a condescending smile of regret, but at the same time a holiday for beginners who are just starting a fire: "What they say, what do you feel now?" But he was still a debt letters to recovery! The value is now at least some anxiety, in turn, although some attention! He

stood there, read, listen to, he said even asked, but it is an afterthought. Triumph self-rescue from a dangerous davivshey - who filled in this moment his whole being, without foresight, without analysis, without guessing and guessing the future, without a doubt, and without question. It was a moment of complete, immediate, purely animal joy.But at this very moment in the office there was a kind of thunder and lightning. The lieutenant, still all shaken irreverent, all glowing and obviously wanting to support the desire of the victims were attacked on all Perun unfortunate "magnificent lady", looking at him since he came with a smile preglupeysheyu.

- And you, and so it is, and that - he suddenly shouted with laughter (mourning lady had already left) - you get what happened last night? and? Again, shame on the street brawl fighting produce.Again and drunkenness. In Gray dreams! In the end, I told you, because I really told you ten times that in the eleventh not'll set! And you again, again, so-and-so you like!

Even paper fell out of the hands of Raskolnikov, and he looked wildly lush lady so unceremoniously finishes;but soon, however, realized what was happening, and immediately start the whole story is very similar to it.He listened with pleasure, even so, I wanted to laugh, laugh, laugh ... All the nerves and jumped.

- Ilya Petrovich! - Began carefully clerk, but stopped to waiting time, because boiled lieutenant could not be for hands, which he knew from his own experience, except.

As for magnificent ladies, first she trembled from the thunder and lightning; but the strange thing: the more numerous and powerful was the curse, it kind of became more polite, so cute makes her smile, facing the terrible lieutenant. She ran to the spot and constantly squat, looking forward to what she was finally allowed to screw his word, and waited.

- No noise, and I do not fight a bull, Mr. kapiten - she suddenly rattled like peas does not wake up with a strong German accent, although smartly in Russia - and no, they do not shkandal prishol drunk, and I'm telling you all this Mr. kapiten, and I'm not guilty ... I have a noble house, Mr. kapiten and noble call, Mr. kapiten, and I always, always, she did not want any shkandal. And they do prishol drunk and then asked again three putilki, and then lifted one leg and began piano nogom igral, and it is not good in a noble house, and he did not lomal Ganz piano, and very, very still and I do not Maniram skazal. And he took him, and began putilku all behind putilkoy tolkal. And then I became a janitor in the near future pozval and Carl prishol, he took Carla

and the profitability and growth of the eye, and Henrietta also profitability and growth of the eye, and I was up to five times the cheek billion. And it's so indelicate a noble house, Mr. kapiten I krichal. And he fled from otvoryal window and stood at the window, like a pig, vizzhal; and that's a shame. And as a window into the street, like a pig, vizzhal; and that's a shame. Fui River-Fui River-Fui River! And Carl for his coat from the window taskal here, however, Mr. kapiten he Zane rock izorval. And then he krichal HE fifteen silver rubles Mans ICC platil fine. And I myself, Mr. kapiten, five rubles he zeynrok platil. And this noble guest, Mr. kapiten any shkandal Dellal! I'm talking shops, you will be a great satire gedryukt because I can in all the newspapers about you all sochinil.

- From the writers mean?

- Yes, sir kapiten, and what makes this noble guest, Mr. kapiten, when a noble house ...

- Well, well, well! Enough! I already told you, saying I told you ...

- Ilya Petrovich! - Again, the clerk said pointedly. The lieutenant looked at him; The clerk nodded slightly.

- ... And you, venerable Laviza Ivanovna, my last tale, and, of course, it was the last time - continued the lieutenant. - If you have at least once in your noble house scandal happens, so I'll most tsugunder how high syllable govoril.Slyshal? So the writer, writer, five rubles "Noble House" Faldo capture? There are writers! - And he cast a disdainful look at Raskolnikov. - The day before yesterday at the hotel and its history: lunch and do not want to pay; "I say, you are in the satire to describe." On the boat, too, the other last week, state councilor respectable family, his wife and daughter called vile words. From the other day in a candy store one pushes him. That's what they are writers, writers, students, heralds ... ugh! And you're gone! I'm here to see you drop by itself ... beware! Heard?

Louisa Ivanovna utoroplennoyu kindly went into a crouch on all sides and, crouching, dopyatilas to the door;but back to the door to a prominent officer, open a fresh face and a great tight blond mustache. It was very Nicodemus Fomich quarterly warden. Louisa Ivanovna hurried to sit down almost to the floor and frequent small steps, bouncing, flew out of the office.

- Once again, the roar of thunder and lightning, tornado, hurricane! - Please and friendly Nicodemus asked Fomich Ilya Petrovich - again stir the heart, boil again! Even the staircase heard.

- Yes INTO! - With precious casually said Ilya Petrovich (and not even in,

and somehow, "Yes shta-ah!") Moving with some papers in the other table and figure distorting shoulders at each step, where a step back and shoulders; - That, sir, if you please, sir, writer, that is, a student who has money does not pay the bills slapping, the apartment is not cleaned, the incessant complaints about them and are happy to join in the statement that I lit a cigarette with them! Sami district despicable act, but, sir, if you please, take a look at them: behold, they are in it very attractive now, Sir!

- Poverty is not a vice, my friend, but it too! It is known, gunpowder, could not move the offense. You something right, offended at him and could not help myself - continued Nicodemus Fomich kindly addressing Raskolnikov - but you are wrong: on and blah ha-a-ar-r-native, I tell you man, but the powder, the powder!Flared, boiled, burned - no! And it's gone! As a result, only one gold heart! His regiment was given the nickname "General powder" ...

- What else is NP-regiment! - Exclaimed Ilya Petrovich, very nice, it's so nice tickled, but still budiruya.

Raskolnikov suddenly wanted to tell them all something extraordinarily pleasant.

- Yes, for pity's sake, Captain, - he said very casually, turning suddenly Nicodemus Fomich - and hearken to my situation ... I am willing to even ask them to apologize, if that is on their side stingy. I am poor and sick student, dejected (he said, "distress") poverty. I am a former student, because now I can not contain myself, but I get the money ... my mother and sister - the first province. I will send, and I will pay .... Mistress of my good woman, but she ozlilas, before I lost my lessons and do not pay for the fourth month, which did not send me to dinner ... And I do not understand that this bill! Now she's with me borrow it requires a letter that I pay her, judge for yourself! ..

- But it is not our business ... - again noticed the clerk ...

- I'm sorry, forgive me, I totally agree with you, but let me explain, and - again took Raskolnikov, referring not to the clerk, and all Nicodemus Fomich, but in every way to handle too, and Ilya Petrovich, although he stubbornly pretended that digs in the papers and contempt not pay attention to him, - Let me explain my role that I live alone for three years, with the advent of the province until ... until ... Well, why should not I admit it, in its all, from the very beginning, I promised that I would marry her daughter, a verbal promise, absolutely free ... It was a girl ... but I liked it. .. Although I was not in love ... In short, young people, that is, I want to say that I'm the mistress

of a lot of credit, and then I went to some of life ... I was very careless ...

- Since you do not need this kind of intimate, milostisdar, and no time - roughly and triumph was interrupted Ilya Petrovich, but Raskolnikov stopped his ardor, though it was very difficult to suddenly speak.

- But let me, let me also, in particular, tell it like it was ... ... and in turn ... but it's too much, I agree with you, tell me - but a year ago, the girl died from typhus I stayed tenant, as he was, and the hostess, she moved to this apartment, said to me ... and said friendly ... it is absolutely confident in me and all ... but what if I give her credit is an hundred and fifteen rubles, only that she thinks I'm in debt. Let C: He said that as soon as I give this paper, he again lend me as much as you like and that will never, ever, in turn - it's her own words - it does not take this article Meanwhile, I'll pay ... And now that I've learned, and I have not lost anything, and she takes to recover ... Well can I say?

- All of these sensitive parts for milostisdar do not concern us, - brazenly snapped Ilya Petrovich - you need to give feedback and commitment and that you were happy to be there in love and all these tragic poses absolutely no worries.

- Well, you ... cruel ... - muttered Nicodemus Fomich, sitting down at the table and sign accepted. He somehow ashamed.

- Write the same - the official said Raskolnikov.

- What to write? - Asked that as a particularly rude.

- And I'll dictate.

Raskolnikov thought the clerk with him casually and contemptuously after his confession, but, oddly enough, - he suddenly felt very strongly all the same to someone else opinion, and this change was once a minute for one minute. If he wanted to think a little, then, of course, would be surprised how he could talk to them, a moment ago, and even put their feelings? And where are these feelings? On the contrary, now, when suddenly the room was filled not quarterly, and especially of his friends, and that did not seem to believe they were not human words, before suddenly emptied his heart. Gloomy feeling painful, endless loneliness and alienation suddenly consciously affected his soul. No meanness of his heart outpourings before Ilya Petrovich, no meanness and poruchikova triumph over him suddenly turned so his heart. Oh, what did he care now to be meanness, for all these ambitions, lieutenants, Germans, penalties, offices and so on. And so on.! If he was sentenced to burn even at this moment, and even then it will not move

even a little sentence listened attentively. Since this is really something completely unknown to him, in a new, unexpected and never experienced. Not that he knew, but he obviously felt the full force of the feelings, which are not only sensitive expansive as ever, but even with nothing else, he could not be more appealing to these people in the quarterly office, and whether it is on -prezhnemu his brothers and sisters, not quarterly lieutenants, and even then it would not be absolutely no reason to reach out to them, and even a way of life; he never had up to this point had not experienced such a strange and terrible feeling. And it's just painful - it was more of a feeling than consciousness than the concept; Direct feeling a painful feeling of all the still life they experienced feelings.

The clerk began to dictate the form of the usual that reviews the case that I can not pay, promised then that (ever), the city is not going to go away, or sell the property, or I will not give, and so on,

- Yes, you can not write, you should pen falls from his hands, - said the clerk, looking curiously at Raskolnikov. - Are you sick?

- Yes ... my head spin ... to say next!

- Yes, everything! sign up.

The clerk took the paper and began another.

Raskolnikov gave the pen, but instead get up and go, put both elbows on the table and clasped his hands over his head. In addition, he scored the nail in the head. A strange thought came to him suddenly: stand up now, go to Nicodemus Fomich and tell him yesterday, all the way down to the smallest detail, then go with them to the apartment and show them things in the corner, into the hole. The desire was so strong that he stood up for execution. "I do not think even for a moment? - Flashed through his mind - no, better, and, without hesitation, and shoulders down." But suddenly he stopped in his tracks: Nicodemus Fomich spoke with fervor Ilya Petrovich, and he flew up to the words:

- It can not be both released! Firstly, contrary to all; Judge for yourself: why do they call the janitor, if that is their business? Inform yourself, or what? Al tricks for? No, it would be too difficult! Finally, the student Pestryakova seen at the gates of both the layman and the janitor at the very moment when he came, he went with three friends and left them at the gate, and at the residence of the respondents in the wipers, even when friends. Well, this will permit to ask if with the intention to go? Koch, so before you go into half an hour old, sitting jeweler and precisely 7:45 on his old woman

went upstairs. Now, to understand ...

- But let me, as they were such a contradiction: they argue that the knock and the door was locked, and three minutes later, when the janitor came out the door unlocked?

- In part, the killer was sitting there and definitely blocked on constipation; and, of course, would have covered it there, if not silly Koch, he did not go to the janitor. And it is precisely in this period, and something had to go down the stairs and slip past them somehow. Koch both hands on the cross: "If I was there, he said, was, he would have jumped out and killed me with an ax." Russian prayer wants to serve, hehe! ..

- The killer, and nobody saw?

- But where is there to see? Noah's Ark - - House told the clerk to listen to his place.

- The thing is clear, the matter is clear! - Hot repeated Nicodemus Fomich.

- No, it's very clear - sealed Ilya Petrovich.

Raskolnikov took his hat and went to the door, but he did not get to the door ...

When he awoke, he saw that he was sitting in a chair that supports this right, some people who left another man with a yellow glass filled with yellow water, and that Nicodemus Fomich stood in front of him and looking at him; He rose from his chair.

- What is it that you are sick? - Rather abruptly asked Nicodemus Fomich.

- They both signed, so nearly led pen - the official said, and sat down in his place, and taking over the paper.

- How long have you been sick? - Shouted Ilya Petrovich from his seat and is also going through the paper.Of course, he is also considered the patient when he was unconscious, but then took off when he woke up.

- Since yesterday ... - Raskolnikov muttered in response.

- And yesterday came out of the yard?

- Exit.

- Sick?

- Patient.

- What time is it?

- At eight o'clock in the evening.

- And where, may I ask?

- On the street.

- Short and sweet.

Raskolnikov snapped sharply, all white, like a handkerchief, not omitting the black eye pain, in their eyes, Ilya Petrovich.

- He barely on his feet worth, and you ... - said it was Nicodemus Fomich.

- It'S Nothing! - How in particular, said Ilya Petrovich. Nicodemus Fomich wanted something more we add, but looking at the clerk, who is also very looked at him in silence. Everything suddenly fell silent. It was weird.

- Well, sir, - concluded Ilya Petrovich - we will not be delayed.

Raskolnikov went out. He could still hear the output, he began a lively conversation in which the louder the voice repeated the question Nicodemus Fomicha ... In the street he really woke up.

"Search, search, search now! - He repeated, slowly walk - suspected robbers!" Daveshny fear gripped him again all from head to toe.

←« »→

←« CHAPTER II »→

"And what if all that were looking for? What if they just yourself and find you?"

But in his room. Anything or anyone;no one was looking. Even Nastasya not pritrogivalas. But ah! How could he leave this morning, all of these things in this hole?

He threw himself into a corner, put his hand under the wallpaper and began to pull things and loaded their pockets. Just turned eight pieces: two small boxes with earrings or something like that - it does not look good; then four small Morocco case. One chain simply wrapped in newsprint. Something else in the newspaper seems to order ...

He poklal all in different pockets in the coat, and the other right-hand pocket of his trousers, trying to make it invisible. Purse and taken at the same time with things. Then he left the room, this time even leaving it wide open.

He walked quickly and decisively, and even felt that the whole is broken, but his mind was with him. He was afraid of the chase, afraid that half an hour after quarter of an hour has come, perhaps, the instruction to follow him; Thus, in no matter what happens, it was necessary to bury the time runs out. We had to deal with, but it was nothing like the forces and at least some arguments ... Where to go?

It was decided long ago: "Throw all in the gutter, and ends in the water, and that's all." So he decided to make one more night in delirium, in those moments when he remembered her, tried several times to get up and go, "as soon as possible, as quickly as possible, and throw it." But the cast was

very difficult.

He wandered along the embankment of the Catherine Canal for half an hour, maybe more, and repeatedly looked at the collections in the ditch, where they met. But I think that it was impossible to carry out the intention: or rafts in most meetings and they laundresses washed linen, or boat approached, and people around the world and swarming, and from all over the waterfront, from all sides, we can see the ads: suspicious that people deliberately went, stopped and something in the water droplets. And also cases did not sink and float? And, of course, so.Everyone see. And without that all is well and look, meeting, looking around as if they just kept it. "Why is it, or I can be, apparently," - he thought.

Finally it occurred, it can not be better to go somewhere on the Neva? There and people are less and less noticeable, and in any case it is more convenient, and most importantly - from local places further. And suddenly asked, as he wandered the whole half hour in anguish and anxiety, and in dangerous places, and that previously could not have invented! And because only half an hour for it all killed reckless that even once in a dream, it was decided in delirium! He became extremely distracted and forgetful, and he knew it. Resolutely he had to hurry!

He went on to Neve V - Fifth Avenue; but the way it came suddenly another thought: "Why Neva Why is water not it better to go somewhere very far away, at least once on the island, and somewhere out there, in a secluded spot in the woods under? Bush - to bury all this and the tree may have noticed "And although he felt unable to just clearly and intelligently discuss at this point, but thought it seemed unmistakable ?.

But also on the island, he was not destined to get there, and it happened again, hanging out with B - Prospect of the area, he suddenly saw the left entrance to the courtyard, furnished completely deaf steny.Sprava immediately upon entering the gate, ran into the yard deaf unbleached wall adjacent four-story building. On the left, parallel to the blank wall, and now also from the gate, was a wooden fence, twenty paces into the yard, and then completely fractured left. It was boring fenced place where lay the materials. In addition, in the recess yard, peeking around the corner of the fence low, sooty, stone barn, apparently part of any studio. Here, of course, was a place, coach or plumbing, or anything of the sort; everywhere, almost at the gates, many blackened coal dust. "That would be where to throw and go!" - Came to him suddenly. Not noticing anyone in the yard, he proshagnul gate and

just saw now near the gate, fence prilazhennoy chute (and are often located in these homes, where many factory, handicraft, cab drivers, and so on.) And in the gutter, that is on the fence was written in chalk in such cases eternal Sharpness "Sdes stanovittsa prohibited WHO." As well, it is good that there is no suspicion that came and stopped. "Everything is so time and lose somewhere in the pile and go!"

Looking around again, he reached into his pocket and, when in the outermost wall, between the gate and the trough, where the entire distance was breadth of the court, he noticed a large rough-hewn stone, oh, maybe one and a half pounds, directly adjacent stone Wall Street. Behind this wall was a street, sidewalk, he could hear passers-by, darted, which is always a lot; gates but no one could see, except Man came from the street, which, however, it may very well happen, but because he had to hurry.

He leaned against the stone, grabbed the top of his tightly with both hands, gathered all his strength and turned the stone. Under this stone formed a small depression; he immediately began to throw it all out of pocket. Purse came to the top, and yet still in the recess area. Then he grabbed a stone, one turn turned it into his former side, and he just came in its original location, it seemed a little higher. But he floated the ground and pressed his foot on the edges. Could not see anything.

Then he left and went to the area. Again, a strong, barely tolerable joy this morning at the office, took possession of it for a moment. "Bury the end And someone who can come in my head to look at this stone was here, perhaps, with the construction of the house is still the same and will lie And even if we find:?.? Who I think it No more! evidence! "- and he laughed. Yes, he remembered afterwards that he laughed nervously, a small, quiet, laughed and laughed all the time, as passed through the area. But when he stepped onto the K - th Avenue, where the third day, he met with the girl, his laughter died. Other thoughts climbed into his head. Suddenly it seemed to him, and that he is now amazingly awful passage of the bench on which he was, after the departure of the girls sat and thought, as well as will be terribly difficult to meet again to barbel, which he then gave twenty cents: "Damn it!"

He was looking around distractedly and spitefully. All his thoughts circled around one now some of the highlights - and he felt that it was really essence of it, and now, just now, he was left alone with the main point - and this is even for the first time after two months.

"And dammit! - He suddenly thought, in a fit of rage inexhaustible.! - Well

begun, and began to hell with it, and a new life as it is, Lord, stupid .. And I lied and napodlichal today How disgusting fawned and flirting morning Fel Ilya Petrovich! And yet, and this is nonsense! I spit on them at all, and what I fawned and flirted! Just do it! Just do it! .. "

Suddenly he stopped; new, completely unexpected and extremely simple question knocked him surprised and bitter:

"If, indeed, all this was done deliberately, and not stupid, if you really had a definite and firm purpose, how is it that you still have not even looked into the purse and do not know what you have, due causing all this pain and took a sneaky, nasty, poor consciously go? Why, you are in the water now wanted to throw a purse, along with all the things that you did not see ... How is it? "

Yes, it is; it's all true. He, however, before he knew it, and in fact not a new problem for him; and when the night was decided to throw in the water, and then the decision was made without any hesitation and objections, and if it's something that should be, as if otherwise is not possible ... Yes, he knew everything and remember everything; yes it is almost yesterday so decided, at the very moment when he was sitting on the trunk and dragged him from the affairs ... But! ..

"That's because I was very ill - he thought grimly, finally - I myself tortured and tormented, and I do not know what I was doing ... And yesterday, and the day before, and all this time ... suffered recover. .. and I will not torture yourself ... Well, it does not get well? Oh, my God! How it bothered me! .. "He walked without stopping. He really wanted to somehow dissipate, but he did not know what to do and what to do. One new, overwhelming feeling came over him, more and more almost every minute: it was some kind of endless, almost physical aversion to anything found and the environment, stubborn, evil, hatred. He had all the nasty counter - it was disgusting their faces, gait, movement.

Just spit someone bitten to think that if someone spoke to him ...

He suddenly stopped when he left Malaya Neva embankment on Vasilevsky Island, close to the bridge. "That's where he lives in this house - he thought - that is, yes, I did Razumikhin himself to come again the same story, as it was then ... And much, but I'm curious :. himself came and easy! went so went here? Anyway, I said ... The third day ... what happened to him after that for another day to go, well, go ahead! As if I really can not leave now ... "

He went up to Razumikhin in the fifth floor.

He was at home in the closet, and at this moment engaged, he wrote, and he opened it. Four months, as they have not seen each other. Razumikhin sat in his tattered rags to robe, slippers on his bare feet, disheveled, unshaven and unwashed. His face expressed surprise.

- What are you? - He said, looking up and down came comrade; then stopped and whistled.

- Is it bad? Yes, you, my friend, our brother outdone, - he added, looking at Raskolnikov's rags. - Yes, sit down just tired, I guess! - And when he fell on the oilcloth Turkish sofa, which was even worse than his own, Razumikhin suddenly saw that his guest was sick.

- Yes, you are seriously ill, you know what? - He began to feel his pulse; Raskolnikov pulled his hand away.

- No, - he said - I have come to this ... I do not have any lessons ... I ... well, I really do not need lessons ...

- And you know what? In the end, you crazy! - He said looking at him intently Razumikhin.

- No, no nonsense ... - Raskolnikov got up from the couch. Rising Razumikhin, he does not think about what happened to him, then, face to face should converge. Now, in an instant, he guessed, has the experience, which is less likely, at this moment, come face to face with someone across the world. All the bile rose in it. He almost choked with anger at himself, just crossed the threshold of Razumikhin.

- Bye now! - Suddenly, he said, and went to the door.

- Yes, you wait a minute, wait a minute, you pervert!

- Do Not! .. - He said again pulls his hand.

- So what the hell you come after that! Are you crazy or what? It's almost a shame .... I will not let you.

- Well, listen, I come to you, because, except you do not know anyone who could help ... start ... because you are their good that smarter, and you can discuss ... Now I see that does not need anything, you do not hear anything ... Services draws and participation ... I myself ... one ... Well, that's enough! Leave me alone!

- Yes, wait, chimney sweep! Absolutely crazy! For me, because, as you want. You see, the lessons and I do not, and do not care, but there are a bookseller Tolkuchem Cherubim, it is very good in its class. I already five trading classes will not change. He pretends izdanitsa and natural produces small book - yes as an expense for you! Some names are where you always felt that

I'm stupid !; I swear, my brother, there are silly me! At present, the direction also climbed; belmesa himself or do not feel well, and I, of course, be encouraged. Here a little over two sheets of text in German - in my opinion, it's silly charlatanism, in a word, is considered to be a man or a woman not a man? Well, of course, turned out to be a triumph of that person.Cherubs on this part of the female prepares the matter; I translate; stretch it to two and a half sheet of six sheets, prisochinim lush title in half a page and let fifty dollars. Go Away! Transfer me six silver rubles from the sheet, for all fifteen rubles get, and I took six rubles in advance. It ended about whales begin to transfer, then the second part of "Confessions," which somehow boring gossip noted'll also translate; Cherub someone said that although Rousseau its kind Radishshev. I certainly do not agree, to hell with it! Well, if you want a second sheet "Man woman?" translate? If you want, so now take the text, take pens, paper - everything is state-owned - and take three rubles: I took forward translation, for the first and the second sheet, then, consequently, three rubles directly to your share and will fall. And the ending leaves - still get three rubles.Why, what else, please, for any of the services do not count on my part. In contrast, only that you have come, I really understand what you are useful to me. Firstly, I spell bad, and secondly, in Germany sometimes seams so that more and more about yourself and make just enjoy and that it is still the best way. Well, who knows, maybe it's not better, but worse ... you take or not?

Raskolnikov silently took the German leaflets article took three rubles and, without saying a word, walked out. Razumikhin looked curiously at him. But even before the first line, Raskolnikov suddenly turned back and returned to Razumikhin, and laid it on the table and the German sheets and three rubles, again, not saying a word, walked out.

- Yes, you have delirium tremens, yes! - Razumikhin roared finally rage. - What are you kidding comedy something! Even me confused ... Why did you come after the Devil?

- Do not ... transfer ... - muttered Raskolnikov is already going down the stairs.

- So, what the hell do you want? - Razumikhin shouted from above. He walked in silence.

- Hey, you! Where do you live?

There has been no response.

- Well, Sher-p-Hg with you! ..

ROBOTS READ

But Raskolnikov has to go out. Nicholas on the bridge, he had more time to wake up completely because of a very unpleasant thing for him. His tightly lashed whip on the back of the carriage driver because he almost fell under the horse, despite the fact that the driver is three or four times, he shouted. Eyelashes so angered him that he jumped to the railing (for some unknown reason, he walked down the middle of the bridge, where to go, not on foot), and gritted his teeth angrily. Circle, of course, heard laughter.

- And for the cause!

- Vyzhiga any.

- Known to be drunk presented so consciously and rises under the wheels; and you are responsible for it.

- Layer, venerable, layer ...

But at the moment, as he stood at the railing and more pointless and angrily watched the retreating carriage, rubbing his back, he suddenly felt that someone puts his hands on the money. He looked elderly merchant's wife in the head and goatskin boots, and her baby girl in a hat with a green umbrella, probably daughter."Please, Father, for Christ's sake." He took it, and they passed.Money twenty cents. On clothes and appearance, they are very capable to take him for a beggar for this collector pennies on the street, and the supply of twenty cents he would probably have been hitting whip, they soften.

He squeezed twenty cents in his hand, walked ten steps and turned around to face the Neva River, in the direction of the palace. The sky was without clouds and water almost blue, that is so rare on the Neva. Dome of the cathedral, which sets out the terms of any no better as looking at it from here, from the bridge, without reaching twenty paces to the chapel, and through the glass clean air and could clearly see even his every decoration. Whip pain subsided, and Raskolnikov forgot about the blow; restless and not absolutely clear thought now exclusively occupied it. He stood and looked long and intently into the distance; this place was particularly familiar with it. When he was studying at the university, as a rule - often comes home - it happened, maybe a hundred times, to stay at the same place, staring at this truly magnificent panorama and almost surprised every time one of his obscure and insoluble impression. Unexplained cold blew it always with this magnificent panorama; dumb and deaf spirit was filled for him this great shot ... was amazed every time he his dark and mysterious impression and lay the answer to it, not trusting myself to the future. And suddenly

he remembered about these former issues and misunderstandings, and it seemed to him that he does not accidentally thought about them now. Oh, one thing that struck him as wild and wonderful, that he was in the same place to stay, as before, as if he really imagine that the same thing may now think, as before, and the same is the same themes and templates for Interestingly, interesting ... so recently. Even it was almost comical, and at the same time compressed chest pain. At a certain depth, bottom, somewhere just seen underfoot, it seemed to him now all former past, and old thoughts, and old problems and old themes and previous experience, and the whole panorama, and he and all ... He seemed to fly somewhere up and everything disappeared in his eyes ... did one involuntary movement of his hand, he suddenly felt his fist clamped twenty cents. He opened his hand and looked at the coin, swung and threw it into the water; then turned around and went home. It seemed to him that he looked like a pair of scissors to cut himself from everyone and everything at this moment.

He came to him in the evening, then a total of six hours. Where and how to get back, he does not remember.Undressed and trembling, like a downtrodden horse, he lay down on the couch, pulled on his coat and immediately forgot ...

He woke up at dusk complete a terrible scream. God, what is this cry! Such unnatural sounds, such howling, wailing, gnashing, tears and curses poboy he had never heard and never seen before. He could not imagine myself such atrocities such a frenzy. Horrified, he sat down and sat on the bed, stopping every moment and torture. But the fighting, shouting and swearing became stronger and stronger. And now, to the great surprise, he suddenly heard the voice of his mistress. She howled, screamed and yelled, slowly, slowly, allowing the words so that it was impossible to discern something begging - of course, that he stopped beating because her mercilessly beaten on the stairs. Became the voice of the beat before the terrible rage and anger that just rattled, but still beat and is also something to say and too early, illegible, and slowly suffocating. Raskolnikov trembled like a leaf, he recognized the voice; It was the voice of Elijah P. Petrovich.Ilya here and click the hostess! He beats her feet, batters her head on the stage - it's clear, you can hear the sounds of screaming over bumps! That is, the light turned over, or what? Can be heard in all the floors, stairs through the crowd, heard voices, exclamations, shoot, bang, slam the door, ran out. "But what, why and how it can be done!" - He repeated, seriously thinking that it was pretty crazy. But no,

he too clearly hear! .. But, then, they came to him now, if so, "because ... it is true of all the same ... Because yesterday ... Oh my God!" He wanted to latch on the hook, but the hand was raised ... and useless! Fear as ice, overlaid his soul, he was tortured, okochenil ... But at the last all this noise, which lasted ten minutes so gradually began to subside. The landlady moaned and sighed, Ilya Petrovich still threatened and cursed ... But in the end, it seems, and he fell silent; Here, too, you can not hear; "Actually, no, Lord!" Yes, there is and hostess, still with a groan and cry ... that slammed the door in her ... That crowd does not agree with stairs in the apartment - aah, argue, echo, then raising his voice to a shout, then drop to a whisper. There must be many of them were; almost the whole house to be saved. "But, my God, to do everything possible! And why, why he came here!"

Raskolnikov fell helplessly on the sofa, but he could not close his eyes; He spent half an hour in such suffering, in such an intolerable sense of boundless horror never experienced.Suddenly bright light shone in his room: Nastasya came with a candle and a bowl supa.Glyadya at it closely and do what he did not sleep, she put the candle on the table and began to lay brought bread, salt, plate, spoon.

- I suppose you have not eaten since yesterday. Certain day proshlyalsya and most lihomanka strikes.

- Nastasya ... that beat the mistress?

She looked at him.

- Who beat mistress?

- Now ... half an hour ago, Ilya Petrovich, assistant chief, on the stairs ... For the fact that he beat her? ... and why? ..

Nastasya silently and frowning consider it and so long looked. He was a very unpleasant view of this, it's scary.

- Nastasia, why are you silent? - Timidly he finally said in a weak voice.

- It is the blood - she finally said, quietly, as if talking to himself.

- Blood! .. What is blood? .. - He murmured, turning pale, and drawing back to the wall. Nastasya continued to stare at him.

- No hostess did not beat - she repeated, strict and firm voice. He looked at her, barely breathing.

- I've heard ... I did not sleep ... I was sitting - even robche he said. - I'm listening ... Parish assistant warden ... on the stairs all ran together, from all apartments ...

- No one came. And it's blood cries out to you. This is when it really is no

way out and bake the liver begins here and it begins to seem ... There will be something, or what?

He did not answer. Nastasya still standing over him, looking at him and did not come out.

- Drink forbid ... Nastasyushka.

She went downstairs and two minutes later he returned with the water in a white mug; but he does not remember what happened next. Only remembered as one drink a sip of cold water and spilled from a cup on the chest. Then unconsciousness.

←« CHAPTER III »→

He, however Well, not that that was unconscious throughout the disease: it was the heat, with delirium and semi-consciousness. Much later he recalled. It seemed to him that he was going around and a lot of people who want to take it somewhere and carry a lot about him argue and quarrel. And suddenly he was alone in the room, all gone, and fear him, and only occasionally slightly opened the door to look at him, threaten him, conspiring about something between a laugh and tease him. Nastasya he often remembered by his side; different and another man, although he is very familiar, but who exactly - he could not guess, and missed it, even cried. Sometimes it seemed to him that he had a month; at other times - that is the same day. But more about that - about how he had completely forgotten; but always remembered something forgotten that it is impossible to forget - tormented, tortured, remembering groaned and fell into a rage or a terrible, unbearable fear. Then he broke away, wanted to run, but always someone stopped him by force, and he again fell into weakness and unconsciousness. Finally, he fully recovered.

It happened in the morning, at 10:00. At this hour of the morning, on clear days, the sun is always held on the longest streak of his right wall and lit the corner near the door. His bed was Nastasia and another person, it is very interesting to study and fully familiar with it. He was a young man in a coat, with a beard and a mind like a doorman. From the half-open door looks hostess. Raskolnikov stood up.

- Who, Nastasya? - He asked, pointing at the guy.

- Look at the end of the day, woke up! - She said.

- Woke up - said the porter. Realizing that he woke up, the owner, to tear

out the door immediately closed them and hid. She was always shy and burden experienced conversations and explanations; She was forty years old, and it was thick and oily, eyebrows and dark-eyed, good from tolstoty and laziness, Sami and very cute. Shy as the need.

- You ... who? - He went to the question, referring to the port. But at that moment the door opened wide again, and leaning a little bit because he was tall, entered Razumikhin.

- What sea cabin - he exclaimed, coming - always forehead bob; too, because the apartment is called! And you, brother, woke up? Now from Pashenka heard.

- Who woke up, - said Nastasya.

- Who woke up - echoed again porter with a smile.

- Who you are, what you please, sir? - I asked, suddenly turning to him, Razumikhin. - I'm here, you see, Vrazumihin; Razumikhin I do not like all the style and Vrazumihin, student, noble son, and he is my friend. Well, who are you?

- I'm the receptionist at our office from the trade Shelopaeva-ies, and in the case, sir.

- Please sit in this chair - Razumikhin himself sat on the other, on the other side of the table. - Is that you, brother, well made, I, woke, - he continued, addressing Raskolnikov. - The fourth day just to eat and drink. Yes, a teaspoon given. I came to you twice led Zosimova. Remember Zosimova? Studied carefully, and you'll say that this is nonsense - in the head or something, like something hit. Nervous delusion of some kind, the diet was bad, says beer and horseradish little release, which is why the disease, but did not pass, and peremeletsya.Zosimov done! Notably began polechivat. Well, since I do not keep - he turned back to the receptionist - all that you explain your need? Note yourself Rodia, they even out of the office for the second time already come; Shortly before it came, and another, and so we have explained. Who is this something before you came here?

- And I believe it tretegodni sir, that's right, sir. This was Alex S.; and in the office, we have, sir.

- But it will potolkovee you, what do you think?

- Yes, sir; they are exactly that with the more impressive.

- This is commendable; Well, go on.

- But Athanasius I. tailors, which read repeatedly were pleased to hear, sir, at the request of his mother, through our office, you pass a - Porter began

directly addressing Raskolnikov. - If you are already a member concept to - thirty-five Rublev give you, sir, how Semen Semenovich Athanasius Ivanovich, at the request of his mother, still way notification. Deign to know, sir?

- Yes ... I remember ... ... clothiers - thoughtfully said Raskolnikov.

- Listen: trading clothiers know! - Razumikhin exclaimed. - How could I not in the concept? And yet, I now notice that you too clever people. Well! Smart voice and pleasant to listen to.

- They are the best and there-with, clothiers, Afanasy Ivanovich, and at the request of his mother, that through them the same way as you have been sent as soon as they are at this time is not denied, seeds and so on S. recent notice from their seats you thirty-five rubles to go, waiting for better with.

- Here in the "waiting for something better" you do best and went out; too bad about "his mother". Well, what do you think ,: in full or in full consciousness, is not it?

- For me, that. Unless the receipt should be-with.

- Scribbling! What do you book as well?

- The book is something here, sir.

- Let's here. Well, Rodia, rises. I will keep thy; podmahni Raskolnikov him a little, take a pen, because his brother, the money that we are now Forest molasses.

- No, - said Raskolnikov, removing the pen.

- What is not?

- I will not sign it.

- Ugh, damn, how do without a receipt?

- Do not ... the money ...

- It does not need the money! Well, that, my friend, that you are lying, I am a witness! Do not worry, please, he's just so ... again voyazhiruet. With him, however, and in fact it happens ... you wise man, and we will keep it, it's just a ride hand, he will sign. Taken a minute ...

- And yet, I'll come another time, sir.

- No, no; why you are worried. You are wise ... Well, Rodia, do not hold a guest ... you see, waiting - and he is seriously willing to be led by the hand of Raskolnikov.

- Leave it, I ... - said he took the pen and signed the book. Porter laid out the money and left.

- Bravo! Now, brother, you want to eat?

- I want - answered Raskolnikov.

\- Do you have soup?

\- Yesterday - answered Nastasya, all standing right there.

\- With potatoes and rice flakes?

\- With potatoes and barley.

\- I know by heart. Bring the soup, and tea came.

\- Bring.

Raskolnikov looked at everything with great surprise and with a blunt senseless fear. He decided to keep quiet and wait for what will happen next? "It seems I'm not delirious - he thought - I think it's really ..."

After two minutes Nastasya gate with soup and announced that now and tea will be. Soup were two spoons, two plates and all tools: salt shaker, pepper, mustard for beef and other, first, in that order, have long had happened. The tablecloth was clean.

\- Not bad, Nastasyushka for Praskovya Pavlovna two bottles pivtsa seconded. We drink, sir.

\- Well, what do you vostronogy! - Nastasya muttered and went to execute the command.

Wildly and continued to get used to the stress of Raskolnikov. Meanwhile Razumikhin sat on his couch, awkward, like a bear, wrapped his left arm around his head, despite the fact that he would have to grow, and the rules brought it to his mouth spoon several times before blowing her that he did not burned. But the soup was just warm.Raskolnikov greedily swallowed one spoonful, then another, and another. But raising a few spoonfuls, Razumikhin suddenly stopped and announced that a further consult with Zosimov.

Nastasya came, carrying two bottles of beer.

\- A cup of tea would you like?

\- I want to.

\- Cathay soon and tea, Nastasya, because of the case, it seems possible without the faculty. But it Pivtsov! - He was sitting in a chair pulled up to his soup, beef and began to eat with gusto, as if he had not eaten for three days.

\- I, brother Rodia, you now every day is here so dinner - he muttered as beef, stuffed his mouth - all Pashenka, your hostess, the owners, I heartily with honors. Of course, I do not insist, and no protests. Here Nastasya with chaem.Eka prompt! Nastya, he loves pivtsa?

\- Ah, well, those for pranksters!

\- A cup of tea?

ROBOTS READ

- Seagull possible.

- Pour. Wait, I'll pour myself; Sit down at the table.

He immediately ordered, poured, then poured a cup of the other, threw his breakfast and sat back on the couch. Nevertheless, grabbed his left hand the patient's head, picked it up and started to drink a teaspoon of tea, again continuously, and is particularly difficult blowing on a spoon, and if in the process poduvaniya and was the most important and vital point of recovery. Raskolnikov was silent and did not resist, despite the fact that I felt really strong enough to stand up and sit on the couch without help, and not just hold hands enough to hold a spoon or cup, but even, perhaps, to walk. But for some strange, almost animal cunning, he suddenly thought to hide until the time of their forces do not hide that kind, if necessary, do not quite understand, and meanwhile listen and find out what's going on here? However, he has not mastered his disgust skhlebnuv ten spoons of tea, he suddenly pulled her head irritably shoved a spoon and fell back on the pillow. Under the head of his now really real pillows - down and clean pillowcases; He also noted and taken into account.

- It is necessary that we sent today Pashenka raspberry jam, drink do - Razumikhin says, sitting in his place again accepted into the soup and beer.

- Where does she get raspberries? - Asked Nastasia, holding five fingers Splayed on a saucer and tea deformation "through the sugar."

- Raspberries, my friend, it will take the bench. Look, Rodia, here without you the whole story took place.When you are so fraudulently received from me and the apartment is not to say that I was suddenly taken such evil that I put you to find and execute. On the same day and nachali.O, I walked and walked, asked asked! That's what I forgot to submit an apartment; However, I do not remember ever, because I do not znayu.Nu old apartment - I only remember that five points home Kharlamov. Search, I was looking for this house Kharlamov - and in fact it turned out that he did not Kharlamov house and Butch - sometimes sounds like something knocks! Well, I got angry. Angry and even went to was not, the next day in the address table, and imagine: in two minutes you saw me there. You are registered there.

- Entries!

- However, in general Kobeleva but could not, when I find. Well, long story. Just as I came down here once all your efforts are made; all, brother, everything, everything that I know; There she saw: and with Nicodemus Fomich met, and Ilya Petrovich showed me, and with the janitor, and Mr. Alexander

G. Zametovym, a clerk at the local office and finally Pashenka - it really was a crown; Here she knows ...

- Usaharil - Nastasya muttered, smiling slyly.

- Yes, you would vnakladochku, Nastasia Nikiforovna.

- Well, you dog! - Suddenly cried Nastasia and laughed. - But I Petrova, not Nikiforov - she added suddenly, when stopped laughing.

- We appreciate sir. Well, brother, not too much to say here, I would first electric jet everywhere are empty, so that all the prejudices in the area once destroyed; but Pashenka won. I, my brother, and did not expect it would be so ... well ... avenantnenkaya? What do you think?

Raskolnikov was silent, though not for a moment to break away from him by his worried look, and now stubbornly continued to look at him.

- And much, - continued Razumikhin, not at all embarrassed silence, as if in response poddakivaya - and very well, all the articles.

- Look at the creature! - Again cried Nastasia, who brought the conversation, apparently inexplicable bliss.

- Very bad, brother, you're at the outset could not get down to business. Since it was not. That is to say, the most unexpected character! Well, about the nature ... And then just like to bring to you a dinner that she did not dare to send? Or, for example, this bill? Yes, are you crazy or something, to sign the bill! Or, for example, that the proposed marriage when another daughter, Natalia Egorovna was alive ... I know everything! And yet, I can see that this is a delicate line, and I settled, I'm sorry. But, speaking about the stupidity of what you think, because Praskovya Pavlovna really, brother, not as stupid as at first glance it can be assumed ,, and ?

- Yes ... - muttered Raskolnikov, looking away, but, realizing that it is cheaper to keep the conversation going.

- Is not it? - Razumikhin exclaimed, apparently pleased that he was told - but then not clever, huh? Of course, all of a sudden character! I, brother, I am lost in the part, I assure you ... Forty-that it will be true. She says - thirty-six and she has every right to. But I swear to you that I judge a moral one metaphysics; here, brother, we played a logo that your algebra! I do not get it! Well, all this is nonsense, and it alone, seeing that you are no longer a student, he studied and lost a suit and death of a young lady, she had nothing to do with you on the appropriate retention feet, suddenly frightened; and since you are on his side, huddled in the corner and does not support the former, it is taken in the head, and you drive from apartment.And for a long

time is the intention of the capital, but the score was sorry. In addition, you are assured that the mother will have to pay ...

- This is me on my meanness ... Mother told me that she just did not ask for alms ... but I lied to my apartment ... and fed - loud and clear Raskolnikov said.

- Yes, it is reasonable for you. Just the thing is that here and abdomen Mr. Chebarov, the court counselor and business people. Pashenka without him nothing would have invented, it is very shy; as well as the business man is not shy and the first thing, of course, ask the question: is there any hope to realize vekselek? Answer: Yes, because there is such a mother that stadvadt-satipyatirublevoy their pension, even if it has not, and only Rodenku help but have a sister that her brother for going into slavery. During this time he founded and ... that moves something? I, brother, now your whole inside story turned out, that's why you have to Pashenka franc when other related leg, and now I'm talking about love ... That's just here it is: an honest and sensitive person admitted and business man listens but eats and then eat. Thus, it has conceded this vekselek claimed payment in this Chebarovu, and he formally demanded not smuschalo.Ya would like him, he knew it all, so to clear his conscience, too, to the plane, but at the time we Pashenka harmony came out, I ordered this thing all stop, that is at the source, a guarantee that you will pay. I, brother, vouched for you, you hear? Called Chebarova, ten silver rubles in his mouth, and the paper back, and now I have the honor to introduce him to you - a word that you now believe - that is, accept it, and ripped me as it should.

Razumikhin submitted a letter of credit; Raskolnikov looked at him and, without saying a word, turned to the wall. Even Razumikhin jarred.

- I see, brother, - he said in a minute - what a fool of myself again stringy. I thought it was you entertain and amuse chatter, and it seems that only the bile caught.

- The fact that I did not recognize you delirious? - Asked Raskolnikov, too, was silent for a minute, and without turning his head.

- Me, and even in a frenzy included on this occasion, especially when I just drives Zametova.

- Zametova? Clerk ..? .. How Come? - Raskolnikov quickly turned away and stared into the eyes of Razumikhin.

- But why are you so concerned about ... What? Wanted to meet you; he wanted to, because we had a lot of you are saying ... Otherwise, from whom I train about you so much learned anything? Nice, brother, it's small,

wonderful ... in his own way, of course. Now shortstop; see each other almost every day. After I moved to this part. You do not know? Just moved. In Lavizy with him a couple of times visited. Lavizu what you remember Lavizu Ivanovna?

- Nonsense, I do something?

- You bet! Does not belong to.

- What am I raving?

- Evosya! What nonsense? Known as nonsense ... Well, brother, now that the time is not lost for the cause.

He rose from his chair and grabbed his hat.

- What nonsense?

- Ek because regulated! I do not for the secret there is no fear? Do not worry: the countess did not say anything. But at some bulldog, but also about the earrings, but some of the chains, but also about MaxMara yes wiper on some, but about Nicodemus Fomich, but about Ilya Petrovich, assistant warden, much has been said. Yes, in addition to your own toed very happy that I wonder a lot of complaints: e-mail, he says, and nothing more. Himself noted in all parts of your socks and will seek their own, washed in perfumery handles with rings, you pass this material. Then just calmed down, and the whole day in the hands of this thing kept; it was impossible to tear. Should be, and now somewhere under the blanket there. And something else on the fringe pants asked why the tears! We're really trying to figure out: that there is still a fringe? It was impossible to make out ... Well, do it! Here, thirty-five rubles; Ten of them get, and an hour or two in his report presented. Meanwhile, the ladies know and Zosima, although without it should be plenty of time to be here, at the twelfth hour. And you, Nastya, often without me ask about drinking Ali is there anything else that you want ... And Pashenka I do now, that it is necessary, I will say. Goodbye!

- Pashenka calling! About clever mug! - Said after Nastasya; then opened the door and listened, but could not resist and she ran down the stairs. It was very interesting to know what he was talking about there with his mistress; and it really was evident that she was fascinated Razumikhin.

As soon as the door closed behind her, the patient dropped the blanket and like crazy, jumped out of bed.With burning, desperately looking forward to it, so they quickly went immediately, without them, and went to work. But why, why is this? - It's as if now, as luck would have it and forget it. "Lord, you tell me one thing: they all know or do not know well, how much they know and

only pretend to tease while I was lying, and there will be a sudden and say that everything is already known, and that they are the only way. .. What to do now? Here are forgotten, as luck, and suddenly forgot, now I remember! .. "

He stood in the middle of the room and looked around in bewilderment painful round; went to the door, opened it and listened; but it is not tak. Vdrug, as if remembering, he rushed to the corner where there was a hole in the wallpaper, everything began to inspect, ran his hand through the hole fumbled, but it is not. He stepped to the plate, opened it and began to fumble in the ashes: pieces of fringe from the trousers and the rags torn pocket and rolled as he threw them, so no one was looking for! Then he remembered the toe, which Razumikhin told seychas.Tem though, here he lies on the couch, under a blanket, but it was packed up and dirty since then, which of course, did not see anything to be seen.

"Ba note .. office .. And why am I in the office, where there agenda Bach .. I mixed:?! It is then required, then I also reviewed the sock, and now ... now I was sick, and then he noticed sign which led him Razumikhin .. -.? he muttered helplessly sitting on the couch. - What is Brad all this happening to me or real seems really ...? And remember: run in pretty bad condition, of course, of course, work Yes ... but where Where is my dress boots are not Kill him Hide And I understand this coat - remember that money on the table, thank you!? !!!! God! This is a bill. .. I'll take money and leave, and another apartment employment, they do not syschut! .. Oh, and the address table? Will find! Razumikhin find. It is better to run very far. .. ... in America, and spit on them! And take the bill. .. it is useful. What else to take something? They think I'm sick! They do not know that I can go, heh, heh! .. I guess your eyes, they know everything! Only would go down the stairs!Well, as they stand on guard there, the police! What is tea? Ah, beer left, half a bottle of cold! "

He grabbed the bottle, which is still a glass of beer and swallowed with delight, as if to put out the fire in my chest. But less than a minute, beer knocked him in the head, and returned to light and even pleasant coolness. He lay down and pulled the blanket. His thoughts were already sick and incoherent, began to falter, more and more, and soon sleep, light and pleasant, grabbed him. I am pleased to have found a place head on the pillow tighter covered with soft cotton blanket that was now on it instead of the old tattered overcoat, sighed softly and went to sleep deep, strong, healthy sleep.

He woke up when he heard that someone had come to him, opened his eyes and saw Razumikhin opened the door wide open and stood in the

doorway, I wonder: to go or not to go? Raskolnikov quickly sat down on the couch and looked at him, as if trying to remember something.

- And do not sleep well, here I am! Nastasya, drag the node here! - Razumikhin shouted. - Now get the report ...

- What time is it? - Raskolnikov asked, looking anxious.

- Yeah cool, brother slept: Evening in the yard, six hours will be. Six hours of sleep a little more ...

- The Lord! Well, that's me! ..

- And what of it! To your health What's the hurry? Today or something? All our time now. I three o'clock waiting for you; come twice, you sleep. By Zosimov twice failed superintending: no home, and more! It will not work! .. In their relations are also absent. I currently moved, just moved, with his uncle. My uncle, because now ... Well, to hell, for the cause! .. Come node Nastya. Here we are ... Well, brother, do you feel?

- I am healthy! I'm not sick ... Razumikhin, you're here for a long time?

- I say three o'clock to wait.

- No, as before?

- What's in the first place?

- When you go here?

- Why, I told you now told Al do not remember?

Thought Raskolnikov. As in a dream he was daveshny. One he could not remember, and looked questioningly at Razumikhin.

- Hm! - He said - do not forget! I imagine now that you are still not in a dream ... Now with fixed ... well, only better. Good for you! Well, yeah, sure! Now remember, that's all. Listen, my dear man.

He began to untie the knot, which seems to be very interesting.

- That, my friend, you would not believe, I especially heart lies. Thus, it is necessary to make a man of you.

: Start from the top. Do you see this hat? - He said, removing a node, and beautiful, but at the same time is a very common and cheap cover. - Allow minutes to try?

- Then, after - Raskolnikov said, waving his exasperation.

- No, brother Rodia not resist, and then it will be; and I will not sleep all night because no measurement accidentally kupil.Prosto! - He exclaimed triumphantly, an example - just to measure the headdress, brother, the very first thing in the suit, a kind of recommendation !. Full of people, my friend, each time forced to shoot their tires, somewhere in the common place where

all the other hats and caps there. Everyone thinks that he is the slave of the senses, and it is only because their nest bird ashamed shy kind of person! Well, Nastya, here are two hats: that of Palmerston (he pulled out of the corner Raskolnikov deformed round hat, which, for some unknown reason, called Palmerston) or yuvelirskaya, and this thing? Bet on, Rodia, what do you think paid for? Nastasyushka? - He said to her, seeing that he is silent.

- Twenty cents, I suppose, considering - answered Nastasya.

- Twenty cents, fool! - He said, offended - now for twenty cents, and you can not buy - eight hryvnia! And this is because wear. It is, however, to the entreaties: wear, next year another gift is given, by golly! Well, now I come to the US Americans, and in high school we called. I warn you - proud of his pants! - And he stood up in front of Raskolnikov of gray, from light summer wool trousers - no holes, no stains, and yet quite tolerable, even wear, so the vest, one color, as required by fashion. And it's shabby, it's true, and the best: softer, more gentle ... You see, Rodia to make a career in the world enough, in my opinion, always observe the season; if in January asparagus does not require a few rubles to the preservation of the purse; However, with respect to the purchase. Today, in the summer season, and I did buy in the summer because the fall season is already warmer question requires so should throw Well ... the more it all, it will be time to break yourself, if not from the efforts of luxury, from -this internal disorder. Well, the prices! How much do you think? Two rubles twenty-five cents! And remember, again with the same condition that they are in the next year you receive another gift! The store Fedyaeva otherwise traded, once paid for life, but because of another time and he will not go. Well, let's start now to boots - so what? In the end, so that it is clear that well-worn, and in a month or two will be responsible, because the work abroad and foreign goods: Secretary last week the British Embassy Tolkuchem reduced; only six days and wore, but the money is needed. Price one ruble fifty kopecks. Successfully?

- Yes Mauger not fit! - Said Nastasya.

- Not suitable! What's this? - And he pulled out an old, deformed, all plastered with dried mud, worn shoes Raskolnikov - I went with a reserve, and I restored a monster on the actual size.The it was all done cardio.And what about the clothes come to an agreement with the owner. That is, firstly, three shirts, canvas, but with a trendy top ... well, eight hryvnia cover, two rubles twenty-five other clothing, a total of three rubles five cents; ruble fifty boots - because it is very good - only four rubles fifty-five cents, but all

five rubles underwear - wholesale trade - just exactly nine rubles fifty-five cents. Forty-five cents on deposits, copper coin, here, sir, if you please - and thus, Rodia, you now restored for a suit, because, in my opinion, your coat is not only still can be, but even a a special kind of nobility: what does it mean to have something Sharmera order! What about the rest of socks and other things to give you; Money is our twenty-five rubles, but Pashenka and paid for an apartment, do not worry; I said, credit boundless. And now, brother, allow you to change underwear, and then, perhaps, the disease only in a shirt and now sits ...

- Leave it! I do not want! - Matt Raskolnikov, who had listened with disgust stress playful correlations Razumihina buy dresses ...

- That, my friend, it is impossible; Well from what I have trodden boots! - Razumikhin insisted. - Nastasyushka, not ashamed, and help me, that's it! - And, despite the resistance of Raskolnikov, he still changed his underwear. He fell to the headboard and two minutes without saying a word.

"As long otvyazhutsya!" - He thought. - What's all the money bought? - Finally he asked, staring at the wall.

- Money? Here you are! Yes, your own personality. This morning was the porter of the tailors, his mother sent; Al and forget it?

- Now remember ... - said Raskolnikov, after a long and gloomy reverie. Razumikhin, frowning with concern looked at him.

The door opened, and a tall and burly man, as if too few are familiar with the type of Raskolnikov.

- Zosimov! Finally! - Razumikhin exclaimed, delighted.

⪻ CHAPTER IV ⪼

Zosimov was tall and fat man with a puffy and pale, colorless, gladkovy-britym person, blond, straight hair, glasses, and with a large gold ring on his finger swollen fat. He was twenty-seven years. He was dressed in a coat energetic light in bright summer trousers, and all of it has been widely different and needles; linen spotless, massive chain clock. His manner slowly, as if slowly and at the same time teaching and cheeky, claims, but it is hard to hide, Gleam minute. All who knew him, found him a man of heavy, but said that he knew his business.

- I, brother, two come to you ... you see, woke up! - Razumikhin shouted.

- I see, I see; Well, as we now feel, eh? - Please Zosimov to Raskolnikov, looking intently at him and sat with him on the couch, in the legs, which immediately collapsed, and as far as possible.

- Yes, all the blues - continued Razumikhin - Linens it now variable, so almost cried.

- It Is Clear; Linen can be and then, as he does not want to ... Pulse nice. Head still hurts a little, huh?

- I'm healthy, I'm perfectly healthy! - Persistently irritable and said Raskolnikov suddenly sat down on the sofa and sparkling eyes, but immediately fell on the pillow and turned to wall.Zosimov followed closely behind him.

- Very well ... all right, - he said listlessly. - Is there anything?

He was told and asked what can be given.

- Yes, it can be given ... soup, tea ... mushrooms and cucumbers, of course, not to give, well, beef is also not necessary, and ... well, so what is there something right! .. - He exchanged glances with Razumikhin.- medicine away, and

all the rest; and tomorrow I'll see ... It would be today ... well, yes ...

- Tomorrow night I go to it! - Razumikhin decided - in the Yusupov garden, and then in the "Palais de Cristal" Let's go.

- Tomorrow, I did not move, and yet ... a little ... well, yes there and see.

- Oh shame, today I just housewarming handle, two steps; It would be it.If I could lie on the couch between us! Do you know anything? - Razumikhin suddenly turned to Zosima, - do not forget to watch, I promise.

- It may be perhaps later. What are you all right?

- Nothing, tea, vodka, herring. Cake will be served: collect them.

- Who's that?

- Yes, all local and all almost new, right - except, perhaps, the old uncle, and it is new: only yesterday arrived in St. Petersburg, there are some tricks; for five years and never see each other.

- Who are you?

- Yes vegetation all my life ... pensionishko county superintendent receives sixty-five years, not worth mentioning ... I, however, love. Porfiry Petrovitch came: a local police officer investigating the case ... a lawyer. Yes, because you know ...

- Also some relative?

- Some of the most distant, so you frowning? What do you quarreled once, so you probably will not?

- And I do not care about it ...

- And best of all. Well, there - students, teachers, official, one musician, an officer noticed ...

- Tell me, please, what could be more common among you, or he - Zosimov nodded at Raskolnikov, - with some Zametovym there?

- Oh, those principles angry! .. And all you something on the principles, as if on springs; including self can not be solved; And, in my opinion, good people - it's the principle, and I know that I do not want anything. Noticed a remarkable man.

- And your hands warm.

- Well, and hands warm, and do not care! So what that warms! - Razumikhin shouted suddenly, somehow unnatural annoying - I thank thee, that he warms his hands? I said that he was only one of its kind of good! And okay, in all kinds of something to watch - so many people of good will it? Yes, I am sure that for me then, but with guts, just something baked onions will, and that if you and I, to boot! ..

- It is not enough; I have for you two ladies ...

- And I'm just for you! Acute yet! Note also, boy, I'm still going to kick it volosenki because it must attract, rather than repel. The fact that people ottolknesh - not correct, especially the boy.With the boy twice gently necessary. Oh, you silly progressive, do not understand! People do not respect yourself hurt ... And if you want to know, so we probably keep one thing in common followed.

- It is desirable to know.

- Yes, in the case of malaria, ie Dyer ... Oh, we get! Yet, at present, not a problem. The bottom line is quite obvious now! We are only a couple succumb.

- What else is there Dyer?

- As I did not tell you? Or not? Yeah, I mean, I just start talking ... it's about the murder of an old woman zakladchitsy, official ... well, here and now Dyer confused ...

- Yes, I'm about to murder your heard and it is not even interested in ... sort of ... one day ... and read in the newspapers! But ...

- Lizaveta something and killed! - Suddenly blurted Nastasia, addressing Raskolnikov. She was always in the room, huddled at the door and listened.

- Lizaveta? - Raskolnikov muttered in a barely audible voice.

- And Lizaveta, the market woman, al do not know? She went here. You still mending his shirt.

Raskolnikov turned to the wall, where the dirty yellow wallpaper with white flowers picked one clumsy white flower, with some brown strokes, and began to consider: how much of it goes that on a piece of zazubrinki and how the dash? He felt that his numb hands and feet, as if paralyzed, but do not try to mix and hard, looking at the flower.

- Well, that Dyer? - With some special displeasure interrupted Zosimov chatter Nastasya. She sighed and stopped.

- And also recorded a killer! - Razumikhin continued with fervor.

- Evidence, why?

- What the hell are the keys! And yet, this evidence, the evidence so, this is not proof that what it takes to prove it! It is in the balance as they took the first suspicions as to tell them ... yes Pestryakova Koch. Ugh! How silly it all, even vchuzhe becomes disgusting! Pestryakov something, maybe today will go with me ... By the way, Rodia, you already know this stuff, even before there was a disease, just on the eve of how you are going down in the office,

when it was said about it. ..

Zosimov looked curiously at Raskolnikov; he did not move.

- And you know what, Razumikhin? I look at you, what you are, but annoying - said Zosimov.

- It is empty and still pull out! - Razumikhin shouted, banging his fist on table.- Because then all that offensive? It's not that they're lying; You can always just a lie; is a wonderful thing because it leads to the truth. No, what a pity that lie, and even his own worship Vrana. Porphyria respect, but ... After that, they, for example, the first thing that knocked confused? The door was locked, and came with the janitor - opens: Well, yeah Pestryakov Koch and killed! This is because their logic.

- Do not worry; they simply detained; You can not ... By the way: I'm from Koch met; he was an old woman bought things late? eh?

- Yes, some rascal! He also buys and notes. Industrialist.To hell with it! I'm angry that you know what to do? On the "routine of their dilapidated, vulgar, warped, evil ... And here, in this one case, a whole new way to open a can. As psychological data can only show you how to get a true journal should." We have, for example, the facts! "Why are not all the facts, at least half the battle, as you know how to deal with the facts!

- Do you know how to deal with the facts?

- Yes, one can not remain silent when you feel the touch feel that this thing can help, if only ... Oh! .. You specify in detail to know?

- Yes, it's a dyer forward.

- Yes, I mean! Well, listen to the story: it is on the third day after the murder, in the morning when they are spoiled, so Koch Pestryakova yes - although those every step proved that the evidence screams! - Suddenly said the most surprising fact. One farmer Dushkin, taverns, front of the house is in the office and brings yuvelirsky case with gold earrings and tells the whole story: "Ran de me Compline, on the third day, around the beginning of the ninth - day and hour! Plunge - Officer Dyer, who to me on the day of running, Mikolaj, and brought me eftu box with gold earrings with stones, and asked them for a mortgage two rubles, and my requirement?, where - announced that the raised panel. More on that I did not ask - Dushkin he says something - and gave him a ticket - that is, the ruble, because de thought I did not, the other is all the same - - drink, and let the best thing I have: you put on de close to take, and announced that al rumors, so I provided. " And, of course, the dream of my grandmother lying like a horse, because

ROBOTS READ

I know, Dushkin, he pawnbroker and hides the stolen goods, and tridtsati-rublevuyu thing is not to "pass away", in Nicholas podtibril. Just chickened out. Well, hell, listen; Dushkin continues: "Farmer eftova, Nikolai Dementieva, syzmaletstva know in our province and district Zaraiskiy because we de Ryazan Mikolaj though not a drunkard, and drinks, and we knew that he was in eftom home runs, color. with Mitrea, and Mitrea they odneh place. And poluchimshi ticket, he immediately traded, drank two cups at the same time, the surrender took it and went, and I Mitrea with him at that hour did not see. And the next the day we heard that Alena Ivanovna and their sister Lizaveta was killed with an ax, and we used to know them, sir, and then took me about Sumlenniy earrings -., because we knew that the deceased gave money for the things that I went to their house and began to carefully study about himself, silent feet, and the first thing asked is whether Mikolaj? Mitra, and said Mikolaj fun came home at dawn, drunk, stayed home for about ten minutes and went out again, and then he did not see Mitra and one finishing work. And they are working on a ladder with the dead, the second etazhe.Slyshamshi all this, we do not have anything to anyone found - said it Dushkin - but about ubivstvo found everything we could and returned home all the same our Sumlenniy. And this morning at 8:00 - that is, it is the third day something, you know? - See Part I Mikolaj not tverezy, and not something that I was very drunk, and the conversation can understand. Sat on a bench, silent. OPRICH it in the tavern at the time was only one person outsider, and even slept on a bench with a friend, acquaintance, but two of our boys with. "I saw, I ask, Mitrea?" - "No, he said he has not seen." - "And is not it?" - "There was, says the third day." - "And Nona Where to stay?" - "And on the sand, said in Kolomna". - "And where, for example, took the earrings?" - "The Panel found" - and he says that this is how it was different, and not looking. "And I heard say that here is the fact that very evening and in an hour, these stairs, happened?" - "No, he said he had not heard," - and he listens, his eyes staring, and he suddenly white, smooth chalk. Etta I told him, look, and he started to get up and hat. That's what I wanted to stop him, "Wait, Mikolaj, saying al not to drink?" And he winked at the boy who kept the door, but because of zastoyki something goes: that's it from me prysnet, but on the street, but to run, but in the alley - and I've only seen it. Then I decided my Sumlenniy, because of his sin, as it is ... "

- You bet! .. - Said Zosimov.

- Stop! End listen! Empty, of course, with all of his quest Nicholas: Dushkin

detained and searched is made, Mitrea, too; poraspotroshili and Kolomna - only the third day suddenly and cause very Nicholas: he was arrested in the area - ing outpost in the hotel. He came back, took the cross, silver cross and asked Shkalik. Dali.Pogodnye a few minutes, the woman went to the barn and sees a break: he was there in the barn belt tied to a beam, made a loop; standing on a tree stump, and wants himself noose around his neck wear, cried the woman scream. ran: "So what do you" - "And do not bring me, says in a certain part, obey in all things the Lord." Well, proper Oner and presented in this format, that's it. Well, that, that, who, how, how many years - "twenty-two" - and so on and so forth.Question: "How to work with Mitrea, who did not see EH stairs here in such and such and such an hour? "The answer:" We know were probably some people, but we are not in the signs. " - "And what l did not hear the noise and other things?" - "I do not hear so special." - "And you know, I was Mikolaj, the same day that this widow on a certain day and time with her sister she was murdered and robbed?" - "Knowing what I know, I know it was not possible for the first time on Pavlitch Athanasius, on the third day, in raspivoshnoy heard.". - "Where? Earrings made of "-" On the found. "-" Why do not show the next day with Mitrea work? "-" Because I Etta fun. "-" Where to go? "-" And there's some-thing in there somewhere. "-" Why run away from Dushkin? "-" Because we really ispuzhalsya then sharpened. "-" What are you afraid of? "-" And in the PMU. "-" How could you be afraid if you do not feel guilty? .. "Well, believe or not, Zosimov, this question has been proposed, and literally in these terms, I know, I'm right-handed! What? What?

- Well, no, but there are some clues.

- I'm not gonna evidence now, I'm talking about the question of how they are something your understanding! Well, damn it! .. Well, it shook, shook, clicked, clicked, well, admitted: ". This is not on the panel, he says, he found, and found Vater, in which we Mitrea anointed one" - "How can such a manner?" - "And so the most manners that we are anointed Etta Mitrea all day to eight hours, going and going, and Mitra took a brush so my face paint and a brush, brush Etta he gave me in the face paint, and run, and I followed him, and I'm running Etta him and cry cry ;. but outside stairs to the road, I ran with a flourish at the janitor and gentlemen, and how many were with him gentlemen, I do not remember how damn janitor for me and another janitor and cursed and Dvornikova woman came out, we are also cursed, and one gentleman at the entrance to the road, damoyu, and we also

cursed because in the space formed Mitek: I Mitya grabbed by the hair and threw it, and began to beat, and Mitya, too, due under me, grabbed me by the hair and began to beat, and we did this not out of malice, but also in all of this so loved and effortlessly, then Mitka oslobodilsya yes, and run, and I followed him, but did not catch and returned to the Vater one -. because nadot be clean. I began to collect and forward Mitrea, can be a good thing. Yes, the door to the room, behind a wall, in a corner, and came to the box.Hours lies in gumage package. Gumagu I took off, I see such mahochkie hooks, hooks, we took Etta - an earring in the box ... "

- For doors? Place behind the doors? Behind the doors? - Cried Raskolnikov, bored, frightened eyes, staring at Razumikhin, and slowly sat down on the couch with his hand.

- Yes ... but what? What happened? What are you? - Razumikhin also rose from their seats.

- It'S Nothing! .. - Pale Raskolnikov answered, falling on the pillow, and again turning to the wall. All were silent for a while.

- Dozed off must stay awake - Razumikhin said finally, looking at Zosimova; he made a slight negative head.

- Well, go on the same way - said Zosimov - what next?

- What's next? As soon as he saw the ring and instantly forgetting apartment and Mitka, grabbed his hat and ran to Dushkin and is known to be received from him the ruble, and he lied that he had found on the panel, and immediately fun. And, as for the murder of former confirms: "Knowing I do not know who was responsible not know, I just heard on the third day." - "Why do you not?" - "In my fear." - "And why wanted to hang himself?" - "From the City Council." - "The thought" - "And in SUE". Well, that's the whole story. Now, do you think that they have learned from here?

- Yes, and think that the track at least some yes, there is. Fact. Well, will not release your Dyer?

- Why do they now have recorded a killer! They also have no doubt ...

- Yes, you are lying, hot. Well, earrings? Recognize that it myself, that if on the same day and hour of the old woman to her chest earrings Nicholas fall into the hands - he must accept that they are somehow so there must have been to get there? That's a lot in this investigation.

- So Random! How to get in? - Razumikhin exclaimed - And you, Doctor, that you, first of all, man must learn and you have a case, the most of any other human nature to know - do not you see, all of these data, for nature is

Nicholas? Do not you see, first, that all that he showed during the interrogation, the truth of God?Tochnehonko and fell into his hands, as he showed. Went on the field and picked up!

- God's truth! However, Well, he admitted that he had lied the first time?

- Listen to me, listen carefully: the caretaker, and Koch, and Pestryakov and even the janitor, cleaner and his wife first, and the man in the street, at that time with her in bed and sat court counselor hook that at this very moment with cabin stood and entered into the driveway in hand with damoyu - all that is eight or ten witnesses unanimously show that Nikolai Dmitri pressed to the ground, lying on him and his tuzil, and he grabbed him by the hair and tuzil. They lie across the road and blocking the passage; abuse from all sides, and they "like little children" (the literal expression of witnesses), lie on top of each other, screaming, fighting and laughing, laughing like a race with the most ridiculous mugs, and catch up with each other as children on the street ran . Heard? Now strictly Note to self: the upper part of the body is still warm, you hear a warm, so finding them! If they are killed, or only one Nicholas, and thus robbed chests burglary, or only attended anything in a robbery, then let me ask you just one question: whether it is a state of mind, that is, the shouts and laughter , childish fight under the gate - with axes, with blood, with a disgusting trick, caution, robbery?Immediately killed, only about five or ten minutes ago - because it goes, the body is still warm - and suddenly, leaving the body and unlocked apartment, and knowing that there are now people are gone, and the production of castings, they are small children, lying on the road laughing all the attention on himself attracted to, and after ten unanimous witnesses there!

- Of course, it is strange! Of course, this is impossible, but ...

- No, brother, not yet, but if the earrings, on the same day and hour he was in the hands of Nicholas actually represent important evidence of dissent against him - but m directly explain his testimony because anothercontroversial dissent - we must we accept into account the facts and exculpatory, and even more so that they are facts convincing. And how do you think the nature of our jurisprudence, can l, or they accept this fact - solely on the basis of only one psychological impossibility alone mood of the soul - because convincing and all beliefs and the facts, whatever they destroyed? No, it will not take any that because de box and found a man wanted to strangle "that could not be, if I do not feel guilty!" That is the main question here is what I'm hot! Understand!

- Yes, I see that you're hot. Wait, I forgot to ask what it is proven that the box with earrings really old chest of a woman?

- Proven - Razumikhin replied, frowning, as if reluctantly - Koch learned a thing is mortgagors, and positively proved that the thing was he.

- Poor. Now we have not seen anyone Nicholas while Koch yes Pestryakov top left, and whether it can be to prove something?

- This is something that no one has seen - Razumikhin replied with annoyance - it is bad; even with Koch Pestryakova ignore them when they are held in the air, although their witness and not a lot of would now mean. "You see, they say that the apartment unlocked, he should have worked, but passes, do not pay attention and do not remember whether there working at the moment or not."

- Hmm. So all this is just an excuse that tuzili each other and laughed. Let us assume that it is a strong proof, but ... Let me now: how are you that explains in general? What explains the discovery of earrings, of course, if he found them, as shown?

- What is the explanation? Yes, what is there to explain: it is clear! At least, the road on which we have to deal with the news, and clearly proved, and it has proven its box. The real killer fell these earrings. The murderer was upstairs when Koch and Pestryakov knock, and sat down on the lock. Koch and went stupid;Then the murderer jumped up and ran down too, because no one else had no way out. Maybe they saw, but did not notice, little did people go? Box he fell out of his pocket when the door was, and did not notice that he had fallen because he did not before he byl.Okno also clearly proves that he was standing there. It's all about!

- Smart! No, brother, it's hard. It's more subtle than most!

- But why, why?

- Yes, because all too successfully come together ... and wove ... as in the theater.

- Oh-oh! - Cried Razumikhin was, but at that moment the door opened, and included a new one who is not familiar with any of the persons present.

←«»→

←« CHAPTER V »→

It was a middle-aged gentleman already years, stiff, stout, with care and capricious person who started, who stood in the doorway, looking around with undisguised surprise, hurt and looks as if asking, "Where I hit it," Unbelief and even with some affectation of fear, almost not even an insult, he looks around and near the low "sea cabin" Raskolnikov. With the same surprise turned and stared in front of Raskolnikov, naked, vsklochennogo, dirty, lying on the couch dirty scarce and still believe it. Then, with the same slow, began to examine the disheveled, unshaven and slovenly figure Razumikhin, which in turn safely survey looked him straight in the eye, without moving from the spot. The tense silence lasted for a minute, and, Finally, as one would expect, there was little change dekoratsiy.Ponimaya should be, according to some, it is, however, a sharp, given that overly strict posture here, in this "sea cabin," absolutely nothing is done, came in r Mr. softened and polite, though not without rigor, said, referring to Zosima and rap each syllable of his question:

- Romanovich Raskolnikov, Mr. student or former student?

Zosimov slowly and may be answered if Razumikhin, who can not be cured, not to warn him:

- And here he lies on the couch! What do you need?

This cavalier "What do you want?" and felled Mr. Prim; he was even almost turn Razumikhin, but still managed to keep himself again and again as quickly as possible turned to Zosima.

- Here Raskolnikov! - Zosimov muttered, nodding at the patient, then yawned, and somehow unusually large number of opened his mouth and

unusually long held him in that position. Then he slowly dragged into his waistcoat pocket, took out the hugest convex blind gold watch, opened, looked just as slowly and lazily dragged them again put.

Raskolnikov himself all the while lying quietly on his back, and it's hard, though without any thought, looking at the newcomer. His face was turned to the side now from the curious flower on the wallpaper was very pale and expressionless terrible suffering, as if he had just suffered a painful operation or released it now from torture. But Mr. logged gradually became aroused in him more and more attention, confusion, mistrust, and even seemed to be afraid of. When Zosimov, pointing at him, said: "This is Raskolnikov," he suddenly sat up quickly, just jumped up and sat on the bed and almost defiantly, but failures and weak voice:

- Yes I Do! I Raskolnikov! What do you want?

Guest looked impressive, and said:

- Peter Petrovich Luzhin. I fully hope that my name will not leave you in the dark.

But Raskolnikov was expecting something completely different, and stared at him and said nothing, as if the name of Peter Petrovich heard him strongly for the first time.

- What? You still do not deign to even get any news? - Peter asked, a few boxes.

In response to this Raskolnikov slowly sank on the pillow, his hands behind his head and stared at the ceiling. Tosca has shown itself in the face of Luzhin. Zosima and Razumikhin yet with great curiosity began to study it, and he finally seemed to be embarrassed.

- I expected and hoped, - zamyamlil it - it's a letter that was already started a little more than ten days, even almost two weeks …

- Hey, what do you all stand at the door, then? - Razumikhin interrupted suddenly - if it is necessary to explain, so sit down, and both of you, with Nastasya, there closely. Nastasyushka, outsiders, let go! Well, here's a chair here! We climb back!

He pushed his chair back from the table, freed some space between the table and knees and waited for a few tense situation in the guest "slipped" into the crack. The moment was chosen so that it was impossible to refuse, and guests raised through a narrow space, slow and stumbling. Achieving a chair, he sat down and looked at Razumihina hypochondriac.

- You will, however, not konfuztes - blurted one - Rodia fifth day already

sick and delirious for three days, and now even woke up and ate with gusto. This here is his doctor sits just looked at him and I Rodkin friend, also a former student and now here with him to nurse; so you do not take us and do not hesitate, and keep you ought to be.

- Spasibo.Obespokoyu not I, but the patient, his presence and conversation? - Peter turned to Zosima.

- N-no, - muttered Zosimov - even entertain can - and yawned again.

- Oh, he has long been in the memory of the morning! - Razumikhin continued acquaintance who had a view of the true innocence that Peter thought, and began encouraging, perhaps in part because it is ragged and insolent introduce students.

- Your mother ... - began Luzhin.

- Hm! - Loudly did Razumikhin. Luzhin looked at him questioningly.

- Nothing, I do not do; Go ...

Luzhin shrugged.

- Your mother ... even when I was with them, the beginning of the letter to you. Coming here, I deliberately missed a few days and will not come to you, so that in fact you can be sure you are informed about everything; but now, to my surprise ...

- I know, I know! - Said Raskolnikov, with an expression of the most impatient annoyance. - Is that you? Groom? Well, I know! .. And it is!

Peter greatly offended, but said nothing. He hurried difficult to understand what it all means? For a moment, the silence continued.

Meanwhile Raskolnikov, slightly turned to him in reply, suddenly began again to consider carefully and with some special curiosity, as if only now did not have time to consider all of this, or as if something new in it struck him: even rose to this from the pillow. Indeed, in general, Peter was struck as something special, namely, something seemed to justify the name "groom", so unceremoniously gave him now.Firstly, it was clear, and even too much, Peter hastened to take advantage of much more days in the capital in time to dress up and decoration in anticipation of the bride, who, however, was quite innocent and legitimate. Even his own, maybe a little too smug, his own mind a pleasant change for the better could be forgiven for such a case, because Peter was on the line of the groom. All his clothes were fresh from the tailor, and all was well, except only that he was too new and too blame known tsel.Dazhe dandy new round hat for this purpose testified Peter a little too respectful to her and also carefully held her in his arms. Even a

couple of lovely lilacs in this zhuvenevskih, gloves showed the same thing, at least, one that they did not set, but were in the hands of the parade. At the same clothes Peter predominant color is bright and yunoshestvennye. It was pretty summer jacket light brown shade, bright light pants, such as vest, just bought fine linen, lawn simple tie with pink stripes, and that the best thing: it was still faced Pyotr Petrovich. Face it, very fresh and even beautiful, and it seemed younger than his forty-five years. Dark mustache nice in the shade it from both sides, in the form of two cutlets, and very well thickened near svetlovybritogo glowing chin. Even his hair, though slightly streaked with gray, combed and curled at the hairdresser, had no idea of this fact there is nothing funny or something silly that, as a rule, with curled hair, gives a person for the inevitable resemblance to German going down the aisle. But if there was anything in it, and a beautiful and solid edges really unpleasant and repulsive, it happened from other causes. Having considered the ceremony Mr. Luzhin, Raskolnikov smiled venomously, lay back and began to continue to look at the ceiling.

But Mr. Luzhin, and refrained himself, seems to have decided not to pay attention to the time, all these oddities.

- I'm sorry, really, really, that you will find in this position - he began with the power to break the silence. - If I knew about his illness, was released earlier. But, you know, the trouble! .. I also have a very important question to my lawyer Senate. Not to mention any of the problems that you guess. Your ie mother and sister waiting from hour to hour ...

Raskolnikov stirred and wanted to say something, his face was some excitement. Pyotr Petrovich stopped and waited, but since nothing happened, then continued:

- ... From hour to hour. Priiskal their apartment for the first time ...

- Where? - Mild said Raskolnikov.

- Very far away, the house Bakaleeva ...

- This Ascension - Razumikhin interrupted - there are two floors below the numbers; merchant Yushin contains; visited.

- Yes, numbering, with ...

- Shockingly awful: dirty, stink, and suspicious place; all that had happened; Yes, and God knows who does not live! .. I myself went to the scandalous case. Cheap, however.

- Of course, I could not collect as much data as himself a new man - a touchy Peter said - but, nevertheless, are two very, very tidy room, as well as

a very short time ... I priiskal already exists, that is the future of our apartment - he turned his Raskolnikov, - and now it finishes; and yet himself closely in numbered, a stone's throw away, Ms. Lippevehzel in the apartment of one of my young friend, Andrew Semenycha Lebezyatnikov; it's just what I Bakaleeva house ...

- Lebezyatnikov? - Raskolnikov said slowly, as if trying to remember something.

- Yes, Andrew Semyonitch Lebezyatnikov service in the ministry. Deign to know?

- Yes ... no ... - answered Raskolnikov.

- Sorry, I thought your question. I was once the guardian of her ... a very nice young man ... and a witness ... I'm glad to meet with young people, because it is to see what's new. - Peter with the hope of all those present.

- It's in what respect? - Asked Razumikhin.

- In the most serious, so to speak, in the very nature of the case - caught Peter, as if happy issue. - I, you know, ten years do not attend Petersburg. All these ideas for our newsletter reform - all this before we touched in the province; but in order to see more clearly, and see everything you need to be in St. Petersburg. Well, my thought is that everyone noticed and learn more by watching the younger generation. And I confess: rad ...

- What is it?

- Your question is extensive. I could be wrong, but I think, I think a clearer view more, so to speak, criticism; more business ...

- It's true - Zosimov hissed.

- You're lying to you, in a business-not - Razumikhin seized. - Efficiently acquired a difficult, but with the gift of heaven do not fly. And we are almost two hundred years, from all things ... to wean Ideas something, maybe wander - he said Pyotr Petrovich - and that's good, though, and children; and honesty even there, despite the fact that there are thousands of scams and stops the business is still no! Efficiently walking boots.

- I do not agree with you - with obvious pleasure Peter said - of course, have a hobby wrong, but we must be indulgent to: Drag shows the fervor of the case and the wrong of the environment in which the business is located.

If done little, look, and time was short. Funds do not say. In my personal opinion, if you want, even something, and does not cover new, useful ideas, spread some new, useful things, instead of the former and romantic Dreamy; Literature takes more mature shade; liquidated and ridiculed many harmful

prejudices ... In a word, we are irrevocably cut yourself off from the past, and this, in my opinion, is really the case, with the ...

- Harden! Recommended - said Raskolnikov.
- What is it? - Peter asked, not hearing, but received no reply.
- It's true - hastened to insert Zosimov.
- Is not that right, sir? - Continuation of Peter, nice to look at Zosimova. - You have to admit - he continued, referring to Razumikhin, but with a touch of triumph and superiority, and almost added: "young man" - that is, prosperity, or as they say now, progress, at least in the name of science and economic so true ...
- The total area!
- No, it is not common place, sir! If for example, I still say "love," and I vozlyublyal, what came out of it? - Continuation of Peter, perhaps with undue haste, - it turned out that I tore his cloak in half, total with its neighbors, and we were both half naked, according to the Russian proverb: "Will you marry several birds at once, but nobody is reached ". Science, however, says: "Love, first of all, I am one, because everything in the world is based on self-inter-est. Loved it yourself, and do fashion, as it should, and your coat will remain unchanged. Economic same truth adds that the larger society and personal files are located, so to speak, whole caftans, the more good reason for this and more it is arranged and a common cause. Therefore, acquiring solely and exclusively myself, I was so acquired, as if everything and I mean, that was a little more proximal torn jacket instead of private, individual bounties, but because of the general prosperity. The idea is simple, but unfortunately too long to wait, eclipsed by enthusiasm and dreamy, but apparently do not need much intelligence to guess ...

- Unfortunately, I neostroumen - Razumikhin snapped - but because perestanemte. I did, and spoke with tseliyu, and that to me all this chatter sebyateshenie, all these continuous, endless common place and yet so all the same, only three years later disgusted that, by golly, red, and when other something that is not what I say in my presence. You certainly made himself hurried to his knowledge, this is forgivable, and I do not blame them. I just wanted to know now who you are, because, you see, in general, has recently caught on so many different manufacturers, and before they are distorted or not touched in their interest that everything that ISPAC. Well, enough!

- Sir, - began Mr. Luzhin, boxes with extreme dignity - if you want to, so unceremoniously must say that I ...

- Oh, for God's sake, have mercy ... Can I! .. Well, enough! - Razumikhin snapped and turned abruptly to continue to talk to daveshny Zosima.

Pyotr Petrovich was so smart to immediately believe the explanation. He, however, decided to leave after two minutes.

- I hope that our acquaintance started now - he turned to Raskolnikov, - after your recovery and the circumstances known to you to strengthen even more ... especially wish you good health ...

Raskolnikov even head did not turn. Pyotr Petrovich began to get up from the chair.

- Killed, of course, the usurer! - He says yes, Zosimov.

- Be sure the usurer! - Echoed Razumikhin. - Porphyry his mind not to let mortgagors and another question ...

- Mortgagors questioned? - Loudly asked Raskolnikov.

- Yes, but what?

- It'S Nothing.

- Where did he get them? - Asked Zosimov.

- Other Koch pointed; other names were written on the package of things, and others, and themselves came as heard on ...

- Well, how smart and experienced, must have channels! What courage! That definition!

- That's just is not so! - Razumikhin interrupted. - This is what you and all the way. And I say - uncomfortable, inexperienced and probably this was the first step! Suppose calculation and deftly channels and unbelievable. Assume also inexperienced and out, that only one case out of trouble, and it's gone, and it's not to do? Why, yes, he and obstacles something, maybe did not expect! And how is business? - Takes ten-dvadtsatirublevye stuff fills their pockets, rummages in women laying in tatters - and in the chest, in the top drawer, in a box, just pure money for fifteen hundred found, except for the tickets! And Rob is that he could not, but only managed to kill it! The first step, I'll tell you, the first step; lost! And not by calculation, but the event twisted!

- It would seem that the recent murder of an old woman official - intervened, citing Zosima, Peter, standing with his hat in his hand and glove, but before leaving and wanted to throw a few key concepts. He apparently fussed about a favorable impression, and vanity overcame prudence.

- Yes I Am. Have you heard?

- As-c, ... in the neighborhood

- In detail, you know?

- I can not tell; but I'm interested in that other circumstance, so to speak, the whole question. Not to mention the fact that the crimes in the lower class in the last five years has grown, not talking about the widespread and rampant looting and fires; strangest of all, for me, that crime and upper classes in the same way and increases, so to speak, in parallel. There, you can hear a former student on the road almost broke; there is advanced, its position in the community, people make false documents; there, in Moscow, caught as many as falsifiers of tickets in the last loan Lottery - and the main participants in the same teacher in the history of the world; they kill our secretary abroad because of the money and mysterious ... And if now this old pawnbroker was killed by one of the mortgagors, this and that, consequently, was a man of high society - because people do not put gold things - - that how do we explain this lack of discipline on the one hand the civilized part of our society?

- Changing economic lot ... - Zosimov said.

- What is the explanation? - Trailer Razumikhin. - But it is too deeply rooted nedelovitostyu and can be explained.

- What do you mean, sir?

- And what posted in Moscow for the lecturer to your question why he forged tickets: "All richer in many ways, and I wanted to get rich as quickly as possible." Exact words do not remember, but the sense that darovschinku, hurry, easy! All ready lived in parentheses strangers walking, chewing. Well, the great hour, all here and declare that looks ...

- But, nevertheless, morality? And, so to say, the rules ...

- Yes, you are fussing about? - Raskolnikov suddenly intervened. - On your left theory!

- How did it on my theory?

- And bring the consequences of what you preached this morning and out, that people can be cut ...

- Oh my God! - Exclaimed Luzhin.

- No, it is not so! - Said Zosimov.

Raskolnikov was lying pale and trembling upper lip and shortness of breath.

- Not at all measure - arrogantly continued Luzhin - economic idea is not an invitation to murder, and if only assume ...

- And the truth is my only weapon that you - suddenly interrupted again

CRIME AND PUNISHMENT

Raskolnikov trembling with anger in a voice that was heard some resentment joy - although yes, what you say his bride ... in the very hour, as from her consent is obtained, that only ... more glad that she was a poor ... because it is more profitable to take his wife out of poverty, then to rule over it ... and reproach that he favored you? ..

- Sir! - Angry and irritable said Luzhin, all blushing and mixed - Sir ... so distort the idea! I'm sorry, but I must say that the rumors have reached you, or rather, brought to you was not a shadow of common ground, and I suspect ... who ... in a word ... this arrow .. One word Your mother ... She already seemed to me at all, however, is its excellent quality, with great enthusiasm and shades of romantic thoughts ... But I still have thousands of miles away from the fact that he is such a perverse imagination can understand and imagine business ... And finally ... finally ...

- And you know what? - Raskolnikov exclaimed, sitting on a bed and looking at him with piercing, sparkling eyes - you know what?

- What is it? - Luzhin stopped and waited for the insult and defiance. The silence lasted a few seconds.

- And what if you have time ... dare to say a word about my mother ... ... then I'll head over heels down the set stairs'll!

- What's with you! - Razumikhin shouted.

- Ah, well, sir! - Luzhin turned pale and bit his lip. - Look, sir, I am, - he said firmly and restraining himself in all respects, but still breathing hard - I have this morning, the first step to solve your dislike, but purposely stayed here to learn more. Much I could just sick and relatives, but now ... you ... ever since ...

- I'm not sick! - Cried Raskolnikov.

- All furthermore, with ...

- Get Out!

But Luzhin was already leaving without finishing it himself, watching again between a table and a chair;Razumikhin this time got to miss it. Not looking at anyone, not even nodded Zosima, which has long been nodding to him to leave the patient alone, Luzhin left, lifting caution in shoulder hat when prinagnuvshis, held at the door. And even bend his back, as he put it, in this case, it carries a terrible insult.

- Can I, do not you? - Said the puzzled Razumikhin, shaking his head.

- Leave me alone, leave me all! - Raskolnikov cried furiously. - Yes, you leave me, finally, the torturers! I'm not afraid of you! I did, and now is afraid

of nobody! Get away from me! I want to be one, one, one, one!

- Let'S Go! - Said Zosimov, nodding Razumikhin.

- Yes, of course it is possible to leave it that way.

- Let'S Go! - Insisted Zosimov and left. Razumikhin thought and ran to catch up with him.

- The worst thing would be if we did not listen - already on the stairs, said Zosimov. - Annoy impossible ...

- What happened to him?

- If you just press it a few more profitable it would be something! Only now he was able to ... you know, it's something on your mind! Something else coming ... What I'm really afraid, and, of course!

- Yes, this gentleman, perhaps something Pyotr Petrovich! By talking it becomes clear that he would marry his sister and that Rodia about this before the disease received a letter ...

- Yes I Am; The devil brought now; may be upset with all this. And you will notice that he is indifferent to everything, all was silent for a single point from which emanates from himself, except for: murder ...

- Yeah yeah! - Razumikhin took - very noticeable! Interested scary. This is the day of his illness frightened in the office at the warden; fainted.

- Are you telling me that this is more in the evening, and I'll tell you something and say. He interested me very much! After half an hour I will come to visit ... inflammation, however, will not ...

- Thank U! And I have Pashenka meanwhile waiting for and I will follow Nastasya ...

Raskolnikov, left alone, and look longingly looked at Nastasya; but she still could not bring himself to leave.

- I'm looking to have a drink now? - She asked.

- After! I want to sleep! Leave me ...

He desperately turned to the wall; Nastasya came.

←«»→

←« CHAPTER VI »→

But as soon as she was gone, he got up, laid the door hook unleashed Razumikhin brought this morning, and they also tie the knot again with the dress and began odevatsya.Stranno say, but he seemed to have suddenly become quite calm; was not crazy nonsense, as before, no panic and fear, as in everything lately. It was the first minute of the strange, sudden calm. His movements were precise and clear, they showed strong commitment. "Today, today! ..", - He muttered under nos.On knew, however, that is still weak, but strong psychological stress came to the world to an obsession, gave him the strength and self-confidence; However, he hopes that falls on the street. Dressed in full, all new, he looked at the money lying on the table, I thought, and put them in his pocket. Money was twenty-five rubles. Also took all the copper coin, the transition from ten rubles Razumikhin, which we spent on the dress. Then calmly took the hook out of the room, down the stairs and looked at the open spacious kitchen: Nastasya stood his back and bent, bloated hostess samovar. She did not hear anything. And who could have predicted that he would be? A minute later he was already on the street.

It was 8:00, the sun was setting. Stuffiness was old; but he greedily inhaled the smelly, dusty, urban air pollution. His head was spinning a little, and some wild energy suddenly shone in his eyes inflamed and his gaunt pale yellow face. He did not know, and do not think about where to go; he knew one thing: "that all this must end today, at one time, now that the home he otherwise can not be canceled, as it does not want to live. " How will end? That the end? This he had no idea and do not want to think. He went thought thought tormented him. He only felt and knew that it was necessary that

all changed in some way, "as if all that," he repeated with desperate, fixed-confidence and determination.

Out of habit, his former general walks, he went straight to the Haymarket. Quick Haymarket, on the sidewalk in front of the store, there was a young dark-haired grinder and spit some very sensitive romance. He was accompanied by standing on the sidewalk in front of his girlfriend, fifteen, dressed as a woman in a crinoline in mantilke, gloves and a straw hat with a bright red pen; it was old and worn out. Street, creaky, but it is nice and strong voice, she sings her song, waiting dvuhkopeechnika magazinov. Raskolnikov stopped at two or three students listened, took the coin and put it in his hand. She suddenly stopped singing in the most sensitive and high notes, just cut off abruptly called organ-grinder, "will be!", And the two trudged on to the next store.

- Love you street singing? - Raskolnikov turned to one, no longer young, a passerby, who was standing next to him in the hurdy-gurdy and had a view of the flaneur . He wildly and surprised. - I love it - Raskolnikov went on, but with a look as if not in the street singing to say - I love the way they sing to the hurdy-gurdy in a cold, dark and damp autumn evening, of course, in oil, when all the passers-by pale green and sick person; or, even better when wet snow, quite directly, without the wind, you know? and through it with gas lights shine ...

- I do not know ... I'm sorry ... - muttered Sir, scared and strange question and Raskolnikov, and crossed to the other side of the street.

Raskolnikov went straight and went to the corner of the Haymarket, where merchants and petty bourgeois woman, then speak with Lizaveta; but now is not. Education place, he stopped, looked around, and turned to the young guy in a red shirt, yawns at the entrance to the barn for storage of flour.

- This is because the trader sells here on the corner, a woman, a wife, huh?
- Any transaction - posted guy down obmerivaya Raskolnikov.
- What's his name?
- Cross and name.
- Oh, and you do not Zaraisky it? Which province?
The guy looked at Raskolnikov.
- We have, Your Excellency, not the province and county, and went brother and I sat at home and I do not know -... I'm sorry, Your Excellency, generously.
- This is a pub on the top that?

- This trahtir and billiards are available; and pryntsessa there ... Luli!

Raskolnikov went through the area. There, on the corner, there was a dense crowd of people, all people. He climbed into the density, looking into his face. It's like something pulled out all start talking. But men do not pay attention to it, and all that is something talked to himself, gathering in groups. He was, I thought, and went right on the sidewalk, to B - mu. After leaving the area, he was in the alley ...

He often took place prior to this short little lane, making a knee, leading from the square to the garden.Recently, he even drew the stick all these places when he fell ill "It was still sick." Now he went about anything without thinking. There's a big house, all under the tavern and other edible-vypiv-atelnymi institutions; They constantly ran out of women dressed as a go "in the neighborhood" - bareheaded and in some dresses. In two or three places are crowded on the sidewalk in groups, mainly due to retirement on the ground floor, where in two steps, you can go down in very different places of entertainment. In one of them, at that time, was the sound of the noise on the street, strum a guitar, singing songs, and it was very fun. A large group of women huddled at the entrance; The others sat on the stairs, the other on the sidewalk, and others stood and talked. In addition, in the street, wandering, loud cursing, drunken soldier with a cigarette and seemed to be somewhere to go, but seemed to have forgotten where. One ragamuffin cursed the other Ragamuffin, and some dead drunk sprawled across street. Raskolnikov stopped a large group of women. They spoke in a hoarse voice, and all were in cotton dresses, shoes and gantry bareheaded. Otherwise, it was in his forties, but there were seventeen years, almost all eye pads.

It somehow took singing and all this clatter and roar, there ... there could be heard among the laughter and shrieks, thin fistula bold and guitar tuning, someone desperately dancing, beating time with his heels. He looked grim and listened thoughtfully, bending the door and peering curiously sidewalk to the porch.

You are my butoshnik prikrasno

You do not hit me in vain! -

crowded thin voice of the singer. Raskolnikov wanted rasslushat, what to sing, it was the whole point.

"Do not go there? - He thought -. Laugh drunk, but then, is not to get drunk drunk!.?"

- Do not go, my dear sir? - Asked one of the women, and the high-pitched

and not very hoarse voice. She was young and did not even disgusting - one of the group.

- You see, pretty! - He replied, sitting and looking at her.

She smiled, praise her very much.

- You are very beautiful, - she said.

- What evil! - Spotted bass another - from the hospital, but was discharged?

- I believe, and the general's daughter, and all the pug nose! - Interrupted by suddenly approached by a man, drunk, in a coat unbuttoned, and yet another tricky laughs Hari. - You see, fun!

- Come on, because not all!

- Complete! Pleasure!

He knocked.

Raskolnikov went on.

- Listen, sir! - Called after the girl.

- What?

She zakonfuzilas.

- I am, dear sir, is always with you and I will be happy to share the clock, and now as a conscience, when you do not intend to. Give me a pleasant gentleman, six cents a drink!

Raskolnikov took a lot got a penny.

- Oh, what a gentleman dobreyuschy!

- What's your name?

- Duklidu ask.

- No, this is what - when I noticed one of the group, shaking his head Duklidu. - That I do not know how to ask for it so! I think a conscience could not ...

Raskolnikov looked curiously at the speaker. It was pockmarked girl, thirty, bruised, with a swollen upper guboy.Govoril and sentenced him calmly and seriously.

"Where is it - thought Raskolnikov, going on - where I read that one sentenced to death, an hour before his death, says or thinks that if he had to live somewhere in height, on a rock, and on a narrow site only two legs can be put - and will circle the abyss, the ocean, eternal darkness, eternal solitude and eternal storm - and remain so, standing in the yard of space, all my life, a thousand years, forever - so it's better to live than to die now!

Only live, live and live! Regardless of how to live - not just to live! .. What is the truth! My God, it's true!Brock man! And the villain that villain for his calls, "- he added later time.

He went into another street, "Bah!" Crystal Palace "! Days Razumikhin says" Crystal Palace ". Just what I wanted to say something? Yes, read on! .. Zosimov says he read in the newspapers ..."

- In the newspapers? - He asked, coming into a very spacious and even create a neat inn a few rooms, but pretty empty. Two or three visitors drank tea, but in the back room sat a group of four people, and drank champagne. Raskolnikov seemed that between them noticed. Nevertheless, at a distance can not be a good look.

"And let them!" - He thought.

- Vodka, you want to? - Asked sex.

- Tea is served. Yes, you can bring me the newspaper, old, that way five consecutive days, and I will give a tip.

- Yes, sir. Here today, sir. And the vodka you want, sir?

Old newspapers and tea were. Raskolnikov sat down and began to look for, "Isler - Isler - Aztecs - Aztecs - Isler - Bartola - Massimo - Aztec - Isler fu ... And it's a sign of the devil: fell down the stairs - tradesman burnt wine! - Fire on the sand - a fire at St. Petersburg - one fire in St. Petersburg - another fire in St. Petersburg - Isler - Isler - Isler - Isler - Massimo ... Oh, that's ... "

He finally found what he wanted, and began to read; Line jumped in his eyes, he said, but then, dochel all "news" and would began to look in the next issue, later addition. His hands were shaking, turning sheets seizure neterpeniem.Vdrug someone sat next to him on his desk. He looked - said the same notification and in the same form, with rings with chains parted in black and curly hair pomaded, a dandy vest and a few shabby coat and dirty laundry. He was cheerful, at least fun and good-natured smile. Brown face it a little inflamed by drinking champagne.

- How! You are here? - He said with a puzzled and in a tone that was familiar with age - and I spoke yesterday Razumihina that you are still not in memory. This is strange! And I was with you ...

Raskolnikov knew he was coming. He put the paper and turn-by-Zametovu. On his lips was a smile and some new irritable impatience showed in that smile.

- I know that you were - he said - I heard, sir. Sock looking for ... you know, Razumikhin you crazy, says that you and he went to Lavize Ivanovna, it's about time you tried to Lieutenant gunpowder flashed, and he still does not understand, remember? Just as it does not seem to understand - it's understandable ... eh?

- And the fact that he is a brawler!

- Gunpowder something?

- No, your friend, Razumikhin ...

- And well you live, Mr. Zametov; good place for duty-free import! Who is now pour the champagne?

- Here we are ... ... I drank and poured!

- Rates! Any use! - Raskolnikov laughed. - Nothing dobreyuschy boy, nothing! - He added, tapping her on the shoulder Zametova - I'm not out of wickedness, "and all loved him, playfully," I say, as your co-worker said something when he Mitya tuzil, here in the case of an old woman.

- How did you know?

- Yes, I have more than you know.

- Quite often lose what you are weird ... It's true, is still very ill. Went in vain ...

- And I seem strange to you?

- Yes I Am. What do you read the newspaper?

- Newspapers.

- Many people write about fires ...-- No, I'm not talking about fires. - Then he looked at the mysterious Zametova; mocking smile curled his lip again. - No, I'm not talking about fires, - he said, winking Zametovu.- And you have to admit, my dear boy, you want to know a lot about what I read?

- I do not want to; I asked. Can not you ask? What do you all ...

- Look, you're an educated man, a literary as well?

- I'm from sixth grade school - said replied with dignity.

- Of the six! Oh, my sparrow! Parted in the rings - a rich man! Phew, that nice little boy! - Here Raskolnikov broke into nervous laughter in the face Zametovu. He stepped back, and not what I was offended, and was very surprised.

- Ugh, that is strange! - Re noticed very seriously. - It seems to me that you are still raving about.

- Delirious? Lies, sparrow! .. So I'm weird? Well, I'm curious about you, huh? Curious?

- Curious.

- That is, that I've read, he was looking for? Look in the end how many ciphers ordered nataschit! Suspicious, is not it?

- Well, tell me.

- Ears open?

- What are the top there?

- When I say that from the top, and now, my dear, I tell you ... no, better: "I admit," ... No, it's not "read to give, and you take off" - that's how! So give an indication of what to read, interesting ... looking for ... spotted ... - Raskolnikov narrowed his eyes and waited - look - and for this and came here - the murder of an old woman official - he finally said, almost in a whisper, bringing extremely their face-to-face Zametova.Zametov looked at him straight in the face, not moving and not pushing his face from his face. Strangest of all it seemed Zametovu, which lasted exactly a whole minutes his silence and even for a moment they looked at each other.

- Well, what to read? - Suddenly he shouted in disbelief and impatience. - For me this thing! Well, what?

- This here is the same old - Raskolnikov went on in the same whisper, not moving exclamation Zametova, - one of which, I remember when they started talking in the office, and I fainted down. What, now you see?

- What is it? This is ... "You know?" - Said said almost in alarm.

Fixed and serious face Raskolnikov turns in an instant, and suddenly he again broke into the same nervous laughter, and in the morning, as if he was completely unable to restrain himself. And at the moment when he remembered the feelings abundantly clear one recent moment when he stood at the door with an ax, constipation jumped, they swore at the door and broke, and he suddenly wanted to cry out to them, argue with them, stick them into the language, taunting them laugh, laugh, laugh, laugh!

- You or crazy, or ... - said notice - and stopped, as if suddenly struck by the thought suddenly flashed in his head.

- Or? This "or"? Well, what? Well, tell me a minute!

- It'S Nothing! - In the heart responds noticed - all nonsense!

Both were silent. After the sudden, epileptic laughter Raskolnikov suddenly thought and sad. He leaned his elbows on the table and leaned his hand to head. He seemed to have completely forgotten about Zametova.The silence lasted a long time.

- What you do not drink tea? Cool - said notification.

- Huh? What? Tea? .. Maybe ... - Raskolnikov took a sip from his glass, put a piece of bread in your mouth and suddenly, looking at Zametova, seemed still remember and shook as though: his face took on a mocking minute original. He continued to drink tea.

- Today, many of these scams divorced - said notification. - Most recently,

ROBOTS READ

I have also read in the "Moscow News" that Moscow whole gang caught fake Monetchikov. Society as a whole was.Forged tickets.

- Oh, that's a long time! I read a month ago - calmly answered Raskolnikov. - So this is what you think it a scam? - He added, smiling.

- How to avoid scammers?

- Is This? These children, blanbeki, not cheaters! All fifty people to sort on goal, but not going to! Is that possible? There will be many, and three, and then with each other every forest itself was sure! And there is one drunk spill the beans, and all the dust has gone! Blanbeki! Rental unreliable people to exchange cash: Sort things so I think the first comer? Well, let's management and blanbekami, let every one million namenyat itself, well, then? The whole life of someone else? Each one another depends on the whole of his life! Yes, it is better to strangle! And they change something he could not: he was in the office to change, got five thousand, and his hands were trembling. Four were counted and placed fifth from each other for granted, but only to avoid pocket so quickly. Well, and provoked suspicion. And all because of the explosion of a fool! Do you think that way can it be? - What hands trembled something? - Caught noticed - no, it's possible, sir. No, I am quite sure that this is not worth possible.Sometimes.

- What's that?

- And you, I think, dunk? No, I would not survive! For a hundred rubles rewarding to go to a kind of horror!Go with a fake ticket - where is it? - In the banking offices where the dog ate - no, I would have embarrassed.Do not you embarrassed?

Raskolnikov suddenly felt bad again "language Stick". Chills, minutes, passing him on the back.

- I would not do that - he started from afar. - That's how I start to change: the first thousand will be taken into account, thus four times around the world, looking at every piece of paper and began to be a thousand; would begin to believe will be considered in the middle, and came to some pyatidesyatirublevuyu, but in the world, it would be a coup, and again into the light - not fake it? "I say, I'm afraid: I have a relative of one of the twenty-five rubles, so recently lost"; and the story could be told here. And what would be considered the third millennium - no, let me, I seem to be there, in the second thousand, seven hundred and properly considered, doubt takes, but fell by one-third, but again, for the second - yes, all the way to all five .and as if in the end, in the fifth of a second so took on a credit card, so back to the light,

but again it is doubtful "variable, please" - yes to sweat clerk would bring, so he gave me a hands, sell something really do not know! End will all finally went to the door and opened - no, sorry, went back to ask about something, explain some get - that's how I would do!

- Ugh, what terrible things you say! - Laughing, said notice. - Only one conversation it all, but in fact, it would probably be tripped. Behold, I tell you, in my opinion, not only we, even polished, desperate people can not vouch for yourself. But why go - here's an example: in our part of something, the old woman was killed. In the end, too, seems to be a desperate chump, in broad daylight at all risks, dare one narrowly escaped - and hands still hesitated to rob failed, could not resist; the case can be seen ...

Raskolnikov as if offended.

- It can be seen! But the catch on, come on, now! - He exclaimed joyfully daring Zametova.

- Well, and caught.

- Who? Do You? You catch? Uprygaetes! This is because what you think: Does a person money or not? It had no money, and suddenly starts spending - Well, is not it? So it's kind of child you puff on it if he wants to!

- This is something that they are doing it - sent notice - kill some difficult life dare, and then once in the pub and popalsya.Raskhody on something and catch them. Yet, like you, cunning. You would not go to the pub, of course?

Raskolnikov frowned and looked at Zametova.

- You seem, razlakomilis and want to know how I did, and here? - He asked with displeasure.

- I want - firmly and said seriously. Something too serious, and he began to speak, to watch.

- Very Much?

- Very Much.

- Okay. Now I have to do - Raskolnikov began, again suddenly bringing her face-to-face Zametova looks back at him and said in a whisper again, so he started at this time. - That's how I would do: I would take the money and things and how I would go there immediately, without anywhere, will go where the blind spot, and only a few fences, and almost no one - Garden -nibud or that. I've seen enough there, even in this court, any such stone, which is in the pecking and half weight somewhere in the corner near the fence that with the construction of the house, maybe lies; raise the stone - a pit should be - yes hole, it will be all the things and money, and in the folded

state. Folded and piled it would be a stone in the form of the first time he lay pinned to the bottom, and leave. Yes, he will not accept 2:58 will not accept - well, look! Was, but everything turned out!

- Are you crazy - why uttered once said, almost in a whisper, too, and somehow suddenly moved with Raskolnikov. Furthermore eyes sparkled; He was terribly pale; The upper lip trembled and jumped. He leaned Zametovu as close as possible, and began moving his lips, saying nothing; This went on for half a minute; he knew what he was doing, but he could not contain himself.Terrible word, how constipation in the door and jump on his lips: is about to fail; about only after going to say more!

- What if I killed the old woman and Lizaveta? - Suddenly, he said - came to his senses.

Zametov wildly looked at him and turned pale as the tablecloth. His face contorted smile.

- Do you think this is possible? - He said in a barely audible voice.

Raskolnikov looked at him angrily.

- Admit it, you believe it? Yes I Do? After all, is not it?

- It's my pleasure! Now, more than ever, I do not believe it! - Said quickly noticed.

- Got you at last! Once sparrow. Thus, I believe it at first, when the now "more than ever, you do not believe?"

- Yes, absolutely not! - Exclaimed noticed apparently confused. - You order something and startled me, that this amount?

- So you do not believe me? And that you are without me talking when I was relieved of his duties? And why me Lieutenant Gunpowder questioned after fainting? Hey, you - he cried sex, getting up and taking his cap - but with me?

- Thirty cents, sir, - he said, running.

- Yes, that's twenty cents tip. See how much money! - He held out a trembling hand Zametovu credit card - red, small blue, twenty-five rubles. Otkudova? Otkudova dress was new? In the end, as you know, it's not a penny! Mistress of something, I think the real question ... Well, enough!

He went out, trembling with some wild hysterical feeling, which at the same time was part of the unbearable pleasure - like dark, very tired. His face was distorted, as if after a seizure. Fatigue increases rapidly. The strength of his excited and came suddenly, with the first push, the first irritating sensation, and just as quickly disappear as weakened feelings.

And we note left alone, sat a long time in the same place, in thought. Raskolnikov accidentally turned his thoughts on some point, and finally made its assessment.

"Ilya Petrovich - a fool!" - He finally decided.

Raskolnikov had just opened the door to the street, when suddenly, on the porch, overlooking the entrance to Razumikhin. And even further, did not see each other, so that almost collided heads. Several times they obmerivali each other eyes. Razumikhin was in amazement, but then the anger, real anger flashed menacingly in his eyes.

- So you've got! - He shouted with laughter. - On the bed to escape! And I did it under the sofa even looking for! Actually went to the attic! Nastasya almost nailed for you ... And this is where! Rodka! What does this mean? Tell the truth! Confess! Do you hear?

- This means that you are bored to death, and I want to be alone - calmly answered Raskolnikov.

- One? If you can not even walk when another face is pale as a sheet, and all of a sudden! Fool! .. What are you in the "Crystal Palace" do? Confess immediately!

- Let go of me! - Said Raskolnikov wanted to convey. It really brought Razumihina about himself: he grabbed his shoulder.

- Empty? How dare you say that "empty"? Yeah, you know what I'm now? I'll get on your hands, tie a knot and the'll take home under his arm, under lock and key!

- Listen, Razumikhin - began quietly and apparently quite calmly Raskolnikov - Can not you see that I do not want your good deeds? And the fact that hunting is to be kind to those who do not care about it ...? So, finally, it is seriously hard to bear? Well, what did you find me in the beginning of the disease? Perhaps I would be very happy to die? Well, I do not really show you today that you torture me, you're tired of me ...!Hunting is really torture people! I assure you that all this prevents recovery seriously, because I always annoys me.

After all went well this morning Zosimov not annoy me! Leave me alone, for God's sake, and you! And what right, finally, you hold me by force? Yes, do not you see that I'm completely filled mind now say? What, what, teach, pray unto me of you, finally, that you do not stick with me and kindly? Let me ungrateful, let me low, just leave me alone, all of you, for God's sake, leave me alone! Go Away! Go Away!

ROBOTS READ

He began quietly rejoicing in advance around the poison, who was preparing to pour out, and ended in a frenzy and breathless, as earlier with Luzhin.

Razumikhin stood, he thought, and let go of his hand.

- Get the hell is! - Quiet and almost wistfully he said. - Stop! - He suddenly roared when Raskolnikov was removed from the site - listen to me. I tell you, all of you, to a man, - talkative and fanfaronishki! Takes you stradanitse - You and him like a chicken with egg nosites! Even steal other authors. No signs of life in your own! Spermatsetnoy ointments you have done and instead of serum! Any of you I do not believe it! The first thing that you should under all circumstances - as if people do not like it! Hundred-oh-oh! - He exclaimed with renewed fury, seeing that Raskolnikov again begins to move in the direction of - listen to the end! You know, I have now come to a housewarming party, maybe too come now, and I left my uncle there - ran now - coming to take. So, if you were not a fool, do not send a fool not terry fool, not a translation from a foreign RODIA ... see, I confess, you're a smart guy, but you're a fool! - So, if you were not a fool, you better come with me tonight to sit than the gift of shoes trample. Okay, so there's nothing to do! I used a chair so soft rolled owners ... Chaishko, the company ... And no, - and couch'll speaking - still lay between us ... And Zosimov will. You come, too?

- No.

- BP-p-dec! - Razumikhin exclaimed impatiently, - you know why? You can not reply to yourself! And anything you do not understand it ... I am a thousand times in the same way with people rasplevyvalsya and resorted back ... be ashamed - and the gateway to the man! So remember, the same house Pochinkova, third floor ...

- Why are you so maybe someone beat you, please, Mr. Razumikhin, for the pleasure of kindness.

- Who? Me! In one fantasy unscrewed the nose! House Pochinkova numbered forty-seven, in a formal grandmother ...

- Do not come, Razumikhin! - Raskolnikov turned and walked away.

- On a bet that will come! - Razumikhin shouted after him. - Otherwise you ... otherwise you do not want to know! Wait, hey! Zametov get there?

- Over There.

- Visit?

- Visit.

- And what?

- Spoke.

140

CRIME AND PUNISHMENT

- About what? Well, to hell with you, may not have. Pochinkova, forty-seven, grandmother, I remember!

Raskolnikov went into the garden and turned the corner. Razumikhin looked after him thoughtfully. Finally, waving his hand, went into the house, but stopped halfway down the stairs.

"Damn it! - He went on, almost aloud, -? He said with meaning, as well as if you ... In the end, I was a fool do you think geeks do not speak with meaning and Zosimov fact, it seemed to me that something to be afraid - he tapped his forehead. - ?! Well, what if ... what if it is possible to start now, utopia ... Oh, I made a blunder you can not "and he ran back to the pursuit of! Raskolnikov, but he disappeared. He spat and returned with rapid steps in the "Crystal Palace" interrogate quickly Zametova.

Raskolnikov went straight on - English Bridge, stood in the middle, at the railing, leaned on their elbows and began to look forward. Farewell, Razumikhin, he was so weak that he barely got here. He wanted somewhere to sit or lie down in the street. Leaning over the water, mechanically, he looked at the last, pink glow of sunset, a number of houses, an oasis in the gathering dusk, a distant window, somewhere in the attic, on the left bank, shone like a flame, the last ray of sunlight that falls into her for a moment, in an oasis of water ditches and seemed carefully looked into the water. Finally, his eyes turned some red circles, came home, passers-by, embankments, crews - all turned and danced around. Suddenly he started, can be saved from fainting again one wild and ugly vision. He felt that someone was standing next to him, on the right, next; He looked - and saw a woman, tall, with a kerchief on her head, with a yellow, oblong, emaciated face and reddish, sunken eyes. She looked at him directly, but apparently did not see anything, and no one else. Suddenly she leaned on the railing with his right hand, raised his right leg and turned her in jail, and then on the left, and ran into a ditch. Dirty water parted for a moment swallowed victim, but a minute later sank to the surface, and it quietly suffered downstream, head and feet in the water, return to the top, with a swollen and huddling over the water, like a pillow, skirt.

- Utopia! Utopia! - Shouted dozens of votes; people came running, and embankments unizyvalis spectators on the bridge, about Raskolnikov, crowded, pressing and crushing him from behind.

- Father, but this is our Afrosinyushka! - I heard somewhere near a poor woman screaming. - Father, save me! Father to pull!

- Marine! Boat! - Shouted the crowd.

141

ROBOTS READ

But the boat was really not worth it: a policeman ran down the stairs descending to the gutter, threw a coat, boots and ran into was a little vodu. Rabota: drowned carried water in two steps from the collection, he grabbed her clothes with his right hand, the left managed to grab pole who gave him one, and immediately drowned woman pulled. She put on a granite slab origin. She quickly recovered, rose, sat down and started sneezing and snorting, senselessly wiping wet clothes by hand. She said nothing.

- Up to hell dopilas, sir, in the room - howled the same female voice, for about Afrosinyushki - Anamniotes also wanted to strangle rope removed. I went to the store now, devchonochka her look left - en sin out!Meschanochka, sir, our meschanochka, near live, the second house on the edge, here ...

People do not agree, the police were busy with other drowned, someone shouted the office ... Raskolnikov looked at everything with a strange sense of apathy and indifference. He was disgusted. "No, disgusting ... water ... not worth it - he murmured to himself. - Nothing happens - he added. - There is nothing to wait for what it is, office ... Why have noticed in the office? Office 10:00 unlocked ... "He turned his back to the railing and looked around him.

"Well, what of it? And maybe"! - Resolutely he said, moved from the bridge and headed in the direction where the office was. His heart was empty and boring. He did not want to think. Even sadness disappeared, no trace daveshney power when he left the house to "finish everything!" Complete apathy to apply in its place.

"Well, this is the result - He thought quietly and sluggishly walked along the waterfront of the ditch. - Nevertheless, I'm done, because I want ... Is Exodus, though still Arshin space will ?! - What Heh, though! ! end End Indeed I say to them, otherwise you will not tell Uh ... hell, and I'm tired:?! somewhere to lie down or sit down to hurry Total ashamed that so very stupid Oh, and do not care about !. it. Phew, what nonsense come to mind ... "

The office had to go straight and second left: it was here in two stages. But when he reached the first turn, he stopped, thought, turn into the alley and went detour through two streets - perhaps without any purpose, and perhaps even more time to stretch and gain time. He went and looked at the ground. Suddenly, as if someone had whispered something in his ear. He looked up and saw that stands in this house, at the very gates. On thisnight, he was not there and did not pass.

Irresistible and inexplicable desire led him. He entered the house, passed through the gateway, the first entrance on the right and began to climb the

stairs to knowing the fourth floor.On narrow and steep stairs was very dark. He stopped at each site and watched with curiosity. In place of the windows of the first floor was completely exposed frame: "It was not," - he thought. The apartment is on the second floor, where they worked Nikolashka and Mitya: "sealed, and again painted door, is given, then the rent." This is the third and fourth floors ... ... Puzzled took him to the apartment door was open wide, there were people who heard voices "Here!"; He did not expect this. Hesitated a little, he climbed the last steps and entered the apartment.

He also again without finishing; were working; it is as if struck. It seemed to him anyway, he still meets the same way as the left, and then, perhaps even dead bodies in the same places on the floor. And now: the bare walls, no furniture; strange somehow! He went to the window and sat on the window sill.

There were two employees, both young men, one older and one much younger. They wallpapered walls with new wallpaper, white, with purple flowers, and the previous yellow, worn and shabby. Raskolnikov as something not very nice; he looked at the new wallpaper hostile, just a pity it was that all this has changed.

The staff is obviously delayed, and now hastily turned his paper and going home. The appearance of Raskolnikov almost drew attention. They are something to talk about. Raskolnikov crossed his arms over his chest and listened.

- Comes him Etta me in the morning, - said a senior junior - ranym-raneshenko, all dressed up. "And what are you telling me limonnichaesh, you are in front of me, I say, apelsinnichaesh?" - "I want to, says Titus Vassilyitch now, still to complete your will." So here it is! And how dressed: magazine, just a magazine!

- What is it, dyadshka magazine? - Asked the young. He obviously had to teach "dyadshki."

- Journal, this is my boy, these paintings, painted, and they are here to adapt the people here every Saturday, by mail from abroad, so that, etc., and someone to dress like men, women and evenly floor. Figure mean.Male gender is increasingly being written in BÃ © kÃ © s, and only for the section of the female, brother, prompters that you give me, and even little ones!

- And the fact that in no eftom Peter! - Enthusiastically shouted Jr. - okro-mya father, mother, everything is there!

- In addition, eftova, my boy, all - didactically decided to make older.

Raskolnikov got up and went into another room, where once stood style

bed and chest of drawers; The room seemed to him terribly small mebeli. Oboi were the same; in the corner of the wallpaper sharply pointed out the place where the icon case with images. He looked up and returned to the window. Senior worker looked at askance.

- What do you want, sir? - Suddenly he asked, turning to him.

Instead of answering, Raskolnikov got up, walked into the hall, took the bell and pulled. Same bell, the same tinny sound! He pulled the second, the third time; He listened and remembered. The former, it was too scary, ugly feeling began to grow brighter and brighter, remember him, he winced with every stroke, and all that was pleasant and comfortable.

- What do you want? Who's that? - Shouted worker, went out to him. Raskolnikov went back to the door.

- Apartments want to hire, - he said - look around.

- Vater night do not hire; and, in addition, you have to come with the janitor.

- Paul then washed; will draw? - Continue to Raskolnikov. - No blood?

- What is blood?

- But this old woman was killed along with his sister. Was the entire pool.

- What kind of person? - Shouted in trouble worker.

- I?

- Yes I Am.

- And you want to know? .. Let's go to the office, there will tell.

Workers with amazement at him.

- We go, it's time to hesitate. Come on, Alyosha. Lock needed - said a senior researcher.

- Come on! - Raskolnikov replied indifferently, and went forward, slowly down the stairs. - Hey, janitor! - He shouted, coming under the gate.

Several people were standing at the entrance to the house from the street, looking at passers-by how the janitor, a woman, a tradesman in a robe and some drugie.Raskolnikov went straight to him.

- What do you want? - Said one of the janitors.

- In the office to go?

- Who was. What do you want?

- Sitting there?

- Sit down.

- And there buddy?

- There was a time. What do you want?

Raskolnikov did not answer and made friends with them, lost in thought.

- Vater expression appeared - said, approaching, a senior fellow.

- What Vater?

- And where we operate. "Why, they say, blood washed? That, says ubivstvo happened and I came to hire." The bell rang, will not cut. And let's say, the office, everything will be proved. Apply.

Janitor with a puzzled frown and looked at Raskolnikov.

- Yes, you are who? - He shouted pogroznee.

- I Romanovich Raskolnikov, a former student and live in Shilya house here in the alley, not far from here, flat numbering fourteen. We ask the janitor ... I know. - Raskolnikov said all this somehow lazily and thoughtfully, without turning around and looking at the darkened street.

- Yes, why Vater is?

- Hours.

- What is there to see?

- But yes take to reduce the office? - Suddenly hit the dealer and said nothing.

Raskolnikov squinted over his shoulder at him, looked and said so softly and lazily:

- Let'S Go!

- Yes, and bring! - Took a good mood trader. - Why is he on this income had this in mind, huh?

- A drunk, not drunk, but God only knows - muttered employee.

- Yes, you what? - Screamed again janitor began seriously angry - why are you stuck?

- Chickened out at the office, then? - He said with a grin Raskolnikov.

- What a coward? Why are you stuck?

- Vyzhiga! - Cried the woman.

- Yeah, what happened to him to interpret - shouted another janitor, a huge man in a coat unbuttoned's and keys in the zone. - Pshol! .. And really burn ... Pshol!

And seizing Raskolnikov by the shoulder, he threw it into the street. He fell, but did not fall, straightened up, looked silently at all the spectators and went on.

- ChudÑ'n man - said the employee.

- ChudÑ'n now are people - the woman said.

- And everything would be reduced to the office - said a trader.

ROBOTS READ

- There's no need to talk - decided large janitor. - How is burning! Sam rises in fact, it is known as contact, not untie ... We know!

"So it or not," - thought Raskolnikov, stopping in the middle of the roadway at an intersection, looking around and around, as if expecting someone last word. But no answer anywhere; everything was dull and dead as stones on which he walked, because the dead, only for him ... Suddenly far, about two hundred yards away, at the end of the street, in the darkness, he saw the crowd, voices, screams. .. Among the crowd was flashed crew ... middle of the street light. "What is it?" Raskolnikov right turn and went into the crowd. He just clung to everything and smiled coldly, thinking that because probably decided by the Cabinet, and knew that it's over now.

←«»→

⟵ CHAPTER VII ⟶

Middle of the street stood a stroller, a dandy and Barsky, drawn by two gray horses hot; Riders were not, and he coachman slezshi goat stood; held the reins of the horses. All around a lot of people crowded in front of the police. One of them was holding a lighted torch, which he bent down and lit something on the sidewalk, in the majority of the wheels. Everyone was talking, shouting, gasp, the driver seemed puzzled, and sometimes repeating:

- What a sin! Lord, what a sin!

Raskolnikov squeezed as possible, and finally saw the object of all this bustle and curiosity. On the ground lay a horse crushed the man unconscious, apparently very badly dressed, but in the "noble" dress, covered in blood. At first glance, the head bleeding; face all beaten up, stripped, deformed. It was obvious that crushed seriously.

- Oh my God! - Due to the driver - as shown here! If it was, I went to Ali shouted to him, and he did not come quickly, evenly. Everyone saw that people lie, and then I train. Drunk candle will not put - we know! .. I see out staggered almost falls - odnovazhdy shouted, but in another, but in the third, and the horses were kept; and he with his head under their feet and fell! Already on purpose, and it was al so very young ... netverez horses, puzhlivye - jerked and he cried, - they are the forest ... that's the trouble.

- This is how it is! - There was someone in the crowd survey evidence.

- Shouted, however, he shouted three times - said another voice.

- In AKURAT three times, all heard! - Shouted the third.

However, the driver was not so sad and scary. It was obvious that belonged to the rich and substantial owner, expect somewhere its arrival; The police,

of course, a lot of attention, how to solve this latter circumstance. Rubble had to be removed in part and in the hospital. No one knew his name.

Meanwhile Raskolnikov squeezed and leaned closer. Suddenly a bright flashlight illuminated face unhappy; he recognized him.

- I know him, I know! - He said, clutching a very forward - it's official, a retired titular counselor, marmalade! He lives here, close by, at a goat ... Doctors quickly! I'll pay, here! - He took the money, and showed the police. He was a great excitement.

The police are satisfied that the learned who crushed. Raskolnikov called himself, gave him and all his strength, as if it were a question of your own father persuaded to move quickly Marmeladova unconscious in his apartment.

- Here, three houses - he sought - a goat house, German, rich ... It is now true, drunk, went home. I know him ... He was drunk ... There he family, wife, children, the daughter of one there.While still in the hospital resistance, and here, right in the same house, the doctor! I pay, pay! .. However, care will have your help now and then he dies in the hospital ...

He even managed to slip unnoticed in his hand; The point, however, it was clear and legally, and in any case it was a close aide. Crushed up and carried; were pomoschniki.Dom goat was thirty paces. Raskolnikov walked behind, carefully kept his head and led.

- Here, here! Stairs should make his head; wrap ... that's it! I'll pay, I thank you, - he murmured.

Katerina Ivanovna, as always, only a minute to spare, immediately rushed to walk back and forth in his small room, from the window to the plate and back, tightly folded arms, saying to himself, and cough. In recent years it has become more and more talk with the senior girls Polechka ten years that, although many of them still do not understand, but it is well understood that he needed a mother, and therefore always looked at her with his big eyes and clever Dodgy enter understands every way. This time Polechka undressed younger brother, who was ill all day to put it to bed. Wait until he changed his shirt, which was supposed to wash the same night, the boy sat on a chair in silence, gravely, erect and motionless, with outstretched legs squeezed together, the heel of the public and toes apart. He listened to what she was saying her mother and sister, pouting, bulging eyes and motionless in the balance, as a rule, have to sit all the smart boys, when they undress, to fall asleep. Still less than perfect girl in rags, standing on the screens, waiting

their turn. Door to the stairs was open to any way to defend against waves of smoke bursts from other rooms and constantly makes a long and painful cough poor consumptive. Katerina Ivanovna seemed to have lost even more weight this week, and red spots on her cheeks burned even brighter than before.

- You will not believe you, and you can not imagine Polechka - she said, pacing the room - how we have fun and richly lived in the house of the pope, and how it ruined me drunk and destroy all of you! Father was a colonel and Civil almost Governor; he only was only one of any stage, so they all went to him and said: "We already have and believe Ivan Mihalitch for our governor." ... When I cough, I ... cough, cough cough ... Oh, cursed life! - She was crying, coughing phlegm and clutching his chest - when I ... ah, when the last ball ... I ... I saw the leader of the landless princess - who then blessed me when I married your father, Paul - then immediately asked, "Is not that cute girl who danced with a shawl at release?" ... (Gaps need to sew something, that would take the needle so now will fix it, and how I taught you and then tomorrow ... cough! Tomorrow ... cough, cough, cough! .. Les RAZO-tears! - she said, straining) ... - Then another from St. Petersburg just arrived kammerjunker Prince graceful.. . dance the mazurka with me, and the next day wanted to come up with a proposal, but I have returned thanks in flattering terms, and said that my heart belongs to an old friend. The other was your father, Paul; Pope furious ... And the water is ready? Well, let's shirt; and stockings? .. Lida - she turned to the little girl - you do so, shirts, sleep in the night; somehow ... yes stockings laid out next to the wash ... At the same time ... What it does not suit lohmotnik drunkard! Shirt carried as wiping some, tore everything ... Everything would be so, at the same time for two nights in a row does not suffer! O Lord! Cough, cough, cough, cough! Again! What's this?- She said, looking at the crowd in the hall and people protesnyavshihsya with some burden for her room. - What is it? What does it bear? O Lord!

- Where to put it? - I asked the policeman, looking around when she was dragged into a room bloodied and unconscious Marmeladova.

- On the couch! Place directly on the couch, head here - shows Raskolnikov.

- Presentation on the street! Drunk! - Someone shouted from the passage.

Katerina Ivanovna stood all pale and hard to breathe. The children were scared. Little Lidochka screamed, ran to Polechka, grabbed her and shook the whole.

With the accumulation Marmeladova, Raskolnikov rushed to Katerina

Ivanovna:

- For God's sake, calm down, do not panic! - He said, tongue twisters - he was crossing the street, he crushed the stroller, do not worry, he wakes up, I said, I am here ... you had to remember ... He wakes up, I'll pay!

- Achieved! - Desperately cried Katerina Ivanovna, and ran to her husband.

Raskolnikov soon noticed that this woman is not one of those who once fainted. Instantly he found himself under the head of the unfortunate theft, which no one has ever thought; Katerina Ivanovna began to undress him, inspect, and vanity is not lost, forgetting herself, biting her trembling lips and suppressing screams, ready to break out of his chest.

Raskolnikov order to convince someone to run for the doctor. The doctor, as it turned out, he lived through the house.

- I sent for the doctor - he said Katerina Ivanovna - do not worry, I'll pay. Is there no water? .. And let the napkin, towel, then as soon as possible; Nobody knows how he hurt ... He was wounded, but not killed, to be sure ... What will the doctor!

Katerina Ivanovna rushed to the window;there is a broken chair in the corner, was erected a large earthen basin of water, prepared for the night washing her husband's and children's underwear.On this night was done washing samoyu Katerina Ivanovna, personally, at least twice a week, and sometimes more often, since reached the point, AC underwear rather almost was not, and it was every member of the family is only one instance, and Katerina Ivanovna could not stand the dirt and agreed to torture yourself better at night and not being able to do when everyone is asleep, to have time in the morning to dry wet laundry on a rope stretched and apply clean, than to see the dirt in the house, she clutched it was for pool wearing it at the request of Raskolnikov, but almost fell with the burden. But he managed to find a towel, soak it with water and began to wash the blood-soaked face Marmeladova. Katerina Ivanovna stood right there, with the pain of breath and holding his arms. She needed help. Raskolnikov began to realize that it may be difficult to do, be sure to move here suppressed. The policeman also stood in disbelief.

- Fields! - Exclaimed Katerina Ivanovna, - run Sonia soon. If you can not find it at home, in any case, tell me that my father was crushed by a horse, and that it was once here ... as a gateway.Most likely, Paul! At the close the handkerchief!

- Hundred etc. Spirit Run! - Shouted the boy suddenly from his chair, and

he said it again plunged into a quiet old direct seat on a chair, rolling his eyes, heels forward and toes apart.

Meanwhile, the room was full, so it was nowhere apple fall. The police left, for example, which remained for a while and tried to lead the audience to dial down the stairs again back to the stairs, except. But from the interior emptied almost all the tenants Mrs. Lippevehzel and initially was crowded at the door, but then the crowd broke into the room. Katerina Ivanovna into a frenzy.

- If I could die in peace he should give something! - She cried the whole crowd - what a performance not found! With cigarettes! Cough, cough, cough! Another sign of the hat! .. And then the one in the hat ... Look! The dead body at least respect!

Cough choked her, but to frighten helpful. Katerina Ivanovna, obviously afraid even; tenants, one after the other, to put back to the door with a strange feeling of inner satisfaction, which is always seen, even the people closest to sudden trouble with their neighbors, and that is not spared no one, without exception, although most sincere feeling of regret and participation.

Behind the door, I heard, however, the voices of the hospital and that there should not be worried in vain.

- Dying is not a trace! - Exclaimed Katerina Ivanovna, and was taken to dissolve the door to break out of them with a zipper, but face-to-door with Mrs. samoyu Lippevehzel, who just managed to hear about misfortune and ran to produce a day. It was very grumpy and disorderly German.

- Oh, my God! - She threw up her hands - your husband drunk horse iztoptal. In the hospital! I am the mistress!

- Amalia Lyudvigovna! I ask you to remember what you say - Katerina Ivanovna began haughtily (with the hostess she always said arrogant tone, so she "remembered his place," and even now can not deny myself the pleasure) - Amalia Lyudvigovna ...

- I told you one-on-you never dare I say shopping Amal Lyudvigovna; I Amal-Ivan!

- You do not Amal-Ivan, and Amalia Lyudvigovna, and since I do not belong to your vile flatterers, as Mr. Lebezyatnikov who's laughing now at the door (really started to laugh and cry, "grappled!"), I always will call you Amalia Lyudvigovna, although it can not understand why you do not like that name. You can see what happened to Semyon Z. Vulikh; he umiraet.Ya ask you to lock the door and do not let anyone here. Give at least die

in peace!Otherwise, I assure you, tomorrow your action will be known the Governor-General. The prince knew I was not yet married and very well remembers Z. seeds that many times courtesy. Everyone knows that the seeds of Z. had many friends and patrons, he left a noble pride, feeling miserable his weakness, but now (she pointed to Raskolnikov) helps us a generous young man, having tools and communications, and which Simon Z. knew as a child and rest assured, Amalia Lyudvigovna ...

All this was very pronounced patter, faster and faster, but the cough once interrupted Katerina Ivanovna's eloquence. At this moment dying woke up and groaned, and she ran to him. The patient opened his eyes, still not recognizing and not understanding, looked at Raskolnikov stood over him. He was breathing hard, deep and rare; on the edge of the lips compressed blood;sweat on the forehead. Not recognizing Raskolnikov, he began to keep track of restless eyes. Katerina Ivanovna looked at him with a sad, but a stern look, and her eyes streaming with tears.

- Oh, my God All his chest crushed! Blood is blood! - She said in despair. - It is necessary to take off his coat all! Turn slightly, Simon Z., if you can - she called him.

Marmalade recognized her.

- Priest! - He said hoarsely.

Katerina Ivanovna went to the window, leaned his forehead against the window frame and cried in despair:

- Oh damn life!

- Priest! - Said to die again and again, after a moment of silence.

- Come and and! - Shouted at him Katerina Ivanovna, he heard screaming and stopped. Shy, sad eyes looking at everything through the eyes; She came back to him and stood at the head of the bed. He calmed down, but not for long. Soon, his eyes rested on a small Lidochka (his favorite), shivering in a corner, in a fit, and looked at him in surprise, Children vigilant.

- And ... and ... - he pointed at her with concern. He wanted to say something.

- What else? - Exclaimed Katerina Ivanovna.

- Bosenkaya! Bosenkaya! - He murmured, pointing to a crazy look bare feet girls.

- Shut up and and! - Riley cried Katerina Ivanovna, - you know why bosenkaya!

- Thank God, the doctor! - Cried happy to Raskolnikov.

The doctor came, neat old, German, looking suspicious appearance; approached the patient, felt his pulse, felt her head and gently by Katerina Ivanovna, undid all the blood-soaked shirt and exposed to the patient's chest. The whole chest was distorted, wrinkled and torn; several ribs on the right side is broken. On the left side, in the heart, it was ominous, large, yellowish-black spot, strong hooves. The doctor frowned. The policeman told him that captured Not crushed in a wheel and dragged, turning thirty paces down the sidewalk.

- It's amazing how he still woke up - she whispered softly Dr. Raskolnikov.

- What do you say? - Asked one.

- Who will die.

- Is there no hope?

- Not the slightest! In its last legs ... It is also very dangerous to have a headache ... Um. Maybe you can open the blood ... but ... it will be useless. After five or ten minutes to die.

- It's better you will discover blood!

- Maybe ... But I warn you, it will be completely useless.

At this time, I heard a few steps, the crowd parted in the hall, and appeared on the threshold priest with additional gifts, gray-haired old man. Behind him was a police officer, even street.The doctor immediately gave him a place, and exchanged a meaningful vzglyad.Raskolnikov persuaded the doctor to wait at least a little bit. He shrugged and walked away.

All retreated. Confession lasted very long. Dying is hardly well understood nothing; say the same thing can only be jerky, vague sounds. Katerina Ivanovna took Lida, took the boy from his chair and went to the corner of the stove, knelt down and put children on their knees in front of him. Only girl trembled; Boy standing on the bare kolenochki, raised a small hand full baptized measured cross and bowed to the ground, bumping his forehead that apparently gave him particular pleasure. Katerina Ivanovna bites her lip and holding back tears;She also prayed from time to time to adjust the shirt on the child and to throw too bare shoulders headscarf girls who took the breast, not on her knees and praying. Meanwhile, the door to the inner room again otvoryatsya curious. The hall is still denser and denser shy spectators, tenants from all over the stairs, without crossing, however, over the threshold of the room. Only one candle is lit the whole scene.

At this point, passing through the crowd, squeezed Polechka quickly ran after her sister. She came in, out of breath from running quickly, took a

scarf, his eyes found her mother came to her and said, "Go met on the street!" Mother knelt down and placed next to nim.Iz crowd, quietly and shyly, she squeezed, and it was strange to her sudden appearance in this room, including poverty, rags, death and despair. She also was in tatters; her outfit was a halfpenny, but painted on the street, the taste and the rules laid down in a special world, with a bright and shamefully outstanding goal. Sonja stopped in the hallway near the threshold, but not to cross the threshold and looked as lost, not knowing, apparently, do not forget about their overbought on the fourth side, silk, here indecent dress color with a long tail and funny, and the huge crinoline, blocking the whole door, and light shoes, as well as ombrelke, unnecessary at night, but it has brought, and funny straw hat with a round brilliant flame-colored pen. From under this boyish cocked wearing looked thin, pale and frightened face with his mouth open and eyes in horror. Sonya was small in stature, eighteen, thin, but pretty cute blonde with beautiful blue eyes. She looked at the bed, at the priest; she breathed too fast walk. Finally whispers some words to the crowd, probably before he departed. She looked down, crossed the step across the threshold and become a room, but again in the doorway.

Confession and communion were over. Katerina Ivanovna went back to the bed of her husband. The priest stepped back and care were invited to say a few words of welcome and comfort Katerina Ivanovna.

- And where I have something to Dana? - Sharp and irritable she interrupted, pointing to the little ones.

- God is merciful; rely on the help of the Most High - began the priest.

- Oh-oh! Merciful, but not for us!

- It is a sin, a sin, madam, - the priest said, shaking his head.

- And it's not a sin? - Cried Katerina Ivanovna, pointing to the dying.

- Maybe those who were unknowingly agree to reward you, even to a loss of income ...

- Do not you understand me! - Riley cried Katerina Ivanovna, waving his hand. - And what reward? He himself, drunk, under the horses reached! What is income? Revenues from him, but only flour. In the end, he, drunk, drank away everything. Yes, we are robbed pub wore them so my life is wasted in the pub! And thank God that he was dying! Loss less!

- You just need to be in the hour of death, and it is a sin, madam, these feelings of great sin!

Katerina Ivanovna was bustling about the patient, she gave him a drink,

wiped the sweat and blood from his head, the restoration of pillows and spoke to the priest, it is sometimes possible to turn to him accidentally.Now she suddenly attacked him almost in a frenzy.

- Oh, my dear! Words so just words! I'm sorry! Here he drank today, no matter how defeated a shirt on him alone, all were, but in pieces, as he fell to sleep, and I would have to dawn in the water to rinse, castoffs let him baby soap, but then dried on the street, but here, as day, and will be darn village - and this is my night .. So what can we say here for forgiveness! And it's easy!

Deep, terrible cough interrupted her words. She otharknulas in a hand-kerchief and put it on display priest, pain, holding his other hand chest. Handkerchief was covered in blood ...

The priest bowed his head and said nothing.

Marmalade was in the last agony; he did not take his eyes off the face of Katerina Ivanovna, bent over him again. He still wanted to say something to her; it was launched, with the power of moving his tongue and saying the words is not clear, but Katerina Ivanovna, I realized that he wanted to ask her for forgiveness, immediately shouted at him imperiously:

- Shut up and and! Do not! .. I know what you mean! .. - And the patient was silent; but at the same time, his eyes wandering down the door, and he saw Sonya ...

Until now, he did not notice her, she stood in the corner and in the shadows.

- Who's that? Who's that? - He said he suddenly gasped in a hoarse voice, all in confusion, horror looking at the door, which had a daughter, and tends to grow.

- Stay down! Lie down and and! - Exclaimed Katerina Ivanovna.

But he had an unnatural strength to rely on hand. He still looked wild and some time in it, as if he did not recognize her. And never before had he seen her in such a suit. Suddenly he recognized her, belittling, killing, ras-franchennuyu and ashamed, humbly waiting for their turn to say goodbye to his dying father. Portray the endless suffering on her face.

- Sonia! Daughter! I'm sorry! - he said, and tried to reach him, but lost his balance, slipped and fell off the couch, right face to the ground; rushed to pick it up, put, but he was already gone. Sonya cried weakly, ran and embraced him and froze in his arms. He died in her arms.

- Achieved its goal! - Katerina Ivanovna exclaimed when he saw the dead body of her husband - well, what do we do now! What I bury it! And what is their something they ever tomorrow, what to feed?

Raskolnikov went to Katerina Ivanovna.

- Katerina Ivanovna - he said it - last week, your late husband told me my whole life and all things ... Be sure that he was talking about you with enthusiasm respect. That evening, when I learned that he was betrayed by all of you and especially you, Katerina Ivanovna, loved and respected, despite his unfortunate weakness with this evening, and we became friends ... Let me now ... Welcoming the duty to promote my late friend. Here ... twenty rubles seems - and if it can serve to help you, then ... I ... in a word, I go - I go ... I, of course, maybe even tomorrow I will come . .. Bye Now!

And he quickly left the room as quickly as possible squeezed into the crowd on the stairs; but in the crowd suddenly faced with Nicodemus Fomich learn about misfortune and wished to get rid of himself. So the scene in the office they are not met, but Nicodemus Fomich immediately recognized him.

- Oh, is that you? - He asked him.

- Died - Raskolnikov answered. - There was a doctor, a priest, all right. Do not disturb a very poor woman, she was already in consumption. Encourage her if what you ... In the end, a good man, I know ... - he added with a grin, looking him straight in the eye.

- And how do you, however, to soak up the blood - told Nicodemus Fomich doing in light of the lantern several fresh spots on the vest Raskolnikov.

- Yes, dunk ... I'm covered in blood! - Said with some special kind of Raskolnikov, then smiled, nodded his head and walked down the stairs.

He walked slowly, slowly, as if in a fever, and without realizing it, one full, new, huge feeling suddenly prihlynuvshey full and powerful life. This feeling can be a feeling of facing the death penalty, which suddenly and unexpectedly announce forgiveness. Half of the stairs caught up with him to return home to the priest; Raskolnikov silently missed it forward by sharing with him a silent nod. But stepping off the last stage, he suddenly heard hurried footsteps behind him. Someone caught up with him. It was Polechka; She ran after him and called him: "Listen Listen"

He turned to her. She ran past the stairs and stood in front of him, step over it. Dim light passed from the yard. Raskolnikov saw a slender, pretty face, but she smiles at him, and having fun as a child, looked at him.She ran to the request, which, apparently, she loved.

- Hey, what's your name? .. And even where you live? - Slowly she asked, breathless voice.

He put both hands on his shoulders and with a kind of joy, looking at her.

He was so nice to look at him - he did not know why.

- Who sent you?

- And I sent my sister Sonia - she replied, still smiling cheerfully.

- I knew that you sent my sister Sonia.

- I and my mother also sent. When my sister Sonia send mother also came and said, "Quickly run, Polechka!"

- Love you sister Sonia?

- I love her more than anyone else! - With a peculiar hardness Polechka said, and her smile became suddenly serious.

- And I love you?

Instead of answering, he saw approaching him face girls and plump lips, naive plot to kiss him. Suddenly thin as matches, arms wrapped tightly around him, her head on his shoulder, and she began to cry softly, pressing his face to his stronger and stronger.

- Pope sorry! - She said after a moment, raising his tear-stained face and hands wiping away tears - all these troubles are gone now - she added suddenly, with a view particularly hard look, it's hard to take the kids when they want to suddenly say, as "the great ".

- My father loved you?

- It is the most favorite Lidochka us - she said very seriously, and not smiling quite as big as they say - because he loved that it is small and, therefore, also, that he was sick, and she always wore goodies, and We read it taught me grammar and the law of God, - she added with dignity - and my mother did not say anything, but we only know that she loves, and dad knew my mother wants me to teach in French, because I have the time, to get an education.

- Do you know how to pray?

- Oh, what, you know how! For a long time; I love that big, pray himself, and Kolya and Lida with her mother aloud; The first "Virgin" to read, and then another prayer: "Lord, forgive and bless sister Sonia," and then again: "Lord, forgive and bless our other papa," because our oldest father has died, and the other, because we pray about it, too.

- Polechka, my name is Rodion; not pray someday I ", and the servant Rodion" - nothing more.

- All of my future life, I will pray for you - hot girl said, and suddenly laughed again, ran to him and hugged him again.

Raskolnikov told her his name, gave the address and promised tomorrow will certainly come. The girl left him in perfect vostorge.Byl the eleventh

hour, when he went outside. Five minutes later he was standing on the bridge, exactly at the same place from which a woman threw herself this morning.

"Enough! - Firmly and he said solemnly, -!?! Other mirages, mock away fears ghosts away .. There is life I just can not live not dead yet my life with God old old woman rest her soul, and - rather, my dear it is time to relax the realm of reason and the light now ... and will, and strength ... and look to compete now - he said haughtily, as if referring to some dark force and causing it. - But I've already agreed to live courtyard space!

... I am very weak at the moment, but ... it seems all diseases are gone. And I knew that it would take when I left this morning. By the way: Pochinkova house is a stone's throw. It would certainly Razumikhin, though not a stone's throw ... let mortgage victory! .. Let entertain - nothing, let them! .. The strength of necessity: no force can take anything; and the force required to produce the same power, that's what they do not know, "- he added, proudly and confidently and went, barely moves his feet from the bridge of pride and self-confidence grew in him every minute of the following. moment when he becomes a man who had been in the previous That, however, happened so special, so that made it Yes, he did not know.? he grasps at straws, he suddenly felt that he "could live there still life that his life is not to die with an old old woman. "Maybe he was too hurried conclusion, but he never thought about it.

"The slave asked Rodion, but remember - suddenly flashed through my mind - well, yes it is ... just in case" - he added, and he immediately laughed at his boyish antics. He was in good spirits.

He easily found Razumihina; in the house Pochinkova new tenant already knew the janitor immediately act on its own. Already half of the ladder could distinguish the noise and live current big rally. Door to the stairs was wide open; hear the cries and spory.Razumihina room was quite large, it was a collection of fifteen people. Raskolnikov stopped in the hallway. There, behind a partition, two master maids bustled about two big samovars of bottles, plates and dishes, cakes and snacks brought to master the kitchen. Raskolnikov sent to Razumikhin. He ran into raptures. At first glance, it was obvious that he was unusually much to drink, and though Razumikhin almost never could get drunk drunk, but this time something was noticeable.

- Listen, - Raskolnikov hastened - I just came to say that you have won a mortgage and that no one knows what might happen to him. Log in, I can

not: I am so weak that now fall. And because hello and goodbye!And tomorrow, come to me ...

- You know, I spend my house! Oh, when you say to yourself that the weak ...

- And the guests? Who is this strange, so now look here?

- This one? Who the hell! A friend of my uncle must have and maybe he came to them ... I leave my uncle;This is a precious person; sorry that you can not currently meet. And yet, to hell with them all! They are no longer with me, and I need to brush up, because, brother, you came by the way: another two minutes, and I'd had a fight there, I swear! Does the game ... You can not imagine to what extent can finally, izovratsya man!Nevertheless, they do not represent? We have something for yourself is not it time? Yes, and let lie, and only then will not lie ... Sit down, I Zosimova.

Zosimov with some even eagerly seized Raskolnikov; it showed some special curiosity; Soon, his face brightened.

- Go to sleep - he decided, considering, if possible, the patient - and the night would be one small thing.Accept? I just now ... poroshochek prepared one.

- At least two - Raskolnikov answered.

The powder was immediately accepted.

- It is very good that you are the owner povedesh - said Zosimov and Razumikhin; - It will be tomorrow see today is very bad: a significant change with daveshny. Live and learn ...

- You know, now that I whispered Zosimov when we left - Razumikhin blurted out, just that they went outside. - I, my brother, you are right to say, because they are fools. Zosimov told me to communicate with you dear, and you get right, and then tell him, because he has an idea ... you're crazy ... or close to that.Imagine that you have to do it yourself! Firstly, you are three times smarter than him, and secondly, if you do not hurt, so you do not care what he has in this game in my head, and, thirdly, it is a piece of meat, and specialty it - a surgeon, frustrated now on mental illness, and about you today finally turned the conversation to Zametovym.

- Said everything that you say?

- All and well done. Now I understand the whole story, and noticed understand ... Well, in a word, Rodia ... the thing is ... I'm not a bit drunk ... But it's nothing ... The fact that this idea. .. you know? they are really on the move ... you know? That is, they have no one dared to express it out loud, because

the game is funny, especially when he took Dyer, it's all over, and was extinguished navsegda.No why they are fools? I was a little beat Zametova - it's between us, brother; Please do not give a hint, you know ,; I noticed that he was ticklish; Lavizy were - but today, today it all became clear. The main thing is that Ilya Petrovich! Then he took advantage of your fainting in the office, and then very ashamed; I know …

Raskolnikov listened eagerly. Razumikhin probaltyvalsya drunk.

- I fainted, because then fell, it was stuffy and smelled of oil paint - said Raskolnikov.

- Another explains! And not one paint: inflammation of the entire month is ready; Zosimov out there! And just like that boy killed now, so you can not imagine! "Pinky says that this man is not worthy!" With respect, that is. He sometimes brother chuvstva.No good lesson, a lesson with him today in the "Crystal Palace", is the acme of perfection! In the end, you're frightened him at first, to convulsions brought! You almost made it again to make sure that all this ugly nonsense, and then suddenly - a language that he put: "At, say, that, take it!"

Perfection! Rubble destroyed now! Master you, by God, so they should be. Oh, I was not there! He was waiting for you right now is terrible. Porphyry also want to meet you …

- And … it's too … And some crazy So I wrote?

- That is not crazy. I, my brother, it seems you are too loose … Startled, you see, it's only now that you alone are interested in this paragraph; Now I understand why interest; knowing all the circumstances … and you are angry, and then woven together with the disease … I, my brother, a little drunk, only God knows he has something to have an idea … I'm telling you, shower Illness prevented . And only spit …

With half a minute both silent.

- Listen, Razumikhin - Raskolnikov said - I want to tell you straight: I'm dead was one officer died … I gave all my money … and in addition to kiss me now one being that if someone I then killed, too, would … in a word, I saw there one of them … with fiery pen … and although I zavirayus; I am very weak to support me … because now the stairs …

- What is it? What happened? - Asked alarmed Razumikhin.

- The head slightly turned, but not the point, but the fact that I was so sad, so sad! just a woman … that's right!Look, what is it? Watch! Watch!

- What is it?

- Do not you see? The light in my room, you see? In between …

They stood up to the last stairs next to the mistress of the door, and in fact, it was obvious from the bottom, in the closet Raskolnikov light.

- Strange! Nastasya, maybe - Razumikhin noticed.

- Do it for the moment I do not have, and she slept for a long time, but … I do not care! Farewell!

- What are you? Yes, I'll take you with me in!

- I know that together will enter, but here I want to shake your hand and say goodbye to you here. Well, let's arm, good-bye!

- What happened, Rodia?

- It'S Nothing; let's go; You will witness …

They began to climb the stairs and Razumikhin thought Zosimov something might be in order. "Oh, I did my Upset chatter!" - He muttered under his breath. Suddenly, going to the door, they heard voices in the room.

- What's up with her? - Razumikhin exclaimed.

Raskolnikov first raised the door and opened it wide, open, and stood on the threshold of his tracks.

His mother and sister sat with him on the couch and waited for half an hour. Why is it a little less than expected and the least thought, in spite of repetition, even today, the news that they are going to go now to come? All these and a half hours, they asked excitedly Nastasia, and now stood in front of them and had to tell them the whole story. They do not remember with fright when they heard that he "ran away today," the patient, and, as can be seen from the history, of course, nonsense! "God, what happened to him!" And cried like flour endured the cross at this hour and a half wait.

Joyful applause greeted the appearance of Raskolnikov. Both rushed to him. But he became as dead; unbearable consciousness suddenly hit him like a bolt from the blue. And his hands were raised to hug them, they could not. Mother and sister clasped him in his arms, kissed him, laughed, cried … He took a step, stumbled and fell to the floor in a swoon.

Anxiety, screams of terror, moans … Razumikhin, who was standing in the doorway to the room, grabbed the patient in his strong arms, and he instantly found himself on the couch.

- Nothing, nothing! - He exclaimed his mother and sister - is weak, this is nonsense! Now only the doctor said that it is much better that he is completely healthy! Water! Well, it's in fact he comes to, well, woke up! ..

And grabbed his hand Dunya, so almost twisted her arms, he bent her

opinion, "it's really him, and woke up."Both mother and sister looked at Razu-mikhin, as Providence, with love and gratitude; they have already heard from Nastasya than it was for their Rodi, during the time of the disease, "flexible young man," as he called it, in the same evening, in an intimate conversa-tion with Dunya, she Pulcheria Alexandrovna Raskolnikov.

←«»→

PART 3
←« CHAPTER I »→

Raskolnikov got up and sat on the couch.

He waved weakly Razumikhin to stop the flow of his rambling and hot consolation for his mother and sister, took them both by the hand and stared in silence for two minutes in one direction or another. Mother was afraid of his gaze. From this point of view rayed before suffering a strong feeling, but at the same time there was something else, even if with uma.Pulheriya Alexandrovna began to cry.

Avdotya Romanovna was pale; Her hand trembled in his hand brother.

- Go home ... with him - he said in a broken voice, not pointing at Razumikhin - until tomorrow; tomorrow ... You were here?

- In the evening, Rodia, - said Pulcheria Alexandrovna - train terribly late. But, Rodia, I would not go now from you! I spend the night here, near the ...

- Do not torture me! - He said, waving his hand in exasperation.

- I'll stay with him - Razumikhin cried - not for the moment does not go away, and to hell with it all my, let us climb the wall! I have the president's uncle.

- What's that, I thank you! - Began Pulcheria Alexandrovna, wringing her hands again Razumikhin, but Raskolnikov interrupted her again:

- I can not, I can not - he repeated irritably, - not torture! Likely to go ... I can not! ..

- Come on, Mom, even leave the room for a moment - Dunya whispered scared - we kill him, it shows.

- Sure Well, I do not look at him, then after three years! - Exclaimed Pulcheria Alexandrovna.

- Wait a minute! - He stopped them again - you can still interrupt, but ... I thought I saw a ball of Luzhin?

- No, Rodia, but he already knows about our arrival. We heard Rodia that Peter was kind enough to visit you today - with some timidity added Pulcheria Alexandrovna.

- Yes ... was so kind ... Dounia, I just now Luzhin said it lowered the stairs and took him to hell ...

- Rodia you! You're right ... you do not want to say - it was the beginning of a frightened Pulcheria Alexandrovna, but stopped looking at Duns.

Avdotya Romanovna looked at his brother and waited on. And already warned about the quarrel Nastasya as she could understand and share, and suffer in disbelief and expectations.

- Dunya - with effort Raskolnikov went on, - I do not want this marriage, but because you have to, and tomorrow, with the first word, Luzhin refused to allow his spirit and does not smell.

- Oh my God! - Exclaimed Pulcheria Alexandrovna.

- Brother, I think you're talking about! - Irritation began Avdotya Romanovna, but immediately put on hold. - You may be, no longer able to, you're tired - she said humbly.

- Delirious? No ... You married Luzhin for me. And I do not accept the sacrifice. And so, for tomorrow, and write a letter ... with failure ... In the morning let me read it, and the end!

- I can not do it! - Offended girl exclaimed. - By what right ...

- Dunya, you are also quick-tempered, come back tomorrow ... Do not you see ... - The frightened mother, rushing Dance. - Oh, it's better uydemte!

- Nonsense! - Shouted drunken Razumikhin - and how would he dare! Tomorrow all this nonsense pops up ... And today he really vygnal.Eto it was so. Well, he's angry rant here ... put their knowledge and left rear hiding ...

- This is true? - Exclaimed Pulcheria Alexandrovna.

- See you tomorrow, brother - with compassion said Dounia, - Come on, Mom ... Farewell, Rodia!

- Hey, sister, - he repeated, followed by collection in the latest effort - I'm not delirious; this marriage - meanness. Suppose I am a scoundrel, and you are not alone ... Someone ... and although I am a scoundrel, but my sister's sister, will not be considered. Or I, or Luzhin! Go ...

- You're crazy! Despot! - Razumikhin roared, but Raskolnikov did not answer, and may not be able to answer. He lay down on the sofa and turned to

the wall in utter exhaustion. Avdotya Romanovna looked curiously at Razumikhin; Her dark eyes sparkled: Razumikhin shuddered under this point of view. Pulcheria Alexandrovna stood and watched.

- I would not want to get off! - She whispered Razumikhin almost in despair - I'll stay here, somewhere ... hold Dunya.

- And spoil everything! - Whispered also from themselves comfort, Razumikhin - vyydemte although stairs.Nastasya, light! I swear to you - he went on a half-whisper, and on the stairs - this morning we have, the doctor and I, I almost nailed! Do you understand? The doctor himself! And he gave way to avoid annoying and gone, and I was left to guard the bottom, and he immediately got dressed and slipped out. Now uliznet, if annoying will, at night, but something did ...

- Oh, what you say!

- And Avdotya Romanovna can not be numbered one without you! Think about where you stand! In the end, it's the villain, Peter, could not better you flat ... And yet, you know, I'm a little drunk and cursed because ...;do not worry ...

- But I will go to the local housewives - Pulcheria Alexandrovna insisted - I will ask her to give me and the angle of Dunya in the night. I can not leave it so I can not!

Having said that, they stood on the stairs, on the ground in front of the hostess samoyu door. Nastasya lit them from the bottom of the stairs. Razumikhin was in an unusual excitement. The other half an hour, watching the house of Raskolnikov, he was very talkative, though, and it was known, but it is fun and almost fresh, despite the terrible amount of alcohol consumed that evening wine.Now, however, his condition was, as some even encouraging, and at the same time as all the wine drunk, and again with a vengeance, hit him in the head. He stood with both ladies grabbed them both by the hand, urging them and representing them with surprising candor reasons, and probably for more persuasion, almost every word of it, tight as a vise, not squeezing them with both hands until the pain and seemed to devour Avdotya Romanovna eyes, it does not hesitate. Pain they sometimes pulled his hands out of the huge paws and bone, but he did not notice what was going on, but even more attracted them to him. If they had told him now for his services, rush down the stairs headfirst, he immediately executed him, not discerning and confident. Pulcheria Alexandrovna, alarmed at the thought of all his views, although he felt that the young man

is very eccentric and too painful squeezing her hand, but as at the same time it was for her providence, and then do not have to ignore all these eccentric details . But in spite of the same concern, Avdotya Romanovna, but not timid character was, but was surprised and almost even with fright met sparkling wild fire brother of his friend, and only the infinite power of attorney, the proposal Nastasia stories about this strange man, keep it on attempts to break out of it and drag it to its mother. She knew, and that, perhaps, they run away and some of them now I can not. However, after ten minutes she calmed down considerably: Razumikhin had all the property not immediately say, whatever it may be in the mood, so that all will soon know with whom they are dealing.

- It can not be the hostess and stuff is awful! - He said, calling Pulcheria Alexandrovna. - Even though you are a mother, and if you stay, then bring it to rabies, and then God knows what will happen! Look, here's what I did: he now Nastasya will sit, and I'll take you both with you, because you can not be on the streets; we are in St. Petersburg on this issue ... Well, not all the same! .. Then you immediately start here and quarter of an hour, I promise, you will receive a report: what is it? sleep or not? and all ostalnoe.Zatem, listen! Then you immediately for myself - I've got guests, all drunk - take Zosimova - a physician who treats him, he now sits with me, not drunk; It did not drink, it never drank! Drag it to the Rodka, and then directly to you, then you get an hour of his two pieces of news - and from the doctor, you know, a doctor; it's not that from me! Kohl bad, I swear I will give myself here as well, and go to sleep spat.Ya here all night, in the hall, and he will not hear, and Zosima'll have to spend the night at his mistress, was at hand. In the meantime better, you or the doctor? After Dr. helpful helpful. Well, then go home! And the hostess is impossible; I might as well you can not be: do not let me down, because ... because she was a fool. She gave me jealous Avdotya Romanovna want to know, and you too ... And Avdotya Romanovna, of course.

This is absolutely, totally unexpected character! However, I am also a fool ... Nothing! Come on! Do you believe me? Well, whether you believe me or not?

- Come on, Mom, - said Avdotya Romanovna - he did the right thing, as promised. He has raised his brother, and if it is true that the doctor agrees to spend the night here, so what could be better?

- So you ... you ... you know what I mean, because you - the angel! - Razumikhin exclaimed in delight. - Bring It On! Nastasia! Trice and sit there with

him with fire; I have a quarter of an hour I will come ...

Pulcheria Alexandrovna, though not entirely convinced, but did not resist anymore. Razumikhin took both of them by the arm and dragged him down the stairs. However, he was worried about her, "although fast and good, but in a state of whether that promise? The fact that he .."

- Oh, I see, you think I like it! - Razumikhin interrupted her thoughts, knowing them and walk with his huge shazhischami on the sidewalk, so that both ladies are unlikely to follow him, which, however, he did not notice. - Nonsense! I mean ... I'm drunk as a fool, but not the point; I do not get drunk with wine. And this is how I saw you, I was wounded in the head and ... Yeah, I do not care Ignore: I was lying; I'm not worthy of you ... I'm not worthy! .. And as you instantly, but here, in a ditch, pour it on his head, two bath water ready ... If you only knew how much I have and I love you! .. Do not laugh and do not be angry! .. We all angry and do not be mad at me! I'm his friend, and, therefore, is your friend. I wish I had a premonition ... ... last year, it was a moment ... However, it's not a hunch because you like the sky fell. And I, perhaps, and all night I will not sleep ... It Zosimov now feared that he did not go mad ... That's why you should not annoy ...

- What you say! - Exclaimed the mother.

- Said the doctor said so himself? - Asked Avdotya Romanovna, frightened.

- I say, but it is not, not at all. He and the drug is given, the powder, I saw, and you came here ... Oh! .. You better come back tomorrow! It is good that we left. An hour later, you're all that he Zosimov otraportuet.Here's one way not drunk! And I'm not drunk ... And why I nahlestalsya? And because the argument is entered, dammit! Curse after all gave not to argue! .. This is nonsense city!

I just can not fight! I left my uncle there, Chairman ... Well, believe it or not: full impersonality and demand this has the most gusto! As if only he would not, however, least of all themselves like! This is something that they have a high progress and reviewed. And even if they lied, they are on their own, and then ...

- Listen, - timidly interrupted Pulcheria Alexandrovna, but it only lends itself to heat.

- Yes, what do you think? - Razumikhin shouted, raising his voice even more - do you think I am, because they're lying? Nonsense! I love it when they lie! Do people only privilege of all organisms. Sovresh not - until you reach the truth! Because I am a man who is lying. Also, the truth does not

get one, do not lie directly in front of fourteen, and perhaps one hundred and fourteen, and it is an honor of its kind; Well, we lie, and what your mind does not know how! You're lying to me, but are in their own way, and then I'll kiss you. Lying in his own way - this is hardly better than someone else's true; In the first case, you are a man, and in the second you're just a bird! The truth will not disappear, but life can be nailed; examples were. Well, what are we now?All that we are all, without exception, on the part of science, the development of thinking, inventions, ideals, desires, liberalism, reason, experience and everything, everything, everything, everything, everything in the first grade predugotovitelnom sit! Liked alien consciousness probav-lyatsya-- velis! Right? So what I'm saying? - Razumikhin shouted, shaking hands and squeezing both ladies - do you?

- Oh, my God, I do not know - said poor Pulcheria Alexandrovna.

- Well, well ... although I do not quite agree with you - seriously said Avdotya Romanovna and immediately shouted to the pain this time he squeezed her hand.

- So Much? You say, what is it? Well, you ... you ... - he shouted in delight - you are the source of goodness, purity of mind and ... perfection! Give your hand, give you too ... Let your, I want to kiss your hand here, now, on your knees!

And he knelt down the middle of the sidewalk, fortunately, this time the desert.

- Stop, I ask you, what are you doing? - Cried too alarmed Pulcheria Alexandrovna.

- Stand up, stand up! - Laughed and worried too Dunya.

- I've never give a hand! That's right, and pretty, and stood up, and let's go! I'm miserable lout, I am not worthy, and drunk, and ashamed ... I love you not worthy, but I bow before you - it is the duty of everyone, if it's perfect stock! I bowed ... That's your number, and, of course, one of Rodion rights that now your Peter went! How dare he have to put these codes? This is a scandal! Do you know someone here allowed? But you are a bride! You are a bride, huh? Well, I'll tell you what your fiance scoundrel then!

- Look, Mr. Razumikhin, you forgot ... - began Pulcheria Alexandrovna.

- Yes, yes, you're right, I forgot myself, ashamed! - Razumikhin caught myself - but ... but ... you can not be mad at me for what I say! Because I honestly say, not because ... um! it would be cowardly; In short, not because I am in you ... um .. Well, so be it, no, I will not say why, I do not dare! .. And we all

now have figured out how he got in, that this man is not of our society. Not because he went, curled in a barbershop, not because he put his mind in a hurry, but because he was a spy and speculator; because he was a Jew and a jester, and it shows. How do you think he's smart? No, he is a fool, fool! Well, couple it to you? Oh my goodness! You see, ladies - he stopped suddenly as he mounted the stairs to the numbering - although they have me there all drunk, but honest, and although we time, because in the end, I too was lying, but in the end Dovre and the truth, because the noble road stand, and Peter ... not a noble way.I though now and scolded severely, but I made them all the respect; although Zametova not respect, love so much, because - puppy!Even this redneck Zosimova because - honest business knows ... But most of all has been said and forgiveness. Excuse me? Right? Well, let's go. I know this corridor, there are; Here, the third numbered, there was a scandal ... Well, where are you here? What are numbered? Eighth? Well, the night the lock, no one is not allowed. Fifteen minutes later I come back with the news, and then another half an hour Zosimov, look!Farewell, run!

- My God, Dounia, it would be? - Said Pulcheria Alexandrovna, anxiety and fear to a daughter.

- Calm down, mom - Dunya said, taking off his hat and mantilku - God Himself sent this gentleman, though he is right with some drink. It can rely on, I assure you. And all that he did for my brother ...

- Oh, Dounia, God knows what will come! And as I dared to leave Rodyu! .. And, in fact, is not imagined to find it! It was hard, though he was not happy, we are ...

Tears welled up in his eyes.

- No, it's not, Mom. You look at, you are still crying. He was very upset big diseases - that's all over and reason.

- Oh, it's a disease! What will happen, something will! And as he spoke to you, Dunya! - His mother said timidly, looking into the eyes of his daughter to read all his idea and already half consoled by the fact that Dunya and protects Rodyu and, therefore, forgive him. - I'm sure he'll come around tomorrow - she added, extorting through.

- And I'm sure he will be tomorrow, and then we'll talk about it ... - cut Avdotya Romanovna, and, of course, it was an obstacle, because there was a point on which Pulcheria Alexandrovna was too afraid to start talking now, Dunya came and kissed her mother. She hugged in silence. Then sat eagerly awaiting the return of Razumikhin and timidly started watching

her daughter, who, with his arms crossed and waiting to start walking back and forth across the room, wondering to himself. This walking from corner to corner, lost in thought, was a common habit of Avdotya Romanovna, and mother always somehow afraid to break at this time thought.

Razumikhin, of course, was ridiculous with his sudden drunk tanned passion for Avdotya Romanovna; but looking at Avdotya Romanovna, especially now that she's gone with his hands crossed on a room, sad and pensive, perhaps many would have apologized to him, not to mention his eccentric state. Avdotya Romanovna was remarkably beautiful - tall, amazingly thin, strong, confident, that was expressed in her every gesture, and that, however, does not take away from her soft and graceful movements. His face was like a brother, but it can even be called a beauty. Her hair was dark brown, slightly lighter than his brother;eyes almost black, shining, proud and at the same time, sometimes minutes, an unusually good. She was pale, but not sickly pale; Her face was radiant with freshness and health. Her mouth was a little small, the lower the same sponge, fresh and scarlet, slightly protruded from his chin - only irregularity in this beautiful face, but gave him the special characteristics and, inter alia, as arrogance. Her face was always more serious than funny, thoughtful; but this man was smiling, as was her laughter, fun, young, selfless! It is understood that hot, frankly, rustic, honest, hard as a hero, and a drunken Razumikhin, never seen anything like it at first glance completely lost his head. For the same case, as if on purpose, for the first time showed him Dunya in a beautiful moment of love and joy of the meeting with his brother. He saw how wavered from her lower lip in disgust in response to the impudent and ungrateful, cruel orders of his brother - and I could not resist.

However, he told the truth when provralsya drunk on the stairs this morning that the eccentric landlady Raskolnikov, Praskovya Pavlovna, his jealous not only Avdotya Romanovna, but perhaps the most Pulcheria Alexandrovna. Despite the fact that Pulcheria Alexandrovna was already forty-three years, her face still retained remnants of the former beauty, and, besides, she seemed much younger than his years, which is almost always women who keep a clear mind, fresh impressions, honest , clean, warm heart to old age. For example, in parentheses, that keep it all the only way not to lose its beauty even in old age. Her hair began to turn gray and thin, small radiant wrinkles have long appeared around the eyes, cheeks and fell on concern dry and sorrow, and yet this man was right. It was a portrait Dunechkinova

face, only twenty years later, but in addition also the expression of the lower jaw, which it is not sticking. Pulcheria Alexandrovna was sensitive, but not cloying, and corresponds to a timid, but up to a point: a lot of it may yield many may disagree, at least from the fact that, contrary to its view, but has always been a trait of honesty, rules and extreme beliefs of which in any case could not get her to cross.

It was twenty minutes after the departure of two Razumihina rang softly, but quickly knock at the door; he retraced his steps.

- Do not go, do not have time! --zatoropilsya it when the door opened - sleeps full Ivanovo, quietly, and God forbid that slept for ten hours. He Nastasya; ordered not to leave me. Now Zosimova'll bring it to you otraportuet, and then you're on the side, the rain, I see a lot.

And he put them in the corridor.

- What is more effective and faithful young man ...! - Cried very glad Pulcheria Alexandrovna.

- It seems that a good man! - Answers to some heat Avdotya Romanovna, starting again to walk up and down the room.

Almost an hour later, the sound of footsteps in the corridor, and another knock at the door. Both women had to wait, this time it is the belief in the promises of Razumikhin; And indeed, he managed to drag Zosimova.Zosimov immediately agreed to throw a feast and go look at Raskolnikov, but the ladies went reluctantly and with great suspicion, not trusting the drunken Razumikhin. But his pride at once reassured and even flattered, he realized that it was really waited as oracle. He sat exactly ten minutes and managed to fully convince and reassure Pulcheria Alexandrovna. He spoke with an extraordinary participation, but restrained and somehow deeply serious, so important to consult a doctor twenty-seven, and not a word dodged the subject and found no desire to engage in a more personal and private relationship with the two ladies. Note also, at the entrance, like a beautiful dazzling Avdotya Romanovna, he immediately tried to not even notice it during the visit, and is intended for Pulcheria Alexandrovna. All this gave him an extraordinary inner satisfaction. Actually sick he put it, that finds him at this point in very good condition.

According to the observations of his patient as a disease, but a bad financial situation in the last months of life, there is still some moral reasons ", so to speak, the product of many complex moral and material influences, anxieties, fears, anxieties, some ideas. .. And other things" . Noting in passing that

ROBOTS READ

Avdotya Romanovna has become particularly listen carefully Zosimov somewhat more prevalent on this subject. At the same anxious and timid question
of Pulcheria Alexandrovna, "although some suspicion of insanity," he replied
with a calm and frank smile that his words have been greatly exaggerated;
which, of course, in a sick noticeable some obsession, something to condemn
mania - because he Zosimov, especially now following this extremely interesting department of medicine - but because it is necessary to remember
that today almost to the patient was not in delirium, and. .. And of course,
the arrival of his family to strengthen, spread and act positively, "if you can
not avoid new special attacks," - he added significantly. And he arose, bowed
solid and welcome, and then blessing heartfelt gratitude, prayers and even
stretching up to him to shake his quest without handle Avdotya Romanovna,
and left very satisfied with their visit and more himself.

- The conversation will be tomorrow; to go, of course! - Razumikhin
sealed, leaving Zosimov. - Tomorrow, as soon as possible, I have to report.

- But what's a nice girl that Avdotya Romanovna! - Zosimov said, almost
licking his lips when both went outside.

- Delightful? You said, delicious! - Razumikhin roared and suddenly
rushed to Zosimova and grabbed him by the throat. - If you ever dare ... Do
you understand? Do you understand? - he exclaimed, shaking him by the
collar and pressed against the wall - you heard?

- Yes, let drunken devil! - Fought Zosimov, and then, when he released
him, looked at him and suddenly zahohotal.Razumihin stood before him
with her hands in the dark and serious reflection.

- Of course, I'm an ass - he said, gloomy as a cloud - but you ... and you
will too.

- Oh, no, my friend, is not the same. I do not dream about stupid things.

They walked in silence, and only coming to the apartment Raskolnikov
Razumikhin deep concern, broke the silence.

- Listen, - he said Zosima - you little cute, but you but all your unpleasant quality also potaskun, I know, but still dirty from. You're nervous, weak
material, you Blazhnov you zazhirel and could not afford to give up - and
that's what I call the mud, because right brings up the dirt. You raznezhil
before, I confess, at least understand how you can be with all this good and
even selfless physician. Sleep on a feather bed (doctor!), And costs for the
patient at night! Three years later, you're really not going to get up in the
hospital ... Oh, hell, this is not the case, and here's the thing: you are now

rented apartment to spend the night, and I (with difficulty persuaded her!) The kitchen is the work in accordance shorter! Not what you think! Now, brother, and the shadow is not ...

- Yes, I do not think.

- Here, brother, shame, silence and modesty, chastity, brutal, and with all this - sighs and melts like wax and melt! Delivery you me from him, for the sake of all the devils in the world Preavenantnenkaya! .. Honored chapter deserve it!

Zosimov laughed more than ever.

- Look at you understand! But why me?

- I assure you, a little care, just tell me which of the slops you want, just sit down and talk together. In addition, you are a doctor, begin to heal from anything. I swear I do not regret it. It has a clavichord stand; I, you know, a little strumming; I've got one song there, Russia is "Zalyus slezmi fuel ..." She really likes - well, with songs and started; But you fortepianah virtuoso meter, Rubinstein ... I assure you will not regret it!

- What did you say to her that promises slapping, or what? Subscription Form? Promised to marry, maybe ...

- Nothing, nothing, absolutely nothing of the sort! And it is not so; it was Chebarov ...

- Well, come on!

- Yes, so you can not get out!

- Yes, why not?

196

- Yeah, something like that is not possible, and more! Now, brother, is the beginning of retraction.

- So why did you get her?

- Yes, I was lured, I would myself lured my stupidity, but it makes absolutely no difference what you or I would just next to someone sat and sighed. Now, Brother ... I can not express it to you, then - well, now you know the math, and now still, I know ... well, begin to pass it integral calculus, actually not kidding, seriously say it will continue to be strong: it will look at you and sigh, and so the whole year in a row. I told her, among other things, a very long time, for two consecutive days of the Prussian House of Lords said (because what it says?) - Just sighed too! About love just do not try - shy to seizures - but also a kind of shows that you can not move - well, beautiful. Awfully convenient; perfectly at home - to read, sit, lie down and write

ROBOTS READ

... I can not even kiss with caution ...

- Yes, I need it?

- Oh, I can not explain in any case! You can see that both of you are perfectly combined with each other! At first I thought of you ... Because you'll end up like this! So if you do not care - earlier il later? Now, brother, like the beginning lies Perino, - oh! and not one Perino! Then pulls; here end of the world, anchor, a quiet refuge, navel of the earth, trehrybnoe foundation of the world, the essence of pancakes, fat cake, evening samovar, quiet sighs and warm katsaveek, superheated lezhanok - Well, that's for sure you were dead, and at the same time and to still alive as well as benefits together! Well, brother, hell, zavralsya, it's time to sleep!Listen: I sometimes wake up at night, well, I'll go and see him. But nothing, nothing, everything is good. Do not worry, and do you, but if you want to go too Razik. But it takes a little, delirium, such as fever, Ali, Ali, that immediately woke me up. However, there can be no ...

⟵ CHAPTER II ⟶

Concern and serious Razumikhin woke up the next day at 8:00. Many new and unforeseen perplexities suddenly found himself in this morning. He had never thought before that ever so wake up.

He remembered everything to the smallest detail yesterday and realized that it has something to do neobydennoe, he took one is still quite unknown to him, and in contrast to the experience though. At the same time, he was clearly aware that the dream of the burning in my head, it is very possible - not possible before he even felt ashamed of her, and he moved as quickly as possible of other more pressing problems and confusion, left him an inheritance after "rastreklyatogo yesterday."

In the worst memories was like it was yesterday, "low and disgusting," and not one that he was drunk, but because scolded in front of a woman, using his position stupidly hasty jealousy, her boyfriend, not knowing, not only their mutual relations among themselves and obligations, but even a person without knowing well. And what right had he to judge him so hastily and rashly?And who invited him to the judge! And how could such a being as Avdotya Romanovna, these unworthy man for money? Consequently, there merits.Numbering? But why is he in fact could find that it is encrypted? In the end, he finished apartments fu ... how it low! And what is the excuse that he was drunk? Silly excuse to humiliate him even more! In the wine - the truth, and the truth, and that's all comments ", that is something all his dirt jealous, cruel heart says!" And this is not acceptable in any case, such a dream to him, Razumikhin? Who is he rather a girl - he drunk and rowdy yesterday bouncer? "How can such a cynical and funny comparison?"

ROBOTS READ

Razumikhin blushed desperately at the thought, and suddenly, as if on purpose, at the same time, remembered how he spoke to them yesterday, standing on a ladder that is jealous his mistress Avdotya Romanovna ... it really was unbearable. For all his power, he slammed his fist on the kitchen stove, injured his hand and knocked one brick.

"Of course - he murmured after a minute, with some sense of self-depre-cation - of course, all these dirty tricks, so as not to draw and make amends now never ... and so, and I do not think anything about it, and, therefore, appear in the silence ... and perform their duties ... and in silence, and ... and do not apologize, and say nothing, and ... and, of course, now all is lost! "

And, well dressed, he carefully examined his costume than usual. Other tips he was not, and if they were, it might put it - ". So purposely did not put" But in any case, a cynic and dirty slut can not stay: he has no right to insult the feelings of other people, especially those and others are themselves in need, and they call ego.Plate her that he carefully removed with a brush. Lingerie has always been tolerated; on this account he was particularly chistoploten.

Washed it this morning cost-conscious - Nastasia found in soaps - washed hair, neck and hands especially. When it came to the question: whether or not to shave his beard (Praskovya Pavlovna was excellent razor retained even after the late Mr. Zarnitsina), the question was answered in the negative, even violently: "Let it remain Well, when I think! I shaved .. . Yes, of course, to think the same thing! No way is not in the world!

And ... and, most importantly, he was so rude, dirty, handling his court; and ... and, say, he knows that, well, a little, but a decent man ... well, so what is there to be proud that a decent man?Everyone should be a decent person, and even cleaner, and ... and yet (he remembers), and accompanied by such transactions ... not that I really unfair, yes, but then! .. And the fact that some of the thoughts happen! um ... and all this put next to Avdotya Romanovna! Well, damn it! And let them! Well, the goal will be such a dirty, greasy, hotel, and do not care! More will be! .. "

In these monologues Zosimov found him, spent the night in the hall Praskovya Pavlovna.

He went home and left in a hurry to look at the patient. Razumikhin told him that he sleeps like a marmot. Zosimov ordered not to wake up, wake up yet. Himself promised to come at the eleventh hour.

- If only he would be home - he added.- Ugh, damn! In the patient has

no power to heal Go! I do not know that he will go to Ali , they come here?

- Those, I think - Razumikhin replied, understand the purpose of the question - and, of course, about his family affairs speak. I'm leaving. You, as a doctor, of course, more than I have rights.

- Not the same spiritual father and I; come and go; And without them many things.

- One bothers me - interrupted, frowning, Razumikhin - yesterday I was drunk, spill the beans to him, dear iduchi about stupid things ... about different ... By the way, that you are afraid that he ... prone to madness. ..

- You and the ladies of the same yesterday spill the beans.

- I know it's stupid! He likes to beat! And it was really you any solid idea?

- Yes nonsense, I say; Some hard thinking! You described it as monomana, when I was to him ... Well, yesterday resist heat, meaning you, these stories are something ... something about malaria; good conversation, when he can himself about this crazy! If only I knew what happened in the office, and there is a suspicion that rascal ... offended! Hmm ... I would not have allowed such a conversation yesterday. In the end, it monomany drops make an ocean, a fable in the people to see the reality ... as long as I can remember, yesterday, in this story Zametova me half the story to find out. What! I know one thing, as a hypochondriac, forty years, not being able to endure the daily taunts table of eight boys stabbed him! And then, all in rags, arrogant quarterly starting the disease, and, as it were suspected! Hypochondriac frenzy! When mad vanity, exceptional! Yes, it is, perhaps, the whole point of the disease and sits! Well, damn it! .. And by the way, it was seen and really cute boy just um ... it's all in vain, he said yesterday. Chatterbox awful!

- But who said Well? I you?

- A purple.

- Well, what Porphyry?

- By the way, do you have any influence on the fact her mother to let her sister? Be careful with him today ...

- Conspiracy! - Razumikhin answered reluctantly.

- And what he did on this Luzhin? The man with the money, he does not seem disgusting ... and yet they do not have a hookah? eh?

- Yes, what you call something? - Razumikhin exclaimed in exasperation - as I know, or barbecue or shisha? Ask yourself, can, and you will know ...

- Ugh, how are you stupid sometimes! Yesterday hops, sitting ... Goodbye; I thank Praskovja Pavlovna his life overnight. Locked himself in his Bonjour

through the doors did not answer, and she got up at 7:00 samovar her across the hall from the kitchen ... I do not secretly awarded to contemplate ...

At 9:00 Razumikhin was in the numbering Bakaleeva. Both ladies were waiting for him for a long time with hysterical impatience. They climbed up to seven hours, or even earlier. He entered the gloomy as night, bowed awkwardly, for what once was angry - at himself, of course. It is calculated without the owner: Pulcheria Alexandrovna and ran to him, grabbed him by both arms and almost kissed them. He sheepishly looked at Avdotya Romanovna; but in this haughty face was at this moment an expression of gratitude and friendship, it is a complete and sudden respect for them (instead of ridicule my views and stimulated, the patient concealed contempt!) that he really, really, it would be easier if met abuse, and it was also embarrassing. Fortunately, it was not ready to talk about the topic, and he clung to rush him.

Hearing that "still did not wake up," but "all right," said Pulcheria Alexandrovna, it was for the better, "because it is very, very, very necessary preliminary talks". Following the issuance of invitations to tea and drink together; they did not drink while waiting for Razumikhin. Avdotya Romanovna call, the call was dirty rags, and he was ordered tea which was finally served, but so dirty and so indecent that the ladies ashamed. Razumikhin vigorously swore were considered, but think about Luzhin stopped, confused and terribly glad when Pulcheria Alexandrovna was showered with questions, finally, without interruption.

Answering them, he said that three-quarters of an hour, constantly interrupted and asked again, and he was able to go through all the most important and relevant facts that are only known from the last year of life, Rodion Romanovich, concluding a thorough account of his illness. However, he missed it, and I had to miss, among other things, about the scene in the office with all its consequences. The story of his eagerly listened to; but when he thought he had finished and satisfied his listeners, it was found that for them it is as if has not yet begun.

- Tell me, tell me what you think ... oh, sorry, I still do not know your name? - Hurry Pulcheria Alexandrovna.

- Dmitri Prokofitch.

- So, Dmitri Prokofitch, I would really, really like to know how to do it ... ... he looks at things now, that is, you know me, how would it tell you that it is best to say that he loves and he does not like? Is it always so grumpy?

What he wants, and, so to speak, dream, if you can? That it now has a special influence on him? In short, I would hope ...

- Oh, Mom, how can all of this so suddenly to answer! - Said Dounia.

- Oh, my God, what I do, so it does not meet Dmitri Prokofitch.

- It is very natural, sir, - said Dmitry Prokofitch. - My mother is not, well, uncle comes here every year, and almost every time I do not know, even on the street, but a wise man; Well, three years of separation took a lot of water. And what can I say? Year and a half, I know, Rodion: sullen, gloomy, arrogant and proud; recently (and possibly sooner) and hypochondriacal suspected. Generous and kind. They do not like to express feelings and cruelty, and to do than words express the heart. Sometimes, however, this is not a hypo-chondriac, but just cold and insensitive to violence, to the right, it is the two opposite nature alternately replaced. Sometimes terribly talkative! All that he did not, all they are prevented, and a lie, do nothing. Not sarcastic, and not because they lacked sharpness, but the exact time he had such a trifle is not enough. Doslushivaet not what they say. Never interested in what all currently interested in.Terrible appreciates herself and seems not without some rights to it. Well, what else? .. I think that your visit will have a positive influence on him.

- Oh, give me a god! - Exclaimed Pulcheria Alexandrovna, exhausted Razumihina Review Rode it.

Finally, pobodree Razumikhin looked at Avdotya Romanovna. He often looked at her during a conversation, but if it is short, only one moment, and immediately turned away. Avdotya Romanovna then sat down at the table and listened attentively, and then stood up and began to walk, as was his custom, from corner to corner, his arms crossed over his chest, secretive, sometimes making his question without interrupting away myshlenie. On also used to doslushivat not what they say. She was dressed in some sort of easy matter temnenky dress, and around his neck was tied white transparent scarf. Largely Razumikhin immediately noticed that the situation of women as well, that in conditions of extreme poverty. Be Avdotya Romanovna dressed like a queen, do not think he will have absolutely no fear; Now, maybe it's because he was so badly dressed, and that he had seen it all miserly Wednesday in his heart possessed by fear, and he began to fear for his every word, every gesture, as it was, of course, ashamed of people no longer believes.

- You said that a lot of interesting things about the nature of his brother

and said ... impartially. It's good; I thought you were in fear before him - said Avdotya Romanovna with a smile. - I think that's true, and that there needs to be a woman - she added thoughtfully.

- I never said that, and in fact, maybe you're right, and just ...
- What?
- Because he does not like anybody; Maybe never love - cut Razumikhin.
- It is not capable of love?
- You know, Avdotya Romanovna, you bad as similar to your brother, even around! - He blurted out suddenly, unexpectedly, but then he remembered that now told her brother about the same, blushed as cancer and terribly embarrassed. Avdotya Romanovna could not help laughing at him.

- About Rodi how you can make mistakes - took a few dive Pulcheria Alexandrovna. - I do not mean to say now Dunya. Peter writes in this letter ... and we thought that with you - may be true, but you can not think Dmitri Prokofitch as fiction, and, as if to say, capricious. His character, which I could never be trusted, even when he was only fifteen years old. I'm sure he's suddenly something can not be done with such things no one ever thought to do ... Yes abound: you know how he and a half years ago, I was amazed, shocked and a bit to kill when even think it had to marry this as her - Zarnitsina daughter, mistress?

- Do you know anything more on this story? - Asked Avdotya Romanovna.
- What do you think - with fervor continued Pulcheria Alexandrovna - then it would stop my tears, my request, my illness, my death, perhaps sadly, their poverty? Will quietly went over all obstacles. And he, if he really does not like us?

- He did and never himself about this story with me did not say - Razumikhin replied softly - but I heard from the Coy Ms. Zarnitsina, who is also one of its kind, and not from storytellers, and that he had heard, perhaps even more strange ...

- And what have you heard? - Asked the two women at once.
- However, nothing special. I just found out that this marriage is absolutely consistent and not only take place in the death of the bride, was the mistress of the most Zarnitsina really do not like ... In addition, they say, the bride is not even a good thing, they say, even ugly. .. And it hurts, and ... and ... and strangely, it seems, with some advantages. Of course, there must have been some merit; otherwise you can not do anything ... No dowry understand, too, but he did not expect a dowry and ... In fact, in this case, it

is difficult to judge.

- I'm sure it was a good girl - briefly noticed Avdotya Romanovna.

- God forgive me, but I'm still glad when her death, although I do not know which of them would have killed each other, shall it he or she? - Concluded Pulcheria Alexandrovna, then carefully, with delays and constant vzglyady-vaniyami on Dunya, which was that, obviously uncomfortable, again began to ask about yesterday's stage between Rohde and Luzhin. This incident, apparently fed up with it, most likely, fear and trembling.Razumikhin told again and again, in detail, but this time he added his opinion and he directly accused of deliberately insulting Raskolnikov Peter Petrovich, this time excusing him very little disease.

- He was supposed to come with the disease, - he added.

- I think so too, - said Pulcheria Alexandrovna killed views. But it is very surprised about Petr Petrovich Razumikhin says of that time as well, and even to love and respect. Hit it and Avdotya Romanovna.

- So you're just what opinion about Peter Petrovich? - I can not help but ask Pulcheria Alexandrovna.

- About the future husband of his daughter, and I could not be of another opinion - firmly and look Razumikhin said - and no one says a vulgar cour-tesy, but because ... because ... well, at least on the fact Avdotya Romanovna that she voluntarily honor choose that person. If I challenged him yesterday, it was because yesterday I was drunk and dirty ... even mind; Yes, crazy, no head, crazy, completely ... and today a shame! .. - He blushed and said noth-ing. Avdotya Romanovna broke out, but did not break the molchanie.Ona not say a single word to the minute to talk about Luzhin.

Meanwhile, Pulcheria Alexandrovna, without his support, apparently was undecided. Finally, haltingly and continually glancing at her daughter, announced that it is now extremely worried about one thing.

- You see, Dmitri Prokofitch ... - she began. - I'll be frank with Dmitri Pro-kovich Dunya?

- Of course, my mother - an impressive noticed Avdotya Romanovna.

- That's what - she hurried, as if from her mountain rises Allow me to report their grief. - Today, very early, we got a note from Petr Petrovich in response to yesterday's notice of arrival. You see, yesterday he was to meet with us, as promised, at the train station. Instead Station sent to meet us some lackey address these ciphers and show us the way, and Peter ordered to tell you that he will come to us here this morning myself.Instead came this

morning from him this note … It is best to read it yourself; there is a point that I am very concerned … now you can see that point … and tell me your honest opinion, Dmitri Prokofitch! You know better than anyone the nature of Rodi and can advise on the best.

I warn you that Dunya allowed everything from the first step, but I, I do not know what to do, and … it's all waiting for you.

Razumikhin unfolded the note marked yesterday's date, and read as follows:

"Gracious Empress Pulcheria Alexandrovna, I have the honor to inform you that the delay occurred suddenly meet you at the pier could not send a man to this end, very agile. Gradually I'm taking my honor to say goodbye to you tomorrow morning will be postponed in the Senate, and not in those cases, prevent visits your home and your son, and Avdotya Romanovna with his brother. And I shall have the honor to visit you and you bow in your apartment is not until tomorrow, at 8:00 in the afternoon, and did not dare we add convincing and will add to my urgent request, Rodion Romanovich and overall this date is no longer, as it is unprecedented and grossly insulted me yesterday when visiting him in sickness and, moreover, that you personally and you need a detailed explanation on certain points, whose desire to learn about your own interpretation. I have the honor to be forewarned that if, contrary to the request, Rodion Romanovich meeting, it will be forced to leave at once, and then blame is over. I write also on the assumption that Rodion Romanovich, who seemed to be so when visiting my patients, two hours later, suddenly recovered and, therefore, leaving the yard, and you can come. Approved by the same in my eyes its own, in a flat one, broken horses, drunkards, from that of the deceased, whose daughter, a girl egregious behavior, released yesterday to twenty-five rubles, under the pretext of a funeral that quite surprised me, knowing what troubles you gathered UIS amount. With that witness their special respect esteemed Avdotya Romanovna, please feeling of reverential devotion

best regards

P. Luzhin. "

- What do I do now, Dmitri Prokofitch? - Said Pulcheria Alexandrovna, almost crying. - Well, as I said Rode did not come? He persistently demanded rejection yesterday Peter, and here and ordered not to take! Yes he purposely came, as you know … and then what will happen?

- Pass in accordance with the decision of Avdotya Romanovna - calmly

and immediately answered Razumikhin.

- Oh, my God, she says ... God knows what she says and does not explain my goal! She says it would be better, it's not what's best, and for some reason, though, of course, you need to Rodia, as well as specially came today at 8:00 and they certainly met ... And I and letters did not want to show him, and somehow made to deceive you, that he can not come ... because he is so angry ... And nothing I do not understand what a drunkard died, and that there is a daughter, and how could he give this daughter all the money last ... what ...

- Who you so much, Mom, - said Avdotya Romanovna.

- He was not yesterday - thought Razumikhin. - If you only knew what it was said yesterday in a restaurant, smart ... ahem! On the dead man, and about some girl he really me saying something yesterday, when we were going home, but I did not understand a word ... And in fact, I did yesterday ...

- Best of all, Mom, let's go to it yourself and there, I assure you immediately see what to do. And besides, this time - God! The Eleventh Hour! - She said, looking at his magnificent gold watch with enamel, hanging from the neck thin Venetian chain and does not really fit the rest of the clothes. "Groomsmen gifts" - thought Razumikhin.

- Oh, it's time! .. It is time, Dunya, it's time! - Aspiring fussed Pulcheria Alexandrovna - still believe that we have from yesterday angry that so long Nadeau.Bozhe my!

Having said that, she hastily threw on her mantilla and wore a hat; Dounia too dressed. Gloves on her were not only worn, tattered, but even that Razumikhin noticed, and even this apparent poverty suit even gave both ladies kind of peculiar dignity that always happens to those who know how to wear poor clothes. Razumikhin watched with awe at the Dun and proud to lead it."It's a queen, - he thought to himself - who was mending her stockings in prison, of course, at this point looked real queen, and even more than in the most magnificent holidays and weekends."

- Oh my God! - Exclaimed Pulcheria Alexandrovna - I thought I would be afraid to meet her son, my sweet, sweet Rode, as now, I'm afraid! .. I'm afraid Dmitri Prokofitch! - She said, looking at him timidly.

- Do not worry, Mom, - said Dounia, kissing her - better believe it. I believe.

- Oh my God! I believe, too, and stay up all night! - Cried the poor woman. They went out into the street.

- You know, Dunya, as soon as I fell asleep a little in the morning, I

suddenly had a dream about the deceased Marfa Petrovna ... and all in white ... came up to me, took my hand, and she shakes her head at me and so strictly, strictly as if convicted ... for good? Oh, my God, Dmitri Prokofitch, you do not know: Marfa Petrovna died!

- No, I do not know what Marfa Petrovna?

- Sudden and! And imagine ...

- Once upon a time, a mother - intervened Dunya - because they do not know who Marfa Petrovna.

- Oh, you do not know? And I thought, you know everything already. You will forgive me, Dmitri Prokofitch, in my opinion these days only for the mind goes. Yes, I think you would want for our Providence, and, therefore, was so convinced that you already know everything. I have a mother and angry ... I do not think I speak so.Oh, my God, you got your right hand! Hurt?

- Yes, trauma, - muttered overjoyed Razumikhin.

- Sometimes I also speak from the heart, so that Dunya corrects me ... But, my God, in which he lives wardrobe! He woke up, though? And this woman, the mistress of it, according to his room? Look, you said that he did not want to show the heart, so that I can be, it serves him right ... my weaknesses? .. Do not you teach me, Dmitri Prokofitch? How do I do with it? You know, I'm just as lost track.

- Do not ask him a lot about anything, if you see that he frowns; in particular, the health of do not ask, do not like.

- Ah, Dmitri Prokofitch how hard to be a mother! But here this ladder ... What a terrible stairs!

- Mom, you even pale, calm down, my dear, - said Dounia, caressing her - he must be happy to see you, and you torture yourself like this - she added, her eyes flashing.

- Wait, I'll come forward, whether awake?

Ladies slowly followed send the stairs ahead of Razumikhin, and when he caught up to the third floor with the hostess door, we noticed that the hostess, the door opened a small crack and two quick black eyes see them as out of the darkness. When his eyes met, the door suddenly slammed shut, and with such a bang that Pulcheria Alexandrovna almost cried out in fear.

⇜≪ ≫⇝

⇜ CHAPTER III ⇝

- Healthy, great! - Fun to meet incoming Zosimov shouted. He was already ten minutes he came and sat in his corner on the couch yesterday. Raskolnikov sat in the corner opposite, fully dressed and even carefully washed and combed, which has long had happened to him. The room was refilled, but Nastasya still managed to pass after the visitors and began to listen.

Indeed, Raskolnikov was almost well, especially compared to yesterday, but was very pale, sullen and distracted. Outside it was like as if a wounded man or vyterplivayuschego some severe physical pain, his eyebrows were knitted, his lips compressed, inflammation of the eye. He spoke little and reluctantly, as if through the power or the performance of duties, and some anxiety from time to time appear in his movements.

Lacked any bandage or cover taffeta on his finger for a complete resemblance to a person who, for example, is very painful to run up a finger or hand injury, or something like that.

Nevertheless, it is pale and sullen face lit up for a moment, as if the lights came on, when his mother and sister, but she added, only the expression of this, instead of the previous melancholy distraction, as if more focused flour. The light faded soon, but remained flour and Zosimov, observe and study his patient with all the young zeal just a beginner polechivat doctor was surprised to see him, with the arrival of relatives, instead of joy, as if a heavy hidden determination to move an hour or two of torture, can not really be avoided. He saw it as almost every word of the conversation that followed, simply touch any wound his patient and open it; but at the same time, he was surprised at today's partially self-control and to hide their

feelings monomana yesterday, because the slightest word expired yesterday, almost crazy.

- Yes, now I can see for myself that almost good - said Raskolnikov, friendly kiss his mother and sister, why Pulcheria Alexandrovna immediately beamed - and not the day before saying this - he added, referring to Razumikhin animals and shaking his hand .

- And I was even surprised him today - started Zosimov who came was very happy because ten minutes later managed to lose the thread of conversation with their patients. - Three or four days, if it goes, everything will be as before, that is, as was the case last month, Ali ... Ali two, perhaps three? It was preparing afar began so ... is not it? Carries now that perhaps they themselves were to blame? - He added with a careful smile, as if still afraid of him with something annoying.

- It may be - Raskolnikov answered coldly.

- I must say - continued Zosimov, razlakomivshis - is your perfect recovery, mainly depends on you now. Now that you are available to talk, I would like to impress upon you the need to remove the original, so to speak, the root causes that influenced the birth of your disease condition, and then cured, it will not be worse. These initial reason I do not know, but you should be aware of. You are an intelligent man and, of course, to watch. I think that the beginning of your disorder partially coincides with the release of your university. You can not stay out of work, and therefore labor and firmly with the task, I think it would be very help.

- Yes, yes, you're absolutely right ... so I'm going to do as soon as possible to the university, and then everything goes like clockwork ... ...

Zosimov began clever tips and partly to the effect of the ladies was, of course, somewhat taken aback when, having finished it and looked at the audience, saw in his face a strong nasmeshek.Tem Still, it lasted a moment. Pulcheria Alexandrovna immediately began to thank Zosimova, especially for the last night of their appearance at the hotel.

- How are you this was at night? - Raskolnikov asked, as if worried. - So you do not sleep after the road?

- Oh, Rodia, is only two hours there. We Dunya and the house that the two had never walked.

- I do not know how to thank him - Raskolnikov went on, suddenly frowned and looked down. - Dismiss the question of money - you're sorry that I mentioned it (he turned to Zosima) - I really do not know that I deserve

this from you so special attention? Just do not understand ... and ... and it's even hard for me, because it is not clear: I will speak frankly.

- There can be annoying - laughed through the block Zosimov - imagine that you are my first patient, well, my brother, is just beginning to practice their first patients as their own children, loves, and some of them almost fall in love. And I'm not rich patient.

- I'm not talking about him - said Raskolnikov, pointing at Razumikhin - as well as, except insults and trouble from me did not see anything.

- Ek lain! You are in a sensitive mood, whether that today? - Razumikhin shouted.

He would see if I was a shrewd, sensitive mood, which was not there, and it was not even something quite the opposite. But Avdotya Romanovna remarked. It's close and anxiously watched his brother.

- About the same you, Mom, I do not dare to say - he continued, if the lesson learned in the morning - today I just could not understand how something like you were here yesterday, exhausted waiting for my return. - Having said that, he suddenly, silently and with a smile, handed sister. But the smile flashed this time present the true sense. Dunya immediately grabbed and shook her hand warmly outstretched, was delighted and grateful. The first time he spoke to her after yesterday's quarrel. Mother's face lit up with joy and happiness at the sight of the final reconciliation and besslovnogo brother and sister.

- Look, I love it! - Whispered Razumikhin exaggerate everything, turning energetically on a chair. - Is it a movement! ..

"And as he goes all right - I think that the mother herself - what his noble impulses, and he just finished delicately All this confusion yesterday with my sister - only hand held out in a moment, but looked good and ... what beautiful eyes and a beautiful face all! .. It's even better Dounia ... But, my God, that his suit as he dressed badly! Athanasius Ivanovich store Vasya, courier, better dressed! .. And so it would be here so that would seem to be, and ran to him and hugged him and cried ... - and I'm afraid, I'm afraid ... What is he, Lord .. This is because, and! says softly, and I am afraid that ! Well, what I fear? .. "

- Oh, Rodia, you would not believe - she suddenly picked up, hurrying to respond to his remarks - as we were yesterday ... Dunya unhappy! Now, when we all went over and done with, and we are all happy again - you can tell. Imagine that we run here to hug you, almost straight out of the car,

and this woman - and, yes that's it! Welcome Nastasia! .. It tells us all of a sudden, you're lying in delirium tremens and just ran away quietly from the doctor, in his delirium, on the street and that you went to look for. You will not believe what happened to us! I just imagine how tragically killed Lieutenant Potanchikov, our friend, the friend of your father - you do not remember, Rodia - also in delirium tremens, and in the same way, and ran into a pit in the yard fell on another day could only pull, and we Of course, even more exaggerated. Wanted to rush to find Petr Petrovich even with it ... because as we were alone, absolutely alone - she drawled in a plaintive voice, and suddenly broke off completely, remembering that to start talking about Peter Petrovich still quite dangerous, despite the "what all this is perfectly happy again."

- Yes, yes ... it is certainly a shame ... - Raskolnikov muttered in response, but with such a scattered and almost inattentive view that Dunya in amazement at him.

- What was it, I wanted more - he went on, with the power of remembering - yes: Please, Mom, and you, Dounia, I do not think I do not want to you today is the first to come in and waiting for you in the first place.

- Yes, it's you, Rodia! - Exclaimed Pulcheria Alexandrovna, too surprised.

"The fact that he, debt, whether that answers us? - Thought Dunya - and made it up, and asked for forgiveness, the service exactly Ali lesson learned by rote."

- I just woke up and wanted to go, so I put a delay; forgot yesterday to tell her ... Nastasya ... zamyt this blood ... only now it was time to get dressed.

- Blood! a little blood? - Alarmed by Pulcheria Alexandrovna.

- It's so ... do not worry. It's in the blood, because yesterday when I walked a few delirious, I came across a crushed man ... official ...

- Delirious? But you still remember - Razumikhin interrupted.

- It's true - as a particularly carefully Raskolnikov answered, - I remember everything, down to the smallest detail, but to go and why I did it, so go there, but he has to say? very well, and I can not explain.

- Too well-known phenomenon - got involved Zosimov - sometimes masterful execution of business, slyly, and management actions initiated action, frustration, and depends on a number of painful experiences. Like a dream.

"But it is perhaps just as well that he was crazy about me thinks" - thought Raskolnikov.

- Why, in this way, perhaps, and healthy as well - said Dounia, anxiously

looking at Zosimova.

- Absolutely remark - he said - in this sense, indeed all of us, and very often, almost like a madman, with a small difference that "sick" several more of our mind, because here we have to distinguish the line.Harmonics people, however, almost no one does; on dozens, maybe hundreds of thousands to one occurs, and then only in a relatively weak copies ...

At the word "crazy" involuntarily grabbed swing on his favorite topic Zosimova all winced. Raskolnikov sat, as if oblivious, lost in thought with a strange smile on his pale lips. He went so far as to think.

- Well, so crushed? I interrupted you! - Razumikhin shouted as quickly as possible.

- What? - As if he woke up - yes ... and dirt in the blood, when he helped translate it into an apartment ... By the way, Mom, I'm the one unforgivable what he did yesterday; really was not in his head. Yesterday I was all the money that you sent me, he gave his wife ... ... funeral. Now a widow, consumptive, miserable woman ... three little orphaned, hungry ... the house is empty ... and daughter ... Maybe you would have given yourself, if only ... I have seen, however, had no right to I must admit, especially knowing how you got yourself dengi.Chtoby help, we must first have the right, not that: "Crevez Chiens, Si Vous n'Ãªtes pas content!" - He laughed. - Yes, Dounia?

- No, not so - Dunya replied firmly.

- Bah! and you ... with the intention! .. - He muttered, looking at her almost with hatred and mocking smile. - I'd have to figure that out ... Well, is commendable; You better ... and you will reach those functions that do not step on it - you will be unhappy, and step - maybe even more miserable you ... And yet, all this nonsense!- He added irritably, annoyed by his forced admiration. - I just wanted to tell you, Mom, I'm sorry - he suddenly and dramatically completed.

- Well, Rodia, I'm sure that whatever you do, all right! - Glad mother said.

- It can not be that - he said, twisting his mouth into a smile. Was silence. Something was busy in conversation, and in silence, and as a sign of reconciliation and forgiveness, and it all felt.

"But surely they are afraid of me" - thought to myself, Raskolnikov, looking askance at his mother and sister.Pulcheria Alexandrovna, indeed, quieter and more timid.

"In absentia, apparently, do not you love them" - flashed through his mind.

- You know, Rodia, Marfa Petrovna died! - Suddenly jumped Pulcheria

Alexandrovna.

- What Marfa Petrovna?

- Oh, my God, yes Marfa Petrovna Svidrigailov! I have so much written to you.

- Ah, yes, I remember ... It was dead? Oh Really? - He suddenly shuddered, as if waking up. - Really dead? Why is this?

- Imagine a sudden! - Hurried Pulcheria Alexandrovna, urged his curiosity - and just at the same time, I sent you a letter, then, even in the same day! Imagine what a horrible person, it seems, was the cause of her death. They say he beat her badly!

- And do they live? - He asked, turning to his sister.

- No, on the contrary, even. With it, he was always very patient, even polite. In many cases, even too indulgent to her character, the entire seven years ... somehow suddenly lost patience.

- So, it was not so bad if seven years was recorded? Dunya you justify it?

- No, no, it's a horrible person! Worse than I did, and I can not imagine - almost with a shudder said Dounia, frowned and thought.

- It happened to them in the morning - went slowly, Pulcheria Alexandrovna. - After she immediately ordered to lay the horse immediately after lunch and go into the city, because it always happens in such cases, went into the city; ate for lunch, for example, with a big appetite ...

- Beaten anything?

- ... It is, however, always had this habit ... and for dinner, not to be late to go, immediately went to the pool ... You see, it's like out there treated bathing; they have there key cold there, and she was bathing in it regularly every day, and once entered the water, suddenly hit!

- You bet! - Said Zosimov.

- And hurt he beat her?

- It's all the same - Dunia said.

- Hm! Yet, hunting you, mama, about such nonsense talk, - irritability, and, as if by accident, said Raskolnikov.

- Ah, my friend, but I do not know what to say too - ran Pulcheria Alexandrovna.

- What are you afraid of, and I'm all? - He said with a wry smile.

- It's true - said Dounia, straight and looking sternly at his brother. - Mom, climbing stairs, even baptized fear.

His face contorted as if cramps.

- Oh, you, Dounia! Do not be angry, please Rodia ... Why you, Dounia! - Said in a confused Pulcheria Alexandrovna - that I really came here all the way to the dream car: as we shall see, as we all let each other ... and was so happy that I did not see the road! Yes I Do! Now I'm happy ... In vain you, Dounia! I do this only too happy to see you, Rodia ...

- Well, my mother - he murmured shyly, not looking at her and squeezed her hand - there is time to say enough!

Having said this, he suddenly turned pale and confused once again one of the last horrible feeling cold dead went through his heart again, he suddenly became very clear and understandable that he now said terrible lie that not only never now was not the time to stop talk to him, but none of the more, and never with anyone, he can not now speak. The impression it was a painful thought so much that he, for a moment, almost completely forgotten, stood up and, without looking at anyone, he out of the room.

- What are you? - Razumikhin shouted, grabbing him by the arm.

He sat down and started to look around in silence; all looked at him in amazement.

- Why are you so boring! - He exclaimed suddenly, unexpectedly, - say something! What actually sit there for you! Well, they say the same thing! Let's talk ... collected and silent ... Well, nothing!

- Thank God! I thought that it is something starts yesterday - said, crossing, Pulcheria Alexandrovna.

- What are you, Rodia? - Asked incredulously Avdotya Romanovna.

- Oh, nothing, one part not remember - he said, and burst out laughing.

- Well, since everyone is so good! And then I thought he was ... - Zosimov muttered, getting up from the couch. - I am, however, the time has come; I'm moving on, maybe ... if you ...

He bowed and left.

- What a wonderful man! - Said Pulcheria Alexandrovna.

- Yes, well, well, educated, intelligent ... - Raskolnikov said with an unknown tongue twister and with some extraordinary revival yet - I do not remember where I first met before the disease ... It seems that met somewhere ... So this is also a good person! - He nodded at Razumikhin - as you, Dounia? - He asked her, and suddenly, it is not known that he laughed.

- Very - said Dunya.

- Ugh, what are you ... Piggy! - Said terribly embarrassed and blushed Razumikhin and rose from his chair.Pulcheria Alexandrovna smiled slightly,

and Raskolnikov laughed out loud.

- Yeah, where are you?

- Me too ... I have to.

- Just do not, stay! Zosimov gone, and you should. Do not go ... And now the time? There are twelve? What are your hours of cute, Dunya! Why are you silent again? All just me, but I'm talking about! ..

- It's a gift to Marfa Petrovna, - said Dunya.

- A predorogie, - added Pulcheria Alexandrovna.

- Ah-ah-ah! which are large, almost ladies.

- I love these - said Dounia.

"So, do not care for the gift" - thought Razumikhin, and who knows that he is happy.

- I thought it was a gift Luzhin - said Raskolnikov.

- No, he did not give Dunya.

- Ah-ah-ah! And remember, Mom, I'm in love once been married and wanted - he said suddenly, looking at her mother who suffered an unexpected turn and the tone with which he spoke about it.

- Ah, my friend, yes! - Pulcheria Alexandrovna exchanged glances with Dunya and Razumikhin.

- Hm! Yes I am! What should I say? Even the little I remember. It's such a patient was, - he continued, as if suddenly think again and looking down - quite sick; loved to feed the poor, and the monastery is still dreaming, and just burst into tears when I started to talk about it; Yes, yes ... I remember ... I remember very much. Ugly is .... I do not really know why I then attached to it, it seems, because it always hurts ... If she still limps al hunchbacked, I would have even more in love with her ... (He smiled wistfully). So ... something stupid spring ...

- No, it's not nonsense spring - with live said Dounia.

He carefully and voltage looked at his sister, but they do not hear or understand her words. Then, deep in thought, stood up, walked over to his mother, kissed her, returned to his seat and sat down.

- Do you love her now! - Touching Pulcheria Alexandrovna said.

- Its something? Now what? Oh yeah ... you're talking about! No. That's it, now just in this world ... and so long ago. And that's all that the circle is not right here ...

He looked at them.

- So you ... just because of thousands of miles to watch you ... And God

knows what we're talking about it!And why do you ask? - He added angrily, and stopped, biting his nails and rethinking.

- How do you bad apartment, Rodia, just a coffin - Pulcheria Alexandrovna said suddenly, breaking the painful silence - I'm sure you're already halfway to the apartment became melancholic.

- Apartment? .. - He replied absently. - Yes, the apartment made a great contribution ... I thought about it ... And if you know, but what you just said, a strange idea, mother, - he added suddenly, a strange grin.

A little more, and this society, these relatives, after three years of separation, the tone of the conversation related at least to complete inability to speak - at last he was very miserable. It was, however, be delayed one thing that way or that way, but of course, it was necessary to solve today - so he decided to further this morning when I woke up. Now he was glad that so as output.

- Listen, Dunya - he began seriously and dry - I certainly apologize for yesterday, but I feel the duty to remind you that with my lord, I will not give. Or I, or I Luzhin.Suppose villain and you do not have to. One anybody. If you marry Luzhin, I immediately stop my sister to consider.

- Rodia, Rodia! But it's still the same as yesterday - sadly exclaimed Pulcheria Alexandrovna - and why do you still call yourself a scoundrel, I can not! And yesterday, the same thing ...

- Brother, - firmly and also dryly Dunya - in all this there is an error on your part. I thought for a night and found an error. All that you seem to suggest that I have someone for someone to sacrifice. Absolutely not. I just for themselves, because for me the most difficult; and then, of course, I would be happy if I can be of service to others, but my determination is not the main motivation ...

"Lee - he thought to himself, biting his nails with anger. - With pride I do not want to admit that I want to show kindness, O, low characters they love, hate ... Oh, how I hate them! ... all! "

- In general, I'm getting married Peter - continued Dunya - because of two evils choose the lesser. I honestly intends to fulfill all that he expects from me, and so that he does not know ... Why do you smile today?

She also broke out, and her eyes flashed with anger.

- To make all of this? - He asked, smiling poisonous.

- Up to a certain limit. And the manner and form in matchmaking Peter immediately showed me what he wanted. He, of course, appreciate yourself,

maybe a little too high, but I hope he appreciates me ... Why are you laughing again?

- Why are you blushing again? You're lying, sister, you are consciously
lying, only one woman only stubbornness put it in front of me ... You can not
respect Luzhin: I saw him and spoke to him. Thus, in order to sell themselves
for money, and therefore, in any event, included a minimum, and I am glad
that you, at least you can blush!

- That's not true, do not lie! .. - Dunya exclaimed, losing all self-control
- I did not marry him, not making sure he appreciates me and cherish me;
not to marry him, without being firmly convinced that it can respect it.
Fortunately, I can see it, perhaps even today. And such a marriage is not
meanness, as you say!

And if you were a man, and if I really decided infamy - is not cruel of you
to talk to me? Why are you asking me heroism, which is something you can
be, do not you? This despotism, it is violence! If I destroy anyone, so just the
one I ... I have no one with a knife! .. What are you looking at me? What are
you so pale? Rodia, what's wrong? Rodia, dear! ..

- The Lord! Brought to faint! - Exclaimed Pulcheria Alexandrovna.

- No, no ... nonsense ... nothing! .. A little dizzy. Do not pass out ... you
observed these fainting! Um ..! yeah ... I mean, what do I want? Yes: how are
you today, make sure that you can respect him, and that he appreciates ...
what if, as you say? You seem to say that today? Or I hear right?

- Mom, show the letter to his brother Peter Petrovich, - said Dounia.

Pulcheria Alexandrovna gave the letter with trembling hands. It is with
great curiosity took him. But before we post, he suddenly somehow looked
with surprise at the Dunya.

- It is strange - he said slowly, as if suddenly struck by a new thought -
yes from what I so hard? With all the crying? Yes marry whoever you want!

He spoke as if to himself, but said aloud, and stared at her sister, as if
puzzled.

He finally turned the letter, keeping the shape of a strange surprise;
slowly and carefully began to read and read in two raza.Pulheriya Alexandrovna was of particular concern; and everyone was waiting for something
special.

- It's amazing to me - he said, after some reflection and transmission of
a letter to his mother, but no one in particular - because it walks, a lawyer,
and the conversation even in his so ... with manners - - and still as ignorant

records .

All mix; is expected.

- Yes, because they are all so write - Razumikhin said sharply.

- Did you read?

- Yes I Am.

- We have shown RODIA, we consulted this morning … - beginning embarrassed Pulcheria Alexandrovna.

- It is, in fact, the judges syllable - Razumikhin interrupted - court papers still written.

- Referee? Yes, judges, business … Not that it is very wrong, and not so much literary; Business!

- Peter and makes no secret that he was in copper money, and even boasted that he paved his way - said Avdotya Romanovna, several new tone offended brother.

- Well, if you boast, but something - I do not agree. You, sister, seems offended that I was out of all letters frivolous remark Drew, and I think that I deliberately spoke about such trifles to go wrong at you with annoyance. On the contrary, I, on the syllable, it happened in a not too much, in this case, the remark. There is one expression: "blame yourself," it is important to come and clear, and, in addition, there is a danger that he will leave immediately if I come. This threat to leave - even the threat of both of you to leave if you are disobedient, and quit now, when he called in St. Petersburg. Well, what do you think: is it possible that the expression in the same way Luzhin offense as if he had written here (he pointed to Razumikhin) Zosimov Ali, Ali of us, who else?

- N-no, - said Dounia, perking up - I do understand that it is too naive and say that it can be not only a master record … That you are well founded, brother. I did not expect …

- It's like the judge expressed in similar judges otherwise can not write, and went rougher than maybe he wanted. Nevertheless, I have to disappoint you some of them: in this letter is one expression, a slander on my account, and rather Petty. I gave money yesterday widow, consumptive and killed, and not "under the guise of a funeral", and directly to the funeral, and not in the hands of his daughter - a girl, as he writes, "flagrant behavior" (and I yesterday for the first time in my I've never seen), namely the widow. In all this I see too hasty desire me razmarat and quarrel with you. Reiterated the same in similar judges, it is too obvious targets opening and with haste

rather naive. He is a smart man, but to act wisely - it draws sumasshedshiy. Vse little man, and ... I do not think he's got a lot appreciated. To inform the same to you solely for your edification, because I sincerely wish you well ...

Dounia did not answer; This decision was made even this morning, she did not wait until the evening.

- So how do you decide RODIA? - Asked Pulcheria Alexandrovna, daveshny more concerned about his sudden, new business tone.

- What is "crucial"?

- Yes, that Peter wrote to you was not with us in the evening, and that he will ... if you come. So how are you going to ...?

- It's certainly not for me to decide, but, first, you if such a requirement is not to offend Peter, and secondly, Dunya, if she will not mind. And I will do so, as you get better, - he added dryly.

- Dunya already decided and I quite agree with her - Pulcheria Alexandrovna hastened to insert.

- I decided to ask you, Rodia, urge definitely be with us on this day, - said Dounia - come?

- I will come.

- I also ask you to be with us at 8:00 - she turned to Razumikhin. - Mom, I invite them too.

- And well, Dunya. Well, it's all what you decide - added Pulcheria Alexandrovna - so be it. And I very easily; I do not want to pretend and lie; It is better to tell the truth ... angry, do not get angry, Peter!

⤙« CHAPTER IV »⤚

At this moment the door opened softly, and into the room, looking timidly into a girl. Everyone turned to her with surprise and curiosity. Raskolnikov did not recognize her at first sight.It was Sofya Semyonovna Marmeladova. Yesterday he saw her for the first time, but at this moment, in such circumstances and in such a suit that was reflected in his mind the image of a completely different person.Now it was modestly and even poorly dressed girl, still very young almost like a little girl, with a modest and dignified manner, with clear, but seemed somewhat scary face. It was very simple house dress, the color of the old, old-fashioned hat; only in the hands was yesterday, umbrella. Suddenly we saw a room full of people, it's not that embarrassing, but quite lost, timid, like a little kid, and even made a motion to go back.

- Oh, it's you ..? .. - Raskolnikov said in utter surprise and suddenly embarrassed.

He immediately realized that his mother and sister known casual, letters Luzhin, a girl "outrageous" behavior. Now only he protested against slander Luzhin, and noted that he had seen this girl for the first time, and suddenly she enters herself. He also recalled that in no case were protesting against the expression: "egregious behavior." All of this is not clear and instantly put his head.But looking closer, he saw that it was downtrodden creature before already downplaying that he felt sorry for nemu.Kogda she made was a movement to escape from fear - it's something like upside down.

- I do not expect - he hurried, stopping the eye. - Do me a favor, sit down. You probably from Katerina Ivanovna. Let's not here, here, take ...

ROBOTS READ

Upon entering Sony Razumikhin, who was sitting on one of the three chairs Raskolnikov, now at the door, stood up to let her enter. Raskolnikov was the first to have its place in the corner of the sofa, where he sat Zosimov, but remembering that the sofa was too unceremoniously place and serves as his bed, was quick to point her in the chair Razumikhin.

- And you sit here, - he said Razumikhin, landing him in a corner, where he sat Zosimov.

Sonya sat down, almost trembling with fear, and timidly looked at the two women. It was clear that she did not understand how she could sit next to them. Realizing this, she was frightened before suddenly stood up again and in excellent confusion turned to Raskolnikov.

- I ... I ... went for a minute, I'm sorry that you're worried - she stammered, said. - I'm from Katerina Ivanovna, and she had no one to send ... And Katerina Ivanovna has ordered you really are asked to be at the funeral tomorrow morning ... for life ... on Mitrofanievskom, and then we are. .. .. Honor dine her to do ... She told me to ask.

Sonia faltered and fell silent.

- I will try in every way ... of course - answered Raskolnikov got up too and too hesitantly and not negotiate ... - Do me a favor, sit down, - he said suddenly, - I need to talk to you. Please - you may be in a hurry - do me a favor, give me two minutes ...

And he pushed her chair. Sonia sat down again and again timidly lost, hurry looked at both ladies and suddenly looked down.

Raskolnikov's pale face flushed; its as if all shuddered; His eyes lit up.

- Mom, - he said firmly and persistently - Sophia Semenovna Marmeladova daughter unhappy Mr. Marmeladova which in my eyes yesterday crushed horse and I already told you ...

Pulcheria Alexandrovna looked at Sonya and slightly squinted. Despite his confusion before persistent and defiant expression Rodi, she could not deny myself this pleasure. Dunya seriously, looking straight into the face of a poor girl and her bewilderment considered. Sonia heard the recommendation was looked up again, but even more confused than before.

- I would like to ask you - addressed her as soon as possible Raskolnikov - as you already decided? Do you not worried? .. For example, the police.

- No, sir, everything went ... It's too obvious, why death; Do not disturb except that residents are angry.

- How Come?

- Not for the body for a long time ... because hot, spirit ... So today, for vespers, the cemetery will be held tomorrow, in the chapel. Katerina Ivanovna did not want to at first, and now she sees that you can not ...

- So today?

- She wants you to do us the honor to be the church funeral service tomorrow, and then we come to it after.

- Funeral she?

- Yes, sir, snacks; she told me thank you for helping us yesterday ... without you really do not have anything to bury. - And her lips and chin suddenly jumped up, but she refrained and resisted, as soon as possible, as soon as his eyes on the ground.

Talk Raskolnikov looked at her. It was slim, very thin and pale face, totally wrong for some vostrenkoe vostrenkim with a small nose and chin. He can not even call and beautiful, but her blue eyes were so clear, and when they were quickened, her face was so good and simple, that involuntarily attracted to her. In her face, and her whole figure was in excess of one feature: in spite of his eighteen years, she seemed almost a girl much younger than his years, almost like a child, and it's not even funny sometimes manifested in some of his movements.

- But can Katerina Ivanovna could not do such a little money, even going to eat? .. - Raskolnikov asked, stubbornly continuing the conversation.

- The coffin was really easy ... and everything will be just as cheap ... We are with Katerina Ivanovna, all designed so that will remain in the memory ... and Katerina Ivanovna really want it to be so. You can not, with comfort ... this ... this is so, because, you know ...

- I know, I know ... of course ... What are you staring at me in the room? Here, too, Mom says that resembles a coffin.

- You gave us all yesterday! - Suddenly said in response to Sonia, some strong and quick whisper, suddenly looking down hard again. Her lips and chin again jumped. It has long been struck by the poor situation of Raskolnikov, and now these words suddenly broke itself. Was silence. Dounia eyes somehow proyasneli and Pulcheria Alexandrovna even looked affably at Sonya.

- Rodia - she said, getting up - of course we had lunch together. Dunya, let's go ... And you would Rodia went, went a little, and then resting, lying, and there soon ... And then we will be tired, I'm afraid ...

- Yes, yes, I will come, - he said, getting up and hurriedly ... - I have,

however, business ...

- Well, of course you will have dinner and discord? - Razumikhin shouted in amazement looking at Raskolnikov, - is that you?

- Yes, yes, I will come, of course, of course ... And you stay for a minute. In the end, it is not needed now, Mom? Or I could take him?

- Oh, no, no! And you, Dmitri Prokofitch, come to dinner, be so kind ,?

- Please come - asked Dunya.

Razumikhin bowed and everything sparkled. For a moment, all in a strange suddenly zakonfuzilis.

- Farewell, Rodia, that is goodbye; I do not want to say "goodbye." Farewell, Nastasya ... ah, again, "Farewell," said! ..

Pulcheria Alexandrovna was about Sonya and worship, but for some reason it was not possible, and hurriedly left the room.

But Avdotya Romanovna, as if waiting queue and, after his mother Sonia, falls out of her attentive, friendly and full bow. Sonia was confused, bowed again utoroplenno and frightened, and some even pain reflected in her face, as if the courtesy and attention Avdotya Romanovna it was painful and agonizing.

- Dunya, Goodbye! - Cried Raskolnikov in the canopy - Give a hand!

- Oh, I served, I forgot? - Dunya replied softly and awkwardly turning to him.

- Well, even forbid!

And he firmly squeezed her fingers. Dounia smiled, blushed, quickly grabbed his arm and went to his mother, too, for some reason, everyone is happy.

- Well, that's nice! - He said Sonia, coming back to himself and clearly looked at her - God rest of the living and the dead still live! Right?Right? Is not it?

Sonia even surprised look on his face suddenly prosvetlevshee; this for a few minutes in silence and stared at her the whole story about her late father left her at that moment suddenly in his memory ...

- Lord, Dunya! - Speak directly Pulcheria Alexandrovna, as took to the streets - it's because now I'm just glad that we have left: it is easier somehow. Well, I thought, yesterday, in the car, that even this will rejoice!

- Again I say unto you, Mom, it's still pretty bad. Can not you see? Maybe suffering for us and worry. One must be indulgent and much, much can be forgiven.

- But you do not forgive! - Hot and jealously immediately interrupted Pulcheria Alexandrovna. - You know, Dounia, I looked at the two of you, you are the perfect portrait of his people and not so much as the soul: you are both melancholic as surly and short-tempered, how lofty and generous ... It can not be that he was selfish, Dunya? yes i do? .. And when I think that we will be in the evening today, so all the hearts and collect!

- Do not worry, Mom, this is what it should be.

- Dunya! Yes, just think what position we are now! Well, if Peter refuses? - Accidentally expressed suddenly poor Pulcheria Alexandrovna.

- So why does it cost after! - Dramatically and contemptuously replied Dounia.

- That's what we did well, now gone, - hurried, interrupting, Pulcheria Alexandrovna - he was somewhere on the case in a hurry; skip even breathe the air ... the horror of his stuffy air ... and where else? Here and in the streets, in rooms without ventilation holes. God, what a city! .. Wait for outsiders to destroy, are something! This is done on the piano, just ... pushing ... this girl I am also very afraid ...

- What is the virgin mother?

- Yes, it's that Sofya Semyonovna something now ...

- What is it?

- I have a hunch, Dunya. Well, believe it or not, as she came in, I'm in the same moment, and I thought that was then, this is important, and sits ...

- Just do not sit there! - Angrily cried Dounia. - What do you with your concerns, Mom! He only knew him yesterday, and now, as entered did not recognize.

- Well, you'll see! .. This confuses me, you'll see, you'll see! And so I was afraid she looks at me, looks, eyes so I just sat there in the chair, remember, started recommending And it is strange to me, so that Peter wrote about it, and he recommends it to us, and even? do you! So, dear to him!

- It is unlikely that he wrote! We also talked about, and wrote, I forgot, huh? And I'm sure she's beautiful ... and all this - nonsense!

- Give it to God!

- And Peter worthless gossip - suddenly snapped Dunya.

Pulcheria Alexandrovna and clung. The conversation was interrupted.

- Look, here's what I have to ... deal - said Raskolnikov, looking out the window ... Razumihina

- So I'll tell Katerina Ivanovna that you would come ... - Sonya hastily,

bowing to leave.

- Now, Sofya Semyonovna, we do not have any secrets, you will not inter-fere ... I would like you to even say a few words ... That's what - he turned suddenly, finishing with just ripped to Razumikhin. - Did you know that ... Like this one! .. Porfiry Petrovitch?

- You bet! Relative. And what is it? - Add that curiously explosion.

- In the end, it is now the case ... Well, here on this murder ... But yester-day you said something ... is it?

- Yes ... Well, what? - Razumikhin suddenly opened his eyes.

- He asked mortgagors, and I also have a mortgage, so dryantso, but the ring Well sister, which she gave to my mind when I left here, but my father's silver watch. All rubles worth five or six, but it is expensive and memory. So what do I do now? I do not want to disappear, especially watches. I am delighted with this morning, the mother asks to look at them when it comes to Duns hours. The only thing that survived after his father. She's sick to do if they are lost! Women! So what to do, teach! I know that it would be necessary to declare part. And is not it better porphyria, huh? What do you think? The point is to be quickly wrought. You will see that before lunch mom to ask!

- It is not part of it, and, of course, Porphyry! - Called to some unusual excitement Razumikhin. - Well, I'm glad! Yes, that is, go around the corner, will probably find you!

- Maybe ... go ...

- And he's very, very, very, very happy to meet you! I told him about you at different times ... And he said yesterday. Come on! .. So, you know the old woman? It is so! .. Be-Do-on-plaster it all turned out! .. Oh yeah ... Sophia Ivanovna ...

- Sofia Semyonovna - corrected Raskolnikov. - Sofia Semyonovna my friend, Razumikhin, and he's a good man ...

- If you have to go ... - Sonia began, not quite looking at Razumikhin, and it is even more confusing.

- And let's! - Decided to Raskolnikov - I come to you today, Sofya Semyonovna, just tell me where you live?

He is not what was lost, and as if in a hurry and avoided her gaze. Sonia gave his address and blushed at the same time. All went out together.

- Do not block if? - Razumikhin asked, climbing the stairs after them.

- Never! .. However, it's really all I want two years to buy the castle - he added casually. - Happy, because people who do not have anything to block?

- He said, laughing, to Sonya.

On the street they stood at the gate.

- You're right, Sofya Semyonovna? By the way, how did you find me? - He asked, as if to tell her something completely different. He still wanted to see her quiet, clear eyes, and somehow it is not able to ...

- Why do you treat polka said yesterday.

- Paul? Oh yeah ... Polechka! It's a little ... .. it's your sister? So I gave her the address?

- Yes, you forgot?

- No ... I remember ...

- I'm talking about you, even the dead, at the same time heard ... I do not know if your name, and he did not know ... And now ... and I found your name yesterday ... Then asked today: Mr. Raskolnikov here, where does he live? .. I do not know that you are also of the residents live ... Good-bye, with Katerina Ivanovna ... I ...

She was awfully glad that finally gone; went sadly taking the time to rush something to leave them out of sight, only to get more of these twenty paces before turning right onto the street and stay at the last, and walking very slowly, someone not looking anything noting, I think do not forget to think about every word, every circumstance. Never, she had never felt anything like it.A whole new world of unknown and vaguely entered her soul. She suddenly remembered that Raskolnikov wanted to go to her now, maybe in the morning, maybe now!

- But I do not now, please, not today! - She murmured with a sinking heart, just someone to someone, like a child in a fright. - The Lord! For me ... in this room ... he will see ... oh!

And, of course, she could not notice at the time to get used to his master, diligently watching her and her carefully. He walked her to the door of the gate. At a time when all three Razumikhin Raskolnikov and she stopped for a couple of words on the sidewalk, a passerby, ignoring them, when suddenly shuddered, accidentally caught on the fly Sony ", and asked Mr. Raskolnikov, where he lives?" He quickly, but looked at all three of them, and especially access to Sonia Raskolnikov; Then she looked at the house and saw him. All this was done at the time, on the go, and a passerby, trying not to show even mind went on, turn down a move as if in anticipation. He waited for Sonia; he saw that they were forgiven and that Sonia will now somewhere under his breath.

"So, where did it I saw somewhere that a person - he thought, remembering the face of Sony ... - you need to know."

When he reached the turn, he moved to the opposite side of the street, turned around and saw that Sonya was about him on the same road, and not noticing anything. When he reached the turn, she just turned on the same street. He went after him, his eyes fixed on the opposite sidewalk; fifty paces, turned the other way, which was Sonia, caught up with her and followed her, staying in five steps distance.

He was a man of fifty, above average, portly, with broad shoulders and steep, which gave him some stooping.He was smartly dressed and comfortable and looked stout gentleman. In his hand was a beautiful walking stick, which he tapped with every step on the sidewalk, and his hands were fresh gloves. Wide, skulistoe his face was very nice, and the complexion was fresh, not St. Petersburg. His hair is still very thick, very bright and slightly graying did, and broad, thick beard, going down with a shovel, even lighter than the hair. His eyes were blue and looked coldly, intently and thoughtfully; red lips. In fact, it was well-preserved man, and seemed much younger than his years.

When Sonia went into the ditch, they were alone on the sidewalk. Watching her, he saw his reverie and distraction. When he reached his house, Sonia turned to the gate, he was behind her, as if a little surprised.Going into the yard, she took a right into the corner, where there was a ladder in his apartment. "Bah!" - Unknown gentleman muttered and started to rise after shagov. Tolko then Sonya noticed him. She went to the third floor, he turned to the gallery and named the ninth cipher, the doors of which were written in chalk. "Capernaum tailor" "Bah!" - Repeat again the stranger, surprised by a strange coincidence, and rang the bell next to the eighth numbered. Both doors were six steps from each other.

- Do you have Kapernaumovs stand! - He said, looking at Sonya and laughing. - He told me yesterday to change the vest. And I'm here beside you, Madame Resslih, Gertrude Karlovna. Something!

Sonia looked at him.

- Neighbors - he continued as a particularly fun. - I'm just the third day in the city. Well, good-bye.

Sonia did not answer; The door opened and she got down on her. She felt somehow ashamed, and as if it obrobela ...

Razumikhin way to Porfiry was particularly excited state.

- That, my friend, is nice - he repeated several times - and I'm glad! I'm glad!

"Yes, what you looking forward to?" - He thought Raskolnikov.

- I do not know that you were too old woman put. And ... and ... it's been a long time? That is, how long have you been at it?

"What a naive fool in the end!"

- When? .. - Raskolnikov stopped, remembering - yes, three days before her death, I was at it, I think.However, I do not buy back things go - he went with some haste and take special care of things - in fact I have only once all silver ruble ... because of this damned nonsense yesterday! ..

About delirious he said, particularly impressive.

- Well, yes, yes, yes - and no one knows that hastily agreed Razumikhin - so that's why you are ... then partly hit ... and you know, you and raving about some rings and chains all paid tribute! .. Well, yes, yes ... It is clear, everything is clear.

"Get out! Eck spread, because they have this idea! After this man is crucified to me, and in fact very glad thatexplain why I'm in the ring in delirium memory! Eck was confirmed in all of them! .. "

- And we found you? - He asked aloud.

- Stun, stun - Razumikhin hurry. - That, my friend, a good guy, you see! A little awkwardly, ie he is a man and the secular, but in another way I say awkward. Small smart, intelligent, very stupid, only some special way of thinking ... incredulous, skeptic, cynic ... inflate love, not that high, and a fool ... Well, the old method of the material ... And he knows ... He knows one thing, last year, killing attempted, in which almost all traces have been lost! Really, really, really want to meet you!

- Yes, why so many?

- It's not so much ... you see, lately, it's how you get sick, I often had many of you remember ... Well, he listened and learned ... that you are the legal and finish the course can not in the circumstances, he said: "What a pity!" I came to the conclusion that ... it all together, it's not one thing; Yesterday saw ... You see, Rodia, I tell you something yesterday talked drunk at home ... so I went to my brother, I am afraid that you are not exaggerating, you see ...

- What is it? The fact that I was crazy once considered? Yes, maybe it's true.

He smiled tightly.

- Yes ... yes ... that is, ugh, no! .. Well, all said that I (and something else

here), it's all nonsense, and with a hangover.

- But why are you sorry! How does this to me all tired! - Raskolnikov said with exaggerated irritability. He is, however, partly feigned.

- I know, I know, I know. Be sure I understand. It's embarrassing to say ...

- And if ashamed, and do not say!

Both were silent. Razumikhin was more than delighted and disgusted Raskolnikov felt it. Disturbed him and that Razumikhin're talking about porphyria.

"It is also necessary to sing Lazarus - he thought, turning pale and knocked heart - .. And of course sing Natural nothing will sing enhancement is not not sing No, it is difficult to not have been unnatural again ... Well, yes, there is how to turn ... let's see ... now ... good or not good, I mean? Butterfly on the candle itself flies. My heart was beating, it's not good! .. "

- This gray house - said Razumikhin.

"The most important thing is that he knows or not Porfiry knows I yesterday that the apartment was a witch ... and asked about the blood? In an instant, you need to know, from the first step, as I have come to know in the face, and- on-Th ... although pancake, yes I know! "

- And you know what? - Suddenly he turned to Razumikhin fraudulent smile, - I, brother, today noticed you in the morning in some unusual excitement is? The Truth?

- What's the excitement? In no emotion - Razumikhin shuddered.

- No, brother, it is true it shows. On chair you are sitting now more than ever to sit once at the tip, and all you cramp potyanul.Prygnul no reason, no reason at all. Then anger, and then suddenly a mug like sweet candy, for some reason. Blushed, especially when you were invited to dinner, you blushed terribly.

- Yes I Am; lie! .. Do you mean it?

- What do you, as a schoolboy, Yulish! Fu, hell, he blushed again!

- What do you pig, but then!

- Yes, you know that embarrassment? Romeo! Wait, I'll tell you in some places today, ha ha ha! Here are my mother and have fun ... someone else or ...

- Listen, listen, listen, this is serious, it's ... What, then, damn! - Razumikhin finally lost, turning cold with horror. - What did you tell them? I, brother ... Ugh, how do you pig!

- Just rose spring! And, as it happens to you, if you only knew; Romeo growth of ten inches! Yes, as you washed today, because the nails removed,

eh? When did this happen? Yes, by golly you lipstick! Bend-ka!

- Pig !!!

Raskolnikov laughed, before it's too seemed to restrain himself could not, with a laugh, and went into the apartment Porfiry Petrovich. Togo and had Raskolnikov: the room could hear them laughing and went still laughing in the hallway.

- Not a word here or I'll break your ...! - Whispered fiercely Razumikhin, seizing Raskolnikov by the shoulder.

≪ CHAPTER V ≫

He entered the room. He entered with a look as if all his strength to resist the then sprinkle with laughter. Behind him, with a completely unbalanced and a ferocious face, red as a peony, lanky and awkward, entered Razumihina ashamed. His face and whole figure really were ridiculous at this point and justified Raskolnikova.Raskolnikov laugh, have not yet submitted, bowed in the middle of the room and looked at them questioningly held hands and shook his hand still visibly extraordinary efforts to suppress their fun and, at as at least two or three words to say, introduced himself. But as soon as he could cause serious look and muttered something - suddenly, as if involuntarily, glanced again at Razumikhin, and then, unable to bear: suppressed laughter broke restless, stronger even sderzhivaetsya.Chrezvychayny brutality with which took the "sincere" Razumihina laughter gave the whole scene sincerest form of entertainment and, most importantly, of course. Razumikhin, as luck would have even helped the cause.

- Ugh, damn! - He shouted, waving his hand, and just hit it on a small round table on which stood dopit cup of tea. All flew and rattled.

- Why should something break chairs, gentlemen, the Treasury after the loss! - Fun cried Porfiry Petrovich.

The scene is as follows: Raskolnikov dosmeivalsya, forgetting his hand, the owner of the hands, but knowing the measure, waited a moment, as soon as possible, and natural tsvet.Razumihin, embarrassed, finally delete the table and broke a glass, darkly looked into pieces and spat turned sharply to the window, where he stood with his back to the audience, with terrible frowning face, looking out the window and seeing nothing. Porfiry

Petrovitch laughed and wanted to laugh, but it was obvious that he wanted an explanation. In the corner sat on a chair notice stood at the entrance of guests and stood waiting, but a smile in his mouth, but bewildered and even seemed not to trust, looking at the whole scene, and Raskolnikov even with some unexpected presence confusion.The Zametova Raskolnikov unpleasantly surprised.

"We need to understand!" - He thought.

- Excuse me - he said, strongly zakonfuzivshis - Raskolnikov ...

- Really, really pleased with, and you are so well incorporated ... Well, he certainly did not want to say hello? - Nodded Porfiry Petrovitch on Razumikhin.

- Honestly, I do not know what he was mad at me. I told him just the way he looks like Romeo and .. and proves nothing else, it seems, was not.

- Pig! - He said, without turning around, Razumikhin.

- For very good reasons were in one word so angry - Porfiry laughed.

- Well, you! Investigator! .. Well, to hell with you all! - Razumikhin snapped, and he suddenly laughed, with a cheerful face, as if nothing had happened, went to Porfiry Petrovich.

- Saturday! All fools; to the point: here buddy Romanovich Raskolnikov, first heard and wanted to know, and secondly, the small business has little to you. Bah!Please note: You are how? Do you think you know? For a long time, it was decided not it?

"What is it!" - Aspiring thought Raskolnikov.

Notice how if zakonfuzilsya, but not much.

- Yesterday you met the same - he said casually.

- So, God delivered from loss: last week asked me terribly, something you Porphyry, introduced himself, and you without me snorting ... Where you have tobacco?

Porfiry Petrovich was at home in a bathrobe, in a very clean underwear and worn shoes. He was a man of about thirty-five years, growth is below average, and even with a full stomach, shaven, no mustache and sideburns, with a tight shaved hair on the big round head, as a particularly convex rounded on the back, thick, round and slightly snub face was the color of the patient, dark yellow and cheerful and even mocking. It would even be good-natured, if not prevent expression of the eyes, with some liquid watery sheen covered almost white, blinking, winking, who exactly, eyelashes. Sight these eyes strangely not in harmony with the whole figure, which had even

something Indian, and gave her something much more serious than at first glance might be expected of him.

Porfiry Petrovitch, when I heard that the guest must his "small business", immediately asked him to sit on the sofa, he sat down at the other end and stared at a party in anticipation of immediate business presentation, with the power and too serious attention that even the hardships and uncomfortable for the first time, especially because of their ignorance, and especially if what you set out on your own do you think, is not in proportion with the extremely important to provide you with information. But Raskolnikov in the short and related words, clearly and accurately explain it to his business and was pleased with himself, so that even had a pretty good view of porphyria. Porfiry Petrovitch also never brought with him in the eye all the time.Razumikhin, place, on the contrary, at the same table, hot and curiously watched the presentation of the case, constantly moving his eyes from that to the other and back again, which is already a bit out of the measurements.

"Fool!" - Cursed himself Raskolnikov.

- You need to place your ad in the police - from a business perspective Porfiry replied - so what, news of a certain incident, that is, about this murder, you ask, in turn, notifies the investigator instructed fact that such and such and such things belong to you, and what you want to buy them ... or there ... yes, you are, nevertheless, write.

- That's what I have at the moment - as much as possible tried zakonfuzitsya Raskolnikov - not really about the money ... and even a little thing ... I can not, you see, now I want to say is that these things are mine, but when will the money ...

- It's like, sir, - answered Porfiry Petrovitch, taking cold clarification about finances - and, indeed, you can chat and if you want to write to me, in the same sense that here the news that such and such announcing my stuff , you are welcome ...

- It's on plain paper? - Raskolnikov hastened to interrupt again interested in the financial part of the business.

- Oh, sorry to! - And suddenly Porfiry Petrovich somehow clearly mocking, looked at him with narrowed eyes, as if he winked. However, this may be the only way seemed to Raskolnikov, because it lasted a moment. At least that's something. Raskolnikov would have sworn he winked at him, God knows why.

"You know!" - This lightning.

- Sorry to bother with such trifles, - he continued, several huddling - things only my five rubles, but they are especially dear to me as the memory of those who have gone on, and I confess that I had learned very scary. ..

- That's how you flew yesterday when I blurted Zosimov that Porphyry mortgagors surveys! - Thread Razumikhin, with obvious intent.

It was already unbearable. Raskolnikov could not stand it and glared at him burned black anger with their eyes. And immediately came to his senses.

- You, my friend, it seems to laugh at me? - He said to him, deftly deal with irritation. - I agree that it may already be too concerned about the kind of thing before your eyes, but you can not take me for it either selfish or greedy, and, in my opinion, these two worthless trinkets may not be trash. I told you that the silver watch, which cost nothing, the only thing left after his father. I laugh, but my mother came - he suddenly turned to Porfiry - and if she knew - he turned away again as quickly as possible to Razumikhin, trying especially voice trembled, - that this watch is missing, then I swear, it will be in despair ! Women!

- Yes, do not! I'm not in the sense ,! I'm exactly the opposite! - Shouted distressed Razumikhin.

"It's good of course, you do not exaggerate? -? The thrill of Raskolnikov himself. - Why is said," women "?"

- Mother came to you? - Ask for anything Porfiry Petrovich.

- Yes I Am.

- When it is, sir?

- Last night.

Porfiry paused, as if considering.

- Things your way and could not gulf - calm and cool he continued. - Because I have long been waiting for you here.

And, as if nothing had happened, he began to carefully expose the ashtray Razumikhin ruthlessly sorivshemu cigarette on the carpet. Raskolnikov shuddered, but Porfiry seemed to be looking up, remains concerned Razumihina cigarettes.

- What? Waiting! Yeah, you know, that he there laid? - Razumikhin shouted.

Porfiry Petrovitch addressed directly to Raskolnikov:

- Your two things ring and watch were in it under a piece of paper in the box on a piece of paper your name clearly marked in pencil, as well as the

number of months when she got them from you ...

- As you are so observant? .. - Awkward smile was Raskolnikov, especially trying to look him straight in the eye; but I could not resist, and suddenly said: - I notice now, because that probably had a lot of mortgagors ... so you would be hard to remember them all ... But you, on the contrary, they are all well and remember .. . and ...

"Stupid! Bad! Why did I receive!"

- And almost all mortgagors now I know, because you're only one, and not satisfied Welcome - Porfiry replied with a barely perceptible shadow of ridicule.

- I'm not very well.

- Have you heard about this, sir. Even heard that, too, were very upset about something. Now you seem pale?

- Not at all pale ... on the contrary, very good! - Roughly snapped angrily and Raskolnikov suddenly changed his tone. Malice in it boils, and he could not suppress it. "And in anger and said something! - Flashed it again. - And why do they torment me! .."

- This is not cool! - Razumikhin took. - Avon breccia! Until yesterday, almost delirious with no memory ... Well, I do not believe he barely on his feet, and Porphyry only when we, I Zosimov yes, yesterday turned away - got dressed and ran quietly and do not play tricks somewhere almost not until midnight, and completely, I tell you, delirium, you can imagine! Wonderful event!

- And it's completely delusional ? Please tell me! - With the gesture of a woman in Porfiry shook his head.

- Uh, I do not believe nonsense! And yet, because you do not believe it! - Too bad escaped from Raskolnikov.But Porfiry Petrovitch did not seem to hear these strange words.

- But how could you leave, if not delirious? - Razumikhin suddenly excited. - How is it going? For what? .. And why secretly? Well, whether or not in the usual sense for you then? Now that all danger has passed, I'm just saying!

- I'm tired of this, I yesterday - Raskolnikov turned to Porfiry with a cheeky grin calling - I was running away from them, to hire an apartment, so that they will not find me, and a lot of money with him in captivity. Mr. Vaughn Zametov saw some money. And that, Mr. noticed clever I was yesterday Ali delirious allow minute argument?

He seems to be strangled, and at this point Zametova. Too eyes, and he

did not want to silence.

- I think you said it is not unreasonable, and even irritable were only clever, too, - said dryly.

- And today I spoke Nicodemus Fomich - Porfiry Petrovitch drunk - I met you yesterday, it is very late, in one apartment, crushed horses, officials ...

- Well, at least it official! - Razumikhin took - well, not crazy, if you were an official? Last money for the funeral the widow to give away! Well, he wanted to help - give fifteen to twenty, well at least three rubles afford to leave, and then all twenty-five and rolled!

- Maybe I'm somewhere treasure found, but you do not know? Here I am yesterday and become generous ... Mr. Wong Zametov knows that I have found a treasure! .. Excuse me - he said with trembling lips to Porphyry - that we have such a trifling bust half an hour to worry about. Tired of reality, is not it?

- Excuse me, sir, on the contrary, with one mind! If you knew how you interest me! Curious and watch and listen ... and I must confess I am very happy that you were happy to finally welcome ...

- Yes, even though some tea! Dry throat! - Razumikhin exclaimed.

- Great idea! Maybe all of us do. And if you do not want to ... more essential before tea, then?

- Get Out!

Porfiry Petrovitch went to order some tea.

Thoughts swirled like a whirlwind in my head Raskolnikov. He was terribly annoyed.

"The main thing is not even hidden, and do not want to stand on ceremony! And the fact that this event, since I do not know what you're talking about me with Nicodemus Fomich? So, I really do not want to hide that follows me, like a pack of dogs so frankly in the face and do not care - he was shaking with rage. -. Well, hit directly, but did not play like a cat with a mouse is not polite, Porfiry Petrovich, because I maybe not-!. . Let C stand up and bryaknu all in your face the whole truth, and see how I despise you! .. - He struggled to breath. - What if I just think that if it's a mirage, and I? I am in all not so inexperience angry, mean, my role is not able to stand? Maybe this is all without any intention? All words their ordinary, but something about them ... It is always possible to tell, but there is something. Why did he just said , "from her" Why Zametov added that I slyly saying? Why do they say that tone? Yes ... tone ... Razumikhin sat there, why does not he

do it? It's an innocent fool nothing ever seems! Again fever! .. Winked at me this morning Porphyry or not? It is true, light-headedness; Why wink? Nerves, and wanted to annoy my Ali tease me? Or is it a mirage, or know! .. not even notice the bold courage ... if you noticed? Zametov changed his mind overnight. I had a feeling that will change his mind! This, for the first time. Porphyry his guest did not believe him, sitting in the opposite direction. Snort! Of course because of me snorting! Of course, before we talk about me! .. Do they know about the apartment, then? Fast too! .. When I told that to hire an apartment yesterday escaped, he missed not rise ...

Deftly about this apartment I screwed up: it is useful! .. In his delirium, he says! .. Ha ha ha! We are talking about the whole evening yesterday knows! On the arrival of the mother do not know! .. And the witch and the number registered on the pencil! Lying .. not damsya! In the end, it's not a fact, it is only a mirage! No, you let the facts! And the apartment is not a fact, and delirium; I know what they say ... They know about the apartment, then? Do not go, do not know! Why did I come from? And that's what I'm angry, so this is probably a fact! Ugh, I'm irritable! And maybe it's good; painful role ... He touches me. Will shoot down.Why did I come from? "

All this, as lightning flashed in my head.

Porfiry Petrovitch returned immediately. He suddenly somehow cheered.

- I have a brother, his head since yesterday ... And all that I somehow unscrew, - he said quite a different tone, laughing, to Razumikhin.

- And what was interesting? I was the last time you the most interesting place down? Who won?

- Yes, no, of course. The eternal questions slipped on vozduseh soared.

- Imagine Rodia that came out yesterday: whether a crime? He said that as hell Dovran!

- Well, is it surprising? The average social problem - Raskolnikov said absently.

- The question was not worded - said Porphyry.

- Not really, it's true - immediately agreed Razumikhin, and slowly getting heated as usual. - You see, Rodion: listen and tell me your opinion. I want to. I got out of the skin with them yesterday and is waiting for you; I told them about you, that you came ... It all started with the opinion of the Socialists. Known species: the crime is a protest against the abnormality of the social order - and only, and nothing else, and there is no reason no longer be allowed - and nothing else! ..

- Here lied! - Cried Porfiry Petrovich. He seemed animated and laughing, looking at Razumikhin, even more than it burned.

- N-nothing is not allowed! - Razumikhin impatiently - I'm not lying! .. I'll show you theirs books: they do not have, because "Wednesday devoured" - and nothing else! My favorite phrase! This immediately implies that if the company normally arrange the time and all the crimes disappear, as it is not something that will protest, and all in an instant become righteous. Nature does not take into account the nature of the cast, nature does not depend on! They did not have humanity, to develop historical, alive to the end in itself, finally turn into normal society, but on the contrary, the social system, coming out of some mathematical head, immediately and arrange all of humanity, and currently do his righteous and sinless before any living process, without any historical and alive! That is why they are so instinctively and do not like the story, "Some of the ugliness in his folly yes" - and all odnoyu only be explained by stupidity! Because he did not want to live the life process: it is not necessary living soul ! Live the life of the soul will require living soul is subject to the mechanics, the living soul is suspicious, the living soul is retrograde! And here, although mertvechinkoy pripahivaet, tires can be done - but not alive, but without the will, but the slave does not become! And it turns out, as a result of the fact that all but one of brickwork as the location of corridors and rooms in the phalanstery reduced! Phalanx something and ready, but the nature of what you should phalansteries not ready yet, life wants life process is not yet complete, early in the cemetery! One through discrete nature can not jump! Logic to predict the three cases and their millions! Cut all the million and one questions all about comfort reduced! The easiest solution to the problem! It is tempting to clear, and I think not! The main thing - to think not! The whole secret of life on two printed pages in the form!

- What to do if you have broken the drums! Hands should be kept, - Porfiry laughed. - Imagine - he turned to Raskolnikov - this is the same yesterday, in one room, six votes, and even pre-watered punch - can you imagine? No, brother, you're lying, "environment" means much of the crime; I say to you, which is confirmed.

- And I know myself that much, but that's what you say, forty dishonors ten-year girl - Wednesday, but he made it?

- And then, it is in the strict sense, perhaps, the environment - with surprisingly noticed the importance of porphyria - a crime against women is

very, very possible to "average" to explain.

Razumikhin little crazy not come.

- Well, I want you now withdrawn - he shouted - that you have white eye-lashes solely because only that Ivan the Great thirty-five fathoms high, and bring clear, precise, progressive and even with a liberal tinge? Dare!Well, you want to bet!

- I agree! Let's listen, please, bring it!

- Why, all pretending to hell! - Razumikhin shouted, jumped up and waved. - Well, is it worth to talk to you!In the end, it's all on purpose, do not you know it, Rodion! Yesterday I took them away, just to fool everyone. And what he said yesterday, my God! And they were glad something to him! .. After two weeks, so it's worth.Last year, assured us, for what is a monk: two months stood his ground! Recently even think, to ensure that he will get married, so that everything is ready for the crown. Even sewed a new dress. We really began to congratulate him.Neither bride, nothing happens: all a mirage!

- And here lied! I sewed a dress before. Me about a new dress and head all podnadut.

- Actually, you're such a prude? - Casually asked Raskolnikov.

- And you thought, no? Wait, I'll keep you - ha ha ha! No, you see, sir, I'll tell you the whole truth. On all these issues, crime, environment, girl, I remember now - and, indeed, has always interested me, - one of your little article: "On crime" .. or how you got there, I forgot the name, I do not remember , two months ago, had the pleasure in "Periodic Speech" reading.

- My article? In the "Periodic Speech"? - I was surprised Raskolnikov asked - I actually wrote six months ago, when the University was released on a book, an article, but I blew it, the newspaper "Weekly speech," not "periodic" .

- And hit the "periodic".

- Why, "Weekly speech" has ceased to exist, because if not printed ...

- That's right, sir; but ceases to exist, "Weekly speech" merged with "peri-odic speech", and therefore your article, two months ago, appeared in the "Periodic Table of the word." Do not you know?

Raskolnikov really knew nothing.

- I'm sorry, yes, you can with the money they are asking for the article! Which, however, have the character!Live in seclusion, so that such things for yourself are not only knows. It is a fact, sir.

- Bravo, Rodka! And I do not know! - Razumikhin exclaimed. - Today, the race to the reading room and numbered to ask! Two months ago? How many? Still'll find! Here's the thing! And do not say!

- And how do you know that my article? She signed the letter.

- At random, and then a few days ago. Through the editor; I know ... very interesting.

- I have seen, as I recall, the psychological state of the perpetrator during the course of the crime.

- Yes, sir, and insist that the act of execution of a crime is always accompanied by illness. Very, very original, but ... I have not actually this part of your Wikipedia interesting, and some thought, missed the end of the article, but unfortunately you spend just a hint, it is not clear ... In general, if you remember, Spend some hint of what is in the world, if some of these people who can ... This is not something that can, and have every right to do all kinds of crimes and offenses, and that for them, even though the law not written.

Raskolnikov smiled gain and deliberate distortion of his ideas.

- How? What's this? The right to a crime? But not because "eaten environment"? - What is even asked Razumikhin fear.

- No, no, not really, because - said Porphyry. - The fact that they are even in all humans article once divided into "ordinary" and "extraordinary". Ordinary must live in obedience and have no right to overstep the law, because they, you know, the usual. Extraordinary and have the right to do all sorts of crimes and otherwise break the law, in fact, because they extremely.So you think if I'm not mistaken?

- How do you? Can not be wrong! - Razumikhin muttered in disbelief.

Raskolnikov smiled again. He immediately realized what was happening and what he wants to correct; he remembered his article. He decided to accept the challenge.

- It is not so with me - simply and modestly he said. - However, I must confess, you will almost certainly said, even if you want, and it's true ... (It was just nice to agree that correctly). The only difference is that I do not insist that extraordinary people necessarily and always had to create all kinds of havoc, as you say. I even think that such an article in the press is not to be missed. I just simply hinted that the "extraordinary" man has the right ... that is not an official right, and he has the right to allow their conscience to go ... other obstacles, and is unique in that only when the execution of his ideas (sometimes saving, perhaps, for all mankind) required. You are pleased to

say that my article is unclear; I am ready to explain to you if possible. I can not make a mistake, assuming that you think about and want; if you please, sir. In my opinion, if the Keplerian and Newtonian discovery of the fact that some combination in no way could be known only to people with the donation of the life of one, ten, a hundred, and so on man, it would be advisable to open or on the way to becoming obstacle, Newton would have been entitled, and even would be obliged ... to eliminate these ten or a hundred people, to make known his discoveries to all mankind. From this, however, does not mean that Newton had the right to kill anyone pleases, counterclaims and cross, or stolen every day in the market. Next, remember me, I develop in my article that all ... well, for example, although legislators and installers of mankind, starting with the oldest, continuing Lycurgus, Solon, Mahomet, Napoleon, and so on, each of the criminals were already one that giving the new law, thereby violating ancient, sacred society and fathers who went, and, of course, did not stop in front of the blood, if the blood (sometimes quite innocent and shed stand behind the ancient law) could help them. It is noteworthy that even that most of these benefactors and installers of mankind were especially terrible krovoprolivtsy. In short, I conclude that all is not so great, but a bit of a rut people go, that is a little even able to say something new, it is necessary, by its very nature, do not forget to criminals - more or less, of the Of Course. Otherwise, it is difficult to get out of their rut and stay in a rut of course they can not agree, again, by their nature, and in my opinion, but still must agree. In short, you see, so far there is nothing particularly new. It is a thousand times was published and read. As for my dividing people into ordinary and extraordinary, I agree that it is somewhat arbitrary, but I have also exact figures do not insist. I only believe in my main idea. She just lies in the fact that the people according to the law of nature, divided generally into two categories: on the lower (common), that is, so to speak, on the material serving only for the birth of a kind, and real people, that is, having a gift or talent, said Wednesday its new word. Division here, of course, endless, but the distinctive features of both discharges rather sharp: the first category, that is material, in general, people are inherently conservative, stately in obedience and love to be obedient. In my opinion, they should be obedient, because it is their purpose, and has no relation to their humiliating. The second category all transgress the law, destroyers or inclined, in accordance with their abilities. Crimes of these people, of course, is relative, and diversity; Most of them require a wide range of applications,

the destruction in the name of better. But if he wants, for his ideas go beyond, even if the body through the bloodstream, it is within you, in all conscience, can, in my opinion, give yourself permission to step over blood - depending, however, on the idea and its size - this note. Only in this sense, I say in my article of their right to a crime. (You remember, we actually started a legal problem). Nevertheless, there is nothing much to worry: the mass is almost never recognized them this right, executes them and hangs up (more or less), and therefore rightly takes a conservative on his appointment, in order, but then, that the next generation , the same weight puts executed on a pedestal and worship them (more or less). The first digit is always - this gentleman, the second level - the future of the Lord. First keep the peace and multiply it numerically; The second move the world and bring it to the goal. And they both have exactly the same right to suschestvovanie.Koroche speaking, I have every right to be equivalent and - Vive la guerre Ã © ternelle, 1 --do New Jerusalem, of course!

- So you still believe the same in the New Jerusalem?

- I believe - Raskolnikov answered firmly; Having said this, and continued throughout his long tirade, he looked at the ground, choosing a place on the carpet.

- A-ah believe in God? Sorry, that so curious.

- I believe - Raskolnikov repeated, looking at Porfiry.

- And, in the resurrection of Lazarus believe?

- Be-believe. Why do you need it?

- Just Believe?

- Literally.

- That's something ... so curious. Excuse me, sir. But let me - contact daveshny - because they are not always the same sentence; in front of each other ...

- Holidays in life? Oh yes, others achieve in life, and then ...

- Themselves begin to execute?

- If you need to, you know, even the best part. In general your witty.

- Thank you, sir. But I will tell you that what would distinguish these extraordinary something from the ordinary? At birth, but the signs are there? I am in the sense that it must be Pobol accuracy, so to speak, on the outside of certainty: I'm sorry that I natural concern practical and well-intentioned people, but if there's clothes, for example, a particular brand, wear anything, the stigma that there if anything? .. Because, you see, if

there is confusion and isolation from one imagines that he belongs to a different category, and start "to remove all obstacles," as you put it quite happily, right here ...

- Oh, this is very often the case! This observation is not even wittier your daveshny ..

- Thank U, ..

- No, sir; but bear in mind that this is only possible error in the part of the first category, that is "normal" people (as I can be very unsuccessfully, to call them). Despite the innate tendency to obedience, by some playfulness of nature, which is not denied even a cow, many of them like to imagine themselves progressive people, "Destroyer" and get into the "new word", and it is quite frankly, sir, really like new they at the same time very often overlooked and even despised as backward and demeaning thinking people. But, in my opinion, may be a significant risk, and you are right, do not worry, because they are never far from this step.For passion, of course, sometimes they can be a whip, to remind them of their place, but no more; and here the artist does not even they themselves posekut, because it is very well behaved; Another one another to provide this service, while others do personally ... Repentance various government hereby impose itself - is good and instructive, in a word, nothing to worry about you ... Such a law is.

- Well, at least from this side, you calmed me even more; But then, again, the problem with: Please tell me how many of these people who have something else to cut right to have "something unusual" it? I, of course, ready to bow down, but agree that badly, sir, if you are really a lot, huh?

- Oh, do not worry, in this - in the same tone Raskolnikov went on. - In general, people with new ideas, even slightly only able to say something new, surprisingly little is born, even strange. What is clear is that the order of birth of people, all these bits and blocks have to be very true and accurately determined by some law of nature. This law, of course, now unknown, but I believe that he exists and can later become known. A huge mass of people, material, for it exists only in the world, finally after some effort, some mysterious yet the process, any intersection of genera and species, as well as produce ponatuzhitsya, finally born, well, at least one of the thousands of although any independent person, even with greater independence comes, maybe one in ten thousand (I'm talking about, of course). Even more broadly - from hundred thousand. Geniuses - million, and the great geniuses, terminators humanity - perhaps after many thousands of millions of people on

earth. In short, the retort in which all this is happening, I was not looking. But, of course, there are certain legal and should be; there can not be so.

- What are you two kidding, are not you? - Razumikhin cried in the end. - You are a fool with each other or not? Sit and make fun of each other! Are you serious, Rodia?

Raskolnikov silently raised his pale and almost sad face and said nothing. And the country seemed to Razumikhin, next to the quiet and sad face, not hiding, compulsive, irritability and impolite sarcasm porphyria.

- Well, brother, if indeed it is serious, then ... You're right, of course, saying that this is not new, and, as we all do a thousand times read and heard; but what really original in all this - and indeed belongs to you, to my horror - is that still blood on his conscience permitted, and, excuse me, with such fanaticism ... It had to be, and most important of your article. After this authorization blood on my conscience, it's ... it's, in my opinion, worse than the official permission to shed blood, legal ...

- It's true - it's awful, sir, - said Porphyry.

- No, you somehow got carried away! There is a bug. I read this ... You got carried away! You may not think so ... I'll read it.

- In the article, there is only hints - said Raskolnikov.

- So, with the so - not to sit Porphyria - I almost became clear, now that you have deigned to look at the offense, sir, but ... excuse me for my young (bother you very, very ashamed!) - You see, with you calmed me this morning with a very wrong about the case of mixing the two bits, but ... I have all the different cases are almost no longer worry about! Well, like any other husband, Ali, a young man imagines that he Lycurgus Ali Mohammed ... - the future, of course - and let's eliminate all obstacles to ... We must, he says, far from hiking and trekking need money ... and start making their campaign to ... you know?

Zametov suddenly snorted from his corner. Raskolnikov even eye on him will be charged.

- I agree - he replied calmly, - that such cases should really be. It is foolish and vain particularly caught the bait, young people in particular.

- You see, sir. Well, how is it?

- And in the same way - Raskolnikov smiled - I am not guilty. So there is and always will be. Here he is (he nodded at Razumikhin) now say that I let the blood. So what? Society because too reference, prisons, forensic investigators, prison - that worry? And look for the thief! ..

ROBOTS READ

- Well, syschem?

- There he and the road.

- You still logical. Well, what about his conscience, then?

- Yes, you matter to him?

- Yes, it is, in humanity, sir.

- Who has it, he suffered because realizes the error. This proposal he - OPRICH prison.

- Well, do something brilliant - Frowning, Razumikhin asked - are the ones who cut right given the fact it does not have to suffer all, even the blood shed?

- Why is the word: be? There is no permission or prohibition. Let suffers if the victim is a pity ... pain and suffering is always required for a broad mind and a deep heart. Truly great people, I think, should feel a great sadness in the world - he added thoughtfully, suddenly, not even in the tone of the conversation.

He looked and looked wistfully at all, smiled, and took his cap. He was too quiet compared to how came this morning and felt it. Everyone stood up.

- Well, scold me or not, do not be angry, but I can not resist - concluded again Porfiry Petrovitch - (! Very much I bother you, sir) let another question for one, just a little, little idea how to miss, but do not forget, ... that

- Well, tell your little idea - a serious and pale, stood before him in anticipation of Raskolnikov.

- We are talking about ... do not really know exactly how to put it ... a little idea too ... igrivenkaya psychological and with ... In the end, here, sir, when you are short article is, - - this, of course, can not be that, hehe! that you do not think, well, at least on a drop - the same people "extraordinary" and say a new word -that is, in your terms, with ... That's right, sir?

- It may be - Raskolnikov answered contemptuously.

Razumikhin took a step.

- If so, sir, of course, you would choose - well, there is due to the fact that some of the failures of life and limit or spospeshestvovaniya something about chelovechestvu-- step hurdle, then? .. Well, for example, to kill rob? ..

And again he suddenly winked his left eye and chuckled - a hair's breadth, as this morning.

- If I went again, and then, of course, would not you say - with a defiant, arrogant contempt answered Raskolnikov.

- No, sir, it's just I'm so interested in this, in fact, to educate his articles

in the literature only in one respect, with ...

"Ugh, it's clear and obvious!" - Aversion thought Raskolnikov.

- Allow you to notice - he replied dryly, - Mohammed Ile Napoleon I do not consider myself ... or anyone else from such persons, investigation, and I can not, without being in, to give you a satisfactory explanation of how I would did.

- Well, the fullness of who we have in Russia by Napoleon himself did not believe? - Familiarity with fear suddenly said Porphyry. Even in the tone of his voice this time something really particularly clear.

- Napoleon I do not have a future, and our Alyona Ivanovna last week with an ax to kill? - Blurted suddenly noticed out of the corner.

Raskolnikov was silent, looking firmly looking at Porfiry. Razumikhin frowned darkly. He was also the first, as if something seems. He looked around. Observed a minute of silence in dark.Raskolnikov turned to leave.

- You go! - Porphyry said softly, very kindly extended his hand. - Very, very glad to meet you. And about your request and have no doubts. So still and write, as I said you.Yes, it is better to go there yourself to me ... one of these days ... but at least tomorrow. I'll be there at 11:00 am So, I guess. And to arrange everything ... talk ... You're like one of the last, there is the former, it may be something we could say ... - he added with a good-natured appearance.

- You want me to formally interrogate, with the whole situation? - Very Raskolnikov asked.

- Why is that? While this is not required. You got it wrong. You see, I do not miss your chance ... and with all mortgagors said ... took testimony from other ... and you, as the last ... Yes, it's way back! - He exclaimed, suddenly something happy - the way of thought, well, that's me! .. - He turned to Razumikhin - because that's what you're asking me if Nikolashka promozolil ears ... well, because he and I know, I know myself - he turned to Raskolnikov, - the guy is clean, why, what can I do, and Mitya had a problem here .. here's the thing, sir, that you are in: then passing the stairs. .. Let me because you were at 8:00, sir?

- In the eighth, - said Raskolnikov, an uncomfortable feeling in the moment that it could not speak.

- So passing something at 8:00, with a ladder, and then does not see, but yes, in the second floor of the apartment otvorennoy - remember? - Two members or at least one? They wrote it, did not notice? It's very, very

important to them! ..

- Dyers? No, have not seen ... - slowly, as if rummaging in his memoirs said Raskolnikov, at the same time, straining every creature and flour out of breath, to realize that it was a trap, and will not see that? - No, not seen, and apartments are unlocked, you did not notice ... but on the fourth floor (it is quite mastered the trap and the Arc) - so be sure to officially moved out of the apartment opposite Alyona Ivanovna ... I remember ... ... I remember ... the soldiers ordered some sofa and pressed me against the wall ... and dyes - no, I do not remember that the dyes were ... and the apartment was locked Nowhere, it seems, was not. Yes I Am; was not ...

- What do you mean the same thing! - Razumikhin shouted suddenly, as if coming to his senses and understanding - why, dyes smeared on the day of the murder, and after three days he was there? What are you asking for?

- Fu! shuffled! - Slapped his forehead porphyria. - Gosh, I have this thing for the mind comes to mind! - He said, as if even apologizing to Raskolnikov, - because we have, so it is important to know if anyone has not seen them on the eighth hour of something in the apartment, then I imagine that you, too, might say. .. pretty confused!

- So we have to be careful - Razumikhin said grimly.

The last words were uttered in the front. Porfiry Petrovitch accompanied them to the door very kindly. And went dark and gloomy outside and a few steps away, without saying a word. Raskolnikov deep breath ...

←«»→

⇜ CHAPTER VI ⇝

- ... I do not believe in that! I can not believe it! - Puzzled Razumikhin repeated, trying by all means to refute the arguments of Raskolnikov. They came to ciphers Bakaleeva, where Pulcheria Alexandrovna and Dunya awaited them. Razumikhin constantly stopped on the way in the heat of conversation, confused and concerned about the fact that they first talked about it clearly.

- Do not believe! - Raskolnikov replied cold and careless smile - you, as usual, did not notice anything, and I weigh every word.

- You suspect because weighed and ... um ... really, I agree, the tone was rather strange porphyria, moreover, that scoundrel comment! .. You are right that it was - but why? How Come?

- At night, he changed his mind.

- But, in contrast, on the contrary! If they had this brainless idea why they would try its best to hide and disguise their cards to then catch ... And now - it is blatantly and carelessly!

- If they had the facts, that is, the real facts, or anything like that reasonable suspicion, they really tried to hide the game: in the hope of winning more (and, indeed, for a long time to really find did!). But they have no facts, no one - all a mirage, all with two ends, one idea fly - so they are trying to bring down a peg. Or maybe he ozlilsya, that no facts broke.Or irritation may be that it is the intention of man ... He seems smart ... maybe scare me like he knows ... That, my friend, his psychology ... And yet, it is disgusting to explain everything.Leave!

- And the offensive, insulting! I understand you! But ... as we now speak

clearly (and it's great that finally spoke clearly, I'm glad!) - Then, of course, I'm telling you now admit that have long noticed that the idea for all this time, of course, a little chutoshnom formed only in the creeping, but for some reason, although creeping! How dare they? Where, where these roots are hidden?If you only knew how much I was furious! As due to the fact that a poor student, mutilated poverty and hypochondria, on the eve of a cruel disease with delusions, already, maybe it starts in (note imagine!), Hypochondriac, proud, knows his worth, and six months in his corner more than one species, in rags and boots without soles - not encountered some kvartashkami and tolerate their abuse; and then suddenly owe nose, overdue bill with the court counselor Chebarovym, rotten paint, thirty degrees Reaumur, stale air, a lot of people, the story of the murder of a man who had been the day before, and all this - on an empty stomach! Yes, how can we not fainted! And this is what all to ground! Damn It! I understand that it is annoying, but in your place, Rodka, I would have laughed all in the eye, or better: on the PLE-shaft would be all up in your face, but thicker, but scattered in all aspects of a couple of dozen splash deftly as they always have to give, but those would have committed suicide. Do not care! Stay strong! It's a shame!

"He, however, it is well thought out," - thought Raskolnikov.

- I do not care? And tomorrow, again questioning! - With bitterness he said - I do with them in explaining the magazine? I and what a pity that yesterday I leaned in a tavern Zametova ...

- Damn it! I will go myself to Porphyry! And so I compress it to a relative ; Allow me to explain everything to the roots! And Zametova ...

"Finally, I guessed!" - The thought Raskolnikov.

- Stop! - Razumikhin shouted, grabbing him by the shoulder suddenly - stop! You lied! I managed: You lied! Well, what's the catch? You say that the question of the workers was to catch See through: Well, if it is you did, could you only said that he saw a greased flat ... and working? On the contrary, did not see anything, even if he had seen! Whoever confesses against me?

- If I was that it did, it really would be, of course, said that he had seen and workers and an apartment - reluctantly and with obvious disgust continued to answer Raskolnikov.

- Why speak against yourself?

- And because only some of the guys, IL, of course, the most inexperienced novices during interrogations directly and row around the castle. Little do people have developed and tested, of course, and if possible, try to

confess in all external and unavoidable facts; But for some reason it looks to others, such indication exists, especially unexpected and screw, which is a completely different meaning to them and give them to put another light. Porphyry could only expect that I, of course, to answer and so, of course, to say that he had seen the probability and thus screw something to explain ...

- Why, he immediately and you said that two days workers could not be, and that, consequently, it was you in the day of the murder, at 8:00. From scratch and will be shot down!

- Yes, it's when he realized that I did not have time to figure out, and there is reason to believe in a hurry to answer yes and forget that the two days workers could not be.

- But how to forget it?

- Total easier! On such things, then let all the easier to slip and smart people. What a cunning man, the less he suspects that it just shot down.Cunning man is in just need to shoot down.Porphyry not as stupid as you think ...

- Brock, it then!

Raskolnikov could not help but laugh. But at that moment it seemed strange to him by his own animation and hunting, which he said that the latter explanation, while the entire previous conversation, he maintained a sullen disgust, probably because of the goals as needed.

"To get a taste of other items!" - He thought to himself.

But almost at the same moment he somehow suddenly became restless, as if a sudden and alarming thought struck him. Alarming increases.They have already reached the entrance to the numbering Bakaleeva.

- Going one - said Raskolnikov, - I'll be right back.

- Where are you? Yes, we have come too!

- I have to, it is necessary; that ... come on in half an hour ... Tell me there.

- Will it be, I'll follow you!

- Well, you want me to torment! - He exclaimed with a bitter disappointment with such despair in his eyes that Razumihina hands dropped.Several times he stood on the porch and watched grimly as he quickly walked towards his alley. Finally, gritting his teeth and clenching his fists, he immediately promised that today just squeeze Porfiry, like lemon, went upstairs and you're worried their long absence Pulcheria Alexandrovna.

When Raskolnikov went into his house, his temples were soaked, and then he was breathing heavily. He quickly climbed the stairs, entered the unlocked apartment and immediately closes the hook. Then, scary and crazy,

ran to the corner, to the very hole in the wallpaper, which then lay things out and put it in a few minutes carefully searched the hole, going through all the nooks and folds all oboj. Finding nothing, he got up and deep breathing. Going up in the morning to the steps already Bakaleeva, he suddenly imagine that any thing, any chain, cufflinks or even a piece of paper in which they were wrapped, marked hands of an old woman, somehow escape, and then lost in some crack, and then suddenly appear in front of him suddenly and convincing evidence.

He stood as if in thought, and the country is reduced, polubessmyslennaya wandering smile on his lips. He finally took his cap and quietly left the room. His thoughts were confused. Thoughtfully, he came under the gate.

- Yes, it is for yourself! - Shouted in a loud voice; he raised his head.

Janitor stood at the door of his cell and pointed straight at him a little man, with a view similar to the merchant, dressed in something like a coat, vest and looks very similar to a woman in the distance. His head was in a greasy cap, hung, and it was all just bent. Flabby, wrinkled face showed his fifties; small, swollen eyes sullenly, sternly and with displeasure.

- What is it? - Raskolnikov asked, coming up to the janitor.

Bourgeois looked at him askance looked at it closely and carefully, slowly; Then slowly turned and, without saying a word, walked out of the gates of the house on the street.

- Yes it is! - Cried Raskolnikov.

- Yes, it's some asked whether the student lives here, you called, who you live. You went there, I showed and he went. You see, you know.

Janitor, too, was in some perplexity, and not very good, and a little more thought, he turned and went up to my room.

Raskolnikov rushed for tradesman and immediately saw that he was walking down the street, the same smooth and leisurely pace, burying his eyes on the ground, as if pondering something. He soon caught up with him, but for some time walked behind; finally caught up with him and looked him in the face side. He immediately noticed it and looked around, but looked down again, and they went for a moment, one beside the other, and, without saying a word.

- You asked me ... the janitor? - And finally, said Raskolnikov, but somehow very quiet.

Bourgeois gave no answer, and did not even look. Again there was silence.

- What do you have to ask ... ... and be silent ... but what is it? - Voice

Raskolnikov interrupted, and the words you do not want to say clearly.

Bourgeois, this time raised his eyes and sinister, dark eyes looked at Raskolnikov.

- Murderer! - He said, suddenly quiet, but clear and distinct voice ...

Raskolnikov walked beside him. His legs were severely weakened suddenly went cold on the back, and a heart for a moment as if to stop; then suddenly caught just slipped off the hook. And they have gone a hundred paces, and again very close to silence.

Bourgeois did not look at him.

- What are you ... what ... who the killer is? - Raskolnikov muttered under his breath.

- You murderer - he said, still separate and impressive, with a smile, as if some hateful triumph, and looked straight into Raskolnikov's pale face and in his eyes pomertvevshie. And then come to a crossroads.Bourgeois left turn onto the street and went without looking back. Raskolnikov remained on the ground and watched him go. He saw that, having already fifty paces, turned and looked at him, still standing motionless in one place. It was impossible to do, but Raskolnikov seemed that he and this time smiled his hated the cold and triumphant smile.

Quiet, easy step with trembling knees and as if terribly chilled Raskolnikov returned and went back to his room. He took off his cap and put it on the table and stood for ten minutes, without stirring. Then helplessly lying on the couch and painfully, with a weak groan, stretched over it; his eyes were closed. So he lay on the half hour.

He did not think about anything. Thus, there were some thoughts or fragments of thoughts, any ideas, without order and communication - the faces of people he had seen in childhood or somewhere met only once, and for which he would never have remembered; In the bell tower - the first church; snooker in a pub and an officer in the pool, the smell of cigars in some basement tobacco shop, tavern, back stairs, quite dark, all bathed in the mud and covered with egg shell, and from somewhere came the bell tolls ... Sunday objects and replace spinning like a whirlwind. Some even liked, and he clung to them, but they go out and do something hit him, but not by much. Sometimes it was good ... Easy chills did not go through, and it was too good to feel.

He heard hasty steps Razumihina voice, closed his eyes and pretended to be asleep. Razumikhin opened the door and stood for a moment in the

doorway, as if thinking. Then calmly walked into the room and cautiously approached the couch. Nastasia was a whisper:

- Do not Zamay; let sleep; then eat.

- Really, - said Razumikhin.

And the caution came out and closed the door behind him. It took another half hour. Raskolnikov opened his eyes again, and cutting back, twisting his arms behind his head ...

"Who is it? Who is it because of the people of the earth? Where was he and what did I see? He saw it all, no doubt.

Where he then stood and watched from? Why is it only now coming out from under the floor? And as he could see - is this possible? Hmm ... .. - Raskolnikov went on, turning cold and shivering - and then that Nicholas found behind the door: it is also possible? Evidence? One hundred thousandth of a dash in the display - is evidence in the Egyptian pyramids! Fly fly, she saw! Could it be that way? "

And he felt disgust, as he became weak, physically weak.

"I should have known - he thought with a bitter smile - and how dare I, knowing yourself waiting ! herself to take an ax and bloody I should have known in advance ... Uh Oh, I knew in advance ..! "- he whispered in despair.

Sometimes he stayed motionless in front of a kind of thought:

"No, these people are not made, there is a gentleman that everything is permitted, breaking Toulon, makes a massacre in Paris, forget the army in Egypt, spends half a million people in the Moscow campaign and finished pun in Vilna, he at death, putting idols - and consequently, all allowed No such people apparently not body bronze. "!

A sudden extraneous thoughts suddenly almost made him laugh:

"Napoleon, pyramids, Waterloo - and skinny nasty receptionist, an old woman, pawnbroker, red gasket under the bed - well, what it is to digest even if Porfiry Petrovitch .. Where are they digest hurt .. Aesthetics: rise if saith under Napoleon bed in the "old woman" Oh, damn! .. "

Minutes, he felt as if delirious, he fell into a feverish ecstasy.

"The old woman is nonsense - he thought hot and impulsively - old woman, perhaps, that the error in this case and the old woman's disease ... I just wanted to cross the fast ... I killed the man I killed ,! principle! Principle is I kill, and do not cross crossed on this side ... just stay and it managed to kill. And this is not possible, it is ... How it works? What a fool this morning Razumikhin Socialists abused? hardworking people and trade, "the general

happiness "has been ... No, my life is given once, and it will never be more, I do not want to wait for the" universal happiness. "I myself want to live and that it is better not to live. Well, I just do not want to go by a hungry mother, clutching the money in your pocket, waiting for "universal happiness." "carry, say, a building block for the happiness and peace of heart, because I feel" Haha me Why did you miss something, I just live one day, I also want to ... Oh, I aesthetic louse, and nothing more, -.!? he added suddenly laughing like crazy. - Yeah, I really louse - he went on, with malice clung to the thought, rummaging in his game and make fun of him - and, of course, the one that, at first, now argue that I louse;because, second, month, all-good Providence bother calling to witness that is not for you, say, the flesh and the lust to be taken, and therefore, a large and pleasant goal - ha ha! Because, thirdly, that justice can be seen to put in execution, weight and measure, and arithmetic: all lice and chose naibespolezneyshuyu, killing her, put her to take as much as I have for the first step, and neither more nor less (and the rest, and then retired to a monastery, in his will - ha ha) ... Because, because I finally louse - he said, gritting his teeth - because he somehow I can be messy even nastier than killing lice, and advance premonition tell myself that this is afterhow to kill! Do you think that with such horror nothing can compare! Oh, vulgarity! Oh, meanness! .. Oh, I see, "the prophet" with a sword on horseback. Allah commands and obey "tremble" creature! Rights, "the prophet" when placed somewhere on the other side of the street choir-p-roshuyu battery and blowing the innocent and the guilty, not even explain udostoivaya! Observe, trembling creature, and - I do not want , because - not your business! .. Oh, no way, no way will not not forgive an old woman! "

His hair was wetted then shudders lips, eyes fixed on the ceiling.

"Mother, sister, how I loved them! Why now I hate them? Yes, I hate them, I hate myself physically close can not stand ... The other day I went over and kissed his mother, I remember hugging ... and I think if she knew that ... it's time to tell her from me is ... Hmm! It must be the same as me - he added, thinking hard, as if struggling to cover his nonsense -. Oh, how I hate the old woman now seems to kill another time when I woke Poor Lizaveta why she was here .. It's weird, but then, why I'm on this !! almost never think accurately and not kill anyone? .. Lizaveta! Sonia! poor, meek, gentle eyes ... Lovely! .. Why do not they cry? Why do not they moan? .. They give everything ... look meek and quiet ... Sonia, Sonia! Quiet Sonya. . "

He forgot himself; It seemed strange that he does not remember how he

could find himself on the street. It was late in the evening. Deepening twilight full moon shone brighter and brighter; but as something special in the air was stifling. Crowds of people walk the streets; artisans and busy people to go home, while others were; smelled of lime dust, standing water. Raskolnikov sad and worried: he is a very good thing that came out with a plan, which is something to do and to hurry remembered, but that was it - he forgot. Suddenly he stopped and saw that on the other side of the street, on the sidewalk, a man stands and waving. He approached them on the street, and suddenly the man turned and walked away as if nothing had happened, his head down, not looking back and not giving the type that called him. "Come on, it's called?" - Thought Raskolnikov, but the train started to catch up. Short ten steps, he suddenly recognized him and - frightened; it was daveshny tradesman, one robe and just bent. Raskolnikov was published; Stukalo his heart; turned into an alley - it still does not look back. "He knows what I'm going after him?" - The thought Raskolnikov.Bourgeois entered the gate of one large doma.Raskolnikov walked as quickly as possible to the gate and looked not look back, if he did not call him? In fact, having a gate and they all have access to the courtyard, he suddenly turned and again exactly as if he waved his hand. Raskolnikov immediately went on the track, but in the yard, so it was not a wimp. Thus, he came here today for the first stairs. Raskolnikov rushed after him. In fact, two stairs above even heard one dimensional, slow steps. Oddly enough, the ladder was as familiar! Get out of the window on the first floor; sad and mysterious moonlight through the glass; Here on the second etazhe.Ba! The same apartment in which workers smeared ... How he did not recognize at once?Steps before the man on the wane, "so he stopped and hid somewhere." This is the third floor; whether to go further? And what is there silence, even scary ... But he went. Noise in his own steps scared and anxious.God, how dark! Bourgeois, right here somewhere lurking in the corner. ! The apartment upstairs opened wide;he thought, and went to the front of it was very dark and empty, not a soul, as if all the imaging .; gently, he tiptoed into the room the whole room was doused with bright moonlight; are all in place: chairs, mirror, yellow sofa and pictures in frames. A huge, round, copper-red looked straight month in the window. "It's so quiet for a month - thought Raskolnikov - this is true, now thinks the puzzle." He stood and waited, waited a long time, and was quieter than a month, more Stukalo his heart, even injured. Nevertheless silence. Suddenly he heard the crackle of dry time, as if broken shard, and everything

froze snova.Razbuzhenny fly RAID suddenly hit the glass and hooted mournfully. At this very moment in the corner between a small closet and window, he saw, as if hanging on the wall of the cloak. "Why, then cloak? - He thought - because he had not been there before ..." He walked slowly and realized that his cloak, as if someone is hiding. He gently took her hand cloak and saw that there is a chair and a chair in the corner sat an old woman, all curled up and bowing his head, so he could not see their faces, but it was her. He stood over her, "afraid" - he thought, gently freed from the loop ax and struck the old woman's head, and other times. But strangely, she did not move with the current, just wood. He was frightened, leaned forward and looked at her but it is still below her head. He ducked and then completely on the floor and looked into her lower face and looked half-dead old woman sitting and laughing - and poured in a low, inaudible laughter all forces attached, that he had not heard seemed her.Suddenly him that the bedroom door opened a crack, and that also seemed to laugh and whisper. Rabies overcame his struggles began to beat an old woman on the head, but with each blow of the ax laughter and whispers from the bedroom sounded stronger and louder, and an old woman in such a way full and heaving with laughter. He escaped, but the whole room is full of people already on the stairs opened, the door is open, and on the court, on the stairs and back down - all the people who head to head, all would - but all crouched and waiting , silent ... His heart hesitated, legs do not move, rooted ... He wanted to scream and - woke up.

He heaved a deep breath - but a strange dream, as if still continues his door was open wide, and stood on the threshold quite unknown to him, and the man looked at him intently.

Raskolnikov is not yet fully open their eyes and immediately closed them again. He lay on his back and did not move. "Sleep is happening or not," - he thought, and a little unnoticed again raised lashes look: the stranger standing in the same place and still look into it. Suddenly he stepped gingerly over the threshold, carefully closed the door, went to the table and waited for the moment - all the while keeping an eye on him - and quiet, no noise, and sat down on a chair next to the couch; put the hat on the side on the floor, both hands, leaning on a cane, his chin on his hands. It was clear that he was willing to wait a long time. How many could be seen flashing through the eyelashes, a man no longer young, dense and thick, blond, with a white beard almost ...

He took ten minutes. It was still light, but it was getting dusk. The room

was complete silence. Even the stairs do not bring a single zvuka.Prosto buzzed and struggled a bit big fly, hitting with a plaque on the glass.Finally became unbearable: Raskolnikov suddenly sat on the couch.

- Well, tell me what you want?

- But I never knew that you do not sleep, and just kind of show - strange stranger replied, laughing quietly. - Arkady Ivanovich Svidrigailov, let me introduce myself ...

PART 4
←« CHAPTER I »→

"Is this the continuation of a dream?" - Think again Raskolnikov. He carefully watched in amazement at the unexpected guest.

- Svidrigailov? What nonsense! It can not be! - He finally said out loud in disbelief.

It seemed guest was not surprised that ejaculation.

- Because of two reasons you go: first, to meet personally wished, as long heard very interesting and favorable conditions for you; and secondly, a dream that did not depart, perhaps, help me in the same enterprise, directly affects the interests of his sister, Avdotya Romanovna. One to change without recommendation, it may, in the yard and it now will not start because of the damage, and with your help, on the contrary, I hope ...

- Poor expect - Raskolnikov interrupted.

- They only arrived yesterday, may I ask?

Raskolnikov did not answer.

- Yesterday, I know. I just himself came only yesterday. Well, that's what I tell you, in this regard, Rodion Romanovich; find it unnecessary to make excuses, but let me say the same thing and that is, in all this, in fact, this particular crime on my part, that is, without sacrificing something and judging reasonable?

Raskolnikov went silently to consider it.

- The fact that in his haunted house defenseless damsel, and "insulted her with his proposal" - IT-S? (Looking ahead himself forward!) Why, imagine that I'm a man, and others Nihil Humanum ... 1 word that I can give in to temptation and fall in love (which, of course, not by the will of our going

on), all the most natural explained. There is a question: I Monster or sacrifice? Well, as a victim? After offering my theme to run with me in America or Switzerland, I most respectfully while experiencing the feelings, and even thought to organize mutual happiness! .. The mind, after all, a passion; I think I ruined myself even more, for pity's sake! ..

- Yes, absolutely not the point - with disgust interrupted Raskolnikov - just easily disgusted you, but you're right or wrong, well here with you and do not want to know and take you, and go! ..

Svidrigailov suddenly laughed.

- But why are you ... But you do not sobesh! - He said, laughing frankly way - I thought cheat, but no, you just point to the very real steel!

- Yes, you are at the moment to continue to deceive.

- So what? So what? - Repeat Svidrigailov, laughing wide open - it Bonne Guerre, one that is called, and most acceptable to cheat .. But still you interrupted me; Anyway, I confirm again, nothing terrible will happen if no place in sadu.Marfa Petrovna ...

- Marfa Petrovna you something too, they say, anyway? - Coarsely chopped Raskolnikov.

- Have you heard about this? As, however, have not heard anything ... Well, about your question really do not know how to tell you, but my conscience is very quiet on subject.That is, I do not think I was afraid of something sort of out there: all this made was in perfect order and complete accuracy: medical studies have not revealed apoplexy, came out of the bath now, after a hearty dinner with drunk nearly a bottle of wine, and nothing more, and discover that it could not ... No, sir, that's what I thought to myself for a while, especially here on the road, sitting in the car: I do not contribute to all this ... Unfortunately, somehow there is irritation or moral Chamberlain something like that? But came to the conclusion that it can not be positive.

Raskolnikov laughed.

- Hunting was so worried!

- Yes, what are you laughing at? You think: I hit only twice ambulance, even the characters do not have ... Do not take me, please, a cynic; I knew exactly how it is confusion on my part, and so on, but I'm also probably know that Marfa Petrovna, possible, and I am glad that I was, so to speak, a hobby. The story of his sister fell to Izhitsa. Marfa Petrovna third day was forced to stay at home; There is nothing in the city, it seems, and tired of it all there with her this letter (a letter about reading what you heard?). And suddenly

these two whip as falling from the sky! The first thing the coach told me to lay! .. I did it, and did not say that women have such cases when very, very glad that insult, despite all the apparent indignation. All these cases they have something; People are generally very, very much like to be insulted, have you noticed? But especially women. I can even say that just do shift.

At one time it was thought Raskolnikov get up and leave, and so put an end date. But some curiosity and even calculation of how she spent with him for a minute.

- Do you like to fight? - He asked absently.

- No, not really - calmly replied Svidrigailov. - And Marfa Petrovna almost never fought. We are very much lived under, and I was always pleased. I used the whip, in all our seven years, only two times (not counting a third case, more likely, however, is ambiguous) for the first time - two months after our marriage, immediately upon his arrival in the village, and here there last case . Do you really think I'm such a monster, retrograde, a serf? hehe ... And by the way: I do not remember you, Rodion Romanovich, a few years ago, in the days of the beneficial publicity, we publicly disgraced nobleman and vseliteraturno - forgot the name! - That German whipped in a car, remember? Again, in the same year, it seems, "an ugly act of the century "happened (well, "Egyptian few nights," read the public, remember? black eyes! Oh, where are you golden days of our youth!) Well, here my opinion, Sir, whipped German, deeply sympathize, because it really is ... sorry for that! But these are things that I can not say that sometimes there are podstrekatelnye «Germans", it seems to me there is no progressivist, that it would be able to vouch for you. From this perspective, no one looked at it, and yet, at this point, and there is a real humane, right, with this!

Having said this, Svidrigailov suddenly laughed again. Raskolnikov was apparent that this is what people who have decided firmly and cunning.

- You must have a few days at the end with no one talking about? - He asked.

- Almost. What: The real miracle that I folding man?

- No, I have to admire that you are folding too man.

- Because the rudeness of your questions are not offended? Is that it? Yes ... Why hurt? As asked and answered - he added with a surprising expression of innocence. - Because I especially doing something almost no interest, in fact, - he continued as a thoughtfully. - Especially now that is not the same is not busy ... However, you can imagine that I like a whiny, especially because

I'm dealing with your sister, he declared.But I'll tell you frankly very boring! Especially these three days, so I was glad that you ... Do not be angry, Rodion Romanovich, but you tell me how it seems awfully strange how. As you wish, but something in you;and now, that is not right at the moment, and now ... Well, I will not, will not, do not frown! I can not bear what you think.

Raskolnikov looked darkly at him.

- You may even be, and shall not be, - he said. - I even think that you are very good society, or at least know how to be the case and decent man.

- Why, I'm no one's opinion is not particularly interesting - both dry and even with a touch of arrogance said Svidrigailov, - and, therefore, why not visit the vulgar when this dress in our climate so comfortable to wear and ... and especially, if natural tend to have - he added, laughing again.

- I have heard, however, that you have a lot of friends here. You are doing what is called "not without ties." Why did you-I in if not for the purpose?

- And you are telling the truth, I have friends - Svidrigailov took no answer to the main point - I've seen; the third day after that refrain, and I know, and I seem to learn. This, of course, dressed decently and the number of people not poor; We walked and peasant reform: forest and meadows, some income and is not lost; but ... I will not go there; and especially tired: I go three days, and did not recognize anyone ... And then there's the city! That is, as written here, please tell me! City clerks and all kinds of seminarians! Yes, I have here had not noticed before, eight years ago, when valandalsya ... In anatomy just now, and I hope that by golly!

- What anatomy?

- What about these clubs, Dyussotov, pointe shoes of your own, or maybe there is progress - well, let it be without us, - he continued, again noticing the problem. - Yes, and hunting sharper something be?

- Have you been to the island?

- How do without it? We had the whole company, naiprilichneyshaya, eight years ago; spent his time; and all, you know, people with manners, why the capitalists. And in fact, we are in the Russian society, the best manners of those who visited the bits - you notice? That's because I'm down in the village. And yet I was then imprisoned for debt, grechonka one Nezhinskii. That sprained Marfa Petrovna, a deal and bought me for thirty pieces of silver thousand. (Just what I had seventy thousand). We combined with her legal marriage, and took it with me immediately to his village as a treasure. She is older than me by five years. Very fond of.Seven years from the village

went. And note that the life of the whole document against me, someone else's name, in these thirty thousand, held, so I think that the rebels - right into the trap! And would have done! In women, it all gets together.

- And if it were not for the document will pull?

- I do not know how to tell you. I have this document almost do not hesitate. I do not want anywhere and abroad Marfa Petrovna herself twice invited me, seeing that I missed. What! Abroad, before I went, and I always feel sick happened. It's not that, but the dawn is engaged, the Gulf of Naples, the sea, watching, and somehow sad. Just the contrary, it's really about something sad No, better than at home: here, at least, in all other guilt, and justified. I would probably now in the expedition to the North Pole went because j'ai le tasting bad, 1 drink and disgusts me, and besides wine is nothing left. Tried. And that, they say, Berg Sunday in the Yusupov garden on a huge ball will fly, travel offers, for a fee, is not it?

- Well, would you fly?

- I? No ... well ... - Svidrigailov muttered, as if really thinks.

"Yes, he is, in fact, is not it?" - The thought Raskolnikov.

- No, the document does not hesitate - Svidrigailov went thoughtfully, - I did not go out of the village. And so the year will be as Marfa Petrovna for my birthday, and I returned the document, moreover, in addition presents a very significant. In fact, it was the capital. "You see how I trust you, Arkady Ivanovich," - and put it right. You do not believe that so to speak You know, because I'm the owner of the village became respectable ?; I know the neighborhood. Books and signed. Marfa Petrovna at first did not approve, and then all was afraid that I remember.

- You Marfa Petrovna, it seems very boring?

-? I could be. Yes, it can be. And by the way, do you believe in ghosts?

- What are ghosts?

- In the ordinary ghosts, in which!

- Do you believe?

- Yes, I think not, pour Vous plaire ... 1 This is not something that is not ...
  - Is that it?

Svidrigailov just looked at him strangely.

- Marfa Petrovna to visit, if you like - he said, his mouth curled into a strange smile.

- How did it go, if you please?

- Yes, three times to come. The first time I saw her on the day of the

funeral, an hour after the cemetery. It was the eve of my departure time zdes. Vtoroy third day on the road, at dawn, at the station Malaya Vishera;and for the third time in two hours ago, in an apartment where I stand in the room; I was alone.

- Really?

- That's right. All three times a reality. Well, let's talk for a minute and go through the door; always at the door. Even now, when I heard.

- Why, I never thought that you, of course, something like this happens! - Said Raskolnikov, and at the same time wondering what he said. He was in great excitement.

- On-Off? As you think? - Asked in surprise Svidrigailov, - yes, really? Well, I did not say that between us there is a common point, right?

- Never say that you do not! - Dramatically and passionately answered Raskolnikov.

- Do not say?

- No!

- I thought he was talking about. The next day, as I walked in and saw that you are lying with his eyes closed and pretend themselves - and immediately said to myself: "This is the same!"

- What it is: the same? The fact that you are doing? - Cried Raskolnikov.

- About what? And really do not know that ... - To be honest, and somehow he got confused, Svidrigailov muttered.

Silent for a moment. The two men looked at each other wide-eyed.

- All this is nonsense! - Angrily cried Raskolnikov. - Well, it tells you when it comes?

- This is what? Imagine the smallest detail, and it is surprising that a man, it's me, and angry. The first time came in (I know I'm tired: Funeral services, with the saints give rest, the lithium snacks - finally in the office alone, lit a cigar, thought), walked through the door: "And you, says Arkady today to trouble and forgot to start the clock in the dining room "and watch the ones I did for seven years, every week the plant itself, and forget -. He always reminded. The next day I go zdes.Prishel in at dawn, at the station, - per night of sleep, broken, sleepy eyes - he picked up his coffee; look - Marfa Petrovna suddenly sitting next to me, holding a deck of cards, "I do not think of you, Arkady, on the road, then?" And she was the mistress guess. Well, it can not forgive myself that not stretched! Fled, fearing here, though, and a bell. I sit today after a crappy lunch pastry, with severe stomach - I

sit, smoke - suddenly again Marfa Petrovna, includes all wearing new silk green dress, with a long tail, "Hello, Arkady Ivanovich, how do you like it! My dress Anisko not sew? ".(Anisko - skilled worker in our village, a former fortress in training in Moscow byla-- beautiful girl). This spinning in front of me. I looked at my dress, looked at her face: "Hunting you, I say, Marfa Petrovna, the little things bother me to walk." - "My God, sir, I really can not bother you!" I tell her to tease her: "I, Marfa Petrovna, I want to marry." - "You are that it will be, Arkady Ivanovich, not much honor for you that you are not having to bury his wife and marry immediately went and chose at least something good, and that in fact, I know -. Neither she nor currently only good people laugh. " Went, and came, and tail, as noise. What nonsense in the end, is not it?

- Yes, you are, in fact, perhaps all lying? - Said Raskolnikov.

- I rarely lie - Svidrigailov answered thoughtfully, as if unaware of the issue being rude.

- First of all, before you will never ever seen a ghost?

- N ... no, I saw once in a lifetime, six years ago. Shary, yard man, I had; only that he was buried, I cried, beside himself: "Shary, the tube" - and I went straight to the hill where I stand pipe. I'm sitting, I think, "He's my revenge," because before we firmly samoyu death quarreled. "How dare you, I say, at the mercy of the elbow I go - there scoundrel" turned left and never came. I did not say Marfa Petrovna. It is a pity that there was a memorial service for him to serve, but ashamed.

- Go to the doctor.

- That's what I do without you understand what is harmful to health, but really do not know what; I think that is probably a healthier you five raz.A not mean that you asked - believe it or not, the ghosts? I ask you: do you believe that there are ghosts?

- No, they will not believe! - With some anger even cried Raskolnikov.

- It usually say ,? - Muttered Svidrigailov, as if to himself, looking to the side and tilted his head a little. - They say, "You're sick, so the fact that you seem to have only one non-existent stupidity." But there is no strict logic. I agree that ghosts are just sick; but this only proves that ghosts can not be none other than the patient, not the fact that they are not alone.

- Of course not! - Irritation Raskolnikov insisted.

- No? You think so? - Continuation of Svidrigailov, slowly, looking at him.
- Well, what if the judge so (that help Single): "Ghosts - that is, pieces and

fragments of other worlds, the beginning of their health, of course, they should not see, because healthy people. Most of the earth's people, and therefore should live life odnoyu here for completeness and order. But a little sick, a little disturbed the normal order on earth in the body, and immediately begins to affect the possibility of another world, and more ill, and contact with the rest of the world even more so when he dies quite human right and go into another world. "I talked about it for a long time. If you believe, and this argument can not believe it.

- I do not believe in the Hereafter, - said Raskolnikov.

Svidrigailov sat lost in thought.

- What if there are some spiders or anything like that - he said suddenly.

"It's crazy," - thought Raskolnikov.

- We have everything here, it seems like an eternity as an idea that can not be understood, something huge, huge! But why should it be great? And suddenly, instead of all this, imagine what will be a small room, as some rural baths, smoky and spiders in every corner, and that's all eternity. I know how it is sometimes imagination.

- And, in fact, do you really do not seem comforting and validity of this! - With a painful sense of Raskolnikov cried.

- Fair Play? And who knows, maybe it's true, and you know, I would, of course, deliberately did! - Answered Svidrigailov, with a vague smile.

Some cold shell Raskolnikov suddenly, with the ugly response. Svidrigailov raised his head, looked at him and suddenly burst out laughing.

- No, this is what you see - he said, - half an hour ago that we have each other, and yet never seen, considered the enemy between us there is an open question; Note ejected and Avon that literature we stopped! Well, not so, I said that we were birds of a feather?

- Do the same service - irritability Raskolnikov went on, - let me ask you as soon as possible to explain and tell me why you have awarded me the honor of your visit ... and ... and ... I'm in a hurry, I do not time, I want to go to the yard ...

- Very well, if you please. Your sister, Avdotya Romanovna, with Mr. Luzhin out, Peter?

- Is it possible to somehow circumvent any question about my sister and did not mention her name? I do not even understand how dare you, when I say her name, if you really Svidrigailov?

- Oh, I went up to her and say, how could I not mention that?

- Ok; say, but soon!

- I'm sure what you mean, Mr. Luzhin, for my wife's relatives have already made their opinion, even if it is half an hour or seen anything about it right and just heard. Avdotya Romanovna he did not pair. In my opinion, Avdotya Romanovna, in this case, sacrificing himself very generous and wasteful for ... for your family. It seemed to me as a result of all that I have heard of you, that you, with your hand, I would have been very satisfied, if the marriage can break without breaking interests. Now, to get to know you personally, I'm confident of that.

- On your part it's all very naive; I'm sorry, I meant to say, sassy, - said Raskolnikov.

- So you express it, I busily in his pocket. Do not worry, Rodion Romanovich, if I wanted to take advantage of, he should not speak so frankly, is not a fool, because I did. On this score will tell you a psychological oddity. Only now do I justify my love for Avdotya Romanovna, said that he was a victim. Well, let me tell you that no, I do not feel love now, n-no, so I'm very very strange, because I really felt something ...

- From idleness and debauchery - interrupted Raskolnikov.

- Actually, I'm a depraved and idle. And yet, your sister has so many advantages that could not, and I do not give in to some impressions. But all this is nonsense, because it now and see for yourself.

- How long does it see?

- Pay attention, even before finally convinced of the third day, almost at the very moment of arrival in St. Petersburg. Nevertheless, even in Moscow thought that I will seek Avdotya Romanovna's hand and compete with Mr. Luzhin.

- I'm sorry you Pererva, do me a favor: could cut and go straight to the purpose of your visit. I'm in a hurry, I have to go to court ...

- With the greatest pleasure. Coming here and now decide to take some ... journey, I would like to make the necessary pre-orders. My children stayed with her aunt; they are rich, and I personally do not hath need of them. And the fact that I'm a father! I myself took only what gave me a year ago, Marfa Petrovna. I've had enough. Unfortunately, we turn to the case itself. Prior to travel, which can be, and this is done, and I want to finish with Mr. Luzhin. Not that I like it very much hated, but through it, however, and it came out, my argument with Marfa Petrovna, when I learned that she had prepared the wedding. Now I want to see Avdotya Romanovna, through you, and perhaps

in your presence, as she explained, firstly, that Mr. Luzhin not only is she the slightest benefit, but is likely to be even visible damage. Then, asking her to apologize to all of these recent troubles, I would like to ask permission to offer her ten thousand rubles and thus facilitate the break with Mr. Luzhin, a break from that, I'm sure she will not mind, will be the only possibility.

- But do you really, really crazy! - Cried Raskolnikov, is not so much angry as surprised. - How dare you say that!

- I knew you shout; but, first, I though not rich, but these ten thousand rubles from me free that completely, absolutely not necessary. Do not take Avdotya Romanovna, so I think I'm even stupider their food. It is time.Secondly, my conscience is completely calm; I am without any calculations show ,. Believe me I do not believe, and then find out that you and Avdotya Romanovna.Everything, I really brought trouble and trouble respect your sister; Therefore, feeling sincere repentance, the heart is the desire - not pay, do not pay me, but just easily do to something advantageous, on the grounds that it is not the same privilege in fact I took only one to do evil . If my proposal was even millions of calculation, I would not recommend it so directly; and I would not suggest only ten thousand, while only five weeks ago offered her bolshe.Krome, I can be very, very soon to marry the girl, and, therefore, any suspicion of any attempts Avdotya Romanovna thus be eliminated. In conclusion, I would like to say that, beyond Mr. Luzhin, Avdotya Romanovna also takes money from the other side ... But do not be angry, Rodion Romanovich, the judge calmly and coolly.

Having said this, he Svidrigailov was very cold and calm.

- I ask you to come, - said Raskolnikov. - In any case, it is inexcusable safely.

- Nima. After that, man to man in this world can not do it alone and evil, on the contrary, has no right to make a crumb good because of the empty formalities accepted. This is ridiculous. In the end, if I, for example, died and left this amount to his sister in his will, of course, she then refused to accept?

- Rather be.

- Well, I have not, sir. And yet, there is not, so be it. Only ten thousand - a wonderful thing for the occasion.In any case, ask to transfer said Avdotya Romanovna.

- No, do not give.

- In this case, Rodion Romanovich, I forced myself to be looking for personal visits, and therefore, worry.

- What if I give you will not look for anything goodbye?

- I do not know, in fact, as you say. See once, I'd really like to.

- Do not expect.

- It Is A Pity. However, you do not know me. Here, perhaps, a more closely.

- Do you think that we get to work more closely?

- And why not? - Said Svidrigailov smiled, stood up and took his hat - I'm not that so very much and is going to bother you here, not even very much hope, though, by the way, your face is still that morning, I was amazed. ..

- Where did you see me in the morning? - Anxiously asked Raskolnikov.

- Accidentally something ... I think you have something on my right ... Do not worry, I'm not a nuisance; and the players get along, and Prince Svirbeyu, my distant cousin and nobles, not tired, and Raphael Madonna Mrs. Prilukov in the album managed to write, and Marfa Petrovna lived continuously for seven years, and in the house Viazemsky at the Haymarket in olden nochevyval and a balloon with Berg, maybe fly.

- All right, sir. Let me ask you, you will soon go on a trip?

- On a trip?

- Well, in "Voyage", it's ... You said yourself ,.

- In flight? Oh yes .. in fact, I told you about the trip ... Well, it's overwhelming question ... If you only knew, however, to ask about anything! - He added, suddenly loud and laughed shortly. - I may be, instead of sailing to marry; I woo a bride.

- Over There?

- Yes I Am.

- If you have the time?

- But Avdotya Romanovna day to see. Seriously ask. Well, good-bye ... Oh, yes! In the end, this is what is forgotten! Pass, Rodion Romanovich, your sister that she would, Marfa Petrovna mentioned three thousand.This is a positive true. Marfa Petrovna ordered a week before his death, and it was me. Week two or three Avdotya Romanovna and money you can get.

- Are you telling the truth?

- Truth. Pass. Well, your servant. I am very close to you stand.

Before leaving, Svidrigailov faced in the doorway with Razumikhin.

←«»→

↞« CHAPTER II »↠

It was really almost eight hours; as hurried Bakaleevu appear before Luzhin.

- Well, who else was? - Razumikhin asked, just went out into the street.

- It was Svidrigailov same owner, in whose house offended sister when they were governess.Through love persecution she came from them and went with his wife, Marfa Petrovna. Asked this Marfa Petrovna then on Dunya forgiveness, and now suddenly died. It is only now talking about it. I do not know why, I am very afraid of this man. He came immediately after his wife's funeral. He is very strange and something decided ... It's like he knows something ... From him we must protect Dunya ... That's what I wanted to tell you, you hear?

- Protection! Well, he can against Avdotya Romanovna? Well, thank you, Rodia, I say so ... We will, we will be protected! .. Where to live?

- I do not know.

- Why do not you ask? Oh, sorry! Nevertheless, to find out!

- Have you seen him? - Raskolnikov asked, after a pause.

- Yes, noticed; firmly adhered to.

- You saw it exactly? Obviously, seen? - Raskolnikov insisted.

- Well, yes, I remember; thousands of you know, I pamyatliv to face.

Again there was silence.

- Um ... something something ... - muttered Raskolnikov. - And you know ... I think ... I think ... that it might be a fantasy.

- Yes, about you? I do not understand very well.

- That's all you say - Raskolnikov went on, twisting his mouth into a

smile - that I possessed; It seemed to me now, maybe I'm really obsessed and just saw a ghost!

- What did you do?

- But who knows! Maybe I'm really hurt, and all that was in those days, everything can be so only in the imagination ...

- Oh, Rodia! Upset you again! .. Yes, he said, how come?

Raskolnikov did not answer, Razumikhin thought a minute.

- Well, listen to my answer, - he said. - I came to you, you sleep. Then dinner, and then I went to Porfiry. Zametov all about it. I would like to start, and nothing came of it it.Everything could not speak that way. They just do not understand and can not understand, but not confusing. I took Porfiry over to the window and began to speak, but then again, why could not he looks away, and I'm looking to the side. I finally brought it to his mug fist and said to break his relative. He just looked at me. I spat and went away, that's all. Very glupo.Tak I Zametovym words. Once you see: I thought, podgadit and me down the stairs, one thought came and struck me that what we are busily? After all, if you were a danger, or there is something of course.But Do you think!You do not have anything to do with it, so do not take care of them; we have over them nasmeemsya then, and I would be in your place them even became mistifirovat. Because they are ashamed, it will be! Spit; it will be possible to beat, and now laugh!

- Of course it is! - Raskolnikov answered. "And what do you say tomorrow?" - He thought to himself. Strange to say, but still did not occur to him, "that Razumikhin think when he finds out?"I thought it was, Raskolnikov looked at him. Imagine the same report on the visit Razumihina Porphyry he was very little interest: then lost so much, and as added! ..

In the hallway, they were faced with Luzhin: he was at 8:00, and sought numbered, so that all three together, but not looking at each other and bowing. Young people went forward, and Peter, for decency, hesitated a few in the audience, taking off his coat. Pulcheria Alexandrovna immediately went to meet him at the door. Dunya met with his brother.

Pyotr Petrovich walked in and quite kindly, though with redoubled strength, bowed to the ladies. Nevertheless, looked like a little lost and still not naydeny.Pulheriya Alexandrovna, too, as if embarrassed, hastened to make all sit around a table on which a samovar was boiling. Dunya and Luzhin fit next to each other at both ends of the table. Razumikhin and Raskolnikov fell to Pulcheria Alexandrovna - Razumikhin closer to Luzhin and

Raskolnikov next to his sister.

Was an instant molchanie.Petr Petrovich slowly pulled batiste handkerchief, which suffered from the spirits, and blew his nose with a view though virtuous, but still a few insults human dignity, and, moreover, who are determined to demand an explanation. He returned to the thought did not take off my coat and go, but a stern and imposing penalties of two women, in order to give time to feel everything. But he did not dare.While people do not like uncertainty, and here it was necessary to clarify if it is so clearly violated his orders, so something will be, and therefore, it is better to know in advance; punish the same time, there will always be, and in his hands.

- I hope that the journey went well? - Officially, he turned to Pulcheria Alexandrovna.

- Thank God, Peter.

- Very nice, sir. And Avdotya Romanovna not too tired?

- I am young and strong, not tired, and the mother so it was very difficult - said Dounia.

- What to do with; our national road is very long.Large so-called "Mother Russia" ... I, if they wanted to, they could not be in a hurry for a meeting yesterday. I hope, however, that all happened without much hassle?

- Oh, no, Peter, we were very discouraged - with special intonation hastened to declare Pulcheria Alexandrovna - and if God seems he has not sent us yesterday Dmitry Prokofitch, we would simply never happened. Here they are, Dmitri Prokofitch Razumikhin - she added, recommending him Luzhin.

- How good it was fun yesterday ... - muttered Luzhin, hostile glance at Razumikhin, then frowned and fell silent.Anyway Peter belonged to the category of people seem to be very amiable in society, and especially for the benefit of the application, but it just is not for them immediately and lose all your money and become more like a sack of flour than brash and gentlemen animates society. All fell silent again, Raskolnikov remained stubbornly silent, Avdotya Romanovna, until the time did not want to interrupt the silence, Razumikhin had nothing to say, so Pulcheria Alexandrovna zatrevozhilas again.

- Marfa Petrovna died, have you heard? - She said, resorting to its fixed assets.

- As heard, sir. At the first hearing has been notified and will even come to you today to inform you that Arkady Ivanovich Svidrigailov, immediately after the funeral of his wife, hurriedly went to St. Petersburg. So, at least you

know exactly what I got.

- In St. Petersburg? This Way? - I asked anxiously Dunya and exchanged glances with his mother.

- Besides, sir, and, of course, not without purpose, taking into account the hasty departure, and, in general, the circumstances leading to.

- The Lord! Of course, he will not leave here Dunya alone? - Exclaimed Pulcheria Alexandrovna.

- It seems to me, is not particularly worried about anything, neither you nor Avdotya Romanovna, unless, of course, we do not want to get into any kind of had a relationship with him. This for me is that I have seen, and now look where he left off ...

- Oh, Peter, you would not believe the extent to which you are now scared me! - Continuation of Pulcheria Alexandrovna. - I'm his only twice seen and it seemed to me, the horror, the horror! I am sure that he was the cause of death of the deceased Marfa Petrovna.

- As it is impossible to draw a conclusion. I have the exact news. Do not argue, perhaps, he was instrumental in the rapid course of things, so to speak, the moral influence of the offense; but as for the conduct and moral characteristics of the person as a whole, I agree with you. Now I do not know whether he is rich, and that she left him Marfa Petrovna; That's what I'll be known in a very short period of time; but, of course, here in St. Petersburg, at least some of the money it will take more than once old. This is the most depraved and dead in the evils of people from all kinds of people! I have a serious reason to believe that Marfa Petrovna, who had the misfortune to fall in love with him and so redeem out of debt, eight years ago, he served in another respect: only hard work and put out their victims were, at Home, a criminal case, a mixture of brutal and, so to speak, fantastic murder for which he is very, very likely to reach Siberia.That that this man, if you want to know.

- Oh, my God! - Exclaimed Pulcheria Alexandrovna. Raskolnikov listened attentively.

- Do you really say that you have accurate information about it? - Said Dounia, strictly and impressive.

- I say only what he heard in secret, late Marfa Petrovna. It should be noted that from a legal point of view, in the case of very dark. Lived here and now, it seems, is home to some Resslih, alien and, in addition, a small pawn-shop, and deal with other things. With this door Resslih Mr. Svidrigailov's

been a long time in some very close and mysterious ways. She lived a distant cousin, niece, seems deaf and dumb girl of fifteen, and even fourteen years, which in this Resslih infinitely hated and blamed each piece; even severely beaten. After she was found in the attic of a boa constrictor. Awarded that samoubiystva.Posle normal procedure affair ended, but later, however, reported that the child was severely insulted ... Svidrigailov. Nevertheless, it was dark, was denounced by other Germans, sad woman and had no confidence; Finally, in fact, the denunciation was not, thanks to the efforts and money to Marfa Petrovna, all limited hearing. But, nevertheless, this rumor was mnogoznamenatelen. You, of course, Avdotya Romanovna, too, have heard the story of a man, Philip, who died from torture, six years ago, when serfdom.

- I've heard that, on the contrary, that he hanged himself, Philip.

- Besides, sir, but led rather to persuade him to a violent death UPS systems, prosecution and punishment of Mr. Svidrigailov.

- I do not know what it is, - said dryly Duns - I just heard some very strange story that Philip is some hypochondriac, some houses philosopher, people said "absorbed" and that he hanged himself more of ridicule instead of r Svidrigailov on poboy. And it is in my behavior to people and people loved him, even if it is in fact also accused of the death of Philip.

- I see that you, Avdotya Romanovna, it became suddenly leaned to his justification, - said Luzhin, mouth twisted in an ambiguous smile. - Indeed, he is a man cunning and seductive ladies that lamentable example of Marfa Petrovna, who died so strange. I just wanted to serve you and your mummy with his advice, because of its new and undoubtedly forthcoming attempts. As far as I am concerned, I firmly believe that this man certainly will disappear again in their duties. Marfa Petrovna, of course, was not going to fix it, referring to the children, and if they left him something, doing something most necessary, malostoyaschee, ephemeral, and that a year is not enough for a man with his habits.

- Peter, I beg you, - said Dounia - perestanemte about Mr. Svidrigailov. This makes me sad.

- He came to me - said Raskolnikov, first breaking the silence.

On all sides cries, all turned to him. Even Peter excited.

- An hour and a half ago, when I was sleeping, he came and woke me introduce myself - Raskolnikov went on. - It was quite separate and quite cheerful and hopeful that I get from it. By the way, he asks for and seeking

a meeting with you, Dunya, and asked me to be a mediator in this interview. He has an offer for you; what it is, he told me. In addition, he informed me positively that Marfa Petrovna a week before his death, was able to leave you, Dunya, bequest of three thousand rubles, and the money you can now get in the near future.

- Thank God! - Exclaimed Pulcheria Alexandrovna and crossed herself. - Pray for her, Dunya, pray!

- It's true - escaped from Luzhin.

- Well, well, what's next? - Hurried Dunya.

- Then he said he was not rich, and all property goes to his children, who are now his aunt. Then that stopped somewhere near me, and where? - I do not know, do not ask ...

- But what does what he wants to offer Dunya? - Asked frightened Pulcheria Alexandrovna. - Did he tell you?

- Yes, he said.

- What is it?

- Then tell me. - Raskolnikov stopped and turned to tea.

Petr Petrovich took out his watch and looked at it.

- We have to go on this case, and thus, it does not hurt - he added, with some dive and started to get up from the chair.

- Accommodation, Peter, - said Dounia - because you're going to sit in the evening. In addition, you yourself wrote that you would like something to talk to my mom.

- Besides, sir, Avdotya Romanovna - impressive Peter said, sitting in a chair, but still holding his hat in his hand - I really want to explain to you, dear and vasheyu mummy, and even very important points. But, as your brother can not explain to me about some of these proposals, Mr. Svidrigailov, and I do not want and can not explain it in another ... ... about some very, very important points. In addition, the capital, and my earnest request has not been implemented ...

Luzhin made bitter stout appearance and silent.

- Please, your brother was not with our meeting, not only by my insistence, - said Dounia. - You wrote that you were offended by his brother; I think it is necessary to immediately find out and you should do it. And if you really insulted RODIA, it must and will ask you for an apology.

Peter immediately zakurazhilsya.

- There are some insults, Avdotya Romanovna, who, with all the good

will, you can not forget, sir.Everything has a threshold beyond which are dangerous; because, once crossed, the gate can not return.

- I do not mean that you actually said Peter - a little impatiently Dunya - well understand that all our future now depends on cleared and settled it all as soon as possible, or not? I'm right, the first word I say, or I can not look, and if you're anything like me cherish it, although it is difficult, and it all has to come to an end today. I say to you that if a brother is guilty, he will ask forgiveness.

- I am surprised that you are putting so much a question, Avdotya Romanovna - worn over Luzhin. - Appreciate and, so to speak, adoring you, I at the same time very, very, I can not love someone from your home. Claiming the happiness of your hand, I can not at the same time commit themselves nesoglasimyh ...

- Oh, leave all this discontent, Peter - with a sense of interrupted Dunya - and so intelligent and honest man, as I have always believed that I want. I have given you much hope, I'm your bride; trust me on this issue, and believe me, I'll be able to judge impartially. The fact that I take on the role of the judge is the same surprise my brother like you. When I asked him today, after your letter, be sure to come to our meeting, I did not tell him about his intentions. Understand that if you do not make peace, I must also choose between you, either you have it. So was the matter with him, and with your hand. I do not want and do not make the wrong choice. For you, I have to break up with his brother; for my brother, I must break you. I want and I know now, probably brother if he told me? And as for you, I get you, I appreciate that you're my husband you me?

- Avdotya Romanovna - zakorobivshis said Luzhin - your words are impor-tant to me, too, I would say more, even insulting, because of the position which I have the honor to hold in relation to you. Not to mention a word about pain and strange comparison, at the same level, between me and ... arrogant young man, with your words, you allow the possibility of violation of this I promise. You say, "or you or is it"? Thus, in this way, showing me how little I mean you ... I can not let that happen when a relationship ... and obligations that exist between us.

- How! - Broke Dunya - I put the interest close to everything that is still dear to me in my life so far has beenall my life, and suddenly you are offended, because I give you a little price!

Raskolnikov silently and smiled sarcastically, Razumikhin all started;

but Peter did not accept the objection;on the contrary, with every word he became irritable and all affectionate, just talk Beginning.

- Love for the future partner, her husband, exceeds the love of his brother - he said moralizing - and in any case, I can not stand on one board ... though I insisted this morning that in the presence of your brother not I want to and I can not reveal everything that was, however, I am now going to appeal to your esteemed mummy necessary explanations for very large for me and offensive points. Your son - he turned to Pulcheria Alexandrovna - yesterday, in the presence of Mr. Rassudkina (? Or so it seems ... I'm sorry, I forgot your name - he graciously bowed Razumihina) insulted me my distorted thoughts that I told you that in a private conversation over a cup of coffee, namely, that marriage with the poor girl had already experienced life sorrow, in my opinion, is more advantageous in the marital relationship than on proven satisfaction, for better morals. Your son deliberately exaggerated the meaning of the words, to funny, accusing me of malicious intentions and, in my opinion, based on their correspondence. Send yourself lucky if you Pulcheria Alexandrovna, it may be to dissuade me otherwise so much respect and soothe. Tell me, then, in terms of what he gave you my words in his letter to Rodion Romanovich?

- I do not remember - escaped Pulcheria Alexandrovna - and convey how she got it. I do not know how you gave RODIA ... Maybe it's something and exaggerated.

- Without your suggestion he could not exaggerate.

- Peter, - with dignity, said Pulcheria Alexandrovna - proof that with Dunya, we are not your words in a very bad condition, this is what we are here.

- Well, Mom! - Dunia said approvingly.

- So, I'm to blame! - Offended Luzhin.

- Here, Peter, you're to blame, Rodion, and you yourself just now lie about it in a letter, - added incentives, Pulcheria Alexandrovna.

- I do not remember having written any lie, sir.

- You wrote - Raskolnikov said sharply, without resorting to Luzhin - that yesterday I gave the money to the widow is not suppressed, as in fact, and his daughter (who until yesterday had never seen). You wrote it to embroil me with their families, and to add to the vile terms of the behavior of girls do not know. All this gossip and meanness.

- Excuse me, sir, - trembling with anger, said Luzhin - in my letter I spread

about your unique qualities and actions carried out in such a way to ask her sister and mother to describe them, I found you, and you have made an impression on me ? As he said in his letter, you get at least a fair line, that is, that you will not have spent the money and the family, even if the accident was not unworthy persons?

- And in my opinion, because you, with all its advantages, is not worth the little finger of that unfortunate girl, in which you throw a stone.

- So you've decided to enter it in the company of his mother and sister?

- I did it too, if you want to know. I put it next to my mother today and Dunya.

- Rodia! - Exclaimed Pulcheria Alexandrovna.

Dunya blushed; Razumikhin frowned. Luzhin smiled sarcastically and arrogantly.

- Kindly look for yourself, Avdotya Romanovna, - he said - is there agreement? I hope that now, when it again and clarified once and for all. I also removed, so as not to interfere with other facilities related to travel and postal secrets (he got up from his chair and took his hat). But, leaving, I believe that in the future I hope that spared such meetings and, so to speak, compromises. You can also ask for especially expensive Pulcheria Alexandrovna, on the same subject, the more that my letter was addressed to you and not someone else.

Pulcheria Alexandrovna little offended.

- Something you absolutely must take his power, Peter. Dunya told you why not fulfill your wish: she had good intentions. Yes, and you write to me, just order. Do we really your every wish to count? And I tell you, on the contrary, you have to come to us to be especially delicate and indulgent because we dropped everything and you trust, come here, and therefore already too much in your power to take place.

- That's not entirely true, Pulcheria Alexandrovna, especially at a time when announcing the inheritance Marfa Petrovna three thousand, that seems to be very useful, in accordance with the new tone that spoke to me - he added sarcastically.

- Based on this observation, we can really suggest that you count on our helplessness - Dunya observed irritably.

- But now, at least, so I can not wait, and certainly do not want to interfere with sensitive proposals Arkady Ivanovich Svidrigailov, he ordered his brother and that, as I see it, you have the capital, and possibly very good

value.

- Oh my God! - Exclaimed Pulcheria Alexandrovna.

Razumikhin could not sit on the chair.

- Shame on you now, sister? - Asked Raskolnikov.

- Shame on you, Rodia, - said Dounia - Peter, come out! - She said to him, pale with anger.

Peter Petrovich, it seems, did not expect such an end. He also hoped for himself, for his power and helplessness of their victims. Do not believe it now. He turned pale, and his lips quivered.

- Avdotya Romanovna, if I go to the door now, with this parting words, then - calculate it - I certainly would not return nikogda.Podumayte carefully! My word hard.

- What insolence! - Dunya exclaimed, quickly rose from his seat - and I do not want you to come back!

- How? So KAP-eg! - Exclaimed Luzhin not believed until the last moment, such a result, and therefore completely lost the thread now - so yourself, sir! But you know, Avdotya Romanovna, I could argue with.

- What right do you have to say so to her! - Hot interceded Pulcheria Alexandrovna - than you can protest?And what are your rights? Well, I'll give you this, my Dunya? Go and leave us all!

We are to blame, that injustice has gone, and I … more

- However Well, Pulcheria Alexandrovna - hot rage Luzhin - You tied my word, from which now give up … and finally … Finally, I was involved, so to speak, through that room …

This latter requirement was before the character of Peter Petrovich, that Raskolnikov, blednevshy anger and efforts to curb suddenly broke, and - laughed. But Pulcheria Alexandrovna lost her temper:

- Expenses? What does it cost? I do not mean that our breasts are you talking about? Why do you keep it for nothing touched. Lord, we are tied and you! Yes, you come to your senses, Peter, is that you have on your hands and feet tied, and we do not have!

- Enough, Mom, please, enough! - Pleads Avdotya Romanovna. - Peter, I beg you, go away!

- I'll go with, but only the last word! - He said, almost completely without it - your mother seems to have completely forgotten that I dare you to take, so to speak, after rumors of the city, in the neighborhood raznessheysya of your reputation. Ignoring public opinion for you and restore your reputation,

too, of course, if I could, really, really, based on salary and even require their gratitude ... And only now opened his eyes! I see myself, that can be very, very acted recklessly, ignoring the voice of the public ...

- Yes, it's two heads or something! - Razumikhin shouted, jumping up from his chair and is already preparing to finish.

- Low and you wicked man! - Said Dounia.

- Not a word! Neither gesture! - Raskolnikov exclaimed, holding Razumihina; then almost point-blank Luzhin:

- Please leave out! - Quiet and alone he said - and not a word more, or else ...

Peter few seconds looking at him with a pale face contorted with rage, then turned and left, and, of course, rarely anyone who carried in his heart so much evil hate this man to Raskolnikov. He, and only he, he is guilty. It is noteworthy that already going down the stairs, he still imagined that the case is still, perhaps, all is not lost, and in connection with the ladies, even "very, very" fixable.

↞ CHAPTER III ↠

The main thing is that he was, until the last minute, did not expect such dominated denouement.He to the latest features, even suggesting the possibility that the two poor and defenseless women could get out of this power. I am convinced that it helped vanity and self-confidence, which is best called narcissism. Peter Petrovich, samples from oblivion, painfully accustomed to admire, he highly valued his intelligence and ability, and sometimes, alone, admiring his face in the mirror. But more than anything in the world he loved and appreciated earned by any means, their money: they equated it with everything that was beyond him.

Recalling now bitterly Duns, that he decided to take her, despite her fame spread thin, Peter spoke quite frankly, and even felt a deep resentment against this "ingratitude." Meanwhile, Swat, then for Dunya, he was pretty sure the absurdity of these rumors, publicly denied most Marfa Petrovna and long since abandoned all cities hotly justifies Dunya. Yes, he did not deny now from the fact that it is already known then. And yet he still thought highly of their determination to raise Dunya herself and thought it was a feat. Pronouncing it now Dunya, he said his secret vozleleyannuyu them the idea to which he often admired, and could not understand how others could admire his feat. Appearing then visit to Raskolnikov, he went with a sense of benefactor, preparing to reap the benefits and to listen very sweet komplimenty.I, of course, now, down the stairs, he thought he was in the highest degree of pain and recognition.

Dunya was it absolutely necessary; give it up for him was unthinkable. Long ago, in a few years, with candy, he dreamed of getting married, but still

prikaplival money and waited. He enthusiastically dreamed, in the deepest secret, well-behaved girl and the poor (of course the poor), very young, very beautiful, noble and educated, very scared, very many have experienced misfortune and completely before he prinikshey, one that would consider it the lives of their salvation, in awe of him, obeyed, he was surprised, and only him. How many scenes, how sweet scene he created in his imagination, this seductive and playful themes, resting in the quiet of the case! And now the dream of so many years of almost lucky beauty and education Avdotya Romanovna struck him; helpless position, which causes it to an extreme. There was even a little bit more of what he wanted: she was proud characteristic, virtuous, education and development over him (he felt it), and such a creature would be slavishly grateful for his lifetime achievement and reverently be destroyed before him, and it's something infinitely and fully power! .. As luck would have it, shortly before, after much thought and expectations, he finally decided to completely change careers and start a wider range of activities, as well as together, little by little, and to a higher society which he had long thought of sensuality. .. In short, he decided to try Petersburg. He knew that women can be "very, very" much to gain. Sharm beautiful, virtuous and educated woman may surprise to brighten your way, bring it to create a halo ... and that's all falling apart! This current is suddenly an ugly gap affected him like a bolt from the blue. It was kind of ugly joke, an absurdity! He is only a modicum pokurazhitsya; he did not even have time to talk, and he was just joking, got carried away and ended so seriously! Finally, because he has loved even in his own Dunya, he had dominion over her in a dream - and all of a sudden! .. No! Tomorrow, tomorrow, all that needs to be restored in order to heal, correct, and most importantly - to destroy this arrogant Greenhorn, a boy who has been around the business. With painful sensation reminds him too somehow unwittingly, Razumikhin ... but, nevertheless, he soon calmed down from this side: "You bet, and it's something to put next to him!" But who is he really seriously afraid - so it Svidrigailov ... In short, it was a lot of trouble.

- No, I am more to blame for everything! - Said Dounia, hugging and kissing his mother - I feel for his money, but I swear, my brother - I never thought it was such an unworthy person. If I could see it earlier, I would have nothing to temptation! Do not blame me, brother!
- God delivered! God delivered! - Muttered Pulcheria Alexandrovna, but

somehow unconsciously, as if not quite an expert in making all that has happened.

Everyone was happy, even after five minutes of laughter. Sometimes only Dunya pale and moved his eyebrows, remembering what had happened. Pulcheria Alexandrovna and could not imagine that he also would be glad; rupture with Luzhin appeared to her in the morning terrible disaster. But Razumikhin was delighted. He did not dare to express it yet, but trembled as in a fever, and if the weight has been lifted from his heart pyatipudovaya. Now he has the right to give them all their lives to serve them ... But you'll never know that now! And yet, he still drove further thought timid and afraid of his imagination. Raskolnikov sat alone in the same place, almost morose and even more scattered.He simply move Luzhin insists, as if everything is now less interested in what happened. Dunya could not shake the idea that he was still very angry at her, and Pulcheria Alexandrovna looked at him with fear.

- What did you say Svidrigailov? - Approached him Dunya.

- Oh, yes, yes! - Exclaimed Pulcheria Alexandrovna.

Raskolnikov raised his head:

- He wants to, of course, give you ten thousand rubles, while claiming a desire to see you once in my presence.

- To See! Not for anything in the world! - Exclaimed Pulcheria Alexandrovna - and how dare he offer her money!

Then Raskolnikov handed (dryly) his conversation with Svidrigailov, omitting the specter of Marfa Petrovna, not to go into this matter and excessive aversion to start any conversation was, but the most necessary.

- What have you told him? - Asked Dunya.

- Firstly, said he did not give you anything. Then he announced that he would by all means, try to find out the date. He assured that his passion for you was a fad, and that he was not now do not you feel ... He does not want you to marry Luzhin ... Generally speaking haltingly.

- As you can explain it myself, Rodia? How did he show you?

- I admit that nothing good comes out of this do not understand.Offers ten thousand, and he said that he was not rich. Announces that he wants to go somewhere, and ten minutes later forgot what he said about this.Suddenly also says he wants to get married and that he, too, to persuade the bride ... Of course, it has a purpose, and probably , i'm terrible. But again, strangely assume that he is so stupid, he set to work, if you have bad intentions ... Of

course, I refused it for you, this money, once and for all. In general, it seemed very strange to me, and … … even with signs of madness. But I could be wrong; it just might be a kind of inflation. Death Marfa Petrovna seems to produce an impression on him …

- God rest her soul! - Exclaimed Pulcheria Alexandrovna - forever, forever for her to pray God! Well, what we have now, Dounia, without these three thousand! Lord, just fell from the sky!Oh, Rodia, because we all morning for three rubles for the soul remains, and we just Dunya and is calculated as if the clock somewhere as quickly as possible, to lay not only take until he figured it out.

Dunya is too impressed offer Svidrigailov. She still stood in thought.

- This is something terrible plans! - Almost she whispered to himself, almost shuddering.

Raskolnikov noticed excessive fear.

- It seems that I have more than once he saw - he said Dunya.

- We will follow! I found him - Razumikhin cried vigorously. - Eyes makes not'll set! I Rodia allowed. He told me himself that morning: "Take care of your sister." And you let me, Avdotya Romanovna?

Dunya smiled and held out her hand, but did not care did not leave her face. Pulcheria Alexandrovna timidly looked at her; However, three thousand, it seems to calm down.

Fifteen minutes later they were all in a lively conversation. Even Raskolnikov, although not speak, but listening carefully. Orated Razumikhin.

- And why, why did you leave! - Complete delight he Enthusiastic speech - and what you will do in the city? And most importantly, all of you together and from each other, it is necessary, as it is necessary - to get me! Well, at least for a while … I, however, take a friend, companion, and, of course, I can assure you that the idea of a great company. Listen, I have to explain in detail everything - the whole project! I have this morning, when nothing happened, so that flashed in my head … That's what: I have an uncle (I'll introduce you; preskladnoy and prepochtenny starichonka!), And he has thousand rubles uncle capital and pension and life is not necessary. The second year he clings to me, so I took from him a thousand, and he would have to pay six percent. I am what I see: he just wants to help me; but last year I was not needed, and this year I'm just waiting for his arrival and decided to take it. Then you give a thousand of your three, and it's pretty for the first time, so we joined. What do we do?

Here Razumikhin began to develop the project and talked a lot about how almost all of our bookstores and publishers know a bit confusing in its product, and hence is poor and publishers, while respectable publications pay off and pass percentage, sometimes significantly . On publishing and something dreamed Razumikhin, for two years and worked on other little knowledge of three European languages, despite the fact that six days ago, said that it was Raskolnikov that German "seams" in order to convince his take on the half-pass operation and the makings of three rubles, and then he lied, and Raskolnikov knew that he was lying.

- Why, why do we miss her when we have one of the most important tools was - their own money? - Hot Razumikhin. - Of course, you need a lot of work, but we will work, you, Avdotya Romanovna, I Rodion ... other publications now give a good percentage! And the main backbone of the company, which will know exactly what to translate. We translate and publish, and learn together. Now I can be helpful, because I have the experience. Within two years, will soon dart and publishers know the whole story: not saints molded pots, believe me! And why, why past the mouth piece to carry! Yes, I know myself, and I keep a secret, working on two or three, so that only a single idea to translate and publish them can take Stu rubles for each book, and one of them, and I thought that for five hundred rubles will not take, and what you think I said to someone, maybe even a usumnitsya Dubie, Lviv Oblast! And what about a real hassle for, printing, paper, sale, is that you take me! All crannies know! Gradually begin, until we reach a large, at least feed themselves than to be, and in any case it's true.

In Dunya eyes sparkled.

- What do you say, I really like Dmitri Prokofitch, - she said.

- Here I am, of course, know nothing, - said Pulcheria Alexandrovna - maybe it's good, but again, because God knows. New something unknown. Of course, we have to stay here, at least for a while ...

She looked at Rodyu.

- What do you think, brother? - Said Dounia.

- I think he has a very good idea, - he said. - About us, of course, to dream in advance is not necessary, but five or six books really can be published with undoubted success. I know myself, composition, be sure to go. As for the fact that he will be able to lead it, so there is no doubt: business sense ... However, you will have more time to come to an agreement ...

- Hooray! - Cried Razumikhin - now standing one apartment in the same

building, from the same owners. This is a special, separate, they did not report numbers, furniture fair price, three Gorenki. Here for the first time and take. I'll look tomorrow pawn and brought the money, and everything will be settled. And most importantly, all three can live together, and Rodia with you ... But where are you, Rodia?

- How Rodia, you're really going? - Even with fright asked Pulcheria Alexandrovna.

- In such a moment! - Razumikhin shouted.

Dunya looked at her brother with incredulous surprise. In his hand was a cap; he was preparing to leave.

- Quite often lose something you just bury me forever to say goodbye Ali - how strange he said.

He seemed to be smiling, but it was not a smile.

- But who knows, maybe the last time you saw each other, - he added casually.

He thought it was in itself, but as has been said aloud.

- What's wrong with you! - Exclaimed the mother.

- Where are you going, Rodia? - Oddly asked Dunya.

- So, I have to - he said vaguely, as if hesitant, he wanted to say. But in his pale face some sharp definition.

- I'm going to say ... here ... I wanted to tell you, Mom ... and you, Dunya, we better go for a while. I feel bad, I will not rest ... I do after I come, it will come when it will be possible .... I remember you and love you ... Leave me alone! Leave me alone! I decided even before ... I thought that maybe ... what would you do to me, and I was not going to die or not, I want to be alone. Forget me at all ... Better ... can not cope with me. If necessary, I will come ... or you'll get. Maybe everything will rise again! .. And now that you love me, give up ... Otherwise, I hate you, I feel ... Goodbye!

- The Lord! - Exclaimed Pulcheria Alexandrovna.

Both mother and sister were in a terrible fright; Razumikhin too.

- Rodia, Rodia! In order to make peace with us, we will continue! - Cried the poor mother.

He turned slowly to the door and walked slowly out of the room. Dunya caught up with him.

- Brother! What are you doing with my mother! - She whispered with a look burning with indignation.

He stared at her.

- Do not worry, I'll come, I'll go! - He muttered under his breath, as if not quite knowing what to say, and left the room.

- Insensitive, selfish evil! - Cried Dounia.

- It su-ma-down, not insensitive! He is crazy! Do not you see? You insensitive after that! .. - Hot Razumikhin whispered over her ear, squeezed his hand.

- I'll be right back! - He said, referring to pomertvevshey Pulcheria Alexandrovna, and ran from the room.

Raskolnikov was waiting for him at the end of the corridor.

- I knew you would not be enough, - he said. - The door to them and be with them tomorrow ... .. they always have. I ... I can not, I will come ... if you can. Farewell!

And, stretching out his hands, he was gone.

- Yeah, where are you? What are you? What is wrong with you? Do you think you can! .. - Muttered completely lost Razumikhin.

Raskolnikov stopped again.

- Once and for all: never about what I did not ask. I have nothing to answer to you ... Do not come near me.Maybe I'll come here ... Leave me and ... do not go. Do you understand me?

The hallway was dark; They stood beside the lamp. For a moment they looked at each other in silence.Razumikhin life remembered that moment. And the lights look like Raskolnikov increases with each passing minute, permeable in his soul consciousness. Razumikhin suddenly shuddered. Something strange, as if passed between them ... Some idea slipped, as if a hint that something horrible, ugly and suddenly realized on both sides ... Razumikhin turned pale as a corpse.

- Do you understand now? .. - Raskolnikov said with pain twisted face. - Gates, go to them, - he added, suddenly and quickly turned around and walked out of the house ...

Now I will not describe what it was that evening at Pulcheria Alexandrovna, as Razumikhin returned to them as they settle down, swore that he should be granted a rest in the disease, swore that Rodia certainly will walk every day, it very, very upset that we must not annoy him; he, Razumikhin, to follow him, he would get Dr. Good, better, a council ... In short, with this evening Razumikhin became their son and brother.

⇐«»⇒

↤« CHAPTER IV »↦

And Raskolnikov went straight to the house on the canal where Sonya lived.The storey house was old and green. He delved down janitor and received from him vague directions, where he lives Capernaum tailor. Found in the corner of the courtyard entrance to the narrow and dark staircase, he finally got up to the second floor and went to the gallery, bypassing his yard. While he was wandering in the dark and at a loss, which can be input in Kapernaumovs, suddenly, three steps away from him, opened the door; He grabbed her mechanically.

- Who's there? - Asked the voice alarm woman.

- This is me ... to you - Raskolnikov answered, and went into the tiny front. Here, on a broken chair in curved brass candlestick, candle stood.

- It's you! O Lord! - Sonya cried weakly and became as dead.

- Where are you? This Way?

And Raskolnikov, trying not to look at her, walked into the room as quickly as possible.

A minute later came with a candle and Sonia, candles and put yourself in front of him became totally confused, all in an indescribable excitement and apparently frightened by his unexpected visit.Suddenly paint ran into her pale face, and tears came to our eyes ... She was sick and ashamed, and sweet ... Raskolnikov quickly turned away and sat down on a chair to stolu. Prezhde than it can achieve a look at the room.

It was a large room, but is extremely low, just give Kapernaumovs, locked the door, which was left in the wall. On the opposite side, the wall on the right, was another door, always locked tight.There were other, neighboring

apartments, with different numbered. Sonin room was like as if the barn, took the form of a very irregular quadrangle, and it gave her something ugly. Wall with three windows on the ditch, haircuts room somehow accidentally, resulting in one corner, terribly sharp, running away somewhere deep, so that it, in low light, even impossible to distinguish good; another angle was too ugly stupid. In all of this large room had almost no furniture. In the right corner, there was a bed; next to it, closer to the door, a chair. For the same wall where the bed was, at the door of the apartment by someone else, was just a message board table covered with a small blue cloth; Around the table, two wicker chairs. Then, at the opposite wall, not far from an acute angle, was a small, simple wooden chest of drawers, as if lost in the void. That's all that was in the room. Yellowish, obshmygannye wallpaper and worn blackened from all angles; should have been here in the winter damp and evaporation. Poverty was visible; bed was not even curtains.

Sonia looked at his guest, so attentively and unceremoniously considers his room, and even started, finally, trembling with fear, just standing in front of a judge and determined their fate.

- I'm late … Eleven o'clock there? - He asked, still not looking up.

- Yes, - muttered Sonia. - Oh, yes, there is! - Suddenly she hastily, as if it was all the result - is now struck … and I heard myself … there.

- I am to you for the last time came - grimly Raskolnikov went on, although it was now only the first - I may be, you will not see …

- Are you going?

- I do not know … tomorrow …

- So you will not be tomorrow at Katerina Ivanovna? - Cracked voice Sony.

- I do not know. All in the morning … not the point: I have come to say one word …

He looked at her pensive look and suddenly noticed that he was sitting, and she was still standing in front of him.

- Why are you standing? Sit down, - he said suddenly variable, quiet and gentle voice.

She sat down. He kindly and almost compassionately looked at her for a moment.

- What do you thin! Get what your hands! Very transparent. Fingers, as if dead.

He took her hand. Sonia smiled weakly.

- I've always been so, - she said.

- When and lived in the house?

- Yes I Am.

- Well, of course! - Briefly he said, and his face and the sound of voices suddenly change. He looked around again.

298

- Are you from Kapernaumovs hire?

- Yes, sir …

- They're at the door?

- Yes … They also have a room.

- All in one?

- One-to.

- I would be in your room at night was afraid - he said grimly.

- The owners are very good, very affectionate - Sonia, still would not like coming to himself and realized - and all the furniture and everything … everything economical. And they are very good, and the children often come to me …

- This is a tongue-tied?

- Yes, sir … He stutters and Chrome too. And his wife, too … Not that stutters, but it seems that not all talk. She is kind, very much. And he was a former serf. A seven children … and only one senior stutters, while others just sick … and do not stutter … And you know, how about them? - She said with some surprise.

- I am your father then told all. He told me all about you … and talk about how you went at 6:00 and came back in the ninth, and how Katerina Ivanovna in her bed on her knees.

Sonia was confused.

- I saw him just now - she whispered hesitantly.

- Who?

- Father. I walked down the street near there on the corner, at 10:00, and if it goes ahead. And just as if it were. I really wanted to go to Katerina Ivanovna …

- Did you go?

- Yes - Sonia whispered sharply again embarrassed and looking down.

- Katerina Ivanovna, because you just can not beat him, his father, then?

- Oh, no, you know what you do not! - With some even fear Sonia looked at him.

- So you love her?

- Her? Yes ka-a-ak same!- Sonia gave a plaintive and suffering suddenly threw up her hands. - Ah! If you have ... you just knew it. In the end, it's just like a child ... After her mind just as obsessed ... with grief. And it was smart ... what ... what kind of generous! You have nothing, I know nothing ... ah!

Sonia said it exactly in despair, worrying and suffering, and wringing her hands. Her pale cheeks flushed again, put it in the eyes of flour. It was obvious that he picked up a lot of what she really wanted to express something, say, to intercede. Some insatiable compassion, if I may say so, to portray suddenly all her facial features.

- Bill! What do you mean it! Lord, beat! And even if the beat, so what! Well, so what? You have nothing, I know nothing ... It's so unhappy, oh, what a miserable! And hurt ... She seeks justice ... it's clean. She believes so in all fairness should be, and requires ... Although torture her, and she will not do injustice. She does not understand how it can not be all that was unfair to the people, and annoying ... As a child, like a child! This is true, honest!

- Would you?

Sonia looked questioningly.

- They're on you're gone. This, however, before it's you, and dead at the same hangover you went to ask. Well, here is what will happen?

- I do not know - sadly said Sonia.

- They will remain there?

- I do not know that they have the apartment; Just heard the hostess said today that he wants to deny, and Katerina Ivanovna says that she will not stay a minute.

- Where is she so boldly? You had hoped?

- Oh, no, do not say so! .. We are one, we live together - suddenly excited again and even annoying Sonia, in the balance, as if angry canary or any other bird. -? And how can it be, that's why, how can this be? - She asked, hot and agitated. - And how much she cried today! In her mind gets in the way, you did not notice? Trouble; then worry about how little that tomorrow was decent, snacks, and all were ... then wrung her hands, coughing up blood, cries, suddenly begins to bang your head against the wall in frustration. But then again, comforted, it is for you all hopes: he says that you are now her assistant and that it somewhere and take a bit of the money will go to his city, with me, and boarding school for noble girls will, but I will matron, and we will have a brand new, beautiful life, and kisses me, hugging, comforting, and believes that it is! so we believe anything fancy! Well, if you

did not contradict him? But it all day today, washes, cleans, repairs, trough itself, with its weak force to pull the room, out of breath, and fell on the bed; but we are still in the ranks of her morning walk, shoes and polka Lena buy because they have collapsed, but we have no money and was not on the calculation, it is severely lacking, and she chose such nice little shoes, because we have a taste that you do not know ... That in the store and started to cry when merchants do not have enough ... Oh, it was a pitiful sight.

- Well, it's clear after you ... So live, - said with a bitter smile Raskolnikov.

- And you do not mind? Do not feel sorry for? - Sonya sharply again - because of you, I know you recently gave himself, but seeing nothing. And if you saw something, Lord! And how many times I had her in tears on the Internet! Yes last another week! Oh, I do! Just a week before his death. I came violently! And how many times I have done it. And now, as a day to remember it hurts!

Sonia even clapped her hands saying, pain memories.

- What do something cruel?

- Yes, I am, I am! I came then - she continued crying - and the dead, and saying, "Look at me, says Sonia, my head is something hurts, read my book here ..." - the kind of book that he, Andrew took Semenycha have Lebezyatnikov life here, for example, he took out all the funny books. And I say, "I must go," and do not want to read, and I went to him, more importantly, that the collars show Katerina Ivanovna; I Lizaveta, suppliers, collars and cuffs brought cheap, nice, fresh and with a pattern. And Katerina Ivanovna liked, she put in the mirror and looked at myself, and really, really enjoyed it, "let me say that they are, Sonia, please." Please ask for and so much she wanted to. But where to put it! So: first, only to recall a happy time! Look at yourself in the mirror, admiring, and indeed, there is something her dress is not something any of the things that's really how many years! And do what she never someone to ask; proud, very soon will, at last, and then ask - because she liked it! And I'm sorry to give "what you say, Katerina Ivanovna?" And he said, "what." Oh, that's not what we would have to tell her! She looked at me, and so it was hard to hard, that I refused, so it was a pity to look ... And it's not hard collar, and for the fact that I refused, I have seen. Ah, so would seem now all gates, all redone all the former words ... Oh, I ... yes! .. You do not care!

- This Lizaveta market woman, you know?

- Yes ... And do you know? - With some surprise asked Sonia.

- Katerina Ivanovna in consumption, in evil; she died - said Raskolnikov,

after a pause, not answering the question.

- Oh, no, no, no! - And Sonia unconscious gesture grabbed both his hands, as if asking not.

- Why it's better Well, so die.

- No, not better, better is better! - Scared and instinctively she repeated.

- Then the children? Where you then take them because they do not it?

- Oh, I do not know! - Sonia cried almost in despair and clutched her head. It was evident that this idea too much time alone broke, and he just got scared again this idea.

- Well, if you say, even when Katerina Ivanovna, now ill and hospitalized svezut you, what then? - Ruthlessly he insisted.

- Oh, you, you! That's what really can not be! - And his face contorted Sony terrible fright.

- How can this be? - Raskolnikov went with a stiff smile - you are not insured? Then what will happen to them? On the street with all the crowd going, she would cough and beg and wall somewhere head-banging, as it is today, and the children crying ... And will fall in parts svezut, the hospital will die, and children ..

- Oh, no! .. God will not suffer! - Finally escaped from the crowded chest Sony. She listened with a request to look at him, and his hands clasped in silent request because it all depended.

Raskolnikov got up and began pacing the room. It took about a minute. Sonya stood with his hands and head, in terrible anguish.

- Stash can not? Set aside for a rainy day? - He asked, suddenly stopping in front of her.

- No, - whispered Sonya.

- Of course not! And try? - He added, almost mockingly.

- Tried.

- A disappointed! Well, yes, of course! This is ask!

And he went back to the room. Another took a minute.

- Not every day you get something?

Sonia was confused more than ever, and paint again hit her in the face.

- No, - she whispered with a painful process.

- Polka probably the same thing will happen - he said suddenly.

- No! no! There can not be! - How desperate Sonia screamed as if she suddenly stabbed. - God, God will not allow such a horror! ..

- Other allows the same.

- No, no! God will protect her, O Lord! .. - I repeat it, beside himself.

- Yes, it can, and God is not at all - with some even gloating said Raskolnikov, laughed and looked at her.

Sony scary face suddenly changed: he ran for seizures. With unutterable reproach she looked at him, trying to say something, but she could not speak and just suddenly sobbed bitterly, his hands over his face.

- You say that the mind interferes with Katerina Ivanovna; Do you mind very dirty - he said after a pause.

It took about five minutes. He continued to walk up and down in silence, without looking at her. Finally, it came to him; his eyes sparkled. He took her by the shoulders with both hands and looked straight into her tearful face. His eyes were dry, inflamed, hot, lips trembled a lot ... all of a sudden he bent down quickly and then lying on the floor, kissed her on the leg. Sonia terrified of him recoiled as from a madman. In fact, he looked just like a madman.

- What are you, what are you doing? In front of me! - She murmured, turning pale and absolutely sick suddenly gripped her heart.

He immediately stood up.

- I do not admire you, I bowed to all human suffering - as wildly he said, and walked to the window. - Listen, - he added, the gate to her in a minute - I just said a criminal, that he should not be one of the little finger ... and what I did to my sister today honor, placing it next to you,

- Oh, what do you tell them! And she? - Sonia screamed in terror - to sit with me! Honor! Why, I ... I ... dishonest great, great sinner! Oh, you said it!

- Do not shame and sin I said, it's about you, but for your great suffering. And you are a great sinner, so, - he added almost enthusiastically - and, above all, so that you are a sinner, that needlessly sacrificed and gave himself. Nevertheless, it is not scary! However, not horror that you live in the mud, which is so hated, and at the same time to know yourself (only worth eyes reveal) that someone you do not help anyone if nothing save! Yes, tell me, finally, - he said, almost in a frenzy - as a kind of shame and such meanness you alongside other extreme and sacred feelings together? In the end, just a thousand times fair and reasonable would be straight into the water and immediately put an end!

- And with them, what will? - Weak demand hurt Sonia looked at him, but at the same time, it is not surprised by his predlozheniem.Raskolnikov looked at her strangely.

He had read in one of her eyes. Thus, in fact in itself already been the idea.

Maybe a lot of time and seriously considering him to despair, as if to put an end once and for up to a serious, that is now almost did not surprise him an offer. Even the harsh words that he did not notice (and therefore reviled him, and his special look at her, she's a shame, of course, also have not noticed, and it was probably for him). But he realized quite what a terrible pain tormented her, and for a long time, the idea of dishonorable and shameful of their position. Well, it would, he thought, for now, to stop her determination to put an end to them? It was only then that he realized exactly what it meant for these poor little orphans, and this pathetic, half-crazy Katerina Ivanovna, with his tuberculosis and Stukanov head against the wall.

However, it was again clear that Sonia with its own character and as a development that it has received, in any case can not be so. However, for him it was a question: why is it already too long can remain in that position and not crazy, if not the strength to jump into the water? Of course, it should be understood that the position of Sony is a phenomenon of random in society, but, unfortunately, not one, but not exclusively. But this is something a chance, some developed this and all previous life may seem right to kill her at the first step towards this is disgusting. That supports it? Not debauchery same? In the end, it's a shame obviously touched her only mechanically; real depravity had not yet reached any drop odnoyu in her heart: he saw it;She stood before him really ...

"She was three roads - he thought - to go into the ditch, get into the crazy house, or ... or, finally, to jump into debauchery, intoxicates the mind and heart okamenyayuschy." The last thought was him all the more disgusting; but he was a skeptic, he was young, distraction and, therefore, cruel and, therefore, can not help but believe that the last exit, that is debauchery, was only probable.

"But really Well, it's true - he exclaimed to himself - and it's very good creation, but to preserve the purity of spirit, deliberately lured Finally, in this complex, stinking pit is drawing has already begun, and do so only she could tolerate It? s not up to the fact that the vice-no longer seems so disgusted No, no, this can not be ?! - he exclaimed, as previously Sonia - no, from the ditch held her still thinking about sin, and they are those who ... If it is still not crazy ... But who said that she was not mad? Is this normal? Is that how can you say? this is a reasonable way we can argue? Is it so you can sit on death just above the stinking pit, which has already attracted her, and waving his arms, and plugging his ears when she talked about the danger?

ROBOTS READ

What is this, I do not be surprised if waiting for? And probably so. Is not it all a sign of madness? "

He stopped at the persistence of this idea. This finding it even more loved than any other. He began to take a closer look at him.

- So you really pray to God something, Sonya? - He asked her.

Sonia was silent, he stood next to her and waited for an answer.

- Why would I do without God once was? - Quickly vigorously she whispered, suddenly caught throwing his sparkling eyes and tightly squeezed her hand in hand.

"Well, there it is!" - He thought.

- Are you God for what he is doing? - He asked, extorting further.

Sonia was silent, as if she could not answer. Weakness in the chest heaving from her all the excitement.

- Shut Your Mouth! Do not ask! You do not deserve! .. - She suddenly screamed and looking sternly at him angrily.

"That's right! This is it!" - He repeated himself aggressively.

- It's all done! - Quickly she whispered, looking down.

"This is the result! This explanation is the result!" - He thought to himself, with an insatiable curiosity regarding it.

With a new, strange, almost painful feeling, he looked into this pale, thin, angular face and wrong, those soft blue eyes, which could flash with such fire, a heavy feeling of energy in that little body still shaking with indignation and anger and it all seemed to him more and more strange, almost impossible. "Simpleton! Fool!"- He kept saying to himself.

On the bedside table lay a book. Every time he goes back and forth, saw her; now went and looked. It was the New Testament translated into Russian. The book was an old, used, bound in leather.

- This is where? - He called her around the room. She stopped at the same place in three steps from the table.

- They brought me - she said, as if unwillingly, not looking at him.

- Who brought it?

- Lizaveta brought, I asked.

"Lizaveta! Strange!" - He thought. All Sonia became for him somehow strange and wonderful, with every minute. He suffered a book to the candle and began to leaf through.

- Where to Lazarus? - Suddenly he asked.

Sonia looked at the ground and said nothing. She was standing a little

sideways to the table.

- On the Resurrection of Lazarus where? Find it for me, Sonya.

She looked at him sideways.

- Do not look back ... in the fourth Gospel ... - she whispered sternly, without moving him.

- Find and read it to me - he said, and sat down, leaned on the table, leaned his head on his hands and stared sullenly away, ready to listen.

"Three weeks later, in the seventh kilometer, welcome, I think he will be there, if not worse ,!" - he muttered under his breath.

Sonia came hesitantly to the table in disbelief when he heard a strange desire to Raskolnikov. Nevertheless, he took the book.

- Did not you read? - She asked, looking at him across the table from under his brows. Her voice was getting tougher and tougher.

- For a long time ... When studied. Read!

- And in the church have not heard?

- I ... do not go. Do you often go?

- N-no, - whispered Sonya.

Raskolnikov smiled.

- I see ... And my father, so I do not go tomorrow to bury?

- Bring It On. I was last week ... Requiem served.

- For whom?

- By Lizaveta. Her ax killed.

His nerves were irritated more and more. His head spun.

- You were one of Lizaveta?

- Yes ... it was just ... it came ... rare ... it was impossible. We read it and said .... She must see God.

It sounded strange to him these words of the book, and again the news: some mysterious meetings with Lizaveta and both - fools.

"So he became a holy fool! Contagious!" - He thought. - Read! - He suddenly exclaimed emphatically and irritability.

Sonya still hesitated. Her heart was pounding. Did not dare, as soon as she told him to read. Almost from the torment, he looked at the "wretched man possessed."

- Why do you need? In the end, you do not believe? .. - Quiet and somehow she whispered breathlessly.

- Read! I want it! - He insisted - as Lizaveta read!

Sonya opened the book and found the place. Her hands were trembling

voice lacked. Twice she has become, and all does not say the first syllable.

"There was also someone sick, Lazarus ..." - she said at last, with an effort, but suddenly, with the third word, a voice rang out and broke, as too taut string. Spirit crossed the chest and embarrassment.

Raskolnikov partly understood why Sonya was hesitant to read it and know more about it, the more so rude and irritable insisted on reading. He knew only too well how difficult it was to give her now and put all their own. He understood that these feelings were actually, as it is a long, maybe the mystery of her, maybe even with a teenager, even in the family, which was his father and stepmother accident mad with grief, among the hungry children, the ugly shouts and reproaches. But at the same time he learned now, and probably learned that even though she missed and was afraid something terrible, starting to read now, but at the same time she wanted to read the most painful, despite the suffering and fears and it is to him that he had heard, and, of course, now - " ! Whatever happened then, "... He read it in her eyes, knew her ecstatic excitement ... She forced herself choking throat spasm, at the beginning of presekshuyu verse her voice, and continued to read the eleventh chapter of the Gospel of John. So dochla it until the 19th verse:

"And many of the Jews had come to Martha and Mary to comfort them concerning their brother Martha heard that Jesus was coming, went and met him: but Mary sat .. home Then said Martha unto Jesus, Lord, if you had been here, my died brother. But now I know that whatever You ask of God, will give you. "

Then she stopped again, shamefully expecting her trembling voice breaks again ...

"Jesus saith unto her, Thy brother shall rise Martha said to him, I know he would rise again in the resurrection at the last day Jesus said to her .. I am the resurrection and the life: he that believeth in me, though he were dead, yet shall he live. And whoever lives and he that believeth in me shall never die. Do you believe this? She saith unto him,

(As if the pain of breathing, Sonia separately and with the power to read, just very publicly admitted):

Yes, Lord! I believe that thou art the Christ, the Son of God, come into the world. "

She was stopped, she quickly rose to his eyes, but soon made herself and began to read more. Raskolnikov sat and listened motionless, paying no

elbows on the table and looking away. Dochli in 32 verses.

"Mary, when they came to where Jesus was and saw him, fell at his feet, and said unto him, Lord, if You had been here, would not have died my brother. And when Jesus saw her weeping, and the Jews who came weeping, he groaned in the spirit, and was troubled. And said, Where have you laid him? They say unto him, Lord, come and see. Jesus wept. Then said the Jews, Behold how he loved him. And some of them said, could not he opened the eyes of the blind, have caused that even this man from dying? "

Raskolnikov turned to her and looked anxiously at her, yes, it is! She already shaking in fact, this heat. He expected. She went to the word's greatest and unprecedented miracle, and a sense of great triumph came for her. Her voice began to call, as the metal; triumph and joy were heard in it and fixed it. Lines mixed up in front of her, because in the eyes darkened, but she knew by heart, she read. When the last verse: "Could not he who opened the eyes of the blind ..." - she lowered her voice, fervently and pas-sionately conveyed doubt reproach and blasphemy against the infidels, the blind Jews, who are now in a minute, thunder, and in the fall, crying and have faith ... "And he, he - too blinded and unbelieving, - he, too, now hear it too confident, yes, yes, now, now, "- dreamed of her, and she trembled with joyful expectation.

. "Jesus therefore again groaning in himself comes to the grave It was a cave, and a stone lay upon it, Jesus said, Take away the stone Marta, sister of the deceased said to him .. Lord, already smells, for four days, as it is in a coffin. "

She vigorously slapped on the floor: four.

"Jesus saith unto her, Said I not unto you that if you believed, you would see the glory of God? Then they took away the stone from the place where the dead was laid. And Jesus lifted up his eyes and said, Father, I thank thee that thou hast heard me. I knew that you always hear me, but I said this for the people standing here, that they may believe that thou hast sent me. Having said that, crying with a loud voice, Lazarus, come forth. And the dead man came out,

(Loudly and enthusiastically read it, shaking and turning cold, as if he had seen in ochiyu):

bound hand and foot with linen cloths; and his face was associated with a handkerchief. Jesus saith unto them, Loose him; let him go.

Then many of the Jews which came to Mary, and had seen what Jesus

did, believed in him. "

Further, she did not read and could not read, closed the book and quickly rose from his chair.

- All of the resurrection of Lazarus - abruptly and harshly whispered she became motionless, turning away, hesitating, as if ashamed to look at him. Ague was until now. The calcine has long been extinguished in curved candles, dim lighting in the room impoverished murderer and the harlot who have come together to read strange eternal book. He took five minutes or more.

- I came to talk about the case - and loudly said, frowning Raskolnikov got up and went to Sonya. She stared at him. His eyes were particularly heavy, and some wild determination expressed in it.

- Today I threw relatives - he said - his mother and sister. I will not go into them now. I tore it all.

- How Come? - How stunned asked Sonia. Daveshny meeting with his mother and sister had left her in the extraordinary impression that she remains unclear. News break she listened almost with horror.

- Now I have one that you - he added. - Let's ... I come to you. Together, we are cursed, and let's go together!

His eyes glittered. "How crazy!" - The idea, in turn, Sonia.

- Where to go? - She asked with fear and involuntarily stepped back.

- How do I know? I only know that one of the ways probably know - and only. One purpose!

She looked at him, and do not understand anything. She knew only that he was terribly, infinitely unhappy.

- No one knows of them, if you need to tell them, - he continued - and I understand. I need you because I have come to you.

- I do not understand ... - Sonia whispered.

- Then realize. You did not do the same? You, too, went ... can cross. You are the owner of the hand to the left, you have destroyed a life ... it (this is!). You might live in the spirit and the mind, and ended at the Haymarket ... But you can not stand, and if you stay alone, go crazy as I am. You are better now, like a madman; Therefore, we go together, on the same road! Come on!

- How Come? Why, you! - Sonya said, strange and rebellious glad his words.

- How Come? Because it is impossible to stay - that's why! Wow, finally judge seriously and directly, rather than the baby cries and shouts that God

will not allow! Well, what would happen if in fact you are in the hospital tomorrow svezut? It is not in the mind, and consumptive, will soon die, and children? Polechka is not to die? Have not seen you here for the children, in the corners, which are sent alms mother ask for? I learned where these mothers live and under what circumstances. The children can not remain children. There's a seven-year depraved and a thief. But children - the image of Christ: "Ring the kingdom of God." He ordered them to honor and love, they are the future of mankind ...

- Well, what do you do? - Hysterically crying and wringing her hands, repeated Sonia.

- What to do? Break that must once and for all, and only: suffering and take over! What? Do not you understand? After understand ... Freedom and power, and most importantly the power! For all the trembling creature, and over all the anthill! .. That's the goal! Remember this! This is my farewell to you! Maybe I'm with you last spoke. If you do not come tomorrow, you will hear everything about yourself, then remember these words are present day. And someday, then, over the years, with life, maybe you will understand what they meant. If I come tomorrow, he'll tell you who killed Lizaveta. Farewell!

Sonia all trembling with fear.

- Do you think you know who killed him? - She asked, ledeneya horror and, looking at him wildly.

- I know ... and I'll tell you who you are! I chose you. I did not come to ask for forgiveness for you, I'm just saying. I have been chosen to tell you this, even when my father was talking about you and when Lizaveta was alive, I thought. Goodbye. Do not let your hands. Tomorrow!

He went out. Sonia looked at him as a madman; but she herself was like a madman, and felt it. His head was spinning it. "Lord, how he knows who killed Lizaveta? What is the meaning of these words? It is terrible that!" But at the same time, the thought never crossed her mind. nothing! nothing! .. "Oh, it must be terribly miserable! .. He left his mother and sister. Why? What happened? And what is it intentions? What did he say to her? He kissed her foot and said ... said (yes, he said it was clear) that without him I can not live ... Oh, my God! "

In the delirium of fever and spent the night Sonia. She jumped up crying sometimes, wrung her hands, then forgotten again a fever dream, and she dreamed Polechka, Katerina Ivanovna, Lizaveta, reading the Gospel and he

... he, with his pale face, with burning eyes ... He kisses her feet, crying ... Oh my goodness!

Behind the door on the right, for toyu samoyu doors that separated the apartment from the apartment of Gertrude Sony Karlovna Resslih had a room intermediate, has long been empty, belonged to the apartment of Mrs. Resslih and gave it out, and that was exhibited at the gate and the label pasted on the glass bumazhechki entrance into a ditch. Sonia has long been accustomed to thinking of the room occupied. And yet, all this time, the door to an empty room and stood Mr. Svidrigailov, hiding, overheard. When Raskolnikov went out, he stood, he thought, on tiptoe to his room, next to an empty room, pushed back his chair and quietly brought him to the door leading into the room Sony. The conversation seemed to him entertaining and memorable, and very, very much - as before, he moved to a chair in the future, tomorrow, for example, not to be in need get back on their feet for an hour and get pokomfortnee, so too in all respects, To get the full benefit.

⤝ CHAPTER V ⤞

The next morning, at exactly 11:00, Raskolnikov went into the house, - the second part in the investigation into the police department and asked to report on themselves Porfiry Petrovitch, he was surprised at how long it took: the past, in at least ten minutes before he was called. And according to his calculations, would seem to be so good for him and pounce.Meanwhile, he stood in the waiting room, and walked past him and took the people who seem not to him was not the case. In the next room, like the office, sat and wrote some of the scribes, and it was obvious that none of them had no idea who or what Raskolnikov? Restless and suspicious eyes followed him around, looking at that is not about him, at least some of the convoy, a mysterious kind assigned to guard him, that he was not there, where? But nothing of the sort: he saw only one office, a little anxious person, then another, some people, and no, there is no need for him, although he now go on all four sides. Harder and harder to support the idea that if indeed this mysterious man yesterday, it was a ghost that appeared out of the ground, knew every-thing and everyone saw everything - so it would give him, Raskolnikov, so now stand and wait quietly? And not waiting for him here until 11:00, while he likes to Welcome? It turned out that the man or not yet reported or ... or just something he does not know himself, his eyes have not seen anything (and how could he see?), And, therefore, all that, yesterday, the incident with him Raskolnikov, again, it was a ghost, exaggerated irritation and his sick imagination. This hypothesis is not even yesterday, during the most intense anxiety and despair, began to strengthen it.Changed his mind and now everything is ready for a new battle, he suddenly felt the shivers - and even

anger boiled in him at the thought that he was trembling with fear hateful Porfiry Petrovich.Total worse for him was to meet this man again, he hated him without measure endlessly, and even feared that his hatred then find themselves. So strong was his indignation that immediately stopped shaking; he is ready to go into the cold and arrogant expression and promised as much as possible to remain silent, looking and listening, at least, this time, at least, is that no matter what, do not beat painfully irritated his nature. At that time he was called to Porfiry Petrovich.

It turned out that at this moment Porfiry Petrovitch in his office alone. His office was a room no more, no less; were in it: a large desk in front of a sofa, soft oilcloth, a bureau, a wardrobe in the corner and a few chairs - all gate furniture, yellow polished. In the corner, in the rear wall, or rather, in the septum was locked door there on, behind a partition, must, therefore, be some other room. At the entrance to Porfiry Petrovitch Raskolnikov immediately closed the door, he went in, and they were alone. He met his guest, apparently, with the most cheerful and affable air, and there are only a few minutes later Raskolnikov, in some respects, saw it, as if confused - he just suddenly misleading or caught on something very solitary and secretive.

- Ah, my dear sir! Here you ... in our neighborhood ... - Porfiry began, holding both his hands. - Well, sit down, sir! Ali, you may not like to call you respect and ... sir ?, - So tout court 1 For an introduction, please do not believe ... And here, sir, on the couch.

Raskolnikov sat down without taking his eyes off him.

"In our region," apology acquaintance, French mot "Tout Court" and so on, and so on - .. All these signs characteristics. "He, however, for me, both hands extended, and no one really did not give needed time" - flashed at him with suspicion. Both look at each other, but only that their eyes met, and with lightning speed from each other.

- I brought you this piece of paper ... something ... hours, sir. So, whether written or rewritten again?

- What? A piece of paper? Well, well ... do not worry, because, sir, - he said, as if hurrying somewhere, Porfiry Petrovitch and has already said this, he took the paper and looked at it. - Yes, just c.Nothing more necessary - he confirmed the same patter and put the paper on the table. Then, a moment later, to talk about the other, and took her back to the table and went over to his desk.

- You seem to be saying yesterday that want to ask me ... Uniforms ... about

my acquaintance with this ... killed? - Raskolnikov began again, - "Well, why do I put this? - flashed like lightning. - Well, why me so much about what to put in it? "- flashed at once another thought like lightning.

And suddenly he felt his suspicion, from one contact with Porfiry, only two words, only two opinions in an instant grew to monstrous proportions ... and it's a terrible danger: irritated nerves, the excitement increases."Problem! Problem! .. Again let slip."

- Yes, yes, yes! Do not worry! Time suffer, suffer with time - muttered Porfiry Petrovich, pohazhivaya and back around the table, but somehow aimlessly, as if throwing it out the window, and then in the office, then back to the table, then avoiding fisheye Raskolnikov suddenly stopped himself on the ground and looked at him straight in the face. It seemed very strange and at the same time it is small, plump and round number as the ball rolled in different directions at once and bounce off the walls and corners.

- We'll do it, sir, there is a time-a! .. Do you smoke? Do you have? Here, sir, cigarettes ... - he went on, giving the guest a cigarette. - You know, I agree with you here, and that my apartment here, behind a partition ... shutter with, and I am now on free for some time. The correction should have been here Coy any organized.It's almost ready ... government apartment, you know, it's a good thing - right? As you think?

- Yes, a good thing - Raskolnikov answered, almost mockingly at him.

- Good thing, good thing ... - repeated Porfiry Petrovitch, and if I had to think of something completely different - yes! Good thing! - I almost cried in the end, he suddenly raised his eyes to Raskolnikov and stopping a few feet away from him. This is stupid repetition of this government apartment is a good thing, too, vulgarity, despite serious and mysterious appearance, he was looking at his guest.

But it is even more anger podkipyatilo Raskolnikov, and he could not resist mocking and rather carelessly call.

- And you know what - he asked suddenly, almost defiantly looks at him as if feeling pleasure from his courage - is there seems to be a legal norm, such as the right method - for all possible research - first start from afar, on trifles, or even serious, but completely alien, so to speak, encourage, or rather entertaining conversationalist, to lull his caution, and then suddenly, surprisingly stun him in the crown is the way some of the most deadly and dangerous question, is not it? It seems to be all rules and teachings are still sacred mentioned?

- Well, well … what do you think, I have a breech of the apartment … yes? - And, having said this, Porfiry Petrovich squinted, winked, something fun and challenging passed over his face, forehead wrinkles are smoothed out, eyes narrowed, particularly stretched, and he suddenly burst into nervous laughter long worrying and swaying his body and looking right in the eyes of Raskolnikov. He laughed himself was somewhat forced herself; but when Porfiry, seeing that he was also laughing, Sunset has a laugh that almost turned purple, then disgust Raskolnikov suddenly gone all caution: he stopped laughing, frowned and looked long and hatred to Porfiry, never taking his eyes off him, in all for his long and as if with the intention of continuous laughter.Negligence was clear, however, on both sides: it seemed that Porfiry Petrovich, how to laugh in the face of his guest, taking laughter with hatred and very little embarrassed by this circumstance, the latter was very important for Raskolnikov He knew that, right, Porfiry Petrovitch and this morning was not ashamed, but, on the contrary, he Raskolnikov caught, perhaps in a trap; that obviously there is something he does not know what purpose; that perhaps all is already prepared, and now, at this moment, to discover and fall …

He immediately went straight to the point, got up and took his cap.

- Porfiry Petrovich, - he said firmly, but with a fairly strong irritability - Yesterday you expressed the desire that I have to come to some kind of questioning. (This is especially uper word: interrogations). I came, and, if necessary, so ask not what really let me go. I have no time, I thing … I have to be at the funeral of the most horses crushed the officer that you know … … well, - he said, and immediately got angry with this add-on, but because once again irritably - I'm tired of all this, with the face, and for a long time already … I'm kind of tired … and it was in one word - almost cried he felt that the phrase about the disease even more out of place - one word, if you please, or ask me or let go now … and if you ask, you will not only as a format! Otherwise excluded; so now forgive, as the two of us now have nothing to do.

- The Lord! What do you mean it! Yes to ask you - wheezed suddenly Porfiry Petrovitch, immediately changing the tone and look and instantly stop laughing - so do not worry, please - he fussed, again rushing in all directions, and then suddenly sit accepted Raskolnikov - suffers, suffers-time s, and all this nonsense of some sort, sir! On the contrary, I'm glad you finally came to us … I accept you as a guest. And for that laugh Damn you, Rodion Romanovich Father, forgive me. Rodion Romanovich? So, you think a priest?

.. Nervous man, sir, you amused me very sharpness of your comments; sometimes, right, shaking like gummilastik, so that the path for half an hour ... Smeshliv sir. On my physique even paralysis fear. Yes, take the same as you?.. I ask you, sir, but I thought that you were unhappy with ...

Raskolnikov was silent, listening and watching, still frowning angrily. However, he sat down, but without releasing the lid.

- I'll tell you one thing, my dear Rodion Romanovich, I say to myself, so to speak, based on the characteristics - continued to fuss about the room, Porfiry Petrovitch and still, how to avoid eye contact with the guest. - I know, man is free, and non-secular views known, and finished with a guy numbness People-S, the seed went and ... and ... and l noticed you, Rodion Romanovich, that we are, we are here in Russia with, and, above all, in our circles of St. Petersburg that if two smart man, but not too familiar with each other, but, so to speak, mutually respect each other, that's how we're with you, sir, have gathered together, then half an hour can not find a topic of conversation - numbness with each other, sit and mutually confusion. We all have things to say, ladies, for example ... in a secular, for example, people with a higher tone, there is always a topic of conversation, c'est etiquette, 1 and the average person, like us - all embarrassed and silent. .. I think it is. Why is it, sir, there, sir? Interests of the population, whether that neither Ali honest, that we are not very deceiving each other and do not want to, I do not know, sir. Huh? What do you think? Yes furazhechku the side, sir, I just want to leave now, right, looks awkward ... I, on the contrary, so pleased ...

Raskolnikov put on his cap, while continuing to remain silent and serious, frowning listen to empty talk and inconsistent porphyria. "But what he really wants to know, that my attention to entertain his drivel?"

- You do not ask for coffee, which has no place; but five minutes of time, why not sit down with a friend for fun - not stopping showered Porphyria - and know with all these responsibilities ... but you, sir, do not get me wrong, I'm still here I go, sir, back so on; I'm sorry, sir, you really hurt terribly, and exercise, so I just need to.All sit and we are so pleased that five minutes ... hemorrhoids, with ... all gymnastics will address; there, they say, the state, and even the actual state secret advisers would jump through verevku-; won in science, and in this century, with ... with ... And what about those local duties, interviews and all this formality ... here you are, sir, now deign to mention the interrogations themselves-with, well .. You know, actually, my dear Rodion Romanovich, these interrogations investigators sometimes

more than the interviewee, confused blow … It is you, sir, with perfect justice and wit now deigned to notice. (Raskolnikov did not notice anything like that) .Sbivaet confused, sir! Yes, tangled! And yet it is the same, all the same, like a drum! Vaughn reform is coming and we are even in the name of something we have renamed, heh, heh, heh! But nothing is something our methods - legal, as witty happy to say - so it's quite agree with you, ser.Nu who say that of all the defendants, even the most homespun Muzhichi does not know what his example, first begin extraneous questions posed to sleep (for your happy expression), and then suddenly and ogoroshat the top of the head with the butt-he-he-he-he! most crown on your likening happy, hehe! so do you really think that I apartment what you want … hehe! Ironic you people. Well, I will not! Oh yeah, by the way, one mot more calls, one thought, other reasons - you also about the form this morning deigned to mention, you know, doprosika then, with … But in what form! Form, you know, in many cases, stupidity, sir. Sometimes just a friendly conversation, and profitable. Form will never leave it, let me assure you, sir; And that, in fact, form, I ask you? The form can not be everywhere confuse the researcher. The investigator in the case, because it is, so to speak, free art, in its own way, with or something like that … heh heh heh! ..

Porfiry Petrovitch turned for a moment the spirit. He took a shower and without tiring, no sense of empty phrases, and then suddenly missed some mysterious phrases and once again slipping into nonsense. Room, he almost ran faster and faster moving thick legs, still staring at the ground with his right hand behind his back and left permanently waving and trying to play a variety of gestures, each time surprising not to approach him. Raskolnikov suddenly noticed that, running around the room, he several times as if stopped by the door for a moment, and, as if listening … "Waiting for him that if anything?"

- And you are right, sir - again took Porphyry, fun, with extraordinary simplicity, in spite of Raskolnikov (causing him to flinch and instantly ready for operation) - in fact, right now, that formami-, that Legal pleased wit to laugh, hehe! Oh, these (some, of course) deep psychological methods of some of our very funny, sir, yes, perhaps useless, sir, if the form is very sorry, sir. Yes, sir … again, I'm talking about the form: Well, take, or rather, I suspect that I'm someone else, a third, so to speak, for criminals, some errand entrusted to me…Vy Get ready for lawyers, Rodion Romanovich?

- Yes, ready …

- Well, here's to you, so to speak, and primerchik for the future - that is, do not think that I should teach you dare: Avon, because you have an article about the crimes of the press! No, sir, and so, as a fact, primerchik dare to imagine - and so I think that, for example, one-third of the offender, well, why, I ask, I'll bother him ahead of time, at least I and the evidence against him was, sir ? Otherwise, I will, for example, zaarestovat quickly, and the other is not of this nature, to the right; So why not allow him to walk around the city, hehe, sir! No, I see you do not quite understand why I told you to portray, Put, I did, for example, too early, because I told him that, perhaps, moral, so to say, Come support, hehe! You laugh? (Raskolnikov did not even think to laugh: he sat with clenched lips, his eyes fixed on sore eyes Porfiry Petrovitch). And yet this is the case, sir, on the other topic, especially because people are manifold with, and, above all, on the one practice. Here you want to say tepericha evidence; Yes, because it is, for example, evidence-C, but it is evidence that the father, two-edged sword, for the most part, with, and in fact I am an investigator, therefore, a weak man, I confess I ,: a consequence, so to speak, mathematically clearly present, I would get a small street, so twice two is four, as! On direct and irrefutable proof will be like! But do not put it in time - at least, I was, and I'm sure it's him - so actually I think I'll have the means to take him further reproof, and why? And because I have it, so to speak, to a certain position, so to speak, psychologically, to identify it and to calm down, so he left me in their shells: finally realizes that he is in captivity. Say, in Sevastopol, now after Alma, some people are smart ear, it was feared that he was going to attack the enemy unit uncovered and immediately take Sevastopol; and when they saw that the enemy would have preferred a regular siege and opens the first parallel, so where they will say that they were happy and relieved some smart people, from: to extremes within two months, the case was delayed because, when properly take siege! Laughing again, again, do not believe me? This, of course, you're right. Right-click to be all right, sir! It's all special cases, I agree with you, the case presented, indeed, private, sir! But in fact, that in this case, Rodion Romanovich kindest, must comply with: after the general case, with that, to which all the legal forms and rules and examples from which they are calculated and recorded in the books not exist, with on its own, that every worker, every, even if, for example, the crime once it actually happens, and once it becomes a very special case with; Yes, because sometimes what: just still looks, sir. Prekomicheskie cases sometimes occur in this way, sir. Yes,

ROBOTS READ

I left the gentleman does one thing: I do not take it and not worry about it, but he knew, every hour and every minute, or at least suspected, that I still know the whole story, day and night, to watch it vigilantly his guardian, and if I have it consciously under eternal suspicion and fear, is not it, by golly, whirlwind, right, sir, it is, yes, maybe even do something that is already twice two is like, so to speak, will have a mathematical form - it's nice to. This guy Sivolap can happen, not to mention with our brother, the modern intelligent man, and even well-known aspects of development, and even more! Because, my dear, it's a very important thing to understand in which parties developed people. And nerves AC nerves, something you have something and forget, sir! It's now sick, so thin, so annoying! .. And some bile, bile in them as much! But this, I tell you, on the occasion of my kind, sir! And what bothers me that he walks through the city unbound! Let, let walk now, let; I already know that he is my zhertvochka and not run away from me! And where to run away, hehe!Abroad, or what? Abroad pole run away, not he, even more so that I follow, and the actions taken. In the depths of the fatherland run, or what? Why do men live there, imagine, hemp, Russia; that way because that modern man has developed prefer jail than foreigners such as our peasants live, hehe! But it's all nonsense and open. What is: escape! It has the form; and, most importantly, it is not so; not at the same time he will not run away from me, that there is no place to escape: I have it psychologically not run away, hehe! What vyrazhenitse something! He is a law of nature, I will not run away, even if it was somewhere to run. Have you seen a butterfly in front of a candle? Well, then it will all be about me as about candles, lace; freedom does not become sweet, will think, confusing a circle confusing as networks, zatrevozhit himself to death! .. Not only that: he gave me some mathematical functions such as ABC, to prepare - just let me that he had just intermission genuine ... And all will be me, giving circles, still narrowing narrowing the range - and - bam !Right in the mouth and will fly, I swallow it, and with that, and it's very nice, sir, heh, heh, heh! You do not believe me?

Raskolnikov did not answer, he sat pale and motionless, still with the same strain of looking into the face of porphyria.

"The lesson well - he thought, turning cold - It's not even all that is not a cat with a mouse, as it was yesterday, and he did not make it useless to me and shows ... It offers :.. Much wiser for it! Here another purpose, what is it? Hey, blah, brother, you're scaring me and crafty! You have no proof, and there

is no yesterday, man! You're just confusing to knock want to annoy me want to prematurely, but in this state, and Swat, only lying, oborveshsya, oborveshsya! But why, why to such a degree tells me? .. on sick or something, my nerves expect? .. No, brother, lying, oborveshsya, although you do something and prepared. .. Well, let's see what you are ready. "

And he refrained himself struggling preparing for the unknown and terrible catastrophe. From time to time, he would throw himself on the spot to strangle porphyria. He still come here, this anger was afraid. He felt his lips, heart pounding, foam caked lips. But he still decided to keep quiet and not say the words before time. He realized that it was the best tactic in his position because he did not slip, and irritate the silent enemy, and perhaps even the same thing he says. At least he hoped so.

- No, I see you do not believe me, sir, I think everything that I am innocent jokes you - took Porphyry, more and more Bezalel and constantly giggling with delight and starts a circle around the room - it is, of course, you're right, sir; and I believe that it is actually God himself arranged that only comic thoughts in other add-ons; Buffon's; but I'll tell you something, and I repeat, sir, that you, my dear Rodion Romanovich, I'm sorry, man, young man, so to speak, not the first youth, primarily because the value of the human mind, for example, all youth.Playful sharpness of mind and abstract thinking, mind you, with the bait. And it is a hair's breadth, as the former Austrian Hofkriegsrat, such as this, I can not judge about the war: on paper, they are Napoleon was defeated and taken prisoner, and even there, in his office, all witty correctly calculated and summed, and see General Mack, and then refuse with his entire army, heh, heh, heh! I see, I see, my dear Rodion Romanovich, you're laughing at me that I was such a civilian, all military history primerchiki choose.What weakness, as the military, and even so I like to read all these military reports ... I was very stingy on my career. I will serve in the army, with the right. Napoleon, then, perhaps, would not have done, but what would be a major, heh, heh, heh! Well, as I have now, my dear, my whole more to say, that there is something special case and the nature of reality, sir, you are my, there are important, and how sometimes cut calculation insight! Hey, listen to the old man, speaking seriously, Rodion Romanovich (saying this is hardly thirty-five Porfiry Petrovitch really as if suddenly all become old: even his voice had changed, and somehow everything he crouched) - for the same person, I'm honest I'm with Frank ... I'm a man or not? What do you think? Oh, it seems like it: like some of the things that you say nothing, but

still useful for it is not required, hehe! Well, then, sir, keep-with: namely, in my opinion, an excellent thing, sir; that is, the natural beauty and comfort of life, and so it seems that the focus can set it so much when it seems sometimes think some bad cop, who also himself fascinated by his imagination, as always, because too, because man, sir! Yes, poor little nature saves investigator, sir, that's the trouble! And about this, and I do not think that the use of wit youth, "Walking through all the obstacles" (as you witty and clever way deign to speak). He is saying, and lied, that is people-with, a special case, since, with Incognito-it, and lied perfectly naihitreyshim way; there would seem to prevail and, and enjoy the fruits of his wit, and he - bam! but something very interesting, in a scandalous place and pass out. That is to say, the disease sometimes too stuffy in the rooms there, but still, sir!Nevertheless, the thought gave! Lied-that's fine, but nature-not count. Won it, deception, somewhere in! At other times, he is drawn away of his playful wit, begins to suspect that he is a fool man, pale, as if on purpose, like in the game, but too natural light that is too close to the truth, and again gave an idea! Although inflate the first time, but during the night and far-fetched, if not a fool. Why, at every turn that way, sir! But for some reason, he starts to work too forward, begins to interfere, and do not ask where to begin to start talking incessantly about what it would be necessary, on the contrary, be silent, various allegory begins at a distance, hehe! Come and ask begins: why de I do not take a long time? heh, heh, heh! And it can happen witty man with a psychologist and writer, sir! Nature Mirror, mirror-with the most transparent, sir! Look at him and admire, that's what, sir! What are you so pale, Rodion Romanovich, not stuffy, if you do not dissolve in the window?

- Oh, do not worry, please - and suddenly cried Raskolnikov laughed, - please do not worry!

Porfiry stood against him, waited and suddenly laughed after him. Raskolnikov got up from the couch, suddenly stopping it completely epileptic laughter.

- Porfiry Petrovich! - He said loud and clear, though hardly stood on shaky legs - I finally see clearly that you are positive to suspect me of murdering that old woman and her sister Lizaveta. For my part I declare to you that all this has bothered me for a long time already. If you find that you have the right to make changes in the law to prosecute pursue; arrest arrest. But laugh myself in the eye and torture yourself, I will not.

Suddenly, his lips trembling, his eyes lit up with rabies, and restrained

voice still sounded.

- Do not let Sir! - He suddenly shouted, struggling pounding his fist on the table - you hear this, Porfiry Petrovich? Do not allow it!

- Oh, God, yes it again! - Cried, apparently in perfect fright, Porfiry Petrovich - Father! Rodion Romanovich!Rodimenky! Father! What's wrong with you?

- Do not allow it! - Exclaimed Raskolnikov was a different time.

- Father, be quiet! In the end, hear, come! Well, then we say to them, I think! - Whispered in horror Porfiry Petrovich, causing her face to face Raskolnikov.

- Do not let not allow it! - Raskolnikov repeated mechanically, but also suddenly perfect whisper.

Porfiry quickly turned and ran to open the window.

- Air miss fresh! Yes, a little bit of water with you, my dear, drink it necessary, sir! - And he ran to the door to order the water, but then in the corner, by the way, found a jug of water.

- Father, ispeyte - he whispered, rushing to him with a carafe - maybe help ... - Funk and most of Porfiry Petrovich so natural that Raskolnikov was silent and wild curiosity began to examine it. Water, however, he did not accept.

- Rodion Romanovich! my dear! So, as you reduce yourself crazy, I assure you, uh-oh! -A-Ah! Drink a minute! Yes, drink at least a little bit!

He still forced him to take a glass of water in his hand. He mechanically raised it to his lips, but on second thoughts, disgust put on the table.

- Yes, sir, pripadochek we had, sir! So you again, my dear, old disease itself back - wheezed with a friendly involving Porfiry Petrovich, however, still some puzzled. - The Lord! But how can you take care of yourself is not? This Dmitri Prokofitch came to me yesterday - I agree, I agree, sir, my character is a sarcastic, nasty, and that's what they brought it! ! .. God came yesterday, after you, we had dinner, talked, talked, I just created a hands; Well, I think ... Oh, my God! From you or something that he will come? Yes Sit down, sir, sit down for Christ's sake!

- No, not me! But I knew that he went to you and that was - Raskolnikov replied sharply.

- Knew?

- I knew that. Well, what of it?

- Yes, the same thing, my dear Rodion Romanovich, I still do not know thy works, all we know, sir! In the end, I know how you Renting an apartment

somehow walked right up to the night when it was dark, but the bell rang, but questioned the blood, but the workers and janitors knocked confused. It's my understanding that the mood of your peace, then-then ... but in the end, that, as you will reduce just crazy, I swear, sir! Twisted!Resentment something in you so very much in full swing, with a noble's, derived from the crime in the first lot, and then from the quarterly, so that you and goes back and forth, so to speak, to say, as soon as possible, and get All time commit because you are tired of this nonsense, and all these suspicions. Is not it? Guess the mood with something? .. Only in this way you will not only themselves, and Razumikhin, I felt; because it is too good for this person, you know. Do you have a disease, but it has the power, disease, and goes to him tack ... I want, sir, that when calm down, I'll say ... yes, take the same father, for Christ's sake! Please, take a break, you do not have to face; so sit down, though.

Raskolnikov sat down; shake of his passes and has performed heat throughout the body. In deep amazement, listening, he was frightened and friendly care for Porfiry Petrovich. But he does not believe a word of it, but felt a strange tendency verit.Neozhidannye words Porphyry about the apartment, he was struck perfectly."How is it that he, therefore, knew about the apartment, then -? He suddenly thought - himself and tells me"

- Yes, sir, it was almost certainly the case, psychological, in our jurisprudence, with a painful case, sir, - continued to patter porphyria. - In addition, one focused on the murder-with, and, as it focused on: all gallyusinatsiyu summarized the facts presented, the description of the circumstances, confused, shot down and all, but what? He inadvertently, in particular, the murder was, but only in part, and he learned that he is a killer spawned homesick, zadurmanilsya, was presented to him, rather povihnulsya, and found that he is a murderer! Yes Government Senate finally, the point is made, and miserable, and was acquitted of charity given. Thanks to the Senate! Ah-ma, ah-ah-ah! Yes, just like that, sir? Thus, you can save and fever, like when he attacks their nerves annoying at night to go to the bells to call to ask about the blood! This is because I studied psychology in general-practice with. Thus, because sometimes a person out of the window from the bell hop Ali pulls, and a sense of something seductive. In addition, with bells and ... Illness, Rodion Romanovich, a disease! His illness became neglected too, sir. I would advise you to an experienced physician, and the fact that you have this fat for you! Brad .. thank you! This is all that you have

just made a nonsense! ..

For a moment, everything began to spin and circle Raskolnikov.

"Really, really - flashed in it - it is now impossible, impossible!" - He pushed the thought, feeling in advance to what extent the rage and fury she can bring it, feeling that rabies can drive you crazy.

- It was not a delusion, it was real! - He said, straining all the powers of his mind to get into the game porphyria. - Wake up, wake up! Do you hear that?

- Yes, I see and hear, sir! You said yesterday that it was not delirious, especially even pressed forward, not delirious! Anything you can tell, I understand, sir! Eh! .. Yeah, listen, Rodion Romanovich, you're my benefactor, well, that even if it is a fact. In the end, whether you're actually here, in fact, is a criminal Ali somehow involved in this damn thing, well, you, for pity's sake, do not stress that not all the nonsense you have done, but, on the contrary, a complete memory? Yes, especially the crowd with such persistence, especially Crowd - Well, maybe, well, it may be that, for pity's sake? Why, on the contrary, in my opinion. In the end, if you feel something, so you just have to emphasize the fact that, of course, he says, in his delirium, right !? Is not it?

Something evil is heard in this matter. Raskolnikov fell at the end of the couch from depleted porphyria and in silence, in the face, he looked puzzled.

- Ali here about Mr. Razumikhin, that is, from himself, if he had to say yesterday, or incitement? Yes, you just have to say that I came from you, and hide it from your instigation! But here you can not hide! You simply based on the fact that your instigation!

Raskolnikov never rested on it. The cold was on the back.

- You always lie - slowly and weakly said he curled his lips into a painful smile - you again I want to show my whole game to know all the answers to my know in advance - he said that he could almost feel that this is not the way it is should weigh the words - to intimidate me ... or you just want to laugh at me ...

He continued to look at him to stop talking, and suddenly again boundless anger flashed in his eyes.

- Lie to you all! - He exclaimed. - You know very well that the best criminal ploy did not hide the fact that you can not hide. I do not believe you!

- Eka Vertunov you! - Porphyry giggled - yes, you, sir, and can not cope; monomania some stuck in you. So do not believe me? And I'll tell you what really believe, I believe that a quarter of the yard, and I'll do it, and believe

in the whole yard because true love you and I sincerely wish you well.

Raskolnikov's lips quivered.

- Yes, sir, I want to finally tell you, sir, - he continued, gently, in a friendly, hand in hand, Raskolnikov, a little above the elbow, - said at last, sir; Watch your illness. In addition, here's the names now arrived; some things you should vspomnit.Otdyh and indulge them, and you just scare them ...

- What do you care? How do you know? Why is it so interesting? You see, therefore, for me, and I want to show it?

- Father! Why are you just as you learned it all yourself! You do not notice that in his excitement, all in front of him to say, and I, and others. With Mr. Razumikhin, Dmitri Prokofitch, yesterday also learned a lot of interesting details. No, sir, that you interrupted me, and I say that in suspicion, with all your mind, you even look at ordinary things deigned to lose. Well, for example, at least on the same topic again, something about bells: yes such utter gem of a kind that, so I will, with hands and feet, and gave me (actually a fact, sir!) the investigator! And you do not see this? Yes, I have a suspect, at least a little bit, I have to do? I, on the contrary, it will be the first to lull your suspicions, and gave me what I already know this fact, distract, so you are in the opposite direction, but suddenly, like an ax in the head (in your same expression), and stuns "And that, say, sir, you have been pleased to make the apartment killed at 10:00 pm, but almost did not even eleven? And why Beller called in? What about the blood into question? Why wipers and knocked in particular, the quarterly lieutenant beckoned? "That's how I have to do if I was at least a modicum of suspicion you. Must be in the form you are reading something off, do a search, and maybe even you and zaarestovat ... So, I'm not a premonition, if to do otherwise! Commonplace you lost and do not see anything, I repeat, sir!

Raskolnikov shuddered all over, so that Porfiry Petrovitch too clearly noticed.

- Lie to you all! - He said, - I do not know your goals, but you still lie ... But now you're not in this sense says that you can not go wrong, and I ... You're lying!

- I'm lying? - Picked up Porphyry seems hot, but keep the most hilarious and sarcastic look and do not seem in the least alarming fact that an opinion about this, Mr. Raskolnikov. - I'm lying? .. Well, as I did to you this morning (I somehow investigator), prompting you to itself and gives all the means to defend himself told you all this psychology summation: "Disease,

say nonsense, was razobizhen; melancholy quarterly yes, "and all this stuff? Huh? heh heh heh! Although this, however - as I say - all these psychological defenses, excuses yes evasions, very inconsistent, and a two-edged sword: "Disease, say nonsense, dreams, myself, I do not remember," it's all so -c, but Why, sir, in the disease, but in delirium all such dreams are mereschutsya and not others? Can actually be the other-a? right? Heh-heh-heh-heh!

Raskolnikov proudly and contemptuously looked at him.

- In a word, - persistently and loudly he said, standing up and pushing some time Porphyria - in a word, I want to know: Do you recognize me completely free from suspicion or ? do not tell Porfiry Petrovich, speak positively and finally and more, now!

- Ek after the commission! Well, that commission with you - cried Porfiry with pretty fun, crafty, and in no way alarmed views. - And what do you know, that you know so much, if you do not start to worry at all!After all, you are a child, give so take fire in your hands! And why are you so worried about? Why do something so that you are asking us, from what reasons? A? heh heh heh!

- I'm telling you - Raskolnikov cried in anger - that I could no longer bear ...

- What is it? Unknown, or what? - Porphyry interrupted.

- Do not yazvite me! I do not want! .. I say to you that I will not! .. I can not and do not want to! .. I hear it!Listen up! - He cried, again hitting his fist on the table.

- Yes, just hush hush! In the end, hear! Serious warning: watch yourself. I kid you not, sir! - Whispered porphyria, but this time in the person was no longer daveshny old wife good-natured and frightened expression; on the contrary, now he just ordered strictly frowned, as if time breaking all the mystery and ambiguity. But it was only on mgnovenie.Ozadachenny was Raskolnikov suddenly fell into a trance now; but oddly enough, he again obeyed orders to speak quietly, although he was the strongest in a paroxysm of rage.

- I do not allow myself to torture! - Suddenly he whispered in daveshny, with pain and hatred instantly conscious to himself that he could not obey orders, and based on this idea even more infuriating - arrest me, I searched, but in order to act in accordance with the form, not I play with, sir! Do not you dare ...

- Do not worry about the same as - Porphyry interrupted with a sly grin

in place, as if even enjoyed admiring Raskolnikov, - I have, sir, is now invited to the house, so quite friendly!

- I do not want your friendship and spit on it! Do you hear that? And it is the same: to take cover and go.Well-tissue, now tell me if you would be arrested?

He grabbed his hat and walked to the door.

- Syurprizik do not want to really see? - Porphyry giggled again, grabbing his elbow a little higher and stop dver.On apparently became more fun and playful, the final conclusion that Raskolnikov himself.

- What syurprizik? What's this? - He asked, stopping suddenly and fearfully looking at Porfiry.

- Syurpriziki-s, behold, the doors, I was sitting, heh, heh, heh! (He pointed to the locked door in the wall that led to his government apartment). - I kept on the lock to escape.

- What is it? where? what? .. - Raskolnikov went to the door and wanted to open, but it was locked.

- Closed-with, that's the key!

In fact, he showed him the key, pulling from his pocket.

- You're lying to you all! - Do not cry Raskolnikov is no longer delaying - lying, Punchinello do not care! - And rushed to withdraw from the door, but chickened porphyria.

- I have everything that I understand everything! - He jumped on it. - You're lying and tease me, so I gave myself ...

- Yes, more, and you can not give yourself, sir, Rodion Romanovitch. In the end, you come into a rage. Do not cry, because I will call people sir!

- You're lying, nothing will! Call people! Did you know that I was sick, and angry, I would like rabies, so I gave myself that your goal! No, you have the facts Give! I understand everything! You do not have the facts, you do not have anything but trashy, worthless speculation zametovskie! .. You know, my character in a frenzy, I Give, and then suddenly stun priests deputies yes ... you are waiting for? and? What are you waiting for? Where? Give!

- Well, then what the deputies with, my dear! Imagine the same person! So much so in form and function, it can not be, as you say, you, my dear, I do not know ... And the form will not go away, others, see for yourself! .. - Muttered Porfiry, listening at the door.

Indeed, at this time the door to the next room heard the noise.

- And in the way! - Cried Raskolnikov - you sent them! .. You're waiting

for them! You thought ... Well, bring here everything deputies, witnesses, what you want ... Come on! I'm ready ready! ..

But this strange occurrence happened, something unexpected, with the usual course of things, which are already, of course, neither Raskolnikov nor Porfiry Petrovich this isolation and could not count.

⇜ CHAPTER VI ⇝

Then, in the memory of this moment, Raskolnikov seemed all in this form.

There was noise outside the door suddenly increased rapidly, and the door opened a little.

- What is it? - Angrily shouted Porfiry Petrovich. - Because I warned ...

For a moment there was no answer, but it was clear that the door was a little man, as if someone had pushed.

- What is it? - With alarm repeated Porfiry Petrovitch.

- Conclusion Bear Nicholas, - heard a voice.

- Do Not! Away! Wait a minute!.. Why he got here! What a mess! - Cried Porfiry, rushing to the door.

- Yes, he's ... - began again the same voice and suddenly stopped.

No more than two seconds, a real fight; then suddenly, as if someone had someone with force pushed, and then some very pale man stepped right in the office Porfiry Petrovitch.

The sight of this man at first sight was very strange. He looked straight in front of him, but how would anyone not seeing. His eyes sparkled with determination, but at the same time the death pallor covered his face, as if he was taken to his execution. Completely white lips trembled slightly.

He was still very young, dressed as a commoner, medium height, thin, with hair cropped in a circle, with thin, as dry facial features. Suddenly, they are repelled by the first man was taken to his room and grabbed his shoulder: it was the convoy; but Nikolai jerked his arm and ran again from him.

At the door zatolpilos several curious. Some of them breaking. All the

above happened almost in an instant.

- Other, too soon! Wait until you have caused! .. What brought him before?
- Muttered at vexation, as if confused Porfiry Petrovich. But Nicholas suddenly dropped to his knees.

- What are you? - Porphyry shouted in amazement.

- Excuse Me! My sin!I'm a murderer! - Suddenly said Nicholas, as if some breath, but loud enough voice.

The silence lasted about ten seconds, just tetanus found at all; even escort not recoiled and no longer suitable for Nicholas and otretirovalsya mechanically to the door and became motionless.

- What is it? - Cried Porfiry Petrovich, leaving an instant consternation.

- I ... killer ... - repeated Nicholas, after a pause droplet.

- How ... you ... How ... Who have you killed?

Porfiry Petrovich apparently lost.

Nicholas paused again drops.

- Alena Ivanovna and theirs sister, Lizaveta, I ... killed ... ax. Blurred found ... - he added suddenly and fell silent again. He is on his knees.

Porfiry Petrovitch stood for a few moments, as if thinking, and then again fluttered and waved his arms to undesirable witnesses. Those instantly disappeared, and the doors of the porch. Then he looked at Raskolnikov in the corner, looking wildly Nicholas, and had started toward him, but suddenly stopped, looked at him, looked away immediately to Nicholas, then again at Raskolnikov, then back at Nicholas and suddenly, as if Hobbies, again attacked Nikolai.

- You told me that his defilement, and then ran forward? - He shouted at him almost angrily. - I did not even ask whether you blurred .. Let's say you killed?

- I read the murderer ... Rent ... - said Nikolai.

- Oh-oh! What have you killed?

- Axe. In the store.

- Oh, hurry! One?

Nicholas did not understand the question.

- One killed?

- One. And Mitya was innocent and all that innocent.

- Do not jump to Mitya something! Eh!

- As you well as you down the stairs, and then run? In the end, you both met wipers?

- This is me for drainage ... then ... ran with Mitko - and, as it hurried to prepare in advance, said Nicholas.

- Well, it is! - Angrily exclaimed Porphyry, - his words not said! - It is as if to himself again and muttered Raskolnikov suddenly saw.

He apparently got carried away with Nikolai before that for a moment he forgot all about Raskolnikov. Now he suddenly came to his senses, it's embarrassing ...

- Rodion Romanovich, sir! Excuse me, sir, - he ran to it - so you can not, sir; please you ... There's nothing ... I ... see what surprises! .. If you please, sir! ..

And he took him by the hand, he showed him the door.

- You do not seem to expect? - Said Raskolnikov, of course, still do not understand anything clear, but highly recommended.

- And you, sir, is not expected. Look to handle something like a shudder! hehe!

- Yes, and trembling, Porfiry Petrovich.

- And I tremble, sir; did not expect, sir! ..

They stood in the doorway. Porphyry impatiently waiting to Raskolnikov went on.

- Syurprizik then do not show? - Said Raskolnikov.

- Says, but the teeth in the mouth of one another knock, hehe! Ironic you man! Well, good-bye, sir.

- I think so forgiving !

- How will God bring with-a-God will bring with! - Muttered Porfiry with a twisted smile.

Walking into the office, Raskolnikov noticed that many looked at him. In the corridor, in the crowd, he could see both the janitors of the house, which he would call it a night to quarter.They standing and waiting for something. But as soon as he came to the stairs when he heard the voice again to Porfiry Petrovich. Turning, he saw that he was caught with him, out of breath.

- One little word, Rodion Romanovich with; there's all this stuff, as God is, but still in the form of something you have to ask, with ... so we'll see you, sir.

And Porfiry stood in front of him with a smile.

- Well, sir, - he said again.

It can be assumed that it was something else I wanted to say, but somehow it does not say.

- And you me, Porfiry Petrovich, sorry about daveshny ... I got excited - started it was quite a good mood, an irresistible urge to show Raskolnikov.

- Not at all, nothing else ... - almost gleefully picked up Porphyry. - I did something with character ... poison me, I confess, I confess! Why, we'll see you, sir. If God, and very, very to see you, sir! ..

- And finally, get to know each other? - Once Raskolnikov.

- And, finally, to know each other - echoed Porfiry Petrovich, and squinted, very seriously looked at him. - Now, with a birthday celebration?

- At the funeral, sir.

- Yeah, I mean, the funeral! Health something shore, health-with ...

- And I do not know what you want from him! - Once Raskolnikov, is already beginning to go down the stairs, but then again, turning to Porfiry - I would like to great success, so, you see that your position comics!

- Why comics, sir? - Immediately pricked up his ears Porfiry Petrovich, too, turned to leave.

- But that is a bad Mikolka you should be tormented and tortured psychologically something on their own, at the moment there he did not recognize; day and night, must have appeared to him: "You're a murderer, you're a murderer ..." - Well, now, when he was already recognized you again on his bones begin to knead, "You're lying, they say, you are not a murderer! He could not you have, you are not my words, you're saying! "Well, then do not post the comic?

- Heh, heh, heh! And notice that I just said Nicholas, that he "did not say a word?"

- How not to notice?

- Heh, heh, heh! Witty, clever, sir. All-you note! It's a playful mind, sir! And something very comical line and hook ... hehe! This Gogol, writer, say, this feature was somewhat higher?

- Yes, Gogol.

- Yes, sir, Gogol, from ... to Bon-bye.

- Before pleasant goodbye ...

Raskolnikov went straight home. Before he was shot down and confused that already come home and throw on the sofa, with a quarter of an hour of rest, just relaxing and trying in any way to collect his thoughts. About Nicholas He took no claim ,: he felt the hit; in recognition of Nicholas there is something inexplicable, amazing, but now he does not understand anything. But recognition of the fact that Nicholas was in force. The consequences of this fact, it has become clear: the lie failed to show, and then take it back. But, at least until such time as he is not free and, of course, have to do something

to make for themselves, because the danger is imminent.

But, nevertheless, to what degree? The situation began to emerge. Remembering rough, full communication daveshny his entire scene with Porfiry, he could once again not to shudder in horror. Of course, he did not yet know all the goals porphyria, could not understand all daveshny their calculations. But part of the game was discovered, and, of course, no one better than he could not understand how awful it is for him to "move" in the game porphyria. A little more and he could pass himself off completely, in fact, already. Knowing the pain of his character, and at first glance right and grabbed his penetration, although Porphyry acted too much, but almost certainly. There is no doubt already Raskolnikov himself and only now too compromised, but the facts have not yet reached; after all it is only relative. But, nevertheless, if he understood it all now? Do not mistake he? Which leads clone Porfiry today? If he had anything cooked today? And what exactly? Is he waiting for something or not? How they would leave today if it were not unexpected disaster came across Nicholas?

Porphyry almost the entire game showed his; Of course, risky, but showed both (all seemed to Raskolnikov), if indeed Porphyry was something else, it would show and then. What is this "surprise"? Ridicule, or what? This meant anything or not? Could it be hiding under something like that, on a positive charge? Yesterday's man? Where he failed? Where is he now? In the end, if anything positive in purple, of course, is in connection with yesterday's man ...

He sat on the couch, hanging his head, elbows on his knees and his hands on his face. Willies continued for the whole body. Finally, he got up, took his cap, thought, and headed for the door.

He somehow had the feeling that, at least for the moment, he almost certainly can be considered safe. Suddenly, in his heart, he felt almost joy: he wanted to rush to Katerina Ivanovna. At the funeral, he, of course, too late, but the funeral is ready, and now, he would see Sonia.

He stopped, thought, and a painful smile on his lips reduced.

- Today! Today! - He repeated to himself - yes, today! So it is necessary ...

A man stood in the doorway, looked silently at Raskolnikov and stepped into the room. He was a close call as yesterday, that in a well-dressed, but in the face and in his eyes a strong change: he now looked like something prigoryunivshis and stood there for a bit, took a deep breath. Lacking only to have it put in the hand to her cheek, and her head twisted to one side, so

that it is absolutely sounds like a woman.

- What is it? - Asked pomertvevshy Raskolnikov.

The man stopped suddenly and deeply, almost to the ground, bowed to him. At least touched the ground right thumb.

- What do you? - Cried Raskolnikov.

- Excuse me - quietly said the man.

- What?

- In the bad thoughts.

The two men looked at each other.

- It's a shame it was. As you say, then come, can jump in and wipers in the quarter called and asked about the blood, I wish I was that vain and left drunk you pochli.I so sad that dared to dream. And remember the address, yesterday we came here and asked ...

- Who came? - Raskolnikov interrupted instantly begins to remember.

- I have something that you have offended.

- So you're out of the house?

- Yes, I'm in the same place at the same time the gate was with them, Ali forgot? We rukomeslo him there from time immemorial. Furriers we commoners, take home work ... First of all, it was a shame ...

Raskolnikov clear that I thought the whole scene on the third day at the gate; he realized that in addition to the janitors stood while some others stood and women. He remembered one voice, offers the right quarter. The man could not speak, he remembered, and even now do not recognize, but he remembers that he even said something to him then turned to him ...

So, therefore, you allow all this horror yesterday. Worst of all would have thought that he really was almost killed, nearly killed himself because of such a small circumstances.Therefore, in addition to hiring an apartment and talk about blood, this man can not say anything to do. Consequently, Porphyry also nothing, nothing, but it is nonsense, nothing but the facts of psychology,which is not near the two ends, nothing positive. So, if you do not show the facts (and they should not be more, do not, do not!), Then ... what can you do with it? What can we condemn it completely, although arrested? And, therefore, Porphyry only now, just now found out about the apartment, but still do not know.

- That you said today Porphyry ... I was coming? - He said, struck by a sudden idea.

- What Porphyry?

- Bailiff research.

- I said. Wiper did not go then I went.

- Today?

- For you, for a moment there. And hear all that he tortured you.

- Where? What? When?

- Yes, right there, behind the walls, all the time spent.

- How? So this is what you have been a surprise? But how could this happen? For God's sake!

- Videmshi I - began philistine - that wipers from my words do not want to go because, they say, it's late, and perhaps even more enraged for evermore, that the hour has come, I was hurt and decided to sleep and began to learn. Razuznamshi yesterday, today went. First come - it was not. Hour stop in front - not a third came - did. Then he ran, some call it, and began to speak in a corner, and then again to me - and began to question and criticize. And many reproaches, and I told him everything and said that yesterday with my words do not you dare me to answer, and that you did not recognize me. And he started running here again, and all beat their breasts, and angry, and ran, and what about you posts - well, says, crawling behind a partition, do not sit right now, do not move, no matter what you have heard and chair I brought myself back, and I was locked; You could say that I love you and ask. What led Nicholas, he gave me after you, and brought: I still say require more'll ask ...

- Nicholas, you ask?

- How did you brought up, and brought me immediately, and Nicholas began to question.

Seller suddenly stopped and again put the bow, touching a finger sex.

- For slander and malice of my forgiveness.

- God will forgive - Raskolnikov replied, and as soon as he said, the merchant bowed to him, but not on the ground, and at the waist, slowly turned and left the room. "Everything has two ends, all things both ways" - repeated Raskolnikov and more than ever, quickly left the room.

"Now we are still arguing," - with evil grin, he said, down the stairs. Malice same applies to himself: he with contempt and shame remembered his "cowardice".

PART 5

← CHAPTER I →

Morning after fatal for Peter Petrovich explanations Dunya and Pulcheria Alexandrovna, brought him a sobering effect on Pyotr Petrovich. He, for his great trouble, was forced to gradually take over the fact a complete and consistent, that only yesterday seemed to him an incident almost fantastic and although self-fulfilling, but still seemed to be no longer possible. Black snake hurt pride all night to suck his heart. Rising from the bed, Peter immediately looked in the mirror. He was afraid if he were not spread beyond the gall night? However, on this side, at this time it was good, and looked at his noble, white and a little fatter recent appearance, Peter even for a moment he was comforted in full conviction to find a bride for himself somewhere else, yes, maybe, even cleaner; but then recovered and spat vigorously to the side, which led to a quiet, but a sarcastic smile on his young friend and roommate Andrew S. Lebezyatnikov. Smile that Peter saw himself and immediately put it to his friend at the expense of the young. He has put a lot of it lately on the account. Doubled his anger when he suddenly realized that he was not to report on the results of yesterday's yesterday Andrey Semenovich. It was the second mistake yesterday, made them recklessly, excessive abundance, in despair ... Then, during this morning, unfortunately, and then the trouble to trouble. Even in the Senate, it is waiting for some kind of failure in the event that he fuss. Especially irritated his boss hired him in the types of first marriage and goes at his own expense: the host, some of the rich German craftsman, would not agree to break just perfect agreement and demanded the full penalty prescribed in the contract, despite the fact that Peter came to him almost flat repair. In addition, the furniture store would not want to

return a single ruble deposit to buy, although not yet in the apartment furnishings. "It is not for me to marry furniture!" - Grind Peter himself, and at the same time once again gave him a desperate hope: "Of course, in fact, everything is so hopeless went and did not we try again?" The thought of Duns again tempting thorn in his heart. With anguish he experienced at this point, and, of course, if we could now only one desire, to kill Raskolnikov, then Peter immediately said it would wish.

"The error was more than that, and that I was not the money that they gave - he thought sadly back in the closet Lebezyatnikov - why the hell I ozhidovel There is even no payment was not, I did not think that their in black holding body? and to bring them to me, looked like providence, and they won! .. Ugh! .. No, if I gave them all the time, for example, fifteen hundred dowry yes for gifts, because there are different boxes , travel bags, carnelian matter and all that crap from Knop yes from the English shop, as would be the case clearer and stronger ... Not so easy to refute me now! They are men of the warehouse, which, of course, would prefer to return to service in the case of failures and gifts, and money, and return something to be sorry and tyazhelenko And conscience is tickled: how, they say, because suddenly get rid of a man who had hitherto been so generous and quite thin ?..! Hmm made a blunder " And, grated again, Peter immediately called fool of yourself - to yourself, of course.

Having reached this conclusion, he returned twice more angry and irritable than the left. Preparing for a wave in the room Katerina Ivanovna partly lured his curiosity. He Coy yesterday heard of the following; I even remember if he was invited; but also for their own troubles, he missed the rest ignoriruetsya.Speshit to know Mrs. Lippevehzel, was busy in the absence of Katerina Ivanovna (located in the cemetery) of setting the table, he learned that the funeral will be celebrations that invited almost all the tenants, which even strangers late that even invited Andrew S. Lebezyatnikov, despite his former quarrel with Katerina Ivanovna, and, finally, Peter himself not only invited, but even eagerly expected, as perhaps the most important guest of all tenants.Amalia Ivanovna herself was also invited with great honor, in spite of all the former troubles, and, therefore, took place and was busy, almost feeling pleasure from it, and in addition was all dressed up, though in mourning, but all new, silk, feathers and dust, and proud of it. All these facts and information provided by Peter some thoughts, and he went to his room, which is in the room Andrei S. Lebezyatnikov, some thought. The fact that he also

learned that among the guests there Raskolnikov.

Andrew S. sat some reason all this morning at home. With that, Mr. Peter Petrovich established some countries, however, partly natural relations: Peter despised and hated it, even to excess, almost from the day he lived, but at the same time as some feared it. He stopped him on his arrival in St. Petersburg is not only a miserly economy, although it was almost the main reasons, but there was another reason. Even in the province he heard about Andrew S., its graduates, as one of the most innovative young progressive and even how to play a significant role in other interesting and incredible mugs. He struck Peter Petrovich. Here are a few powerful, all-knowing, despise and subjecting all circles have long frightened Pyotr any special fear is, however, unclear. Of course, he himself, and even in the province, could not do anything because to do so, though, for precise concepts. He heard all that exists, especially in St. Petersburg, some progressives, nihilists, reformers, and so on. And so on. But, like many, exaggerated and distorted the meaning and significance of these names to the absurd. First of all, he was afraid, for several years, reproof, and this was the main basis of its permanent, exaggerated concern, especially with dreams of transferring its activities in St. Petersburg. In this respect, he was, as they say, scared, because sometimes frighten small children. A few years ago in the province, even if only to arrange his career, he met two cases seriously reproach provincial fairly significant persons for whom he still clung to him and patronized. One case ended rebuking man as highly controversial, and the other was a little off very hard. That's why Peter says, arrived in St. Petersburg, just to find out what is happening and, if necessary, in any case, to run forward and zaiskat on "our younger generations." In this case, "hoping he Andrei S. and when you visit, such as Raskolnikov knew somehow rounded known phrase from someone else's voice …

Of course, he quickly managed to see in Andrew S. poshlenkogo very rustic and man. But this does not discourage, and called Peter Petrovich. Even if it is certain that all progressive same fools, and even then it would not stop worrying. In fact, all these teachings, thoughts, systems (which Andrey Semenovich so jumped on him and) he could not be so. He had his own goal. He's just hurry up and immediately find out what and how it happened? In the power of these people or not valid? There is something to fear in fact it or not? Oblichat him if he was here, something will happen or not oblichat? And if oblichat, for what it is, and what is actually now condemn?

ROBOTS READ

Not only that: is it possible somehow to imitate him and immediately podn-adut them if they are really strong? Should or should not it? Is it possible, for example, something podustroit in his career was through their own? In short, the next hundreds of questions.

This is Andrew S. was overgrown and scrofulous little man of small stature, somewhere to serve and oddly blonde with a mustache, in the form of meatballs, which he very proud.Moreover, he almost constantly aching eyes. His heart was rather bland, but it is very stubborn, and sometimes even very arrogant - is compared with the figure of him, almost always came out funny. In Amalia Ivanovna, was considered, however, in the number of tenants is quite an honor that is not drunk and regularly paid for kvartiru.Nesmotrya all these qualities, Andrew S. was really stupid. He lent progress and "our young generation" - passion. It was one of those countless and raznolichnogo Legion vulgar, dohlenkih noobs and dictators around the dropout rate, which of course instantly adhere to the most fashionable walking idea immediately humiliate him blink caricature everything they sometimes sincerely serve.

However, Lebezyatnikov, despite the fact that he was very Dobrenky, too, began to partially tolerate his roommate and former trustee Peter Petrovich. Do this on both sides as a chance and mutual. Because he was a simpleton Andrey Semenovich, but still started to look at what Peter is inflates and secretly despises and that "it's not quite a man." He tried to imagine him Fourier system and Darwin's theory, but Peter, especially in recent years, started listening a little too sarcastic, but in recent years - so even became a battleground. The fact that he, by instinct, began to penetrate that Leb-ezyatnikov not only poshlenkoe and stupid man, but, perhaps, a liar, and that no, he had no connection poznachitelnee even in his own circle, but only heard something about thirds vote; Moreover, some of his business, propaganda, can not know very well, because something gets off too and too much to be a witness against him! Incidentally, we note in passing that Peter in these ten days, willingly accepted (especially at first) by Andrew S. even very strange praise, that is, did not object, for example, and if promal-chival Andrew S. explained his desire to contribute to the future and soon a new device " Commune "somewhere on the street Meshchanskaya; or, for example, does not interfere with Dunya, if that, from the first months of mar-riage, happy lover; or baptize their unborn children, and so forth., and so on. - All of the sort. Peter Petrovich, according to his custom, was not opposed to such qualities attributed to him and allowed himself to praise even so

- before it was nice to praise.

Petr Petrovich exchanged for some reason this morning about five percent of the tickets sitting at the table and counted the stack of credit cards and the series. Andrew S., almost never happened money, walked around the room and made himself look that looks at all of these beams with indifference and even contempt. Peter never would, for example, do not think that really Andrey Semenovich can look for that kind of money with indifference; Andrew S., in turn, reflected bitterly that in fact actually Peter may be able to think about it, but still nice, probably tickle and tease the occasion of his young friend posted a bundle of banknotes, reminding him of his insignificance and if all of the difference existing between both of them.

He found him at this time unprecedented irritable and inattentive, despite the fact that he, Andrew S., let it develop in front of him his favorite theme of the new institution, a special "commune". Brief objections and comments, tears Peter Chikanov between his knuckles on the accounts, breathed samoyu yavnoyu and with the intention rude mockery. But the "humane" Andrei Sergeyevich attributed mood Peter impression yesterday's break with Dun and want to quickly say on the subject: he had something to say which-in this regard and the progressive expansion, which can comfort him honorable friend and "certainly" benefit from its further development .

- What's the funeral is arranged ... the widow, then? - Suddenly asked Peter, Andrew S. searching the most interesting place.

- As if you do not know ,; I made yesterday spoke to you on the same subject and developed the idea of all these rites ... Yes, she also invited you, I've heard. You talked to her yesterday ...

- I did not expect that it would be a bad place fool to wake up all the money received from that other fool ... Raskolnikov. Even wonder now passing: There cooking wine! .. Called a few people - God knows what! - Continuation of Peter, questioning and suggests that conversation, as if with a kind tseliyu. - What? You say that, and I was invited? - Suddenly, he added, raising his head. - When is it? I do not remember, sir. However, I will not go. I was there? Yesterday, I spoke only with her death, an opportunity to get it as an impoverished widow official annual salary in a lump sum. So it's not for him, if she invites me? Hehe!

- I'm not going to go - said Lebezyatnikov.

- You bet! Personally chipped. Clearly, it is a shame, heh, heh, heh!

- Who secede? Who? - Suddenly frightened and even blushed

ROBOTS READ

Lebezyatnikov.

- Yes, what you say, Katerina Ivanovna something a month ago, or what! I have heard, sir, yesterday, with ... That's just so they belief something! .. And the woman question podgulyal. Heh-heh-heh!

And Peter, as if comforted, and began again to press accounts.

- It's all nonsense and slander! - Broke Lebezyatnikov that constantly ran reminders about this story - and it really was not! It was another ... You did not hear; gossip! I was then defended. She first looked at me with claws ... She told me all tore his mustache ... Anyone can, I hope, will help to protect their identity. Also, I will not let anyone to ... In accordance with the principle of violence. Because almost despotism. Well, I was, and stand in front of her? I just pushed it.

- Heh, heh, heh! - Continue to laugh wickedly Luzhin.

- Are you being bullied because they are evil and angry ... But this is nonsense, and very, very not related to women's issues! You do not understand; I even thought that if it is recognized that a woman is equal to man in everything, even in view of (which is said), it should have been, and there should be equality. Of course, I then thought that such a question, in fact, should not be, because the fights and should not be, and that fought in the future society would be unthinkable ... and that is strange, of course, to seek equality in this fight . I'm not that stupid ... but to fight, however, and there ... that is after will not, and now there is something ... ugh! damn! You sobesh! I do not because I do not go to the funeral, which was trouble. I just do not go on the principle not to participate in the commemoration of the vile superstition, that's what! Nevertheless, we could go, so just laugh ... But it is a pity that the priests not.And is, of course, go.

- That is to sit on someone else's bread and salt, and then spit on her form, and those who had been invited. Is that it?

- Do not give a damn, and protest. I am a useful purpose. I can indirectly contribute to the development and promotion. Everyone has a responsibility to develop and promote, and perhaps sharper, the better. I can throw the idea, grain ... From this seed will grow fact. What have I done to offend them? First, offended, and then look at myself that I brought them uslugu.Von were accused Terebevu (which is now in the commune), that when she left the family and ... give it up, then wrote the father and mother does not want to live among the prejudices and enter into a civil marriage, and that if it was too rough, fathers, that they may be spared, write softer. In my opinion, it's

all nonsense, and do not need to softer, on the contrary, on the contrary, where the protest. Vaughn Varentsov seven years with her husband lived, threw two children, once snapped her husband in a letter: ". I know that you could not be happier, I'll never forgive you, you deceived me, hiding from me that there is another order of society and communities. Recently I learned all this from one generous man who gave himself and with him, and looking at some of the community. Simply put, because I think it's unfair to deceive you. Be as you like it. Do not expect me, you're too late. I want to be happy. "That's how to write such a write!

- This Terebeva, the same one which you then said that in the third civil marriage?

- Just a second judging for real! Yes, even in the fourth, if only in the fifteenth, it's all nonsense! And if I ever regretted that my father and mother died, of course, now.Several time I even dreamed that if they were still alive, how would I beat my protest! Deliberately wrong ... Is that just any "cut a slice," ugh! I would show them! I would surprise them! Indeed, it is a pity that no one else has!

- To the surprise of something? Hehe! Well, let it be as you want - interrupted Peter, - and this is what Tell me: because you know the daughter of the deceased, then there are very bad! It's really perfect that say about it, huh?

- Well, is it? In my opinion, it is, in my personal opinion, this is the normal condition of the woman. Why not? This distinguons. 1 In today's society it is certainly not normal, because of the need, but in the future, it is perfectly normal, because free. And now she had the right: she was suffering, and that was its foundation, so to speak capital, which she had every right to imet.Konechno in the future of the Company do not have to;but his role will be marked with a different meaning, in connection with the orderly and rational. As Sofya Semyonovna personally, now I look at her actions as an energetic and embodied protest against the social structure of society and deeply respect her for it; enjoy looking at it!

- And I also told you something and survived it from ciphers!

Lebezyatnikov even rage.

- This is another gossip! - He shouted. - Very, very bad it was! It really is not so! It's all Katerina Ivanovna, you lied because I do not understand! And I'm not quite incitement to Sofya Semyonovna! I'm just easy to develop it completely selflessly, trying to provoke her protest ... I only protest was necessary, and in itself Sofya Semyonovna could not stay here in numbered!

- In the commune, and, in the name?

- You all laugh, and very bad, let me tell you this notice. You do not understand! In the commune of roles not. Commune and arranged for such roles were not. In the commune of this role will change all of the submission of its essence, and it's stupid, it would not be smart here, in the present circumstances, unnatural, and will quite naturally. It all depends on the conditions under which and the environment in which people.Everything from the environment, but the person does. And Sophia Semenovna, I'm in trouble now that you can serve as proof of the fact that she never thought that I was his enemy and abuser. Yes I am! I seduce her now in the commune, but only very, very different reasons! What you're funny? We want to make your commune, especially, but only on broader grounds than the previous one. We went further in their beliefs.We do not deny! If Dob rose from the grave, I would argue with him. And Belinsky be rolled up! Meanwhile, I continue to develop Sofya Semyonovna. It's a beautiful, beautiful scenery!

- Well, something beautiful nature and use, as well? Hehe!

- No, no! Oh, no! On the contrary!

- Well, that and the other way around! Heh-heh-heh! Eck said!

- Yes, I believe in it now! Yes, because for some reason, I would begin to hide in front of you, please, tell me? On the contrary, even for me it is strange to me is somehow hard with fear chaste and shy!

- And you, of course, develop ... hehe! prove to her that all this nonsense modesty? ..

- Not at all! Not at all! Oh, how about you as even stupid - sorry - understand the word: development! N-Nothing-not understand! My God, you're still not ready ...! We are looking for the freedom of women, and you have one in mind ... Bypass entirely a matter of chastity and female modesty, as things in themselves are useless and even cause harm, I'm really, really recognize her chastity with me, because it's - - it all desires, all her rights. Of course, if she told me, she said, "I want you," I would consider myself a very lucky girl because I really like; but now, now, at least, of course, no one has ever treated her more polite and courteous than I, more respect for her dignity ... I wait and hope - and more!

- Did you give her the moment something better. I bet it's here that you never thought of.

- N-nothing, then you do not understand, I said! This, of course, its position, but that is another question!completely different! You simply despise

her. Seeing that mistakenly considered worthy of contempt, you have to deny the human being as a human look at it. You do not know what a character! I'm just really annoyed that he recently as something completely stopped reading and did not take me more books. The First Cut. It is a pity also that for all his energy and determination to protest - which she proved once again - he still seemed a little independence, so to speak, independence, a little denial completely break away from the other prejudice and stupidity .... Although she understands other issues . It's great, for example, understood the question to kiss his hands, that is, that a man insults a woman inequality if kisses her hand. This issue was discussed at us, and I immediately gave her. Union workers in France she also listened attentively. Now I say to her question of free entrance to the room in the future society.

- What is it?

- Was discussed in recent years, the question of the right to membership in the commune move to another member in the room, male or female, at any time ... and decided that has ...

- Well, he or she held at the time of the necessary requirements, hehe!

Andrei Sergeyevich even angry.

- And you all about it, about these damned "needs"! - He exclaimed with hatred - ugh, I'm angry and annoyed that, saying the system you mentioned, it is premature to these damned needs Damn! This is a stumbling block for all of you love, and above all - increases the heart, not knowing what's going on! And just because it is necessary! It is because some pride! Ugh! I have several times argued that the whole issue can express beginners only as at the end when he really believes in the system when it is developed and directed people.And, please tell us what you find such shameful and despicable even landfills? I am the first, I am willing to clean latrines, whatever you want! There is not even no sacrifice! That's just work, noble, useful activities of the company, which is worth any other, and is much higher, for example, the activity of Raphael or Pushkin because it useful!

- A noble, noble, - heh, heh, heh!

- What is "noble"? I do not understand such expressions in the sense of human activity. "Noble", "generous" - all this nonsense, nonsense, old superstitious words that I deny! All that is useful to humanity and noble!

I know only one word: useful ! Giggle, as you like, but it's true!

Peter laughed. He finished reading and hid the money. Nevertheless, some of them for any reason, there is still on the table. This is "the question of

garbage pits" served several times, despite its banality, reason for the gap and differences between Peter Petrovich and his young friend. All the nonsense that Andrew S. very angry. Luzhin prevented against that soul, and at this point he would especially like to annoy Lebezyatnikov.

- You are out of your failure yesterday so angry and connections - finally broke Lebezyatnikov that, generally speaking, in spite of its "independence" and all the "protests" somehow did not dare to speak out against Peter Petrovich, and still saw before him some familiar with in previous years, the veneration.

- And you better tell you that minute - arrogant and angrily interrupted Peter - if you can, with … or should I say that, so if you are missing with the aforementioned young lady to ask him now just a minute here, in this room? It seems that they are really the gate to the cemetery … I hear … I rose to go to see her, sir, really something, sir.

- Yes, why? - Asked in surprise Lebezyatnikov.

- Well cc necessary. Today and tomorrow I eat here, so I would like to say to her … But, maybe, and here, while explaining. Nevertheless, even better. And you, probably, and god knows what to think.

- I have absolutely nothing … I think that the only way to ask, and if you have a case, there is nothing simpler than its cause. Now I will go. And rest assured, I will not bother you.

Indeed, five minutes later returned with Lebezyatnikov Sony. This happened in utter surprise and, as usual, timidly. She always shy in such cases, and was very afraid of new people and new acquaintances, and was afraid before, since childhood, and now more than ever … Peter met her "kindly and politely," but with some shade some fun acquaintance, decent, but according to Peter Petrovich, this respectable and decent man like him, for such young and a few interesting things. He rushed her to "encourage" and he put the table in front of him. Sonya sat down, looked around - at Lebezyatnikov money lying on the table, and then suddenly again on Pyotr Petrovich, and kept her eyes on him more, just riveted to it. Lebezyatnikov headed for the door. Petr Petrovich stood up, Sonya beckoned to sit down and Lebezyatnikov in the doorway.

- It has Raskolnikov? He came? - He asked in a whisper.

- Raskolnikov? There. What? Yes, there … Now only came, I saw … And what?

- Well, I ask you especially to stay here with us, and do not leave me alone

with this girl …. trifling things, and bring God knows what. I do not want to Raskolnikov has passed … Do you understand what I'm saying?

- Oh, I see, I see! - Suddenly realized Lebezyatnikov. - Yes, you're right … This, of course, in my personal opinion, you are far from lacking in your fears … but you still have right.Certainly, I'm staying. I'll be here at the window, and I will not bother you … I think you have the right …

Pyotr Petrovich returned to the couch and sat down in front of Sonia, looked at her and suddenly took a very strong, even more strict form ". Say, you do something that she does not think about it, ma'am" Sonia finally embarrassed.

- First, you'll please excuse me, Sophia Semenovna, dear, before your mother … So in fact you think? Instead you have native Katerina Ivanovna something? - Peter began very hard, but, nevertheless, quite gently. It was obvious that he has the most friendly intentions.

- Similarly, with so; instead of mother-to-- quickly and timidly said Sonya.

- Well, that's my excuse in front of her, that I, as appropriate, independent, forced to save, and I'm not on your damn … that is, at the funeral, despite the appeal of his dear mother.

- So-c; I say, sir; Now, sir, - and Sonya hurriedly jumped up from his chair.

- However, not all, sir, - Peter stopped her with a smile on her naivete and ignorance of propriety - and there is little you know me, my dear Sophia Semenovna, if you think that because of this matter concerning me one cause I'll bother to call and personally to him a man like you. The purpose of my friend with.

Sonya hastily Sat Gray and iridescent credit card, do not remove from the table, again flashed in her eyes, but she quickly turned away from their faces and raised it to Pyotr Petrovich: it suddenly seemed terribly indecent, especially her to look at other people's money. She looked at the golden eyes were lorgnette Peter, which he held in his left hand, and at the same time on the big, massive, very beautiful ring with a yellow stone that was on the middle finger - but suddenly, and took him from the eyes not knowing really what to do over, stared straight into the eyes of Peter Petrovich. After a while, more solid than before, he continued:

- It happened to me yesterday, in passing, to throw a word or two with the unfortunate Katerina Ivanovna.Two words were enough to realize that she is in a state - unnatural, if one may say so …

- Yes, sir … in unnatural with - slowly struck Sonia.

- Or, easier and more intuitive to say - in a patient.

- Yes, sir, it is easier to understand and … yes, sir, bad-ies.

- So-c. Thus, with a sense of humanity, and-and-and, so to speak, of com-passion, I would like to be on his side, something useful, waiting for the inevitable fate of her unhappy. It seems a poor family, and all up to you now only one, and it depends.

- Let me ask you - suddenly stood Sonia - this is what you are pleased to say yesterday about the possibility of retirement? Because she told me yes-terday that you took her pension acquired. It is true, sir?

- Not at all, sir, and even a kind of absurd. I only hinted about time helps widow died in service of the official - if only to patronage - but it seems to me that your deceased parent not only to curry favor with the term, but not even fed recently. In short, the hope, though it may be, but very ephemeral, because neither in fact, the right does not help in this regard does not exist, and even vice versa … And this is already retired conceived, heh- hehe ! Lively Lady!

- Yes, sir, about retirement … Because she's trusting and kind, and kind-ness believes all things, and … and … and … have a mind of it … Yes, sir … izvinite- with, - said Sonya, and then got up to leave.

- Excuse me, you do not listen, sir.

- Yes, sir, do not listen, sir, - muttered Sonia.

- So good to sit, sir.

Sonia zakonfuzilas bad and sat down again for the third time.

- It is better to see once their position, accidents minors, we would like - as I said - something, as far as possible, be helpful, that is what is called a power, not more. You can, for example, to arrange in favor of its membership, or, so to speak, lottery … or something like that - as always in such cases, organized, or at least close and outsiders, but in general, you want to help people. That's what I intended to say. It would be possible to.

- Yes, sir, good to … God bless you for it, with … - Sonya murmured, look-ing at Peter Petrovich.

- Is it possible, sir, but … we have to … then you can start today. See you tonight, collusion and set, so to speak base. Come see me here at 7:00, that way.Andrew S. hope will also participate with us … But … there is one thing that you must first carefully mention. For this reason I interrupted you, Sofya Semyonovna, my challenge here.That, sir, it is my opinion - that the money is impossible, and dangerous to give into the hands of Katerina Ivanovna; The

proof of these things - it's the same today's funeral. Not having, so to speak, one peel urgent food the next day and ... well, shoes, and everything can be bought today Jamaican rum, and even seems to Madeira and-and-and coffee. I saw goes. Tomorrow again all of you will fall on the last piece of bread; it's funny, sir. And so the subscription, in my personal opinion, should be done in such a way that the poor widow, so to speak, and not about the money, and will know, for example, only you. So what I'm saying?

- I do not know, sir. It is only now, with so ... this time in my life ... she really wanted to remember, honor render, memory ... and she is very smart, sir. And yet, as you, sir, and I am very, very, very ... they will get you ... and you ... God and orphans, with ...

Sonia has not finished, and wept.

- So-c. Well, keep in mind, sir; And now deign to accept, on behalf of their relatives in the first case, the feasible amount from me personally. Very, very sorry that my name is not mentioned. There is ... having, so to speak, he worries, no longer able to ...

Peter gave Sonia ten credit card, carefully unfolded. Sonia took broke out, jumped up, muttered something and began to take leave as soon as possible. Petr Petrovich solemnly escorted her to the door. She finally ran out of the room, all excited and exhausted, and the gate to Katerina Ivanovna in complete confusion.

Throughout this stage Andrew S. stood at the window, and then walked across the room, not wanting to interrupt the conversation; When Sonya left, he suddenly came to Peter Petrovich and solemnly held out his hand:

- I heard everything, and all saw - he said, emphasizing the last word. - This is noble, that is, I would say, humanely! You want to escape thanks, I've seen! And although I confess to you, I can not sympathize with the principle of private philanthropy, because he not only does not eradicate the evil in the bud, but even feeds even more, but I can not admit that looking at your action with pleasure - Yes, yes, I like it.

- Uh, it's all nonsense! - Peter muttered, a little excitement and somehow get used to Lebezyatnikov.

- No, nothing more! A man insulted and angry, like you, and yesterday's event at the same time able to think about the suffering of others - such a man by his actions ... though he does social mistake - nevertheless ... worthy of respect! I did not expect from you, Peter, the more that you think about! How else to prevent you from your ideas! How to care for example, you have

this failure yesterday - said Andrew S. Dobrenky, again feeling the increased proximity of Pyotr Petrovich - and that what you really what marriage, legal marriage, precious, dear Peter? Well, if you want to beat me, and I'm glad that I'm glad he did not succeed, you are free, you are not very much and died for humanity, I am glad ... You see, I told you so!

- Besides, sir, that your civil marriage, I do not want to wear the horns and raise other people's children, this is what I-legal marriage hath need - to say something, said Luzhin. He was something particularly busy and thoughtful.

- Children have? You touched on children? - Andrew S. winced Warhorse heard military pipe - children - the social question and the question of primary importance, I agree; but the issue of children be resolved otherwise. Some even completely deny children, as well as any hint of the family. We'll talk about the children after that, now we get the horns! I confess to you, that's my weakness. This is bad, hussar, Pushkin expression unthinkable in the future lexicon. And that horn? Oh, what nonsense! What horns? Why horns?What nonsense! On the contrary, in a civil marriage, then they would not be! Horns - it's just a natural consequence of any legal marriage, so to speak, his amendment, protest, so in that sense they are not even humiliating ... And if I ever - provided absurdity - I'll be legally married, then I will be happy even your rastreklyatym horns; I then say to his wife: "My friend, I still love only you, but now I respect you, because you can protest!" You laugh? This is because you can not break away from prejudices! Heck, I realize that it was an inconvenience when deceived by law; but it is only a consequence of the vile vile actually where humiliated and more. When the horns are placed openly, as in a civil marriage, even if they do not exist, they are impossible to lose and even the name of the horns. On the contrary, your wife will show you how well she respects you if you are unable to resist her happiness and well developed, not to avenge her new husband.Heck, I sometimes dream that if I was married, ugh! if I were married (civil whether, in accordance with the law, if, in any case), I think he gave his wife a lover if she had it for a long time will not start. "My friend, - I would say - I love you, but even beyond that want you to respect me - that" It's because I'm saying? ..

Peter chuckled listen, but without much enthusiasm.

←«»→

⟪ CHAPTER II ⟫

It would be difficult to determine the precise reasons for which disappointed the head Katerina Ivanovna was born the idea of these stupid way. In fact, they put it aside and have been for almost ten rubles from the twenties, received from Raskolnikov's actually the funeral Marmeladova. Perhaps Katerina Ivanovna consider themselves bound by the dead man to honor his memory "right" to know all the tenants and Amalia Ivanovna especially, that he was "not just as good, maybe even better, with" and that none of the They do not have right in front of him, "turn up their noses." Maybe it was more likely to have influenced the special pride of the poor, because of which, under certain social rituals needed in everyday life for all, many poor people look at the last effort and spend the last penny of savings just to be "better than other "and not" condemn "them somehow those and others. It is likely, and that Katerina Ivanovna wanted on this case, at the moment when it seemed the whole world, what's left to show all these "empty and unpleasant tenants," which is not only "knows how to live and to know how to make, "but not even for a fraction and was raised and educated was" noble, one might even say, in the aristocratic Colonel House, "and, of course, not in order to cook, sweep the floor and wash himself clothes for children night. These paroxysms of pride and vanity, and sometimes visit the poorest and most downtrodden people and, at times, turning them into irritability, irresistible necessity. And Katerina Ivanovna and not developed: it can be completely kill the circumstances, but to score his moral backbone, intimidation and submit his will, it was impossible. In addition Sonya very carefully about her saying that she mind to intervene. Positively and finally, it is still, however, it was

impossible to say, but in fact as recently as last year, her poor head was too tired to at least partially intact. Strong development of consumption, as the doctors say, too, contributes to the madness of mental abilities.

Win in the plural and diverse varieties were not, Madeira , too: it was exaggerated, but the wine was. Were vodka, rum and Lisbon, all the nasty quality, but just enough. Of the dishes except the scullery, there were three or four dishes (by the way, and pancakes), all with kitchen Amalia Ivanovna, and in addition put back two samovars perspective afternoon tea and punch. Purchases told himself to Katerina Ivanovna, with one passenger, some pathetic Pole, God knows that lived at Madame Lippevehzel, who immediately loaned to send Katerina Ivanovna and ran all day yesterday, and all this in the morning with a head and protruding tongue, it seems particularly noticeable was trying this latter circumstance. For every little thing that he always sought the most Katerina Ivanovna ran even look at it in the arcade, called her incessantly: "pani horunzhina", and finally tired of her as radishes, though at first she said that without it " helpful and generous "person, it will be quite lost. In material nature Katerina Ivanovna quickly to dress the first comer and cross to the best and brightest colors, flattered him so that others were even ashamed to come to the praise of the various circumstances that do not exist at all, and honestly and sincerely believe in their greater reality, then suddenly, at once, give up, break down, spit and blow pushes the person with whom he is just a few hours ago, literally worshiped. Nature of the characters she giggled, cheerful and calm, but continuous misfortunes and failures, before she furiously began to desire and demand that all live in peace and joy, and did not dare to live differently, that the easiest dissonance in life is the slightest failure Steel cause almost immediately into a frenzy, and she at one point, after the bright hopes and fantasies did not curse fate, throw up everything that came to hand, and banging his head against the wall. Amalia Ivanovna, too, suddenly acquired as something extraordinary significance and extraordinary respect for Katerina Ivanovna, just because it may be that they have started the funeral and that Amalia Ivanovna wholeheartedly decided to take part in all the troubles she has undertaken to lay the table, bring bed linen, crockery, etc .. and in the kitchen to cook the dish. Its authorized and left on their own Katerina Ivanovna herself going to the cemetery. In fact, everything was cooked to fame: the table was laid, even fairly clean, dishes, forks, knives, cups, glasses, cups - all this, of course, was a team, raznofasonnoe and varied, from a variety of tenants, but it was

known up to one hour in his place, and Amalia Ivanovna, feeling perfectly executed business, met a refund even with some pride, all dressed up, wearing a cap with new mourning ribbons and black dress. This pride, though deserved, not like for some reason, Katerina Ivanovna, "in fact, accurately and without Amalia Ivanovna and a table would not be able to cover!" And her too, and a hat with new tapes not like ?! "I'm not proud of, if, God forbid, it's stupid German hostess and she agreed to help his mercy to the poor tenants grace I humbly ask you to Papa We Katerina Ivanovna, who was a colonel, and almost to the governor's desk was covered with some time on the forty so that any Amalia Ivanovna, or should I say Lyudvigovna, go to the kitchen and did not allow ... "However, Katerina Ivanovna not tolerate no time to express their feelings, but decided in his heart that Amalia Ivanovna, of course, have to besiege today and remind her of her real place, but it's God knows about me dream, meanwhile, is also treated her just cold. Another problem is also partly contributed to the annoyance of Katerina Ivanovna: the funeral of the residents were invited to attend the funeral, except for the Polish girls who have run and at the cemetery, almost no one was; as a result of the same, that is to snack, they were all very small and poor, many of them are not even in the form, so some things. Which of them are older and more impressive, all of them, as if on purpose, as if by agreement, stingy. Pyotr Petrovich Luzhin, for example, we can say, the strength of all the tenants, did not appear, and last night Katerina Ivanovna was able to tell the story of every person in the world, that is, Amalia Ivanovna, polka, Sonia and Polish girl that noble, generous person with and vast connections with the state, a former friend of her first husband, was held in the house of his father, who promised to use all means to ensure her considerable pension. Note here that if Katerina Ivanovna and praise someone's connection status and is without interest, without any personal calculation, completely disinterested, so to speak, from the fullness of the heart, from the simple pleasure to praise and to give more price hvalimomu, and Luzhin, probably, "taking his example," do not appear "nasty villain Lebezyatnikov." "I do this, what about yourself think? His mercy is by invitation only, and that is because he Peter in the same room each and it was not so awkward to invite." Was not the same and one ton lady with her "overripe maiden," her daughter, who was living all week with only two in the numbered Amalia Ivanovna, but several times already complained about the noise and clamor rises from the room Marmeladov, especially when he died return

home drunk, which, of course, it was already known to Katerina Ivanovna through Amalia Ivanovna, when another war with Katerina Ivanovna and threatening to expel the entire family, screaming with laughter, they were concerned about "the noble tenants whose foot wrong. " Katerina Ivanovna deliberately set now to invite this lady and her daughter, whose "feet, as if it is not necessary", especially because so far, in random encounters, she arrogantly turns away - and so she knew that here "noble thoughts and feelings, and invite, not remembering evil," and they saw that Katerina Ivanovna, and not to the number of shares used to live. This, of course, is to explain to them at the table, as well as the province of the late Pope, and at the same time indirectly pointed out that there was nothing to look away when they met, and that it was extremely stupid. Do not get too thick and Lieutenant Colonel (in fact, retired captain), but it turned out that he had "no back legs" since yesterday morning. In short, were the following: polyachok, then plyugavenkim clerk without speeches in oily coat, acne and nasty smell; then another deaf and nearly blind old man who once served in some post office, and that someone, from time immemorial, and for some unknown reason, stored in Amalia Ivanovna. Was too drunk retired Lieutenant essentially Providing official with indecent and loud laughter, and "Imagine", without a vest! Someone sat down at the table, not even bow to Katerina Ivanovna, and finally, one person, because of the lack of clothes, was dressed in a robe, but it was wrong to such an extent that the efforts of Amalia Ivanovna and the Pole has his recall . Polyachok, however, brought with it another some two other Polish girl who has never lived in Amalia Ivanovna, and that no one has yet to see numbered. All this is extremely frustrating annoying Katerina Ivanovna."Who, then, are all ready?" Even the children in order to get a seat at the table has planted, already occupied the room, and covered them in a corner chest and small, sitting on a bench, and Polechka as big had to look after them, feed them and destroy them "as precious children, "spouts. In short, Katerina Ivanovna did not want to meet with a doubling of the importance and even arrogance. Particularly strict she looked down, and some asked to sit at the table. Given some reason, that for all no-show should not be responsible Amalia Ivanovna, she suddenly began to treat her to an extreme casually that she immediately noticed and to the extreme it was a dive. Such a beginning boded no good end. Finally sat down.

Raskolnikov came almost at the same moment as the gate of the cemetery. Katerina Ivanovna awfully glad to see him in the first place, because

it was only "educated guest" of all the guests and, "as it is known, two years preparing to take the local university professors", and secondly, because it immediately and respectfully apologized to her that, in spite of all desire can not be at the funeral. She was so jumped on him and put it on the table next to him on the left (right sat Amalia Ivanovna), and despite the continuous hassles and troubles that correctly dish was spread out and get it all, despite the painful cough, which is constantly interrupted, and choked it, and it seems particularly entrenched in these last two days, constantly turned to Raskolnikov and whisper to him in a rush to pour out all the accumulated feelings in it and all his righteous anger could not wake up, time to change the anger is often the most interesting, the most uncontrollable laughter of the guests, but mostly samoyu mistress.

- Over the Cuckoo's fault this. You know, I say about her, about her! - And Katerina Ivanovna nodded his mistress. - Look at her eyes widened, feeling that we are talking about it, but he can not understand, and eyes to hatch. Fu, the owl! ha-ha-ha! .. Hee-hee-hee! And she wants to show off her hat! hee-hee-hee! Have you noticed she still wants everyone to think that it protects and makes me the honor to attend. I asked her how decent, invite people better and that the friends of the deceased, and see who she brought: some clowns!chumichki! Look at this face with unclean: it is some snot on two legs! And these polyachishki ... ha ha ha!Hee-hee-hee! Nobody, nobody here had never seen, and I've never seen before; Well, why they came, I ask you? Sedately sitting side by side. Ban ,! - She suddenly shouted one of them - you have pancakes? Get more! Drink beer, beer! Vodka do not want? See: jumping, bows, look, look, he must be very hungry, the poor! Nothing, let edyat. Otsutstvie noise, at least, just ... just right, I'm not afraid of silver spoons hostess! .. Amalia Ivanovna! - She suddenly turned to her, almost aloud, - if it pokradut spoon, I can not answer for them, I warn you in advance! Ha-ha-ha! - An explosion in it, turning again to Raskolnikov, again nodding his lover and enjoy their antics. - I do not know, again, I do not understand! Sitting mouth Cuckoo, see: owl, real, Sychiha new ribbons, ha ha ha!

Here again, the laughter turned into an intolerable cough, which lasted five minutes. On the scarf several blood sweat on his forehead. She silently showed the blood on Raskolnikov and barely otdyhnuvshis, once whispered to him again the extraordinary animation and with red spots on her cheeks:

- Look, I gave her the most subtle, it can be said to invite this lady and her daughter, you know, I'm saying?There should behave in the most sensitive

way to act the most skillful way, and she did so, it is a fool, this arrogant creature, this tiny provincial, just because it seems to be there, and the widow of Major came to petition for pensions and hem studs in public places, it's fifty-five years Surma, belitsya and rosy (known) ... and such that not only loves to appear, but not even sent an apology, if she can not come, as in such cases the most common courtesy calls ! I can not understand why he came, too, Peter? But where Sonia? Where to go?Ah, here it is finally! Sonya, where he was? I'm surprised that you even at the funeral of his father, to casually. Rodion Romanovich, let her near him. Here's your place, Sonia ... take what you want. The filler is better. Now bring the pancakes. And the children were given? Polechka, all you have there? Hee-hee-hee!Well, well. Be smart, Lenya, and you, Nick, do not tell legs; sit like a noble child should sit. What do you say, Sonia?

Sonia immediately rushed to give her an apology Peter, trying to speak out loud for all to hear, and have the choicest respectful expression, even purposely podsochinennye on behalf Lazarev wrote. She added that Peter said, especially to convey that he was, as he will probably soon come to talk about matters in private and agree on what can be done and to take in the future, and so on., and so on.

Sonia knew it dies, and appease Katerina Ivanovna, flatter her, and most importantly - the pride will be provided. She sat next to Raskolnikov, who hastily bowed and looked curiously at him. However, at other times, as something to avoid and look at it and talk to him. It was as if even distracted, though, looking in the face of Katerina Ivanovna to please her. Neither she nor Katerina Ivanovna was not in mourning, due to lack of duty; Sonia was some brown, darker, and Katerina Ivanovna only her dress, cotton, temnenky with stripes.News about Peter Petrovich went like clockwork. After listening to an important Sonya, Katerina Ivanovna with the same importance asked how health Peter? Then immediately and almost aloud, whispered to Raskolnikov that it would be strange indeed respected and decent man like Peter, fall into such "extraordinary company," although all his devotion to his family and to his old friendship with her dad.

- That is why I am particularly grateful to you, Rodion Romanovitch that you do not disdain my bread and salt, even in such a situation - she added almost aloud - but I am sure that only your special friendship my poor dead prompted you to keep your word .

Then she proudly and with dignity and studied their guests with

extraordinary care suddenly asked loudly across the table with a blind old man, "if he wants to continue hot, and if he was allowed to Lisbon?" The old man did not answer, and he could not understand what he was asked, although neighbors jokingly even started to shove it. He just looked around the mouth circle cuckoo than the more common fire pleasure.

- That fool! Look, look! And this led him? As for Peter Petrovich, I was always sure of - continued Katerina Ivanovna Raskolnikov, - and, of course, do not like it ... - sharp and loud and with a very strict view she turned to Amalia Ivanovna, why she even shy - not look like your overdressed shlepohvostnits, whose dad cook in the kitchen did not take, and the deceased husband, of course, they would have done honor to receive them, and that for her kindness inexhaustible exception.

- Yes, sir, with love drinks; loved him with beer, sir! - Shouted suddenly resigned Regulation, draining the twelfth glass of vodka.

- The late husband really was this lack, and everyone knows that - and suddenly grabbed him Katerina Ivanovna - but it was a good and noble man who loved and respected his family; one evil to goodness it too much confidence in all kinds of depraved people and even God knows whom he did not drink, those who even the soles of his no cost! Imagine that Rodion Romanovich, pocket gingerbread member found: dead drunk, but the children remember.

- Pe-tush-ka? You were happy to say, NE-tush-ka? - Providing shouted Mr.

Katerina Ivanovna did not deign to reply. It's something to think about and sighed.

- Now you're probably thinking, like everyone else, I'm too hard on him was - she continued, turning to Raskolnikov. - But it is not so! He respects me, he gave me a very, very respected! Good was a man! And so sometimes felt sorry! Sits, used to look at me from the corner, so I'm sorry to be, I would cuddle and then think to myself, "weasel, and he gets drunk again," only more or less rigor and can accommodate.

- Yes, sir, there was a torn-vortex-C, happened repeatedly with - again laughed position and poured a glass of vodka still.

- Not only ragged whirlwind, but even a broom would be useful to do with the other fools. I am not talking about the dead! - Providing snapped suddenly Katerina Ivanovna.

Red spots on her cheeks burned stronger and stronger, her panting. Another minute, and she was ready to start the story. Many giggled a lot,

apparently, is that nice. Providing began to push and whispered something to him. They obviously wanted to pit.

- Step-azvolte and ask you about something - began to supply - that is, for whom ... noble ... you were pleased to now ... And yet, it is not necessary! Nonsense! Widow! Widow! Sorry ... Paz! - He knocked again vodka.

Raskolnikov sat and listened in silence and disgust. He ate only out of politeness really touching parts that constantly puts on his plate Katerina Ivanovna, and then only, so as not to offend her. He stared at Sonya. But Sonia becomes anxious and anxiety; She also felt that awaken peacefully over, and watched with irritation fear Katerina Ivanovna. Incidentally, it was known that the main reason for both beginner ladies, so contemptuously treated with an invitation to Katerina Ivanovna, it was Sonia. She heard from the mother herself even offended invitation Amalia Ivanovna and asked the question: "How could she sit next to this girl? your daughter "Sonia had a presentiment that Katerina Ivanovna somehow already know what it is but an insult to her, Sonia, Katerina Ivanovna meant more than an insult to her personally, her children, her father, in a word, fatally injured, and Sonya knew too Katerina Ivanovna now will not rest "until he proves this shle-pohvostkam, that they are both", and so on. d., and. those, unfortunately, someone sent from the other end of the table Sonia plate with a cast on it, black bread, two hearts pierced by an arrow. Katerina Ivanovna, and immediately broke out loudly remarked across the table to the forwarded rate "drunk ass." Amalia Ivanovna, too, had a premonition that something was wrong, but at the same time deeply offended by the arrogance of Katerina Ivanovna to distract unpleasant mood of society in the opposite direction and, incidentally, to raise himself to general opinion, the beginning of a sudden with no of any of this, told me that to know it, "Karl from the pharmacy," went into the cabin at night, and that "The driver wanted ubival and Carl his ocean, ocean prosil, that he did not ubival and plakal and hands slozhil and ispugal, and fear his heart pronzil. "Katerina Ivanovna, though smiled, but then he noticed that Amalia Ivanovna should not be in Russian jokes to tell. This is even more offended and replied that she "Vater Aus Berlin Bull ocean, ocean shelovek important and all hands went into his pocket." Easy funny Katerina Ivanovna broke down and laughed horribly, so that Amalia Ivanovna had already begun in the past to lose patience and hard fixed.

- Here Sychiha something! - Whispered again Katerina Ivanovna Raskol-nikov, almost ridiculous - to say wore his hands in his pockets, but it turned

out that he reached into his pocket, hee-hee! And I noticed that you, Rodion Romanovich, once and for all, that all these Petersburg foreigners, that is, more importantly, the Germans who come to us otkudova something stupider than we all come! Well, you see, well, we can talk about that, "Karl from the pharmacy fear pronzil heart," and that he (jerk!), Rather than to tie the cabin, "Hands slozhil and plakal and ocean prosil." Oh, durynda! And it thinks it is very moving, and has no idea how she is stupid! In my opinion, this drunken Providing much smarter than she is; at least, it is clear that a drunkard, a former propyl mind, and yet it is staid, serious ... Look, sitting, eyes hatched. Wicked! Wicked!Ha-ha-ha! Hee-hee-hee!

Surprised, Katerina Ivanovna at once fascinated in different parts, and suddenly began to talk about how to provide retirement, using it will certainly lead to his hometown of T ... Guesthouse for Noble Maidens. This was not mentioned Raskolnikov samoyu Katerina Ivanovna, and she immediately became involved in the most seductive details. It is not known when suddenly he found himself in the hands of the same "certificate of merit" which Raskolnikov notice Marmeladov dead, explaining to him in the tavern that Katerina Ivanovna, his wife, with the release of the Institute, danced with a shawl, "the Governor and others."Certificate of Merit is, obviously, was now to serve as proof of the right to have the best Katerina Ivanovna board; but more importantly, was built for this purpose, to finally cut "as overdressed shlepohvostnits" when they came to the wake, and clearly show them that Katerina Ivanovna of the most noble ", one might even say aristocratic house, Colonel's daughter and therefore probably better than the other adventurers who gave birth to so many lately. "Certificate of Merit immediately went to the hands of drunken guests Katerina Ivanovna did not interfere, because it really was detected, En TOUTES literature, [black and white - fr.] that she was the daughter of the court counselor and gentleman, and, consequently, in fact almost polkovnika.Ignite daughter, Katerina Ivanovna immediately spread to all parts of the future of beauty and quiet life in t ... bytya, school teachers, who she invited to study at your board, one venerable old gentleman, Mango Frenchman who taught at French even the most Katerina Ivanovna at the institute and which even now living out his life in t ... and will probably go to her very similar charge. He came, finally, the case and Sony », which went to the T ... Katerina Ivanovna and will be around to help. " But suddenly someone snorted at the end of the table. Katerina Ivanovna, though once tried to pretend not to notice the neglect occurred at the end

of the table laughing, but then deliberately raising his voice began to speak about the animation of the undoubted abilities Sofya Semyonovna serve as her assistant ", its gentleness, patience, selflessness nobility and education, "and patted Sonya on the cheek, and, standing, passionately kissed her twice. Sonia broke out, and Katerina Ivanovna suddenly burst into tears, immediately noticed about myself, "she is nervous fool, and that too upset that it was time to finish, and as an appetizer really over, then spread to tea." At this very moment, Amalia Ivanovna, was finally offended by the fact that during the whole conversation, she did not take the slightest participation and that it is not even listening, suddenly took a chance on the last attempt, and with hidden longing, dared to tell Katerina Ivanovna one very intelligent and thoughtful note that in the future a guest house should pay special attention to the clean underwear girls (di veshe), and that "should nepremen Bull is one of those good women (Lady Di), to Caras on linen watched" Vo Second, "that all young girls quietly at night, no one reading the novel number." Katerina Ivanovna was very upset and very tired, and it was pretty tired to wake up immediately "cut" Amalia Ivanovna that she "grinds nonsense" and does not understand ; that concerns about de veshe transaction housekeeper, not BOARDING SCHOOL headmistress;and how to read novels, so it's just another indecent, and that she asks her zamolchat. Amaliya Ivanovna flushed and furious, she noticed that she was only "good zhelal" and that she was "a lot of good zhelal ocean" and that she "apartments for long, so do not Geld platil." Katerina Ivanovna immediately "siege" of her, saying that she was lying, saying that "good zhelal", because yesterday when silence lay on the table, she was tormented by her apartment. This is very consistent Amalia Ivanovna noticed that she was "priglashal these ladies, but these ladies are not prishol because those ladies, noble ladies and can not prishol to the noble ladies." Katerina Ivanovna at once, "said that" her that since she chumichka, you can not judge what is true nobility. Amalia Ivanovna not demolished, and immediately said that she "Vater Aus Berlin Bull ocean, ocean shelovek important and both hands on the pocket, and went all the way Dellal: poof, poof" And in fact, present their Vater, Amalia Ivanovna jumped up from chair, put his hands in his pockets, puffed out his cheeks and began to publish a vague sounds mouth like poof-poof, with a loud laugh all the tenants who deliberately encouraged Amalia Ivanovna its approval, pending the battlefield. But he could not stand Katerina Ivanovna, and immediately publicly "tapped" that Amalia Ivanovna perhaps never

Vater-it was not, and that only Amalia Ivanovna - St. Petersburg Chukhonka drunk and probably somewhere, especially in Cook veins and perhaps even worse. Amalia Ivanovna blushed as cancer and screamed that it was maybe Katerina Ivanovna "not Vater Bull, and that he Boules Vater Aus Berlin, and still wore a long coat and all Dellal: poof, poof, poof!" Katerina Ivanovna with contempt say that its origins are well known, and that this very laudable sheet specified in block letters that her father was a colonel; and that the father of Amalia Ivanovna (if it was not some kind of father), probably some Petersburg Finn, milk is sold; or rather, all that my father was not at all, because what else is still unknown, the name Amalia Ivanovna My father Ivanovna or Lyudvigovna? Here Amalia Ivanovna, finally, into a rage and slammed his fist on the table and started screaming that she Amal-Ivan, not Lyudvigovna her Vater "name was Johann and he Burmeister Bull", and that Katerina Ivanovna Vater "absolutely never Burmeister Bull." Katerina Ivanovna rose from her chair and violently, apparently calm voice (though all pale and deep breast lifts), remarked to her that if she ever again dare only "compare equally with their shoddy faterishku her dad, she Katerina Ivanovna. break her cap and trample him with their feet "Hearing this, Amalia Ivanovna ran around the room, crying hard, and that she was the mistress to Katerina Ivanovna," at the moment sezzhal dwelling house "; then rushed out to rip off the table silver spoons. Rose noise and roar; children cried. Sonia rushed to spend Katerina Ivanovna; but when Amalia Ivanovna suddenly shouted something about a yellow card, Katerina Ivanovna, and let Sonya pushed Amalia Ivanovna, to immediately withdraw its threat, a hat, a reality. At this moment the door opened and in the doorway suddenly seemed Peter Luzhin. He stood and strict, sharp eyes scanning the entire company. Katerina Ivanovna rushed to him.

←«»→

↞« CHAPTER III »↠

- Peter! - She cried - at least protect you! Teach this stupid creature that dares to treat him as a noble lady in trouble, it is the court ... I said to myself, the Governor-General ... She will answer ... I remember the bread and salt of my father, the orphans.

- Excuse me, ma'am ... I'm sorry, I'm sorry, ma'am, - brushed Peter - your dad, you know, I had the honor to know ... I'm sorry, ma'am! (Someone laughed out loud), and your incessant feuds with Amalia Ivanovna, I'm not going to participate, with ... I need ... and his desire to explain immediately, with stepdaughter, Sophia Ivanovna ... ... It seems so, sir? Let go of something ...

And Peter, having won in the direction of Katerina Ivanovna, went to the opposite corner, where there was Sonya.

Katerina Ivanovna stopped and stayed just dumbfounded. She could not understand how could Peter deny the bread and salt her dad. Inventing the time this bread and salt, it is already very firmly believed her. And hit his business, a dry, full, even some threats contemptuous tone of Pyotr Petrovich. And somehow gradually silenced when it appears. Besides the fact that it is "serious business and" people are too strict is not in harmony with society, moreover, it was obvious that it was for something important came, probably, any emergency reason could bring him in such company, and that, therefore, now that something will happen, it will. Raskolnikov, who was standing next to Sonya, stepped aside to let him; Peter did not seem to notice ego.Cherez moment appeared on the threshold and Lebezyatnikov; in the room, he did not enter, but stopped too, with some special curiosity, almost

with surprise; listened, but seemed a long time for something he could not understand.

- Unfortunately, I have to interrupt, but it's very important, sir, - said Peter as a general and no one in particular - I'm happy even with the public. Amalia Ivanovna, I humbly ask you, as the owner of the apartment, pay attention to my subsequent conversation with Sophia Ivanovna. Sophia Ivanovna, - he continued, turning to the right very surprised and scared in advance Sonia - from the table of my room, my friend, Andrew S. Lebezyatnikov immediately after your visit, disappeared belonged me state centesimal credit cards dignity. If, however, in any way, you know, and show us where he is now, I assure you, I promise, and I take to witness all that unique, and the end. Otherwise, I will refer to enforcement action seriously, ... have to blame yourself, sir!

Perfect silence in the room. Even the children were crying subsided. Sonia was dead, pale, looking at Luzhin and could not answer. She did not seem to understand. A few seconds passed.

- Well, what about it? - Asked Luzhin, looking at her.

- I do not know ... I do not know ... - weak voice finally said Sonia.

- No? You know? - asked Luzhin, and paused for a few seconds. - Think, mademoiselle, - he said sternly, but still, as if exhorting, - discuss, I agree to give you more time to see think.Kindly C: if I was not so sure, it really is, of course, from my experience, would not risk so directly accuse you; because for such a direct and transparent, but false or erroneous charges only I, in a sense, is responsible. I know that, sir. This morning, I exchanged for their needs, about five percent of the tickets for the amount of the par-three thousand rubles.Calculation I wrote in my wallet. Arriving home, I - Witness Andrew S. - began to count the money and count two thousand three hundred rubles, put them in your wallet and purse in the side pocket of his coat. On the table there were about five hundred rubles, banknotes, as well as between the three tickets, one hundred rubles each. At this point, you have arrived (my call) - and all the time I was in utter confusion later, so that even three times, including conversation, got up and hurried to leave for some reason, even though our conversation was not yet over. Andrew S. can all confirm this. You probably Mademoiselle, will not refuse to confirm and declare that I have called thee Andrew S., solely in order just to talk to you about orphans and helpless position of your relative, Katerina Ivanovna (which I could not come to the funeral), and how it would be useful

to organize it in favor of something like subscriptions, lotteries or similar. You thanked me and even shed a few tears (I'm telling you all how it was that, firstly, to remind you, and secondly, to show you that in my memory will not be blotted no sign). Then I took ten credit card and handed it to you on its own behalf, on behalf of their relatives, and in the types of first helps. All of this can be seen Andrew S .. Then I held you to the door - all the same, with your hand, confusion - and then, when he was alone with Andrei Semenovich and talks with him about ten minutes left Andrew S. I turned back to the table with a lie on it with money, in order to count them, postpone, as predicted by me before actually. To my surprise, one hundred ruble tickets, among other things, there was not. Please same judge: Andrew S. suspect I can not, sir;offers even ashamed. To make a mistake in the long run, I also could not because, for a moment, before you came, were all the bills, I found the result is correct. You must recognize that remembering his embarrassment, hurried away and you hand in hand, while on the table; Taking finally into account your social status and related habits, I am, so to speak, with horror, and even against my will, was forced to stop on suspicion - of course, bad, but - fair, sir! I'll add more and repeat that, despite my apparent confidence, I realize that after all, in this indictment, I will present some risk for me. But as you can see, I did not leave in vain; I rebelled, and I'll tell you why: unique, ma'am, just because of your ingratitude! How? I invite you to the interests of the poor cousin of yours, I give you alms perhaps ten rubles, and you immediately, now I have to pay for all such actions! No, sir, it's not very good, sir! Needs a lesson, sir. Judge for the same; In addition, as a true friend, I ask you (for best friend can not have any at the moment), come to your senses! Otherwise, I will work tirelessly! So what?

- I did not take you, - whispered in horror Sonia - you gave me ten rubles, here to take them. - Sonia took out his handkerchief, found knot untied it, took out a gold coin and held out her hand Luzhin.

- And in the other hundred rubles, and you do not recognize? - Reproachfully and insistently he said, without taking the ticket.

Sonia looked around. They all looked at her with such a terrible severe ridicule, hateful person. She looked at Raskolnikov ... he stood against the wall, her hands folded crosswise, fiery eyes and looked at her.

- Oh my God! - To wrest from Sony.

- Amalia Ivanovna, it will be necessary to bring to the attention of the police, and therefore humbly ask you to send a janitor for the time being

- quietly and even affectionately said Luzhin.

- Goat-der-barmgertsige! I knew she voroval! - Amalia Ivanovna clasped her hands.

- Did you know him? - Luzhin caught - so already before at least some reason to conclude so. I ask you, honorable Amalia Ivanovna, to remember your words, however, in the presence of witnesses.

On all sides rose suddenly speaks loudly. All movements.

- Ka-ah! - Cried suddenly, coming to his senses, and Katerina Ivanovna - just dropped - rushed to Luzhin - how! You accuse her of stealing? This Sonya something? Ah, rascals, scoundrels! - And rushed to Sonya, she is in the grip, hugged her withered hands.

- Sonia! How dare you take from him ten rubles! Oh, silly! Give here! Let me now these ten rubles - here!

And, snatching the paper Sonia, Katerina Ivanovna crumpled it in his hands and threw it in the face backhand Luzhin. Pellet hit in the eye and bounced to the floor. Amalia Ivanovna rushed to raise money. Peter angry.

- Keep that in mind! - He exclaimed.

At the door, at that moment, it seemed near Lebezyatnikov and several others, among whom were looking at both beginners and ladies.

- How! Crazy? That's what I'm crazy? Dur-cancer! - Cried Katerina Ivanovna. - Sam deceive you connect judges, low man! Sonia, Sonia to take money from him! This is what Sonia thief! Yes, it still gives you, fool!- And Katerina Ivanovna laughed hysterically. - Have you seen eh you, fool? - To throw it in all directions, showing everyone in Luzhin. - Like you, too!? - She saw the mistress - and you're there, kolbasnitsa confirms that he is "voroval", meaning that you Prussian chicken leg in a crinoline! Oh, thank you! Oh, thank you!Yes, it's out of the room and not go and how you came, you bastard, Rodion Romanovich near here and the village! Production .. it! Kohl she did not go anywhere, so the money should be given her! But seek, look, look! Only if you can not find, then excuse me, dear, answer! By the emperor, for the emperor, the king, in order to avoid, compassion, feet brooches, right now, today! I - an orphan! I let them! Do you think that will not be allowed? You're lying, I'll go! I'll go-oo! It is you that gentle, calculated? You're on something hoped it? Yes, I, my brother, but Oborveshsya lively! Look at him now! Look, look, well, look !!

And Katerina Ivanovna, in a frenzy, plucking Luzhin, dragging it to Sonia.

- I'm ready, and answer ... but uymites, ma'am, uymites! I also see that

you are brisk! .. This ... this ... this how-to? - Muttered Luzhin - it should be a police officer with ... although, however, and now witnesses than enough ... I'm ready to ... But in any case it is difficult person ... because of sex ... If using Amalia Ivanovna ... although, however, so do not do it ... It's a how-to?

- Who do you want? Let those who want one and looking for! - Exclaimed Katerina Ivanovna - Sonia, reversing their pockets! Here, here! Look, monster, here are empty, there lay a handkerchief pocket is empty, you see! Here's another pocket, here, here! You see! You see!

And Katerina Ivanovna not that snatched and grabbed and two pockets, one after the other, outside. But from the second to the right, suddenly jumped out of his pocket a piece of paper in the air and described a parabola, fell at the feet of Luzhin. This is all seen; many cried. Petr stooped, picked up a piece of paper with two fingers on the floor, took all the shape and distribution. It was a hundred rubles credit cards, folded in the eighth share. Peter circle around the hand showing all the tickets.

- Thief! Won with flats! Polis, Polis! - Amalia Ivanovna cried, - they must prognal Siberia! Get out!

On all sides flew exclamations. Raskolnikov was silent, staring at the Sony, occasionally, but quickly transforming them into Luzhin. Sonya stood in the same place as the unconscious: it was not even close and surprised. Suddenly filled with paint over its entire surface; she screamed and closed by hand.

- No, it's not me! I did not take! I do not know! - She cried, tearing the heart cry and rushed to Katerina Ivanovna. She grabbed her and hugged her tightly, as if to protect her from all the breast.

- Sonia! Sonia! I do not believe! You see, I do not believe it! - Screaming (despite all the evidence) Katerina Ivanovna, shaking it in his hands, as a child, kissing her countless times, catching her hands and bright and kissing them. - I hope you have! What stupid people! Oh my God! You silly, silly - she said, referring to all - yes you do not know, do not know what the heart of what this girl! She'll take it! Yes, she would give up her last dress, to sell, to walk barefoot, and give you, as you will need, this is it! She and yellow ticket was because my children with the same hunger disappeared, sold himself to us! .. Oh, dead, dead! Oh, dead, dead!See? See? Here's your funeral! O Lord! Yes protect it, as what you stand it! Rodion Romanovich! What do you say, why not stand up? You, too, but, believe me? Pinky, you do not deserve it, everything, everything, everything, everything! O Lord! Yes

Protection Well, finally!

Crying, poor, consumptive, lonely Katerina Ivanovna did seem a strong impact on the audience. There was so unhappy, so much suffering in this curved pain, dry consumptive face, these dry, dry lips in the blood, screaming hoarse voice, is bitterly crying like a baby crying in this trusting child, and at the same time a desperate plea to protect it, that seemed to regret all failed. At least Peter immediately regretted .

- Madam! Madame! - He exclaimed impressive voice - with you, this fact does not apply! Nobody would dare you accuse intent or agreements, the more that you are doing and find eversion pocket: consequently, nothing predpolagaetsya.Ochen, very ready to regret if, so to speak, poverty and inspired Sofya Semyonovna, but beyond that, Mademoiselle You would not want to admit it? Shame afraid? The first step? Missing, maybe? The point, of course, c; very friendly, with ... But, but, for what he had to deal with as such! The Lord! - He asked all present - GentlemenRegretting, so to speak, condolences, I think I'm ready to forgive, even now, despite getting personal insults. Yes serve Mademoiselle, shame you imagine a lesson for the future - he turned to Sonya - and I will go farther in vain, and it will be so, stop. Enough!

Pyotr looked at Raskolnikov. Their eyes met. Burning eyes Raskolnikov was ready to burn it. Meanwhile Katerina Ivanovna seemed nothing more and nothing heard, she hugged and kissed Sonia like crazy. Children are also wrapped around all sides Sonya their little hands and Polechka - do not quite understand, however, that this - it seemed a whole, and in tears, overwrought with sobs and hiding his swollen from tears beautiful face on his shoulder Sony.

- How is it low! - There was suddenly a loud voice in the doorway.

Peter glanced quickly.

- What meanness! - Repeat Lebezyatnikov, looking into his eyes.

Pyotr Petrovich even seemed to flinch. This notice everything. (Then think about it). Lebezyatnikov entered the room.

- Do you dare me to put the witnesses? - He said, approaching Peter.

- What does this mean, Andrew S.? What are you talking about? - Muttered Luzhin.

- This means that you ... the accuser, that's what it means to my words! - Hot Lebezyatnikov said looking sternly at him with her eyes half-blind. He was terribly angry. Raskolnikov and stared at him with eyes as if catching

and weighing every word. Again there was silence. Peter even almost lost, especially at first.

- If you let me ... - he said, stammering, - but what is it? You think you are?

- I have something in mind, sir, but you're so ... rascal! Oh, how low! I listened to everything, everything that I purposely waited to see everything, because I confess that even now it is not quite logical ... But what you all did - I do not understand.

- Yes, I did it! You stop your stupid talk in riddles! Or you can drunk?

- It is you, the lowest man, maybe drinking, not me! I never quite vodka drink, because it's not in my beliefs! Imagine, he, with his own hands put a ticket hundred rubles Sophia Semenovna - I've seen, I testify, I swear!He, he! - Repeat Lebezyatnikov, referring to one and all.

- Yes, you're crazy or not, punk? - Cried Luzhin - she in front of you, there - she's here, now, for all confirmed that for ten rubles, except anything from me does not work. How could I tell her what?

- I've seen seen! - Screamed and confirmed Lebezyatnikov - and though it is against my beliefs, but I'm ready to take this very hour in court any oath, because I saw you it quietly! I was just something stupid, I thought you slipped from business! At the door, saying goodbye to her when she turned to her and when you shook hands with one hand, on the other hand, the left, and you put it quietly in the pocket a piece of paper. I have seen! Visiting!

Luzhin pale.

- What you're lying! - Boldly he exclaimed, - and, as you might, standing at the window, read the article?You are currently on ... podslepye eyes. You love it!

- No, not imagined! And while I was away, but I still have all seen it, and even if the window is really hard to see a piece of paper - you speak the truth - but I, for a special occasion, I knew for sure that this is the ticket hundred rubles because when you have to give Sofya Semyonovna ducat - I saw - at the same time you picked up a ticket to one hundred rubles (that I saw because I was standing next to, and as I was once one thought, it is because I have not forgotten what you have in your hands the ticket). You lay down and held it in his hand all the time. Then again, I forgot, but when you get to stand up, then shifted from right to left and nearly dropped; Then I remembered again, because I came here again, the same idea, namely that you want from me softly, her kindness to do. You can imagine how I started looking - well, I saw how you managed to stick it in your pocket. I saw, I saw, I swear!

CRIME AND PUNISHMENT

Lebezyatnikov nearly choked. On all sides were heard various cries, simply means that the more surprising, but I heard screams, and took a threatening tone. All zatesnilis Pyotr Petrovich. Katerina Ivanovna rushed to Lebezyatnikov.

- Andrei Sergeyevich! I was wrong about you! Protect her! One you for it! She is an orphan, God has sent you! Andrew S., my dear, my dear!

And Katerina Ivanovna, almost do not remember what I did, fell on her knees.

- Game! - Shouted in rage rage Luzhin - the game, you still grind, sir. "I forgot, remember, forget about it," - that is! So I deliberately planted? For what? For what purpose? What is common to me is ...

- For what? This is exactly what I do not understand what I say true fact, it's true! Before I am not mistaken, vile, criminal you are a person who, remember that I immediately to mind when the question arose at the time, I thank you and give you a sting. What exactly do you put it in your pocket unnoticed? That's why to get? It is only because they wanted to hide from me, knowing that I deny the opposing beliefs and private charity, nothing radical healing? Well, have decided that you really I was ashamed to give such large amounts, and, in addition, may be, I thought that he wanted to surprise her with a surprise to her when she is in your pocket hundred rubles. (Because other benefactors are very fond of his affairs distributed in such manner, I know). Then I thought, well, you want to try, that is, whether there is to find, thank you? Then, you want to avoid gratitude and, well, as they say, on the right hand, and did not know a word ... somehow that way ... Well, a little eh I thought then occurred to me, so I put it all to think about it, but still thought it indelicate to find in front of you that I know the secret. But, nevertheless, I immediately came to mind again another question: what Sophia Semenovna before noticing, perhaps, God forbid, lose money; That's why I decided to go here, cause it and notify it in the pocket of one hundred rubles. Yes passing took first place in the cipher Mrs. Kobylyatnikovym, to bring them "positive overall conclusion of the method," and especially recommend the article Piderita (and, incidentally, also Wagner); then here, and here, in history! Well, like, if I could have all these thoughts and reasoning, if I really do not see what you put it in his pocket a hundred rubles?

When Andrew S. ended his long-winded arguments logical conclusion to the depot speech terribly tired, and even sweat dropped litso.Uvy it in Russia and can not explain a decent (not knowing, however, no other language), so

that all as- at once, exhausted, even if lost after his lawyer feat. However, he made it an unusual effect. He spoke with such passion, with such conviction that he, apparently, all considered. Peter felt that something was wrong.

- What do I care that you have come back some silly questions - he exclaimed. - This is not proof, sir! You can all sbredit in a dream, that's all, sir! And I tell you that you are lying, sir! Lies and slander against any evil on me, and it is for naserdke, because I do not agree with your freethinking and godless social proposals, that's what, sir!

But turn not taken advantage of Peter. On the contrary, it was the murmur from all sides.

- And this is where you dropped in! - Shouted Lebezyatnikov. - You're lying! Call the police, and I'll take the oath! Only one can not understand why he took a chance on such a low thing to do! About miserable, vile man!

- I can not explain why he took the risk of such an act, and, if necessary, he will take the oath! - Said in a firm voice, finally, Raskolnikov and stepped forward.

He was apparently strong and calm. All at once it became clear the mere sight of him that he really knows what it is, and that came to a decision.

- Now I do everything myself, to understand - Raskolnikov went on, speaking directly to Lebezyatnikov. - From the beginning of history, I began to suspect that some cruel joke; I began to suspect, due to some special circumstances, the only one I know of that I now explain everything: they all work! You, Andrew S., your precious sign finally understood me. I ask everyone to pay attention to everything this gentleman (he pointed to Luzhin) has recently courted a girl, and she was my sister, Dunya.No, arrived in St. Petersburg, he was the third day, when our first date, quarreled with me, and I chased him, so that there are two svidetelya.Etot people very angry ... the other day, I did not know that it is worth to you numbered, Andrew S., and that, therefore, the same day as we had a falling out, it is also the third day, he was a witness, as I was, as a friend of the late Mr. Marmeladova, his wife Katerina Ivanovna some money for the funeral. He immediately wrote a note to my mother and told her that I gave all the money is not Katerina Ivanovna, and Sophia Semenovna, and at the same time in the most heinous expressions of the nature of these ... Sofya Semyonovna that hint at the nature of the relationship to my Sofia Semyenovna. All this, as you know, to embroil me with his mother and sister to impress on them that I generously with baser purposes of their last money they help mne.Proshloy night, when her

mother and sister, and his presence, I restored the truth, proving that gave money to Katerina Ivanovna for the funeral, and not to Sofya Semyonovna and that Sophia Semenovna the third day, I still was not even a sign, and even in the face have not seen it. In this case, I added that he, Pyotr Petrovich Luzhin, with all its benefits, is not worth one little finger Sofya Semyonovna, of which he speaks so bad. His own question: if I put Sofia Semyonovna next to my sister? - I said that I did it on the same day. Angry that his mother and sister do not want to slander him, to quarrel with me, he said, word for word, began to tell them unforgivable insolence. Was the final break, and he was kicked out of the house. All this happened last night. Now I ask special attention: imagine that if he were able to prove now that Sophia Semenovna - a thief, then, firstly, it would prove to his sister and mother, who was almost right in his suspicions; he rightly angry for what I put on a par with my sister and Sofya Semyonovna; that by attacking me, he defended, and therefore defend the honor of my sister, and his bride. In short, through it all, he could not even again embroil me with my family and, of course, hoping to re-enter in their favor. Not to mention the fact that he took revenge for me personally, because it has reason to believe that the honor and happiness of Sofya Semyonovna is very dear to me. That's his whole calculation! This is how I understand this thing! That's the whole reason, and the other can not be!

One way or almost finished his speech Raskolnikov, frequently interrupted by applause the audience to listen to, however, is very blizko.No, despite all the breaks, he said sharply, quietly, accurately, clearly, firmly. His sharp voice, his tone convinced and stern face produced an extraordinary impact on everyone.

- Well, it's true! - Glad confirmed Lebezyatnikov. - It must be so, because he just asked me how something came to our room Sofya Semyonovna, "You're here, I can not see you among the guests of Katerina Ivanovna?" He called me to do to the window and asked quietly. Thus, it is, of course, had to have you here!Thus, it is all true!

Luzhin was silent and smiled contemptuously. Nevertheless, he was very pale. He seemed to think about how it can be vyrvatsya.Mozhet, he would gladly dropped everything and went, but at this point it was almost impossible; it meant simply to recognize the legitimacy vzvodimyh charges and that he actually slandered Sofya Semyonovna. In addition, the public, and has signature too worried. Providing though, however, and not everyone understands all cried more and offered some very unpleasant for Luzhin

measures. But there were not drunk; got together and gathered from all rooms. All three poles fucking hot and he cried incessantly: "Pan laydak!", And other threats murmured in Polish. Sonya listened with stress, but as it's not exactly understand woke up from fainting. It just does not take his eyes off Raskolnikov, feeling that all this protection. Katerina Ivanovna, panting and hoarse and found himself in a terrible fatigue. All stupider Amalia Ivanovna stood slack-jawed and nothing at all meaning. She saw only that Peter somehow caught.Raskolnikov asked to speak again, but he did not give complete: all the screaming and the crowd Luzhin with insults and threats. But Peter was not a coward. Seeing that the case against Sony has completely lost, he simply resorted to arrogance.

- Excuse me, gentlemen, let; not close, let go! - He said he makes his way through the crowd - and do me a favor, do not threaten; I assure you that nothing will happen, do not shy do not, with, on the contrary, you, ladies and gentlemen, the answer is that violence covers a criminal case. Thief more exposed, and I will continue, sir. The Court is not so blind and ... not drunk, sir, and do not believe the two sworn atheists, freethinkers and violators accusing me of personal revenge, that they themselves, foolishly, I confess ... Yes, sir, let C!

- To immediately your spirit was not in his room; if you do, please stop, and everything in between us over!And when I think that I embossed leather, he laid out the whole two weeks ...! ..

- Why, I'll tell you, Andrew S., now says that moves when you held me; Now I will only add that, fool with. I wish you heal your mind and your eyes podslepye.Allow me, ladies and gentlemen, sir!

He squeezed; Providing but do not want to let him go so easily, with just one curses: he grabbed a glass from the table, swung and threw it at Pyotr Petrovich; but the glass flew straight at Amalia Ivanovna. She cried out and lose volume Providing balance, fell heavily under the table. Pyotr Petrovich went to his room, and half an hour later he had not been in the house. Sonia, timid by nature, and before she knew it was easier to destroy than anyone else, not to mention hurt her, just could not with impunity. However, up to this point, he did not seem to her that you can somehow avoid disaster - attentive, meekness, submissiveness to all. Her disappointment was too hard. This, of course, with patience and almost without a murmur could move everything - even that. But in the first minute was too hard. Despite the triumph and his defense - when was the first fright and the first tetanus,

when she realized and understood, it is clear - the feeling of helplessness and resentment painfully hesitate to her heart. Since in hysterics. Finally, unable to stand, she rushed out of the room and ran home. It was almost now for retirement Luzhin. Amalia Ivanovna, when she with a loud laugh now hit the glass, too, could not stand in someone else's holiday hangover. Screaming like crazy, she rushed to Katerina Ivanovna, believing that it's all my fault:

- Down with the apartments! At The Moment! Marsh! - And with that, start grabbing everything that came her hand any of the things that Katerina Ivanovna, and throw off the floor. Almost already killed nearly fainted, pants, pale, Katerina Ivanovna jumped up from the bed (which was dropped in exhaustion) and rushed to Amalia Ivanovna. But the struggle was too unequal; she pushed her as a feather.

- How! Not only that shamelessly slandered - this thing, I have now! How! On the day of the funeral of her husband being driven to the apartment, after my bread and salt, in the street, with the orphans! But where I'm going! - Yelled sobbing and gasping, poor woman. - The Lord! - Not to cry, she suddenly flashing eyes - very well not fair! Who are you protecting, since we are not an orphan? But we'll see! There is a light in the judgment and righteousness, I syschu! Now, wait, godless creature! Polechka, to stay with the children, return II. Wait for me, even on the street! See whether there is in the world is not it?

And they cast on the head of a green dradedamovy scarf, which was mentioned in the story later Marmeladov, Katerina Ivanovna pushed through the crowd of drunken disorderly tenants are still crowded into the room, and with shouts and tears ran into the street - with the aim of uncertainty where -So now immediately, and in that the validity has been found. Polechka huddled in fear with children in a corner of the chest, where the covering as a small, trembling, began to wait for the arrival of the mother. Amalia Ivanovna rushed across the room, screaming, crying, threw everything that came or her to the floor and Buyan.Residents who yelled into the woods, who for firewood - others agreed that they could, in place of the event;others argued and quarreled; other songs sucked ...

"And now it's time for me - thought Raskolnikov -. Well-tissue Sofya Semyonovna, let's see, what do you say now!"

And he went to the apartment Sony.

⇐« »⇒

⟨⟨ CHAPTER IV ⟩⟩

Raskolnikov was an active and energetic defender against Luzhin Sony, despite the fact that he wore his own horror and suffering in the soul. But suffered so much in the morning, he was just happy to get a chance to change their impressions, becomes unbearable, not to mention how much personal and heart the desire to stand up for your Sony. In addition, he had in mind terribly worried about it, especially the minutes, the upcoming meeting with Sonia, he had to tell her who killed Lizaveta, and foresaw a terrible torment yourself, and only shook hands. So when he exclaimed, coming out of Katerina Ivanovna, "Well, what do you say now, Sofya Semyonovna?" That was obviously still in some externally excited vitality, tone and a recent victory over Luzhin. But strange happened to him. When he came to the apartment Kapernaumovs, I felt a sudden fear of emasculation. In meditation, he stopped at the door with a strange question: "Do I have to influence who killed Lizaveta" The question was strange, because he suddenly, at the same time, he felt that he can not only talk, but even postpone this Currently, though it is not possible. He did not know why this is not possible; he just felt it, and it hurts the consciousness of his impotence before necessity almost crushed him. This does not mean, of course, and not to suffer, he quickly opened the door and looked on the verge of Sonia. She was sitting with his elbows on the table and covered his face with his hands, but seeing Raskolnikov, stand up and went to meet him, as if waiting for him.

- What will happen to me without you it was! - Quickly she said come along with him among the rooms. Apparently, she just wanted to get him and tell him. Then waited.

Raskolnikov went to the table and sat down on the chair from which she had just stood up. She stood before him in the corner, in the balance as yesterday.

- What, Sonia? - He said, and suddenly felt that his voice trembles - because it all depends on the "social status and ownership that habit." You now understand what it is?

Suffering is reflected in her face.

- Do not tell me yesterday! - She interrupted. - Please, I do not start. And so, a torment ...

It is as fast as possible smiled, fearing that maybe he does not like a reproach.

- I do stupid ottudova left. What now? Who would want to go, but I thought it was him ... you go.

He told her that Amalia Ivanovna drives them to the apartment and that Katerina Ivanovna ran somewhere "to seek the truth."

- Oh my God! - Sonia snapped up - let's quickly ...

And she grabbed mantilku.

- Always the same! - Raskolnikov exclaimed in exasperation. - You only have to keep in mind that they are! Stand by Me.

- And ... Katerina Ivanovna?

- And Katerina Ivanovna, of course, you do not pass, it will come to you if you already ran out of the house - he added irritably. - Koli you will not find, because you will be to blame ...

Sonia agonizing indecision sat down on a chair. Raskolnikov was silent, staring at the ground and pondering something.

- Let us now Luzhin did not want to - he said, not looking at Sonya. - Well, if he wants, or something included in the calculations, because he hid you in jail is not going to happen, I Lebezyatnikov yes! Huh?

- Yes, - she said in a weak voice, - yes! - She said, absently, and in anxiety.

- But I really could not happen! Lebezyatnikov, he was quite by accident. Sonia was silent.

- Well, if the prison, what then? Remember what I said yesterday?

She again said nothing. He waited.

- I thought you scream again: "Oh, do not say stop!" - Raskolnikov laughed, but somehow difficult. - Well, again silence? - He asked after a moment. - Because it is necessary to say something? Thus, I was curious to know how you would now be allowed one "issue", says Lebezyatnikov. (He seems to

get confused). No, really, I'm serious. Imagine Sonia, you have to know all intents Luzhin will know in advance (ie, probably) that through them would have died quite Katerina Ivanovna, and children, in addition you also (as you can think of that as well , to the trunk). Polechka well ... because it's exactly the same. Well; So if suddenly all this is now your decision to give one or live in a world that is Luzhin to live and do abomination, or dying Katerina Ivanovna? How would you choose: which of them die? I beg you.

Sonia anxiously looked at him: it is something special in this unstable and heard something from a distance corresponding word.

- I have a feeling that you have something to ask - she said, looking at him curiously.

- Well, let; but, nevertheless, how to solve it?

- Why do you ask that it is impossible? - Sonya said with disgust.

- So, it's better Luzhin to live and do abomination! And you did not dare to solve this problem?

- Why, I do not know of Divine Providence can not ... Why do you ask, you can not ask? Why such empty questions? How can it happen that it depended on my decision? A judge who put me here: who should live who do not live?

- Oh, how divine providence mixed up, so you can not do anything - Raskolnikov muttered grimly.

- They say the right to say what you want! - Sonya cried from pain - again you something you roll ... you just come to torment!

She broke down and wept bitterly suddenly. In a dark melancholy, he looked at her. It took about five minutes.

- But you're right, Sonia, - he said quietly at last. He suddenly changed, treated, sassy and powerless-defiant tone disappeared. Even his voice suddenly weakened. - Sam, I told you yesterday that did not come to ask for forgiveness, and almost immediately began that forgiveness ... I mean Luzhin and Providence for myself ... I said that I asked for forgiveness, Sonia ...

He tried to smile, but something impotent and unfinished said in a pale smile. He bowed his head and closed his hands over his face.

And suddenly, strangely, suddenly feeling a caustic hatred for Sonia went through his heart. As would be surprised and scared that feeling, he suddenly raised his head and looked at her; but he met on the restless until flour eye care; was love; I hate it vanished like a ghost. This is not what it was; he took one feeling to another. It just means that it has come a minute.

He closed his hands over his face and bowed. Suddenly he turned pale, rose from his chair, looked at Sonya and say instinctively moved her bed.

At that time, it was an awful lot like, in its way, one when he was behind the old woman, already allocates an ax out of the loop, and felt that even "point can not lose any more."

- What is it? - Asked Sonia terribly shy.

He could not speak. He's very, very wrong is supposed to declare himself did not understand what to do about it now. She quietly walked over to him and sat on the bed beside and waited, never taking his eyes off him. Her heart was pounding and freezes. Became unbearable, he turned to her dead pale his face; His lips curled helplessly, noting that some say. The horror was the heart of Sony.

- What is it? - She said, gently pulling away from him.

- Nothing, Sonia. Do not be afraid ... Nonsense! Of course, if the judge - is nonsense - he muttered with a view of themselves beside a man in delirium. - Why only you, I have come to torment? - He said suddenly, looking at her. - Right. How Come? I still ask myself this question, Sonia ...

It can be, and asked myself this question a quarter of an hour ago, but now spoke in complete impotence, barely aware of himself and feeling smooth tremors throughout the body.

- Oh, how you suffer! - From the suffering she said, looking at him.

- All nonsense! .. That's what Sonia (he suddenly somehow smiled, somehow pale and powerless, two seconds), - you remember that yesterday I wanted to tell you?

Sonia anxiously waited.

- I said, leaving, perhaps, say goodbye to you all, but what if I come today, I'll tell you ... who killed Lizaveta.

Suddenly she shivered all over.

- Well, I came to say.

- So you really do yesterday ... - barely whispered it - how do you know? - Quickly she asked, as if suddenly coming to his senses.

Sonia began to breathe with difficulty. Face became paler and paler.

- I know.

She paused for a moment.

- It was found that regardless of whether it? - she asked timidly.

- No, it was not found.

- So how do you about it know? - Again, almost inaudibly she said, and

again after almost a minute of silence.

He turned to her and looked at her.

- Guess, - said he was still twisting and powerless smile.

Similarly, convulsions ran over his body.

- Yes, you ... me ... that you're scaring me like that ...? - She said, smiling like a child.

- So, I'm with him a great friend ... if I know - Raskolnikov went on, relentlessly continuing to look into her face, as if he already could not take his eyes - he Lizaveta is ... I do not want to kill ... He accidentally killed ... her ... He wanted to kill the old woman ... when she was alone ... and came ... And then came Lizaveta ... here ... and he killed her.

He took another scary moment. And all looked at each other.

- So you can not guess what? - Suddenly he asked, feeling as if rushed down from the bell tower.

- N-no, - whispered almost inaudibly Sonia.

- Look good.

And once again he said it, one former, familiar feeling suddenly froze my soul: he looked at her and suddenly, in her face, as if he saw the face of Lizaveta. He vividly recalled the expression of Lizaveta, when he approached her with an ax, and she moved away from him to the wall with his hand, with a totally childish fright in the face by a thread like little children when they suddenly start chego-something to be frightened, and -prezhnemu look uneasily on their frightening object suspended back and stretch forward a little hand, ready cry.Almost same thing happened now with Sonia: just do nothing, with the same fright, she looked at him a few days, and suddenly, his left hand, a little, a little, put his fingers in his chest and slowly began to climb out of bed, more and more it pulls to one side, and all was still at him. Horror and suddenly told him the same fear appeared in his face as he looked at her, and almost even with the same childish smile.

- Guess? - He whispered at last.

- The Lord! - Terrible cry burst from her chest. She fell helplessly on the bed, face in the pillow. But a moment later rose quickly, quickly moved closer to him, grabbed him by both hands and squeezing them like a vice, thin fingers again became motionless, as if glued to look at his face. This last, desperate look she wanted to look and catch at least some last hope for himself. But there was no hope; there was no doubt they exist; it was so ! Even later, when she remembered that moment, she felt strange and wonderful,

why sheimmediately saw that there is no longer any doubt? In the end, she could not say, for example, that it is something like this apprehension? Meanwhile, now that he had just told her that she felt as if she really likethis thing had a premonition.

- Well, Sonia, that's enough! Do not torture me! - Said he was hurt.

He really, really do not think so open to it, but it turned out well.

As if she does not remember, she jumped up and, wringing her hands, reached the middle of the room; but quickly came back and sat down next to him, almost touching his shoulder to shoulder. Suddenly, as if pierced, she shuddered, screamed and ran, not knowing why, on his knees.

- What do you have that you did it to yourself! - Desperately she said, and jumped from his knees, embraced him and hugged him tightly clenched hands.

Raskolnikov drew back with a sad smile looked at her:

- It is strange that you Sonya - hug and kiss when I told you about it. Do not you remember yourself.

- No, no, you are unhappy now no one in the whole world! - She exclaimed, in a frenzy, he did not hear his comments, and suddenly began to cry bitterly, hysterically.

It has long been familiar feeling wave flooded his soul and soften it again. He did not resist him, two tears rolled from his eyes and hung on the eyelashes.

- So do not leave me, Sonya? - He said, almost looking forward to it.

- No, no; Never ever! - Exclaimed Sonya - after you go, everywhere I go! Oh my God! .. Oh, I'm miserable! .. And why, why did not I know you before! Why did not you come before? Oh my God!

- It happened.

- Now that's something! Oh, what to do now! .. Together, together! - She repeated, as if in a trance, and hugged him again - in hard labor with you go! - It seemed suddenly shuddered, former, hateful and almost arrogant smile on his lips reduced.

- I, Sonia, even in labor, you may not want to go, - he said.

Sonia looked at him quickly.

After the first, passionate and painful sympathy for the unfortunate murder again terrible idea struck her. In variable tone of his words, she suddenly heard the killer. She looked at him in surprise. She does not know, nor why, and how, and what it was for. Now all these questions again flashed in

her mind. Again, she did not believe: "He was a murderer But it is possible !?"

- Yes it is! Yes, where I stand! - She said in a deep confusion, as if not yet come to himself, - yes you, you areso ... this could be solved? .. Yes it is!

- Well, yeah, rob. Come on, Sonya! - How is tired and even as if with vexation he said.

Sonia stood as if stunned, but suddenly exclaimed:

- You were hungry! You know ... to help her mother? Yes I Do?

- No, Sonya, no - he muttered, turning away his head - I was not so hungry ... I really wanted to help her mother, but ... it's not quite right ... do not hurt me, Sonia!

Sonia clapped her hands.

- Of course, it all really! My God, it's true! Who can believe it? .. And as you give yourself in the past and killed to rob! Ah .. - she exclaimed suddenly, - money that Katerina Ivanovna gave money ... ... God! X and money ...

- No, Sonya, - he interrupted hastily, - money was not the same, calm down! Mom money is transferred through one merchant, and I got them sick, that same day, he gave Razumikhin saw ... ... and he's got for me ... my money, my own, my real.

Sonya listened with disbelief and all the forces trying to figure out something.

- And those money ... However, I do not even know if you have money, and something - he added softly, as if lost in thought - I pulled out of the bag and then the neck, suede ... full, tight purse so ... yeah, I have not looked into it; there was no time to be ... Well, still some cufflinks chain yes - I am all these things and purse on another yard on B - m prospectus under a rock buried the next morning. All there is now.

Sonya listened hard.

- Well, why ... what you said Rob, while they did not take anything? - Quickly she asked, clutching at straws.

- I do not know ... I have not decided - to take or not to take the money - he said again, as if in thought, and suddenly realized quickly and briefly smiled. - Oh, what nonsense, I blurted now, huh?

Sonya wondered: "Not crazy right" But as soon as she left her no, it's not. It's all right, it is not understood!

- You know, Sonia, - he said suddenly, with some inspiration - you know, I tell you what: if I only killed the fact that he was hungry - he continued, emphasizing each word and mysterious, but, honestly speaking, looking at

her - I would now ... happy he was! I know that you did!

- And what do you, what do you actually - he cried for a moment with some even despair - what you eat, if I confessed, and now badly done? Well, you're in this stupid triumph over me? Ah, Sonya, because I come to you now!

Sonia again to say something, but she said nothing.

- That's why I called you yesterday with him, that one you have me and left.

- Where is called? - Timidly asked Sonia.

- Do not steal and do not kill, do not worry, not for this - he smiled bitterly - we, the people, strife ... And you know, Sonia, I'm only now just realized where I called you yesterday? And yesterday, when called, I do not know where. For one and called One came not leave me. Do not leave, Sonia?

She squeezed his hand.

- And why, why, I told her why I opened it! - In despair, he exclaimed in a minute, with endless torment, looking at her - that's what you want me to explain, Sonia, to sit and wait, I see it; and I tell you? Nothing, because you do not understand, but not tormented all ... because of me! Well, you cry and hug me again - well, that you hug me? For the fact that I do not deserve to lose it to another "to suffer and you will be easier for me!" And you can love such a scoundrel?

- Do you think that you also do not suffer? - Cried Sonya.

Again, the same feeling waves broke into his soul, and again for a moment to soften it.

- Sonia, my heart is evil, you will notice it: it can be a lot to explain. That's why I came to this evil. There are those who would not have come. And I'm a coward and a scoundrel ...! But ... let them! All this is not that ... now we have to say, and I do not know how to start ...

He stopped and thought.

- Oh, the people we strife! - He exclaimed again - not a couple. And why, why I come! Never forgive myself!

- No, no, it's good to come! - Exclaimed Sonya - it is better to let me know! Much better! He looked at her pain.

- And what, indeed! - He said, as if far-fetched - it's there, because it was! That's what I wanted to be Napoleon, and killed because ... Well, now you understand?

- N-no, - naively and timidly whispered Sonia - just ... talk, talk! I know, I own all understand! - She begged him.

- Do you understand? Well, let's see!

He stopped and thought for a long time.

- The main thing I asked myself when this question: What if, for example, in my place, and there was Napoleon would not have to start a career or Toulon nor Egypt, nor go through the Mont Blanc, and instead of all these beautiful and monumental things simple, easily one any funny old woman, legistratorsha, the deal should be killed, so from the trunk to steal money from it (for a career, you know?), well, so decided whether he will have access to it, if there was no no alternative? Corrupted or not because it's too much ... and not monumental, and sin? Well, I tell you that this "issue" I suffered an awful lot of time, so I'm terribly ashamed when I finally realized (suddenly somehow) that not only did not flinch, but even thought it would not come it is not a monumental ... and do not even realize what he was doing: that is, to warp? And even if he was not the only other way it would have been strangled, so pop in and will not give without any thought! .. Well ... I got out of the reverie ... ... strangled such power ... And this is a hair's breadth from it! You funny? Yes, Sonia, there is only funny thing is that maybe it's because it was ...

Sonia was not at all funny.

- You better tell me right ... no examples - even robche and almost inaudibly she said.

And he turned to her, unfortunately looked at her and took her hand.

- You're right again, Sonya. It's all nonsense, because nearly one-chatter! You see, you know that my mother almost nothing. Sister trained, accident, and sentenced to hang governess. All their hopes were only for me. I learned, but to keep yourself in the university could not and then was forced to retreat. If even so stretched, then for ten years, twelve (when turning in good circumstances), I could still hope for some teacher or director with a salary of one thousand rubles ... (He spoke as if he knew). By the time her mother had dried from care and sorrow, and I still will not have to comfort her, and my sister ... well, my sister and I could even worse happen! .. And the hunt of a lifetime and pass all turns away from it all, forget about the mother and sister of the crime, for example, to transfer with respect? For what? For oh, yes, they were buried, the new accumulate - and wife children, then penniless and without a piece of vacation? Well ... well, so I decided, seizing money the old woman, to use them in my early years, not torturing his mother to give yourself University, the first steps after university - and it's all good,

radically, so it's absolutely all new career and make a new, independent way to be ... Well ... Well, that's all ... Well, of course, that I killed the old woman - it's bad, I did ... Well, enough!

At some helplessness he trudged to the end of the story, and hung his head.

- Oh, this is not the case, it is not - in anguish cried Sonia - and how is it ... no, that's not true, is not it!

- It can be seen that it is not so! .. And I honestly told the truth!

- Yes, something is true! My God!

- I just killed a louse, Sonya, useless, nasty, destructive.

- This is a man-louse it!

- Why, I know that this is not a louse - he said, looking at her strangely. - And yet, I'm lying, Sonia, - he added - has long been lying ... It's not that; You are right. Really, really, really, there are other reasons! .. I had no one told Sonia ... The head is now very sore.

His eyes were feverish. He almost began to rave; restless wandering smile on his lips. Through the excited state of mind already showed terrible impotence. Sonia knew how he suffers. She also felt dizzy. And oddly enough, he said, as if he knew something, but ... "But of course! What! Oh, God!" And she wrung her hands in despair.

- No, Sonia, it is not so! - He again began suddenly raised his head, as if startled by the sudden turn of thought and re-submit it - not that! Better .. assume (yes, that's really the best!), Suppose that I am proud, envious, angry, mean, vengeful, well ... and maybe more prone to madness. (Oh, let it all at once! Oh madness has already said, I noticed ,!) I have told you this morning that the university can not contain themselves. You know what I could and could not? Mother sent to in order to do what is necessary, and shoes, dress and bread I made myself, probably! Lessons output; half ruble offered. Powered same Razumikhin! Yes, I ozlilsya and do not want to. This ozlilsya (nice word!). I was like a spider in his corner scored. You were in my kennel, I saw ... And you know, Sonia, that low ceilings and cramped rooms shove soul and mind! Oh, how I hated that kennel! Yet out of it is not desirable. Deliberately do not want to! Within a few days did not go out, and do not want to work, and do not even want to have all lied. Bring Nastasia - sing, do not bring - and the day will be held; The purpose of anger did not ask! At night, no fire, lying in the dark, and do not want candles. We should have known, I sold books; and on the table from me, on the Bonds so on laptops, on my

finger and now the dust. I liked it better to lie down and think. Nevertheless, I think ... and I have had such dreams, strange, different dreams, which have nothing to say! But then I also start to think that ... No, it is not so! Once again, I'm not telling you! You see, I did everything I ask myself, why am I so stupid that if others are stupid, and if I really know for sure that they are stupid, I do not want to be smarter? Then I learned, Sonya, if you wait until all become smarter, it will be too long ... Then I found out that it will never be that people are not variables, and does not alter them to anyone, and not worth the trouble spend! Yes it is! It's their law ... law, Sonia! That's it! .. And now I know, Sonia, that someone strong and strong in mind and spirit, and the ruler over them! Who dares much that they are right. Who can spit more, they have both legislative and who more than anyone dared, he's all right! So still and will always be carried out! Only the blind can not tell!

Raskolnikov, saying that though, looking at Sonya, but I'm still more: to understand it or not. Fever completely engulfed him. He was in some grim delight. (In fact, it's too long with no one to say that!) Sonya understood that this gloomy catechism was his faith and the law.

- I think if Sonia - he continued with enthusiasm - that power is given only to those who dare to bend over and take it. Here is just one: it is necessary to decide! Then I thought to invent one, for the first time in his life, which no one had ever before me did not invent! No One! I suddenly clear as the sun, imagine that it is not only still not solved, and I do not dare, passing by the absurdity of it all, just gets everything just the tail and shake the hell out! I ... I wanted to dare and killed ... I just wanted to dare, Sonia, is the whole reason!

- Oh, do not worry, do not worry! - Sonia exclaimed, clasping her hands. - You have moved away from God, and God struck you, damn betrayed! ..

- By the way, Sonya, when I'm in the dark and lied to me all thought it was the devil confused me? eh?

- Shut Your Mouth! Do not laugh, blasphemy, nothing, nothing, you do not understand! Oh my God! It's all right, he does not understand!

- Shut up, Sonya, I do not laugh, because I know myself that I was pulling the devil. Shut up, Sonya, do not worry! - He repeated grimly and persistently. - I know everything. All this I changed my mind and peresheptal myself when I was lying in the dark ... All this I have to argue with them, to the smallest features, and know everything, everything! And so tired, so tired of me, all this chatter! I wanted to forget everything and start all over again, Sonia, and stop talking! And you think I'm a fool went to the

head? I went as a wise guy, and that's what I'm ruined! And do you really think that I do not know, for example, at least the fact that if we started to ask ourselves the question: Am I right l in power? - It is, therefore, not have the right to rule.What if I ask a question: whether a person is a louse? - It is, therefore, I do not louse man for me , and a louse, for whom it was not the slightest idea who comes and goes straight, no question ... If I suffered for many days, Napoleon went there or not? - Is not it so clearly felt that I was not Napoleon ... All, all the torments of all this chatter I survived, Sonia, and all her shoulders shake sorry that I wanted to kill Sonya without casuistry, kill for himself, for himself alone ! I do not want to lie in it, even yourself! Not help his mother, I killed - nonsense! Not that I killed to get the money and power to become a benefactor of mankind.Nonsense! I just killed; kill yourself, just for myself, and there, if I become someone's benefactor, or the life of a spider caught in nets for all and all living juices sucked me at the moment, still had to be., It not money, as long as I had, Sonia, when I killed; not so much money is needed, and the other ... that's all I know now ... Do not get me wrong: it may be going the way, I never repeat murder. I had to learn again and again pushed my hand: I should have known then, and as quickly as possible to find out whether I louse, like everything else, or people? Will I be able to cross or not! Do not be afraid to bend over and pick it up or not? I'm trembling creature or the right to have ...

- Kill? Kill something right there? - Sonia clapped her hands.

- Oh, Sonia! - He exclaimed in exasperation, as there was something she said, but contemptuously silent. - Do not interrupt me, Sonia! I would like to show you only one thing: that God knows I then pulled out, and even after I explained that I had no right to go there, because I was exactly the same louse as all! He lied to me, so I come to you now! Welcomes guests! If I was not a louse, that if I come to you? Listen, when I went to the old woman, I just try to go ... Know!

- And killed! Killed!

- Why do you kill something? It's so kill? Is it going to kill, as I was then! Have I ever told you how I was ... I killed the old woman? I'll kill myself, not old! There are so again, and you throw it away yourself forever! .. And this damn old woman killed, but I do not ... Enough, enough, Sonia, that's enough! Leave me - suddenly he shouted convulsive anguish, - leave me!

He leaned his elbows on his knees, and mites, squeezed with his hands down.

- Ekoe suffering! - Broke the painful cry Sonya.

- Well, what do I do say! - He asked, suddenly raised his head and the ugly face contorted in frustration, looking at her.

- What to do! - She exclaimed, suddenly jumped up, and her eyes full of tears, until now, suddenly flashed. - Stand Up! (She grabbed him by the shoulder, and he sat down, looking at her almost in amazement). Come now, this minute, stand at a crossroads, bow, kiss, first, the land which thou hast defiled, and then bow around the world, on all four sides, and say everything out loud: "I have killed" Again, God will send you life. Go? Go? - She asked him, trembling, as if in a fit of capture both hands clenched in their hands and looking at his eyes shot.

He was surprised and impressed by her sudden enthusiasm.

- You mean the hard work or something, Sonya? Pass, while they themselves want? - Darkly he asked.

- Suffering and take them to redeem themselves, this is what we need.

- No! I will not go into them, Sonia.

- And live, live, how are you? Live it with you? - Cried Sonya. - Can we now? Well, how are you going to talk to the mother? (Oh, something with them, with them, which will be now!) Yes, I am! In the end, you really left his mother and sister. This is because a lot of the same shade cast. Oh, my God! - She was crying - because he already knows everything myself! And, of course, as without a live person! What has happened now!

- Do not be a child, Sonya, - he said quietly. - What am I being unfair to him? Why go? What do they say?All this is just one ghost ... They do millions of people trouble, and even revered as a virtue. Rogues and rascals, Sonia! .. I will not go. And I say: I killed, but did not dare to take the money and hid under a rock? - He added with a grin edkoyu. - So in fact they are the same me laugh, let us say, a fool not to take it. A coward and a fool! Never mind that they do not understand, Sonya, and unworthy to understand. Why should I go? I will not go. Not a child, Sonia ...

- Torment, flour - she repeated, in a desperate plea holding out her arms to him.

- I may be a more focused, - he said grimly, as if lost in thought - maybe I'm still a man and not a louse, and haste to condemn myself ... I still charges.

Arrogant smirk on his lips reduced.

- A kind of flour wear! Why, the whole life, your whole life! ..

- Get used to it ... - he said grimly thoughtfully. - Listen, - he said in a

minute - full cry, it's time to business: I have come to tell you that I am now looking to catch ...

- Ah! - Sonia cried terribly.

- Well, what are you crying! She wants me to go to prison, and now scared? Only that I did not damsya them.I'm still with them extortion, and do nothing. They have no real evidence.Yesterday I was in great danger, and I think that many have been lost; Today the same thing better. All evidence of their two ends, ie their allegations, I in my favor as I can draw, you know, and I will return ?; because now I know ... But I go to jail for sure. If more than one time, you can, and today will be planted, perhaps, perhaps, more and planted today ... But it's nothing, Sonya: sit, and let out ... because they have no real confirmation and does not give the word. And the fact that they have, you can not throw a man. Well, pretty ... I just want you to know ... with my sister and mother, I'll try to do something like this to calm them down and not scare my sister ... Now, however, it seems, must be provided ... Therefore, the mother ... Well, that's all. If, however, careful. You'll be up to me to go to jail, where I sit?

- Oh, I will! I will!

Both were sitting side by side, sad and dead, as if after a storm washed up empty beach alone. He looked at Sonya and felt that a lot of it was her love, and oddly enough, he suddenly became hard and painful, so that his love. Yes, it was strange and terrible feeling! Jump to Sonia, he felt that his whole hope and outcome of the whole; he thought, lay at least part of their suffering, and all of a sudden, now that all my heart turned to him, he felt, and he knew that he was an unprecedented unhappier than he was before.

- Sonia - he said - it is better not to go with me when I'm sitting in jail.

Sonia did not answer, she cried. A few minutes passed.

- There is a cross on you? - Suddenly she asked, as if suddenly remembered. At first he did not understand the question.

- No, because not? Here, take this, cypress. I have another left, copper, Lizavetin. We Lizaveta crosses changed, she told me his cross, and I gave her my scapular. Now I'm going to wear Lizavetin, and it's you.Take ... because my! In the end, my! - She begged. - However, after suffering go together and cross the go! ..

- Give! - Said Raskolnikov. He did not want to disappoint her. But he immediately took his outstretched hand cross.

- Not now, Sonia. Better than - he added, to reassure her.

- Yes, yes, better, best - she took with enthusiasm - as you go on suffering, and then put on. Come to me, I will put on you, pray and go.

At this moment, someone knocked on the door three times.

- Sofia Semyonovna, can you? - I heard someone very familiar gentle voice.

Sonia rushed to the door in a fright. Mr. Lebezyatnikov blonde face peered into the room.

⟪ CHAPTER V ⟫

Lebezyatnikov was kinda worried.

- I am to you, Sofya Semyonovna. Excuse me ... I thought that you will find - he turned suddenly to Raskolnikov, - that is, I do not think so ... ... but I just thought that ... There we Katerina Ivanovna with mind - he abruptly suddenly Sonia, leaving Raskolnikov.

Cried Sonia.

- That is, it is, at least, so it seems. But ... we do not know what to do, that's what, sir! Gate - it somehow seems to have been ruled out, might come ... at least so it seems ... She ran to the head of Seeds Zakharych, he was not at home; He dined with some very general ... Imagine, she waved where dinner ... This is another common, and imagine - still insisted that caused major Seeds Zakharych, yes, I think that even the -this table. Can you imagine what happened there. This, of course, was deleted; and she said that she cursed him and something in his empty. He can not even imagine ... as it does not take? - I do not understand! Now she tells everyone, and Amalia Ivanovna, but it is difficult to understand, with shouts and beat ... Oh, yes, he says, and shouts that since everything is now thrown, it will take the children and go into the street, wearing a barrel organ and children will singing and dancing, and she, too, and collect money, and every day window all go ... "May said, look how precious children bureaucratic father through the streets of beggars to go!" Children of all strokes are crying. Lenya teaches singing "Little Farm" boy dance, Polina Mikhailovna, too, tearing all the dresses; making them some hats as an actor; she wants to carry the bowl to bash, instead of music ... Do not listen ... Imagine how it is? It is simply

impossible!

Lebezyatnikov still more, but Sonia, listen to him hardly breath, suddenly grabbed mantilku, hat and ran from the room, putting on the go. Raskolnikov followed her, Lebezyatnikov it.

- Be sure to stop them! - He said Raskolnikov, leaving him on the street - I just do not want to scare you Sofya Semyonovna and said, "seems", but there is no doubt. This, they say, these shocks in consumption, jump on the brain; sorry I do not know the drug. Nevertheless, I tried to convince her, but she would not listen.

- You told her about the strikes?

- It's not all about the beats. Although she did not understand. But I say that if logically convince a person that, in fact, he was not going to cry, he will stop crying. That is clear. And your belief that stops?

- It's too easy, it would be to live, - answered Raskolnikov.

- I'm sorry, I'm sorry; Of course, Katerina Ivanovna is quite difficult to understand; but did you know that in Paris serious experiments have already taken place in connection with the possibility of cure crazy acting independently of logical persuasion? One professor there, recently deceased scientist seriously thought that I may lechit.Osnovnaya idea that particular disorder in the body there is a madman, and that madness, so to speak, a logical error, error in judgment, wrong view of things. He gradually denied patient and imagine reaching, say, the results! But since then, he has used and the soul, the results of this treatment are exposed, of course, the question ... At least, so it seems ...

Raskolnikov has long been a favorite. Level Drew to his house, he nodded and turned Lebezyatnikov the road. Lebezyatnikov woke up, looked around and ran on.

Raskolnikov went into his room and stood in the midst of it. "Why did he come back here?" He looked at them obsharkannye yellow wallpaper, dust your sofa ... From the courtyard came some sharp, continuous knocking; something where as hammering a nail some ... He went to the window and stood on tiptoe and long, with a view to emergency attention, looked at dvor. No yard was empty, and there was seen pounding. Left wing can be seen here and there an open window; on window sills were pots of geraniums rare. Outside the windows was posted linen ... All this he knew by heart. He turned away and sat down on the couch.

Never, never before had he felt so terribly lonely!

Yes, he again felt that perhaps, really hate Sonia, and now that made her unhappy. "Why did he go to her to ask her to tears? Why did he grab his life? Oh, despicable!"

- I will stay one! - He said suddenly - and it will not go to jail!

Five minutes later he raised his head and smiled strangely. It was strange, he thought: "Maybe in jail is really better," - he thought suddenly.

He could not remember how long he stayed at home with the crowd in his mind vague thoughts. Suddenly the door opened and in walked Avdotya Romanovna. At first, she stopped and looked at him from the doorway as he used to Sonia; then went and sat on a chair against it, at yesterday's place. He silently and somehow without thought looked at her.

- Do not be angry, brother, I have only one minute - said Dounia. Her expression was thoughtful, but not heavy. His eyes were clear and quiet. He saw it with love came to him.

- Brother, I now know what all . all I Dmitri Prokofitch explained everything and told. You persecuted and tortured silly and sneaking suspicion … Dmitri Prokofitch told me that there is no danger, and that nothing you with such horror takes. I do not think so, and to fully understand how outraged you in everything, and that he may leave traces of indignation forever. That's what I'm afraid. For the fact that you left us, I do not judge and do not dare to judge, and I'm sorry that I blamed you before. I for myself feel that if I had such great sorrow, I would have gone to all.Mom, I'm about it did not say, but I will talk about you constantly and speak on your behalf, you will come very soon. Do not suffer because of it; I reassure her; but you will not be subjected to torture - come at least once; Remember that she is the mother! And now I just came to say (Dunya began to rise from their seats), that if in case, I'm what you need me or if you need me … all my life, or something … click me, I Attending, Farewell!

She abruptly turned and walked toward the door.

- Dunya! - Raskolnikov stopped her, got up and walked over to her - it Razumikhin, Dmitri Prokofitch, a very good man.

Dunya blushed slightly.

- Well! - She asked, after waiting a minute.

- He is a man of action, hard-working, honest and capable of much love … Goodbye, Dunya.

Dunya blushed, then suddenly alarmed:

- Yes, this is my brother, we really ever leave you so desire … I do?

- It does not matter … goodbye.

He turned away from her and went to the window. She stopped and looked at him nervously entered the alert.

No, it was not cold to her. It was a moment (last) when he wanted to hug her and say good-bye to her, and even to say it, but even her hands do not dare file:

"Then again, perhaps shudder when I remembered that I have now embraced her, tell her that I stole a kiss!"

"And survive this or not survive - he added a few minutes to myself - No, he will not stand;?. how would not withstand a couple never survive …! "

And he thought of Sonia.

From the window of breath freshness. The yard is not as bright shining light. He suddenly took his cap and went out.

Of course, he could not, and did not want to take care of their disease state. But all this incessant anxiety and all this horror world could not pass without consequences. And if he was not lying still in the midst of this, it may be, simply because it is an internal, continuous anxiety kept him on his feet and conscious, but somehow artificially, for a time.

He wandered. The sun was setting. Some special longing beginning to affect him lately. This is not anything particularly pungent, burning; but it came from something permanent, eternal, foreboding bad years this cold, deadening melancholy presentiment of some eternity in "Arshin space." In the evening hours, usually even stronger feeling began to torment him.

- Here with such stupid purely physical ailments, according to some sunset and hold to make a nonsense! Not that Sonia, but Dunya go! - Muttered he hated.

He was proclaimed. He looked around; Lebezyatnikov rushed to him.

- Imagine that I was with you, looking for you. Imagine that it is carried out her intention and took her children! We Sofya Semyonovna hardly find them. She gets into the pot, forcing the children to sing and dance. Children cry. Stop at the intersection and shops. They were stupid people work. Come On.

- And Sonia? .. - Anxiously asked Raskolnikov hurried after Lebezyatnikov.

- Just in a frenzy. This is not to Sofya Semyonovna in a frenzy, and Katerina Ivanovna; Indeed, Sofya Semyonovna in a frenzy. And Katerina Ivanovna absolutely insane. I'm telling you, completely crazy. Take them to the police. Can you imagine how it would operate … Now they have to ditch

- ING bridge, very close to Sofia Semyonovna. Close.

On the ditch, not very far from the bridge and short the two houses of the house where she lived Sonia, a bunch of people crowding. Especially boys and girls came running. Hoarse voice breaks Katerina Ivanovna heard from the bridge. Indeed, it was a strange sight that might interest a public street. Katerina Ivanovna in her old dress and shawl dradedamovoy broken straw hat, knocked ugly piece on the side, was really into this madness. She was tired and breathless. Exhausted by his consumptive face looked stradalnee than ever (except for the street, the sun always seems to be consumptive sick and disfigured than at home); excited state, but can not stop it, and it became every moment more irritation. She rushed to the children, shouting at them, persuade, teach them right away when people love to dance and sing, he began to explain what he was doing, come to despair of their stupidity, beat them ... Then, finishing rushed to the public; If you notice a bit of well-dressed man stopped to look, then immediately gets up to explain that here, they say, what led children "noble, one might even say aristocratic house." If you hear laughter in the crowd or some zadiratelnoe mot, then immediately pounced on the courage and began to scold them. Some, however, laughed, others shook their heads; All General was curious to see the frightened children possessed. Pots, which said Lebezyatnikov not; at least Raskolnikov did not see; but instead of knocking the pan Katerina Ivanovna began to clap to the beat of his hands dry when they are forced to sing and polka Lenya and Kolya dance; and even indulges herself to sing, but every time I paused for a second note from painful cough, why again in despair, cursing his cough, and even cried. Most relied on myself crying and afraid Kohli and Leni. Deystvitelno, was an attempt to dress the children in costume, dress up as street singers. The boy was dressed in something red and white turban, he portrayed himself in Turku. On Lenya costumes were not; was only put on the head of a red knitted cap of worsted (or, more simply, cover) at the end of Seeds Zakharych, and stuck a piece of white ostrich feather hat, still belonged to his grandmother Katerina Ivanovna and keep still in the chest, in the form of family rarity. Polechka was in his usual odezhdy.Ona timidly looked at her mother and lost, not to deviate from it, hide your tears, guess what madness mother and anxiously looked around.Street and the crowd went terribly ispugalas.Sonya tirelessly Katerina Ivanovna, weeping, begging her to return home permanently. But Katerina Ivanovna was relentless.

- Come on, Sonya, come on! - She cried patter, slowly, gasping and

coughing. - She did not know what to ask, just a kid! I already told you that I will not return to that drunken German. Let them see everything, all of St. Petersburg, and children begging noble father, who served his entire life in faith and truth, and it can be said to have died in the service. (Katerina Ivanovna was able to establish this fantasy and believe blindly). Let, let the bad generalishka sees. And you're stupid, Sonya: Now there's something to tell me? We will be very torn and do not want to! Ah, Rodion Romanovitch, it's you! - She cried, seeing Raskolnikov and rushing to him - explain to you, please, this fool, that nothing can be done smarter! Even organ-grinders mined, and will feature all of us at once, they will know that we are poor noble family of orphans, the poor, and only this place generalishka lose, you'll see! Every day under the window at him go, and it will be the emperor, I'll be on my knees, it will all be set out and show them: "Protect, father," He is the father of orphans, he is merciful, protection, see, and it generalishku ... Lenya! TENEZ-Vous Droite! 1 You Kohl's now going to dance again. What do you hnychesh? Whining again! Well, what are you afraid, you fool! O Lord! what I do with them, Rodion Romanovitch! If you only knew what they were stupid! Well to do with! ..

And she said, almost in tears (that did not stop her continuous and unin-terrupted knock), showed him whimpering children. Raskolnikov tried to convince her to come back and even said to think in order to act on the feel-ings that it is indecent to walk the streets as organ-grinders to go, because she prepares herself in the girls boarding school headmistress ...

- Apartments, ha ha ha! Nice diamonds around the corner! - Cried Katerina Ivanovna, laughing immediately after sunset cough - no, Rodion Romano-vitch held dream come true! All our cast! .. And it generalishka ... You know, Rodion Romanovitch, I let him inkwell - here in the servants' quarters, by the way on the table stood next to the sheet on which were painted, and I signed, blank, and fled. Oh, vile, vile. Yes, and do not need Now I will feed them himself, nobody bow! We tortured her enough! (She pointed to Sonya). Polechka, which were collected, show? How? Only two pennies? Oh, despi-cable! Do not give anything, just run after us, his tongue hanging out! Well, what a fool laughs? (She pointed to one of the crowd). This is because the Kolka such stupid to mess with him! What do you want, Polechka? Speak to me in French, Parlez-Moi franGais. 1 In the end, I have taught you, because you know a few phrases! .. Otherwise, how to distinguish between what you noble family, raising children, and not like all the organ-grinders; not

"Petrushka" we present some of the streets and sing the noble romance ... Oh yeah! What are we going to sing something? I interrupt you all, and we ... You know, we stopped here, Rodion Romanovitch to choose what to sing, - such that Cole and could dance ... because all that we have, you can imagine without preparation; you must come to an agreement, so that everything is fine to rehearse, and then we'll go to the Nevsky, where many more people of high society, and we will immediately notice: Lenya knows "Farm" ... Just everything "Little Farm" yes "Little Farm" and all of his singing! We should sing something much more noble ... Well, you have come to the fields, even if you're a mom helped! Memory, I do not, I would have thought! Not "Hussar is based on the sword" to sing, in fact! Oh, let's sing in French "CINQ su"! 2 I have taught you so taught the same thing. And most importantly, because it is in French, you will immediately see that you are children of the nobility, and it will be much more touching ... You can even: "Malborough s'en va-t-en guerre", as it's pretty children song, and is used in all the aristocratic houses, when a lull children.

Malborough s'en va-t-en guerre,
Ne Sait Quand reviendra ...

she began to sing ... - No, it's better to "Cinq sous!" Well, Nick, the handle on the hips as soon as possible, and you, too restless Lenya in the opposite direction, and we will sing and polka podhlopyvat!

Cinq sous, Cinq sous,
Pour Monter Notre mÃ © nage ...

Hee-hee-hee! (And she turned cough). The right dress, Polechka, shoulders down, - she said through coughing, otdyhivayas. - Now, do you need to keep yourself well and fine leg for all to see that you are children of the nobility. I then said that the bra to be larger than the incision, and that the two fabric. It was you, then, Sonya, with his advice: "In short yes shorter" it was that every child disfigured ... Well, again, all of you cry! Why are you, stupid! Well, Nick, begin as soon as possible, as quickly as possible, as quickly as possible - Oh, it's enfant terrible! ..

Cinq sous, CINQ su ...

Again soldier! Well, what do you want?

Indeed, through the crowd protesnyalsya police. But at the same time a gentleman in official uniform and greatcoat, a solid official fifty years, the Order on the neck (in the past it was very nice to Katerina Ivanovna and influenced the police), approached and silently gave Katerina Ivanovna three ruble banknotes dollars. His face expressed genuine compassion. Katerina Ivanovna adopted and politely, even ceremoniously, bowed to him.

- Thank you, sir, - she said haughtily, - reasons that prompted us ... take the money, Polechka. You see, there is also a noble and generous people, immediately ready to help the poor lady in distress. You see, sir, precious orphans, one might even say, the most aristocratic connections ... And it generalishka sat and ate grouse stamped their feet ... I was worried it ... "Your Excellency, I say, to protect the orphans , very knowledgeable, say, the late Seeds Zakharych, and his own daughter despicable villains from the date of his death, defamatory ... "Again, this is to protect soldiers! - She cried officer - that this soldier rises to me? We really escaped from one of Meshchanskaya here ... well, what do you say that business, you fool!

- Because the streets is prohibited sir. You do not misbehave.

- Sam, you bully! I still love to go hurdy-gurdy, you care?

- As for the barrel organ must have permission, and you yourself, and thus with people banging. Where are you going next Lodge?

- How permission! - Cried Katerina Ivanovna. - Today I buried my husband, permission!

- Ma'am, ma'am, calm down - began official - Come on, I'll see you in a crowd ... Here you are unwell indecent ... ...

- Sir, sir, you do not know anything! - Exclaimed Katerina Ivanovna - we go on Nevsky - Sonia, Sonia! But where is she? Crying too! What's wrong with all of you! .. Kolya, Lenya, where are you? - She suddenly cried out in terror - stupid kids! Kolya, Lenya, and where they are! ..

It so happened that Kolya and Lenya, fearing to the last degree street crowd and recommendations obsessed mother, seeing, finally, a soldier who wanted to take them somewhere and lead, suddenly, as if by agreement, grabbed her hand and ran away. With screaming and crying poor Katerina Ivanovna rushed to catch up with them. Ugly, and it was a pity to look at her, running, crying, gasping for breath. Sonia Polechka and rushed to her.

- Gates, Gates them, Sonia! About stupid, ungrateful children! .. Fields! Catch them ... For you, I ...

She stumbled over the entire term and fell.

- Crashed into the blood! Oh my God! - exclaimed Sonya, leaning over her.

All ran all zatesnilis circle. Raskolnikov and Lebezyatnikov fled from the first, official too hurried, followed by a policeman growled: "Ah-ma!" and waving his hand, expecting that everything will turn out, busily.

- Go! went! - He broke up the narrow circle of people.

- Die! - Someone shouted.

- Crazy! - Said another.

- Lord, save me! - One woman said, crossing himself. - Devchonochka something with the child zlovili it?Won in the lead, senior caught ... You see, sbalmoshnye!

But with the right to distinguish Katerina Ivanovna, I saw that it was not broken stone, as Sonya thought, and that blood stained the pavement, gushing from her chest throat.

- I know, you see - and muttered Raskolnikov official Lebezyatnikov - is consumption, c; bleeding, and thus crush. With one of my relatives who have recently occurred in that way, and half cup ... suddenly ... What, however, do now die?

- Here, here, come here! - Begged Sonia - I live here! .. That this house, second here ... For me, hurry, hurry!.. - Threw it all. - For the doctor went ... Oh, my God!

Thanks to the efforts of the official business it was settled, even the police helped carry Katerina Ivanovna.Made it with Sonja almost dead, and laid on the bed. Bleeding is still going on, but it seems to be starting to revive. Entered the room again, with the exception of Sony, Raskolnikov and Lebezyatnikov, officials and police to disperse the crowd beforehand, some of which are accompanied to the door. Polechka entered, holding hands, Kolya and Lenya, shaking and crying. And agreed Kapernaumovs: he limped curve strange man with a bristly, standing straight hair and mustache; his wife, who was for some time for all scared, and some of their children, persons with stiffness constant surprise and open mouths. Between this door with the entire audience appeared suddenly and Svidrigailov. Raskolnikov looked at him, not knowing where he was, and next to him in the crowd.

Speaking of doctors and priests. Although the official Raskolnikov whispered that seems doctor becomes superfluous, but ordered to send. He ran down to Capernaum.

Meanwhile Katerina Ivanovna breath during the blood moving. It looked

painful, but a closer look at and permeable pale and trembling Sonya, her handkerchief to wipe them with beads of sweat from his forehead;Finally, asked to raise sebya.On was put on the bed, holding both sides.

- Children, where? - She asked in a weak voice. - You brought them, Paul? About stupid! .. Well, what do you run ... Oh!

Blood still closed withered lips. She led eye circles, looking:

- So how do you live, Sonia! Never something I was not you ... led ...

She looked at the suffering:

- We Issosali you, Sonia ... Fields Lenya, Nick, come here ... Well, here they are, Sonia, all take their ... hands ... and I've had enough! .. Cum ball! G'A! .. Put me give even die in peace ...

She threw a pillow.

- What? The priest? .. Do not ... Where you once ruble? .. I do not sin! .. God must have just ... He knows how I suffered! .. And not just so, and do not need it! ..

Restless delirium, covering her more and more. Sometimes she started running his eye circles, learned all for a moment; but again, replace the consciousness of stupidity. She hoarse and hard to breathe, something like gurgling in his throat.

- I told him: "Your Excellency! .." - He shouted otdyhivayas after each word - this Amalia Lyudvigovna ... ah! Lenya, Kolya handle on the hips, hurry, hurry, slipping, slipping, pas de basque! getcha feet ... Be graceful child.

Du You Diamanten und Perlen ...

Like what? It would have been singing ...

Du you die schÃ∮nsten Augen,
MÃ¤dchen, was Willst du Mehr?

Well, yes, but it's true! was Willst du Mehr, - invent the same, stupid! .. Oh, here's another:

In the midday heat in the valley of Dagestan ...

Oh, how I loved to madness ... I loved this song, Polechka! .. You know, your father ... even groom Phewa ... Oh, the days! .. It would be, I wish we sing!

Why, here's how ... I forgot ... yes, we recall, too? - She was full of excitement and enhance grow. Finally, it is terrible, hoarse voice shouted she started screaming and gasping at every word, with this in mind, increases the fear:

In the heat of the day! .. In the valley! Dagestan ..! ..
With lead in his chest! ..

Your Excellency! - Suddenly she screamed heart-rending cries and bursting into tears, - the orphans!Knowing the bread and salt end Seeds Zakharych! .. You could even say aristocratic! .. G'A! - She suddenly shuddered, opamyatovavshis and with some horror of view, but immediately knew Sonya. - Sonia, Sonia! - Softly and tenderly she said, as if surprised that he saw her in front of you - Sonia, dear, and you're here?

Picked it up again.

- Enough! It's time ..! .. Farewell, poor wretch! Counties .. nag! .. Overexert-smiling! - She cried desperately and hateful and hit his head on the pillow.

He was again forgotten, but it did not last long last oblivion. Pale yellow, withered face threw it back back, mouth open, his legs stretched out convulsively. She took a deep, deep breath and died.

Sonia fell on her corpse, grabbed her by the arm and stopped and, clinging to the head dry chest of the deceased. Polechka fell at the feet of the mother and kissed them, crying bitterly.Kolya and Lenya, still do not understand what happened, but in anticipation of something very terrible, hugged each other with both hands and shoulders, looking into each other's eyes, suddenly together again, opened their mouths and began to cry.Both were still in suits: one in the turban, the other in the skullcap with an ostrich feather.

And how does this "Certificate of Merit" suddenly found himself on the bed next to Katerina Ivanovna? He lay on the pillow; Raskolnikov saw him.

He went to the window. For him, jumped Lebezyatnikov.

- Died! - Said Lebezyatnikov.

- Rodion Romanovich, the two of you have the right to pass the word - came Svidrigailov. Lebezyatnikov immediately buckled and delicately effaced. Svidrigailov surprised Raskolnikov still taken away in a corner.

- All this fuss, that is, the funeral and stuff, I'm taking. You know, there would be money, but because I told you that I have an extra. These two chicks and this polka I put in some places better orphans and put on each, to adulthood, one thousand five hundred rubles of capital Sofia Semyonovna

absolutely dead. Yes, and it will pull out of the pool because a good girl, is not it? Well, you and tell Avdotya Romanovna that her ten thousand here, and I've used.

- What are the goals as you razblagotvorilis? - Asked Raskolnikov.

- Oh-oh! Man incredulous! - Laughed Svidrigailov. - Because I said that I had money in addition. Well, just for humanity, is not allowed as well? This is not a "louse", as it was (he pointed to the corner where she was dead) as the old pawnbroker. Well, you see, well, "Luzhin whether, in fact, live and do abomination, or she dies?" And do not help me, do not you "Polechka, for example, in the same place on the same road goes ..."

He said this with a view of winking, cheerful deception, not taking his eyes off Raskolnikov. Raskolnikov turned pale and froze, hearing their own expression, said Sonia. He quickly stepped back and looked at Svidrigailov wildly.

- In the ... you know why? - He whispered, barely taking a breath.

- Why am I here, through the wall, Madame Resslih stand. Here Capernaum, and there Madame Resslih, an old friend and dedication. My neighbor.

- Do You?

- I - continued Svidrigailov, rocking with laughter - and I can assure you, honor, my dear Rodion Romanovich, surprisingly you are interested in me. In the end, I said that we were going together, you predicted it - well, that agreement. And you will see that I am folding man. Look what happened to me, you can continue to live ...

PART 6
←« CHAPTER I »→

Raskolnikov came to a strange time only fog suddenly fell in front of him and put it in a hopeless and heavy solitude. Remembering this time, then, for a long time later, he knew that his mind sometimes as though dimmed, and that it lasted, with some intervals, up to the final catastrophe. It was convinced positively mainly erroneous, then, for example, in terms of time and some accidents. At least, remembering afterwards and trying to understand myself, I remember that he had learned a lot about myself, posted information received from strangers. One event it is mixed, for example, on the other hand; Others believe that the investigation of the accident, which existed only in his imagination. Sometimes it had hurt him excruciating anxiety, panic and even reborn. But he also remembered that there were moments ,, hours or maybe days full of apathy, took possession of him, as it were, in contrast to earlier fears - apathy, similar to other morbidly indifferent state of dying. Typically, in these last days he as if trying to escape from a clear and complete understanding of their situation; other vital facts, demanded an immediate explanation, especially his burden; but how glad he was free and escape from other problems, forgetting that threatens, however, complete and inevitable death in his position.

Particularly disturbed him Svidrigailov: you could even say that he seemed to be focused on Svidrigailov. So bad for him too clearly expressed words of Svidrigailov, Sonya apartment in death minute Katerina Ivanovna as to impair the normal course of his thoughts. But, despite the fact that this new fact is extremely concerned, Raskolnikov is somehow not in a hurry, explaining things. Sometimes, suddenly finds himself somewhere

in a remote and secluded corner of the city, in some miserable hotel one at the table, in meditation, and barely remember how he got here, he suddenly remembered about Svidrigailov he suddenly very clear and disturbing to realize that it would be necessary, as soon as possible to come to an agreement with that person, and that can finally decided to do. One day, somewhere behind the outpost, he even imagined that here waiting for Svidrigailov and that they set the date. Another time he woke up before dawn, somewhere on earth, in the bushes, and almost did not realize how wandered here. However, in these two or three days after the death of Katerina Ivanovna he met twice with Svidrigailov, almost always in the flat at Sony, where he came as something without a purpose, but almost always in a minute. They always exchange short words, and never spoke of major points, as if between them, because by itself and the conditions to be silent about this for some time. Katerina Ivanovna's body was still lying in a coffin.Svidrigailov arranged funerals and bustle. Sonia was also very busy. At the last meeting Svidrigailov Raskolnikov explained that the children of Katerina Ivanovna he once made, and made a success; that he was so aloof attitude to find a man with the help of which you can put all three of them orphans, immediately, in very good places for them; that deferred money for them too much help as orphans with capital to put much more easily than the poor orphans. He said something about Sonya and promised to somehow come to the most recent Raskolnikov and mentioned that he "would like to consult, it is very necessary to say that there are such things …" This conversation took place in the hall, stairs. Svidrigailov Raskolnikov looked into the eyes and suddenly, after a pause, and in a low voice, he asked:

- What are you, Rodion Romanovitch such did not? That's right! Listen to and watch, and did not seem to understand. You are invited. Here, let's talk: a pity that a lot of things, and that of others, and it … Ah, Rodion Romanovitch - he added suddenly, - all people need air, air, air-to-it … First it!

He suddenly stepped aside to allow entrance to the priest and deacon stairs. They went to serve a memorial service.By order of Svidrigailov, requiems were served twice a day, gently.Svidrigailov went on his way. Raskolnikov stood, he thought, and he went for an apartment priest Sony.

He stood in the doorway. Service began quietly, politely sad. In the consciousness of death and death is always a sense of presence for him was something heavy and mystically terrible childhood; And for a long time he did not hear a requiem. Yet there is something else, too horrible and restless.

He looked at his children: they all stood by the coffin, on his knees, crying Polechka.Za them, quietly, as if timidly crying, praying Sonia. "But these days she never looked at me and did not say a word to me," - suddenly thought Raskolnikov. The sun shone brightly on the room; incense rose clubs; the priest read "Give rest, O Lord." Raskolnikov stood the entire service. Blessing and farewell, the priest in the country vzglyadom.Posle service Raskolnikov went to Sonya. She suddenly took both his hands and dropped her head on his shoulder. This short gesture even struck Raskolnikov, with perplexity; it was very strange, how? The slightest disgust is not the slightest aversion to it, not the slightest tremor in his hand! It really was a kind of infinite self-abasement. So, at least, he understood it.Sonia did not say anything.Raskolnikov shook her hand and went out. He was terribly difficult. If it were possible to go anywhere at this point and remain alone, even for a lifetime, he thought it would be greatly appreciated. But the fact that it recently, though almost always had one, I could not feel that he is one. Happened to him to leave the city, leaving the high road, even once he went into some woods, but the place was hidden, the more I realized, as if someone close and disturbing presence, is not that terrible, but somehow very annoying so quickly returned to the city, mixed with the crowd, entered the tavern restaurants, went to Tolkuchy at the Haymarket. It would be very much easier and even personal life. In the tavern, in the evening, singing songs: he sat for an hour, listening, and remembered that he was very nice. But in the end he suddenly became restless again; repentance is suddenly began to torment him: "Here, sit, listen to songs, but maybe something I have to do" - as if he thought. However, he knew right away that this is not one of his concerns; Was that require immediate resolution, but that you understand any words could not convey. All in some tangle unwound. "No, it's better to have some fight! Better Porfiry again ... or Svidrigailov ... Hurry to support the call someone attack ... Yes! Yes!" - He thought. He left the hotel and ran almost over. The thought of Dance and mother brought him suddenly, for some reason, as if panic. This is something the night before the morning he woke up in the bushes, on Krestovsky all izdrognuvshy, as in a fever; He went home and came already in the early morning. After a few hours of sleep the fever was gone, but he woke up too late: it was two o'clock in the afternoon.

He recalled that the designated day of the funeral of Katerina Ivanovna, and was glad I did not attend them. Nastasya brought him there;He ate and drank with pleasure, almost impatiently. His head was fresh, and he relaxed

than in the past three days. He even thought briefly, the same wave of panic. The door opened and in walked Razumikhin.

- Ah, there is, therefore, not sick! - Razumikhin says, took a chair and sat down opposite Raskolnikov. He was alarmed and did not try to hide it. He spoke with obvious irritation, but without haste and without raising his voice, especially. You may think that it gave some special and even exceptional intention. - Listen, - he said decisively - to me there to hell with you all, but from what I see now, I see clearly that I can not understand ,; Please do not think that I have come to the question. Not all the same! I do not want!Sam now all reveal all their secrets, so I still listen to something, maybe I will not spit and leave. I just found out personally and finally: It is true, first of all, you're crazy? About you, you see, there is a belief (well, there, somewhere), you can be crazy or very inclined. I confess to you, I've been pretty much inclined to support this point of view, first of all, judging by your stupid and partly vile actions (unexplained), and secondly, the recent behavior of his mother and sister. Only a monster and a scoundrel, if not crazy, could do it for them, as you have done; and, therefore, you're crazy ...

- How long have you seen them?

- At The Moment. And since you have not seen? Where you shlyaesh-sya, please tell me, I can do for you three times came. Mother is sick since yesterday seriously. Gathered together unto thee; Avdotya Romanovna was retention; listen wants nothing: "If he says he is sick, if he has the mind gets in the way, which will help him as no mother?" We all came here because I did not throw it to us as one. For the most calm your door begging. Entered you do not, here it is Sat Stayed ten minutes we stood over her in silence. He got up and said: "If he comes out of the yard, and, consequently, a healthy mother and forgotten so indecent and shameful mother standing in the doorway affection, as handouts, begging. "The main gate and took to her bed, now in full swing," I see, said she has time. "She believes that it is something - this is Sofya Semyonovna, your fiancee, or lover, I do not know. I immediately went to Sofya Semyonovna, because, brother, I wanted everyone to find out - come take a look: coffin stands, children cry. Sofya Semyonovna mourning them trying. You do not. Looked apologized and Avdotya Romanovna message. All, however, it is not nonsense, and there is not it, or rather the whole, therefore, the madness. But here you sit and boiled beef zhresh, just three days did not eat. This, for example, and there are crazy, but at least you have a word with me did not say, but you're not crazy ...! This I swear. First of all,

not crazy. So to hell with you, because there is some mystery, some secret; I break over your head secrets do not intend to. So just went cursed - he concluded, getting up - take heart, and I know what I do now!

- What do you want to do?

- Do you care what I want to do now?

- Listen, you zapesh!

- Why ... why do you know that?

- Well, here's another!

Razumikhin paused.

- You've always been a very intelligent man, and never, never you do not go crazy - he said suddenly with fever. - It's like this: I take a drink! Farewell! - And he began to walk.

- I'm on to you, the third day, it seems, with my sister said Razumikhin.

- About me! Yes ... this is where you can see the third day? - Razumikhin suddenly stopped, even a little pale. It can be assumed that his heart slowly and with a voltage pounding in my chest.

- She came here, alone, sitting here talking to me.

- Is This!

- Yes she is.

- What do you say ... I want to say about me, then?

- I told her that you're a very good, honest and hardworking person. What do you love her, I told her, because she knows herself.

- She knows?

- Well, here's another! Wherever I went, it will not be with me no matter what happens - you are left with them Providence. I am, so to speak, to release them for you, Razumikhin. I say this because I know how much you love her, and convinced of the purity of your heart. I also know that she can not love you, and even, perhaps, too fond of. Now decide how you know best - should or should not you drink.

- Rodka ... You see ... Well ... Oh, shit! And you do something where you want to go? You see, if it's all a secret, let them! But I ... I know a secret ... I am sure, of course, some terrible stuff and nonsense, and that you are all one and started. And yet, you are a great man! Great man! ..

- I just wanted to let you add, you're broke, you very well now be judged by these mysteries and secrets do not recognize. Leave time, do not worry. All in good time, you'll know exactly when it is needed. Yesterday I had one person said that the need to air a person, the air, the air! I want it now and

find out what he meant by that.

Razumikhin stood in thought and in the excitement and something to think about.

"It's a political conspirator, I think, and he on the eve of a decisive step - he should!

Can not be otherwise, and ... and Dunya knows ... "- suddenly he thought to himself.

- So you're going to Avdotya Romanovna, - he said, shouting words - and you do want to see a man who says he needs more air and the air ... and, therefore, the letter ... it's also something same - he concluded as if to himself.

- What letter?

- She received another letter today, it is very alarmed. Very Much. Too even. I'm talking about you - please be quiet. Then ... then said that perhaps we are soon parted, I then started something hot to thank; then went to his room and locked.

- She received a letter? - Thoughtfully asked Raskolnikov.

- Yes, a letter; and you do not know? Hmm.

They were both silent.

- Farewell, Rodion. I, brother ... there was one time ... and indeed, good-bye, see, there was a time ... Well, good-bye! I also have to go. I will not drink. Now ... not lying!

He was in a hurry; but leaves, and, of course, almost closed the door, he suddenly opened it again and said, looking away:

- By The Way! Remember, this is murder, well, this is what Porphyry old woman, then? Well, you should know that this killer look, confessed himself, and all the evidence presented. This is one of those very workers, dyes then, imagine, remember, I still defended them here? If you think that this whole fight scene and laughing on the stairs with his friend when they somehow scrambled janitor and two witnesses, he purposely arranged it for the call. What is the trick of how the presence of mind to the puppy! Hard to believe that, yes, he explained that he had confessed to everything! And I somehow vlopalsya! Well, in my opinion, it's just a genius pretense and resourcefulness, the genius of the legal removal - and, therefore, there is nothing particularly surprising! Do not be such? And he could not resist the nature and confessed, so I gave him for it even more to believe. Probably ... But somehow I did something I vlopalsya! For them to climb the wall!

- Tell me, how did you know what and why are you so interested? - With visible emotion Raskolnikov asked.

- Well, here's another! Why I am interested! Responding to a question ,! .. And I learned from porphyria, among others. However, almost all of it and learned.

- From porphyria?

- From porphyria.

- What ... what is it? - Fearfully asked Raskolnikov.

- He was well explained to me. Psychologically explained in his own way.

- He explained? And explain myself to you?

- Sam, himself, bye! Then it was that Coy will say, but it is now. ... There was a time when I thought that ... Well, that; then! .. Why do I now drink. You and me without wine is poured. Drunk because I Rodka!Without wine drunk now, but about good-bye; I will come, very soon.

He went out.

! "It's a political conspirator, probably most likely - finally decided to Razumikhin himself slowly down the stairs - A sister sucked ;. It is very, very likely to be the nature of Avdotya Romanovna My go ... And because it also. I hinted. For many, she said ... and the word ... hint, it all comes out that way! And how else to explain all this confusion? Hmm! I thought ... Oh, my God, I was pleased. Yes, sir it was an eclipse, and I am guilty before him! He then light in the corridor, the eclipse has brought me. Ugh! That's disgusting, rude, vile thought on my part! Well done Mikolka admitted that ... And now the former, as everything is explained! This disease is the fact that his country, all such acts, even earlier, before, even at the university, he was always gloomy, sullen ... But what makes this letter now? Here, perhaps, something too. From this letter? I suspect ... Um. No, I'll find out everything. "

He remembered and knew all about Dunya, and his heart sank. He jumped up and ran.

Raskolnikov, as Razumikhin left, stood up, turned to the window, pushed into a corner to the other, as if unaware of their misfortune nursery ... and sat on the couch. This all would like to update and re-fight - then the result has been found!

"Yes, it means that the result has been found! And that, too, all stolen and connected, it became painfully push, intoxication assault of some kind. From the stage with Mikolka Porphyry he began to choke without logging in distress. After Mikolka on a the same day, was the scene of Sony,

he led and finished it at all, not at all, as I could imagine myself in front of ... weak, then immediately and radically! Together! And in the end, he had agreed with Sonia, he agreed, agreed to the heart, as he is one on one with such a thing in the soul can not live! And Svidrigailov? Svidrigailov secret ... Svidrigailov troubles him, however, but somehow the wrong side. With Svidrigailov, maybe even too must fight. Svidrigailov may also be the result, but Porfiry is another matter.

So Porphyry himself also explained Razumikhin, psychologically he explained! Again his damn psychology began to fail! Porphyry something? Yes porphyria believe even for one minute that Mikolka guilty then between them was then, after this scene, face to face, to Mikolka that you can not find the correct interpretation except one? (Raskolnikov several times these days flicker and remembers scraps whole scene with Porfiry, in general, it would not be able to make memories). Were at that time uttered such words between them, were the movements and gestures, they shared such views, it was said that Coy voice to such an extent that only after that did not Mikolka (which Porphyry heart of the first word and gesture guess) Mikolka not shake the very foundations of their beliefs.

And how! Even Razumikhin began to suspect! The scene in the hallway, in the lamp, it is not passed in vain.Here he rushed to Porfiry ... But why should this be something to inflate it so? That its purpose is to prevent their eyes from Razumihina on Mikolka? In the end, of course he's up to something; there is an intention, but what? However, since that morning was a long time - too much, too much, and Porphyry was no hearing, nor spirit. Well, it's certainly worse ... "Raskolnikov took his cap and thoughtfully out of the room. The first day, during all this time, he felt, at least in his mind." We must put an end to Svidrigailov, - - he thought - and that no matter what, as soon as possible: this, too, seems to be waiting for me to come to him myself. "And at this moment such hatred suddenly rose from his weary heart that maybe he could kill someone from the two :. Svidrigailov or Porfiry At least, he felt that if not now, then he can do it. " We'll see, we'll see, "- he repeated to himself.

But as soon as he opened the door to the hallway, when suddenly faced with the very porphyry. It was part of him. Raskolnikov was dumbfounded for a moment. Oddly enough, he was not surprised purple and almost scary. He has just started, but quickly, instantly ready. "Maybe insulation! But as he went quiet as a cat, and I have not heard anything? Is listening"?

- Unexpected visitor, Rodion Romanovitch - exclaimed, laughing, Porfiry Petrovich. - How long are going to wrap up, I'm going through, I think - why not go five minutes to visit. Somewhere along? Do not delay. Only here cigarettes, if you will.

- Yes, sit down, Porfiry Petrovich, sit - sit Guest Raskolnikov, a seemingly happy and friendly view that the right to wonder if I could look at myself. Some Finally, vyskrebyvalis foam! Sometimes people suffer in this way half an hour of mortal fear of the thief, and how it will make him a knife to her throat, finally, because there is no fear will pass. He sat down right in front of Porphyry and smignuv, looked at him. Porfiry narrowed his eyes and began to smoke.

"Well, I told you, I'll tell you - as if he wanted to jump out of the heart of Raskolnikov. - Well, well, why do not you tell?"

⫷⫷ CHAPTER II ⫸⫸

- In the end, these cigarettes! - Finally, said Porfiry Petrovitch finished lights and otdyhnuvshis - injury, damage to clean, and I can not get behind! Cough, sir, to tickle the very beginning, and shortness of breath. I know a coward, sir, went the other day B - well - each patient for a half hour at least considering; so even laughed, looking at me, and Stukal, and listened to - you said, among other things, tobacco is not good; easily expanded. Well, I'll throw it? What can replace it? I do not drink, sir, it's trouble, heh-heh-heh, do not drink anything, the trouble! This is because relatively Rodion Romanovitch, everything is relative!

"The fact that he, in his old tape is assumed that there!" - Aversion thought Raskolnikov. All recently the scene of the last goodbye, he suddenly thought, feeling a wave and then prihlynulo to his heart.

- But I have come to you in the evening of the third day; You do not know, -? Continued Porfiry Petrovitch, looking around the room - the room in this very entered. Too, like today, I pass - give, I think, vizitik give him anything. I walked in and the number of wide open; looked around and waited, and your maid did not report - released. Do not block?

Raskolnikov's face clouded over and over again. Porphyry accurately guessed his thoughts.

- Explain come, my dear Rodion Romanovitch explain, sir! And should explain to you, sir, - he said with a smile, and even a little banged his hand on the knee of Raskolnikov, but almost at the same moment, his face suddenly serious problem and mine; even if the sadness was covered, to the surprise of Raskolnikov. He had never seen and did not know he was a man. - Strange

scene took place the last time between us, Rodion Romanovitch. This is, perhaps, in our first meeting took place between us, too strange scene; but then ... Well, now it's all 12:59! Here I can be, and very guilty before leaving; I can feel it, sir. In the end, we both broke something, you remember that you sing and podkolenki nerves tremble, and my nerves podkolenki sing and shake.And you know, somehow, even dishonest, and then between us, not a gentleman. But we are still gentlemen; that is, in any case, first of all lords; it is necessary to understand, sir. After all, remember what happened before ... there's even a pretty indecent, sir.

"Well, this is it, someone take me?" - I was surprised Raskolnikov asked himself, lifting his head and all eyes looking at Porfiry.

- I thought that by revelation to us now better - continued Porfiry Petrovitch, head thrown back a little, and with downcast eyes, as if not wanting to embarrass him look at his former victims, as if ignoring their old methods and tricks - Yes - with such suspicions and such scenes can not last long. Let us then Mikolka, but I do not know what will be achieved between us.this damn meschaninishka Sat with me during section - can you imagine? Of course, you already know this; Yes, and I know myself that he later came to you; But what if you suggested that it was neither of whom I did not send in anything else I have not ordered. Ask why did not order? And, as you say, it's all very me then how would pristuknulo. I just ordered the wipers and send.(Janitors, you may have noticed, passing). Then I thought, swept, so alone, fast as lightning; too much, you see, I was convinced that Rodion Romanovitch. Give, I think, at least for a while and miss one, but another to grab the tail - something, but something extreme, do not miss it. Irritability you very much, Rodion Romanovitch, by nature, sir; even too much, sir, for all something different basic properties of your character and heart, which I flatter myself, partly understand, sir. And, of course, I could, even if the judge does not always the case with people who make you and blurted out the whole story. It happens, however, especially when the last person brought the patient, but, in any event, rarely. What I could tell. No, I think I would dash!even if most mahochkuyu dash, only one, but only so that so that you can take your hands so much that is not what one is psychology. Because I thought that if a person is guilty, then of course you can, in any case, something significant to expect from him; allowed even at the most unexpected result calculated.The character of his time, I counted Rodion Romanovitch primarily with the character! Hoping means a lot to you then.

- Yes you are ... but what you are now somehow all say so - and finally muttered Raskolnikov did not even realize a good question. "What he says - he lost himself - really really innocent to take me?"

- So says? Come to explain, so to speak, the sacred duty of honor. I want you to explain everything to the ground, as it were, the whole story of it all, then, so to speak, from the defilements.Many I had you go, Rodion Romanovitch. I'm not a monster, sir. After all, the same thing, and I understand what it's all drag yourself man, dejected, but proud, imperious and impatient, especially impatient! I, in any case, a man most noble honor, sir, and even with the rudiments of nobility, with, though not agree with you in all your beliefs about what has long been considered to declare in advance, directly and frankly, because first all do not want to cheat. Knowing you, you felt affection. You can, of my words burst out laughing? Have the right, sir. I know that you and I, at first glance do not like, because, in fact, and not on the fact that love with. But keep in mind what you want, but now I want, for its part, by all means to make amends print and prove that I'm a man with heart and sovestyu.Chestno speaking, sir.

Porfiry Petrovich paused with dignity. Raskolnikov felt a surge of new fear. The idea that Porphyry says that his innocent suddenly start to frighten him.

- Honestly all right, and if I had become almost necessary - continued Porfiry Petrovitch; - I think that even superfluous. And it is unlikely I can, sir. Thus, as explained in detail? Initially, the rumors went. The fact that it was hearsay and from whom and when ... and for whatever reason, in fact, he came to you - also, I think too much. Personally, I started with a random, one completely random, which may be substantially and could not be - what? Hmm, I think, too, there is nothing to talk o.Vse it, and rumors and chance, coincided in time, when I thought of one. I confess frankly, because if we assume, as in all - this is my first time on you and atakoval.Oni there, say, an old woman a sign of things and so on, and so on - all this nonsense, sir. Such details can nachest hundred. I also had the opportunity to then find out details about the scene in the office quarter, as well as random, and not something as casually as a special narrator, the capital, which, unwittingly, it is surprising that the scene osvoili.Vse because it is one -on-one with one-on-one with Rodion Romanovitch, dear! Well, that was not to turn in a certain direction? Of the one hundred rabbits never was a horse every hundred suspicion was not evidence because it is as the English proverb says,

but it's just common sense, sir, and passion is something trying to cope with the passions, because the investigator and the person-in. Then I remembered, and your short article in zhurnaltse you remember, in the first, then your visit to the details of it says something. I was bullied, but it is for you to continue to call. I repeat, you are impatient and very ill, Rodion Romanovitch.What you are brave, arrogant, serious and ... felt too much all felt it, I have long known, sir. I know that all of these feelings, and your short article I read in another. In the sleepless nights and in a trance she conceived, and podymaniem Stukanov hearts with enthusiasm depressed. And it's dangerous depression, proud enthusiasm of youth! I was bullied, and now you say that awfully fond of at all, that is, as an amateur, first, young, hot pen sample. Smoke, fog, string sounds in the mist. Article absurd and your fantastic, but it flickers such sincerity in her young pride and integrity, courage in despair; she grimly article, sir, yes, it's good, sir. Your article that I read, and postponed, and ... how shall I say something and thought, "Well, this man did not come!" Well, as you say, now, after that in the past was not to get carried away and then! Oh my God! Do you think I have something to say? Is there anything I now argue? I just noticed. What's there to think about? There is nothing that absolutely nothing and may substantially nothing. Oh, and take part in this way to me, the investigator does not even indecent: I won Mikolka on hand, and the facts - we have what you want, but the facts! And he also brings his psychology; they should pozanyatsya; because there is life and death. What am I now to explain all this? And so you know, and your mind and heart are not charged me for evil, then the behavior. Not maliciously sincerely say, sir, hehe! Do you think I did not have time to search? Was-was-with, hehe, was, sir, when you are a patient lying in posteli.Ne officially, but not his face, and he was, sir. Until recently, the hair you have, the apartment has been checked at first even a trace; but - umsonst! [vain! . (It)] I think, now this man will come, he will come, and very soon; Kohl is guilty, so be sure to come. Another will come, and it will come. Do you remember how Mr. Razumikhin began to speak with you? This is what we had to make sure that you are happy, because we consciously and spread the rumor that he speaks to you and Mr. Razumikhin kind of person who will not support outrage. Mr. Zametovu especially your anger and your courage to open his eyes ran: well as in the tavern suddenly bryaknut: "I have killed" too bold, sir, too cocky, sir, and if I think he's guilty, he feared fighter ! Since then, and thought, sir. In anticipation, sir! We are waiting for you to go all

out, and then you Zametova just crushed ... and after all, the thing that this whole damn psychology ends! Well, I'm waiting for you, you see, and God gives you - go! So I knocked and heart. Eh! Well, why did you come? Laughter is that your laughter, as if it is on, remember, because it was through the glass, then I think everything, and I did not expect such a special way, and your laugh would not have noticed. That's what it means in the mood for something to be. And Mr. Razumikhin that then - ah! stone, stone-something, remember, stone, here are the things by which something to hide? Well, that's exactly see it somewhere in the garden - in the garden, because you said, Zametovu something, and then I have something for the second time? And the way we started this article on your touch as you become the state - is the fact that every word of his double takes, just another beneath it sits! Well, Rodion Romanovitch, so that, and I reached the poles, and how to hit him in the forehead, and came to. No, I say, that's me! In the end, if you want all this, I say, as long as possible can be no other way to explain even more naturally come out. Flour, sir! "No, I think I'd better dash .." Yes, I heard about these bells is so still and measured, even trembling prohvatit. "Well, I guess that's it hyphen! This is it!" And then I do not want to reasoned. A thousand rubles per minute I gave my only you in your eyes , and see how you, a hundred steps meschaninishkoy next to go, after you "killer" in the eyes said, and nothing from him for a hundred steps, did not dare to ask ! .. Well, something this cold in the spinal cord? Bells is, in some disease, half delirious something? Thus, Rodion Romanovitch, and after, and it is interesting that I am with you, if joking? And why are you at the moment come? In the end, you are pushing, but, by God, and if we do not apply Mikolka, then ... well, then Mikolka remember? Well remembered? In the end, it was thunder, sir! This thunder clouds, lightning! Well, I met up with him? Boom that that no matter stolechko not believe myself, if you please! But where! Only after you, when he became very, very smoothly other objects to respond, so I was surprised, and then he either did not believe a penny! That's what it means to become stronger as adamant. No, I think, Morgen free! What is already here Mikolka!

- Razumikhin I just said that you now accuse themselves Nicholas Razumihina sure ...

He captured the spirit, and he did not finish. He listened to the unspeakable excitement, like a man to bite through it, from the refuse. He was afraid to believe and not to believe. In still ambiguous words he avidly sought and

caught something more accurate and definitive.

- Mr. Razumikhin something! - Cried Porfiry Petrovich, just loved all the dumb question Raskolnikov - heh, heh, heh! Yes, Mr. Razumikhin and had to be removed: two of them are third not poke your nose. Mr. Razumikhin non-s, and the stranger, came running to me all so pale ... Well, God bless him, he's here to get involved! And nothing Mikolka Do you know what kind of story, in the form as it is, I understand it? First of all, it is a minor child, and not so much a coward as well as, for example, if an artist of some of them. Yes, sir, you do not laugh, I interpret it. Innocent and receptive to everything. Heart; science fiction. He and sing and dance, fairy tale and he says so to speak, that from other places come together to listen. And go to school, and laugh till you drop, because Thumb show and get drunk senseless, not that of corruption, as well as bands when the drink, like a kid again. Then he stole, and that's how he does not know; because "if on the ground over the fact that for a stolen?" Did you know that he is from the dissenters, rather than something that schismatics, but simply sectarian; in his way was the second, and it recently, for two years, in the village, with some old man was under the spiritual principle. All this, and I Mikolka from Zaraisky recognized him.Yes kudy! just wanted to flee into the wilderness! Zeal prayed to God at night, Old Book, "truth" is read and read. Petersburg he acted strongly, especially women, and wine.Receptive-ies, and the old man, and forget about everything. I know this is one artist liked to go, he began, but this thing and go! Well, obrobel - hanged! Run! What to do with the concept, which was held by the people of our yuridistike! Even more frightening, because the word "condemn". Who is to blame! Here's what the new courts say. Oh, would give God! Well, in prison and remembered something, it is clear now fairly old; The Bible also came again. You know, Rodion Romanovitch that there are other means of them "suffer?" This is not something that someone else, and so easy to "suffer necessity"; suffering, which means it take, and the authorities - so the bolee.SB in my humble once concluded within one year in prison on the stove at night all read the Bible, and read well, so carried away, you know, actually, so that for no reason at all grabbed a brick and threw the head, without any resentment on his part. And threw something: on purpose yards past took to produce any harm! Well, we know that the end of a prisoner who rushes into his arms with the authorities, "accepted, it means suffering."So I suspect that now that Mikolka wants to "take the pain" or something like that. This is me, perhaps even on the facts

as I know, sir. He just does not know what I znayu.chto not allowed, or something that people of this fantastic people out? Yes, totally! Senior now again began to act, especially after the cycle to remember something. And yet, he tells me that everything will come. You think you stand? Wait another will unlock!From hour to hour wait that comes from the testimony of debris. I loved this Mikolka and explore its doskonalno.A you think! Hehe! Elsewhere something very smoothly replied, obviously, received the necessary information, deftly prepared; as well as on other matters as well as in a puddle, nichegoshechko does not know, does not know, and he himself does not know, he did not know! No, my dear Rodion Romanovitch is not Mikolka! That's fantastic, dark, modern business, our time, and when the heart is dizzy rights; when tsituetsya phrase that blood "refreshing"; when all life is preached in comfort. Then book with dreams, theoretically stimulation of the heart; Here we see the definition in the first stage, but the definition of a special kind - fear not, as a mountain or fell from the bell tower fell, and the crime for some reason does not seem to come with his feet. The door behind him, forgot to close, and killed, two died, according to the theory. Died and take the money failed, and that he was able to capture, then demolished stone.

Not only that, this is what made the meal, sitting outside the door, and the doorbell rang and explosion - no, that's just an empty apartment, half delirious, remember the bell goes cold again spinal experience necessary ... Well, for example, in the case of illness, and here's another: killed, but an honest man he appreciates people despise, pale angel walks - not so Mikolka, my dear Rodion Romanovitch is not Mikolka!

These last words, after all is said and so similar to the renunciation was too unexpected. Raskolnikov shuddered as if transfixed.

- So ... who killed ...? .. - He asked, unable to stand, panting. Porfiry Petrovitch even started back in his chair, as if we were so unexpected, and he was amazed at the question.

- As someone killed? .. - He said, as if in disbelief - so you killed, Rodion Romanovitch! You and killed, with ... - he said, almost in a whisper, fully convinced voice.

Raskolnikov got up from the couch and stood there were a few seconds, and then sat down without saying a word. Small cramps suddenly passed over his face.

- Sponge something again, as if startled - muttered if even with the participation of Porfiry Petrovich. - You got me, Rodion Romanovitch do not

seem to understand, sir, - he added, after a pause - and because they were amazed. I just came from the fact that it's all said and then lead to open.

- It was not me killed - was Raskolnikov whispered, as if afraid of small children when they took place.

- No, it's you, sir, Rodion Romanovitch you, sir, and no one else - strictly and seriously Porfiry whispered.

They both fell silent, and the silence lasted long enough even for ten minutes. Raskolnikov leaned his elbows on the table and silently ruffled his hair with your fingers. Porfiry Petrovich sat quietly and waited.Raskolnikov looked contemptuously at Porfiry.

- Again, you're old, Porfiry Petrovich! All these your tricks: how do you get tired, really?

- Uh, completeness, I now stunts! Another would be the case if there are witnesses; and that in fact we have one-on-one whisper. You see, I'm not coming to you in the management and catch you like a hare. Al recognizes not - at this point I do not care. As for me, I am convinced that without you.

- And if so, why did you come? - Raskolnikov asked irritably. - I will ask the first question, if you think I'm guilty, then why do not you take me to jail?

- Well, that's the question! Point is the answer: First, you still directly under arrest me unprofitable.

- How profitable! If you believe ,, so you'll have ...

- Hey, I'm convinced ,? After all this time be my dream, sir. Yes, and I have to take a break will put there?You know, if asked himself. I cite, for example, to testify against you meschaninishku, and you say to him? "You're drunk or not Who saw me with you, I'll just drunk and tried, and yes, you were drunk," - well, I have something to say even more to your else plausible than him because of his testimony only psychology - his face and even indecent - and you somehow get to the point, because the drink, you bastard, bitter and too well known. Yes, and I'll tell you frankly admitted several times that a two-edged sword of psychology, and that the second end of something else will, and much more likely, and, moreover, against you, and I have nothing, And though I still put you even imagine that I came here (not human) forward you to declare, but still just telling you (also remove the person), for me it will not be profitable. Well, and secondly, because I have come to you ...

- Well, yes, in the second? (Raskolnikov still choking).

- Because, as I do, and announced this morning, I feel obliged to you an explanation. I do not want you to be my Monster deserved, especially

because you sincerely believe me, I do not believe it.As a result, third, and come to you with open and direct demand - to put recognition. This you will be countless more profitable and beneficial to me too - because from the shoulders down. Well, to be honest, or not on my side?

Raskolnikov thought.

- Listen, Porfiry Petrovich, because you yourself say, one psychology, and in the meantime entered into mathematics. Well, if you're doing wrong now?

- No, Rodion Romanovitch, I was not mistaken. In dash. A dash of something that I have found since then, sir; The Lord sent!

- With a dash?

- I will not say that, Rodion Romanovitch. And, anyway, now I have no more delay; will be set to. So you judge: I now really do not care, and consequently, I just for you. Frankly, it would be better, Rodion Romanovitch!

Raskolnikov smiled wickedly.

- It is not only ridiculous, it's so shamelessly. Well, even if I was guilty (which I do not say), well, why should I be with you to admit that you really say that I'm there for you to resign?

- Ah, Rodion Romanovitch not quite believe the words; may not be entirely alone! It's just a theory, but still my sir, but I will tell you by what authority? I can be myself and you that even now with the skin. You have not so I take and lay out, hehe! Second case: as what benefit? Yeah, you know what you vosposleduet for this conclusion? In the end, you will also appear, if anything at this moment? You just tried for it! When one crime already took it all confused? And I'll tell you what, I swear to God, so "out there" to forge and arrange it so that your appearance will be as unexpectedly. All this psychology we do destroy all suspected you become nothing, so that your crime as obscuring some imagine, because, frankly, it's vertigo. I am an honest man, Rodion Romanovitch, and will keep his word.

Raskolnikov was silent and sadly bowed his head; He thought for a long time and finally smiled, but his smile was already tender and sad:

- Oh, no! - He said, as if quite openly with porphyria. - Not worth it! I do not need all your contributions!

- Well, that's what I was afraid of! - Passionately, as if involuntarily exclaimed Porphyry - that is what I was afraid that you do not need our conclusions.

Raskolnikov sad and impressive look at him.

- Hey, life is not squeamish! - Porphyry continued - a lot of it will still

be ahead. How to avoid punishment, since it is not necessary! Striving for you man!

- What will be the front lot?

- Life! You are a prophet, you know, a lot eh? Seek and ye shall find. YOU CAN God for it and waited. And it's not forever, Network ...

- The penalty will be ... - Raskolnikov laughed.

- What a shame bourgeois whether that scary? It can be as frightened, but I do not know - because young! Yet you should not be afraid of Ali there to be ashamed of surrender.

- Oh, do not care! - Whispered contempt and disgust Raskolnikov, as if not wanting to talk. He stood up again, just wanted to go somewhere, but sat down again in the visible despair.

- Just do not give a damn! Lost faith, and I think that I have a butter; yes a lot eh you live then? Many well understand something? Theory invented, and ashamed that failed, that is not really very original work! It turned out that somewhere, it's true, but you somehow have not yet hopeless wretch. This is not such a villain! At least not for a long time he cheat again came to the last post. I, whom you admire? I admire you for one of them, which, while reducing the intestine, and it will be so with a smile looking at tormentors - if only faith god IL godsend. Well, look, and you will live. You primarily has long needed to change the air.Well, suffering is good too. Affected. Mikolka something, maybe it is right that wants suffering. I know that not veruet-sya - and you do not philosophize slyly; gave their lives directly, without thinking; do not worry - right on the beach will produce and deliver on its feet. On the beach? How should I know? I just believe that you live more. I know that you are my words as ratseyu currently taking remember; Yes, it can, after the revocation comfortable ever; say. Another good thing is that you just killed the old woman. And you invented another theory, so maybe even a hundred million times uglier thing to do! Even God can not thank; As you know, maybe you God for that and sorry. Do you have a big heart to be less fearful. High performance is forthcoming scary? No, it's a shame a coward. Kohli made such a move, so be brave. Here justice. Here carry me, that's right. I know you do not believe, and by golly, the life force. Himself after slyubitsya. You now only need air, air, air!

Raskolnikov shuddered.

- Yes, it's who you are - he said - that you are a prophet? From the height of this majestic tranquility you me premudrstvuyuschie utters prophecies?

ROBOTS READ

- Who I am? I pokonchenny people, not more. A person may be feeling and compassion, perhaps, Coy and who knows what, but it's completely finished. And you - another article: God has prepared you for life (and who knows, maybe you have so only the smoke passes, nothing will). Well, you are in a different category of people will pass? Comfort is not a pity that you do something, something with your heart? Well, you can be too long no one sees? No matter the time, and in fact you are. Become the sun, and all that you see. The sun should be primarily the sun. Why are you smiling again: I'm such a Schiller? And I'm sure I had podolschayus you now! And then, maybe, actually podolschayus, heh, heh, heh! You tell me, Rodion Romanovitch word something, perhaps, and I do not believe, perhaps even do not believe - so my character, I agree; Only now add that, as far as I lower face, and I honestly seems to be able to judge!

- Do you think that when I was arrested?

- Yes, a day or two and a half Ali can still give you a ride. Just think, my dear, pray to God at this. Yes, and cheaper, by golly, it is advantageous.

- But what if I run? - In a strange smile, asked Raskolnikov.

- No, do not run away. The guy runs away to escape sectarian fashion - the waiter thought that someone - because it is only the tip of the finger, to show how the midshipman of the hole so that it is for life whatever you want to believe. And you do not, your theory no longer believe - that you ran away? And then you run away? In the future, it is difficult and unpleasant, you should first of all life and situation specific, air, respectively; Well, if your air? . Escape the gates themselves without us, you can not do. I and ambush you in jail lock - well, a month, well, two, maybe three to sit, and then all of a sudden, and, mark my words, he will be as well, and as perhaps and very unexpectedly. Themselves more than an hour will not know what will come of guilt. I even here'm, that you are "suffering managed to take"; me your word that you do not believe me now, and themselves at the bus stop. Because suffering, Rodion Romanovitch a great thing; You are not looking at the fact that I do not otolstel, do not need to, but I know; do not laugh at this, in suffering an idea.Mikolka something right. No, do not run away, Rodion Romanovitch.

Raskolnikov got up and took his cap. Porfiry Petrovitch also rose.

- Walk going? The evening will be something good, but the storm would not be here. And yet, and better, if only updated ...

He also took his cap.

- You, Porfiry Petrovich, please do not take the head - with the harsh insistence said Raskolnikov, - I confessed to you segodnya.Vy, people, countries, and I listened to you from curiosity.And I have nothing confessed ... remember this.

- Oh, yes, I know, remember - ish, because even trembling. Do not worry, my dear; Thy will be done. Walk a little; just too much, you can not walk. In any case, I have and still you prosbitsa, - he added, lowering his voice - it schekotlivenkaya and important: if, that is, just in case (which, however, I do not believe, and I believe that you have to be completely incapable), if the case - well, just in case - you will come to hunt in forty to fifty hours somehow to fight different way to go - this is the way to treat yourself to raise the (ridiculous assumption, but oh, how I forgive you this), leave a brief but careful attention. Thus, these two lines, only two strochechki, and in the stone a mention: Noble will, sir. Well, good-bye ... Good thoughts, good beginnings!

Porfiry went out, somehow bent, as if not to look at Raskolnikov. Raskolnikov went to the window and waited with irritable impatience, when, on the calculation, which will be released on the street and leave.Then ran out of the room.

<«»>

⤙ CHAPTER III ⤚

He took the time to Svidrigailov.What he could have hoped for from this man - he did not know. But this man was hiding some power over him. Aware that time, he could not calm down, and now the same thing, and it's time.

Dear one question especially tormented him was Svidrigailov Porphyry?

How could he say and what he swore, - no, not there! He thought again and again recalled all visits porphyria, realized there was not, of course, it was not!

But if you have not already, you will or will not do this to Porfiry?

Now, at the moment it seemed to him that would not work. How so? He could not explain it, but even if I could explain, but now he will not be on this particular puzzle. All this tormented him, and at the same time he was somehow not up to etogo.Stranno say, but no one can be, would not have believed, but his immediate fate, he somehow weak, absent-mindedly concerned. He was tormented by something else, much more importantly, the state of emergency - it is about, not about those who have, but something else, something important.Besides, he felt boundless moral fatigue, though his mind this morning worked better than in their last days.

And worth eh now, after all that has happened, try to win all these new challenges miserable? As soon as Mademoiselle, for example, try to intrigue, to Svidrigailov did not go to Porfiry; explore, learn, spend time on some Svidrigailov!

Oh, how he was tired of it all!

And yet he still was in a hurry to Svidrigailov; I do not expect it something from him new instructions, the solution? And at straws, because there

is not enough! No luck eh, not instinct brings whether what they together? Maybe it was just fatigue, despair, I may not Svidrigailov but someone else, and the only way Svidrigailov got here. Sonya? And why is he now went to Sonia? Again, ask her tears? Yes, and he was afraid, Sonia. Sonia was an uncompromising verdict, decision unchanged. Here - or her way, or. Especially at a time he was unable to see her. No, better to try Svidrigailov What is this? And he could not admit it really is something that has long been, as it was necessary.

Well, however, that may be common between them? Even evil can not be the same from them. This man is very, moreover, it was unpleasant, obviously very dissolute, certainly cunning and deceptive, can be very angry. About him to go to such stories. Nevertheless, he sought for the children of Katerina Ivanovna; but who knows what, and what does it mean? This person always has some intentions and projects.

Flashed continuously during all these days Raskolnikov another thought and terribly worried about him, even though he tried to chase it away, so it was hard for him! He sometimes thought: Svidrigailov everything revolves around him, and now it turns out; Svidrigailov knew his secret; Svidrigailov has designs on Dunya.And if they now have? Almost certainly we can say that , yes. And if now, having learned his secret and thus gain power over him, he wants to use it as a weapon against Dunya?

This idea sometimes, even in sleep, tormented him, but for the first time appeared to him to consciously bright as now, when it came to Svidrigailov. The idea that led him into a dark rage. Firstly, even if that something will change, even in his own position, he should immediately reveal the secret Dunya. It should, perhaps, force yourself to be distracted from Dunya any misstep. Letter? This morning Dounia received some letter! From St. Petersburg, she could get the letter? (Luzhin Really?) But Razumikhin guards; Razumikhin, but does not know anything. Perhaps we need to open and Razumikhin? Raskolnikov thought with disgust about this.

"In any case, we must see Svidrigailov as soon as possible - he thought to himself, finally - thank God, it is not necessary items, such as the merits ;. But if, if only he is capable, if Svidrigailov something intriguing against Dunya - then ... "

Raskolnikov before tired after all this time, for the entire month, that he could not deal with such matters now anyway, as only one solution: "Then I'll kill him," - he thought in cold feeling squeezed his despair.Heavy heart;

ROBOTS READ

He stopped in the middle of the street and began to look around: how it goes and where it went? He was on - skom Avenue, a few steps in thirty or forty Haymarket, which was held. The entire second floor of the house to the left was busy restaurant. All the windows were wide open; Pool, in accordance with moving figures in windows, was packed. In the hall shed singers, called the clarinet, violin and thunderous bass drum.Women's screams could be heard. He wanted to go back, wondering why he turned --sky Avenue, when suddenly, at one extreme otvorennyh windows of the restaurant, I saw, sitting at the window, at the tea table, with a pipe in his mouth, Svidrigailov. It's scary to the horror hit him. Svidrigailov observed and examined it in silence and that too immediately struck Raskolnikov seems to get up to catch the sly leave until he was spotted. Raskolnikov immediately pretended as if he did not notice it and looks deep in thought, to the side, and he continued to follow his corner of his eye. His heart was beating anxiously. That's right: Svidrigailov obviously do not want to be seen. He took the phone from his lips, and was going to hide; but standing up and pushing back his chair, probably suddenly noticed that Raskolnikov sees and watches. Between them there was something like a scene of their first meeting at Raskolnikov, during sleep. Sly smile appeared on his face Svidrigailov and more extended. They both knew what to see and watch each other. Finally Svidrigailov laughed out loud.

- Well, well! come too, if you like; here i am! - He shouted out the window. Raskolnikov went to the hotel.

He found him in a very small back room with one window, adjacent to the great room, where a table for twenty desperate cries songbirds, drinking tea merchants, officials and all the people. Somewhere heard the sound of balls billiards. On the table in front of Svidrigailov stood an open bottle of champagne and a glass half full of wine. The room was still a boy organ-grinder, with a small hand organ, and a healthy, rosy-cheeked girl in a striped skirt and belly in a Tyrolean hat with ribbons, singer, eighteen years old, that despite the choral song to another room, singing to the accompaniment of a rather hoarse organschika contralto, some lackey song ...

- So beautiful! - Cut her off at the entrance Svidrigailov Raskolnikov.

The girl immediately stopped and stood in respectful expectation. She sang her rhymes lakeyschinu also with some serious and respectful person in the shade.

- Hey, Philip, a glass! - Shouted Svidrigailov.
- I will not drink wine - said Raskolnikov.

- As you wish, I'm not for you. Drink, Kate! Today, nothing else is needed, come on! - He poured her a glass of wine and put a small yellow ticket. Katya drank a glass of time, as women drink wine, it does not stop, twenty sips, bought a ticket, kissed Svidrigailov's hand, which he very seriously committed to kiss, and left the room, and behind him and pulled the boy from the body. Both of them were taken from the street.Svidrigailov weeks and lived in St. Petersburg, and it was all about him at some patriarchal leg. Inn waiter, Philip, too, was already "familiar" and podobostrastnichal. The door was locked; Svidrigailov in the room was at home and had it, perhaps in a few days. The restaurant was dirty, trashy and not even mediocre.

- I come to you, and you were looking for - began Raskolnikov - but why now I suddenly turn on - English prospectus with the hay! I never fail to get here, and I do not come. I turn to the right with Senna. And the way you are. Rotation only, here you! This is strange!

- Why do not you just say it's a miracle!

- Because it is, perhaps, just in case.

- After some time all these people! - Svidrigailov laughed - not recognized, even though the inside and believed in a miracle! After much yourself say that "maybe" just in case. And what about all cowards his own opinion, you can not imagine, Rodion Romanovitch! I do not mean you. Do you have your own opinion and is not afraid to have it. Meanwhile, you and enticed my curiosity.

- More than anything else?

- Yes, and this fact is sufficient.

Svidrigaïlov was evident in the excited state, but only a droplet; wine he drank half a cup and nothing more.

- I think you come to me before know that I can have what you call my own opinion, - said Raskolnikov.

- Well, then, is another matter. We all have our steps. And lo and behold I say to you that you seem to be these last two or three days sleeping. I tell you this himself appointed restaurant and there is no miracle was not that you just came; He explained all the way, said the place where he stands and looks in which you can catch me here. Remember?

- I forgot - responded with surprise Raskolnikov.

- I believe. I told you twice. Address minted in your memory mechanically. You turned here and mechanically, and more strictly to the address without knowing it. I say something to you, then there is no hope that you

understand me. Very you say that, Rodion Romanych.Da, that's another thing: I am convinced that a lot of people in St. Petersburg, Walking, talk to themselves. This half-mad city. If we had a science, doctors, lawyers and philosophers could do extensive research over Petersburg, each in their specialty. Rarely where so many gloomy, sharp and strange effects on the human soul, as St. Peterburge.Kakie climatic effect!Meanwhile, the administrative center of the whole of Russia, and his character should be reflected at all. But this is not so, and I have repeatedly looked at you sideways. You leave the house - still keep my head straight.With its twenty steps you go down, hands folded. You look, and apparently, neither before nor on the sides have not see anything. Finally, begin to move lips and say to yourself, sometimes you let go of his hand and read, finally, to stop in the middle of the road for a long time. That's too bad, sir. Maybe you are someone and notices but me, and even it is not profitable. I, in fact, all the same, and I can not be cured, but of course you know what I mean.

- Did you know that for me next? - Raskolnikov asked, looking at him curiously.

- No, I do not know - as if in surprise Svidrigailov replied.

- Well, then leave me alone - frowned and muttered Raskolnikov.

- Well, we'll leave you alone.

- Tell me, if you come here to drink himself to me was administered two times that I have come here, why are you now when I looked out the window from the street, hiding and wanted to leave? I noticed it very well.

- Heh, heh, heh! And why did you, when I stood in the doorway, lying on the couch with her eyes closed and pretended to sleep, you do not sleep? I noticed it very well.

- I could ... reasons ... you know it yourself.

- And I could have my reasons, even if you have not learned.

Raskolnikov dropped his right elbow on the table, propped his right hand under his chin and looked at Svidrigailov. He thought his face, which always struck him before. It was a strange face, like a mask, such as: white, pink, pink, red lips, with light-brown beard and a fairly thick blond hair yet. His eyes were too blue, and look at them as something too heavy and immobile. Something was terribly uncomfortable in this beautiful and very young, judging by his years, his face. Clothing Svidrigailov was a dandy, summery, easy, in particular, he was wearing underwear. On his finger was a huge ring with expensive stone.

- Yeah, same for me, and you still have to mess around too - said Raskolnikov, going with a convulsive look directly into the open - although you can be the most dangerous man, if you want to hurt, but I do not want break yourself more. I'll show you right now that this is not so cherish one another, as you probably think.You know, I come to you only say that if you keep it original intention of my sister, and if he thought nothing of use, which is open late, I'll kill you before you plant me in jail. My word is true: you know that I'll be able to keep it. Secondly, if you want me to say something - because I do it all the time, it seemed as if you want me to say something - something to announce soon, because time is expensive and can be very soon will be too late.

- Yes, this is where you are in such a hurry? - Asked Svidrigailov, looking at him curiously.

- We all have our steps - grimly and said impatiently Raskolnikov.

- You are now called to be frank, and to the first question and refuse to answer - said Svidrigailov with a smile. - Do you still think that I have some goals and, therefore, looking at me with suspicion. Well, it is quite clear in your polozhenii.No no matter how much I wanted to get together with you, I did not bother to disabuse you of the contrary. Honestly, the game is not worth the trouble and tell you something about something I did not intend such a feature.

- Why am I so, then you need? In the end, you took care of me?

- Yes, just as a curious thing to observe. I liked you a fantastic nature of your position - that's it! Also, you brother lady that I was very interested, and, finally, the man at the time I was an awful lot, and often heard of you, where did they come to the conclusion that you have a great influence on her; is not that enough? Heh-heh-heh! However, I must admit that your question is very difficult for me, and I was hard on him to answer you. Well, for example, because you went to me is not enough that the case, but for something new? Is not it?Is not it? - Insisted Svidrigailov fraudulent smile - well, imagine yourself well, then, I did something else Ehav here in the car, you also expressed the hope that you also tell me something new , and you should do the same I will be able to borrow something! This is what we are rich!

- What is it borrowed?

- What can I say? Did I know what? See in which traktirishke sit all the time, and it is the content of my heart, it's not something to enjoy, and it is necessary to sit down somewhere. Well, at least this poor Katya - see? .. Well,

ROBOTS READ

I would, for example, even a glutton, club deli, and that in fact this is what I have! (He pointed to the corner where on a small table, on a tin plate, were the remnants of a terrible steak with potatoes). By the way, you had dinner? I eat and do not want to. Wine, for example, do not drink. Except champagne, no, yes and champagne all night on the glass, and then a headache. This I now set, ordered to bring, because I'm going somewhere, and you will see me in a special mood. Because I'm just now and hid like a schoolboy, I thought you stop me; but it seems to me (he took out his watch), I can spend an hour with you; now half pyatogo.Poverte, at least there was something; Well, the owner to be, well, my father, well, Ulan, photographer, journalist ... n-nothing, no special! Sometimes even boring. Right, I thought you told me something new.

- Who are you and why are you here?

- I am who? You know ,: nobleman, served two years in the cavalry, and then just hang around here in Petersburg, then married Marfa Petrovna and lived in the village. Here is my biography!

- You seem to be a player?

- No, what I player. Schuler - not a player.

- You were sharper?

- Yes, it was sharper.

- Well, you beat?

- Boxes. So what?

- Well, then, can duel ... and indeed, alive.

- Do not contradict you, and that not philosophize mastering. I confess to you, I'm here more women came quickly.

- Only that buried Marfa Petrovna?

- Yes, - smiled frankly wins Svidrigailov. - So what? You seem to find anything wrong, I'm talking about women like that?

- I mean, I feel bad or not corruption?

- In the debauchery! Well, where are you! And yet, in order to respond to you before about women in general; I know what he says. Tell me what I'm going to restrain themselves? Why women leave, if I ever have a hunter? At least activity.

- So you're here only one debauchery and hope?

- Well, well, well, and debauchery! They were given the debauchery. Yes love, at least, a direct question. In this spot, at least, something permanent, even based on the nature and may not be fancy, it kindled charcoal perpetual

blood abides forever igniter, and that for a long time, and over the years, maybe not so soon zalesh .You must recognize that this activity of its kind?

- What is there to be happy? This disease, and dangerous.

- And that's where you are! I agree that it is a disease, like all passing through the measure - and, of course, have to go through a measure - but it is, firstly, to one side, the other way, and secondly, of course, in all hold the measure calculation, though vile, but what do you do? Without it, because in this way, to shoot, will likely have. I agree that an honest man should be boring, but back then, but ...

- And you could shoot?

- Here you go! - Aversion said Svidrigailov - do me a favor, do not talk about it, - he added hastily, and even without boasting, which showed in all his previous words. Even his face seemed to have changed. - Recognize fatal weakness, but what I am afraid of death and do not like to talk about it. You know, I kind of mystic?

- Ah! ghosts Marfa Petrovna! Well, let's go on?

- Well, they do not think; St. Petersburg was not yet; To hell with them! - He exclaimed with some annoying.- No, let's about it ... yes, indeed ... Hmm! Eh, a little time, I can not stay with you for a long time, it is a pity!It will say something.

- And what have you, woman?

- Yes, a woman, as an unintended one case ... No, I do not mean that.

- Well, this whole situation is an abomination to you is no longer valid? Already lost the power to stop?

- And you, and the power of the application? Heh-heh-heh! You are surprised me, Rodion Romanovitch, even though I knew beforehand that it would be so. You're talking about me depravity and aesthetics! You - Schiller, you - an idealist! All this, of course, as it should be, and should be surprised if it were otherwise, but, nevertheless, somehow still very strange ... Oh, sorry, that time is short, because you are exposed to prelyubopytny! And by the way, do you like Schiller? I'm awfully fond of.

- But you, however, braggart! - With some disgust said Raskolnikov.

- Well, by God, no! - Svidrigailov replied, laughing - and, by the way, do not argue, even a braggart; but then why not pofanfaronit, when it is safe. I spent seven years in a village near Marfa Petrovna, but because now attacking intelligent man like you - for smart and very curious, very happy to communicate, and, in addition, they drank half a glass of wine and have

at least kakuyu- mind amazed. And most importantly, there is one thing I really mount, but I keep silence .... Where are you going? - With fright suddenly asked Svidrigailov.

Raskolnikov began to rise. To make it difficult, and stuffy, and somehow embarrassed that he came here. In Svidrigailov he found in an empty and useless villain in the world.

- Oh-oh! Sit, stay, - pleaded Svidrigailov - yes tell them to make themselves even tea. Sit Well, I will not talk about himself, that is. I'll tell you something. Well, I'll tell you, I was a woman, let your style, "saved"? It will even answer your first question, because this person - your sister. You can tell? Yes, and kill time.

- Say, but I hope you ...

- Oh, do not worry! In addition, Avdotya Romanovna, even in such a bad and let a man as I can inspire just one deepest respect.

←« CHAPTER IV »→

- You know, it may be (yes, indeed, I told you I) - are Svidrigailov - I'm sitting here in prison for the huge amount of the debtor, and not having the slightest means to pay for it. There's no need for this, as I later bought Marfa Petrovna; You know the extent to which a woman can sometimes madness to love? It was an honest woman, and very reasonable (although completely uneducated) .Would you think that this is a very honest and jealous woman decided later, after many scenes of hysterics and reproaches for some contract with me, who sang all the time in our marriage. The fact that she was much older than I am, moreover, always wore a slice of mouth or something. I had so many disgusting in my heart and a kind of honesty to tell her straight out that absolutely faithful to her, I can not be. This rec-ognition led her into a frenzy, but it seems that my brutal frankness of her somehow, like, "Well, he said he does not want to cheat, if in advance, says:" - well, for a jealous woman is the first vesch.Posle many tears an unwritten contract between us: first, I will never leave Marfa Petrovna and always will be her husband, and secondly, without her permission may be separated in any place; Thirdly, constant mistress ever; Fourthly, this Martha Petrovna gave me sometimes hay girls, but not only with her secret knowledge; Fifth, God forbid that I loved a woman in our class; Sixth, in case, God forbid, I will attend any passion, and most seriously, I have to show it to Marfa Petrovna. On this last Marfa Petrovna was, however, kept quiet; It was a smart woman, and therefore she could not help looking at me like slutty wasteful unable to true love can not. But an intelligent woman and a jealous woman - two very different things, and it's just the trouble. However, judging impartially

about some people must renounce certain preconceived opinions and every-day habits of ordinary people about us and objects. Your judgment, more than anyone, 'I have a right to expect. Maybe you have already heard a lot about Marfa Petrovna was ridiculous and absurd. Indeed, there were some very funny ways; but I tell you frankly that I sincerely apologize for the numer-ous ills that I was the cause. Well enough, I think, for a very decent Oraison funÃ¨bre [Praise (fr.).] tender wife tender husband. When we quarreled, I, for the most part, quiet and non-irritating, and it is almost always dzhen-telmennichane reached the goal; it affected her, and she even liked it;there were times that she was proud of me even. But your sister has not done. And how is it that she ventured to take such a beautiful creature in his house as a governess! I explain that Marfa Petrovna was an ardent and impres-sionable woman and that just simply fell in love with herself - literally fell in love - with your sister. Well, yes and Avdotya Romanovna something! I understand very well at first glance that it was bad, and - what do you think? - Decided not to look at her. But Avdotya Romanovna herself took the first step - believe it or not? Do you believe, too, that Marfa Petrovna got to the point that even angry with me first for my persistent silence about her sister, because I did not care for her constant admiring praise Avdotya Romanovna? I do not understand what she wanted! And, of course, Marfa Petrovna told Avdotya Romanovna me the whole story. She had the unfortunate habit of telling everyone all our family secrets and continually complaining of me; as you can skip this new and wonderful friend? I believe that they have a conversation, and there was no way for me, and, of course, without a doubt, Avdotya Romanovna learned all these dark, mysterious tales that I attribute ... I bet you do that -So in this case, too, heard?

- Heard. Luzhin accused you that you were even the cause of death of the child. Is this true?

- Do me a favor, leave it alone vulgarity - disgust and exasperation pleaded Svidrigailov - so if you want to know about all this nonsense I ever tell you otherwise, but now ...

- Speaking about some footman in your village, and that if you were also the cause of something.

- Do me a favor, enough! - Interrupted again impatiently Svidrigailov.

- This is not the waiter that you have come after the death of the pipe to fill ... more themselves told me? - Irritating increasingly Raskolnikov.

Svidrigailov looked at Raskolnikov, and flashed in his eyes that moment,

like lightning, evil grin, but Svidrigailov kept and very politely said:

- It's the same thing. I see that you, too, all very interested and mail for the debt, at the first opportunity, on all counts, to satisfy their curiosity. Damn It! I see that really seems to someone face romantic. Judge the extent to which I have to thank the deceased after Marfa Petrovna for what she was talking to my sister about me, as a mysterious and curious. I do not dare to judge the impression; but in any case, it was useful to me. With all the natural aversion to me Avdotya Romanovna and despite my usual dark and repulsive appearance - she felt sorry for me, finally, sorry missing person. And when the girl's heart would be a pity, then, so, of course, is simply too dangerous for her. Here it is, and they want to "save", and feelings, and rose, and called for more noble goals, and to revive a new life and work - well, we know that you can namechtat so. I immediately realized that the bird flies in the network itself, and, in turn, is ready. You seem to be frowning, Rodion Romanovitch? Not at all the case, as you know, did not do anything. (Gosh, how much I drink wine!) You know, I've always wanted from the beginning, that fate has not given birth to his sister in the second or third century AD, somewhere daughter sovereign prince, and whether there is a governor or proconsul in Asia Minor. This, no doubt, would have been one of those who suffered martyrdom, and, of course, will smile when her chest was burning red-hot pincers. She would have gone to that end, and in the fourth and fifth centuries have left in the Egyptian desert and would have lived there for thirty years, living on roots, ecstasies and visions. She was just what he craves and demands that for someone to any meal as soon as possible to take and not give her the food, so maybe a window. I heard something about a gentleman Razumikhin. It is small, say, a moderate (as indicated by its name, a seminarian should be), well let and protects your sister. In general, I think I figured it out, and I think that the very honor. But then, that is at the beginning of dating, you know, there's always something reckless and stupid, you look so not what you see. Damn it, why is it so good? I do not blame! In short, I started with the most compelling sensory impulse. Avdotya Romanovna awfully chaste, incredibly and phenomenally. (Please note, I tell you this about your sister as a fact. It is chaste, perhaps, disease, despite her broad intelligence, and it hurt her). Here we had one girl Paracha, Paracha eyed, fresh from another village, hay girl, and I've never seen before - a very beautiful, but incredibly stupid: in tears, howled the whole yard, and there was a scandal. One day, after dinner, Avdotya Romanovna purposely

find me one in an alley in the garden and with flashing eyes demanded of me that I should leave the poor Parasha alone. It was almost the first two of our conversation. Of course, I thought it was an honor to meet her wishes, trying to pretend to be overwhelmed, confused, well, played the role of bad. Start chat, mysterious conversations, sermons, teachings, prayers, umalivaniya even tears - would you believe it, even tears! Such is the power coming from the other girls passion for propaganda! I, of course, all the blame on his fate, pretended to hunger and thirst of light and, finally, even the most progress and stable means to win a woman's heart, means that no one would ever cheat and that acts decisively on each one, without any exceptions. This tool is known - flattery. There's nothing in the world more difficult directness, and there is nothing easier than lest.Esli only one simple one-hundredth of counterfeit notes, dissonance occurs immediately, and after him - the scandal. If flattery, even until the last notes of all false, then it nice and listened, not without pleasure; albeit with coarse pleasure, but still fun. And no matter how tough it was flattery, it is sure, at least half seems right. And this is for all the events and walks of life. Even virgin can be seduced by flattery. But there is nothing ordinary people and say nothing. Without laughter can not afford to remember how I once seduced one devoted to her husband, children and her virtues, her mistress. How fun it was and how little work! The lady was very virtuous, at least in their own way. My whole strategy was that I was just crushed every minute and fell in front of her chastity. I shamelessly flattered, and only then, that I managed to get a handshake, even a glance, reproach myself that it was I tore it out of her power, she resisted, she resisted, so I probably never would have got if I had was not so wicked; that she, in her innocence, did not foresee the hype and succumbed accident, that not knowing, not knowing, and so on, and so on. In short, I achieved everything, and my lady was very sure that she is innocent and chaste and performs all debts and liabilities, and died unexpectedly. And how did she get mad at me when I told her, in the end, that is, in my sincere conviction, he was just looking for fun as I did. Poor Marfa Petrovna too awful to succumb to flattery, and if I just wanted to, of course, wrote her estate would all be over in her lifetime. (However, I have a lot of drinking wine and chatting). I hope that you will not be angry if I mention now that the same effect began to come true and Avdotya Romanovna. Yes, I did was stupid and impatient and spoiled the whole thing. Avdotya Romanovna several times before (and as soon as something especially) really hate the look of my mind, if you believe

in it? In short, they are stronger and accidentally broke some fire that frightened her, and she finally began to hate. Needless to tell the details, but we parted. And here I was stupid. Let openly make fun of all these propaganda and appeals; Paracha again appear on the scene, and this is not one - in a word, started an uproar. Oh, if you saw Rodion Romanovitch, once in your life in your sister's eyes, as they can sometimes shine! It's nothing that I have now drunk, and now a glass of wine drunk, I'm telling the truth; I assure you that this view I have dreamed; the rustle of her dress, I finally could not stand it. Right, I thought it was made by me with epilepsy; I never thought that I could come to such a frenzy. In short, it was necessary to make peace; but it was impossible. And imagine what I did then? To what extent is the stupidity of rabies can lead a man! Never take anything in a rage, Rodion Romanovitch. Hoping that Avdotya Romanovna, in fact, like a beggar (oh, sorry, I do not like it ... but does it really matter if expressed the same concept?) In short, living works of their hands, that its content and mother and you (oh, hell, frowning again ...), I decided to offer her all my money (up to thirty thousand, and then I was able to carry out) the fact that she ran with me even here in St. Petersburg. Of course, I would have sworn eternal love, bliss and so on, and so on. Believe me, I ran before, she told me, slaughter or poison Marfa Petrovna and marry me - it will be done immediately! But all ended in disaster, you know, and can judge whether rabies could I go, to find out what Marfa Petrovna then took the most terrible of this order, Luzhin and almost unique wedding - is, in fact, it would be something Same thing, as I suggested. Right? Right? Is not it? I noticed that you have something listened very carefully ... interesting young man ...

Svidrigailov impatiently pounded his fist on the table. He blushed. Raskolnikov saw clearly that a glass of champagne and two times that he drank, sipped almost unconsciously affected him painfully - and decided to take the opportunity. Svidrigailov was very suspicious of him.

- Well, after I fully believe that you came here, referring to my sister - he said Svidrigailov directly and openly, to annoy him even more.

- Oh, completeness, - and if I had caught myself Svidrigailov - I tell you ... and besides, your sister can not stand me.

- Yes, it is, and I am convinced that he can not, but it is not.

- Do you believe that he can not? (Svidrigailov narrowed his eyes and smiled ironically). You're right, she does not love me; but never charged in the affairs of the former between husband and wife or lover and mistress.

ROBOTS READ

There is always a corner that is always around the world remains unknown and known only to them two. You represent that Avdotya Romanovna at me with disgust watching?

- According to some words in your during your story, I notice that you are now his views and intentions to save more Dunya course lousy.

- How! I ran the following words and phrases? - Prenaivno Svidrigailov suddenly frightened, not paying any attention to the epithet bestowed on his designs.

- Yes, they have pulled out now. Well, what do you like so afraid of? What are you so afraid of now?

- I'm afraid and scared? Afraid of you? Chances are you afraid of me, Cher Ami. [(. FR). Dear friend] What, however, the game ... And yet, I ohmelel, I see it; almost blurted again.To hell with wine! Hey, the water!

He grabbed the bottle and unceremoniously thrown out the window. Philip brought the water.

- It's all nonsense, - said Svidrigailov, wetting a towel and put it to his head - and I'm one word can break all your suspicions to dust wipe. Oh, you know, for example, that I'm getting married?

- Have you talked to me before.

- I can tell? Forgot. But then I could not say yes, because even the bride has not seen; I just wanted to. Well, now I really have a bride, and the deed is done, and if it's just not put off, I would certainly take you to see them at once - because I want to ask your advice. Hey, you devil! Only ten minutes from the end. See, look at the clock; And yet, I tell you, because it's an interesting story, my marriage is something in its own way - where are you? Again go?

- No, I will not go now.

- Just can not get away? Let'S See! I'll take you there, however, show the bride, but not now, and now you will soon be time to go. You're right, I'm gone. You know, it Resslih? It is Resslih, which I now live - and? Do you hear? No, what do you think, here, about which they say that the girl was something in the water, in the winter, and then - well, can you hear it hear? Well, she told me all this up; You said something so boring, entertaining time. And I'm gloomy, depressed person. What do you think jolly? No, grim: do no harm, and sit in the corner; sometimes three days, without saying a word. Resslih this rascal, I tell you this because it keeps the mind: I'm bored wife throw and go, while his wife goes to her, it's her and put into circulation; This layer, i.e., so above. Yes, says one such relaxed father, a retired officer,

sitting in a chair, and the third year of the feet are not moving. Yes, says the mother, intelligent lady, the mother of something.Son somewhere in the province does not help.

Daughter got married and did not visit, and at the hands of two young nephew (his little), but without completing the course, the girl from school, their youngest daughter, only sixteen month, a month and it is possible to question. This is for me something. We went; since they have a ridiculous; Introducing: the landowner, a widower, well-known names, such compounds, the capital - well, that I am fifty and she is not sixteen? Who looks at it? But it's interesting, is not it? In the end, it's tempting, ha ha! You should have seen how I talked with my dad so with his mother! It is necessary to pay just to see me at this time. Turns out she crouches, well you can imagine, even in a short dress, unopened bud flushing in the morning (they said it, of course). I do not know how you feel about a woman's face, but, in my opinion, these sixteen years, these children's eyes, tears of shame and shyness - In my opin- ion, it is better than beauty, and she must teach and images. Svetlenkie hair and lamb lokonchiki whipped, full lips, red, legs - lovely! .. Well, first met, I announced that in a hurry for family reasons, and the next day, the third day, that is, and has blessed us. So come, so now her lap, and so it does not come down ... Well, break forth as the morning, and I kiss every minute; mother, of course, assume that it is, say, your husband, and it is required, in a word, raspberries! And this state of modern law of the groom, it may be better in marriage. There is what is called La la nature et al Rita vÃ © ©! [nature and the truth (fr.).] Ha ha! I told her twice - which is not a stupid girl; sometimes it stole glances at me - azhno will burn. And you know, her face as Madonna by Raphael. In the end, the Sistine Madonna fantastic person, his face mourn- ful religious ecstasy are not caught my eye? Well, in this case. Only that we are blessed, I the next day and a half thousand bought her a diamond dress together so pearly silver dressing box - is as big with all kinds of things, so that even her face shone with my Madonna. Yesterday I sat on my knees, and I think rather too cavalierly - blushed and began to shed tears, but she did not want it to light up the whole. All gone for a minute, as we had stayed there alone, she suddenly flung open at the neck (the first time), embraces me with both hands, kissing and swears that she will be obedient, faithful, and good wife, she would make me happy, that devote all his life, every minute of his life, all, donate, and for all that he wants me to just one of my respect and over I said, "Nothing, nothing, no gifts!" You have to admit that he had

heard nothing of such confessions from the angel of sixteen, in muslin dress with whipped lokonchikami, with a blush of shame and the Virgin with tears of delight in his eyes - have to admit that it's pretty tempting zamanchivo. Posle? After all, what it takes, eh? Well, because it will cost? Well ... well ... well, listen, let's move on to my fiancee ... not now!

- In short, this monstrous difference in age and development, and excites your sensuality! And you really can make such a marriage?

- And then what? Sure. Everyone thinks of himself, and all the more fun and alive, who knows best how to deceive himself. Haha! What are you, in effect, it is so eager about? Why, sir, I am a sinful man. Heh-heh-heh!

- But you have children of Katerina Ivanovna. But ... well, you had your reasons ... I now understand everything.

- I love children, I love children - laughed Svidrigailov. - At the moment I can not even tell you one interesting episode, which is still ongoing. The first day I came here, I visited various haunts, well, after seven years and nabrosilsya.Vy probably noticed that I have my own company was in no hurry to meet with old friends and acquaintances. Well, as long as possible and without interruption. You know, Martha P. country, I was tortured memories of all these mysterious places and places where, who knows, he may find much. Damn! Drunk people, educated young people from inactivity burns in unfulfilled dreams and reveries, mutilated theories ; Jews came and accumulate money, and everything else debauchery. I got a dance called the evening - Cloaca awful (and I love it cloaca gryaznottsoy), well, of course, can-can, and some do not have any at the time, and it was not. Yes, sir, in this progress. Suddenly, look, girl, thirteen, bonuses dressed, dancing with a virtuoso; Other front of their colleagues. In the same wall sits on a chair at her mother. Well, you can imagine that the cancan! Girl embarrassed blushes finally takes his offense and began to cry. Virtuoso catches it and starts to twirl and pose in front of her, all around and laugh - I love these moments in our audience, even if the cancan - laughing and shouting: "And this, so it is, but do not take the kids!!" Well, I do not care about something, and do not care: it is logical al illogical they comfort themselves! I once had my plan, sat down to his mother and began by saying that I, too, a stranger, and here it is ignorant that I could not distinguish their advantages and nourish dostodolzhnogo respect; let it be known that I have a lot of money; invited to leave his carriage; driving home, he met (in some closet from tenants, just arrived). I announced that my friend, and she and her daughter can not take

as honor; I know that they have no house, no home, and have come to ask for something at some presence; We offer services, money; I know that they went to the evening the mistake of thinking that the real dance class; I offered to promote education of their young girls, French and dancing. Accept with enthusiasm, consider it an honor, and still sign ... Want to go - but not now.

- Enough of your vile, anecdotes, depraved, vile, sensual man!

You know, I purposely tell you what you need to hear your screams. Pleasure!

- Nevertheless, I made myself at this point is not that funny? - Angrily muttered Raskolnikov.

Svidrigailov laughed heartily; Finally, he called Philip, paid and started to grow.

- Well, yes, and I was drunk, Assez CAUSA ©! [and right (fr.)] - he said - enjoy!

- No wonder you do not feel pleasure - Raskolnikov cried, rising too - for issharkavshegosya Libertine talk about these adventures exception - with reference to some monstrous intention in the same way - not fun, and even under these circumstances, and such a person, like me ... Kindle.

- Well, if so - even with some surprise Svidrigailov Raskolnikov said, considering - if so, then you are honest cynic. The material at least has a huge. Can realize many, many ... Well, you do, and the fact that many can. Well, then, really. I sincerely regret that I spoke to you a little bit, but you can not get away from me ... That's just wait ...

Svidrigailov left the restaurant. Raskolnikov it. Svidrigailov was not, however, a lot of hops; in the head just for a moment struck, hops and go every minute. He was something very concerned about, something extremely important, and frowned. Some expectations seem to worried about it and worried. With Raskolnikov at the last minute he somehow suddenly changed in every moment becomes rough and mocking. Raskolnikov noticed all this and was in trouble. Svidrigailov became very suspicious of him; he decided to go after him.

Back down on the pavement.

- You are right, and left me, or maybe vice versa, just - forgive, Montplaisir, one joyful goodbye!

And he went straight to the Haymarket.

⇐«»⇒

←« CHAPTER V »→

Raskolnikov went after him.

\- This is it! - Svidrigailov exclaimed, turning - I seem to say ...

\- This means that now you will not go away.

\- What-oh-oh?

And stopped for a moment, and both looked at each other as if meryayas.

\- From all your half drunk stories - dramatically reduce Raskolnikov, - I concluded positively, you are not only left their dastardly plans for my sister, but even more than ever they are busy. I know that this morning my sister got some letter. All you could not sit still ... you think you can dig in the way of any woman; but it does not mean anything. I personally would like to make ...

Raskolnikov himself barely able to determine what it is like now, and what he wanted to make sure that he personally.

\- Here's how! And if you want, I will press the police?

\- Cry!

They stood for a moment with each other to retreat. Finally people Svidrigailov changed. Making sure that Raskolnikov was not afraid of threats, he suddenly took the most cheerful and friendly appearance.

\- It is a kind! I consciously about your business, you did not say, though of course I was tormented by curiosity. Case fantastic. Was postponed to another time, yes, of course, you can tease and dead ... Well, let's just say in advance: now only point home to grab the money; then lock the apartment, take a taxi and the whole evening on the island. Well, where are you me?

\- I'm currently in the apartment, and then not with you, but Sofya

Semyonovna, sorry, that was not at the funeral.

- This is the way you want, but Sofya Semyonovna not at home. She took all the children of a lady, a noble lady, old lady, my longtime friend and former mistress in some orphanages institutions. I am fascinated by this lady, making her the money for all three chicks Katerina Ivanovna, moreover, places and donated more money; finally told her the story of Sophia Semyonovna, even with all the honors, hiding nothing. The effect produced indescribable. That's why Sofya Semyonovna and had to appear today, right in the - th hotel where temporarily out of the country, there is my mistress.

- Requirements: No, I'll go all the same.

- As you wish, but I somehow wrong mate; I am! Here we are at home. For instance, in my opinion, because you look at me suspiciously, that I myself was so thin and still do not bother you with questions ... do you understand? You thought it was an amazing thing; I bet it is! Well, that and be sensitive after.

- And listen at the door!

- Oh, you mean it! - Laughed Svidrigailov, - yes, I would be surprised if, in the end, if you missed it without comment. Haha! I though something and realized from the fact that you then ... there ... and screwed Sofya Semyonovna told himself, but, nevertheless, what is it? Maybe I'm completely at a time, and nothing really I can not ponyat.Obyasnite, for God's sake, my dear!Enlighten the most modern principles.

- Nothing you could not hear everything that you're lying!

- Yes, I do not mean that it is not about (although I have, however, something and heard), no, I'm talking about the fact that you are all ohaete ohaete yes! Schiller, you hesitate a minute. And now at the door and listened. If so, click Yes, and declare to the authorities that here, they say, and it happened to me this incident: in the theory of small entry errors. If you are sure that you can not listen at the door, and you can starushonok luschit anything for your pleasure, so go somewhere in America as soon as possible! Flee, young man! Maybe there's still time. I sincerely say. Money or something, is not it? I will give way.

- I do not think about it - it was Raskolnikov interrupted with disgust.

- I understand (you, but do not worry, if you want, and do not say a lot); I understand that your question within: moral, or what? civil and human rights issues? And you poboku them; why they tell you something right now? Hehe! Then it's a citizen and a man? And if this is so, and do not put; There

is nothing that we do not shoot yourself berem.Nu; Al does not want that?

- You seem to be purposely want to tease me that I'm just now for you …

- Here's an eccentric, yes, we really came Welcome stairs. See, this is where the entrance to Sofia Semyonovna, look, not one! You do not believe me? Ask Kapernaumovs; it gives them a key.Here she herself Madame de Capernaum, huh? What? (She was a bit dull) gone? Where? Well, now you hear? There he is not up to the end, perhaps the evening. Well, now let me. In the end, you want to see me? Well, we at me. Madame Resslih not home. This woman is always in trouble, but a good woman, I assure you … Maybe it would be helpful for you if you were a little more reasonable.Well, if you see: I take five percent box office (now I have them many more!), and the money-changers from today poboku go. Well, you see? Over time, I lose nothing. Bureau locked, locked apartment, and we are again on the stairs. Well, want naymemte taxi! I'm on the island. You would not want to go? Here I take this stroller on Elagin that? Opt Out? Not survive? Prokatimtes not nothing. It seems that the rain is not nothing, after top …

Svidrigailov was already seated in a wheelchair. Raskolnikov decided that his suspicions, at least for the moment, are unfair. Without answering a word, he turned and walked back to the Haymarket. If he turned at once, dear, you had to see how Svidrigailov, after driving no more than a hundred paces, paid with a sidecar, and he was on the sidewalk. But he did not see and could go around the corner. Drew his deep aversion to Svidrigailov. "And I could at least for a moment expect something from this crude villain of this voluptuous profligate and a scoundrel!"- He cried involuntarily. It is true that the decision to Raskolnikov spoke too hastily and carelessly. There was in general a situation Svidrigajlova that at least gave him at least some of the original, if not enigmatic. With regard to all these sisters, then Raskolnikov was still probably convinced that Svidrigailov would not leave her alone. But too heavy and intolerable becomes to think and rethink!

As was his wont, he was the one in twenty steps into a deep reverie. Having ascended to the bridge, he stopped at the railing and looked at the water. Meanwhile over it was Avdotya Romanovna.

He met her at the entrance to the bridge, but it was without consideration. Dunya never met him in the street and was so struck by fear. She stopped and did not know: whether or not to call him Suddenly she noticed quickly fit the Haymarket Svidrigailov ?.

But he seemed to be approached carefully and mysterious. He went up to

the bridge and stopped on the roadside, on the sidewalk, trying by all means, that Raskolnikov had not seen. Dunya he saw and began to make his characters. It seemed to her that he signs it begged her not to scream brother and leave him alone, and called her to him.

So Dunja did. She walked slowly around his brother and close to Svidrigailov.

- Come quickly - Svidrigailov whispered to her. - I do not want to Rodion Romanovitch knew about this date. I warn you that I sat with him not very far from here, in the tavern, where he found me himself, and is unlikely to get rid of it. He knows the reason for my letter to you and suspects something. Oh, of course, you do not open it? And if not you, then who?

- Here we go again turned the corner - interrupted Dunya - now we will not see his brother. I declare to you that I will not go with you further. Tell me everything here; All that can be said on the street.

- First of all, he can not say, on the street; Secondly, you have to listen and Sofya Semyonovna; Third, I will show you some of the documents ... Well, finally, if you decide not to come to me, I refuse any explanation and immediately leave. At the same time, I ask you not to forget that a very curious secret of your beloved brother completely in my hands.

Dunya hesitated and piercing look at the Svidrigailov.

- What are you afraid! - Say good - the city is not a village. And in the village of harm more you tell me what I have, but here ...

- Sofia Semyonovna warned?

- No, I do not say a word to her, and not even quite sure whether it home? Nevertheless, likely at home. She buried her cousin today: not a day for guests to walk. Until the time when I did not want to talk about it, and even partly regret what you said. There is the slightest indiscretion already denunciation. I live here, here, in this house, here we come. This janitor of our house;janitor knows me very well; Thus, he bows; he sees that I'm going with the lady, and, of course, able to see your face, and it's good for you, if you are very afraid, and I suspect. Unfortunately, I was so rude. I myself live by tenants. Sofya Semyonovna lives with me, wall to wall, also from local residents. The entire floor of the driver and passengers. What are you afraid of as a child?Or am I really so very terrible?

Svidrigailov's face twisted into an indulgent smile; but he was not smiling. His heart and breathing Stukalo spiral chest. He spoke loudly on purpose to hide his growing excitement; Dunya, but did not have time to notice this

special excitement; too irritated her remark that she was afraid of him as a child, and he was afraid for her.

- Even if I know that you are a man without honor ... but I'm not afraid. Go ahead - she said, apparently calm, but her face was very pale.

Svidrigailov stopped in apartments Sony.

- Let the handle, whether at home. Nope. Disclaimer! But I know that she can come very soon. When she came out, it not only as a lady of his orphans. Their mother died. I also got involved and dispose of. If Sofya Semyonovna will not be back in ten minutes, I'll send it to you most of all if you want today; Well, this is my lucky number. Here are my two rooms. Behind the door is my mistress, Mrs. Resslih. Now, listen, I'll show you my main documents: from my bedroom here, this door leads to a completely empty two rooms that are for rent. Here they are ... that you need to look more carefully ...

Svidrigailov occupy two furnished rooms are quite spacious. Dunya incredulously looked around, but did not notice any decoration or arrangement of rooms, even if it could be seen that Coy, for example, that the apartment Svidrigailov comes as something between the two is almost uninhabited apartment. Sign in to it was not from the hallway, and two rented room is almost empty. From the bedroom as Svidrigailov otomknuv locked door with a key, showed Dunya too empty, to rent an apartment. Dunya was stopped at the door, not knowing what she was invited to watch, but Svidrigailov hastened with an explanation:

- Here, look here, in this second large room. Please note that the door was locked. Chair next to the door, only one chair in both rooms. I brought him out of his apartment, to make it easier to listen to. Oh, now the door table Sofya Semyonovna; There she sat and talked with Rodion Romanovitch. So I listened, sitting on a chair, two nights in a row, both times for two hours - and, of course, could not learn something, what do you think?

- You overheard?

- Yes, I heard ,; Now let me; here and get nowhere.

He led Avdotya Romanovna back to my first room that served as his room, and invited her to sit on a chair. He was sitting at the other end of the table, at least seven feet from her, but probably in his eyes already shone same flame that is as scary as Duns. She shivered and looked puzzled. Her gesture was involuntary; She apparently did not want to show distrust. But a secluded area apartment Svidrigailov finally hit her. She wanted to ask,

whether at home, at least, his mistress, but she did not ask ... pride. In addition, as a disproportionately greater suffering than fear for himself, was in her heart. She suffered intolerable.

- Here's your letter, - she said, putting it on the table. - Is it possible that you're writing? You allude to a crime committed by his brother, though. You too clearly implying you do not dare make excuses now. Know that I am before you heard about this silly tale, and I do not believe that one iota. It is disgusting and ridiculous suspicion. I know the story of how and why she invented.You can not have any evidence. You promised to prove that say the same thing! But know in advance that I do not believe you! Do not believe it! ..

Dunya says hurriedly, haste, and for a moment the color rushed to her face.

- If you do not believe, then maybe it's true that you dare come to me one? Why have you come? Out of curiosity?

- Do not torture me, talk, talk!

- It goes without saying that you are a brave girl. Frankly, I thought you were asking Mr. Razumikhin accompany you here. But neither you nor the terms that you have not been, I still watched, he bravely as, so to save Rodion Romanovitch. Nevertheless, all the divine in you ... As for your brother, I'm telling you? You have just seen it for yourself. What?

- Not the same one that you base?

- No, not in this, and in his own words. Here two nights in a row he came to Sofya Semyonovna. I showed you where they were sitting. He told her his full recognition. He is a murderer. He killed the old woman employees, creditors, which itself pledged thing; Also killed her sister, a market woman named Lizaveta, was accidentally included in the murder of sisters. He killed them both with an ax, which brought with him. He killed them, robbing, and plundering; Coy took the money and some things ... It's all gone, word for word, Sofya Semyonovna, and that one knows the secret, but the murder was not involved either in word or deed, but rather horror, but as you are doing now. Do not worry, she will not let him.

- That can not be! - Muttered Dunya pale pomertvevshimi lips; she gasped, - can not be, no, there is no reason, no reason ... It's not a lie! Lies!

- He robbed, that's the whole reason. He took the money and things. However, he, in his mind, do not take any money or things, and blew them somewhere under a rock, where they are now lezhat.No it's because he did not dare to use.

- Do you think it is possible that he could steal, rob? The fact that he could

only imagine it? - Dunya exclaimed, jumping up from his chair. - Because you know, you know? Can he be a thief?

She just umalivala Svidrigailov; she forgot all her fears.

- Here, Avdotya Romanovna, thousands and millions of combinations and sorting. Thief steals, but as he himself knows that he is a scoundrel;but I have heard of noble people, almost broke, so who knows, maybe he really thought that decent deal! Of course, I would not have believed himself, as if you, if I got the part. But his own ears, I think. He Sofya Semyonovna and explained all the reasons; but she could not believe my ears at first, but eventually felt that his eyes, his own eyes. He personally handed her.

- What are the reasons ...!

- The fact is, for a long time, Avdotya Romanovna. Then, as you put it, a kind of theory, the same thing that I find, for example, that the evil one is acceptable if the main objective is good.

Only evil and one hundred good deeds! It also, of course, sorry for the young man with a sense of dignity and self-esteem with exorbitant know what will happen, for example, while only three thousand, and his career, the whole future in his life is formed in different ways, and at the same is not These three thousand people. Add to that the irritation from hunger, from nearby apartments, out of the mud, the bright beauty of consciousness of their social position, as well as with the provisions of the sisters and mother. Forest all the fuss, pride and vanity, as if God knows, maybe with good tendencies ... I do not blame him, do not worry, please ,; and it's none of my business. There was also one private teoriyka - so the theory itself - on which people are divided, you know, to the material and special people, ie those people for whom, in the uppermost position, the law is not written, and which themselves constitute the laws and other people, materiyalu then litter.Nothing, so-so teoriyka; UNE Tha © Ori Comme UNE Autre. Napoleon drew it horrible that, in fact, led him to see so many brilliant people on one evil without looking, and went through without hesitation. He seems to imagine that he is a genius - it really is time for sure. It was badly damaged and now suffers from the idea that the theory that he could write, and move on to something without thinking and can not, therefore, a person is not shining. Yes, and it is for a young person with dignity and humiliating, in our age, especially ...

- Remorse? Do you deny it, then every moral sense? But is he?

- Ah, Avdotya Romanovna, now all dizzy, that is, by the way, he never

ordered something special was not.Russian people are generally broad people, Avdotya Romanovna, broad, their land, and extremely prone to fantasy, indiscriminate; but the trouble to be wide without special genius. Do you remember how much we have in the same manner and on the same topic to talk to you alone, sitting in the evening on the terrace in the garden, each time after dinner. Nevertheless, you got me in this very broad prohibition. Who knows, maybe at the same time and said, as he lay there, thinking about her, yes. We have an educated society, especially because there is no sacred traditions, Avdotya Romanovna, Is someone currently on the books will be ... Ali from the chronicles bring something. But it's more scientists and, as you know, kind of all caps, so that even secular people and indecent.However, in my opinion, you know. I do not blame firmly. I myself op, and stick to it. Yes, we have said many times, I even had the pleasure of my judgment interest you ... You're very pale, Avdotya Romanovna!

-. I have this theory know him, I read his article in a magazine about people who are still allowed ... I brought Razumikhin ...

- Mr. Razumikhin? Article of your brother? In the magazine there such an article? I do not know.There must be something interesting! But where are you, Avdotya Romanovna?

- I want to see Sofya Semyonovna - said in a weak voice Dounia. - Where to go for it? Maybe they come, of course, I now want to see her. Let it ...

Avdotya Romanovna could not agree; it literally gasped.

- Not Sofia Semyonovna be canceled till night. I think so. She had to come very soon, if not, then it is too late ...

- Oh, you're lying I see ... you lied ... you lied! .. I do not believe you! Do not believe it! Do not believe it! - Cried Dunya in this madness, completely losing his head.

Almost fainted in the chair, which she hastened to replace Svidrigailov.

- Avdotya Romanovna that with you, wake up, here is water. Otpeyte one mouthful ...

He splashed water on her. Dunya started and woke up.

! - To act decisively. - Svidrigailov muttered to himself, frowning - Avdotya Romanovna, calm down! Know that he has friends. We will save him help. Want, I'll take it abroad? I have the money in three days I'll get a ticket. And what about the fact that he killed, he made a lot of good deeds, so that everything is cleared, Calm down. A great man can still be.Well, with you? How do you feel?

- Angry man He even mocks. Let me ..

- Where are you? But where are you?

-. For him, where is he? Do you know? Why is this door locked? We came here through the door, and now it's locked. When you have time to fix it with a key?

. - It was impossible to yell at all the rooms that we're talking about, I do not sneer; I speak only the language dostatochno.Nu where you go it? Or do you want to put it? You could bring him into a rage and he betrays himself sebya.Imeyte in mind that watching too, has fallen on the trail. You only betray him. Wait, I've seen him and talked with him now. it can still be saved. Wait, sit, think together I order and I called you to talk about it and think about it alone. Yes, take the same!

- How you can save him Can I save?

Dunya village. Svidrigailov sat down beside her.

- It all depends on you, on you, on you, - he said with shining eyes, almost in a whisper, stumbling or even uttering certain words with emotion.

Dunya in fear of him next. He, too, was trembling.

- You ... one of your words, and he is saved! I ... I saved him. I have money and friends. I immediately send him, and he will have a passport, two pass-port. One of his mine. A friend I have friends, I have business people ... Do you want to? I'll take you to another passport ... your mother ... Why do you Razumikhin? I love you too ... I love you forever. Let me kiss the edge of your dress, come on! Give! I can not hear, it makes a noise. Tell me, do it! I'll do anything. I can not do. What you believe, I'll believe. I'm all done! Do not look, do not look at me like that! Did you know that you are killing me ...

He even began to rave. With him something suddenly felt as if his head suddenly hit. Dunya jumped up and ran to the door.

- Open and you! Open you! - She shouted through the door, calling some-one a handshake and a door.- With the same open E. Do not have one?

Svidrigailov got up and came to his senses. Spiteful and mocking smile slowly squeezed on shaky even lips.

- There's no one at home - quietly and deliberately he said - the owner went and wasted effort to shout themselves only worried for nothing.

- Where is the key to open the door, now low man!

- I lost the key, and I can not find it.

! - Ah! So this violence - Dunya cried, pale as death, and threw herself into a corner, where the table screen as quickly as possible, what happened

in his hand. She did not scream, but she looked at his tormentor and vigilantly watching his every dvizhenie.Svidrigaylov also did not budge and stood against him at the other end of the room. He even regained control of himself, at least from the outside. But his face was still pale. mocking smile never left him.

- You just said "violence," Avdotya Romanovna. If violence, then you can judge for yourself, I made a decision. Sofya Semyonovna is not at home; Kapernaumovs up very far, five locked rooms. Finally, I have at least twice as strong as you, and besides, I have nothing to fear, because you and then you can not complain, do not want you to betray your brother really Yes and no will not assume that you: so why one girl went to a lonely man in the apartment? So, even if his brother and the victim, there is nothing to prove that violence is very difficult to prove, Avdotya Romanovna.

- Brock! - Dunya whispered indignantly.

- As you wish, but please note I said only a hypothesis. In my personal opinion, you're absolutely right :. violence - an abomination, I said only that on your conscience, absolutely nothing will remain, even if. .. Even if you want, and save his brother voluntarily, I offer you. You simply means that obey the circumstances, well, power, finally, if you really can not do without this word. Think about it; fate of your brother and your mother in your hands. I'll be your slave ... all my life ... I'll be waiting here ...

Svidrigailov sat on the couch, away from Dunya eight. For there was no doubt in his unwavering determination. Besides, she knew it ...

Suddenly she pulled out a revolver, cocked it and put her hand with a revolver on the table.Svidrigailov jumped.

- Yes, so that's how! - He exclaimed in surprise, but wickedly grinning - Well, it changed the course of events! You got me greatly facilitates the task yourself, Avdotya Romanovna? But where you have a gun, I do not whether Mr. Razumikhin? Bah! Yes, my revolver something! an old friend! And I had it while looking for! .. Our village shooting lessons, which I had the honor to give you have not been in vain.

- Not your revolver, and Marfa Petrovna, whom ye slew, the villain. You do not have to own at her house, I took it as it was suspected that you can do. Do not be afraid to step in one step, and I swear I'll kill you!

Dunya was in a frenzy. She was holding a gun at the ready.

- Well, brother? Out of curiosity, I ask, - said Svidrigailov, still standing on the spot.

- Denunciations, if you want! Do not move! Do not go! I'll shoot you poisoned his wife, I know that you yourself are a murderer! ..

- And you firmly believe that I poisoned Marfa Petrovna?

- Do you have any! You told me himself hinted; you told me about the poison ... I know that you went after him ... you did ... This, of course ... you bastard!

- Even if it were true, so because of the same ... you would you have the same cause.

- You're lying! I hate you always, always ...

! - Hey, Avdotya Romanovna visit forgotten in the heat of propaganda already inclined and melted ... I've seen on the hinges; I remember the night when the moon is something else nightingale whistle?

- You're lying (Rabies shone in the eyes of Dunya) lie, a slanderer!

-? LSU. Well, maybe, and lying. Women Lied about these little things do not remember. (He laughed). I know that shot, zverok cute. Well, shoot!

Dunya raised the revolver and the dead pale, bleached and trembling lower lip, with shining like fire, big black eyes, looked at him, daring, measurement and waiting for the first motion with his hand. He had never seen her so beautiful. Fire that flashes from her eyes at that moment, when she raised the gun, just burned it, and his heart ached with pain. He took a step, and a shot rang out. Bullet brushed his hair and hit the back wall. He paused and grinned:

- Bitten by a wasp! Right in the head tags ... What is it? Blood! - He took a handkerchief to wipe the trickle of blood on his right temple; ., Probably a little bullet grazed the scalp. Dunya lowered the revolver and looked at Svidrigailov not in fear but in some wild confusion It's as if she has no idea what she had done, and that it's done!

- Well, Miss! Shoot more, I think - Svidrigailov said softly, still smiling, but somehow gloomy - so I will have time to grab before you vzvedete cause!

Dunya started quickly cocked and again raised the revolver.

- Leave me alone! - She said in despair - I swear I'll shoot again ... ... I'll kill you! ..

- Well ... three steps, and you can not kill. Well, do not kill ... then ... - His eyes sparkled, and he stepped out in two stages.

Dunya shot, flash in the pan!

-. Charging dirty! It's nothing. Do you still have the cap right, I'll wait.

He stood before her in a corner and waited and looked at her with dikoyu

definition, inflammation, passionate, hard look. Dunya realized that he would rather die than let her go. "And ... and, of course, she would kill him now, a few steps away! .."

Suddenly she threw the gun.

- Quit! - Said Svidrigailov with surprise and deep breathing. Something like once departed from his heart, and may not burden a mortal fear; Yes, and it is unlikely he felt at that moment. He had to get rid of other, more sad and gloomy feelings that he could not identify in full force.

He went to the Dun and quietly hugged her hand on her waist. She did not resist, but, trembling like a leaf, looked at him with pleading eyes. He had to say something, but his lips curled, and he could not pronounce.

! - Let me go - Begging said Dounia. Svidrigailov shuddered: he was as you do not let it slip as daveshny.

- So you do not like? - He asked quietly.

Dunya shook her head.

- And ... can not you? .. Never? - Desperation he whispered.

- Never! - Dunya whispered.

He took a moment of terrible, dumb struggle in the soul Svidrigailov. Untold glance he looked at her. Suddenly, he removed his hand, turned away, quickly went to the window and stood before him.

He picked up another point.

- Here's the key! (He took it out of the left pocket of his coat and put it on the table behind him, without looking, and without resorting to Duns) .Vozmite, go fast! ..

He stubbornly stared out the window.

Dunya went to the table to take the key.

- Faster! Hurry! - Re Svidrigailov, still not moving and not looking back. But this "soon" is obviously sounded a terrifying note.

Dunya understood it, grabbing the key, rushed to the door, opened it and quickly pulled out of the room. After a minute, like a madman, forgetting himself, ran to the ditch and ran to the - of the bridge.

Svidrigaïlov stood still in the box for three minutes; Finally, slowly turned, looked around and quietly passed his hand over his forehead. strange smile twisted his face, pathetic, sad, weak smile, a smile of despair. The blood has dried, washed his hand; He looked at the blood with malice; . Then soak a towel and washed the temple Revolver Dunya dropped and flew to the door, suddenly caught his eye. He picked it up and examined it. He was a small,

ROBOTS READ

pocket-size three defeats gun older devices; . it has two charges and one capsule. Once it was possible to shoot He thought, put the gun in his pocket, took his hat and went out.

←« CHAPTER VI »→

All that evening to ten hours he spent at various restaurants and chases, moving from one to another. Find somewhere and Katya, who again sang another song servants about how someone "a rascal and a tyrant"

Kate kissed.

Svidrigailov watered and Kate, and organ-grinder, and composers, and footmen, and two rows pisarishek. With the help of these clerks he contacted, actually, because they were both with crooked noses, one nose curve to the right, and the other left. He struck Svidrigailov. They pulled him out, finally, some pleasure garden, where he paid for them and for input. This garden was a thin, three years and three tree bush. In addition, it was built "vakzal" essentially a tavern, but it could be obtained, and tea, and in addition there were several tables and green chairs.Choir bad singers and some drunken Munich German as a clown with a red nose, but kak it is very boring to entertain the audience. Officials had quarreled with some other officials and started a fight. Svidrigailov was chosen their judge. He tried them for the past quarter of an hour, but they shouted that there was no way something unintelligible.Most all, it was the fact that one of them stole something and even managed to immediately sell part of hiding a Jew; but sales did not want to share with a friend. It turned out that, at last, the goods sold was tea-spoon owned station. At the station, missed him, and he began to take on the dimensions of hlopotno.Svidrigaylov paid for the spoon, got up and walked out of the garden. It was about ten o'clock vechera.On did not drink all that time not a drop of wine, and everything just asked myself at the station tea and then more for the order. Meanwhile, the evening was stuffy and dark.

ROBOTS READ

By ten o'clock pulled from all sides scary clouds; thunder, and rain poured down like a waterfall. Drops of water fall is not so, and a flood of gushing onto the ground. Lightning flashed every minute, and you could count to five times for each of the glow. All drenched to the skin, he came home, locked the door and opened his desk, took out all his money and broke two or three documents.Then, putting money in his pocket, he wanted to change her dress, but looking out the window and listen to the thunder and rain, waved his hat and left without blocking the apartment. He went straight to Sonia. It was in the building.

She was not alone; around him were four small children Kapernaumovs. Sofya Semyonovna gave to drink their tea. She silently and respectfully met Svidrigailov with surprise looked him izmokshee dress, but did not say a word. All children immediately ran to the indescribable horror.

Svidrigailov sat down to the table and sat down next to Sonia asked. She timidly prepared to listen.

- I, Sophia Semenovna, may leave for America - said Svidrigailov, - and, as we meet with you is probably the last time I came Coy any orders sdelat. Nu, this lady you saw today? I know that she said that there is nothing to tell. (Sonia also had to move and blushed). It is widely known times. As for the sisters and a brother to you, they really take it easy and the money owed to them, I gave a friend, receipt, which must be in good hands. You, however, these proceeds to take you, just in case. Well! Well, now it's all over. Here are three of the five per cent of the ticket, only three thousand. It you take you actually own, and let it so between us and will, no one knew that there would be no you have not heard. They need you, because, Sofya Semyonovna, so to live, anyway - is bad, and you do not need no more.

- I'm with you, as well, and the orphans, sir, and the dead - hurried Sonia - what if I'm still a little bit so thankful that ... I do not think ...

- Uh, fullness, completeness.

- And this money, Arkady Ivanovich, I am very grateful, but I do not need them now. I guess that one zavsegda nourish, do not consider ingratitude: if you beneficial, money ...

- You, you, Sofya Semyonovna, and please, without further ado, because even for me somehow. And you'll need. Rodion Romanovich two ways: either a bullet in his forehead, or Vladimirka.(Sonia wildly looked at him and shivered). Do not worry, I know everything from him, and I'm not a chatterbox; will not tell anyone. Is that you taught him well, so he came up and said. The

fact that he will be much more profitable. Well, how Vladimirka - it's there, and you do to him? Is not it?Is not it? Well, if so, then it means that the money that you need. For him, the same need, you know? Giving you, I do not care what to give him. In addition, you promised, and that Amalia Ivanovna to pay the debt; I heard. What are you, Sofya Semyonovna, so thoughtlessly all such contracts and commitments to take? After Katerina Ivanovna is obliged German, and not you, and you do not care for a German woman. So the world can not survive. Well, if you have when someone asks - well, tomorrow or the next day - and about me about me (and you will be asked something), I now come to you, and not to mention the money is not shows and does not affect the fact that I gave you, to anyone. Well, now goodbye. (He got up from his chair). Rodion Romanovitch onions. By the way: keep-ka money time, at least from Mr. Razumikhin.You know, Mr. Razumikhin? Of course, you know. It's small, so-so. Carry-ka to him tomorrow or ... when the time comes. Until hide.

Sonia also jumped up from his chair and looked at him warily. She wanted to say something, to ask something, but it is in the first few minutes did not dare, and do not know how it started.

- How did you ... how are you, sir, but now in the rain and go?

- Well, America is so afraid of rain, hehe! Farewell, my dear, Sophia Semenovna! Live and live a lot, you will be useful for drugih.Kstati ... Tell me, Mr. Razumikhin that I have commanded to worship. So still and pass Arcadia, say I. Svidrigailov bows. Yes, all mean the same thing.

He went out, leaving Sonia in astonishment, in fear and in some obscure and heavy suspicion.

It later emerged that the same evening at 12:00, and he made another very eccentric and unexpected visit.Rain still continued. All wet, he went at 11:20 in a cramped apartment parents of his bride, on Vasilevsky Island, in the third line, the Small prospectus. Hardly walk and was first produced great confusion; but Arkady, when he wanted was a man with a very charming manner, so that the original (although, in fact, very witty) think parents wisely bride that Arkady Ivanovich, probably, to have somewhere nahlestalsya drunk a lot and not themselves remember - immediately fell in itself. Relaxation parent rolled in a chair Arkady Ivanovich compassionate and wise mother of the bride, and, as usual, immediately proceeded to the Khoi-how far matters. (This woman never made a direct question, and always indulge in the first smile and rubbing his hands, and then, if it was necessary to learn something and, of course, is true, for example: when will appoint Arkady

wedding, and then began a curious and almost greedy questions about Paris and life there, and the court may then reached in the manner and to the third line of Vasilievsky Island). In other cases, all of this, of course, inspired a lot of respect, but this time Arkady appeared particularly impatient and strongly wished to see the bride, though he had already reported at the beginning of the bride went to sleep uzhe.Konechno, the bride was. Arkady directly told her that at the time, if one very important reason to leave St. Petersburg, and, therefore, brought her fifteen thousand rubles in silver in various tickets, asking them to accept him as a gift while he was going to give her a trifle before the wedding. In particular, the logical connection immediately send gifts, and of course to come in the rain, and at midnight, of course, these explanations do not show, but that, however, done very smoothly. Even need Ohana and Achan, interrogation and surprisingly became somehow suddenly unusually moderation and restraint; but thanks were the most ardent and even supported reasonable mother's tears. Arkady Ivanovich stood up, laughed, kissed the bride, patted her on the cheek, confirmed that will come soon, and noticing her small eyes, though childish curiosity, but at the same time very serious, dumb question, I thought, kissed her on the other time and then sincerely podosadoval in mind that the gift will go immediately to maintain reasonable under lock and key materey.On went out, leaving all in an unusually excited state. But tender-hearted mother immediately, and the whisper of a tongue twister, allowed several major misunderstanding, namely, that a man of great Arcadia, a man with chores and with constraints, the rich man - God knows what is in his mind, and went even to think, and to think even gave money, and hence it is not surprising. Of course, it is strange that he is all wet, but the British, for example, eccentric, and all the higher tones do not look at what they say, and do not stand on ceremony. Maybe he even intentionally so goes to show that he is not afraid of anyone. And most importantly, it's a word not to tell anyone, because God knows, but what will happen, and money as soon as possible under lock and key, and, of course, the best of that Theodosius sat in the kitchen, and most importantly far, far away, no need to explain anything bastard Resslih, and so on, and so on. We sat and whispered two hours. The bride, however, went to bed much earlier, surprised and a little sad.

And Svidrigailov rovnehonko between midnight passed through --kov bridge towards the other side of St. Petersburg. The rain had stopped, but the wind rustled. He began to tremble, and one minute with some special

curiosity and even with the question looked at the black water of the Little Neva. But soon he seemed very cold to stand above the water; He turned and walked to the --oy avenyu.On was endless --omu prospectus for a long time, almost half an hour, and not only break in the dark wooden bridge, but not something to stop the curiosity to look for the right-hand side of the street. This is where, at the end of the avenue, he saw something recently passed by, one of the wooden hotel, but extensive, and her name when he remembered something like Adrianople. He was not wrong in his calculations: this hotel in a desert looked like they have spots, it's impossible not to find, even in the dark. It was a long wooden blackened building, which, despite the late hour, still glowing light and notice some recovery. He came and who met him in the hallway beggar asked numbered. Ragamuffin, looking Svidrigailov, shook himself, and immediately took him to a remote cipher, stuffy and cramped, somewhere at the end of the corridor, in a corner, under the stairs. But others were not; they were all busy. Ragamuffin looked.

- Tea? - Asked Svidrigailov.

- Is it possible, sir.

- Still there?

- Veal with vodka, with a snack.

- Bring the beef and tea.

- And nothing else is needed? - Asked even in some bewilderment Ragamuffin.

- Nothing, nothing!

Ragamuffin removed completely disappointed.

"Well, there must be room - Svidrigailov thought -. As I do not know that I probably also have the form back from somewhere kafeshantana, but expensive curious story, but then who will stop here and spend the night.?"

He lit a candle and looked numbering more. It was a closet, a little earlier, even almost to the height of Svidrigailov, in a single window; the bed is very dirty, just painted table and chair occupied almost the entire space. The walls looked like as if knocked together from boards with wallpaper obshar-kannymi already dusty and ragged, their color (yellow) to guess it was still possible, but the figure was impossible to discern any.One of the walls and the ceiling was reduced Nakos, as usual, in the attic, but here on this shelf was a staircase. Svidrigailov put a candle, sat on the bed and thought. But it is strange and continuous whisper, sometimes rises almost to a shout, in the next cabinet, finally drew his attention. That did not stop whispering since

he entered. He listened: someone abused and almost tearfully blamed each other, but only heard one voice. Svidrigailov stood up, shielding the candle with his hand, and on the wall immediately flashed well;He walked over and looked. In numbered a little more than his own, had two visitors. One of them without his coat, with extremely curly head and red, sore face, standing in the oratorical pose, legs spread for balance, and striking his hand on his chest, the other pathetic reproach, that the poor and even rank on itself does not, he pulled it from dirt, and that when he wants, and then can throw him out, and that all this sees only one finger of God. One suggestion was sitting on a chair and had the kind of person who wants very sneeze, but it failed. He sometimes lamb and dull eyes, looked at the speaker, but obviously had no idea what was going on, and hardly anything else could hear of.Dying candles on the table, stood almost empty carafe of vodka, wine glasses, bread, glasses , crockery and cutlery with cucumbers have long been drinking tea. After a thorough seeing this picture, Svidrigailov blankly walked away from the slit and sat on the bed.

Ragamuffin, gates with tea and veal, could not help but ask again: "should not have anything else," and after not hearing again the answer is no, permanently deleted. Svidrigailov fell tea to warm up, and drank a glass, but I could not eat a piece, perfect for a loss of appetite. This apparently started fever. He took off his coat, zhaketku, wrapped in a blanket and lay down on the bed. He was annoyed, "everything will be better this time to be healthy," - he thought, and smiled. The room was stuffy, a candle was burning dimly in the court of the wind rustling, somewhere in the mouse angular scrapers, and the whole room smelled of mice and something skin. He was lying as if asleep: the idea was replaced by the idea, he seemed very much like to see at least something to cling especially imagination. "It's under the window should have some garden - he thought - the trees rustle, as I do not like the sound of trees at night, in a storm and in the darkness, feeling bad," And he remembered now by Petrovsky Park, disgust did not even think about it . He remembered how, and - Cove Bridge and Malaya Neva, and again, it becomes as cold as this morning, as he stood over the water. "Never in my life I do not like water, even in landscapes - he thought again and again suddenly smiled a strange thought - in fact, it seems that now everything will be the same thing about all this aesthetics and comfort, and here - So read and looked like a beast that is sure to put himself chooses ... in such a case. It would be easy now to Peter, I guess it seemed dark, cold, hehe! Almost

pleasant needed! By the way?. .. why I did not put out the light (He blew it) Neighbors on the wane - he thought, seeing no light in daveshney cracks -. Currently, Marfa Petrovna, now I wish you and welcome, and dark, and this place and originality minute. But it is now, it has not come ... "

He suddenly remembered why something like this in the morning, an hour before the examination implementation plan Dunya, he recommended Raskolnikov entrust her guard Razumikhin. "In fact, I'm probably the forest for their own enthusiasm has said Raskolnikov guess. Shunned, however, this Raskolnikov! Many dragged on themselves. Rogue may be more by the time povyskochit nonsense, and nowtoo much as he wants live What about this item, these people -. scoundrels well, to hell with him, and he wants me. "

He does not sleep. Gradually daveshny Dounia images began to appear in front of him, and all of a sudden shiver passed through his body. "No, it is really necessary now to give up - he thought waking up - must be something else to think about this strange and funny: not one I've never had a great hatred, even revenge never particularly wanted and it ,. bad sign, a bad sign say neither loved nor hot! - too bad sign and I only now she promised - fu, hell, and even, perhaps, and ground to me somehow ... "He paused again and then gritted his teeth Dounia image appeared before him in the balance, as it was when shooting for the first time, terribly frightened, dropped the gun and pomertvev, looked at him, so he had twice to grab her, and she will not hand raised in defense, if he is not recalled. He remembered him at the moment just felt sorry for her, as if squeezed his heart ... "E! Damn! Again these thoughts, all this should leave, quit! .."

He forgets; ague decline; suddenly as if something ran under a blanket on hand and foot. He shuddered: "Ugh, damn, it's almost a mouse - he thought - that I veal left on the table ...!" He hated to open, get cold, but then again something unpleasant shorknulo leg; He tore off blanket and lit a candle. Trembling with feverish cold, he bent down to inspect the bed - there was nothing; he shook the blanket and sheet suddenly jumped mouse. He ran to catch it, but the mouse does not run out of bed, and flashed zigzagging in all directions, slipped from his fingers, ran across his hand, and suddenly threw himself under his pillow, and he threw a pillow, but in an instant felt something, he jumped in his chest, shorkatsya body and have him under his trembling rubashkoy.On nervously and woke up. The room was dark, he was lying on the bed, wrapped up this morning, in a blanket under the window the wind howled. "That's disgusting!" - He thought angrily.

ROBOTS READ

He got up and sat on the edge of the bed, his back to the window. "It is better not to sleep" - he decided. From the window, however, was cold and damp; without getting up, he nataschili blanket and wrapped himself in it. He did not light the candles. He did not think about anything, and I do not want to think; but wants to stand up for each other, flashed excerpts of thoughts, without beginning or end, and without communication. As if he dozed off. Do cold, darkness there, whether dampness, whether wind, howling at the window and shakes the trees, caused him some stubborn fantastic inclination and desire - but it all began to represent color. He caused quite a landscape; light, almost hot day, holiday, the Day of Pentecost. Rich, luxurious rustic cottage in the English style, all overgrown with fragrant flowers flower beds planted with ridges extending around the house; veranda overgrown with vines, overgrown ridges rose; bright, cool staircase covered with rich carpets, furniture with rare flowers in Chinese banks. He stressed in a jar with water, windows, bouquets of white and tender nartsizov, relying on their bright green, fat and long stems with a strong aromatic odor. He even move away from them did not want to, but he climbed the stairs and entered a large, high hall, and again, and then everywhere in windows around the open door to the terrace, terrace itself, everywhere there were flowers.The floors were strewn with freshly cut herbs, the windows were open, fresh, light, cool air enters the room, the birds are chirping under the windows, and in the midst of the hall, covered with white satin linen cloths on the tables were coffins. This tomb was lined with white and trimmed with white ruffles grodenaplem thick. Garlands of flowers wrapped around it on all sides. All the colors lying in his girl in white tulle dress with folded pressed against his chest, as if carved from marble rukami.No her loose hair, light brown hair were wet; wreath of roses twined head. Strict and already ossified profile of her face was the same as that made of marble, but the smile on his pale lips was full of some nedetskiy, boundless grief and great complaint. Svidrigailov knew the girl; No picture, no candles had the coffin and could not hear the prayers.This girl was a suicide - drowned. She was only fourteen years old, but she has a broken heart, and it will destroy itself, insults hurt, fear and surprise young, childlike mind, zalivsheyu undeserved shame her angelically pure soul and run the last cry of despair, not heard, and frankly ignored dark night, in darkness, in a cold and wet, while the wind howling ...

Svidrigailov woke up, got out of bed and went to the window. He groped found the latch and opened the window. Wind rushed furiously in his little

room and close as frosty rime plastered face and veiled odnoyu shirt chest. Under the window, must have really been something like the garden and seems to be too fun;probably the day here Phewa songbooks and make tea for stole.Teper, with trees and shrubs sprays of glass, it was dark in the basement, so it is hardly possible to distinguish only a few dark spots showing objects.Svidrigailov, bending and leaning on the window sill and looked for five minutes, without stopping in this mist. Among the darkness of the night and it was a gun shot, then another.

"Signal water goes! - He thought - in the morning peak, where the lowest place on the streets, flooding basements and cellars, basements occur in rats, and the rain and the wind people start swearing, wet and drag your trash in the upper floors ... And something what time? "And I think he's somewhere near, is, and as if hurrying to go all out, the clock struck three. "Hey, so an hour there be light Why wait, I'm going to go, go straight to Peter :? Somewhere Choose a large shrub, all bathed in the rain, so little shoulder hurt and millions obdadut spray entire head. .." He walked away from the window, locked it, lit a candle, pulled on his jacket, coat, put on his hat and went out into the corridor with a candle to find somewhere to sleep in the closet between trash and candles candle torn, pay him for numbering and out of the hotel. "The best time and the best way to choose!"

He walked around for a long time and a long narrow corridor without finding anyone, and will have a loud click when in a dark corner, between the old and the closet door, he saw a strange object that seemed alive.He bent down with a candle and saw the child - a girl of five years, not more, as izmokshem scrubber rag platishke, shaking and crying. She did not seem afraid of Svidrigailov, but looked at him with a dull surprise her big black little eyes and occasionally sobbing like children who were crying for a long time, but no more, and even comforted, and yet, no, no, and again all of a sudden sob. Girls face was pale and haggard; he froze from the cold, but "it get here? Well, here it is hidden and does not sleep through the night." He began questioning her. The girl suddenly came to life and quickly faltered him something for their children language. Was something about the "Mamas", and that "mamasya plibet" On some dish that "lyazbilya" (robbery). Teenage girl talking incessantly; you can guess from all these stories, it's unloved child, whose mother, any drunken cook, probably because of the local hotels also kill and intimidate; She broke Mothers cup and that scared before that ran the night before; long, probably hiding somewhere in the yard, the rain finally got here,

hid behind a closet and sat there in the corner all night, crying, shivering from the damp, darkness and fear, now that I'm sorry for all of this will take beat.He her up, walked over to his cipher, planted on the bed and began to undress. Holi bashmachonki her bare feet were so wet, as if the night lying in a pool. Stripped, he laid her on the bed, covered and fully wrapped in a blanket with his head. She immediately fell asleep. When he finished everything he again thought grimly.

"Here's another even think to contact! - He suddenly thought with a heavy and angry feelings. - What nonsense!" In annoyance he took the candle to go and look at what was ragged and get out of here. "Hey, girl!" - He thought with a curse, opened the door, but returned again to look at the girl if she sleeps and sleeps? He carefully lifted the blanket. The girl was fast asleep and have a blissful sleep. She warmed up under the covers, and the paint was spilled on her pale cheeks. But oddly enough, this paint was designated as brighter and stronger than normal children can be dropped. "It's hectic blush" - thought Svidrigailov - a blush wine, just as if it had been given to drink a whole glass. Red lips just burn pyshut; but what is it? He suddenly felt that her long black eyelashes, as if startled and flash, as if lifted, and from the looks of their cunning, sharp, some children do not winking eye as she is awake and pretending. Yes, that's right: her lips parted in a smile; the tips of the jaws to tremble, as if still holding back. But now it has ceased to hold back; laughter is obviously laughter; something daring, causing light in this case is not the baby's face; this debauchery, that person camellias, sassy face sales Camellia frantsuzhenok.Zdes quite openly, opened both eyes: they surround his fiery eyes and shameless, they call him laugh ... something infinitely ugly and humiliating was that laughter in those eyes, in all this dirt in the face of the child. "The fact that five years -! Whispered in this horror Svidrigailov - it ... what is it?" But now she turns to him all the glowing face, stretches out his hands ... "Oh shit!" - I cried in horror Svidrigailov, raising his hand over it ... But at the same time awake.

He is in the same bed, just wrapped in a blanket; The candle does not burn, and only in the windows of a white full-time.

"Koshemar all night!" He stood up angrily, feeling that the whole is broken; his bones ached. In the courtyard of a sufficiently dense fog and can not see anything. At the end of the fifth hour; overslept! He got up and put on his coat and zhaketku still wet. Feeling a revolver in his pocket, he took his hat and handling; Then he sat down, took out a notebook and the title

of the most notable piece, written in a large number of rows. Re-read them, he thought, his elbows on the table. Revolver and notebook were there at the elbow. Flies woke up and settled on the untouched veal, which is still on the table. He looked at them, and finally, with his free right hand began to catch a fly. As long as he is not tired, but he could not catch.Finally, I found myself in this interesting pursuit, he started, got up and left the room firmly. A minute later he was on the street.

Milky, thick fog lay over the city. Svidrigailov walked along the slippery dirty wooden bridge toward the Minor Nevy.On imagined raised high water per night Malaya Neva Petrovsky Island, wet track, wet grass, wet trees and shrubs, and finally, the same bush ... he angrily began to consider the house to think about something else. Neither the passer or cabin do not occur along the avenue. Dull and dirty looked bright yellow wooden houses with shutters closed. Cold and wet prohvatyvali his body, and he was trembling. From time to time he came across Lavochne and vegetable signs and carefully read each of them. There was a wooden bridge. He had already caught up with a large stone house. Dirty, izdrogshaya dog with its tail between its legs, ran on his way. Some are dead drunk, in an overcoat, face down, lying across the pavement. He looked at her and walked away. High tower flashed to the left. "Bah! - He thought - but it is also the case, why Peter at least on the official witness ...?" He almost smiled and thought about the new turn in - cal street. And then it was a big house with a tower. In large closed gate of the house was leaning against his shoulder, little man, wrapped in a gray coat and a soldier in copper ahillesovskoy helmet. Slumbering eyes, looked coldly he came Svidrigailov.On his face was seen that eternal cranky regret that so gloomy imprint on everything, without exception, people of the Jewish tribe. Both of them, Svidrigailov and Achilles, for some time in silence, looked at each other. Achilles finally seemed irregularities that people are not drunk, and stood before him in three steps, looking straight and says nothing.

- Zee Zee hundred zdesya you-on can do? - He said, still not moving or changing their position.

- Oh, nothing, brother, hello! - Said Svidrigailov.

- Zdesya not the place.

- I, my brother, the food in foreign countries.

- In foreign countries?

- In America.

- In America?

ROBOTS READ

Svidrigailov took out the revolver and cocked it. Achilles raised his eyebrows.

- Zee Zee сто twenty-four hours (jokes) not zdesya place!

- But why not place?

- So-so, not a hundred places.

- Well, brother, it's all the same. The location is good; If you ask, and answer, that he went in, say, America.

He put the gun on the right temple.

- A zdesya impossible not zdesya place! - Achilles started, expanding more and more students.

Svidrigailov pulled the trigger.

←«»→

← CHAPTER VII →

On the same day, but at night, at seven o'clock, Raskolnikov came to the apartment of his mother and sister - in the same apartment building where they gave Bakaleeva Razumihina.Vhod the stairs was a street. Raskolnikov went up, still holding a step back, as if hesitating: to enter or not? But he would not have turned around for anything; the decision was made. "In addition, all the same, they still do not know - he thought - and I'm already used to the idea of an eccentric …" his suit was terrible: it's dirty, spent the night in the rain, ragged, exhausted . His face was almost disfigured by weariness, bad weather, physical exhaustion, and almost daily struggle with himself. Throughout the night he spent in solitude, God knows where. But at least, he decided.

He knocked on the door; he opened his mother. Dounia was not at home. Even while the maid was not. Pulcheria Alexandrovna at first speechless with amazement joyful, and then grabbed his arm and dragged him into the room.

- Well, there you are! - She said, stammering with joy. - Do not be angry with me, Rodia, I'm so stupid you meet, with tears, that I laugh instead of cry. You think I pay? No, I'm happy, and so I have this silly habit: a flood of tears. This is me with the death of his father, of the total payment. Sit down, dear, tired, must see. Oh, you got dirty.

- I was in the rain yesterday, mother … - began Raskolnikov.

- No, no, no! - Snapped Pulcheria Alexandrovna, interrupting him - you think I'm so now and start questioning the woman the previous habit, do not worry. I understand, I understand everything, now I really learned in

the local and the right, it can be seen that there is a reasonable. I once and for all, where I understand your concern and ask you reporting judge? You probably only God knows what kind of business plans and in the head, or if there is thought to proceed; so me and you push the lever: about than, say, what do you think? I ... Oh, my God! But what I'm talking back and forth like mad ... I'm here, Rodia, your article in a magazine I read the third time, I brought Dmitri Prokofitch. So I gasped when she looked up, it was stupid, I think to myself, that it does, and this is the key to unlocking things! It can, new thoughts in my head at that moment; he reflects them, I had to suffer and feel ashamed. I read, my friend, and, of course, many do not understand; Yes, it is, however, as it should be: where am I?

- Show me, Mom.

Raskolnikov took the paper and looked at your article. No matter how contrary it is his position and status, but he felt something strange and bit-ingly-sweet feeling experienced by the author, the first time he saw himself printed than twenty-three years old and injured. This went on for a moment. After reading a few lines, he frowned, and a terrible sadness gripped his heart.All his spiritual struggles of recent months remind him again. With disgust and annoyance, he threw an article on the table.

- But, Rodia, no matter how stupid I am, but I still can tell you very soon become one of the first people, if not the first in our scientific world. And they dare to think about you, you're crazy.Ha ha ha You do not know - because they thought! Ah, low worms, but where they understand what the mind! And it is also a little Dunya not believe - that! The dead man, your father twice sent in magazines - the first verse (and I had a laptop I've ever show), and then the whole story (I had asked him to give me rewrite), and even as we pray and take - do not take! I Rodia, six or seven days ago killed, despite your dress, how you live, what you eat and what you are going. And now I see that again was stupid, because you want everything now I get one once, intelligence and talent. It is now you, so do not want to now more important things to do ...

- Dunya was not at home, his mother?

- No, Rodia. Very often he can not see out of the house, leave me alone. Dmitri Prokofitch, thanks to him, comes to sit with me and all of you say. He loves and respects you, my friend. About her sister not to say that it was really so very disrespectful to me. I do not zhaluyus.Ona has its own char-acter, I have my own; He had some of his secrets bred; Well I have secrets

from you Number Of course, I am firmly convinced that Dunya too clever and, in addition, both me and loves you ... but I do not know what all this will lead. Here you are doing right now I am glad that Rodia that went, and that's what this trip; come, I say, and without you, brother, and where you deign to spend time? You got me, Rodia, very much, and do not spoil: Can you - Well, you can not - there is nothing to do, and so wait. In the end, I still will know that you love me, with me, and that's enough. I'll be here to read the works, I do not hear about you all, but no, no - and you come to visit yourself why better? After all, that is no longer to calm the mother, because I see ...

Here Pulcheria Alexandrovna suddenly burst into tears.

- Again, I do! Do not look at me, you fool! Oh, my God, I'm sitting - she exclaimed, jumping up from their seats - because of coffee, and I'll never treats! This is because some selfish old woman, what does it mean. Now, now!

- Mom, leave it, I'll go. I did not come. Please hear me out.

Pulcheria Alexandrovna timidly approached him.

- Mom, no matter what happens, not what you would think of me or heard, what would you say to me, no, you'll love me as much as it is now? - Suddenly he asked the fullness of the heart, as it were, without thinking about his words and not weighing them.

- Rodia, Rodia that to thee? But how do you ask you can! Who of you I say something? Yes, I do not believe those who come to me or just run.

- I'm here to assure you that I have always loved, and now am glad that we are alone, even glad that Dounia not - he went to the same impulse - I came to tell you straight out that even if you are unhappy with the will, but taki know that your son loves you more than himself, and now that everything that you thought of me, I do not like hard and you, all of this was not true.You I'll never stop loving ... What Well, it is; I thought that it should be done this and start ...

Pulcheria Alexandrovna silently hugged him, clutching his chest and cried softly.

- What happened, Rodia, I do not know - she said at last, - all this time I thought we were just annoy you, but now I see around that you prepare a great sorrow, because you and toskuesh. I foresee a long time RODIA. Forgive me for talking about it; still thinking about it, and I do not sleep at night. On this night, your sister and all have been lying in delirium, and all of you to remember. Rasslushala I do something, and do not understand anything. All morning before the execution went expecting something, and

this anticipation wait! Rodia, Rodia, where are you? You go, regardless of the fact that somewhere?

- Meals.

- That's what I thought! Why, I can go with you if you need it. And Dunya; she loves you, she loves you, and Sofya Semyonovna, maybe, let's go, if necessary; You see, I am ready even her own daughter to take it. Dmitri Prokofitch help us together ... but ... where are you going? ...

- Goodbye, Mom.

- As today! - She exclaimed, as if she had lost forever.

- I can not, I have to go, I have to ...

- And I can not be with you?

- No, you're on your knees and pray to God for me. Your prayer may come to that.

- Let me cross over you, bless you! That's right, that's right. Oh, my God, what we do!

Yes, he was glad that he was very glad that no one was there, they were alone with his mother. As if all of this terrible time again softened his heart. He fell to his knees in front of her, he kissed her feet, and both embraced and wept. And she was not surprised and did not ask for this time. It has long been understood that the son of something terrible happening, and now it's some terrible moment for him.

- Rodia, my dear, you are my firstborn, - she said, sobbing, - that you are now the same as was small, just come to me as well and hugged and kissed me; even when we lived with his father and bedovali You comforted us by the one who was with us, and I buried my father - how many times we take with you, as it is now, at the grave of his crying. And the fact that I was crying, the mother of heart disease known in advance. As soon as I first saw you, in the evening, I remember when we first came here, everything in your opinion one assumption, since my heart trembled and then, and today, as you opened the door, looked, well, I think, be seen came the fateful hour. Rodia, Rodia, you're not going now?

- No.

- Are you still talking?

- Yes ... I come.

- Rodia, do not be angry, I did not dare ask. I know that I do not dare, but two simple words, tell me, where are you going?

- Very far.

- What is, then, that the service, career, or something, is not it?

- That God would send ... just pray for me ...

Raskolnikov went to the door, but she held him and desperate look in his eyes. Her face contorted in horror.

- Enough, mother - said Raskolnikov, deeply regretting that you like to come.

- Not forever? In the end, there is not forever? Eventually, you will come tomorrow come?

- Well, well, goodbye.

He finally managed to escape.

The evening was fresh, warm and clear; the weather cleared up early in the morning. Raskolnikov went to his apartment; he was in a hurry. He wanted everyone to finish before sunset. Up until not want someone meeting. Going up to his apartment, he noticed that Nastasya, looking up from a samovar, closely following him and accompanies his eyes. "Oh, if there is anyone with me?" - He thought.He currently Porphyry disgust. But when he reached his room and opened it, he saw the Dunya. She sat alone, deep in thought and seems to have long been waiting for him.He stood in the doorway proeme.Ona got off the couch and sat down in fear before him. Her eyes, still looking at him, portrayed the horror and the infinite sadness. And judging he knew right away that she knows everything.

- Well, I come to you, or to go? - He asked incredulously.

- I sat all day at Sophia Semyonovna; We were waiting for you both. We thought you were, of course, where you came from.

Raskolnikov walked into the room and sat down on a chair, exhausted.

- I somehow weak, Dunja; so very tired; and I would like anything at this moment to control himself perfectly.

He raised his disbelief in her eyes.

- Where have you been all night?

- I do not remember well, you see, my sister, I finally wanted to go out and many times approached the Neva; I remember that. I wanted to finish, but ... I do not dare ... - he whispered, again glancing suspiciously Dunya.

- Thank God And, as we were afraid to do it, I Sofya Semyonovna! So you still believe life: thank God, thank God!

Raskolnikov smiled bitterly.

- I do not believe, and now with her mother, hugging, crying; I do not believe, and asked her to pray for themselves. God knows how to do it, Dunya,

and I do not understand it.

- You mother was? You and she said? - Dunya exclaimed in horror. - Do not you say?

- Poor people, and suffering ready to go! Once you go next?

- I'm going. In The Moment.Yes, to avoid this shame, I wanted to drown myself, Dunya, but the idea is already on the water, which, if I thought I was still strong, let the shame, and now I will not be afraid, - he said, looking forward. - It's pride, Dunya?

- Pride, Rodia.

As if the fire flashed in his dull eyes; He was just glad that he is still proud.

- Do not you think, sister, I just chickened out of water? - He asked with a smile hideous looking at her face.

- Oh, Rodia, completely! - Bitterly cried Dounia.

Lasted two minutes of silence. He sat with his eyes and looked at the ground; Dounia was at the other end of the table and looked at it longingly. Suddenly he stood up:

- It's too late, it's time. I'm going to give myself. But I do not know what I'm going to give myself.

Large tears streaming down her cheeks.

- Are you crying, my sister, and you can lend me a hand?

- Do you doubt?

She hugged him tightly.

- You iduchi to suffering, not washed away half of his crime? - She cried, holding it in his hands and kissed him.

- Crime? What crime? - He exclaimed suddenly, at some sudden rage - I killed a nasty, pernicious louse old woman lender does not need, who killed forty forgive sins, which sucked the juice is poor, and it is a crime? I do not think about it and wash it I do not think. And all I poked from all sides: "crime, a crime" Only now I see clearly the absurdity of my cowardice, now, how many have decided to go into this unnecessary shame!Just my meanness and mediocrity to be made, perhaps even of the benefits as suggested … Porphyry! ..

- Brother, brother, what are you talking about! But you have shed blood! - Dunya exclaimed in despair.

- All that shed - he almost caught up in a frenzy - which flows always flowed in the world, like a waterfall, which poured like champagne, and crowned in the Capitol, and then called the benefactor of mankind. Yes, you

just look carefully and make out! I myself would like nice people and made hundreds of thousands of good deeds instead of one of stupidity, not even stupidity, but just uncomfortable, because the whole idea was not as stupid as it seems now, the failure ... (In case of failure all seem stupid!) etoyu stupidity I just wanted to put myself in an independent position, the first step you need to do to get the funds and there would still have been deleted immeasurably rather use ... But I, I could not resist the first step, because I - - scoundrel's the whole point! And yet your eyes will not look if I could, I would have been crowned, and now into the trap!

- But it is not so! Brother, what are you talking about!

- Ah! not the form but not as aesthetically good shape! Well, I really do not understand why people in the thrash bomb regular siege, more respectable form? Fear Aesthetics first sign of weakness! .. Never, ever more clearly, I did not know about this, as it is now, more than ever, I do not understand my crime! Never, never was I strong and committed than it is now! ..

Paint even hit his pale, gaunt face. But saying last exclamation, he accidentally met the gaze of the eyes Dunya, and how much flour for himself, he met with this point of view, that involuntarily came to his senses.He felt that after all the suffering of these two poor women. Nevertheless, it is a reason ...

- Dunya, dear! If I am guilty, forgive me (though I can not forgive, and if I'm guilty). Farewell! We will not argue! It's time. Do not go with me, I beg you, I still have to go on and on ... And now immediately sit down next to her mother. I implore you to do it! This latest, greatest, my request to you. Do not leave it all the time;I left her in the lurch, it is unlikely to take: he either dies or goes mad. Good to be with her! Razumikhin will be with you; I told him ... Do not cry for me, I will try to be brave, and to be honest, all my life, although I murderer.Maybe you ever hear my name. I do not osramlyu you see; I prove ... now on a date - he hastened to conclude, again noticing the strange look in his eyes when Dunya last words and promises him. - What are you crying? Do not cry, do not cry; not really quite the same parting! .. Oh yes, wait, I forgot! ..

He walked over to the table, took one thick, dusty book, opened it and pulled out a small position between the sheets portretik, watercolor on ivory. It was a portrait of his daughter mistress, his former fiancee, who died of a fever, the very country girl who wanted to go to a monastery. For a moment he looked at him and painful expressive face, kissed the portrait and gave Dunya.

- That's it, and I talked a lot about it, with its one - he said thoughtfully, - her heart, I said a lot of what later happened so ugly. Do not worry - he turned to Dunya - she did not agree was just like you, and I am glad that she is no more. The main thing, the main thing is that now all go to the next, divided into two parts - he exclaimed suddenly, again returning to his sorrow - everything, everything, and I'm ready? Do I want it myself? This, they say, because my tests need to be! Why all these meaningless tests? The fact that they are better I will understand, and then milled flour, idiotic, in senile impotence after twenty years of hard labor, than they now know and what I then live? Why am I now, I agree to live this way? Oh, I knew that I was a scoundrel, where I am now, at dawn, standing on the Neva!

And finally came. It was hard to dance, but she loved it! She went, but came back fifty paces, turned back to her. It is also to be seen. But when he reached the corner, and he turned; the last time they met views; But when he saw that she was looking at him, he willingly and even angrily waved her go, and he abruptly turned the corner.

"I am angry, I see it - he thought to himself, ashamed of his irritation by minute gesturc Dance -.! But why did they love me so, if I do not deserve Oh, if I was alone, and no one loved me and I would have never loved anyone! Would not it be just that! It is interesting to make these future fifteen? - twenty years have resigned my soul that I am delighted with men whimper, calling himself the entire word robber Yes, it is, it is! To do this, that they expelled me now, that's what they need, and ... That's all they scurry down the street back and forth, and because each of them a scoundrel and a thief has his nature and worse - an idiot and try to get around me a link, and they all went mad with noble indignation Oh, how I hate them all! "!

He thought deeply about, "how this process can take place in such a way that it finally before all of them without the humble reasoning, persuasion put up! And then, why not train? Of course, the way it should be. Twenty years of continuous oppression will not achieve the final? water wears away the stone. And why, why live after that, why I go now that I know myself that all this is just a way of books, and nothing else! "

He hundredth time, perhaps, ask yourself this question, since last night, but still went.

←«»→

←« CHAPTER VIII »→

When he went to Sonya, twilight had already begun. All day Sonia waited for him in a terrible excitement. They waited together with Dunya. She came to her early in the morning, remembering the words of yesterday Svidrigailov, Sonya "knows about it." We will not pass on the details of the conversation and the tears of the two women, and how much they agreed with each other. Dunya from this meeting, at least made one consolation is that my brother will not be alone: for her, Sonia, first he came with his confession; In it, he was looking for a man when he needed a man ,; it will also follow him where to send destiny. She did not ask, but I knew it would be so. She looked at Sonya even with some awe and at first almost embarrassed her this sense of awe with which she was treated. Sonja was ready even almost cried she, on the other hand, considered himself unworthy to even look at Duns. Fine image of Dunya, when she falls out of her with care and respect during their first meeting in Raskolnikov has since remained forever in her heart, as one of the most beautiful and unattainable visions of her life.

Dunya finally broke down and left Sonya wait his brother in his apartment; it all seemed to be there before he comes. Left alone, Sonya immediately began to suffer from fear at the thought that maybe he really committed suicide. The same was afraid and Dunya. But both of them all the day vying discouraged each other all the arguments that it can not be, and have been quieter while they were together. Now, just separated, and both became one it just to think about it. Sonia recalled yesterday Svidrigailov told her that Raskolnikov two roads - Vladimirka or ... She knew, but his vanity, arrogance, self-esteem and lack of confidence. "Maybe only cowardice and fear

of death can make him live?" - She thought that, at last, in despair. The sun was setting at the same time already. It was a sad sight window and looked at him - but the window was seen only one capital unbleached wall of the neighboring house. Finally, when in fact it has reached a perfect conviction in the death of an accident - he went to his room.

Cry of joy burst from her chest. But closely at his face, she suddenly turned pale.

- Well, yes! - He said, grinning, Raskolnikov, - I am for your crosses, Sonya. The very same you sent me into the intersection; Well, how came down to it, and a coward?

Sonia looked at him. It seemed strange to her that tone; cold shiver ran through her body was but a moment later she knew that tone, and these words - it was imaginary. He said something, looking at it as something in the corner and just avoided looking her straight in the face.

- I see Sonia decided that in this way, it may be more beneficial. There's not a fact ... Well, long story, and nothing. I only know that angry? I shame that all this is stupid, cruel hari surrounded me now, will be stared at me with his burkaly, asking me their stupid questions that need to be responsible - to be pointing the finger ... Phew! You know, I do not go to Porfiry; it bothers me. I would prefer my friend go gunpowder, it is not surprising that the effect of its kind to achieve. And we should be colder; I also became bile lately. You will not believe, I shook my sister is now almost a fist just for this, she turned one last time to look at me. Disgusting - a kind of state! Oh, how I got! Well, that's where the passes?

It was as if he did not own. He even on the spot could not resist one minute on any subject, can not concentrate; his thoughts popped up one after the other, he said, his hands trembling slightly.

Sonia silently pulled out of the drawer two crosses, cypress and copper, cross, crossed it and put it on the cross chest cypress.

- It is, therefore, a symbol of the cross to take over, hehe! And, of course, I have a little pain! Cypress, it is vulgar; Copper - is Lizavetin, you treat yourself - Show me? So it ... it was at that moment? I also know how the two crosses, silver and shoulder. Then I threw my chest old woman. It would be as it is now, right, and they will carry me ... And yet, I lie all forget about this case; scattered I somehow! .. You see, Sonia - I, in fact, and then come to you to alert you to know ... That's it ... I'm just then, because he came from. (Hmm, I, however, thought it more to say). But you and she wanted me to go,

well, that's going to go to jail, and your wish will come true; Well, why are you crying? ? And you, too, okay, is complete; oh, it's hard for me!

Feeling, however, was born in it; His heart sank, looking at her. "That is, it is, then what? - He thought to himself, -? I have something that she that she was crying, that's going to change, as a mother or Dunya nurse will be mine!"

- Crosshair, pray at least once - trembling, timid voice asked Sonia.

- Oh, please, it's just the way you want! And with all my heart, Sonya, from the heart ...

He wanted, however, to say something else.

He crossed himself several times. Sonia grabbed a scarf and threw it on the head. It was a green scarf dradedamovy, probably the one who mentioned it Marmalade "family." Raskolnikov flashed about this idea, but he did not ask. In fact, he began to feel terribly distracting and somehow terribly alarmed. He was afraid of this. He was suddenly struck by the fact that Sonia wants to go with him.

- What are you! Where you go? Wait, wait! I am alone, - he cried with vexation and fainthearted, almost rage, went to the door. - And what is the environment! - He muttered, going out.

Sonia was left in the room. He did not even say goodbye to her, he forgot all about it; One sarcastic and rebellious doubt boils in my heart.

"Yeah right, as if all this? - Again, he thought, down the stairs - you can not do more to stop and all along ... and not to go?"

But he still was. He suddenly felt conclusively that there is nothing to ask yourself questions. Out on the street, he remembered that not only Sonya, she was in the middle of the room, in her green shawl, not daring to move with his cry, and paused for a moment. At the same time, the thought suddenly brightly lit it - just waiting to hit him completely.

? "Well, why, why I came to her now I said to her, for business, for how this matter at all No, and do not care Declare that ?! I'm going, so that the need I like! what I? In the end, no, is not it? After all, now led her like a dog. Cross or something, I really took away from him? Oh, how low I have fallen!

No - I tear it should be, I am afraid to see her have to look like her heart ache and suffer! We had though about something to cling to linger, to look at the man! And so I dared to hope for themselves, so dream about themselves, poor me, I'm worthless scoundrel, rascal! "

He walked along the embankment of the ditch, and was too close to him.

But when he reached the bridge, he suddenly stopped and turned on the bridge, to the side, and went to the Haymarket.

He eagerly looked around left and right, looking at the voltage for each subject and nothing could focus; All vyskolzalo. "It's a week, a month after I provezut somewhere convict these cars on the bridge for some reason I look at this ditch - remember this? - Flashed through his mind. - That's a sign, I will read these very? Letters It says: "Tavarischestvo", well here and I remember, and a letter, and look at it through the month, is the most well: I somehow look like I'm going to feel and think ?.. God, how things should be low, all these worries ... my gift! Of course, all this should be interesting ... good ... (ha ha ha! that I think!) I was?! child to do, I'll show off in front of him well, I'm ashamed of myself Fu as noise Here thickness - German, and should be - that pushed me: Well, if he knows who pushed a woman to? child begging, curious as to what she thinks I'm happier than I . And that it would appeal to curiosity. Bach, survived a penny in his pocket, where? On to ... hell, my mother! "

- Save your god! - I heard a plaintive voice poverty.

He went to the Haymarket. He is unpleasant, very unpleasant to deal with people, but he was right there, where you could see all the people. He would give anything in the world to be alone; but he felt that no minutes will not be alone. The crowd bezobraznichal drunk: he still wanted to dance, but he still will collapse on the way. He was surrounded. Raskolnikov pushed his way through the crowd, a few minutes staring at a drunken and suddenly short and clipped laughed. After a while he forgot about it, did not even see him, though, and looked at him. He moved to the end, I do not remember where it is located; but when he came to the middle of the square, it suddenly occurred to me, in one motion, one feeling came over him immediately grabbed his whole - body and mind.

He suddenly remembered the words of Sonia: "Go to the crossroads, bow to the people, kiss the earth, because you have sinned, and in front of her, and tell the world aloud:" I am a murderer! "" .He Tremble, remembering him. And before already crushed desperate anguish and worry about it all the time, but especially in the last hours, he rushed to the possibility of this whole, new, full of feeling. One goes to him suddenly rose on fire in the soul odnoyu spark and suddenly, as the fire spread to all. All at once softened, and tears flowed. As it was, and he fell to the ground ...

He knelt among the area, bowed to the ground and kissed the dirty

ground, with pleasure and happiness. He stood up and bowed a second time.

- Look nahlestalsya! - Says the guy next to him.

Was laughter.

- He's going to Jerusalem, brothers, children, their homeland is forgiven, the world worships, the capital of St. Petersburg and kissed the ground - added some drink from the middle class.

- The boy is still young! - Threaded third.

- From expensive! - Someone noticed, firm voice.

- Nona they can not tell who is noble and who is not.

All these answers and conversations are stored Raskolnikov, and the words "I killed" may be ready to take off his tongue froze in it. He is quiet, but then, after going through all these cries and not looking back, went straight down the alley toward the office. One vision flashed before him dear, but he was not surprised by it; he had a premonition that the way it should be. At that time, when he was in the Haymarket, bowed to the ground a second time, turn left, about fifty yards away, he saw Sonya. She hid from him in one of the wooden houses standing on the square, so it was accompanied by all his mournful procession! Raskolnikov felt and understood at the time, once and for all that Sonia is now with him forever, and will follow him to the ends of the earth, wherever he went no luck. His heart turned over ... but - that he had reached the fateful place ...

He quite cheerfully went into the yard. We had to climb to the third floor. "At the moment, is still growing," - thought on.V general, it seemed to him that before the fateful moment is still far, a lot of time left, a lot can still change your mind.

Again garbage, the same sheath of spiral staircases, the door opened again, wide strips, again dishes, of which carries the smoke and stench. Raskolnikov as there was. His legs were numb and buckled, but walked. He stopped for a moment to catch his breath, to recover, to get a man. "And why, why -? he thought suddenly made sense of their movement. - If you really need to drink this cup, that's not all really matter that unpleasant better? -. In his mind flashed at the moment the figure of Ilya Petrovich Gunpowder.? - Is it really there is no other Can Nicodemus Fomich turns now and go to the headman himself for an apartment?? at least cost way home. .. No, no! It's shot in the locker gunpowder! Drink, drink, so all at once ... "

Feeling cold and a little as I can remember, he opened the door to the office. At that time there were very few people standing janitor and even

some commoner. Caretaker and looks out of his septum. Raskolnikov went into the next room. "Maybe you still can not speak," - flashed it. There is one type of individual scribes privately coat and matching to write something in the office. In the corner sat the other clerk. Zametova was not. Nicodemus Fomicha, of course, was not.

- There's nobody there? - Was asked Raskolnikov, referring to the man at the table.

- And what are you?

- Ah-ah-ah! I have never heard of opinion is not visible, and the Russian spirit ... as there is a fairy tale ... forgot! M-May n-Patsch-Ten! - Cried suddenly a familiar voice.

Raskolnikov shuddered. Before him stood Gunpowder; he suddenly came out of the third room. "It's very fate - thought Raskolnikov - Why is he here?"

- For us? What? - Exclaimed Ilya Petrovich. (He was, apparently, in excellent and even a modicum of the excited state of mind). - If in the case, it is too early to complain. I'm on the case ... And yet, I can. I confess to you ... how? how? Sorry ...

- Raskolnikov.

- Well: Raskolnikov! And, of course, you could assume that I forgot! You, too, please do not take me for it ... Rodion Ro ... Ro ... Rodionych, so it seems?

- Rodion Romanovitch.

- Yes, yes, yes! Rodion Romanovitch, Rodion Romanovitch! That's what I wanted. Even several times asked.I confess to you, so sincerely sorry that we did, you ... I said then, I have learned that the young writer and scholar ... and even, so to speak, the first steps ... Oh, my God! But who among the writers and scientists originally made the original steps! My wife and I - we both respect for literature, and his wife - so passionately! .. Literature and Art! It would be fair, and anything else you can buy the talent, knowledge, intelligence, genius! Hat - well, for example, this means that hat? Hat is Hell, I'll buy it from Zimmerman; but under the hood is stored hat covered, so I do not buy it, sir! .. I admit that I even want to go to you to explain, but I thought that maybe you ... But do not ask, you do whatever you want? For you to say come home?

- Yes, mother and sister.

- Even if the honor and good fortune to meet his sister - educated and charming lady. I confess that I was sorry that we did with you before you got excited. The incident! And the fact that I was going to do about your fainting,

some eyes - what is the most brilliant way to explain! Bigotry and intolerance! I understand your anger. Maybe the family arrived changing a flat?

- N-no, I just ... I went to ask ... I thought that I would find Zametova.

- Oh yes! Once you have made friends; heard from. Well, Zametova we did not - did not catch. Yes, sir, we lost Lukashenko! Since yesterday, the box office is not available; moved ... and go, even with all perebranilsya ... so even rude ... Windy Boy, nothing more, and may even hope to serve; yes that come with them, with the youth of our brilliant! Exam or something, some want to save, but only because we would like to talk pofanfaronit and the examination is over. This is not something that, for example, you're there, Mr. Ali Razumikhin, your friend! Your career - Scientists often and you do not get knocked failure! You all the beauty of life, we can say, - Nihil Est, ascetic monk, hermit! .. For you, a book, a pen behind his ear, scientists are studying - that's where your spirit soar! I myself have a few notes ... Livingston pleasure to read?

- No.

- I read it. Today, however, many nihilists distribution; Yes, because this is understandable; just something that, I ask you? And yet, I'm with you ... because you're certainly not a nihilist! Answer frankly, honestly!

- N-no ...

- No, you know you're with me frankly, you do not hesitate, as if to himself alone! Other services, and another thing ... You thought I was going to say: friendship, no, sir, I do not think! Not friendship, and a sense of human and civil rights, a sense of humanity and love of God. I can be an officer, and in the post, but a citizen and a man I always feel obliged to give an account of themselves and here ... You were happy to talk about Zametova. He said soskandalit something in the style of French institutions in indecent for a glass of champagne or Don - that's what your comment! And I can be, so to speak, was burned to the dedication and high emotions and, in addition, have a value, but rank ranking! He is married and has children. Is acting as a citizen and man, and one who, may I ask? Treat you as a person, meaningful form. These midwives too much paste.

Raskolnikov raised his eyebrows questioningly. According to Ilya Petrovich obviously recently released from the table, knocked and rained down in front of him for the most part as empty sounds. But part of it is somehow understood; He looked and did not know what it's all over.

- I'm talking about these girls clipped - continued talkative Ilya Petrovich,

ROBOTS READ

- I called them myself and midwives believe that the nickname is quite satisfactory. Hehe! Climb to the academy, learning anatomy;Well, tell me, I'm tired, I'll get well, treat yourself to a virgin? Hehe!

Ilya Petrovitch laughed very pleased with his witticisms.

- This is, for example, excessive desire for education; but after cleaning, as well as beautiful. Why not abuse?Why insult the noble personality, as does the villain noticed? Why he insulted me, I ask you? Here's how these suicide spread - is you can not imagine. All this at home all the money and kills himself. Girls, boys, old men ... So this morning reported that the newly arrived gentleman. Neil and Neil Pavlitch Pavlitch! as it is, my lord, which was reported this morning, shot something in St. Petersburg?

- Svidrigailov - hoarse and calmly said someone from the other room.

Raskolnikov shuddered.

- Svidrigailov! Svidrigailov shot! - He exclaimed.

- How! You know Svidrigailov?

- Yes ... I know ... He recently came ...

- Well, recently arrived, his wife lost, people zabubennogo behavior, and suddenly shot, and so scandalous that it is impossible to imagine ... left in his notebook a few words that he dies on his mind, and asks, Who is to blame for his death. The money is said to have. You know how you like?

- I ... sign ... my sister lived in their house governess ...

- Ba, ba, ba ... But you tell us, what can I report it. And you do not know?

- Yesterday I saw him ... he was drinking wine ... ... I do not know.

Raskolnikov felt that he would like something fell and crushed him.

- You once again like pale. We have here a stale spirit ...

- Yes, I have to go, sir, - muttered Raskolnikov - sorry, worried about ...

- Oh, for pity's sake, as you want! Pleasure accepted, and I'm glad to say ...

Ilya Petrovich even hand held out.

- I just wanted to ... I Zametovu ...

- I understand, I understand, and fun.

- I am very happy ... ... goodbye, with ... - Raskolnikov smiled.

He went out; He shakes. His head was spinning. He felt no stand on their feet. He started down the stairs, leaning against the wall with his right hand. It seemed to him that some janitor with a book in his hand, pushed him, climbing to meet him at the office; that some dogs barking poured somewhere on the first floor, and the woman left him with a rolling pin and screamed. He went downstairs and out into the yard. Here in the yard,

near the exit, pale, all pomertvevshaya, Sonia and wildly, wildly at him. He stopped in front of her.Something sick and exhausted reflected on her face, something desperately. She clasped her hands. Horrible, lost smile on his lips sokraschayutsya.On stood, smiled and turns up again in the office.

Ilya Petrovich sat down and began rummaging through some papers. Before him stood the same man who had just pushed Raskolnikov, climbing the stairs.

- Ah? Thank you again! Left something? .. But what about you?

Raskolnikov with pale lips, with a fixed stare quietly approached him, went to the table and stared at his hand, wanted to say something, but could not; there were only a few incoherent sounds.

- You are sick, chair! Here, sit down on a chair, sit down! Water!

Raskolnikov sat down, but did not take his eyes off the face of a very unpleasant surprise Ilya Petrovich. Both time looking at each other and zhdali.Prines water.

- This is me ... - began Raskolnikov.

- Drink water.

Raskolnikov took his hand and calm water, with the arrangement, but clearly said:

I killed the old woman and then the clerk, and her sister Lizaveta with an ax and robbed.

Ilya Petrovich opened his mouth. Came running from all directions.

Raskolnikov repeated his testimony.

←«»→

EPILOGUE
⟪ CHAPTER I ⟫

Siberia.On bank of a wide, desolate river stands the city, one of the administrative centers of Russia; a fortress to fortress prison. In prison for nine months, a prisoner in exile convict the second category, Rodion Raskolnikov. From the day of his transgression is almost half a year.

Proceedings in the case he passed without much difficulty. Offender firmly, precisely and clearly supported his testimony, without confusing circumstances not soften them in his favor, without distorting the facts, not forgetting the smallest details. He spoke with the latest features the entire process of murder: the mystery clarified mortgage (wooden plank with metal strips), who was killed in the hands of an old woman; a detailed account of how the murdered took the keys, these keys are described, stacking and described what it was filled; even some of the individual objects located in it; explained the riddle of the murder of Lizaveta; talked about how he came and knocked Koch, and then the student passes all they talked among themselves; he, criminal, and then ran down the stairs and heard the screeching and Mikolka Mitki; as he hid in an empty apartment, came home, and finally, the stone in the yard, on Voznesensky Prospect, under the gate, by which all were found and purse. In short, the case came out clear. Investigators and judges were very surprised by the way, that he hid the purse and belongings under a rock not to use them, and, above all, the fact that he does not remember the details of all the things they actually stolen, but even among them wrong, This, in fact, the fact that he never opened his wallet and did not even know exactly how much money in it, it seemed incredible (in the wallet turned three hundred and seventeen silver rubles and twenty three

cents, from long lying under a rock Some of the best, the biggest, the paper is very spoiled). Long sought to find out why it is the defendant in this one circumstance lies, whereas in all other recognized voluntarily and truthfully? Finally, some (especially from psychologists) have made even the possibility that he does not really look into the purse, and therefore do not know what was in it, and not knowing, and demolished under a rock, but immediately from this and come to concluded that the majority of crimes could not have happened for some temporary insanity, so to speak, with painful delusions of murder and robbery, in the absence of other purposes and payments to defined benefit plans. Here, by the way, came the latest fashionable theory of affect, so they often try to apply in our time to other criminals. In addition, hypochondriacal state long Raskolnikov was stated in the accuracy of many witnesses, Dr. Zosimov, his former comrades, Mistress, slave. All this contributed significantly to the conclusion that Raskolnikov was not quite like an ordinary murderer, a thief and a robber, but there is something else. To the great chagrin of defending this view, the criminal himself almost did not try to defend himself; Last question: what can convince him to kill, and this led him to commit a robbery, he said very clearly with samoyu rough exactly what was the cause of his bad situation, his poverty and helplessness, a desire to strengthen the first steps of his career with the help of life at least, three thousand rubles, which he expected to find in killed. He decided to kill because of their thoughtless and cowardly nature, irritable, moreover, difficulties and failures. On the same question, prompting him to surrender, said simply that it was a sincere pokayanie. Vse almost rude ...

Sentence, but then, was more merciful than you would expect, judging by the crime committed, and, perhaps, precisely because the offender not only did not want to make excuses, but even as he expressed a desire to be more to blame themselves. All countries and especially the circumstances of the case were taken into account. Painful and miserable condition of the offender to commit a crime or questioned. The fact that he did not use robbed, often attributed to the action, to awaken repentance, often insufficiently robust state of mental capacity at the time of the crime. Circumstance accidentally killing Lizaveta even served as a model for strengthening the latter assumption: a man commits two murders and at the same time forgets that the door was not locked worth it! Finally, voluntary surrender, at the very time when it is very confusing because of false testimony to the fallen spirit fanatic (Nicholas) and, in addition, when the real culprit is not only clear evidence,

but even the suspicion was almost no (Porfiry Petrovitch fully kept his word), it all ultimately helped to mitigate the fate of the accused.

Declared, moreover, quite unexpectedly, and other circumstances, strongly advocated by the defendant. A former student Razumikhin dug up from somewhere and information provided evidence that the criminal Raskolnikov, during his time at the university, of the last means of helping one of their own poor and consumer university friend and almost kept it for six months.When he died, he went to the survivors and relaxed old father of the deceased partner (who keep and feed his father for his work with almost thirteen years) finally put the old man to the hospital, and when he, too, died, and they buried him. All of this information has a positive influence on the decision about the fate of Raskolnikov. Herself a former lover of his late mother of the bride Raskolnikov Zarnitsina widow, also showed that, when they still lived in another house at Five Corners, Raskolnikov in a fire in the night, pulled out of one apartment, already tanned, two young children, and burned at the same time. This fact has been carefully researched and is well supported by many witnesses. In short, over the fact that the culprit was awarded the second category of hard work in just eight years, with respect to surrender and to facilitate Some blame the circumstances.

At the beginning of Raskolnikov's mother became ill. Dunya and Razumikhin found it possible to take her away from St. Petersburg to the court all the time. Razumikhin chose the city for rail and a short walk from St. Petersburg to be able to regularly monitor all the circumstances of the process and at the same time as often as possible to see Avdotya Romanovna. Disease Pulcheria Alexandrovna was a strange, nervous and was accompanied by a kind of madness, if not completely, then at least chastichno.Dunya goal last meeting with his brother, discovered that his mother was very sick, feverish and delirious. That same evening, she in cahoots with Razumikhin that answer questions his mother about his brother, and even came up with him, for his mother, the story about leaving Raskolnikov somewhere far away, on the border of Russia, a private team that takes it Finally, money and fame. But they were surprised that all of this than it Pulcheria Alexandrovna, neither then nor later did not ask. On the contrary, it was more the whole story about the sudden departure of his son; she tearfully tells how he came to her to say goodbye; while giving hints to know that only one known to her many very important and mysterious circumstances, and that many Rodi very powerful enemies, so it should still go underground. As for his future

career, she also seemed to her undeniable and shiny when will some hostile circumstances; Razumihina sure that her son would eventually even the human condition, which proves his article and his brilliant literary talent. This article is read continuously, sometimes even read aloud, almost did not sleep with her, but still, where she is now Rodia, hardly in doubt, despite the fact that, apparently fled with her to talk about it - that that only may bring her hypochondria, there finally be afraid of this strange silence Pulcheria Alexandrovna some points. For example, she did not complain that there are no letters from him, whereas before, does not live in the city, and only lived odnoyu hope and expectation of a hurry to get a letter from her lover Rodi. The latter circumstance was too much bother and inexplicably Dunya; It occurred to him that his mother may have a premonition of something terrible in the fate of her son and is afraid to ask, do not learn something even worse. In any case, Dounia saw clearly that Pulcheria Alexandrovna did not sound state of mind.

Once or twice, but it so happened that she changed the subject so that it was impossible to answering it, let alone where he is now Rodia; when the answers did not want to leave unsatisfactory and suspicious, she suddenly became very sad, sullen and silent, which lasted a very long time. Dounia saw at last that it is difficult to lie and make up, and came to a final conclusion that it is better to completely silent on some points; but more and more it became clear evidence that poor mother suspected something terrible. Dounia remembered, among other things, the word brother that her mother listened to delirium, the night before this last fateful day, after her scene with Svidrigailov if he had heard something then? Often, sometimes after several days or even weeks morose, gloomy silence and silent tears, the patient somehow revived hysterically and suddenly began to speak out loud, almost continuously, about his son, about their hopes for the future ... it was very strange sometimes Fantasies . Her amused, she agreed (it can be clearly seen that its consent and only to amuse her), but she still says ...

Five months after the surrender followed his criminal sentence. Razumikhin saw him in prison, when only it were possible. Sonia too. Finally followed and separation; Dunya brother vowed that such a separation is not forever; Razumikhin too. In a young and hot head Razumihina firmly entrenched in a future project to put three or four years, if possible, even the beginning of the future state, to save even more money, and go to Siberia, where the soil is rich in all respects, and employees, people and capital

not enough; live in the same city, where he will Rodia, and ... all together to start a new life. Saying good-bye, everyone was crying. Raskolnikov over the past few days have been very thoughtful, many asked about his mother constantly worried about her. Even a lot of her tormented, fearing that Dunya. Learn more sickly mother's mood, he became very gloomy. With Sonia he was somehow especially negovorliv all the time. Sonia, with the money to her Svidrigailov long gathered and made to follow the party of convicts in which it will be sent. It was never a word was not mentioned between her and Raskolnikov; but both knew that it would be so. Most recently, he smiled strangely goodbye fiery sisters identity and Razumikhin about their happy future when he gets out of prison, and predicted that a painful condition of the mother will end soon in trouble. He finally went to Sonya.

Two months later, Dunya married Razumikhin. The wedding was sad and quiet. Of the guests was, however, Porfiry Petrovitch and Zosimov. All the latest Razumikhin had the look of a man who was determined. Dunya believed blindly that he will fulfill all his intentions, and could not believe it: the man could see the iron will. By the way, he listened to the university lectures again to complete the course. They both were drawn every minute plans for the future; as firmly counted in five years is likely to move to Siberia. For those long hoped there Sonya ...

Pulcheria Alexandrovna gladly blessed daughter in marriage to Razumikhin; but after marriage became as if even sadder and problems. To give her a nice moment, Razumikhin told her, among other things, the fact of the student and his decrepit father and that Rodia was burned and was even sick, who escaped death last year, two babies. Both news brought already problematic because of Pulcheria Alexandrovna almost ecstatic state. She constantly talked about it, join the conversation on the street (though Dunya constantly accompanied her). In public cars, stores, catching at least some listeners, he hit the conversation to his son, in his article, he helps students, was burned in the fire, and so on. Dounia did not even know how to hold it. Oh, the danger of such an enthusiastic, morbid mood, one that has already threatened calamity that someone can remember the name of Raskolnikov in the first case, the court and talk about it, except. Pulcheria Alexandrovna even seek to find the mother of two children rescued from the fire and will definitely go for it. Finally, concern has risen to its extreme limits.Sometimes she suddenly burst into tears, often sick and delirious in the heat. One day, in the morning, she announced bluntly that she should soon arrive

calculations RODIA, she remembers him goodbye told her, he noted that it was in the first nine months we can expect from it. Became everything to clean the apartment and prepare for the meeting was to finish assigns a number (your own), scrape off the furniture, wash and put new curtains and so on. Dunya was alarmed, but was silent, and even helped her arrange the room to get it brother.After alarm day in the ongoing fantasies, in joyful dreams and tears, night and the next morning she was sick already feverish delirium. Fever opened. Two weeks later she was dead. In his delirium had fled from his words that could draw the conclusion that it is much more suspect in son's terrible fate than even expected.

Raskolnikov long time did not know about his mother's death, although correspondence with St. Petersburg was established from the very beginning of its location in Siberia. Got it through Sonia, who wrote carefully each month in St. Petersburg in Razumihina and carefully every month received from St. Petersburg response. Letters Sony seem at first Dunya and Razumikhin something dry and unsatisfactory; but in the end they both found it impossible to write better, because both of these letters, the result is still the most complete and accurate picture of the fate of their unfortunate brother. Letters were placing Sony samoyu everyday reality, simple and clear description of the situation throughout the life of the convicted Raskolnikov. There has been no statement about her own hopes, no secrets about the future, or describe their feelings. Rather than explain his mental mood and the entire interior of his life were some of the facts, that is, his own words, detailed news about the state of his health, he wants that, when we meet, how to ask her what she ordered and so on.All the news reported in great detail. The image of an unhappy brother in the end he did, drew clear and precise; there can be no mistakes, because all the facts were true.

But few could bring an appreciative Dunya and her husband on the news, especially in the beginning. Sonia constantly reported that he was constantly sullen, neslovoohotliv and even almost no interest in the news, she tells him every time he gets letters from; sometimes he asks about his mother; and when she saw that he was awaiting the truth is finally told him about his death, then, surprisingly, even the news of his mother's death on him no matter how badly acted, at least so it seemed in its external form, She said, among other things, that, despite the fact that he seems to be so absorbed in himself and from all kinds of block - a new life, he took a very direct and simple; he clearly understands his position, nothing close to it is

better not to expect does not have unreasonable expectations (which is so characteristic of his position), and almost nothing surprises among the new environment, so little resemblance to anything previous. She said that his health condition is satisfactory. He goes to work, which does not shy away from and which are not guessing. Almost indifferent to the food, but the food, except on Sundays and public holidays, so much that, finally, he willingly took from her, Sonia, some money to make in their daily tea; And what about all the others asked her not to worry, saying that all these worries about it just to annoy him. Next Sonia said that putting him in jail with all; the insides of their barracks she had not seen, but comes to the conclusion that close, ugly and unhealthy; that he slept on benches, under the sub-genres of felt, and the other does not want to give himself. But he lives so rude and poor not on any preconceived plan or intention, and so easy to neglect and indifference to the outside of his fate. Sonia directly wrote that he, especially in the beginning, and not just interested in her visits, but even almost a shame it was neslovoohotliv and even rude to her, but at the end of these visits, it became a habit, and even almost a necessity, so it is very homesick when she was sick for a few days and could not attend. She sees him on holidays at the gate or convicted in the guardhouse, where he was summoned to her for a few minutes; weekdays at work, where she comes to him, or in workshops or in brick factories, or in sheds on the bank of the Irtysh. Sonia notice myself that she was able to get some even dating and patronage; that it is engaged in sewing, and so the city is almost no milliner, then became in many homes even necessary; not only to note that, through it, Raskolnikov was mandated protection that he had oblegchaemy work, and so on. Finally came the news (Dunya even take some special joy and anxiety in her last letters) that he avoids all that hard work in prison is not pleasant; He was silent for a few days in a row and became very pale. Suddenly, in the last letter Sonia wrote that he fell ill seriously and is in the hospital, in the House of prisoners ...

←«»→

⟵ CHAPTER II ⟶

He had been ill for a long time; but not the horrors of convict life without work, without food, without a shaved head, and not a patchwork dress broke it on! that it was for all these torments and torture! On the contrary, he even was glad to work: physically exhausted at work, he would at least earn their few hours of restful sleep. And what does it mean for him food - empty soup with cockroaches? Student, during his previous life, he often does not have that. His clothes were warm and adapted to its way of life. Staples, he did not even feel it. If he is ashamed of his shaved head and a half jacket? But to whom? Previous Sonia? Sonya was afraid of him, and in front of it, if he was ashamed of?

So what? He was ashamed even before Sonia, who broke for contempt and abuse. But not shaved head and shackled he was ashamed: his pride was hurt badly; he fell ill from wounded pride.Oh, how happy he was, if he could have himself to blame yourself! Then he destroyed everything, even shame. But he judged himself severely, and cruel conscience did not find particularly terrible guilt in his past, except for a simple mistake that can happen to anyone. He was ashamed of what he, Raskolnikov, who died so blindly, hopelessly boring and stupid for some phrase of blind fate, and shall adopt and submit to the "nonsense" of the sentence, if he wants something to calm yourself.

Anxiety aimless and purposeless in the present and in the future one continuous victims who did not take - that's what he had in the world. And what's up with him after eight years, it will be only thirty-two years, and you can start again, even live! Why does he live? What to keep in mind ,? To strive for? To live, to exist? But he is a thousand times before and was ready

to give his life for the idea, hope, even to the imagination. One has always been there for him a little; He always wanted more. Maybe only one force of desire, and he thought he was then a man who allowed more than others.

And though fate had sent him to repentance - burning remorse, broken hearts, drives away sleep, such remorse, from the terrible suffering that coming up with a loop and a jacuzzi! Oh, he would love to see it! Flour and tears - it is also life. But he did not repent of his crime.

At least, he could be angry at his stupidity, because he was angry at first ugly and stupid actions of their own, which led him to prison. But now, even in prison, released, he was again discussed and thought about all his previous actions and did not find them so stupid and ugly, as they seemed to him that fateful time before.

"What's that - he thought - my idea was stupid other thoughts and theories, swarming and colliding with each other in the world, as it should need only look at the case completely independent, wide and free of everyday influences? You look, and then, of course, my idea was not so ... strange. On the negative and the wise men in a silver penny, why should you stop halfway!

Well, that my actions they feel so ugly? - He said to himself. - The fact that he - a crime? What does the word "crime"? My conscience is clear. Of course, a criminal offense; Of course, violated the letter of the law and shed blood, well, take the letter of the law of my mind ... and pretty! Of course, in this case, even many benefactors of mankind, will not inherit power, but grabbed her own, must be made in the very first of its steps. But those people have taken out your steps, because they are right, and I could not bear it, and therefore I had no right to afford this step. "

Here's one he confessed to his crime: only that he did and made a confession.

He also suffered from the thought: why did not he kill himself? Why is it then stood over the river and preferred to confession? Is there such a force in the desire to live and so hard to overcome it? Beat well Svidrigailov afraid of death?

He torments asked myself this question and could not understand that too, when standing over the river, perhaps a premonition in themselves and in their deep convictions lie. He did not understand that this is a premonition of the future may be a harbinger of a turning point in his life, the future resurrection in the future, a new outlook on life.

Rather, he admitted that only one stupid instinct burden that he was not supposed to break, and he again failed to cross (for being weak and insignificant). He looked at his fellow prisoners and asks how they all loved the same life as they cherished it! It seemed to him that in prison it even more love and appreciate and value it more than freedom. What terrible torment and torture have not transferred some of them, such as a tramp! It's too much for them can mean any one ray of sunshine, dense forest, somewhere in the cold desert unknown key, which is celebrated in the third year and a date with this tramp dreams as a date with his mistress, sees him in a dream, green grass around him, the birds were singing in the bushes? Looking further, he saw examples of even more inexplicable.

In prison, his entourage, he certainly did not notice much, and do not want to completely ignore. He lived as a downcast eyes: it's disgusting and unbearable to watch. But in the end it became a lot to surprise him, and he somehow involuntarily began to notice something before and had no idea ,. In general, however, and became the most surprising of his terrible, that unbridgeable gulf between him and all these lyudom. It seemed that he and they were of different nationalities. He and they looked at each other with suspicion and vrazhdebnostyu.On know and understand common causes of this division; but never admitted it before, that these reasons were in fact so deep and strong. In prison and exiled Poles, political prisoners. They just thought that all the people for fools and flakes and despised them down; but Raskolnikov could not watch because he saw clearly that they are ignorant in many respects much smarter than most Poles. There were also Russian, too, too despised this nation - one officer and two former seminarian; Raskolnikov clearly noticed and error.

It also did not like, and avoided all. He even began to hate the end - why? He did not know that. Despised him, laughed at him, laughed at his crime, those who were much his crime.

- You're a gentleman! - Tell him. - You were there with an ax to walk; not lordly thing.

During the second week of Lent came to his turn to prepare for Communion with the barracks. He went to the church to pray with drugimi.Iz the fact that he did not know that - once had a quarrel; all at once attacked him violently.

- You're an atheist! You are not a god you believe in! - Shouted at him. - Kill you need.

ROBOTS READ

He never talked to them about God and faith, but they wanted to kill him as an infidel; He was silent and did not mind them. One inmate was brought to him in a decisive madness; Raskolnikov awaited him calmly and silently: eyebrows do not move, nor one tittle of his face did not flinch. The guard had come between him and the killer - no blood be shed.

Insoluble for him was another question: Why are they all so fond of Sonia? She did not spare them; they rarely met with her, sometimes works only when she came for a moment to see him.Meanwhile, everyone knew her, knew that she followed him followed, knew how she lives, where he lives. Money she did not give them, especially services not rendered. Only once, at Christmas, she brought the whole prison alms: cakes and roll. But little by little between them and Sonia became a little more intimate relationship: she wrote them letters to their families and sent them to the post office. Their families and relatives, who came to the city, to the left, at the direction of, in the hands of Sonia things for them and even money. Their wives and mistresses knew her and approached her. And when she was at work, coming to Raskolnikov, or met a party of convicts, going to work - all took off their hats, all bowed: "My mother, Sofya Semyonovna, you are our mother, tender, disease!" - He said that these rough, branded convicts who create small and thin. She smiled and otklanivayus and they all loved it when she smiled.They loved it even walk, turn around to take care of it as it goes, and praised her; even praised her for what she was so small, I did not even know that praise. For her, even went for treatment.

He was in the hospital the entire end of Lent and Holy. Already recovered, he remembered his dreams, even when lying in a feverish and delirious. He dreamed of a disease, if the whole world is doomed to sacrifice some terrible, unheard and unseen plague coming from the depths of Asia to Europe. All of them were killed, except for a few, a very few are chosen. There were some new Trichinella, microscopic creatures live in the bodies of humans. But these creatures were spirits, gifted intelligence and will. People take them to him, immediately became possessed and mind. But never, never people do not consider themselves so intelligent and steadfast in truth, as has been infected. Never thought his unshakable belief, their scientific conclusions, their moral convictions and beliefs. Whole villages, whole cities and nations have been infected and sumasshestvovali. All of them were in trouble and do not understand each other, everyone thinks that it is one and the truth, and suffered, looking at the others, beat his breast, cried and wrung his hands. I

do not know who and how to judge, could not agree that is an evil that good. I do not know whom to blame, whom to justify. People kill each other in some kind of senseless rage. The transition at each other whole armies, but the army in the campaign, suddenly began to torment themselves failed rows, the soldiers threw themselves at each other, injected and cutting, biting and eating each other. In cities all day to sound the alarm: all summoned, but who and why is calling, no one knew, and they were all in trouble. Left most ordinary ship, because each offered their thoughts, their amendments, and could not agree; stopped farming. In some places, people ran together, agree together on anything, vowed not to leave - but then he started something completely different than it is now assumed to himself, began to accuse each other, fighting and cutting. Start a fire, famine. Everything and everyone dies. Ulcer grew and moved farther and farther away. Save the world could only a few people, it was clean and elected intended to start a new race of people and a new life, renew and cleanse the land, but no one and nowhere to be seen these people, no one heard their words and voices.

Raskolnikov was tormented by the fact that it is meaningless drivel so sad and so painful echoes in his memoirs that for so long does not pass the impression these goryacheshnyh dreams. It was the second week after Easter; were warm, clear, spring days; in the House of prisoners opened the windows (lattice, which went under the hour). Sonja, during the whole time of his illness, he can see only twice in the building; every time I had to ask permission, but it was difficult. But she often went to the hospital courtyard, under the windows, especially at night, and sometimes it's just a minute to stand in the yard and even from far away to look at the window chamber. One day, in the evening, almost fully recovered Raskolnikov fell asleep; Waking up, he accidentally went to the window, and I could see in the distance, at the hospital gate, Sonya. She stood there as if waiting for something. Something like piercings at the time of his heart; He shuddered and quickly moved away from the window. The next day, Sonia did not come on the third day, too; He noticed that her waiting anxiously. Finally, he was discharged. Arriving at the jail, he learned from the convicts that Sofya Semyonovna ill, is at home and not go out.

He was very restless, sent for her to handle. He soon learned that her illness is not dangerous. Education turn it so craves, cares, Sonia sent him a note written in pencil, and notified him that it is much easier that it is empty, a slight cold and that soon, very soon, will come to work for him. When he

read the note, and his heart was beating hard and painful.

The day was clear and warm again. Early in the morning, at 6:00, he went to work on the river bank, where the barn was constructed firing kiln for plaster and where he knocked. Go only three employees. One of the prisoners took the convoy and went with him to the castle for a tool; Another was of wood and cast into the furnace. Raskolnikov walked out of the barn to the shore, and sat down on hinges log barn and began to look at the broad river and desert. On the high bank opens a wide area. On the far other side barely audible songs could be heard. There, bathed in sunshine boundless steppes, imperceptible point blackened nomadic yurt. Was freedom and lived other people do not like local, it would be most like time stood still, just not passed the age of Abraham and his flock. Raskolnikov sat staring fixedly without stopping; thought that his move to the dream, in contemplation; he was not thinking about anything, but some are concerned about his pain and anguish.

Suddenly found myself next to him Sonya. She came weakly and sat down beside him. It was still very early in the morning chill did not give. She wore a poor old burnous and green scarf. Her face still showed signs of the disease, thin, pale, haggard. She is friendly and happily smiled at him, but, as usual, held out her hand timidly.

She always held out his hand shyly, sometimes not filed at all, as if afraid he would alienate her. He was always as if in disgust and took her hand, always just met her with annoyance, sometimes stubbornly silent at all times during their visit. It so happened that she trembled before him and went into deep mourning. But now their hands are not separate; He quickly looked and looked at her, not reprimand looked down at the ground. They were alone, they have not seen. The guard at the time turned away.

As it happened, he did not know, but suddenly something like catch it and how to throw himself at her feet. He cried and hugged her knees. For a moment she was terribly frightened, and yet her face was half dead. She jumped up and, trembling, staring at him. But immediately, in the same moment she realized. Her eyes lit up endless happiness; she knew, and she did not doubt that he loves infinitely loves her and that she was in the last moment ...

They wanted to say but could not. Tears were in their eyes. They were both pale and thin; but in these patients and pale faces have shone the dawn of a renewed future full of resurrection to a new life. They rose love heart

infinity consists of one source of life for the heart of another.

They laid wait and be patient. They are still seven years; As long as unbearable as flour and infinite happiness! But he rose again, and he knew it, he felt quite all his update existing, and she - she did not have anything except her, and lived his life!

That same evening, when she was locked barracks, Raskolnikov lay on his bunk and thought about it. On this day, he even seemed as if all the convicts, who were his enemies, already looked at him differently. He even spoke to them, and he said quietly. He remembered it now, but it's the way it should be: If not all change now?

He thought about it. He remembered how he was constantly tormented her and broke her heart; remembered her pale, thin face, but it almost did not torture, and now these memories: he knew that the infinite love he now atone for all his suffering.

And all this, all the flour at last! Everything, even his crime, even a sentence and a link seemed to him now, in the first flush, some external, oddly enough, not even happened to him this fact. He, however, could not this evening for a long time and constantly about anything to think, focus on something thought; yes he did, and will not allow now consciously; he had just come felt. Instead dialectic life and consciousness to come up with something completely different.

Under his pillow lay the Gospel. He took it mechanically. This book belonged to her, was the same with which she read to him about the resurrection of Lazarus. At the beginning of hard labor, he thought she was tortured religion, will talk about the gospel and to impose his book. But, to his great surprise, she never talked about it, not even offered him the Gospel. He asked him to shortly before his illness, and she silently brought him a book. Until now, he did not disclose.

He did not disclose it now, but the thought flashed through him, "her beliefs may not be now, and my beliefs Her feelings, her aspirations, at least ...?"

She, too, the whole day was agitated and even into the night again fell ill. But she was so happy that I was almost afraid of his happiness. Seven years, only seven years old! At the beginning of his happiness, at other times, they were both willing to look at these seven years as seven days. He did not even know that a new life is not in vain, that he gets that it should be more expensive to buy and pay for this great feat of the future ...

ROBOTS READ

But here begins a new story, the story of the gradual renewal of a man, his history of the gradual degeneration of the gradual transition from one world to another, meeting new, hitherto completely unknown reality. This can create a new topic of the story - but our present story ended.

MCH.\E  TR.\SLTD

CONTENTS

PART 1   **1**

CHAPTER I   1
CHAPTER II   8
CHAPTER III   22
CHAPTER IV   33
CHAPTER V   43
CHAPTER VI   52
CHAPTER VII   63

⟨⟨»⟩

PART 2   **73**

CHAPTER I   73
CHAPTER II   88
CHAPTER III   98
CHAPTER IV   110
CHAPTER V   119
CHAPTER VI   129
CHAPTER VII   147

⟨⟨»⟩